Today's *College* Students

AC SS
Adolescent Cultures, School & Society

Joseph L. DeVitis & Linda Irwin-DeVitis
GENERAL EDITORS

Vol. 57

The Adolescent Cultures, School & Society series
is part of the Peter Lang Education list.
Every volume is peer reviewed and meets
the highest quality standards for content and production.

PETER LANG
New York • Bern • Frankfurt • Berlin
Brussels • Vienna • Oxford • Warsaw

Today's *College* Students

A READER

Pietro A. Sasso & Joseph L. DeVitis, Editors

PETER LANG
New York • Bern • Frankfurt • Berlin
Brussels • Vienna • Oxford • Warsaw

Library of Congress Cataloging-in-Publication Data

Today's college students: a reader / Edited by Pietro A. Sasso, Joseph L. DeVitis.
pages cm. — (Adolescent cultures, school and society; Vol. 57)
Includes bibliographical references and index.
1. College students—Social conditions—21st century.
2. Education, Higher—History—21st century.
I. Sasso, Pietro A. II. DeVitis, Joseph L.
LA186.T63 378.1'9800905—dc23 2014009386
ISBN 978-1-4331-2395-5 (hardcover)
ISBN 978-1-4331-2394-8 (paperback)
ISBN 978-1-4539-1356-7 (e-book)
ISSN 1091-1464

Bibliographic information published by **Die Deutsche Nationalbibliothek**.
Die Deutsche Nationalbibliothek lists this publication in the "Deutsche Nationalbibliografie"; detailed bibliographic data are available on the Internet at http://dnb.d-nb.de/.

The paper in this book meets the guidelines for permanence and durability of the Committee on Production Guidelines for Book Longevity of the Council of Library Resources.

29 Broadway, 18th floor, New York, NY 10006
www.peterlang.com

Printed in the United States of America

Dedication

To my parents, friends, and family, who supported me through the process of planning, editing, and formatting this text; and to those who still actively listen to the student voice in consideration of their lived experiences. This empathy toward the student narrative is the real *ethos* of higher education. It is to these practitioners and researchers that the pages of this text owe so much.

—PAS

To A.L. Addington, a university administrator who actually enhanced students, faculty, and staff; and to Richard Raskin, who ignited my social consciousness when I was a college freshman. They added to my adventures in academe more than they know.

—JLD

Acknowledgments

Credit is due to the wonderful students of the graduate program in the student affairs and college counseling program at Monmouth University during the development of this text. They helped edit many of the chapters and provided timely, constructive feedback representing the student voice. We would also like to acknowledge our contributors, who utilized a contemporary, critical lens to address significant issues affecting the college student experience. Finally, we are grateful to the Peter Lang staff for its able, efficient, and caring treatment of our work throughout this project.

Contents

Introduction

Pietro A. Sasso and Joseph L. DeVitis

> *I went to college because I didn't have anywhere else to go and it was a fabulous hang. And while I was there I was exposed to this world that I didn't know was possible.*
> —Tom Hanks

> *I loved [college] for what it provided me access to: bonds with people I grew to cherish. And nothing was better than working toward my dreams alongside people I loved who were doing the same.*
> —Liz Murray, *Breaking Night: A Memoir of Forgiveness, Survival, and My Journey From Homeless to Harvard* (2011)

Typically, college admissions websites and brochures create exorbitant optimism about higher education. They mirror the excitement and energy of first-year student welcome weeks, residence hall move-in days, and the initial anxiety of adult learners scurrying to find their classroom locations. Yet the distance between this description and the actual student experience often reflects a less sanguine narrative. That narrative—set between the margins of catalogues, policies, procedures, protocols, strategic plans, grants, retention reports, financial statements, and assessment data—paints a less ideal portrait of college life, one in which the students we presumably serve seem to be peculiarly left out of sight.

As a profession and an industry, higher education—like most institutions—is hardly infallible. Its long, often contentious history has moved from a focus on *in loco parentis* (in place of parents) to *alma mater* (caring mother) to *caveat emptor* (buyer beware). Similarly, contemporary colleges have shifted to a kind of McDonaldization, privileging capitalist rationales for university management in the name of efficiency and "progress" (Hayes & Wynyard, 2002). More and more, this dominant corporate model plagues the spatial and temporal landscape of postsecondary education. In all this, we are again compelled to ask: Have we largely forgotten the student? In presenting this volume, we hope to offer a significant counterpoint, one that might revivify the main reason for any university's existence: to educate students as persons in their full totality.

In 1910, former U.S. and Princeton University President Woodrow Wilson stated:

> The great voice of America does not come from the seats of learning, but in a murmur from the hills and the woods and the farms and the factories and the mills, rolling on and gaining volume until it comes to us from the homes of the common [sic]. Do these murmurs come into the corridors of the university? I have not heard them. (Link, 1975, p. 365)

Echoing this sentiment, we believe that Wilson's grave message remains alive today. We still need to be more sensitive to students' experiences and more willing and able to respond to their needs. We need to step back, reflect, and become more understanding of students as individuals. This means we also need to step back from our unquestioning idolatry of administrative and legislative efficiency. It offers no real panaceas for what ails today's college students.

* * *

This book affords an extensive, in-depth overview of America's contemporary undergraduate students. As editors, we faced a challenging task in that there are over 20 million of them in our institutions of higher education. About one-third are the traditional college age (18–22), and some 25% are older than 25. Part-timers comprise over one-third of the country's student body; approximately 60% attend four-year public and private colleges, and the rest attend community colleges and for-profit schools (Johnson, 2013).

In addition to their sheer numbers, these students bring mind-boggling diversity with them. Just as there are myriad kinds of colleges and universities, different student groups and identities abound on our campuses: African American, Latino/a, Native American, Asian, White, Middle Eastern, Indian, students with disabilities, residential, nonresidential, first-generational, distance learners, and so on. Accordingly, we have sought to present rich, descriptive, interpretive, and normative analyses of a wide variety of student types. Indeed, we believe that this emphasis sets our work apart from other books on college students that do not cover such a broad spectrum of student populations. In so doing, we have attempted to avoid stereotyping any particular group(s). Thanks in large part to our thoughtful contributors, we trust that effort has succeeded. It is our sincere hope that the chapters in this volume will provide readers (especially college students) with informed insights on counterparts who may be similar to or different than themselves.

We also acknowledge our privileged past and seek a more hopeful, egalitarian future in the wake of such challenges as mental health, substance misuse, and the good and ill represented in advanced technologies. In addition, as social inequality rises and a deep recession has taken its toll, financial aid is becoming harder to find, especially at state schools (Folbre, 2010; Newfield, 2008), and astounding tuition hikes make many parents and students shake their heads in despair. Their disappointment might be even more pronounced at universities that unduly privilege faculty research over any commitment to undergraduate teaching.

Throughout this book, we invite students, their instructors, and other college/university practitioners to be mindful of the crucial, yet sometimes overlooked, connection between extracurricular campus activities and the academy's cardinal aim of learning. All of us in higher education should expect our pursuits to be, in John Dewey's (1938) words, "educative" rather than non-educative or mis-educative. To forget that out-of-classroom programs should sustain educational moments is to sabotage why colleges exist. *Both* social interaction and individual critical reflection are vital to worthwhile collegiate experiences.

Our philosophy of education harkens back to the professional vision of adopting the "student personnel point of view" (American Council on Education, 1949), that is, the need to see the student "as a whole" in all her dimensions—physical, social, emotional, and spiritual, as well as strictly academic. Learning can occur in many settings, though the university is perhaps the most perfected laboratory for its practice in a more or less organized form. Indeed, college commencement, meant to be a "beginning," should remind all of us who work in academe that our ultimate goal is to equip students for life *after* college as well as *during* college:

> Educate our students as whole people, and they will bring all of who they are to the demands of being human in private and public life. The present and future well-being of humankind asks nothing less of us. (Palmer, Zajonc, & Scribner, 2010, p. 153)

And what should postsecondary institutions do with and for their students? A concerned report issued by the University of Michigan (President's Commission Report on the Undergraduate Experience, 2002) offers a coherent set of recommendations:

1. Make the campus more interconnected, integrated, and permeable.
2. Connect students to the community and the world.
3. Treat the undergraduate career as a life-course journey, both intellectually and socially.
4. Equip undergraduates with good maps and good guides for their journey.
5. Create a student community that is diverse, inclusive, adventurous, and self-reflective.
6. Provide resources and nurture practices that renew the faculty commitment to undergraduate education and enhance faculty-student interaction. (pp. 11–14)

At the same time, some recent critiques of American higher education paint a rather dismal portrait of how little learning may actually be occurring on our campuses (Arum & Roksa, 2011; Bok, 2007). Their findings underscore the need to tie social activities to engaged learning experiences. Since undergraduates spend, on average, about 15 hours per week in the classroom, it is imperative that student life professionals prepare ample educative encounters for student activities across the quadrangle. Ideally, they should include students themselves in their planning and execution so that they can be real actors in their own learning—one that requires reflection and judgment.

Meanwhile, we urge college and university personnel to wean students away from an overarching contemporary obsession: the consumer society. Too many students today "live in an age of convenience and consumption. A college education has been commodified, understood as yet another acquisition to be made rather than a process in which you engage" (Crone & MacKay, 2007, p. 18). That is, students should gain from intangible, yet felt, activities *themselves,* and not just from more tangible material products. Knowing the difference is to be able to differentiate between "to be" and "to have." Admittedly, student affairs practitioners face countless difficult challenges. They are working with students in all manner of transition, whatever their age:

> Students are adjusting to newfound freedom, with more control over their schedules, selection of activities, choice of friends, food consumption, and myriad similar choices large and small. At the same time, there is often a loss of family contact, exposure to religious, racial, sexual, or cultural differences that may be disconcerting. (Radison & DiGeronimo, 2004, p. 11)

For traditional undergraduates, the transitional phases of college life can be especially problematic as they "learn to individuate from parents, to establish social relations, to settle into their sexuality, to decide how they will deal with drugs and alcohol, and to rise to financial, intellectual, and social demands" (Pistorello, 2013, p. 10).

To engage with such students requires a special person: one who has flexibility, commitment, and an uncanny ability to deal with ambiguity. In some ways, these are the very kinds of capacities that William Perry (1970) outlined in his seminal study on the intellectual and ethical development of college students themselves. The halls of academe demand that kind of maturation from us all. This means that we, who serve in higher education, must also practice deep self-reflection if we are to be effective agents of student development.

In the end, it may really be the power of diversity on college campuses that leads to many of the educational goals that we yearn for in student growth: the formal and informal social interactions, bonded in reflective learning, that help build social and academic success. In this we can celebrate together, especially those of us who have savored so many "bright college years":

> How many of us would have predicted, in the 1950s or 1960s, that so great a number of talented and dissimilar students would be studying together and learning from one another after so brief a passage of time? No similar transformation has ever before taken place in the long history of higher education, either in this country or elsewhere. (Rudenstein, 2001, p. 47)

That blessed diversity must be protected, indeed augmented, against present and potential legal and social barriers with the most compelling moral suasion we can muster—for the benefit of *all* students, today and tomorrow.

References

American Council on Education. (1949). *Student personnel point of view.* Washington, DC: Author.

Arum, R., & Roksa, J. (2011). *Academically adrift: Limited learning on college campuses.* Chicago, IL: University of Chicago Press.

Bok, D. (2007). *Our underachieving colleges: A candid look at how much students learn and why they should be learning more.* Princeton, NJ: Princeton University Press.

Crone, I., & MacKay, K. (2007). Motivating today's college students. *Peer Review, 9*(1), 18–21.

Dewey, J. (1938). *Experience and education.* Indianapolis, IN: Kappa Delta Pi.

Folbre, N. (2010). *State U: Why we must fix public higher education.* New York, NY: New Press.

Hayes, D., & Wynyard, R. (Eds.). (2002). *The McDonaldization of higher education.* New York, NY: Praeger.

Johnson, J. (2013, September 14). Today's typical college students often juggle work, children, and bills with coursework. *The Washington Post,* p. C8.

Link, S.A. (Ed.). (1975). Address to Princeton University alumni, Pittsburgh, Pennsylvania (April 17, 1910). In *The papers of Woodrow Wilson* (Vol. 20, p. 365). Princeton, NJ: Princeton University Press.

Murray, L. (2011). *Breaking night: A memoir of forgiveness, survival, and my journey from homeless to Harvard.* New York, NY: Hyperion.

Newfield, C. (2008). *Unmasking the public university: The forty-year assault on the middle class.* Cambridge, MA: Harvard University Press.

Palmer, P.J., & Zajonc, A., & Scribner, M. (2010). *The heart of higher education: A call to renewal.* San Francisco, CA: Jossey-Bass.

Perry, W.G., Jr. (1970). *Forms of intellectual and ethical development in the college years: A scheme.* New York, NY: Holt, Rinehart, and Winston.

Pistorello, J. (2013). *Mindfulness and acceptance for counseling college students: Theory and practical applications for intervention, prevention, and outreach.* Reno, NV: Context Press.

President's Commission Report on the Undergraduate Experience. (2002). *The second chapter of change: Renewing undergraduate education at the University of Michigan.* Ann Arbor, MI: Board of Regents of the University of Michigan.

Radison, R., & DiGeronimo, T.F. (2004). *The college of the overwhelmed: The campus mental health crisis and what to do about it.* San Francisco, CA: Jossey-Bass.

Rudenstein, N.L. (2001). Student diversity and higher education. In G. Orfield (Ed.), *Diversity challenged: Evidence on the impact of affirmative action* (pp. 31–48). Cambridge, MA: Harvard Education.

Part One

Student Diversity

ONE

Historical and Contemporary Challenges Faced by African American Undergraduate Students

Ufuoma Abiola, Marybeth Gasman, Thai-Huy Nguyen, Andrés Castro Samayoa, and Felecia Commodore

Completion of higher education is critical for African American students. A college education serves a private and public good by providing economic and social benefits both to individuals and to society as a whole (Institute for Higher Education Policy, 2006). Individuals with more education tend to have higher salaries, higher savings, more leisure time, and better health/life expectancy (Institute for Higher Education Policy, 2006). However, for African American students, the U.S. higher education system is not providing the same benefits as compared to White students (Institute for Higher Education Policy, 2006; Long & Riley, 2007). In this chapter, historical and contemporary challenges faced by African American undergraduate students are examined. The argument begins with a discussion of K–12 education and family background and then moves to issues of access and enrollment, persistence and retention, and graduation. This topic is of importance because projections indicate that, by 2014, more than 40% of graduating high school seniors will be people of color; by 2015, students of color will represent 37% of all postsecondary enrollments, and 80% of the new undergraduate students will be African American, Hispanic, or Asian/Pacific Islander (Institute for Higher Education Policy, 2006). In order for African American students to survive, thrive, and ultimately graduate from college, postsecondary educators must offer high-quality, customized institutional programs and practices for these students.

History of African American Education

Despite efforts to deny them access to education, African Americans have sought learning opportunities, albeit informally, since their arrival in the United States. During slavery, free African

Americans in the North enrolled in the few colleges willing to admit them, such as Oberlin and Dartmouth. Richard Humphries, of Philadelphia, established the Institute for Colored Youth (later Cheyney University) to educate free African Americans. Following the close of the Civil War and the end of slavery, African American and White missionaries created small colleges to educate African Americans, providing both teacher training and religious instruction. Most jobs for African Americans were menial, and those who were college educated were limited to teacher and preacher positions, as these were the only professional jobs available. Historically Black Colleges and Universities (HBCUs) are responsible for educating the African American middle class as we know it, preparing African American scientists, doctors, nurses, teachers, and business people. These institutions educated over 90% of African Americans for nearly 100 years, since predominantly White institutions (PWIs) did not welcome African Americans on their campuses (Gasman, 2007; Gasman, Lundy-Wagner, Ransom, & Bowman, 2010).

The Supreme Court's 1954 *Brown v. Board of Education* decision, although directly pertaining to K–12 education, had a significant impact on higher education for African Americans in that it very slowly opened the doors to PWIs by dismantling segregation in the nation (Gasman, 2007). Although legally admitted to PWIs, African American students had to fight countless battles in order to gain admission and to gain rights as students through the early 1980s. Some African Americans were forced to face hostile college environments in which faculty and administrators, as well as other students, challenged their intellect and humanity daily (Gasman, 2007). Although the experiences of African American students have improved, there are still myriad challenges. But despite these challenges, African Americans have made great strides in terms of higher education, leveraging their education to contribute to society in important ways (Gasman, 2007; Gasman et al., 2010).

K-12 Underpreparation and Family Background

In examining contemporary experiences of African American students in college, the barriers and issues influencing their access to postsecondary opportunities must be acknowledged. African American students' experiences in the K–12 environment remain deeply marginalizing and, indeed, affect their college readiness. On average, African American students enter college highly underprepared on several levels (Kao & Thompson, 2003). They have a greater likelihood of graduating from poorly funded secondary schools that possess few opportunities for students to recognize and reach their full potential (Kao & Thompson, 2003; Perna & Titus, 2005). In these under-resourced schools there is a shortage of qualified teachers to prepare these students for college English and mathematics, both of which are general education requirements for the associate's degree or to transfer to bachelor-level, degree-granting institutions. Moreover, institutional practices such as tracking, which "is the process whereby students are divided into categories so that they can be assigned in groups to various kinds of classes," have been shown to constrain African American students' opportunities for achievement in high school and for a college education (Oakes, 1985, p. 3).

African American students are more likely than White students to come from lower-income homes with non-college-educated parents, which can starve students of the economic and cultural capital needed to pursue higher education (McDonough, 1997). Having college-educated parents, especially ones actively involved in their child's academic life (Perna & Titus, 2005), is not only related to higher aspirations in students and a greater likelihood of college enrollment, but also means that they have the financial resources (Orr, 2003) to take advantage of programs and tutorials that can enhance their likelihood of being admitted to a selective institution.

Data from the U.S. Department of Education suggests that the average freshman graduation rate[1] for African American students is 62%, which is 19% lower than the graduation rate for their White peers (NCES, 2011b; 2012). Explanations for this discrepancy are many, though studies suggest that indicators for future education achievement are influenced by factors such as parental education, teacher preparation (Aud, Fox, & KewalRamani, 2010), and neighborhood composition (Sharkey, 2009), to name just a few. The multifactorial elements influencing African American students' future collegiate success are important reminders of the ways in which postsecondary success is deeply entwined with the K–12 system, a sobering reminder that coalition building across educational tiers remains a work in progress in the United States.

Access and Enrollment

Between 1976 and 2011, African American undergraduate enrollment grew by 50% (NCES, 2012). Currently, of 18 million students enrolled in undergraduate programs, African Americans make up 15% of this total. Despite substantial gains in the past 35 years, disparities in postsecondary education continue to exist along racial and ethnic lines. White enrollment has decreased slightly since 2009, and yet Whites continue to make up 59% of the undergraduate population (NCES, 2012). According to the Center on Education and the Workforce at Georgetown University (Carnevale & Strohl, 2013), "the postsecondary system mimics and magnifies the racial and ethnic inequality in educational preparation it inherits from the K–12 system" (p. 7). Granted, increased African American enrollment may be considered an indication of diminishing educational inequality. However, the choices African American students make to attend certain institutions and the challenges they continue to face during their collegiate journey bear testament to the reality that gains in enrollment alone do not guarantee postsecondary success.

In our nation's large and complex systems of higher education, African American undergraduates primarily enroll in less selective and open-access colleges and universities, or institutions with historical missions to serve African American communities. The most common open-access institution is the community college—for which African Americans make up 16% of enrollment as opposed to 13% at 4-year institutions. Additionally, 105 HBCUs enroll 11% of the nation's African American students, despite the fact that they make up less than 3% of all U.S. postsecondary institutions (Gasman et al., 2013). HBCUs, which provide a nurturing environment with ample student support and same-race role models, remain a viable option for many African American students.

For many African American students, both social status and racial identity play a large and critical role in their choice to pursue postsecondary education and their selection of which college to attend. A study by Orr (2003) has shown that even after controlling for social class, racial identity has a significant effect on educational achievement as measured by standardized exams. For instance, in the past 20 years the gap in SAT-Critical Reading scores for African Americans and Whites has hovered around 100 points; a similar pattern exists for the mathematics section (NCES, 2011a).

Graduation from high school may mark students as competent and ready for college, but in reality, many African American students attend community colleges because they were not given adequate preparation for a 4-year institution. Community college offers a plethora of avenues, including remedial education for students to begin their path toward completion (Goldrick-Rab, 2010). For many students of color and non-traditional students who leave high school underprepared for the rigors of a 4-year institution, attending a community college represents a singular opportunity to earn a college degree. However, enrollment in community colleges does not always guarantee successful transfer to a 4-year institution. Many students find themselves stuck in the system and leave with a multitude of units, but not a degree (Shaw, 1997).

Wassmer, Moore, and Shulock (2004) found that community colleges with larger shares of African American and Latino students had a much lower transfer rate. Conversely, their study also suggests that community colleges with higher transfer rates had more resources and a strong focus on academic preparation; these institutions had a higher enrollment of Whites and Asians (Wassmer et al., 2004). In other words, even within the community college system, African American students continue to face challenges that constrain their opportunities to progress along the educational pipeline.

Access alone, however, does not mean that African American students will enroll in college or persist to graduation. With rising tuition and the additional costs associated with a college degree (room and board, textbooks, transportation, health insurance), college affordability continues to be a significant barrier to African American students. St. John, Paulsen, and Carter (2005) state that the recent changes in financial aid (reduction in federal, state, and institutional grants and scholarships) have a greater effect on African American students than they do on Whites. Tuition and financial aid are closely associated with the types of colleges that African American students choose to attend, whereas the same constraints matter less for Whites (St. John, Paulsen, & Carter, 2005). More recently, loans are making up a larger proportion of financial aid packages (Long & Riley, 2007). Not only is the relationship between loans and enrollment negative for African American students (Perna, 2000), but there is also growing concern that the increase in loans may, in the long term, outpace meaningful and sufficient opportunities needed to pay them off. According to Long and Riley (2007), more full-time African American students (58%) take out federal and private loans to finance their college education than any other racial or ethnic group. In 2010, 15.1% of the nation lived in poverty, and African Americans exceeded the national average by almost 13% (National Poverty Center, 2013). Not only are African American students coming from far more disadvantaged homes, but they and their families also face a more difficult task in financing a college education (National Poverty Center, 2013). Despite the large number of institutions that can provide greater access to African American students, the current state of the financial aid structure calls into question the benefits of a college degree in such a volatile economy.

Persistence and Retention

Campus Racial Climate

Student success within postsecondary settings is highly correlated with institutional environments. The seminal work by Sylvia Hurtado (1992) on campus racial climate has become a benchmark for assessing campus success in addressing racial tensions and creating a hospitable environment not only for African American students, but for all students negotiating their racial identities in a diverse environment. In a meta-analysis updating Hurtado's seminal work, Harper and Hurtado (2007) provide nine themes in a multi-sited qualitative study across a racially heterogeneous group of students (n=278). In their findings, Harper and Hurtado (2007) acknowledge the deleterious effects of "the pervasiveness of Whiteness in space, curricula, and activities" (p. 18) on college campuses, as well as the "infrequency with which race-related conversations occurred on campus" (p. 16). These findings are highlighted as crucial factors influencing African American student success at predominantly White campuses. Institutional heterogeneity throughout the United States, however, is indicative of the myriad environments available for African American students in their postsecondary pursuits. Research consistently demonstrates that environments such as those provided at HBCUs enable students not only to explore their racial identities, but to develop the necessary competencies for academic success as well (Gasman et al., 2010).

Infused with a historical mission to serve African American communities (Gasman, Baez, & Turner, 2008), enrollment in an HBCU allows students to accrue several educational benefits. First, institutional climates at HBCUs are centered upon the academic and professional achievement of African American students (Allen, Jewell, Griffin, & Wolf, 2007; Brown & Davis, 2001). This means that, first, every decision, strategy, and intervention is driven by the desire to see every student on that campus reach his or her full potential. Second, the cultivation of this climate specifically includes hiring faculty members (Hubbard & Stage, 2009) and staff members of color (Hirt, Strayhorn, Amelink, & Bennett, 2006) who understand their students' backgrounds and can provide consistent mentoring. Third, curriculum and student leadership activities are developed and employed to demonstrate to students the value of their own histories and cultures predicated on the belief that such provisions will strengthen and deepen their academic engagement and ultimately provide them with the support they need to succeed (Nelson Laird, Bridges, Morelon-Quainoo, Williams, & Holmes, 2007; Palmer & Gasman, 2008).

Transfer Students

Community colleges serve a large number of low-income students and students of color (Hagedorn, Maxwell, & Hampton, 2001; Pascarella & Terenzini, 1991). The literature speaks to African American students' collegiate experience and their challenges in transferring between institutions. Transfer rates of students by racial/ethnic group show disparities. Wassmer, Moore, and Shulock (2004) found that, after accounting for all other factors that affect transfer rates, institutions with higher percentages of African American or Latino students have lower 6-year transfer rates, whereas those with a larger percentage of Asian American students have higher transfer rates. Blau (1999) found that African American transfer rates were positively related to school size, meaning that "the larger the school the higher the transfer rate" (p. 528). Income was also found to be positively related to the transfer rate of Black students. Communities that were largely African American and affluent were likely to have high transfer rates. This suggests that the African American middle class has begun to use the 2-year college to pursue college degrees (Blau, 1999). Altogether, more must be understood about the unique experiences of African American transfer students, particularly those transferring from 2-year colleges to 4-year colleges. Their voices are often missing from the research on African American college students (Wassmer et al., 2004).

Hawley and Harris (2005) found that there are numerous variables that play a role in community college students being retained and persisting as opposed to dropping out. One of the highest predictors of dropout is the amount of developmental education courses a student must take (Hawley & Harris, 2005). This was found to be true across all racial/ethnic groups. English proficiency was also found to be a problem. This finding points to retention issues for African and Caribbean ESL students who are identified as Black/African American—necessitating the acknowledgment of the heterogeneity of African American students' backgrounds and experiences (Hawley & Harris, 2005).

Similarly, the length of time between completion of high school and entry into college presented itself as a barrier to retention (Hawley & Harris, 2005). Hawley and Harris (2005) make the case for a counterintuitive finding, namely, that the motivation to transfer to a 4-year institution is a strong predictor of students dropping out, especially in their first year. This finding is interesting and begs the question as to how community colleges communicate their role and ability to serve as a pipeline to 4-year institutions.

Other predictors tagged students who suspect they will have trouble financing college and who have employment responsibilities outside of college (Hawley & Harris, 2005). Various strategies have been explored to increase African American student retention at community colleges, particularly African American males (Glenn, 2003). More must be learned about this specific group of students in order to bolster the completion rates of African American students in community colleges.

Achievement and Learning

The literature on African American college student achievement and learning spans various areas. Often this literature focuses on the varying experiences at different types of institutions. Though there is no differential impact on African American students' degree completion between institutional types, the experiences that students have at these institutions may vary (Kim & Conrad, 2006). These are the experiences that affect student learning. Cokley (2000) found that there was no significant difference in African American students' academic self-concept between PWIs and HBCUs, though African American students attending HBCUs reported more positive experiences at their institutions as compared to those who attended PWIs. Regardless of institutional type, academic self-concept for African American students increased as GPA increased (Cokley, 2000). Class status was a predictor of academic self-concept (Cokley, 2000), and student-faculty relationships also played a role in positive academic self-concept (Cokley, 2000).

Integration is an important part of increasing retention rates for all students (Tinto, 1997). For students of color in particular, programs such as freshman seminars, mentoring, and diversity-friendly campus climate help to foster such integration (Szelenyi, 2001). Nelson Laird and colleagues (2007) found that African American students at HBCUs experienced significantly higher rates of engagement than African American students at PWIs. African American seniors at HBCUs reported gaining more in terms of outcomes (e.g., acquiring a broad general education, thinking critically and analytically, and understanding oneself and people of other racial and ethnic groups); this being true, levels of satisfaction for African American seniors at both institutional types were similar (Nelson Laird et al., 2007).

Same-Race/Cross-Race Faculty Mentors

Faculty-student mentoring relationships prove to be beneficial to the success of students of color. Many institutions are aware of this and provide some kind of mentoring program or faculty relationship for students to access. For faculty of color, this obligation is often found when it comes to students of color, who find access to faculty-student mentor relationships with same-race faculty to be beneficial to their academic success (Turner, 2002). In fact, African American students at HBCUs interacted with faculty more than did their counterparts at non-HBCUs (Nelson Laird et al., 2007). HBCUs tend to have a more racially and ethnically diverse faculty than PWIs, and one could infer that this may be the reason for such high rates of interaction (Gasman et al., 2013).

Lee (1999) found that African American students were more concerned with having a mentor in their career field than having a mentor of the same race, and thus could establish productive and fruitful mentor relationships with cross-race faculty. Some students even reported having less-than-positive interactions with same-race faculty (Lee, 1999). What is most important is that there is reciprocity in the mentor relationship (Lee, 1999). This does not mean that there are no challenges involved in the cross-race mentoring relationship. Johnson-Bailey and Cervero (2004) found that there are six common issues that come with these relationships: trust between mentor and protégé, acknowledged and unacknowledged racism, visibility and risks pertinent to minority faculty, power and paternalism, benefits to mentor and protégé, and the feeling of "otherness" in the academy (Johnson-Bailey & Cervero, 2004). Cross-race mentoring relationships should be encouraged on campuses, but to be beneficial to both parties—particularly African American students—sensitivity to their unique experiences must be understood and acknowledged in these relationships.

Graduation

There is a large disparity in the graduation rates between African Americans and Whites in U.S. postsecondary institutions. According to the most recent NCES data regarding undergraduate graduation rates (NCES, 2011b), African Americans earned 10% of the baccalaureate degrees in 2010, whereas Whites earned 70.8% of them in the same year. These statistics reveal the alarmingly disproportionate rate of graduation between African Americans and Whites—that is, African Americans overall are graduating from college at a far lower rate than Whites. There are also fewer African American males earning undergraduate degrees than African American females, as African American male students are often less prepared for rigorous college-level work (Harper, 2012; Lundy-Wagner & Gasman, 2011). African American male college completion rates are not only the lowest between genders but are also the lowest among all racial/ethnic groups in U.S. postsecondary education (Harper, 2012; Strayhorn, 2010). Further stark statistics show that the percentage of African American males enrolled in the academy in 1976 stayed the same in 2002, when African American males comprised only 4.3% of students (Harper, 2012; Strayhorn, 2010).

At highly selective postsecondary institutions there are high rates of graduation for African American students. Harvard University, Amherst College, Princeton University, and Brown University have an African American student graduation rate of over 90% (*Journal of Blacks in Higher Education,* 2005/2006). Yale University, Georgetown University, Dartmouth College, and the University of Pennsylvania have an African American graduation rate of 85% or more

(*Journal of Blacks in Higher Education,* 2005/2006). The graduation rates of African Americans at elite PWIs are, in part, a result of the orientation and retention programming and practices on campus designed to aid African American students in acclimating to these spaces. Kuh, Cruce, Shoup, Kinzie, and Gonyea (2008) state:

> These practices include well-designed and implemented orientation, placement testing, first-year seminars, learning communities, intrusive advising, early warning systems, redundant safety nets, supplemental instruction, peer tutoring and mentoring, theme-based campus housing, adequate financial aid including on-campus work, internships, service learning, and demonstrably effective teaching practices. (p. 556)

Having a significant number of African American enrollees, offering culture-rich programming with African American student organizations to enhance a sense of community on campus, and providing peer-mentoring opportunities between African American freshmen and upperclassmen increases the African American student graduation rate (*Journal of Blacks in Higher Education,* 2005/2006). Also, campuses located in urban areas or areas where African Americans have a significant presence have higher rates of graduation for African American students (*Journal of Blacks in Higher Education,* 2005/2006). Institutions with large endowments that enable them to support low-income African American students also have higher African American graduation rates (*Journal of Blacks in Higher Education,* 2005/2006).

In terms of African American post-baccalaureate outcomes, academic achievement at an undergraduate institution is the most significant predictor of entry into a graduate program for both genders (Bedard & Herman, 2008). However, African American women are seeking graduate education at higher rates than African American men (Perna, 2004). "During a 30-year period (1977–2007), Black men experienced a 109% increase in post-baccalaureate degree attainment, compared to 242% for Latino men and 425% for Asian American men; the comparative rate of increase for Black women was 253%" (Harper, 2012, p. 3). Financial aid also influences post-baccalaureate attendance. For low-income students, who can be negatively affected by the cost of tuition, financial aid can incline them toward attending school (Berkner & Chavez, 1997). For African American students, financial aid is particularly important, as it is a major deciding factor in whether to enroll in a graduate program or join the workforce (Davis et al., 2010). It is noteworthy that African American students who attended an HBCU for their undergraduate degree are just as likely to pursue a graduate degree as African American students who attended a PWI (Eagan et al., 2010; Zhang, 2005). Overall, African American students who acquire baccalaureate degrees earn wages significantly higher than African Americans who drop out of college, with a median income that is almost on a par with Whites of comparable education (*Journal of Blacks in Higher Education,* 2005/2006).

Conclusion

Current research continues to emphasize the importance of highlighting African American students' heterogeneity across intersecting identity markers such as gender, socioeconomic status, sexuality, and religious affiliation (Stewart, 2009). Indeed, institutional variability alone already provides ample opportunity for a multiplicity of experiences for African American students. To presume that a synthesis of African American students' collegiate experiences can be truncated is beyond the scope of any research agenda. It is more compelling, instead, to identify the patterns emerging within the multiple groups of African American students. Emerging trends can guide future research agendas. For example, there is a need to further enhance our understanding of the experiences of gay, lesbian, bisexual, and transgendered African American students, about which there exists scant literature (Patton, 2011). Additionally, there is a critical need to improve and support the experiences of African American males, whose participation in higher education in 2009 was 31.8% less than African American women (Harper, 2012). Thus the aim of this chapter has been to give a broad overview of the trends in African American higher education with the goal of informing those interested in strengthening the experiences of African American students.

Note

1. The National Center for Education Statistics (NCES) defines the "average freshman graduation rate" as the proportion of public high school freshmen who graduate with a regular diploma four years after starting 9th grade.

References

Allen, W.R., Jewell, J.O., Griffin, K.A., & Wolf, D. (2007). Historically Black colleges and universities: Honoring the past, engaging the present, touching the future. *Journal of Negro Education, 76*(3), 263–280.

Aud, S., Fox, M.A., & KewalRamani, A. (2010). *Status and trends in the education of racial and ethnic groups.* Washington, DC: National Center for Education Statistics, U.S. Government Printing Office.

Bedard, K., & Herman, D.A. (2008). Who goes to graduate/professional school? The importance of economic fluctuations, undergraduate field, and ability. *Economics of Education Review, 27*(2), 197–210.

Berkner, L., & Chavez, L. (1997). *Access to postsecondary education for the 1992 high school graduates* (NCES 98–105). Washington, DC: National Center for Education Statistics, U.S. Government Printing Office.

Blau, J.R. (1999). Two-year college transfer rates of black American students. *Community College Journal of Research & Practice, 23*(5), 525–531.

Brown, M.C., & Davis, J.E. (2001). The historically Black college as social contract, social capital, and social equalizer. *Peabody Journal of Education, 76*(1), 31–49.

Carnevale, A.P., & Strohl, J. (2013). *Separate and unequal: How higher education reinforces the intergenerational reproduction of White racial privilege.* Washington, DC: Georgetown University.

Cokley, K. (2000). An investigation of academic self-concept and its relationship to academic achievement in African American college students. *Journal of Black Psychology, 26*(2), 148–164.

Davis, K.E., Johnson, L., Ralston, P.A., Young-Clark, I., Colyard, V., Fluellen, V., & Rasco, M.R. (2010). Perceptions, experiences, and use of resources as selected HBCU students transition to graduate and professional roles in family and consumer sciences. *Family and Consumer Sciences Research Journal, 39*(1), 107–118.

Eagan, M.K., Garcia, G.A., Herrera, F., Garibay, J., Hurtado, S., & Chang, M.J. (2010, June). *Making a difference in science education for underrepresented students: The impact of undergraduate research programs.* Paper presented at the annual forum of the Association for Institutional Research, Chicago, IL.

Gasman, M. (2007). *Envisioning Black colleges: A history of the United Negro College Fund.* Baltimore, MD: The Johns Hopkins University Press.

Gasman, M., Baez, B., & Turner, C.S.V. (Eds.). (2008). *Understanding minority-serving institutions.* Albany, NY: State University of New York Press.

Gasman, M., Lundy-Wagner, V., Ransom, T., & Bowman III, N. (2010). Unearthing promise and potential: Our nation's historically Black colleges and universities. *ASHE Higher Education Report, 35*(5), 1–134.

Gasman, M., Nguyen, T., Castro Samayoa, A., Commodore, F., Abiola, U., Hyde-Carter, Y., & Carter, C. (2013). *The changing face of historically Black colleges and universities.* Philadelphia, PA: University of Pennsylvania, Center for Minority Serving Institutions.

Glenn, F.S. (2003). The retention of Black male students in Texas public community colleges. *Journal of College Student Retention: Research, Theory and Practice, 5*(2), 115–133.

Goldrick-Rab, S. (2010). Challenges and opportunities for improving community college student success. *Review of Educational Research, 80*(3), 437–469.

Hagedorn, L.S., Maxwell, W., & Hampton, P. (2001). Correlates of retention for African-American males in community colleges. *Journal of College Student Retention, 3*(3), 243–263.

Harper, S.R. (2012). *Black male student success in higher education: A report from the National Black Male College Achievement Study*. Philadelphia, PA: University of Pennsylvania, Center for the Study of Race and Equity in Education.

Harper, S.R., & Hurtado, S. (2007). Nine themes in campus racial climates and implications for institutional transformations. *New Directions for Student Services, 2007*(120), 7–24.

Hawley, T.H., & Harris, T.A. (2005). Student characteristics related to persistence for first-year community college students. *Journal of College Student Retention: Research, Theory and Practice, 7*(1), 117–142.

Hirt, J.B., Strayhorn, T.L., Amelink, C.T., & Bennett, B.R. (2006). The nature of student affairs work at Historically Black Colleges and Universities. *Journal of College Student Development, 47*(6), 661–676.

Hubbard, S.M., & Stage, F.K. (2009). Attitudes, perceptions, and preferences of faculty at Hispanic serving and predominantly Black institutions. *Journal of Higher Education, 80*(3), 270–289.

Hurtado, S. (1992). The campus racial climate: Contexts of conflict. *Journal of Higher Education, 63*(5), 539–569.

Institute for Higher Education Policy. (2006). *Convergence: Trends threatening to narrow college opportunity in America*. Retrieved from http://www.ihep.org/assets/files/publications/a-f/convergence.pdf

Johnson-Bailey, J., & Cervero, R.M. (2004). Mentoring in Black and White: The intricacies of cross-cultural mentoring. *Mentoring & Tutoring: Partnership in Learning, 12*(1), 7–21.

Journal of Blacks in Higher Education. (2005/2006, Winter). Black student college graduation rates remain low, but modest progress begins to show. *Journal of Blacks in Higher Education*, (50), 88–96.

Kao, G., & Thompson, J.S. (2003). Racial and ethnic stratification in educational achievement and attainment. *Annual Review of Sociology, 29*(1), 417–442.

Kim, M.M., & Conrad, C.F. (2006). The impact of historically Black colleges and universities on the academic success of African American students. *Research in Higher Education, 47*(4), 399–427.

Kuh, G.D., Cruce, T.M., Shoup, R., Kinzie, J., & Gonyea, R.M. (2008). Unmasking the effects of student engagement on first-year college grades and persistence. *Journal of Higher Education, 79*(5), 540–563.

Lee, W.Y. (1999). Striving toward effective retention: The effect of race on mentoring African American students. *Peabody Journal of Education, 74*(2), 27–43.

Long, B.T., & Riley, E. (2007). Financial aid: A broken bridge to college access? *Harvard Educational Review, 77*(1), 39–63.

Lundy-Wagner, V., & Gasman, M. (2011). When gender issues are not just about women: Reconsidering male students at Historically Black Colleges and Universities. *Teachers College Record, 113*(5), 934–968.

McDonough, P. (1997). *Choosing colleges: How social class and schools structure opportunity*. Albany, NY: State University of New York Press.

National Center for Education Statistics (NCES). (2011a). College Entrance Examination Board, *College-bound seniors: Total group profile [national] report*, selected years, 1986–87 through 2010–11. Retrieved from http://professionals.collegeboard.com/profdownload/cbs2011_total_groupreport.pdf

National Center for Education Statistics (NCES). (2011b). *Digest of education statistics: 2011*. Washington, DC: U.S. Department of Education. Retrieved from http://nces.ed.gov/programs/digest/d11/tables/dt11_300.asp?referrer=report

National Center for Education Statistics (NCES). (2012). *Digest of education statistics: 2012*. (NCES Report No. 2012-263). Washington, DC: U.S. Department of Education.

National Poverty Center. (2013, August 28). *Poverty in the United States*. Retrieved from http://www.npc.umich.edu/poverty/

Nelson Laird, T.F., Bridges, B.K., Morelon-Quainoo, C.L., Williams, J.M., & Holmes, M.S. (2007). African American and Hispanic student engagement at minority serving and predominantly White institutions. *Journal of College Student Development, 48*(1), 39–56.

Oakes, J. (1985). *Keeping track: How schools structure inequality*. New Haven, CT: Yale University Press.

Orr, A.J. (2003). Black-White differences in achievement: The importance of wealth. *Sociology of Education, 76*(4), 281–304.

Palmer, R.T., & Gasman, M. (2008). "It takes a village to raise a child": The role of social capital in promoting academic success for African American men at a Black college. *Journal of College Student Development, 49*(1), 52–70.

Pascarella, E.T., & Terenzini, P.T. (1991). *How college affects students: Findings and insights from twenty years of research*. San Francisco, CA: Jossey-Bass.

Patton, L. (2011). Perspectives on identity, disclosure, and the campus environment among African American gay and bisexual men at one historically Black college. *Journal of College Student Development, 52*(1), 77–100.

Perna, L.W. (2000). Differences in the decision to attend college among African Americans, Hispanics, and Whites. *Journal of Higher Education, 71*(2), 117–141.

Perna, L.W. (2004). Understanding the decision to enroll in graduate school: Sex and racial/ethnic group differences. *Journal of Higher Education, 75*(5), 487–527.

Perna, L.W., & Titus, M.A. (2005). The relationship between parental involvement as social capital and college enrollment: An examination of racial/ethnic group differences. *Journal of Higher Education, 76*(5), 485–518.

Sharkey, P. (2009). *Neighborhoods and the Black-White mobility gap*. Retrieved from http://www.pewtrusts.org/uploadedFiles/wwwpewtrustsorg/Reports/Economic_Mobility/PEW_SHARKEY_v12.pdf?n=1399

Shaw, K.M. (1997). Remedial education as ideological battleground: Emerging remedial education policies in the community college. *Educational Evaluation and Policy Analysis, 19*(3), 284–296.

St. John, E.P., Paulsen, M.B., & Carter, D.F. (2005). Diversity, college costs, and postsecondary opportunity: An examination of the financial nexus between college choice and persistence for African Americans and Whites. *Journal of Higher Education, 76*(5), 545–569.

Stewart, D.L. (2009). Perceptions of multiple identities among Black college students. *Journal of College Student Development, 50*(3), 253–270.

Strayhorn, T.L. (2010). When race and gender collide: Social and cultural capital's influence on the academic achievement of African American and Latino males. *Review of Higher Education, 33*(3), 307–332.

Szelenyi, K. (2001). Minority student retention and academic achievement in community colleges. Retrieved from http://files.eric.ed.gov/fulltext/ED451859.pdf

Tinto, V. (1997). Colleges as communities: Taking research on student persistence seriously. *Review of Higher Education, 21*(2), 167–177.

Turner, C.S.V. (2002). Women of color in academe: Living with multiple marginality. *Journal of Higher Education, 73*(1), 74–93.

Wassmer, R., Moore, C., & Shulock, N. (2004). Effect of racial/ethnic composition on transfer rates in community colleges: Implications for policy and practice. *Research in Higher Education, 45*(6), 651–672.

Zhang, L. (2005). Advance to graduate education: The effect of college quality and undergraduate majors. *Review of Higher Education, 28*(3), 313–338.

TWO

Understanding and Meeting the Needs of Latinas/os in Higher Education

Cristobal Salinas, Jr.

It is projected that by 2050 Latinas/os will comprise 29% of the U.S. population (Pino, Martinez-Ramos, & Smith, 2012). Given the historical position and growing population of Latinas/os, it is essential to highlight the impact of the Latina/o population on the United States and to critically analyze the Latina/o students' experience in higher education. Latina/o students face barriers to higher education that include racial identity development, underrepresentation inside and outside the classroom, lack of same-race/ethnicity faculty and staff, family, and community transition. In this chapter, the author identifies possible theoretical frameworks that can enhance Latina/o students' development and describes best practices to facilitate effective engagement and learning.

Latinas/os: A Growing Population

The 2010 U.S. Census reported that more than half of the growth in the total population of the United States between 2000 and 2010 can be attributed to an increase in the Hispanic population. Latinas/os are the largest and fastest-growing marginalized population in the United States (Castellanos, Gloria, & Kamimura, 2005), logging an increase of 43% in this period (Pew Hispanic Center, 2011).

"Hispanic" and "Latina/o" are controversial terms used to categorize millions of people of varied racial, ethnic, national, and cultural heritage. The label Hispanic signifies an individual of Cuban, Mexican, Puerto Rican, South or Central American, and/or other Spanish cultural origin, regardless of race (Delgado-Romero, Manlove, Manlove, & Hernandez, 2006). Latinas/os are defined as individuals of Mexican, Latin American, or Caribbean heritage living in the United States (De Luca & Escoto, 2012). It should be noted that not all individuals may identify as Hispanic or Latina/o; most Latinas/os in the United States identify according to their country of origin or their parents' country of origin

(Retta & Brink, 2007). According to a 2010 U.S. Census Bureau report, more than 48.5 million people declared themselves to be of Hispanic origin. Of those who claimed Hispanic origin, 31.8 million were Mexican, 4.6 million were Puerto Rican, 1.7 million were Cuban, and 12.3 million listed themselves as Other Hispanic or Latina/o. Latinas/os number 50.5 million—16% of the U.S. population—and comprise the largest minority group in the United States.

The Latina/o population is growing, thereby enhancing its potential effect on society as a whole—in economics, health care, government, and education. By 2050, the Latina/o working-age population will have increased by 18 million over 2000 (Pino et al., 2012). As that population continues to grow and enters the workforce, it will be necessary to encourage more Latina/o high school students to enroll in higher education. It is projected that by 2030 Latinas/os will constitute the majority of elementary and high school students (Martinez & Aguirre, 2003), so colleges and universities are likely to see increased Latina/o enrollments.

"The 1.5 Generation" in Higher Education

Undocumented students come from society's most vulnerable segments, those marked by racism and poverty. There are an estimated 65,000 undocumented students (children born abroad who are not U.S. citizens or legal residents) who graduate from U.S. high schools each year. These children are guaranteed an education in U.S. K–12 public schools, but they are not guaranteed higher education (see also Russell, 2011; Salinas, 2013). According to an Urban Institute report, between 7,000 and 13,000 undocumented students enroll in college nationwide each year (Diaz-Strong, Gómez, Luna-Duarte, & Meiners, 2011). Many of these students face legal and financial barriers to higher education and limited opportunities for success because of segregation and unequal resources—such as the challenges of migration and discrimination and little or no access to financial aid. As a result of these challenges, students have generally depended on employment, limited scholarships, and family contributions.

Undocumented students are also known as the "1.5 generation" because they fall somewhere between the first and second generation of their national and cultural heritage. These 1.5 generation students "are not first-generation immigrants because they did not choose to migrate, but neither were they born and spent part of their childhood outside of the United States" (Gonzales, 2009, p. 7).

While the U.S. Census Bureau (2012) does not collect data on undocumented immigrants, it does offer an estimate of this group's numbers. In 2004, the bureau believed that there were 34 million undocumented immigrants residing in the United States. The Pew Hispanic Center (Passel & Cohn, 2008) estimates that there are approximately 11.9 million undocumented people in the United States (comprising 4% of the nation's total population). As of 2006, 56% of undocumented individuals were from Mexico, 22% from Central and South America and the Caribbean, 13% from Asia, 6% from Europe and Canada, and 3% from Africa or "Other" (Huber, Malagon, & Solorzano, 2009).

Historical Context of Latinas/os in Education

Higher education in the United States has a history of exclusion when it comes to marginalized and targeted populations (Thelin, 2011). Latina/o students are no exception and are still "seeking to have their educational needs met in a system that has often rejected them" (Marx & Larson, 2012, p. 261). Nonetheless, they have shared a long history of overcoming barriers.

The Latina/o community has demonstrated extraordinary achievements in the arts, business, education, government, labor, literature, military, science and technology, sports, and many others areas. Kanellos (1997) provides the following examples of Latinas/os making an impact in higher education and other areas:

- In 1513, the Escuela de Gramática (Grammar School), established in Puerto Rico, became the first school in an area that became part of the United States.
- In 1811, the first Spanish-language reading textbook for elementary school was published in the United States.
- In 1859, the College of San Miguel in Santa Fe became the first college in the territory of New Mexico dedicated to the higher education of Hispanics.
- In 1894, Manuel García was the first Mexican American to graduate from the University of Texas.
- In 1970, the Chicano Study Research Center at the University of California at Los Angeles became the first university-based Hispanic research center.
- In 1978, Dr. Tomás Rivera (1935–1984) became the first Hispanic chancellor of the University of California system.
- In the U.S. Supreme Court's 1982 *Plyler v. Doe* case, children of undocumented workers in Texas were given the right to free public education.
- In 1988, Lauro Cavazos became the first Hispanic U.S. Secretary of Education.
- In 1989, Elsa Gómez became the first Hispanic woman to be named leader of a 4-year arts college when she assumed the position of president of Kean College in New Jersey.

Latina/o leadership in education has created opportunities for success in higher education for today's Latina/o students. Even though Latinas/os have made an impact on the U.S. educational system, it is still unclear why Latina/o students are not successfully retained and graduated at the same rate as other populations.

The Latina/o Student Experience

Latina/o students are often classified as a single group, even though they come from many different countries, each with its own unique culture and traditions. Oftentimes we hear generalizations such as "all Latinas/os are Mexican." This is an example of how Latina/o students are "Mexicanized" and lumped into a single group (Gandara & Contreras, 2009). Similarly, Latina/o students are more likely to be "Cubanized" in Florida or "Salvadoranized" in Washington, DC.

Latina/o students enjoy both the privileges and challenges of constructing identity development by combining one or two races/ethnicities, and they sometimes choose one over the other (i.e., Mexican, Mexican American, Chicana/o, Latina/o, or Hispanic). In addition, they have to choose other social identities: "An intersectional approach to identity allows for recognition of all social identities when constructing identity development" (Salinas & Beatty, 2013, p. 24). Intersectionality is "an analytical lens that allows for the integration of multiple identities" (Gallegos & Ferdman, 2012, p. 55). Talking with Latina/o students about social identities can lead to an examination of the intersectionality of social identities, family, history, traditions, and subcultures—all of which may be important to them. Gender identity/expression, sexual orientation, size/appearance, age, social/economic class, religion/spirituality, race/ethnicity, (dis)ability, educational background, language, immigration status, and other social identities are valuable but uncommon in discussions with Latina/o students.

Latina/o students and their families are placed at a disadvantage in the college admissions process and the overall college experience for a variety of reasons. These may include being first-generation students and coming from low socioeconomic backgrounds and non-English-speaking families (Gandara & Contreras, 2009). Latina/o students are challenged to explain aspects of the higher education system to their families—for example, financial aid, the academic curriculum, and leadership involvement. The admissions and financial aid processes do not easily translate into Spanish; thus, how do Latina/o students describe the terminology and the educational system to their parents? Most important, how do Latina/o students translate their own experiences? Many Latina/o parents do not speak English or have a minimal understanding of the students' college experience. When Latina/o students repeatedly have to translate their educational experiences, they can experience a feeling of "cultural loss" or "crossover." These students might ask themselves the question: "Am I no longer a Latina/o?" After having to constantly repeat their college experiences, the cultural loss or crossover feeling can occur because students might feel invisible to society, family members, and sometimes even the student-self.

Human life constructs and uses cultural terms. It creates understanding of and meaning for the cultural lexicon through interpersonal interactions (Ainslie, 2009) and experiences, and humans perform/live within multiple and current positions of privilege and oppression (Patton, Shahjahan, & Osei-Kofi, 2010). In situations where loss is unclear, incomplete, or partial, "cultural loss" occurs because of the degree to which mainstream American culture varies as a function of countless factors: location, language, friends, and family. Further, "crossover" is a process in which beloved people, places, and things are left behind (Falicov, 2009). When cultural loss or crossover occurs, Latina/o students have to constantly monitor if they have lost themselves or if they have lost their culture. They may even question whether they are no longer Latina/o, Hispanic, Chicana/o, or American because they might feel invisible to society, family members, and themselves, often as a result of having crossed intellectual, psychological, and emotional boundaries.

The college journey is often puzzling to Latina/o students, especially when they first arrive on campus. They may face academic or social challenges related to time management, financial concerns, homesickness, depression, choosing a major, oppression, and discrimination because of their immigrant status, language, skin color, and appearance. It may be a struggle for Latina/o students to leave their families and community behind to attend college. For many of them it is hard to navigate their educational career, since they often have to create their own path to success without guidance from family members who themselves did not seek higher education or grow up in the United States. Latina/o students are "often the first in their families to go to school" and therefore "cannot rely on their families for information" (Gloria & Castellanos, 2012, p. 83).

The literature tells us that family and community are important to Latina/o students. Many Latina/o students are expected to help the family, especially if there are younger siblings. They also are expected to serve as translators for their parents if their parents do not speak

English. In addition, for students coming from low socioeconomic backgrounds, their moving out often places yet another financial burden on the family.

Communicating in Spanish with other Latina/o students is highly important. Spanish-speaking students are challenged to speak Spanish, as there is often a lack of representation of Spanish-speaking Latina/o administrators, faculty, and staff. This also limits mentorship, role models, educational curricula, and programming for Latina/o students. Because of the challenges and oppression that Latina/o students typically face, they may experience other internal questions: What does racism mean? Where is the sense of Latina/o community in the United States? How have Latina/o leaders and scholars made an impact in the United States? Are society and communities run mostly by Caucasians (Salinas & Beatty, 2013)?

Latina/o students need a welcoming and safe space to celebrate their culture and the intersectionality of their social identities. They require a commitment of support, academic resources, and preparation if they are to succeed in a diverse environment, especially at Predominately White Institutions (PWIs). In addition, colleges and universities should provide a space where administrators, faculty, and staff are involved in the success of Latina/o students, and where students create and call their college experience "a home away from home."

Theoretical Framework

Familia, respeto, simpatía, personalismo, cultural fatalism, religion, and spirituality (Canul, 2003; Hernandez, 2005; Marin & Marin, 1991; Ontai-Grzebik & Raffaelli, 2004; Santiago-Rivera, Arredondo, & Gallardo-Cooper, 2002; Sue & Sue, 1990) are aspects of Latina/o culture that influence the values and behaviors of Latina/o students and create a world inherently different from that of sometimes-naïve academic leaders. Latina/o students' marginalization through the rejection of their cultural values and a lack of a sense of belonging within PWI structures can "evoke painful personal histories and a strong historical consciousness of being excluded" (Gonzales, 2001, p. 132).

Gonzales, Salinas, and Evans (2011) outline two prominent approaches to understanding Latina/o student identity development: Ferdman and Gallegos's (2001) model of Latino identity development and Torres's (1999) bicultural orientation model. Ferdman and Gallegos identify six orientations that Latinas/os use in constructing and presenting their identities. These identities are influenced by several factors, including family, reference group, educational experiences, peer interaction, and physical appearance. Torres's model offers a four-quadrant typology based on the individual's level of acculturation in relation to his/her ethnic identity. Torres's (2003) research suggests that the identity of Latina/o students is shaped by the environment in which they grew up, family influence, generational status, self-perception, and status in society. Changes in identity can result from cultural dissonance and diverse relationships in college, which impact long-term leadership development and professional socialization processes.

There is a strong need to support Latina/o students through culturally appropriate means to increase enrollment, retention, and graduation rates of Latina/o students and to enhance their potential leadership options. Villalpando (2004) suggests that Latino Critical Theory (LatCrit) is another way by which administrators, faculty, and staff can "fully understand and more appropriately respond to the academic and sociocultural needs" (p. 42) of Latina/o students. LatCrit provides a framework for recognizing patterns, practices, and policies of racial inequality that continue to exist in more indirect and covert ways, and helps to dismantle them and remove them as barriers to the success of Latina/o students.

Latina/o Student Engagement

Student engagement is critical to the success of Latina/o students inside and outside the classroom. "What students do during college counts more for what they learn and whether they will persist in college than who they are or even where they go to college" (Kuh, Kinzie, Schuh, & Whitt, 2010, p. 8). It is necessary to engage Latina/o students in critical conversations, research opportunities, study groups, and social activities with administrators, faculty, staff, and peers to promote active learning. Administrators, faculty, and staff must maintain high expectations for Latina/o students and continue to respect their diverse talents and learning preferences.

Engaging Latina/o students in programs and curricula can be challenging. The challenge occurs when administrators, faculty, and staff are unaware of the issues and struggles faced by Latina/o students. Success for Latina/o students is determined by a positive cultural climate once they enroll and participate in culturally relevant activities (Longerbeam, Sedlacek, & Alatorre, 2004). In order to understand the experience of Latina/o students, one may begin by asking: "What is the experience of Latina/o students (and other social identities) at a hegemonic campus?"

Latina/o students' social identities affect their engagement and academic performance. There is a need to document not only effective educational practices inside and outside the classroom, but also to document the unique challenges faced by Latina/o students. Institutions need to assess their campus and classroom climates for Latina/o students, distribute the data, and take responsibility for educational quality and more effective organization of students' academic and social experiences (Kuh et al., 2010).

"Students learn firsthand how to think about and solve practical problems by interacting with faculty inside and outside the classroom. As a result, teachers become role models, mentors, and guides for lifelong learning" (Kuh et al., 2010, p. 207). Accessible and responsive faculty and staff influence and empower Latina/o students. Linking students, faculty, and staff enriches the educational experience. In order to continue promoting Latina/o students' success, institutions should provide more faculty training and development; recruit, hire, and retain Latina/o faculty and staff; and create Latina/o affinity groups for faculty and staff to provide more visibility, role models, and mentors for Latina/o students.

Self-discovery occurs when Latina/o students are challenged by the intersection of race and culture and the way in which society believes Latina/o students should explore an institution. It is the institution's responsibility to provide Latina/o students with opportunities to collaborate with faculty on research projects, to engage in peer mentorship, to validate race/ethnicity, to create Latina/o learning communities and advisory committees to ease the transition to college, and to help them build loyalty to the institution so that it will engage them until graduation and, later, profit from their contribution as active alumni.

Best Practices for Latina/o Students' Success

It is important for Latina/o students to learn about the complex nature of their own social and cultural identities and leadership possibilities within a created safe space. College campuses need to rethink their practices and provide an environment in which individuals of diverse backgrounds intentionally interact. The overarching goal should be to provide opportunities for collaboration across racial boundaries that challenge students to explore other cultures.

Such a mission, if successful, will help mold them into better professionals, better people, and better citizens of the world.

Retention of Latina/o students has been one of the top priorities of many college administrations. Campus programming should address these concerns, using Astin's (1996) and Tinto's (1993) theoretical constructs. Astin's (1996) theory of student involvement and Tinto's (1993) theory of student departure identify factors that contribute to research practices and assessment activities related to first-year programs and courses. Astin's theory suggests that student involvement is a function of three forms: involvement in academics, involvement with faculty, and involvement with student peer groups. Together these three levels of involvement can contribute to student engagement, retention, and overall satisfaction. Tinto's theory of student departure suggests that students who are not successfully integrated into the college environment will eventually leave the campus.

In 2012, staff and students from Iowa State University's Multicultural Student Affairs Office developed the Latina/o Leadership Retreat, an overnight retreat for freshman and sophomore Latina/o students interested in building their leadership skills and connecting with other Latina/o students. Using a strengths-based approach, the retreat has three foci: building community among Latina/o undergraduate students, developing and cultivating leadership capacity among the Latina/o student population on campus, and promoting social justice awareness. Student leaders coordinate the retreat each year by urging the previous year's participants to take a leadership role on the planning committee. During the retreat, students participate in activities that promote self-awareness regarding their strengths—including cultural strengths—followed by "scenario" workshops in which they have the opportunity to work together in small teams as well as in a large-group format to address actual campus dilemmas experienced by Latina/o students and student organizations (Lozano, 2013).

The University of Texas at Austin is currently in its third year of implementation of the Project MALES student-mentoring program. MALES fosters discussion and relationship-building among male undergraduate mentors and male high school students in the local school district. This model is a research-informed initiative that highlights mentoring as a way to leverage social capital among males of color at various points in the educational pipeline. The goal is to build a stronger college-focused culture among this group of students (Project MALES, 2013). The basic structure entails a "near-peer" mentoring philosophy, with college freshmen being paired with high school freshmen to allow for longer-term bonds to develop. The mentoring model takes a dynamic and intergenerational approach to promoting achievement and retaining male students of color both in secondary and postsecondary educational settings. This model brings together three key groups: male professionals as role models, current Latino male college students (both upperclassmen and first-years), and younger Latino male students in local high schools (Project MALES, 2013).

USC El Centro Chicano was funded at the University of Southern California in 1972. For over 40 years, it has fostered a vibrant community of critically thinking, socially conscious Chicana/o and Latina/o leaders who provide students with personal, social, and academic support through graduation and beyond. El Centro offers student advocacy, personal support, assistance for Latina/o student groups, and transition beyond USC programming (El Centro Chicano, 2013). The *Latino Resource Handbook & Planner*, written in 2005, provides information about El Centro's programs; 20+ Latina/o student undergraduate and graduate organizations; Latina/o faculty and staff; scholarships, research, and internship opportunities; graduate school assistance; tips for new students; and other key resources.

In addition, the Latino Floor: El Sol y La Luna residential program is designed to ease the transition to college for freshmen Latina/o students and empower them to become campus leaders (El Centro Chicano, 2013). The Black & Latino New Student Symposium, Latino Trojan Family Reunion, and the Latino Student Empowerment Conference all focus on providing students with the tools needed to succeed at USC through workshops by student leaders, faculty, staff, and alumni. Other culturally enriching and empowering programs include La Posada: Celebrating Latin American Holiday Traditions and Giving Back, L.A. Power Trips, the Latino Honor Society, and Project ReMiX: Exploring the Mixed Race Generation—each with the aim of offering students and their families a sense of community, value, pride, awareness, consciousness raising, and knowledge about their identities (El Centro Chicano, 2013).

Excelencia in Education, a not-for-profit organization promoting Latino success in higher education, is committed to a better understanding of what is effective in increasing Latina/o students' success on college campuses, as well as identifying evidence-based practices. *Excelencia* in Education compiles an annual list of honors programs and departments that increase academic opportunities and enhance achievement for Latina/o students. The examples of excellence are based on practices that serve as resources for programs and institutions considering efforts to improve service, practice, and success for Latina/o students in higher education (*Excelencia* in Education, 2012).

College campuses need to invest in more programs that provide individualized support, academic resources, and preparation for graduate school or the professional world. These programs should be structured to enhance, encourage, and support students' academic, social, and cultural activities throughout their collegiate careers. In order to promote continuous learning, achievement, and integrity, programs should be designed to help Latina/o students adapt to college life, meet the institution's challenge of academic growth, take advantage of opportunities that aim to enhance social and leadership skills, and broaden perspectives that develop an appreciation for diversity—all the while becoming competent professionals and contributing citizens of the world.

Conclusion

Continuous reflection on the historical context of the Latina/o community will lead to learning, discovering, and filtering the meaning of powerful anti-discriminatory vocabularies. Administrators, faculty, and staff have the obligation to support and learn about the developmental experiences of marginalized and targeted populations by engaging in work that attempts to improve the climate for those populations in academic settings and society—with a purposeful emphasis on the Latina/o community.

As Cesar Chavez said, "You cannot un-educate the person who has learned to read. You cannot humiliate the person who feels pride. You cannot oppress the people who are not afraid anymore." We must continue to educate each other about feelings, beliefs, and attitudes regarding Latina/o students by asking the appropriate questions. Do colleges perpetuate stereotypes? They need to create safe spaces in which to discuss beliefs and stereotypes, engage in active learning, and develop critical thinking about stereotypes and inequalities in the Latina/o community. How does one promote equity? Finally, universities need to empower faculty and staff groups to understand and use cultural values to develop more optimal learning environments for the Latina/o community. How can they approach Latina/o students in a more culturally relevant manner?

"Education status is an important determinant of academic achievement in the United States" (Pino et al., 2012, p. 18). Latina/o faculty are key to a successful college experience for Latina/o students (Pino et al., 2012); more Latina/o mentors in higher education are needed to help support success for Latina/o undergraduate and graduate students. This chapter has encouraged administrators, faculty, and staff to engage in and learn more about the reality and challenges that Latina/o students face. Working with a historically marginalized and oppressed community is hard work. Administrators, faculty, and staff need to advocate for the Latina/o community to ensure both Latina/o student success and America's own success in the future.

References

Ainslie, R.C. (2009). The plasticity of culture and psychodynamic and psychosocial processes in Latino immigrant families. In M.M. Suárez-Orozco & M.M. Páez (Eds.), *Latinos remaking America* (pp. 289–301). Berkeley, CA: University of California Press.

Astin, A.W. (1996). Involvement in learning revisited: Lessons we have learned. *Journal of College Student Development, 37*(2), 123–133.

Canul, K.H. (2003). Latina/o cultural values and identity and the academy: Latinas navigating through the administrative role. In J. Castellanos & L. Jones (Eds.), *The majority in the minority* (pp. 167–175). Sterling, VA: Stylus.

Castellanos, J., Gloria, A.M., & Kamimura, M. (2005). *The Latina/o pathway to the Ph.D.: Abriendo Caminos.* Sterling, VA: Stylus.

El Centro Chicano. (2013). *Establishing El Centro Chicano.* University of Southern California, Los Angeles. Retrieved from http://sait.usc.edu/elcentro/about/history/establishing-el-centro-chicano.aspx

De Luca, S.M., & Escoto, E.R. (2012). The recruitment and support of Latino faculty for tenure and promotion. *Journal of Hispanic Higher Education, 11*(1), 29–40.

Delgado-Romero, E.A., Manlove, A.N., Manlove, J.D., & Hernandez, C.A. (2006). Controversial issues in the recruitment and retention of Latino/a faculty. *Journal of Hispanic Higher Education, 6*(1), 34–51.

Diaz-Strong, D., Gómez, C., Luna-Duarte, M.E., & Meiners, E.R. (2011). Purged: Undocumented students, financial aid, polices, and access to higher education. *Journal of Hispanic Higher Education, 10*(2), 107–119.

Excelencia in Education. (2012). *What works for Latino student success in higher education.* Washington, DC: Author.

Falicov, C.J. (2009). Ambiguous loss: Risk and resilience in Latino immigrant families. In M.M. Suárez-Orozco & M.M. Páez (Eds.), *Latinos remaking America* (pp. 274–288). Berkeley, CA: University of California Press.

Ferdman, B.M., & Gallegos, P.I. (2001). Racial identity development and Latinos in the United States. In C.L. Wijeyesinghe & B.W. Jackson II (Eds.), *New perspectives on racial identity development: A theoretical and practical anthology* (pp. 32–66). New York, NY: New York University Press.

Gallegos, P.I., & Ferdman, B.M. (2012). Latina and Latino ethnoracial identity orientation. In C.L. Wijeyesinghe & B.W. Jackson II (Eds.), *New perspectives on racial identity development: Integrating emerging frameworks* (pp. 51–80). New York, NY: New York University Press.

Gandara, P., & Contreras, F. (2009). *The Latino educational crisis: The consequences of failed social policies.* Cambridge, MA: Harvard University Press.

Gloria, A.M., & Castellanos, J. (2012). Desafíos y bendiciones: A multiperspective examination of the educational experiences and coping responses of first-generation college Latina students. *Journal of Hispanic Higher Education, 11*(1), 82–99.

Gonzales, G.R. (2009). Young lives on hold: The college dreams of undocumented students. *College Board.* Retrieved from http://advocacy.collegeboard.org//sites/default/files/young-lives-on-hold-college-board.pdf

Gonzales, M.J. (2001). *Generational transmission of organizational inheritance in a corporate setting: A case study* (Unpublished doctoral dissertation). Washington State University, Pullman.

Gonzales, M.J., Salinas, C., & Evans, N. (2011, November). *Re-conceptualizing higher education leadership development for Latino/a graduate students: Converting aspiration to attainment.* Paper presented at the Association for the Study of Higher Education Conference (ASHE), Charlotte, NC.

Hernandez, F. (2005). *The racial identity development of selected Latino school principals and its relation to their leadership practice* (Unpublished doctoral dissertation). University of Wisconsin, Madison.

Huber, L.P., Malagon, M.C., & Solorzano, D.G. (2009). Struggling for opportunities: Undocumented AB 540 Latina/o education pipeline. *UCLA Chicano Studies Research Center, 13*, 1–13.

Kanellos, N. (1997). *Hispanic firsts: 500 years of extraordinary achievement*. Detroit, MI: Visible Ink Press.

Kuh, G.D., Kinzie, J., Schuh, J.H., & Whitt, E. (Eds.). (2010). *Student success in college: Creating conditions that matter*. San Francisco, CA: Jossey-Bass.

Longerbeam, S.D., Sedlacek, W.E., & Alatorre, H.M. (2004). In their own voices: Latino student retention. *NASPA Journal, 41*(3), 538–550.

Lozano, S.A. (2013). *Re-imagining Latina/o student success at ISU: Student perspective on leadership development*. (Unpublished capstone). Iowa State University, Ames.

Marin, G., & Marin, B.V. (1991). *Research with Hispanic populations*. Newbury Park, CA: Sage.

Martinez, R.O., & Aguirre, A. (2003). Resource shares and educational attainment: The U.S. Latino population in the twenty-first century. In D.J. Leon (Ed.), *Latinos in higher education* (pp. 37–55). Oxford, UK: Elsevier Science.

Marx, S., & Larson, L.L. (2012). Taking off the color-blind glasses: Recognizing and supporting Latina/o students in a predominantly White school. *Educational Administration Quarterly, 48*(2), 259–303.

Ontai-Grzebik, L., & Raffaelli, M. (2004). Individual and social influences on ethnic identity among Latino young adults. *Journal of Adolescent Research, 19*(5), 559–575.

Passel, J., & Cohn, D. (2008, October 2). Trends in unauthorized immigration: Undocumented inflow now trails legal inflow. Pew Research Hispanic Center. Retrieved from http://www.pewhispanic.org/2008/10/02/trends-in-unauthorized-immigration/

Patton, L.D., Shahjahan, R.A., & Osei-Kofi, N. (2010). Introduction to the emergent approaches to diversity and social justice in higher education. *Equity & Excellence in Education, 43*(3), 265–278.

Pew Hispanic Center. (2011). *Hispanics account for more than half of nation's growth in past decade. Census 2010: 50 million Latinos.* Retrieved from: http://www.pewhispanic.org/2011/03/24/hispanics-account-for-more-than-half-of-nations-growth-in-past-decade/

Pino, N.W., Martinez-Ramos, G.P., & Smith, W.L. (2012). Latinos, the academic ethic, and the transition to college. *Journal of Latinos and Education, 11*(1), 17–31.

Project MALES. (2013). *Project MALES mentoring to achieve Latino educational success*. University of Texas at Austin. Retrieved from http://ddce.utexas.edu/projectmales/mentor-program/

Retta, E., & Brink, C. (2007). *Latino or Hispanic panic: Which term should we use?* Cross Culture Communications. Retrieved from http://www.crossculturecommunications.com/latino-hispanic.pdf

Russell, A. (2011). State policies regarding undocumented college students: A narrative of unresolved issues, ongoing debate and missed opportunities. *American Association of State Colleges and Universities*, 1–10.

Salinas, C. (2013). Social justice from a point of view of an 8-year-old boy. *Living in Color: Broad, A Feminist & Social Justice Magazine, 55*(1), 70–72.

Salinas, C., & Beatty, C. (2013). Constructing our own definition of masculinity: An intersectionality approach. In Z. Foste (Ed.), *Looking forward: A dialogue on college men and masculinities* (pp. 24–29). Washington, DC: College Student Educator (ACPA); Standing Committee on Men and Masculinities.

Santiago-Rivera, A.L., Arredondo, P., & Gallardo-Cooper, M. (2002). *Counseling Latinos and la familia: A practical guide*. Thousand Oaks, CA: Sage.

Sue, D.W., & Sue, D. (1990). *Counseling the culturally different: Theory and practice*. Hoboken, NJ: Wiley.

Thelin, J.R. (2011). *A history of American higher education*. Baltimore, MD: Johns Hopkins University Press.

Tinto, V. (1993). *Leaving college: Rethinking the causes and curse of student attrition*. Chicago, IL: University of Chicago Press.

Torres, V. (1999). Validation of a bicultural orientation model for Hispanic college students. *Journal of College Student Development, 40*(3), 285–298.

Torres, V. (2003). Influences on ethnic identity development of Latino college students in the first two years of college. *Journal of College Student Development, 44*(4), 532–547.

U.S. Census Bureau. (2010). *Resident population by Hispanic origin and state*. Retrieved from http://www.census.gov/prod/2011pubs/12statab/pop.pdf

U.S. Census Bureau. (2012). *International immigration*. Retrieved from http://www.census.gov/population/intmigration/about/faq.html#Q3

Villalpando, O. (2004). Practical considerations of critical race theory and Latino critical theory for Latino college students. *New Directions for Student Services, 2004*(105), 41–50.

THREE

Native American Students in Higher Education

Robin Minthorn and Heather J. Shotton

Introduction

Understanding the lived experiences of Native American college students in higher education is important as administrators, faculty, staff, and current graduate students in higher education seek to better serve and support all college student populations. The following chapter will encourage conversation and learning about Native American students in higher education, including the general experiences of Native students, building community on campus, and transitioning back home ("giving back"). Finally, the chapter will offer recommendations for improving how colleges and universities serve Native American students. It should be noted here that research continues to emerge regarding the Native American college student experience; therefore, there are no citations for some statements, as supporting research does not currently exist. Statements are instead informed by the authors' experiences as Native scholars who have spent several years working with Native students in higher education.

General Experiences of Native American College Students

This section will address the general experiences of Native American college students in order to afford a better understanding of the challenges facing this population. Issues such as lack of representation, invisibility, and encounters with stereotypes will all be addressed, as well as the diversity of Native students and their shared experiences in higher education. Each of these topics serves to provide perspectives on Native American college students and their shared experiences.

Being Invisible or Least Represented

Discussions of Native Americans in higher education are often centered on the issue of representation—or, more appropriately, underrepresentation. In fact, numerous authors have addressed the issue of underrepresentation of Native American college students (Pavel, 1999; Snyder, Dillow, & Hoffman, 2008; Snyder, Tan, & Hoffman, 2004; Tierney, 1992). Though enrollment of Native students in institutions of higher education has more than doubled in the last 30 years (NCES, 2007), Native American students remain underrepresented and account for only 1% of the total college student population in the United States (Aud et al., 2011). While underrepresentation is a serious concern, by itself it does not fully capture the deeper issue of Native Americans in postsecondary education—that of invisibility. Underrepresentation addresses one piece of the puzzle, namely, enrollment of Native American students. However, invisibility more adequately addresses the multiple ways in which Native students are often excluded from the higher education landscape.

The issue of invisibility of Natives in higher education is a long-standing concern. In U.S. institutions of higher education, particularly Non-Native Colleges and Universities (NNCUs), Native American students are rendered invisible in multiple ways. Shotton, Lowe, and Waterman (2013) explain that, as Native people, "we are often excluded from institutional data and reporting, omitted from the curriculum, absent from the research and literature, and virtually written out of the higher education story" (p. 2). Furthermore, Native American students are often lumped in with other underrepresented populations (i.e., African Americans, Asian Americans, Latinas/os), and their unique status as citizens of sovereign nations is ignored. This exclusion of Native Americans, either by omitting or ignoring the population altogether, has a detrimental effect on Native American students and perpetuates a message that they do not have a place in higher education.

Fryberg and Townsend (2008) explain that invisibility is a much more intentional act that moves beyond the issue of lack of representation and involves an active "writing out" of the story of a particular group. Moreover, the "writing out" of certain groups serves to maintain and perpetuate a status quo that benefits the dominant group (Fryberg & Townsend, 2008). The invisibility of Native Americans perpetuates an ignorance of Native Americans in general and Native American students in particular. The result is a lack of serious dialogue about appropriate solutions for serving Native students (Shotton, Lowe, & Waterman, 2013). Moreover, NNCUs often fail to recognize the unique status of Native American tribes as sovereign nations—and Native students as citizens of those sovereign nations—causing them to miss the mark altogether when it comes to this particular population.

When the historical relationship between tribal nations and educational systems is examined, one can begin to understand this pattern of invisibility. Historically, the relationship between education and tribal nations has been tenuous; education, as a matter of early policy, was utilized as a tool to erase Native American people and to eradicate the "Indian problem." Today, Native Americans continue to confront attempts to erase the acknowledgment of their existence. Historical education policy toward Native people sanctions the idea that we are not supposed to be here, and the issue of invisibility in higher education continues to perpetuate this message.

On any given NNCU campus, Native American students are hard-pressed to find their place within the institution because, when they look in the institutional mirror, they do not see their own reflections. They are excluded from institutional imagery, and oftentimes when they are represented, it is in negative, stereotypical ways (e.g., mascots or historical images).

Additionally, Native Americans are erased from institutional memory, where the role of Native people in the story and history of the institution is ignored or omitted. This is particularly troubling given that many of our campuses are linked in some way to tribal populations, yet many institutions still refuse to acknowledge the place of Native Americans in their stories. When institutions of higher education fail to include Native Americans in their stories, they perpetuate the message that there is no place for Native Americans and that they do not belong.

Misconceptions and Stereotypes

One of the consequences of invisibility is that misconceptions abound about Native American students in general, particularly in NNCUs. The relative invisibility of Native Americans in general means that most Americans form their views of Native American people from information acquired indirectly from sources such as the media (Fryberg, Markus, Oyserman, & Stone, 2010). Considering that most Americans have not had direct, personal experience with Native Americans (Pewewardy, 1995), it is not surprising that Native students come up against stereotypes and misconceptions on NNCU campuses. These misconceptions, such as that Native students attend college for free, that all tribes have casinos, or the belief that Native Americans share one common culture, are all challenges Native American students must face at NNCUs. Such misconceptions can be encountered in the classroom, with faculty and administrators, or with other students. Moreover, such encounters are often further exacerbated by experiences with stereotypes and hostile campus environments.

Experiences with stereotypes and racism are not uncommon for Native American students. In fact, research points to the fact that racism is prevalent on college campuses and that many university policies are not supportive of Native American students (Castagno & Lee, 2007; Pewewardy & Frey, 2002, 2004). Kirkness and Barnhardt (1991) indicate that racism and institutional discrimination serve as barriers for Native American students. Exposure to stereotypes has also been found to undermine positive feelings of worth and lead to lower self-esteem in Native American students (Fryberg et al., 2010). Struggles with racism and stereotypes are common experiences for many Native American students, and they must be addressed if we are to better serve this population. If NNCUs are to improve the college experience of Native American students, they must work to acknowledge, understand, and confront misconceptions and stereotypes—both those that are personally held and those that are perpetuated by the institution. This is a vital step in creating an inclusive and welcoming environment for Native American students and for fostering their academic success.

Diversity of the Native Students and Common Experiences

One of the most important things to understand about Native American students is that they do not represent one singular culture or experience. Native American students represent various tribes and come from varied backgrounds. One must understand that "Native people live on reservations, in border towns, and in urban areas. Many are traditional, many are not, and many practice their traditions in addition to Christianity. There is no one physical characteristic that sets Native people apart" (Shotton et al., 2013). The Native American population is very diverse, with over 560 federally recognized tribes in the United States (*Federal Register*, 2010), and each tribe has its own distinct culture, language, and history. It is thus important to recognize that the current and historical experiences of Native Americans vary greatly (Brayboy, Fann, Castagno, & Solyom, 2012).

While there is not a single Native American culture or experience, there are some shared experiences as they relate to Native Americans and higher education. It has been well documented that Native American students arrive at NNCUs with unique cultural perspectives that are not always consonant with the dominant Western culture of the academy (Benjamin, Chambers, & Reiterman, 1993; Huffman, 2001, 2010; Reyhner, 1992). This cultural conflict is thought to reveal a clash between the values, behaviors, and political economic power possessed by Native American students and mainstream educational institutions (Huffman, 2003). Often when a Native student enters an NNCU, he/she encounters a disruptive cultural experience (Tierney, 1992). Cultural conflict has been well documented. However, more recent research has pointed to the important role that culture plays in the success of Native students (Deyhle, 1995; Huffman, 2001, 2003, 2010; Jackson & Smith, 2001; Waterman, 2007, 2012). Many scholars have argued that Native American students draw upon their cultural identities as sources of strength in order to succeed in college (Huffman, 2003, 2010; Jackson & Smith, 2001; Waterman, 2007, 2012). Thus, it must be understood that culture is a central part of the experiences of Native students in higher education (Shotton et al., 2013).

In addition, family, community, and spirituality have all been found to be important for Native students (Benjamin et al., 1993; Guillory & Wolverton, 2008; HeavyRunner & Marshall, 2003; Kirkness & Barnhardt, 1991; Waterman, 2012). In particular, the value of community is key for many Native students. The importance of community can be tied to students' home community as well as the campus community, particularly the Native campus community. Waterman (2007, 2012) found that staying connected to one's home community is an integral part of Native student persistence. On campus, ties to a Native community serve to provide a safe space for Native American students to express who they are and provide much-needed support (Shotton, Yellowfish, & Cintron, 2010). Community often serves as an anchor and source of support for Native American students, keeping them tied to their tribal culture and supporting their identity and experience as Native American persons in higher education. Considering the significant role of community for Native students, it is imperative that college personnel understand how to build community for Native American students on campus.

Building Community on Campus

The following section will highlight services that administrators, practitioners, and current graduate student affairs professionals can use that work to benefit Native American students in higher education. They include leadership experiences/opportunities, mentorship/peer mentoring, Historically Native American Fraternities and Sororities (HNAFSs), connecting to Native faculty (and allies), and home-going. Each of these forms of service has been shown to have a positive impact on Native American students in higher education when they are present and supported on campus.

Leadership Experiences/Opportunities

There is a growing need for more culturally relevant conceptions of leadership in programming practices and student organizations that assist Native American college students (Williams,

2012). Oftentimes on NNCU campuses, leadership development programs and student affairs departments utilize Western modes of leadership, and those theories and models have typically excluded the Native American college student population (Williams, 2012). This predicament calls for a better understanding of how leadership concepts and development are viewed within the Native American student community. Minthorn (2014) identifies three values that are important for Indigenous leadership across Native college student leaders within five geographic regions in the United States: the importance of being committed, community, and collaboration. Not only is it vital to understand what values of leadership Native students bring with them to campus; it is also imperative to be sensitive to the impact of programming, workshops, and conferences that target Native students. For example, a conference that seeks to serve Native students should focus on creating positive self-images, providing Native role models, and building Native community (Minthorn, Wanger, & Shotton, 2013).

There are numerous opportunities available for Native American college students to gain leadership experience within Native student organizations on campus and nationally within their own disciplines through internships, which allow them to acquire practical skills while giving back to their tribal or broader Native community. Some of these opportunities include currently existing Native American student organizations that range from general, cultural, and social groups to discipline-specific organizations, as well as Native student centers. There are also national internship programs such as the Washington Internship for Native Students (WINS), the American Indian Science and Engineering Society (AISES), the Udall Internship program, and tribal-specific summer internship opportunities (e.g., the Cherokee Nation, Osage Nation, and Navajo Nation) that exist to provide college students with experience in developing their career and leadership skills.

Leadership development is an important aspect of the college student experience, and this is true for Native American college students as well. Because of the unique perspectives of the Native American student, it is important that NNCUs gain a better understanding of how leadership development is viewed within the Native student community. When NNCUs begin to take a more active role in understanding the values attributed to Indigenous leadership for Native college students and what works for this student population surrounding leadership development, it can engender empowerment of Native American college students on campus (Williams, 2012).

Mentorship/Peer Mentoring

Peer-mentoring programs have been found to have a positive impact on Native American college students and their persistence in higher education (Anagnopoulos, 2006; Gloria & Robinson Kurpius, 2001; Jackson, Smith, & Hill, 2003; Shotton, Oosahwe, & Cintron, 2007). Peer mentoring for Native college students has been done through formal mentoring programs on campus that match lower- and upper-class students with similar (or identical) tribal affiliation, academic majors, or interests, such as peer-mentoring programs that have been created at the University of Oklahoma and Oklahoma State University. These peer-mentoring programs also provide opportunities for Native college students to gather on a regular basis for social, cultural, and academic-related activities. Peer-mentoring programs afford active engagement of Native American college students. This may include students who strongly identify with their cultural identity, students who do not strongly identify with their cultural identity, and/or students who are not academically prepared for college when they enter institutions of higher education. There are also opportunities for Native American faculty and allies on campus to participate and mentor upperclassmen and graduate students who may also want guidance as they prepare for their professional careers. Peer-mentoring programs specifically designed for Native American college students can help increase participation on campus and provide a sense of belonging that is often missing in current campus programming (Shotton et al., 2007).

There are other mentoring programs that exist on NNCU campuses that are not peer-mentor specific, but discipline-specific or college- or department-based. For instance, there are programs in psychology, medicine, nursing, and Native American Studies in which the mentoring of Native American college students is done with current faculty or professionals to ensure their success on (and off) campus.

It is important for Native American student centers, multicultural programs, and student affairs offices to support these initiatives and provide the necessary fiscal and physical resources for them (whether peer mentoring or academically based) to ensure a strong foundation and to engage Native American students, faculty, and staff on campus. Mentoring and outreach to Native American college students helps to strengthen the social, cultural, and academic connections that are needed for them to persist and be successful as they graduate and transition back to their communities.

Historically Native American Fraternities and Sororities (HNAFSs)[1]

In the last 20 years there has been an evolution in the Historically Native American Fraternity and Sorority (HNAFS) movement in terms of providing an alternative to traditional Greek organizations (Oxendine, Oxendine, & Minthorn, 2013). This alternative is one that incorporates Native American cultural values into the mission, purpose, and activities of fraternities and sororities. Often, the founding of each HNAFS was aimed at addressing issues of retention and missing pieces of Native student support on campus (Oxendine et al., 2013). There are currently seven known HNAFSs in the United States. Some have achieved a national presence with multiple chapters on NNCUs, including Alpha Pi Omega, Inc. (est. 1994), Phi Sigma Nu, and Gamma Delta Pi (est. 2001) (Oxendine et al., 2013).

There are strengths that HNAFSs bring to the greater Greek community by adding diversity and richness to the purposes and functions of these organizations. Some of the benefits of HNAFSs are that they foster retention, provide support systems, promote cultural identity on campus, and serve the local and surrounding tribal communities (Oxendine et al., 2013). Yet there are also barriers that HNAFSs have encountered on their own campuses and in local communities in defying "stereotypical" ideas of what a Greek organization is and incorporating Native American cultural values into Greek life. There will doubtless continue to be growth and a stronger presence of HNAFSs on NNCUs. It is important that student affairs and Greek advisory boards and staff acquire a better understanding of their impact on Native college students and find ways to support—and enrich—their contributions.

Connecting to Native Faculty (and Allies)

The role and impact that Native and non-Native faculty and staff have on the academic and social integration of Native students is underestimated (Belgarde, 1992; Falk & Aitken, 1984; Tippeconnic & McKinney, 2003; Tippeconnic Fox, 2005; Wright, 1985). For Native American students, a perceived lack of support from non-Native faculty and staff (in terms of interaction and mentorship) is shown to negatively impact their success as students (Mihesuah & Wilson, 2004; Pavel & Padilla, 1993). This highlights the need for non-Native faculty and staff to become familiar with the issues and concerns of Native students (Hornett, 1989). Such efforts can greatly increase the success and confidence of Native students while building a stronger connection to the institution itself (Jackson et al., 2003). Native and non-Native faculty play a critical role in Native student academic persistence, particularly when they seek to understand the concerns and issues that Native students face and demonstrate their support for and connection with Native students (Brown & Robinson Kurpius, 1997).

Positive faculty and staff interaction, demonstration of institutional commitment to supporting Native American students through services, and providing an inclusive campus climate all increase academic persistence (Garrod & Larimore, 1997). Building relationships with other students, staff, and faculty, as well as with the campus itself, is essential for Native American students to feel accepted and welcomed and to be more likely to become engaged. When the institution demonstrates a commitment to being supportive and honoring Native students' cultural values as strengths, the relationship to the institution is deeply connected and aligned with Native student tribal and cultural values (Huffman, 2001).

Home-Going

Home-going is often viewed separately from the college setting and the on-campus experience of students, and the importance of home connections for Native American students is widely misunderstood by faculty, student affairs professionals, and administrators (Waterman, 2012). However, for Native American students, home-going has been found to be an important part of their overall experience, both on and off campus (Waterman, 2012). Families and support networks are critical. Many students draw their strength and motivation to persist from families; this includes the desire to make life better for their families and even the goal of not letting their families down (Guillory & Wolverton, 2008). The home or tribal community of Native American college students helps them persist because they receive emotional, spiritual, and financial support that encourages them to achieve their higher education goals (Bowker, 1992; HeavyRunner & DeCelles, 2002). As NNCUs acknowledge the important roles that family, community, and support networks play with regard to academic persistence, they enhance the likelihood that Native students will maintain cultural ties to their community and benefit from a social support system while away from it (Guillory & Wolverton, 2008). "Home and community validate the participants' indigenity by serving as a bridge between Native and non-Native cultures" (Waterman, 2012, p. 201).

As mainstream higher education institutions increasingly recognize the needs of various student populations, the inclusion of the voice and needs of Native American students is essential. This requires faculty, staff, and institutions to be open to the desire of Native students to return home for ceremonies and family emergencies, and to renew themselves through their family and tribal support systems (Waterman, 2012). Incorporating broad definitions of families, facilitating relationships between students and their home communities, and recognizing the culture and values that each student brings to campus are all important factors associated with enhancing Native student success in higher education (Jackson & Smith, 2001; Jenkins, 1999; Tippeconnic Fox, Lowe, & McClellan, 2005a, 2005b).

Transitioning Back Home (Giving Back)

The college experience of Native American students must be viewed in a holistic way. Unfortunately, we often center our discussions on the transition to college and the experiences of Native students while in college, and little attention has been paid to their transitions back home. Because "home for Native Americans has a special meaning connected to 'place'" (Waterman, 2012, p. 196), it is important that we consider the return home as a vital aspect of the overall experience of Native American students, particularly with regard to the value of reciprocity.

Reciprocity has been acknowledged by a number of scholars as a key factor in the success of Native American students in higher education (Brayboy, 1999; Garcia, 2000; Garrod & Larimore, 1997; Guillory, J., 2008; Guillory, R.M., 2002; Jackson et al., 2003; Kirkness & Barnhardt, 1991; Lintner, 1999; Shotton, 2008; Waterman, 2007). For many Native American students, the desire to obtain a university degree is "often linked to aspirations with much broader collective/tribal considerations" (Kirkness & Barnhardt, 1991, p. 4). Underlying the value of reciprocity is the desire to give back in an effort to advance the tribe or community. Within many tribal cultures, emphasis is placed on the value of generosity, which is usually displayed through informal and formal means of giving and sharing, wherein success depends more on the extent to which an individual shares accumulated wealth (Badwound & Tierney, 1988). Thus, for many Native American students, notions of achievement differ considerably from the individual perspective of mainstream culture. Many tribal cultures emphasize the group over the individual and the ethic of cooperation and group commitment (Deyhle, 1995; Lamphere, 1977; Swisher, 1990). From this perspective, individual achievement is connected to the betterment of the group (Deyhle & Swisher, 1997).

Because reciprocity plays a key role for many Native American students, it is important to understand how Native students transition back into their communities. Reflecting deep-rooted values of reciprocity, they often cite a desire to use their degrees to "give back" to their tribes or communities (Brayboy, 1999; Garcia, 2000; Garrod & Larimore, 1997; Guillory, J., 2008; Guillory, R.M., 2002; Jackson et al., 2003; Kirkness & Barnhardt, 1991; Lintner, 1999; Shotton, 2008; Waterman, 2007). They see their degrees and experiences in higher education as an opportunity to gain knowledge that is needed within their tribes or home communities. Native students possess a strong desire to utilize their education to better their home communities, strengthen their tribes, and contribute to the overall nation building of the tribal nations they represent.

Education is not just a tool for their own personal gain, but to be used to strengthen their tribes and home communities. However, the transition back home for Native American graduates is not always easy. Justin Guillory (2008) acknowledged that the transition of Native students back into the community after graduation is sometimes met with challenges—namely, tensions with family, places of employment, or the community. Consequently, it has been recommended that community mentors play an important part in Native graduates' re-entry into tribal communities (Guillory, J., 2008). Additionally, given the important role that community plays for Native students, it seems pertinent for institutions to find ways to help them remain connected to their tribal communities.

Maintaining connections to community has been found to be a significant factor in the academic success of Native American students (Waterman, 2012). It has been suggested that institutions of higher education should develop programs to connect Native students to tribal communities so that they can interact with tribal leaders, elders, and community members, and as a means of reinforcing and maintaining students' tribal connections (Minthorn et al., 2013). This concept can be further extended to transitioning back into a tribal community, where a continued connection to tribal communities may help in aiding the transition for Native students post-graduation.

Recommendations

This chapter has provided an overview of the general experiences and current status of Native students in higher education, as well as ways to help Native American college students transition back to their home communities once they graduate. This information will enable administrators, faculty, staff, and graduate students in higher education to understand the lived experiences of Native college students. In the following section, three specific recommendations will be offered on how to better serve and support Native American college students, as well as how to create a "safe place" on campus, including tribes as partners, the importance of advisory boards, and cultural competency training of staff and faculty on campuses where Native students are present (see also Guillory, 2009).

Tribes as Partners

One of the first recommendations to any group of personnel in higher education is to emphasize the critical role of connecting Native American students to their tribal nations. Native students have sacrificed living and being in their tribal communities to pursue a higher education. Therefore, it is important that colleges and universities recognize the necessity to build healthy and reciprocal partnerships with the tribal nations their students represent and the tribal nations located near the university. If there are not already partnerships in place, a good first step is to ask current Native American college students whom to contact (whether that be a tribal higher education director or tribal leader) to begin to build a relationship. Initial contact can be done through the Native American student affairs department, multicultural affairs department, and/or upper administration. Meetings with these individuals should be undertaken in order to build a reciprocal relationship to benefit both the institution and the tribe, and to provide support to future and current tribal citizens at that university or college. Formal agreements should be put in place to hold the institution accountable to tribal nations through a commitment to partnership.

Forming partnerships with tribal nations that Native American college students represent will help them see the commitment that the institution has in valuing who they are and their needs as tribal citizens. The formation of relationships to tribal nations within close proximity to the university conveys a commitment from the institution to invite them to the table for decision making and to ensure that their students' needs are met. It also acknowledges the tribes' vital role in the educational process. Tribal partnerships and healthy connections to their home communities are important pieces in seeing Native American college students succeed in their academic journey.

Advisory Boards

The second recommendation for universities and colleges is to consider the creation of advisory boards to support and serve the needs of Native American college students. A tribal advisory board, for instance, may be composed of tribal nations that are within a short distance of the university (Francis-Begay, 2013). This type of advisory board could report on new initiatives and opportunities to mutually serve tribal partnerships, as well as keep up with the current state of Native American college student demographics and events (Francis-Begay, 2013).

Another type of advisory board might be a Native American roundtable that includes Native student organizations, faculty/staff organizations, and Native American studies departments that meet on a regular basis to disseminate information on events and opportunities and to address issues surrounding Native Americans on campus. A combination advisory board that includes tribal officials and representatives from Native American student organizations and departments might also be formed to include potential partnerships, opportunities, and updates on events and concerns within the university and tribal communities. One final recommended advisory board would address the situation in which the capability of including regular involvement of tribal nations does not exist, or there is low representation of Native Americans on campus. Such an advisory board would bring together campus departments that impact the success of Native college students; this would include designating an ally in admissions, financial aid, the registrar's office, residence life, and student affairs who would work to advocate for Native American students on campus. This includes inviting some Native students to be on the advisory board so that their experiences and voices can be heard.

The composition and type of advisory board will depend on the needs of the community and the institution; as it develops, all those involved should decide on the purpose, role, and frequency of meetings to ensure that the success of Native American students is achieved. Advisory boards on college campuses that include tribal nations, community, and departments on campus should serve to better understand the community's needs. But, more important, they will be in a better position to support and serve Native students on campus as well as in their transition home after graduation (Francis-Begay, 2013).

Cultural Competency Training for Staff and Faculty

The final recommendation is for university and college campuses to develop and implement cultural competency training for staff and faculty, specifically in working with Native American colleges, students, and tribal communities. Institutions can utilize multiple resources for this type of training. If there are Native American faculty members on campus, student affairs workers could inquire about their willingness to work with administrators to develop and deliver this training (Brayboy et al., 2012). Such training could address the various functions of serving Native American college students, including the roles of faculty and staff within departments, faculty teaching, and working with Native American college students at various levels of postsecondary education. Targeting cultural competency training to educate staff and faculty for specific purposes will provide them with information on how to better work with Native students in different capacities (Brayboy et al., 2012). Another component of cultural competency training of staff and faculty is the way in which faculty and departments approach research with tribal communities and create partnerships with tribes. The more aware faculty and staff are of the needs of Native students and ways of working with tribal communities, the more likely it is that allies for Native students will be developed, thus increasing their success in their higher education journey.

Conclusion

In this chapter, an overview of the general experiences of Native American college students in higher education has been provided by addressing the issues of being invisible on campus, the stereotypes and misconceptions about Native Americans in college, and the complex diversity the Native student population represents. We have also highlighted the important role of building community on campus for Native students in areas such as leadership development, peer mentoring, HNAFSs, connecting them with faculty (and allies), and the role that home-going plays in Native students' success on campus. A deep understanding of the importance of helping Native American college students transition back home and stay connected to their tribal communities is essential in serving Native students holistically. Finally, three recommendations have been made that would impact the campus climate and experiences of Native American college students by creating tribal partnerships, advisory boards, and opportunities for cultural competency training for faculty and staff on campus. It is crucial that administrators, faculty, staff, and graduate students understand the unique experiences of Native American college students, the values they bring with them, and how to better serve and support them. After all, the ultimate goal is ensuring a successful collegiate experience that will ultimately impact both the students and their communities.

Note

1. This term was used initially by Jahansouz & Oxendine (2008) and later in Oxendine, Oxendine, & Minthorn (2013).

References

Anagnopoulos, C. (2006). Lakota undergraduates as partners in aging research in American Indian communities. *Educational Gerontology, 32*(7), 517–525.

Aud, S., Hussar, W., Kena, G., Bianco, K., Frohlich, L., Kemp, J., & Tahan, K. (2011). *The condition of education 2011* (NCES 2001-033). Washington, DC: U.S. Department of Education, National Center for Education Statistics.

Badwound, E., & Tierney, W. (1988). Leadership and American Indian values: The tribal college dilemma. *Journal of American Indian Education, 28*(1), 9–15.

Belgarde, M.J. (1992). *The performance and persistence of American Indian undergraduate students at Stanford University* (Doctoral dissertation). Retrieved from *Dissertation Abstracts International, 53*, 05A.

Benjamin, D.P., Chambers, S., & Reiterman, G. (1993). A focus on American Indian college persistence. *Journal of American Indian Education, 32*(2), 24–40.

Bowker, A. (1992). The American Indian female dropout. *Journal of American Indian Education, 31*(3), 3–21.

Brayboy, B.M. (1999). *Climbing the ivy: Examining the experiences of academically successful Native American Indian students in two Ivy League universities* (Unpublished doctoral dissertation). University of Pennsylvania, Philadelphia.

Brayboy, B.M.J., Fann, A.J., Castagno, A.E., & Solyom, J.A. (2012). *Postsecondary education for American Indian and Alaska Natives: Higher education for nation building and self-determination. ASHE Higher Education Report, 37*(5). San Francisco, CA: Jossey-Bass.

Brown, L.L., & Robinson Kurpius, S.E. (1997). Psychosocial factors influencing academic persistence of American Indian college students. *Journal of College Student Development, 38*(1), 3–12.

Castagno, A., & Lee, S. (2007). Native mascots, ethnic fraud, and interest convergence: A critical race theory perspective on higher education. *Equity and Excellence in Education, 40*(1), 3–13.

Deyhle, D. (1995). Navajo youth and Anglo racism: Cultural integrity and resistance. *Harvard Educational Review, 65*(3), 403–444.

Deyhle, D., & Swisher, K. (1997). Research in American Indian education and Alaska Native education: From assimilation to self-determination. In M.W. Apple (Ed.), *Review of Research in Education* (Vol. 22, pp. 113–194). Washington, DC: American Educational Research Association.

Falk, D.R., & Aitken, L.P. (1984). Promoting retention among American Indian college students. *Journal of American Indian Education, 23*(2), 24–31.

Federal Register. (2010, October 1). 75(190), 60810-60814.

Francis-Begay, K. (2013). The role of the special advisor to the president on Native American affairs. In H. Shotton, S. Lowe, & S. Waterman (Eds.), *Beyond the asterisk: Understanding Native students in higher education* (pp. 81–94). Sterling, VA: Stylus.

Fryberg, S.A., Markus, H.R., Oyserman, D., & Stone, J.M. (2010). Of warrior chiefs and Indian princesses: The psychological consequences of American Indian mascots. *Basic and Applied Social Psychology, 30*(3), 208–218.

Fryberg, S.A., & Townsend, S.S.M. (2008). The psychology of invisibility. In G. Adams, M. Biernat, N.R. Branscombe, C.S. Crandall, & L.S. Wrightsman (Eds.), *Commemorating Brown: The social psychology of racism and discrimination. Decade of Behavior* (pp. 173–193). Washington, DC: American Psychological Association.

Garcia, F.M. (2000). Warriors in education: Persistence among American Indian doctoral recipients. *Tribal College Journal, 11*(3), 46–48, 50.

Garrod, A., & Larimore, C. (1997). *First person, first peoples: Native American college graduates tell their life stories.* Ithaca, NY: Cornell University Press.

Gloria, A., & Robinson Kurpius, S. (2001). Influences of self-beliefs, social support and comfort in the university environment on the academic nonpersistence decisions of American Indian undergraduates. *Cultural Diversity and Ethnic Minority Psychology, 7*(1), 88–102.

Guillory, J. (2008). *Diverse pathways of "giving back" to tribal community: Perceptions of Native American college graduates* (Doctoral dissertation). Retrieved from ProQuest Dissertations & Theses database. (AAT 3379393).

Guillory, R.M. (2002). *Factors related to Native American students' persistence in higher education: A comparative analysis of student and state and university officials' perceptions* (Unpublished doctoral dissertation). Washington State University, Pullman.

Guillory, R.M. (2009). American Indian/Alaska Native college student retention strategies. *Journal of Developmental Education, 33*(2), 12–38.

Guillory, R.M., & Wolverton, M. (2008). It's about family: Native American student persistence in higher education. *Journal of Higher Education, 79*(1), 58–87.

HeavyRunner, I., & DeCelles, R. (2002). Family education model: Meeting the student retention challenge. *Journal of American Indian Higher Education, 41*(2), 29–37.

HeavyRunner, I., & Marshall, K. (2003). "Miracle survivors": Promoting resilience in Indian students. *Tribal College Journal, 14*(4), 14–18.

Hornett, D. (1989). The role of faculty in cultural awareness and retention of American Indian college students. *Journal of American Indian Education, 29*(1), 12–18.

Huffman, T.E. (2001). Resistance theory and the transculturation hypothesis as explanations of college attrition and persistence among culturally traditional American Indian students. *Journal of American Indian Education, 40*(3), 1–23.

Huffman, T.E. (2003). A comparison of personal assessments of the college experience among reservation and nonreservation American Indian students. *Journal of American Indian Education, 42*(2), 1–16.

Huffman, T.E. (2010). *Theoretical perspectives on American Indian education: Taking a new look at academic success and the achievement gap.* Lanham, MD: AltaMira.

Jackson, A.P., & Smith, S.A. (2001). Postsecondary transitions among Navajo students. *Journal of American Indian Education, 40*(2), 28–47.

Jackson, A.P., Smith, S.A., & Hill, C.L. (2003). Academic persistence among Native American college students. *Journal of College Student Development, 44*(4), 548–565.

Jahansouz, S., & Oxendine, S. (2008). The Native American fraternal values movement: past, present, & future. *Perspectives,* (Spring), 1.

Jenkins, M. (1999). Factors which influence the success or failure of American Indian/Native American college students. *Research and Teaching in Developmental Education, 15*(20), 49–52.

Kirkness, V., & Barnhardt, R. (1991). First nations and higher education: The four Rs—respect, relevance, reciprocity, responsibility. *Journal of American Indian Education, 30*(3), 1–15.

Lamphere, L. (1977). *To run after them: Cultural and social bases of cooperation in a Navajo community.* Tucson, AZ: University of Arizona Press.

Lintner, T. (1999). Cycle starters: American Indian doctorates as role models. *Tribal College Journal, 10*(3), 46–49.

Mihesuah, D., & Wilson, A. (2004). *Indigenizing the academy: Transforming scholarship and empowering communities.* Lincoln, NE: University of Nebraska Press.

Minthorn, R.S. (2014). Perspectives and values of leadership for Native American college students in non-Native colleges and universities. *Journal of Leadership Education, 13*(2), 67–95.

Minthorn, R.S., Wanger, S., & Shotton, H. (2013). Developing Native student leadership skills: The success of the Oklahoma Native American Students in Higher Education (ONASHE) conference. *American Indian Culture and Research Journal, 37*(3), 59–74.

National Center for Education Statistics (NCES). (2007). *Postsecondary institutions in the United States: Fall 2006 and degrees and other awards conferred: 2005–06.* Washington, DC: U.S. Department of Education.

Oxendine, D., Oxendine, S., & Minthorn, R. (2013). The historically Native American fraternity and sorority movement. In H. Shotton, S. Lowe, & S. Waterman (Eds.), *Beyond the asterisk: Understanding Native students in higher education* (pp. 67–80). Sterling, VA: Stylus.

Pavel, D.M. (1999). American Indians and Alaska Natives in higher education: Promoting access and achievement. In K.G. Swisher & J.W. Tippeconnic (Eds.), *Next steps: Research and practices to advance Indian education.* Charleston, WV: ERIC.

Pavel, D.M., & Padilla, R.V. (1993). American Indian and Alaska Native postsecondary departure: An example of assessing a mainstream model using national longitudinal data. *Journal of American Indian Education, 32*(2), 1–23.

Pewewardy, C. (1995 , November). *The Americanizing of "Pocahontas": Misconceptions and assimilation of an American Indian heroine.* Paper presented at the National Indian Education Association Annual Convention, Tucson, AZ.

Pewewardy, C., & Frey, B. (2002). Surveying the landscape: Perceptions of multicultural support services and racial climate at a predominantly White university. *Journal of Negro Education, 71*(1–2), 77–95.

Pewewardy, C., & Frey, B. (2004). American Indian students' perceptions of racial climate, multicultural support services, and ethnic fraud at predominantly White universities. *Journal of American Indian Education, 43*(1), 32–60.

Reyhner, J. (1992). American Indians out of school: A review of school-based causes and solutions. *Journal of American Indian Education, 31*(3), 37–56.

Shotton, H.J. (2008). *Pathway to the Ph.D.: Experiences of high-achieving American Indian females* (Unpublished doctoral dissertation). University of Oklahoma, Norman.

Shotton, H.J., Lowe, S.C., & Waterman, S.J. (Eds.). (2013). *Beyond the asterisk: Understanding Native students in higher education.* Sterling, VA: Stylus.

Shotton, H.J., Oosahwe, E.S.L., & Cintron, R.C. (2007). Stories of success: Experiences of American Indian students in a peer-mentoring retention program. *Review of Higher Education, 31*(1), 81–108.

Shotton, H.J., Yellowfish, S., & Cintron, R. (2010). Island of sanctuary: The role of an American Indian cultural center. In L.D. Patton (Ed.), *Culture centers in higher education: Perspectives on identity, theory, and practice* (pp. 49–62). Sterling, VA: Stylus.

Snyder, T.D., Dillow, S.A., & Hoffman, C.M. (2008). *Digest of education statistics 2007* (NCES 2008-022). Washington, DC: National Center for Education Statistics, Institute of Education Sciences, U.S. Department of Education.

Snyder, T.D., Tan, A.G., & Hoffman, C.M. (2004). *Digest of education statistics 2003* (NCES 2005-025). Washington, DC: U.S. Department of Education.

Swisher, K. (1990). Cooperative learning and the education of American Indian/Alaskan Native students: A review of literature and suggestions for implementation. *American Educational Research Journal, 29*(2), 36–43.

Tierney, W.G. (1992). *Official encouragement, institutional discouragement: Minorities in academe—The Native American experience.* Norwood, NJ: Ablex.

Tippeconnic, J.W., & McKinney, S. (2003). Native faculty: Scholarship and development. In M. Benham & W. Stein (Eds.), *The Renaissance of American Indian higher education: Capturing the dream* (pp. 241–256). Mahwah, NJ: Lawrence Erlbaum.

Tippeconnic Fox, M.J. (2005). Voices from within: Native American faculty and staff on campus. In M.J. Tippeconnic Fox, S.C. Lowe, & G. McClellan (Eds.), *Serving Native American students* (pp. 49–60). San Francisco, CA: Jossey-Bass.

Tippeconnic Fox, M.J., Lowe, S.C., & McClellan, G.S. (2005a). From discussion to action. In M.J. Tippeconnic Fox, S.C. Lowe, & G. McClellan (Eds.), *Serving Native American students* (pp. 95–98). San Francisco, CA: Jossey-Bass.

Tippeconnic Fox, M.J., Lowe, S.C., & McClellan, G.S. (Eds.). (2005b). *Serving Native American students* (*New directions for student services*, no.109). San Francisco, CA: Jossey-Bass.

Waterman, S.J. (2007). A complex path to Haudenosaunee degree completion. *Journal of American Indian Education, 46*(1), 20–40.

Waterman, S.J. (2012). Home-going as a strategy for success among Haudenosaunee college and university students. *Journal of Student Affairs Research & Practice, 49*(2), 193–209. doi:10.1515/jsarp-2012-6378

Williams, R.S. (2012). *Indigenizing leadership concepts through perspectives of Native American college students* (Unpublished doctoral dissertation). Oklahoma State University, Stillwater.

Wright, B. (1985). Programming success: Special student services and the American Indian college student. *Journal of American Indian Education, 24*(1), 1–7.

FOUR

Asian American College Students

Samuel D. Museus and Varaxy Yi

Asian American college students are a frequently misunderstood population. Nevertheless, over the past 15 years, a growing body of research has shed light on Asian American college students' realities in higher education. In this chapter we utilize this literature to provide a brief overview of some critical contexts and realities that shape the Asian American experience in college and can inform institutional policy and practice aimed at serving this increasingly visible population. First, we discuss important historical contexts that help shape Asian American students' experiences in college. We then provide an overview of some important demographic contextual realities that shed light on the condition of the communities from which Asian American students come. Next, we discuss the racial contexts within which Asian American students navigate college and university campuses. Finally, we illuminate some of the realities that Asian American students encounter on college campuses and their response to those challenges.

Before moving forward with our discussion, a few caveats are warranted. First, it is impossible to provide in a single chapter an overview of the contextual and experiential realities of Asian Americans in higher education with sufficient depth or breadth. For a more complex and comprehensive treatment of the subject of Asian American students in college, we refer readers to more extensive collections and reviews of research on this population (Ching & Agbayani, 2012; McEwen, Kodama, Alvarez, Lee, & Liang, 2002; Museus, 2009, 2013b; Museus, Antonio, & Kiang, 2012; Museus, Maramba, & Teranishi, 2013). Second, it must be made clear that there are, in fact, several Asian American subgroups (e.g., Southeast Asian Americans, low socioeconomic Asian Americans, undocumented Asian Americans, sexual orientation minority Asian Americans) that have distinct experiences which are not sufficiently captured in the current discussion. For more specific analyses of these subpopulations, we refer readers to the small but rapidly expanding body of empirical research on these Asian American subgroups (Buenavista & Chen, 2013; Buenavista, Jayakumar, &

Misa-Escalante, 2009; Chhuon & Hudley, 2008; Kiang, 2002, 2009; Museus, 2011b, 2013b; Museus & Vue, 2013; Narui, 2011; Pepin & Talbot, 2013; Vue, 2013).

Historical Context: Waves of Migration

The immigration of Asian groups to America took place in two waves, each of which is characterized by different groups immigrating into the United States (Hune, 2002; Okihiro, 1995). The first wave, consisting of approximately 1 million Asian Americans, began in the 1840s and continued until the 1930s (Hune, 2002; Tamura, 2001). It included Asian Indians, Chinese, Japanese, Koreans, and Filipinos who entered the continental United States and were laborers on the transcontinental railroad, as well as some who migrated to the islands of Hawaii to work on plantations. Many of these groups settled into and helped develop the western states by opening up small businesses. However, during this period, these groups faced limited political and legal rights and economic exploitation.

The second wave of Asian American immigration occurred after the 1965 Immigration Act (Chan, 1991). During this period, both skilled and unskilled workers entered the United States to fill jobs in needed areas such as hospitals and garment factories. This second wave of immigration also included refugees from Southeast Asia who fled the countries of Cambodia, Vietnam, and Laos to escape political unrest and persecution in the 1970s. While many East and South Asian Americans immigrated with higher levels of education and professional skill, most Southeast Asian American refugees came from agrarian backgrounds and had minimal education. Moreover, having fled Southeast Asia as a result of war, persecution, and genocide, significant trauma has continued to affect this community.

Since the first wave of Asian immigration in the 1800s, the Asian population has grown exponentially and still continues to increase rapidly, as previously noted. Each wave has brought vastly different ethnic groups with a range of historical contexts, and it is apparent that the realities of the different groups' journeys to America have been characterized by salient differences. While some groups chose to migrate to the United States to fill necessary roles in highly professionalized occupations, other groups were forced to escape their home countries. The experiences of various ethnic groups migrating to America were vastly different, and their present situation in larger American society continues to be shaped by these historical realities.

Demographic Contexts: Growth, Diversity, and Inequality

Researchers have noted that the Asian American population is characterized by rapid growth, vast diversity, and significant inequalities (Museus, 2013a, 2013b). These three characteristics have implications for higher education institutions when creating programs to foster and support Asian American student success, and we discuss them in greater detail herein.

Asian Americans are the fastest-growing racial group in the United States. According to the U.S. Census (2011), the Asian American population increased by 43% between 2000 and 2010. Geographically, the Asian American community is heavily concentrated in the West, but has grown in every major region of the United States, with the Midwest and South experiencing the most growth in their Asian American communities. Moving forward, the national Asian American population is slated to double in size by the year 2050.

In addition to rapid growth, the Asian American population is characterized by substantial diversity. This population encompasses over 24 distinct ethnic groups, with the 10 largest being Chinese (22%), Filipino (20%), Asian Indian (18%), Korean (10%), Vietnamese (10%), Japanese (8%), Pakistani (2%), Cambodian (2%), Hmong (2%), and Thai (1%) (Museus, 2013a). The Asian American population also encompasses a wide array of cultures, languages, generational statuses, religions, socioeconomic statuses, poverty rates, education attainment levels, occupations, political orientations, and other traits (Hune, 2002; Museus, 2009, 2013a, 2013b). Despite common misconceptions that all Asian Americans are the same, today's Asian American college students represent many different ethnic groups with distinct languages and cultures.

Finally, inequalities within the Asian American population are significant. Despite a general view that all Asian Americans are doing well economically, educationally, and occupationally, the reality is that certain ethnic groups within the population face drastic economic, educational, and occupational disparities. In fact, while some ethnic groups have very high educational achievement rates (e.g., Asian Indian and Taiwanese), other groups (e.g., Hmong, Cambodian, and Laotian) have higher rates of poverty, lower attainment rates, and high rates of unemployment (Museus, 2013a). For example, while the average Asian American poverty rate is 12.6%, rates of poverty for Hmong (37.8%), Cambodian (29.3%), Laotian (18.5%), and Vietnamese (16.6%) populations are much higher. Similarly, Asian American bachelor's degree attainment rates reveal drastic ethnic disparities. Whereas Asian Indian (76%) and Taiwanese (72%) Americans attain bachelor's degrees at over double the rate of the national population, Hmong (14%), Cambodian (13%), and Laotian (12%) Americans hold bachelor's degrees at less than half the rate of the overall population (28%).

The Asian American population will continue to grow and diversify. Yet, as a result of misconceptions, Asian American students are often excluded from research, policies, and programs that target underserved populations. The reality is that the demographic profiles of many ethnic groups—such as Cambodian, Hmong, and Laotian Americans—do warrant targeted policies, programs, and practices to better serve these populations.

Racial Contexts: Racial Ideologies and Racial Oppression

Historical examples abound of the ways in which the Asian American community has been forced to contend with deeply embedded and ongoing systemic racial oppression in society (Museus, 2013b). Indeed, since the first waves of Chinese immigrants came to the United States in the 1800s, reactions toward Asian Americans have been characterized by xenophobia. Although celebrated as hard workers during this period (in contrast to African Americans), the Chinese laborers who worked on the Central Pacific Railway experienced a sharp negative shift in sentiment toward their community during economic downturns (Wu, 1995). This led to the first race-based exclusionary law, the Chinese Exclusion Act of 1882, which barred Chinese workers from entering the country. During this period, Chinese immigrants experienced xenophobia and mob-like violence, and were prevented from securing employment. This act was renewed two times for 10-year periods and then indefinitely until the Immigration Act of 1965.

Other laws were subsequently passed that curtailed the entry of Asians into America. In the early 1900s, the influx of immigrants from Japan was met with increased anti-Japanese sentiment. In 1907, for example, the Gentleman's Agreement prohibited Japanese laborers from entering the United States. Another immigration law was passed in 1924 that banned all Asian immigrants, except Filipinos, from entering the country. Several decades later, anti-Japanese sentiment led to the internment of over 125,000 Japanese Americans during World War II.

More recently, South Asian Americans have experienced similar xenophobia and discrimination as a result of the anti-Islamic sentiment that followed the terrorist attacks on the Twin Towers on September 11, 2001. The attacks led to race-based fear and hatred toward the Muslim and Middle Eastern communities within the United States, and immigration laws again have been used to justify the detention and deportation of thousands of Muslim and Middle Eastern men (Elver, 2012). For example, within the first month after the attacks, there were over 300 cases of violence and discrimination against the Sikh community, despite its lack of ties to the Islamic faith (The Sikh Coalition, n.d.). The experiences of South Asian communities today mirror those of the Japanese who were persecuted during World War II.

Several dominant racialized stereotypes have shaped American society's misperceptions of Asian American college students throughout history. The "forever foreigner" myth, for example, has been deeply embedded in societal views toward Asian Americans. The forever foreigner stereotype is reflected in assumptions that all Asian Americans are foreign-born, and it refers to the exclusion of Asian Americans from dominant conceptualizations of what is viewed as "American" (Kim, 1999; Lowe, 1996; Saito, 1997; Volpp, 2001). This stereotype also suggests that Asian Americans are incapable of full integration into American culture and society. Moreover, closely related to the forever foreigner myth is the "yellow peril" myth, or the misconception that Asian Americans are a threat to the United States (Espiritu, 1992; Lowe, 1996). Sometimes the yellow peril myth is gendered, depicting Asian American men as hypermasculine sexual threats (e.g., Fu Manchu) or Asian American women as untrustworthy sexual deviants (e.g., dragon ladies) (Eng, 2001; Espiritu, 1992). The yellow peril stereotype has fueled military fears, such as the anti-Japanese American sentiment during World War II or the post-9/11 anti-Islamic discourse, as well as economic concerns and anxieties, including the fear of the power of Japanese automobile companies during the 1970s and 1980s.

Today, the model minority myth—or the misconception that all Asian Americans achieve universal and unparalleled academic and occupational success—is arguably the most pervasive stereotype assigned to Asian Americans (Museus, 2009, 2013b; Museus & Kiang, 2009; Suzuki, 2002). The model minority myth rose to prominence in the 1960s as a tool for conservative groups to discount civil rights activists' claims that racism was partially responsible for the struggles of people of color (Suzuki, 1977; Uyematsu, 1971; Wu, 1995). Although it can be perceived as benign on the surface, scholars have discussed how this myth is still used to discount the racial challenges faced by other populations of color, how it masks important inequalities and problems within the Asian American community, and how it leads to its exclusion from educational research, policy, and practice (Museus, 2009, 2013b; Museus & Kiang, 2009; Suzuki, 2002). Southeast Asian Americans (Cambodians, Hmong, Laotians, and Vietnamese) are stereotyped both as model minorities and as inferior minorities who are dropouts, welfare sponges, and gang members (Museus, 2008, 2013b; Ngo & Lee, 2007). Therefore, Southeast Asian Americans occupy a unique space in the discourse on Asian Americans because their experiences are shaped by these two polarized academic stereotypes.

The experiences of Asian American men and women are shaped by sexualized racial stereotypes as well (Eng, 2001; Espiritu, 1992; Prasso, 2005; Shek, 2006; Sue, Bucceri, Lin, Nadal, & Torino, 2007). Asian American men are often portrayed as unthreatening, asexual, effeminate, and socially awkward nerds in American contexts (Eng, 2001; Shek, 2006). These stereotypes have historically been used to emasculate Asian American men (Eng, 2001), and their presence in contemporary society persists in a variety of forms (Museus, 2013b). The impact of this emasculation on Asian American men can be so profound that it has been called a form of racial castration (Eng, 2001). Alternatively, Asian American women are often stereotyped as hypersexual and submissive sex objects (Cho, 2003; Prasso, 2005). These stereotypes show up in images of lotus blossoms, geishas, and prostitutes, and continue to permeate the contemporary media.

It is important to note that these stereotypes can intersect to shape Asian American college students' experiences. On a national and institutional level, the forever foreigner and yellow peril myths can converge with the model minority myth to engender fears of hyper-successful foreigners taking over American education (Saito, 1997; Takaki, 1989). It could be argued that some manifestations of these fears are recent news media attention and YouTube rants arguing that Asians are "taking over" the top universities in North America, which we discuss in greater detail below, as well as recurrent accusations that elite institutions discriminate against Asian Americans in the admissions process to limit their presence on those campuses (Museus, 2013b; Museus & Iftikar, 2013). In addition, the ways in which these racial contexts shape the everyday experiences of Asian American students will be discussed in the following sections.

Cultural Context: Community and Campus Connections

The bulk of the evidence on Asian American college students' experiences suggests that their cultures of origin—including their communities and families—play a significant role in shaping their pathways to and through higher education (Museus, 2011b, 2013a, 2013b; Museus, Lam, Huang, Kem, & Tan, 2012; Museus & Quaye, 2009; Ngo & Lee, 2007). A few examples of the ways in which Asian American culture and communities shape these students' experiences in college include parental influence, community support, and cultural engagement on campus.

First, research indicates that Asian American undergraduates' parental expectations, encouragement, and support are among the most salient factors influencing these students' educational success (Chhuon & Hudley, 2008; Kiang, 2002, 2009; Museus, 2011b, 2013a, 2013b). In some cases, however, these experiences can become complicated. Parents can push students into choosing majors that might not be the best fit for them, and excessive pressure that makes students feel like they cannot meet their family's high expectations of academic success can eventually diminish their motivation (Museus, 2011b, 2013c).

Second, education scholars have written about how Asian American communities can create academic support structures that facilitate Asian American students' pathways to college (Zhou & Kim, 2006). There is also evidence that Asian American community structures such as community advocacy organizations can influence the experiences of Asian American students in significant ways (Museus, Lam, et al., 2012). For example, community organizations can provide spaces in which meaningful curricular and co-curricular learning experiences take place and help educate Asian American college students about the realities of their communities and how those realities are shaped by educational policies and programs.

Finally, when postsecondary institutions engage Asian American cultural communities in meaningful ways, they can have a profound impact on the experiences of Asian American students (Kiang, 2002, 2009; Museus, 2008, 2011c; Museus, Lam, et al., 2012; Museus & Quaye, 2009). Specifically, when postsecondary educators provide spaces for Asian American college students to connect with people from their own cultural communities, curricula and programming that offer opportunities for these students to learn about their own ethnic communities, and opportunities for these undergraduates to give back to their communities of origin through community service, service-learning, and problem-based research activities, they can construct environments in which Asian American students may thrive in college (Museus, 2013b).

In sum, educational policies, programs, and practices that bridge the gap between Asian American students' cultural communities and their experiences on campus can—and do—shape these undergraduates' experiences in profound ways. By constructing such meaningful cultural community connections, college educators can minimize the Asian American students' experiences with racial barriers in college, to which we now turn.

Racial Realities of Asian American College Students

There is ample evidence that racism plays a significant role in shaping Asian American college students' experiences. Indeed, while Asian American students face many of the same challenges as other college students—finding friends, learning how to navigate their respective campuses, staying caught up in math and science homework, and so forth—racism shapes the Asian American experience in college in unique ways. We discuss a few of these ways in this section.

First, evidence suggests that Asian American undergraduates are more likely to encounter racial hostility and harassment than their White counterparts (Ancis, Sedlacek, & Mohr, 2000; Buenavista & Chen, 2013; Buenavista et al., 2009; Cress & Ikeda, 2003; Kim, Chang, & Park, 2009; Kotori & Malaney, 2003; Museus & Park, 2012; Museus & Truong, 2013; Park, 2009; Suyemoto, Kim, Tanabe, Tawa, & Day, 2009; Vue, 2013). This hostility and harassment can manifest in a variety of ways, including experiences with racial profiling from police, racial slurs, and racial bullying. In extreme cases, racial hostility toward Asian Americans leads to physical violence and even death, such as when a White supremacist opened fire on and murdered Won-Joon Yoon, a Korean American student at Indiana University, in 1999.

Second, Asian American college students report experiencing negative pressure as a result of the stereotypes mentioned above (Lewis, Chesler, & Forman, 2000; Museus, 2008, 2013b; Museus & Park, 2012). For example, Asian American undergraduates have reported that the model minority myth places excessive pressure on them to conform to the stereotype, makes them feel like they should not or cannot seek help, leads to their disengagement in the classroom, and is associated with misconceptions that they are all socially awkward math and science nerds. In addition, Southeast Asian American college students have reported being stereotyped as "ghetto" or lacking in academic values (Museus & Park, 2012). Finally, there is some indication that sexualized racial stereotypes shape the experiences of Asian American students (Cho, 2003; Museus & Truong, 2013; Tran & Chang, 2013). Indeed, Asian American women face racialized sexual harassment as a result of the misconception that all Asian American women are hypersexual, submissive, and docile (Cho, 2003; Museus & Truong, 2013). And Asian American men experience the aforementioned emasculating stereotypes that lead them to engage in violent, hypermasculine activity to counter those misconceptions (Tran & Chang, 2013).

Third, Asian American students experience substantial racial isolation in college, and this can negatively influence their satisfaction and ultimate success (Lewis et al., 2000; Museus & Park, 2012; Park, 2009). Even on campuses with significant Asian American student populations, an Asian American student can experience isolation within subcultures (e.g., Greek life) and ethnic isolation, feeling as though he or she is the only one or one of just a few students from their own cultural communities on campus (Museus & Park, 2012; Park, 2009; Vue, 2013).

Finally, Asian American undergraduates feel pressure to conform to stereotypes that otherize them as different from members of the mainstream culture of their campuses and pressure to assimilate to fit into that culture (Lewis et al., 2000; Museus, 2013b; Museus & Park, 2012). The pressure to assimilate into the mainstream on campus causes several additional problems for Asian American college students because it leads to pressure for students to sever ties with their own cultural communities and families—who have significant, positive influences on these students' sense of self and success—in order to adapt to the dominant campus culture (Museus, 2013b; Tierney, 1999).

Racial Resistance Among Asian American College Students

In response to the systemic and individual racism experienced by Asian Americans, there have been many instances of the Asian American community collectively mobilizing to combat racial oppression. During the Civil Rights Movement of the 1960s, for example, Asian Americans mobilized to create the "yellow power" movement (1966–1975), which was a collective effort to seek freedom from systemic racial oppression (Uyematsu, 1971). This movement led to increased Asian American engagement in political and social activism, the creation of a collective pan-ethnic Asian American consciousness, the growth of pan-ethnic Asian American coalitions, and the emergence of ethnic studies programs.

The San Francisco State College (SFSC) strike of 1968–1969 was a microcosm of the larger social movements of the 1960s (Umemoto, 1989). Several environmental factors created the conditions for the SFSC strike. First, the California Master Plan led to decreased access to the most selective institutions in the public higher education system in California. Second, the interests of communities of color and students of color converged. For example, growing awareness of racial problems in the Asian American community coincided with an increased racial consciousness among Asian American undergraduates at SFSC. Finally, when the Third World Liberation Front (TWLF), a coalition of ethnic student organizations, demanded a Black Studies program, the demands were denied by the SFSC administration. This led to increased tensions on campus and, eventually, the strike.

The SFSC strike ended in negotiations and concessions by the campus administration. In establishing the first school of ethnic studies in the nation, the administration made a commitment to create more than 22 faculty positions (Umemoto, 1989). The SFSC strike story offers a reminder of the struggles that Asian Americans have shared with other communities of color. The strike also provides a critical historical context for the emergence and purpose of ethnic studies in higher education. Today, although limited in their number and reach, Asian American studies programs across the country offer spaces in which faculty, staff, and students work together to counter dominant systems of racial, class, and gender oppression, while providing Asian American and other students with education that is relevant to their communities, creating spaces where these students feel valued, and constructing conditions for them to feel supported and thrive within larger education systems that are not designed for them (see, for example, Kiang, 2002, 2009; Museus, Lam, et al., 2012). As such, some Asian American undergraduates, in collaboration with faculty and staff, engage in acts of racial resistance in Asian American Studies programs on a daily basis.

In contemporary America we have witnessed multiple incidents that have sparked widespread activism among Asian American students. Further, the growing incidence of racial oppression and efforts to battle that racism among Asian American college students has recently appeared in the digital arena (Museus, 2011a). Indeed, examples of racism targeted at Asian American college students are not difficult to find on the Internet (see, for example, Museus & Truong, 2013). In 2011, for example, Alexandra Wallace, a White student at UCLA, posted a short YouTube video called *Asians in the Library*. Wallace vented her frustration over Asian students using their cell phones in the library in the wake of a devastating earthquake and tsunami in Japan. She presented herself as a "polite, nice American girl" in contrast to the "hordes of Asians" who should use "American manners," and she used a mock-Asian accent to say "Ching chong, ling long, ting tong" (Lee, 2011). The video was viewed over 1.5 million times. Soon after Wallace posted the video, responses in the form of videos, parodies, and blog posts rapidly multiplied at UCLA and across the nation, denouncing Wallace's racist remarks and denigrating her for posting them. Wallace eventually issued a public apology, but the video had already gone viral and the damage to her reputation had been done. She decided to drop out of college.

The Wallace incident provides a salient example of the increasing role of social media in efforts to perpetuate and combat racism targeted at Asian American college students. Indeed, the reach and anonymity of the Internet allows for a variety of xenophobic and racist ideals to be shared, and these digital environments can become part of the campus climate experienced by Asian American college students (Museus & Truong, 2013). Moreover, while Asian American students likely encounter a plethora of racist and xenophobic content distributed by way of Twitter, Facebook, blogs, and forum discussions, the digital responses to these incidents among Asian American students and other community members have also been substantial. These digital efforts to combat racism are a new sign that Asian American college students and community members are constructing a collective voice and engaging in advocacy.

Conclusion

The historical, demographic, and racial contexts of Asian Americans within the United States are critical to understanding the experiences of Asian American students in college. These contexts can aid college administrators in the creation of policies and programs that address the realities that these students face. Indeed, the differences in immigration histories within the group help to explain the disparity in socioeconomic, educational, and occupational attainment within the Asian American population. Moreover, racial contexts that are characterized by dominant and oppressive overgeneralizations of Asian American communities continue to shape Asian American college students' realities. Fortunately, Asian American college students have engaged—and continue to engage—in the collective raising of Asian American racial consciousness to racial resistance.

References

Ancis J. R., Sedlacek, W. E., & Mohr, J. J. (2000). Student perceptions of campus cultural climate by race. *Journal of Counseling and Development, 78*(2), 180–185.

Buenavista, T.L., & Chen, A.C. (2013). Intersections and crossroads: A counter-story of an undocumented Pinay college student. In S.D. Museus, D. Maramba, & R. Teranishi (Eds.), *The misrepresented minority: New insights on Asian Americans and Pacific Islanders, and their implications for higher education.* Sterling, VA: Stylus.

Buenavista, T.L., Jayakumar, U.M., & Misa-Escalante, K. (2009). Contextualizing Asian American education through critical race theory: An example of U.S. Pilipino college student experiences. In S.D. Museus (Ed.), *Conducting research on Asian Americans in higher education* (pp. 69–81). New Directions for Institutional Research, No. 142. San Francisco, CA: Jossey-Bass.

Chan, S. (1991). *Asian Americans: An interpretive history.* Boston, MA: Twayne.

Chhuon, V., & Hudley, C. (2008). Factors supporting Cambodian American students' successful adjustment into the university. *Journal of College Student Development, 49*(1), 15–30.

Ching, D., & Agbayani, A. (2012). *Asian Americans and Pacific Islanders in higher education: Research and perspectives on identity, leadership, and success.* Washington, DC: NASPA Foundation.

Cho, S.K. (2003). Converging stereotypes in racialized sexual harassment: Where the model minority meets Suzie Wong. In A.K. Wing (Ed.), *Critical race feminism: A reader* (pp. 349–356). New York, NY: New York University Press.

Cress, C.M., & Ikeda, E.K. (2003). Distress under duress: The relationship between campus climate and depression in Asian American college students. *NASPA Journal, 40*(2), 74–97.

Elver, H. (2012). Racializing Islam before and after 9/11: From melting pot to Islamophobia. *Transnational Law & Contemporary Problems, 21*(1), 119–174.

Eng, D.L. (2001). *Racial castration: Managing masculinity in Asian America.* Durham, NC: Duke University Press.

Espiritu, Y.L. (1992). *Asian American panethnicity: Bridging institutions and identities.* Philadelphia, PA: Temple University Press.

Hune, S. (2002). Demographics and diversity of Asian American college students. *New Directions for Student Services, 2002*(97), 11–20.

Kiang, P.N. (2002). Stories and structures of persistence: Ethnographic learning through research and practice in Asian American Studies. In Y. Zou & H.T. Trueba (Eds.), *Advances in ethnographic research: From our theoretical and methodological roots to post-modern critical ethnography* (pp. 223–255). Lanham, MD: Rowman & Littlefield.

Kiang, P.N. (2009). A thematic analysis of persistence and long-term educational engagement with Southeast Asian American college students. In L. Zhan (Ed.), *Asian American voices: Engaging, empowering, enabling* (pp. 21–58). New York, NY: NLN Press.

Kim, J. (1999). The racial triangulation of Asian Americans. *Politics and Society, 27*(1), 105–138.

Kim, Y.K., Chang, M.J., & Park, J.J. (2009). Engaging with faculty: Examining rates, predictors, and educational effects for Asian American undergraduates. *Journal of Diversity in Higher Education, 2*(4), 206–218.

Kotori, C., & Malaney, G.D. (2003). Asian American students' perceptions of racism, reporting behaviors, and awareness of legal rights and procedures. *NASPA Journal, 40*(3), 56–76.

Lee, E. (2011, March 22). Did UCLA and NYT overreact to student's "Asians in the library" video? *Huffington Post.* Retrieved from http://www.huffingtonpost.com/edward-lee/did-ucla-and-nyt-overreac_b_838841.html

Lewis, A.E., Chesler, M., & Forman, T.A. (2000). The impact of "colorblind" ideologies on students of color: Intergroup relations at a predominantly White university. *Journal of Negro Education, 69*(1–2), 74–91.

Lowe, L. (1996). *Immigrant acts: On Asian American cultural politics.* Durham, NC: Duke University Press.

McEwen, M.K., Kodama, C.M., Alvarez, A.N., Lee, S., & Liang, C.T.H. (Eds.). (2002). *Working with Asian American college students.* New Directions for Student Services, No. 97. San Francisco, CA: Jossey-Bass.

Museus, S.D. (2008). The model minority and the inferior minority myths: Understanding stereotypes and their implications for student involvement. *About Campus, 13*(3), 2–8.

Museus, S.D. (2009). A critical analysis of the invisibility of Southeast Asian American students in higher education research and discourse. In L. Zhan (Ed.), *Asian voices: Engaging, empowering, and enabling* (pp. 59–76). New York, NY: NLN Press.

Museus, S.D. (2011a). Asian American millennial college students in context: Living at the intersection of diversification, digitization, and globalization. In F. Bonner & V. Lechuga (Eds.), *Diverse millennial students in college: Implications for faculty and student affairs* (pp. 69–88). Sterling, VA: Stylus.

Museus, S.D. (2011b). Mixing quantitative national survey data and qualitative interview data to understand college access and equity: An examination of first-generation Asian Americans and Pacific Islanders. In K.A.

Griffin & S.D. Museus (Eds.), *Using mixed-methods approaches to study intersectionality in higher education* (pp. 63–75). New Directions for Institutional Research, No. 151. San Francisco, CA: Jossey-Bass.

Museus, S. D. (2011c). Using cultural perspectives to understand the role of ethnic student organizations in Black students' progress to the end of the pipeline. In D. H. Evensen & C. D. Pratt (Eds.), *The end of the pipeline: A journey of recognition for African Americans entering the legal profession*. Durham, NC: Carolina Academic Press.

Museus, S.D. (2013a). *Asian American students in higher education*. New York, NY: Routledge.

Museus, S.D. (2013b). Asian Americans and Pacific Islanders: A national portrait of growth, diversity, and inequality. In S.D. Museus, D.C. Maramba, & R.T. Teranishi (Eds.), *The misrepresented minority: New insights on Asian Americans and Pacific Islanders, and their implications for higher education*. Sterling, VA: Stylus.

Museus, S.D. (2013c). Unpacking the complex and multifaceted nature of parental influences on Southeast Asian American college students' educational trajectories. *Journal of Higher Education*, *84*(5), 708–738.

Museus, S.D., Antonio, A.L., & Kiang, P.N. (2012). *The state of scholarship on Asian Americans and Pacific Islanders in education: Anti-essentialism, inequality, context, and relevance*. Honolulu, HI: Asian American and Pacific Islander Research Coalition.

Museus, S.D., & Iftikar, J. (2013, April 27–May 1). *AsianCrit: Toward an Asian critical theory in education*. Paper presented at the Annual Meeting of the American Educational Research Association, San Francisco, CA.

Museus, S.D., & Kiang, P.N. (2009). The model minority myth and how it contributes to the invisible minority reality in higher education research. In S.D. Museus (Ed.), *Conducting research on Asian Americans in higher education* (pp. 5–15). New Directions for Institutional Research, No. 142. San Francisco, CA: Jossey-Bass.

Museus, S.D., Lam, S., Huang, C., Kem, P., & Tan, K. (2012). Cultural integration in campus subcultures: Where the cultural, academic, and social spheres of college life collide. In S.D. Museus & U.M. Jayakumar (Eds.), *Creating campus cultures: Fostering success among racially diverse student populations* (pp. 106–129). New York, NY: Routledge.

Museus, S.D., Maramba, D.C., & Teranishi, R.T. (2013). *The misrepresented minority: New insights on Asian Americans and Pacific Islanders, and their implications for higher education*. Sterling, VA: Stylus.

Museus, S.D., & Park, J.J. (2012, November). *The significance of race and racism in the lives of Asian American college students*. Paper presented at the Annual Meeting of the Association for the Study of Higher Education, Las Vegas, NV.

Museus, S.D., & Quaye, S.J. (2009). Toward an intercultural perspective of racial and ethnic minority college student persistence. *Review of Higher Education*, *33*(1), 67–94.

Museus, S.D., & Truong, K.A. (2013). Racism and sexism in cyberspace: Engaging stereotypes of Asian American women and men to facilitate student learning and development. *About Campus*, *18*(4), 14–21.

Museus, S.D., & Vue, R. (2013). A structural equation modeling analysis of the role of socioeconomic status in Asian American and Pacific Islander students' transition to college. *Review of Higher Education*, *37*(1), 45–67.

Narui, M. (2011). Understanding Asian/American gay, lesbian, and bisexual experiences from a poststructural perspective. *Journal of Homosexuality*, *58*(9), 1211–1234.

Ngo, B., & Lee, S. (2007). Complicating the image of model minority success: A review of Southeast Asian American education. *Review of Educational Research*, *77*(4), 415–453.

Okihiro, G.Y. (1995). *Privileging positions: The sites of Asian American Studies*. Pullman, WA: Washington State University Press.

Park, J.J. (2009). *When race and religion hit campus: An ethnographic examination of a campus religious organization* (Unpublished doctoral dissertation). University of California, Los Angeles.

Pepin, S., & Talbot, D. (2013). *Negotiating the complexities of being Asian American and lesbian, gay, or bisexual.* In S.D. Museus, D.C. Maramba, & R.T. Teranishi (Eds.), *The misrepresented minority: New insights on Asian Americans and Pacific Islanders, and their implications for higher education* (pp. 272–293). Sterling, VA: Stylus.

Prasso, S. (2005). *The Asian mystique*. New York, NY: Public Affairs.

Saito, N.T. (1997). Alien and non-alien alike: Citizenship, "foreignness," and racial hierarchy in American law. *Oregon Law Review*, *76*, 261–345.

Shek, Y.L. (2006). Asian American masculinity: A review of literature. *Journal of Men's Studies*, *14*(3), 379–391.

Sue, D. W., Bucceri, J., Lin, A. I., Nadal, K. L., & Torino, G. C. (2007). Racial microaggressions and the Asian American experience. *Cultural Diversity and Ethnic Minority Psychology*, *13*(1), 72–81.

Suyemoto, K.L., Kim, G.S., Tanabe, M., Tawa, J., & Day, S.C. (2009). Challenging the model minority myth: Engaging Asian American students in research on Asian American college student experiences. In S.D. Museus (Ed.), *Conducting research on Asian Americans in higher education* (pp. 41–55). New Directions for Institutional Research, No. 142. San Francisco, CA: Jossey-Bass.

Suzuki, B.H. (1977). Education and the socialization of Asian Americans: A revisionist analysis of the "model minority" thesis. *Amerasia Journal*, *4*(2), 23–51.

Suzuki, B.H. (2002). Revisiting the model minority stereotype: Implications for student affairs practice and higher education. *Working with Asian American College Students* (pp. 21–32). New Directions for Student Services, No. 97. San Francisco, CA: Jossey-Bass.

Takaki, R. (1989). *Strangers from a different shore: A history of Asian Americans* (Rev. ed.). Boston, MA: Little, Brown.

Tamura, E.H. (2001). Asian Americans in the history of education: An historiographical essay. *History of Education Quarterly, 41*(1), 58–71.

The Sikh Coalition (n.d.). *Fact sheet on post-9/11 discrimination and violence against Sikh Americans.* Retrieved from http://www.sikhcoalition.org/images/documents/fact%20sheet%20on%20hate%20against%20sikhs%20in%20america%20post%209–11%201.pdf

Tierney, W. G. (1999). Models of minority college-going and retention: Cultural integrity versus cultural suicide. *The Journal of Negro Education, 68*(1), 80–91.

Tran, M., & Chang, M.J. (2013). To be mice or men: Gender identity and development of masculinity through participation in Asian American interest fraternities. In S.D. Museus, D.C. Maramba, & R.T. Teranishi (Eds.), *The misrepresented minority: New insights on Asian Americans and Pacific Islanders, and their implications for higher education* (pp. 68–92). Sterling, VA: Stylus.

Umemoto, K. (1989). "On strike!" San Francisco State College strike, 1968–69: The role of Asian American students. *Amerasia Journal, 15*(1), 3–41.

U.S. Census Bureau. (2011). *Overview of race and Hispanic origin: 2010.* Washington, DC: Government Printing Office.

Uyematsu, A. (1971). The emergence of yellow power in America. In A. Tachiki et al. (Eds.), *Roots: An Asian American reader* (pp. 9–13). Los Angeles, CA: University of California Press.

Volpp, L. (2001). "Obnoxious to their very nature": Asian Americans and constitutional citizenship. *Asian Law Journal, 8*, 71–85.

Vue, R. (2013). Searching for self, discovering community: An examination of the experiences of Hmong American college students. In S.D. Museus, D.C. Maramba, & R.T. Teranishi (Eds.), *The misrepresented minority: New insights on Asian Americans and Pacific Islanders, and their implications for higher education* (pp. 214–234). Sterling, VA: Stylus.

Wu, F.H. (1995). Neither Black nor White: Asian Americans and affirmative action. *BC Third World LJ, 15*, 225.

Zhou, M., & Kim, S. (2006). Community forces, social capital, and educational achievement: The case of supplementary education in the Chinese and Korean immigrant communities. *Harvard Educational Review, 76*(1), 1–29.

• I have learned so much about Asian-American students that I never even thought of.

FIVE

Today's Asian Indian College Student

Sudha Wadhwani

Today's Asian Indian college students represent multiple subgroups that reflect the complexity and diversity of the United States and the Indian subcontinent. Successive waves of Indian immigration to the United States have contributed to a rich and heterogeneous Indian American population (Tummala-Narra, Alegria, & Chen, 2012). Indian students' family immigration history and experiences surrounding their adjustment and acculturation processes are critical in determining the context and complexity of their identity development, impact on self-esteem, and issues related to social identity and belonging that may influence their college experience. Contemporary Indian college students are juggling multiple identities and engaging in the process of creating a dynamic, multicultural identity (Inman, Constantine, & Ladany, 1999; Tummala-Narra, 2009; Tummala-Narra, Inman, & Ettigi, 2011) that integrates Indian, Euro-American, and global perspectives.

The development of ethnic and racial identity is a fluid process. Racial identity refers to the level of the student's identification with his/her racial group (Helms, 1995). Ethnic identity refers to the student's sense of belonging and connection to his/her ethnic group and the cultural norms of that group (Ibrahim, Ohnishi, & Sandhu, 1997; Phinney, 1996). Students of Indian descent may identify in multiple ways at any given point in time, and this may change in the course of their college experience. Learning how students self-identify is important to understanding where they may be in their racial and ethnic identity development process. This dynamic self-perception is more important than what box they check. They could identify as Asian Indian, Indian, South Asian, Asian, Asian American, Indian American, East Indian American, or simply American. There have been generational differences through the decades in common identifiers used in the media or literature that also may impact how a student identifies. The term(s) they use to describe themselves and the people they tend to associate with are likely to be influenced by how "Indian" or "American" they feel in their acculturative identity development process.

Asian Indians may or may not be included in research focused on "Asian Americans" (Durvasula & Mylvaganam, 1994). They are typically grouped into the category of South Asian, about which there is a growing body of literature (Tummala-Narra, 2013). The South Asian subcontinent is typically understood to include India, Nepal, Pakistan, Bangladesh, and Sri Lanka. It is important to keep in mind that India alone is so incredibly diverse, with multiple geographic and language groups (e.g., Punjabi, Gujrati, and Sindhi, among others), as well as multiple religions (e.g., Hindu, Muslim, Jain, Sikh, Buddhist, and Christian). Indians are often erroneously grouped with Southeast Asians, who are from Thailand, Vietnam, Myanmar, Cambodia, Malaysia, Indonesia, and the Philippines—countries diverse in their own right and with incredibly different cultures and histories than India. It is important to view such overgroupings with caution, given the large range of diversity of each country. Conceptualizing all the peoples, cultures, and countries across the vast Asian continent and Asians as a whole may lead to misconceptions that would not be helpful in addressing the needs of individual Indian students (Tummala-Narra et al., 2012). However, some research on Asians as a whole may include or be relevant to the experience of Indian students, particularly if other, more specific cultural literature is not available.

The Asian Indian college student's level of acculturation is a critical variable in determining the cultural conflict he or she may experience in the college years. Acculturation refers to the extent to which ethnic minorities adapt to their host culture, as well as the level to which they maintain their culture of origin (Berry, 1980). It has been found that low acculturation to the host culture is associated with greater incidence of problems and more severe challenges among Asians in general, given the greater level of cultural conflict (Leong, Kim, & Gupta, 2011). The emotional difficulties associated with adapting to the challenges of a new culture can cause acculturative stress, which can be exacerbated or mitigated by a multitude of factors related to the nature of the individual's immigration experience (Roysircar-Sodowsky & Maestas, 2000). For example, experiencing discrimination and social isolation can increase an individual's level of acculturative stress, leading to possible mental health difficulties such as depression (Tummala-Narra et al., 2012). On the other hand, family and peer support can serve to buffer an individual's perceived discrimination, mitigating his or her experience of acculturative stress that would otherwise lead to symptoms of depression (Tummala-Narra et al., 2012).

Given the diversity within the Indian community, it is important to use caution when making generalizations or assumptions about the student sitting before you, whether as a therapist, dean, advisor, professor, or other support provider. This chapter will discuss themes that may create conflict for Indian students attending colleges and universities in the United States. Keeping these cultural issues in mind, it is important that the support provider determine where each student fits along a spectrum of acculturation with regard to the various issues presented. It is important to take an emic perspective (Sue & Sue, 1990), meeting students in their cultural world(s) and assessing their cultural conflict, while taking care not to over- or undergeneralize each student's presenting concerns. Understanding the cultural issues and potential areas of conflict and confusion the Indian student experiences could assist the support provider in not over- or underpathologizing the student seeking help. In addition, developing a recognition of the complex factors that may impact the student's college experience could provide the empathy and support the student needs in order to move forward in resolving his/her identity confusion, cultural conflict, or other presenting issues.

Concepts related to identity development, self-esteem, and separation-individuation exemplify the bicultural aspects of the Asian Indian college student experience. These concepts reflect Western-bound, Euro-American perspectives (Tummala-Narra, 2013) that intersect with Indian cultural norms that traditionally emphasize a collective family identity over an individualistic definition of being. Whether the Asian Indian student is presenting with clear cultural conflict concerns or not, a range of acculturation and cultural variables are undoubtedly critical factors in understanding the student's presenting concerns and need to be considered in order to provide culturally competent support. Cultural nuances are embedded to varying degrees in all aspects of students' college developmental process, including their choice of major, career path, social relationships and decision making, the way in which they negotiate the allocation of their time, and so forth. Disregarding cultural variables could hinder the process of providing support and leave the student feeling misunderstood and isolated, which could lead to a premature termination of the support program participation or supportive relationships.

Immigration History of Asian Indians in the United States

Masood, Okazaki, and Takeuchi (2009) report that South Asians are among the fastest-growing Asian immigrant groups in the United States, with Asian Indians being the second-largest Asian immigrant group in the United States (18.6% of total Asians in the United States are Asian Indians; American Immigration Law Foundation (AILF), 2002; Inman & Tummala-Narra, 2010; Mehrotra & Calasanti, 2010; cf. Tummala-Narra, 2013). Many Asian Indians entered the United States after the Immigration and Naturalization Act of 1965, which allowed increased entry for professional Asian Indians and their families (Durvasula & Mylvaganam, 1994). These immigrants were highly educated physicians or scientists with mastery of the English language. They came to America, the "land of opportunity," to realize their dreams of building a prosperous life for their families. It was common for the man to come to the United States, secure a position and place to settle, and then either send for his family or go back to India to marry and return to the States with his new bride. Later, in the 1980s, through the Family Reunification Act, the more professional Asian Indians who were already settled in the United States sponsored the immigration of their family members, causing a bimodal distribution of Indian immigrants in the country. The members of this second immigrant wave created small businesses and vocational trades in hopes of becoming financially stable and realizing their own dreams of achieving a comfortable family life in American society. Adaptation may have been more challenging for the latter group, since they were not as educated or as well versed in English, and thus had limited financial resources (Prathikanti, 1997). Their adjustment would be influenced by many factors, including where they settled in the United States, the context of their immigration experience, associated challenges, and any acculturative stress they endured (Aktar, 2011; Inman, 2006; Tummala-Narra, 2009).

Asian Indian immigrants have continued to migrate to the United States steadily since 1966, with almost two-thirds of the Asian Indian immigrant population arriving after 1990 (AILF, 2002; Mehrotra & Calasanti, 2010; U.S. Bureau of the Census, 2007; cf. Tummala-Narra, 2013). The multiple waves of immigration have created a strongly diverse group of South Asians in the United States that varies in educational level, socioeconomic status, and language proficiency (Tummala-Narra, 2013). In addition to a history of different pre-immigration contexts, each of these cohorts may experience unique challenges and social pressures as they acclimate to the United States and engage in their acculturation process, which will be experienced and responded to differently across immigrant generations (Bhattacharya & Schoppelrey, 2004; Tummala-Narra et al., 2012). Across the literature, first-generation Asian Indians are typically described as those born and raised in India until the age of 18, while second-generation Asian Indians are described as those born and raised in the United States or those who migrated to the United States in their childhood—that is, prior to age 18 (Tummala-Narra et al., 2011).

Today's Indian college freshmen were born in 1995 and came of age in the post-9/11 era. Just when those of the initial immigrant generations were making progress in being acknowledged as "American," 9/11 triggered increased nationalism and mistrust of foreigners, particularly immigrant groups with brown skin or accents. Those groups are often misunderstood and discriminated against, along with other Asians and Middle Eastern immigrant groups, particularly Muslim and Sikh religious subgroups (Ahluwalia & Pellettiere, 2010; Inman, Yeh, Madan-Bahel, & Nath, 2007; Tummala-Narra, 2013; Tummala-Narra et al., 2012). Current Indian college students were either born in India and entered the United States as small children, or were born after their parents emigrated to the United States. Depending on multiple variables surrounding their immigration and acculturation process, including where the family settled, these young adults may have been raised in homes that maintained traditional Indian values and lifestyles. They may now be faced with new challenges as they adjust to a greater level of independence and establish their identities in the college setting. Given the diversity of today's college students and the fact that they came to the United States at different points, it is critical to assess the individual student's particular immigration history and how it impacts his or her college experience.

The College Developmental Process for the Asian Indian Student

Second-generation Asian Indians are approaching adulthood as products of two very distinct cultural systems. While Indian students may face particular stressors related to their own acculturation process, they also face stressors shared by other minority students as well as college students as a whole. Grayson (1989) argues that students who do not disengage effectively from their parents cannot fully invest in college life and acquire the skills needed to live independently in society. It is clear that Grayson's developmental theory is based on a Western worldview. As seen through this lens—that is, without considering cultural differences—many Asian Indian students would be viewed as developmentally backward, since concepts of separation and individuation are not consistent with Indian culture (Viswanathan, Shah, & Ahad, 1997). On the other hand, it would be unrealistic for Indian families to expect that their Asian Indian college students would not individuate somewhat when they are in a situation in which that is the norm. In some cases, Asian Indian parents may not understand the need for adaptation to the host culture, leading them to do whatever they feel is necessary to prevent such individuation in an effort to safeguard the survival of family life. (In some cases they may even send their pre-teen and adolescent children to India to keep them from internalizing American influences and to preserve more traditional Indian values.) Even in Western cultures, many families have difficulty adjusting to the effects of their children's independence on the family system; however, these struggles would naturally be exacerbated in families adhering to an Eastern collectivist belief system. Given these two contradicting cultural views of development, it is critical to view the Indian American college student's developmental process through a bicultural lens. College personnel need to develop an understanding of specific aspects of the Asian Indian culture and how they may conflict with the developmental models on which American psychotherapy and higher education are based. This knowledge will assist them in assessing whether an Indian student who initially appears to be developmentally behind in terms of separating from his or her family is actually having developmental difficulties or is, in fact, behaving in a manner that is culturally conforming. In some cases these students may present as conflicted because their desire for independence may be at odds with their family's views of how their role within the family system should continue, despite their move to college. It is important that providers are knowledgeable about these complex cultural issues so that they can respond sensitively and competently.

Nguyen (2006) argues that second and later generations of racial and ethnic minorities raised in the United States may be at greater risk for challenges to their well-being and mental health. The Asian Indian student's acculturation process and way of identifying is likely to be impacted by his or her experience in elementary school, middle school, the childhood neighborhood, high school, and so on. Whether the student's hometown was predominantly Indian or whether it was more integrated or mostly White is an important factor. Also, it would be helpful to learn about his or her experience as a person of Indian descent (e.g., whether his or her cultural identity was received well and accepted by peers, or was a source of rejection and shame). It will be important to assess whether the student's experience back home was different or similar to the experience at college. For example, was the student the only Indian in his or her school and is now in a school with a large Indian student community? Or was the student raised in a community with a large Indian presence and is now one of the only Indian students in his or her college or university? Also, how often the family visited India provides information as to how assiduously the connection to the home culture was preserved. In addition, the frequency of visits or phone calls (including Skype) by family from India provides information on how much impact the extended family in India has on a day-to-day basis. Having older generations in the home also affects the level of cultural conflict and any acculturation gap the student may experience.

For Asian Indian students, the stressors of college can be exacerbated by pressure from the Indian culture regarding academic expectations, contact with family, and social restrictions with peers. They may face conflict because of the competing values of the American and Asian Indian cultures. Ramisetty-Mikler (1993) described considerable differences between the two cultures that are likely to lead to the need for a shifting of family roles and potential conflicts during the acculturation process, including the perception of time, role of religion and philosophy of life, and family structure. Asian Indian students often experience a disconnect between the demands of their family (i.e., Asian Indian norms and values) and the environmental pressures to individuate and seek independence (i.e., American norms and values) (Durvasula & Mylvaganam, 1994; Segal, 1991; Varma, 1988). These students may face the following challenges: interpersonal (e.g., socializing with peers, time spent in family activities, dating, marriage) (Durvasula & Mylvaganam, 1994; Varma, 1988); educational (e.g., choosing a major and future occupation); and emotional (e.g., feeling torn between loyalty to their family and desire for exploration and independence) (Varma, 1988). For example, these students may feel a conflict between building relationships with their college peers and responding to demands to attend family functions. They may experience anxiety as a result of family pressures to partake in an arranged marriage when they are in a secret relationship that would not meet the approval of their parents (Sodowsky & Carey, 1988). They may second-guess their academic and vocational decisions because of family pressures to go into the medical field when they would prefer to pursue a field that would not meet with their parents' approval. Understanding their interpersonal, educational, and emotional needs, as well as the nature of the Asian Indian family system, is crucial to providing culturally consistent services.

Learning about students' membership in groups and organizations can serve as a springboard to exploring deeper aspects of their cultural, racial, and ethnic identity. It can also provide a window onto their immigration and acculturation process. Given that ethnic and racial identity development is a fluid process throughout life, with college being a time of exploring issues of identity and belonging, the role the Indian culture plays in students' college life is likely to evolve along various points in their college experience. Throughout their 4 (or so) years of college, Indian students may explore and connect with different groups and peers, whether related to their ethnic/cultural/religious identity or to other aspects of their identity (e.g., particular interest, hobby, or subject). Whether students are or are not involved in student cultural or religious organizations may provide insight into their level of connection to their Indian identity and where they are in the process of acculturation or ethnic identity development. Some Indian students may feel at home in the Indian Culture Club on campus, while others may not. Some may be more connected with their religious identity/group and may feel more comfortable in the Muslim or Hindu (or Sikh, etc.) cultural organizations, while others may feel that they do not fit in with peers in their respective religious organization. Yet other students may choose to have friends from multiple minority or international backgrounds and join other minority organizations (e.g., Asian Student Organization, International Student Organization). In addition, some students may not feel a particular connection to their ethnicity, race, or religion, and may focus on having friends from diverse backgrounds who share other commonalities, such as an interest in math, gaming, art, or a particular sport, for example.

Within-group differences will also impact whether an Indian student joins a particular organization or chooses to connect with other Indian students. In qualitative interviews with Indian college students, the distinction between "ABCDs" ("American Born Confused Desis") and "FOBs" ("Fresh Off the Boats") was repeatedly described as a distinction within the Indian student community between second- and first-generation Indian students respectively (Wadhwani, 2000). Tummala-Narra (2013) states that conceptions of the culture of origin and the mainstream culture are evidenced in self-identity labels and indicate one's relationship to the culture of origin and to the mainstream culture. These self-identifiers and memberships provide a window onto the student's sense of authenticity and belonging to each respective community. A student who is a more recent immigrant from India may not feel a sense of belonging in the Indian student organization, for example, if the membership consists more of second-generation Indian students. Many second-generation Indian students stated that being Indian seemed to keep them grounded and influenced the choices they made about focusing on studies over drinking and partying. Interestingly, these students were found to be even more involved in the Indian community than a sample of Asian International students, of which only one-third reported active participation in cultural and religious organizations on campus (Kenney, 1994).

Some Indian students may purposely choose not to be involved in the Indian student community on campus and make a conscious decision not to have Indian friends. These students may be concerned that participating in Indian social groups will exclude them from socializing with non-Indian students. Several Indian students interviewed expressed concern that non-Indian peers would perceive their membership in Indian or Asian student organizations as "self-segregation" and assume they did not want to socialize with non-Indian peers (Wadhwani, 2000). Contextual factors may also impact how they choose to identify and with whom they want to associate. For example, their experience will be impacted by whether they are living in a geographic area that feels unsafe (particularly post-9/11) or in a college community that they perceive to be not accepting of difference. Tummala-Narra, Inman, and Ettigi (2011) suggest that second-generation Asian Indians may internally identify as more "American" and not want to identify as "other," highlighting their minority status in a racialized society. Racism-related stress can influence Indian students' racial and ethnic identity, as these negative perceptions of their Indian identity can be internalized and create a sense of shame and self-hatred (Helms, 1995; Inman, 2006). These challenges are of particular concern to Indian college students, for whom a sense of acceptance and belonging is critical to self-esteem and adjustment to college. Indian college students may be particularly sensitive to how they are perceived by others (Tummala-Narra & Claudius, 2013a), because they are at a critical point in identity development when they are trying to connect with others and determine where and to what groups they belong.

The Indian Student's Family Context

Given that the concept of separation-individuation is based on a more Western (Euro-American) perspective, Indian students may be expected to continue their level of involvement with their families during the college years. This would be in contrast to the path of their Euro-American peers, who are in the process of individuating from their families of origin (Tummala-Narra, 2013; Viswanathan et al., 1997). Although intergenerational conflict may be common for all students regardless of ethnicity, the experience may be different for Asian Indians (and possibly students of other South Asian backgrounds), especially at the college level. For example, students of all ethnic backgrounds may have conflicts with their parents about curfew, social activities, time with family, dating/relationships, grades, and majors; however, certain elements of the Indian culture may exacerbate the intensity of these conflicts for Indian college students. Wakil, Siddique, and Wakil (1981) report conflicts related to sex role development, dating, and marriage among Asian Indians. Kurian (1986) states that intergenerational conflict is likely to arise in relation to individual freedom, gender-based double standards, cultural identity, cultural assimilation, dating, marriage, and social change. Sodowsky and Carey (1987) describe parent-child cultural conflicts related to dating and marriage. Lee (1997) states that intergenerational conflict among Asian families often occurs over dating, marriage, educational goals, and career choice. Mehta (1998), who has studied the relationship between acculturation and mental health in first-generation immigrants, has revealed the need to determine how second-generation Asian Indians cope with the acculturation process and interact with their parents to resolve intergenerational conflict, particularly in relation to dating and marriage.

The level of acculturation gap (Prathikanti, 1997) in the family system will influence how much of an issue certain cultural variables will be for the individual. If the student's parents are quite acculturated and open to dating, choice of major/career, or socialization options, there may be less of a conflict for the Indian college student. In addition, some students may have a strong and clear attachment to their family customs, religion, and culture, and not have an interest in participating in typical aspects of college life (social groups, range of majors, etc.). If their views and choices are consistent with those of their parents, their adjustment to college will be less complicated by confusion and cultural conflict.

Asian Indian families are quite different from Euro-American families in terms of norms and structure (Durvasula & Mylvaganam, 1994; Shon & Ja, 1982). The Asian Indian family is not focused on individual members; rather, family members are expected to sacrifice their individual needs for the benefit of the family as a whole. It would be considered selfish and shameful not to make sacrifices for the sake of family, since the concept of self is actually a collective self that includes the family (Steiner & Bansil, 1989; Viswanathan et al., 1997). Each member has a clearly defined role within the hierarchical family system designed to make it function successfully, and that role is based on norms of interdependence, obedience, and conformity (Segal, 1991). Children are viewed as the fruit of the parents' life work (Durvasula & Mylvaganam, 1994), as well as a reflection of the larger extended family system. According to Lee (1997), across Asian cultures the individual is the product of all the generations of his or her family, and personal action reflects not only on the self but also on the family as a whole. Members have an ethical responsibility to the family that can be quite demanding; however, they also have strong loyalty, since the family is a tremendous source of support and pride (Ramisetty-Mikler, 1993). First-generation immigrants (i.e., the parents), who may be holding on to the ways of life they left behind in their home country, may set limitations on their children's exposure to Western lifestyles, leaving the children at the meeting point of two quite different cultures. As Indian families are assimilating into American society, many are becoming less authoritarian and increasingly allow children's input in decision making (Sodowsky, 1985). However, they are still likely to be influenced by traditional cultural norms of how a family should function.

Lee (1997) discusses five types of immigrant families within the Asian culture: the traditional family, the cultural-conflict family, the bicultural family, the Americanized family, and the interracial family. In the "traditional family," all members were born and raised in Asian countries. In the "cultural-conflict family," members hold different cultural values, since each member came to the United States at a different point in his or her development. For example, grandparents who came later in their lives would retain their traditional beliefs, whereas children raised in the United States would be more "Americanized." In this type of family, Lee argues, there is considerable stress due to intergenerational conflicts, because each generation has different values and expectations. Traditional parents expect their children to be respectful and obedient, focusing on their role as hardworking students. In contrast, the child's American peers may have more opportunity to participate in family decisions, engage in recreational activities, build a sense of self-reliance and autonomy, and be assertive and open with opinions and ideas. This would not be encouraged in the Asian household, where the child must deferentially comply fully and without question. The third type of family Lee refers to is the "bicultural family," in which the parents are well acculturated and quite familiar with the American culture because they were either raised in urbanized (i.e., "Westernized") locales in their home country or were actually born in America themselves. These families are usually bilingual, professional, and middle or upper class. The relationship between parents in the bicultural family is more egalitarian, decision making is a joint endeavor, and children are allowed to join family discussions, thereby merging several Eastern and Western cultural beliefs. The fourth family type, the "Americanized family," consists of parents and children who were all born and raised in the United States. Finally, in the "interracial family," the Asian individual has married outside the Asian culture. Given the diversity among these families, the level of difficulty a student experiences will likely be related to the type of family in which he or she was raised.

It is important to understand the student's family system and role in his or her family. There is considerable diversity among Indian families in terms of acculturation and level of cultural or religious practice, ranging from less to more traditional in terms of beliefs, values, and family norms. This diversity will, in turn, impact restrictions and rules laid out by the family. In terms of connection to family, it would be helpful to assess how often the student calls home, goes home, and is expected to engage in family functions and activities while in college (particularly if he or she is close to home). Expectations on the part of family to continue to partake in family affairs in the same way as back in high school could lead the Indian college student to feel torn between home and school social lives and commitments. There is likely to be more family connectedness and expectation for the Indian student than for the average American student, given Asian Indian norms of interdependence. It has been found that Indian students typically remain integral to family life rather than becoming developmentally "individuated," "autonomous," or "independent," as is commonly the case in Western families when children go to college (Ramisetty-Mikler, 1993). There is an expectation for the Asian Indian college student to continue his or her role in the family even though he or she is now in college. The student's birth order and the acculturation of siblings may also be factors in his or her cultural conflict and adjustment to college. For example, an older sibling may have paved the way, rebelled, or followed the culturally conforming path, leading this student to feel pressured to conform to parents' desires or to feel unable to take a different path. In other cases, the student may be the oldest child and would not want to make things harder for the younger siblings.

In interviews with Indian college students, many subjects reported maintaining two separate lives—home and school—that they described as a practical solution to maintaining the peace and keeping everyone happy (e.g., family and self) (Wadhwani, 2000). It may be that living in these two worlds is working fine for them and that they have found a way to negotiate them. Secrecy appeared to be their reported method of balancing their parents' wishes and their own, particularly in relation to dating practices (not so different from LGBTQ students across cultures, who have not yet come out to their parents and go back into the closet when at home). There is no doubt that some level of secrecy is involved in parent-child relationships across cultures. In American culture, the secrecy may be related to drug use or poor grades. However, it appeared that secrecy was a common form of relating (or not relating) between Indian American students and their parents in this sample. The specifics of what is kept secret—dating, going to a party with friends—seemed different in this population. (Most American adolescents and college students are allowed to date and go out with friends, so they do not need to keep it a secret.) It could be that maintaining secrecy was essentially a way for some Indian students to balance the two cultural systems—their actions did not cause conflict in the family, yet their own needs were also being met. These students may not see it as deceit, but more as a pragmatic strategy of compartmentalizing to make everyone happy.

It is likely that the more restrictive the parents, the more the potential for secrecy. In turn, secrecy inevitably affects the quality of the parent-child relationship, and the student either gets caught or experiences feelings of guilt and shame that could lead to further distress. Although secrecy may be an effective approach for some Indian students, evidence suggests that having a more open relationship with parents, including more communication, is associated with more positive mental health outcomes across immigrant cultures (Cho & Haslam, 2010). Indian students have been described as perceiving considerable differences in their relationships with their parents as compared to their American peers, stating that their American peers were able to have more open relationships with their parents. Asian Indian students perceived their parents to be more restrictive and conservative than American parents (Wadhwani, 2000). This is consistent with the markedly different theories of separation-individuation within the two cultures. For certain Indian students, it was found that secrecy from parents caused inner turmoil and guilt, feelings of exhaustion from maintaining two separate lives, and anxiety about the risk of being found out (Wadhwani, 2000). There is an element of risk involved when one chooses to maintain two separate lives, and this can be very stressful. If and when these cultural worlds collide—such as during breaks, in the summer, when parents visit campus, upon graduation, or if there are other students from home attending the same college—these students may suffer heightened cultural conflict to the point of experiencing anxiety or panic symptoms, or even presenting in a state of crisis. In addition, the burgeoning social media phenomenon has changed the culture of communication and privacy for today's college students. As a result of Facebook, Instagram, blogging, and the like, it has become more challenging for students to keep the two worlds separate. Information that in the past could have been maintained at a private level now can be publicized in ways beyond one's control, leading to a potential blurring of the student's two worlds. These challenges could increase an Indian student's anxiety and confusion surrounding balancing his/her college and family worlds.

Indian students have reported a decline in their family contact as they settle into college. For instance, they see their parents increasingly less after their first year (Wadhwani, 2000), which indicates that some level of separation-individuation has taken place. It may be that the same developmental changes do occur in this population, but at a more gradual pace such that students would be more individuated by the time they complete their college education. In other words, while they remain students, they are considered to have the same dependent role in family life, but this gradually shifts in the course of their college experience. After completion of college, women in particular are expected to move to the next phase of life to become part of their husband's family (the more traditional route, if the family is less acculturated) or to continue on a trajectory toward being a more independent adult (if the family is more acculturated).

Even at the college level, it is common for Indian parents to want their offspring to be an integral part of the family and to try to influence their social and dating practices (Prathikanti, 1997). Although Indian parents may apply restrictions in the hope of protecting and strengthening their son or daughter's Indian identity, there is a concern that they could, in fact, be driving their children farther away from the culture and the family, while at the same time alienating them from their American peers. These restrictions may lead Indian students to experience internal struggle and emotional distress in their adjustment to college life, given their inability to connect with other students and maintain interpersonal peer relationships.

The "Acculturation Gap": Juggling Family and School/Self

When a family migrates to America, the parents may try to maintain the homeland culture and keep their child from "Americanizing." However, it is inevitable that, in the new context, other cultural norms will infiltrate the family system. Prathikanti (1997) states that in families where there are discrepant levels of acculturation, intrafamilial cultural conflicts may occur because of an "acculturation gap" that would exacerbate the "generation gap" found across all cultures. In response, parents may adopt an even more conservative and rigid stance in order to reinforce the values of the native culture. It may be that students who experience the most conflict are those whose parents met the most discrimination or had difficulty assimilating into the host culture and, thus, held on to a stronger Indian cultural identity (Sodowsky & Carey, 1988) rather than develop a flexible integration of their homeland culture and American attitudes (Cross, 1971). Students who have less acculturated parents, but are more acculturated themselves, are more likely to have a conflict with their parents, since there is more of an "acculturation gap." They may have more difficulty balancing their own wishes with those of their parents, since the two would be more dissonant.

The "acculturation gap" creates a further divide than does the "generation gap" that all college students face. Students' connection and loyalty to family is often in conflict with their desire to fit into the college world. Often, Indian parents attempt to shield them from the perceived negative influences of American college life that take them away from their religious functions, studies, and focus on academics, family, and career, which is the culturally normative focus for this phase of life. There is no place for social groups, student activities, partying, or dating, as these are often perceived as distractions from the family and impediments to the student's success.

According to Eastern belief systems, the family's needs supersede individual needs. However, Indian American college students have usually been raised in a Western society in which peers normatively consider their own wishes. That is not to say that the family is not important in Western cultures, or that there isn't variation among families; however, there is a clear emphasis on respecting individual needs, wishes, and boundaries. Given these dissimilar cultural norms, Indian American students would need to strike a balance by negotiating with their parents and coming to some sort of compromise, with give-and-take on both ends indicating a merging of the two philosophical systems. Most Indian American students interviewed indicated that there were difficulties in balancing their family and school lives. Some students reported coping with the discrepant cultural worlds by maintaining a separate social life at college that they did not disclose to their parents, but at the same time conforming to their parents' wishes when they went home on weekends. Others dealt with these challenges by giving in to their parents and neglecting their own needs (which would be the more culturally appropriate route) or defying their parents openly (which would be antithetic to cultural norms of obedience and respect for authority). Although these methods of managing their relationships with their parents may in some ways be adaptive, all of these approaches may also eventually create internal conflict, guilt, and distress that could place these students at risk for future emotional difficulties (Wadhwani, 2000).

Connection to extended family here in the United States and in India is an important variable in Indian students' acculturation process. The importance of image, the reflection on the family, and even the marriageability of other family members (immediate and extended) in the United States or in India could be a concern for individuals or for their parents. Their choices and academic success or failure could impact many others in their collectivistic family system. Again, there is such diversity within the Indian community that this may not be an issue for some; for others, however, this could be a very real barrier to seeking help and creates great concern, given the strong cultural stigma of mental health treatment. Students may not be focused as much on themselves as on other family members. The influence of family comes not only from the immediate family but also, in many cases, from family back in India by way of phone or Skype. With the emergence of Skype in recent years, Indian students and their families may be in more contact with relatives in India than in the past and receive a greater level of pressure from family back home. Indian students report that family members who reside in a very different society may seem judgmental and unsupportive, when in fact they are from another world and do not understand the students' real experience. With that said, it should be noted that, because of globalization factors, the family back home may be more Americanized than the family here in the United States that has maintained the level of tradition found in the India they left behind decades ago.

Dating and Marriage

Dating is an area where there are clear cultural norms and striking differences between the values of the American and Asian Indian cultures. Dating and courtship, per Western style, and premarital sex are not permitted in the Asian Indian culture (Durvasula & Mylvaganam, 1994), particularly for women (Saran, 1985). Prathikanti (1997) states that parents may fear that dating will lead to premarital sex or loss of the family's cultural identity through interracial marriage. They may want to protect their child and the family as a whole for the future, without understanding the conflicting feelings their child may be experiencing. Conversely, the child may feel frustrated by not being able to attend social activities as do the majority of his or her peers. Basham (1996) states that, in the original Vedic tradition, the first quarter of one's life should be dedicated to study and moral development, the second to work, marriage, and experiencing the joys and struggles of life, the third to turning over family and vocational responsibilities to the next generation, and the fourth to contemplation and spiritual inquiry. The expectations stemming from this Vedic tradition proscribe behaviors that are normative among the U.S. college population, which leads many Asian Indian students to date in secret. This secrecy speaks to the traditional parental influence and/or avoidance of conflict with parents, and it may illustrate a difficulty in negotiating the two cultures. On the other hand, these students have determined that secrecy, which keeps their two lives safely separate, is the best way to negotiate their cultural conflict (Wadhwani, 2000).

Sodowsky and Carey (1988) examined views on interracial dating among first- and second-generation Asian Indian immigrants. They found that less acculturated subjects showed greater disapproval of their children dating American peers and specifically felt they should not go out on dates or to dances with American peers of the opposite sex. Alternatively, subjects who were non-married students and identified as bicultural-integrated or mostly American were approving of dating American peers. Based on these findings, the authors suggested the possibility of intergenerational conflict wherein second-generation Asian Indians feel dissatisfied about not being allowed to date Americans. Based on interviews with Indian college students, it was found that, depending on level of acculturation, some Indian students anticipated having an Indian partner in the future because it would make life much easier for them. Some students who were dating non-Indian partners (and had generally not disclosed this to their families) stated that they considered the relationship to be temporary and would want an Indian partner when they were ready for a more serious relationship (and thus would not inform their parents of their dating until that point). One subject stated that when she was with her Indian boyfriend she did not need to explain why her parents were the way they were, whereas it had been more of an issue with her former non-Indian boyfriends, who did not understand Indian family issues (Wadhwani, 2000).

In interviews with Indian college students on the topic of arranged marriage, a majority of them indicated a preference for some sort of compromise between—or hybrid of—arranged marriage and American forms of courtship in which they would be willing to be introduced to someone by their parents but would want to get to know the person before making the final decision. Some stated they would be fine with this type of arrangement if they were to reach a certain age and not have found someone on their own. Although many students believed in more Americanized marriage practices, a considerable number were open to some diluted form of arranged marriage. In terms of dating, Indian students reported that they would not tell their parents about the person they were dating, even if the person met their parents' criteria (e.g., same ethnicity, religion, education, or status), because they were concerned their parents would push them to marry. This focus on marriage rather than allowing the dating process is qualitatively different from the approach of Western culture. In fact, American parents would probably want their children to be sure before choosing to marry and would feel they were marrying too soon in the relationship if the couple had not spent some time dating (Wadhwani, 2000).

It should be noted that, even in more traditional arranged marriages, the person may have the final pick of a selection of candidates chosen by the family. How strictly this procedure is followed will depend on within-group differences as well as differences between families. Most often, the final decision is made jointly with the family (Durvasula & Mylvaganam, 1994; Viswanathan et al., 1997), possibly accompanied by pressure to follow the recommendations of family friends or extended family who may have been involved in the process. Nevertheless, it is safe to say that, even in more progressive families who practice arranged marriage, the couple is not likely to date or get to know each other to the degree found in Western courtship practices. Often they will meet on just a few occasions in the company of other family members (Prathikanti, 1997). According to Durvasula and Mylvaganam (1994), the concept of arranged marriage dictates that the child (who is an adult) marry a person who is chosen by the parents based on social (i.e., caste) and cultural compatibility, factors believed to yield a successful marriage. Marriage is considered to be an alliance between two families rather than two individuals (Viswanathan et al., 1997). Assessing whether the student's parents were arranged is a relevant factor in determining family norms and views surrounding arranged marriage, although this is strongly impacted by the parents' immigration and acculturation experience after coming to the United States. It is important to remember that there are within-group and individual differences; thus, certain students may have had forebears who did not fit the more general Indian norms. It would be helpful to determine the context and response of the extended family toward their parents' marriage (for example, if it was a "love marriage" or cross-cultural marriage).

The negotiated version of arranged marriage described by Indian American students seems to include "getting to know the person" (i.e., dating) before making a decision and being "individually" compatible, indicating that they have been influenced by American cultural norms. However, they are willing to accept their parents' input in meeting the person, which indicates a clear Indian cultural influence. Thus, the approach seems to be a true hybrid of the two conflicting belief systems (Wadhwani, 2000). Similarly, in interviews with Indian-American women ages 20 to 30 who had "one foot in each culture," Gupta (1999) found that "they are weaving conflicting marital traditions into a new pattern, one they can live with…negotiating a bicultural identity" (p. 121).

Major and Career

Coping with educational/career norms and expectations are common presenting concerns for Indian students, in many cases serving as areas of entry for them to seek help, since there is less cultural stigma associated with academic concerns than emotional or mental health concerns. Asian Indian college students have been found to report cultural conflict related to academics (e.g., studying, grades, major, profession, or choice of college). Ramisetty-Mikler (1993) states that achievement and education are status symbols in Indian society. A job becomes one's identity (and, by definition, the family's collective identity), and the family is supposed to play a critical role in career decision making. The child's role is to bring honor to the family through his or her achievements, while loyalty and shame reinforce expectations and behavior (Durvasula & Mylvaganam, 1994). Indian students often report pressure from their parents to major in science-related fields as opposed to liberal arts. It may be that their parents, as a result of their immigration experience, brought with them a fixed notion of what constitutes success and stability (Prathikanti, 1997; Roysircar, Carey, & Koroma, 2010; Wadhwani, 2000).

Parents' career status and immigration history are likely to influence educational and career expectations for their child in a way that the student has likely internalized. As is the case with other immigrant groups, Indian parents may not understand or believe that there are alternative ways to be successful in the United States, since they have a strong cultural bias toward careers that provide stronger financial security. These parents most often mean well and only want the best for their child, but may inadvertently be pressuring their child into a crisis. Indian parents are found to focus on majors that are more secure and practical because they want their children to be financially stable and not have to face the obstacles that they did. It is important to note that the concept of loving what you do and deriving passion from your work is a very Western concept that is at odds with what Indian students are hearing at home. Culturally, one's career is to provide for the family and may not be something a person enjoys or loves. It is important to recognize the inconsistent messages that students are receiving (from family vs. college resources) and assist them in negotiating this cultural conflict, both within themselves and with the family.

Initially, Indian immigrants with scientific and medical skills were recruited to the United States in recognition of their advanced abilities (Sodowsky & Carey, 1988). They were provided the opportunity to come to the United States for career advancement and a "better life," and in this way their training in science-related fields opened doors for them. These parents want the same opportunities for their children and do not want them to be limited in any way. They believe a science-related or medical position will provide financial and job security (Roysircar et al., 2010). Students may not understand this concern and feel pressured when in fact they would prefer to pursue other careers, but still may feel a sense of loyalty and a desire to please their parents. Students may feel pushed to major in science-related fields to fulfill the wishes of their parents, whom they perceive to have sacrificed so much to come to this country for the educational and career opportunities available to their children. In this way, Indian students may feel externally and internally compelled to push through and persist in a major or career path that may not be a good fit for them. Their parents may not even be aware of their children's academic difficulties. Students may feel a sense of shame about keeping their progressive failure from their parents. This in turn may create inner turmoil, as they are loath to disappoint their parents, who unknowingly exert pressure or express expectations (without knowing how much the student is in fact struggling). Indian parents may not recognize these signs or may feel it inappropriate to push their students to overcome their struggles and focus on their studies and do well. A student's persistent failure may cause further distress and symptoms of depression. Again, because of cultural stigma, first-generation parents may not see these as indicators of a problem or may deny them.

This cultural conflict regarding majors may be similar for Asians in general, but this is not the case for all students. Liberal arts majors are actually quite popular among the general college population. Across cultures, parents' careers are likely to influence selection of majors among students to some degree. Indian students have also been found to feel pressure from parents to focus on their work and not engage in extracurricular activities, while at the same time they learn from college professionals that it is important to engage in student activities and be well-rounded, like many of their American peers (Wadhwani, 2000). It is important for support providers (e.g., deans, advisors, counselors, etc.) to be aware of what cultural factors may be impacting Indian students, in order to support them in negotiating the potentially dissonant messages they may be receiving from home and college fronts.

Model Minority Myth

As with other Asian groups, there is often an assumption that the Indian student is smart, science/math inclined, studious, and on the path to becoming a physician, an engineer, or some sort of scientist. The internalized expectations of the model minority myth can be concerning because they perpetuate the pressure to conform to a certain standard that may not be the best fit for the individual. The student may feel a sense of shame and failure secondary to being perceived as a disappointment to his or her family and culture, leading to potential self-esteem issues, anxiety, depression, helplessness, and even hopelessness. This dissonance can lead students to feel confused and persist—despite repeated failures—when a major turns out to be unsuitable, feeling the need to work harder in order to appease the parents and other family members. They may compare themselves (or be compared) to siblings or cousins in the extended family system who have conformed to these model minority expectations, leading to further feelings of inadequacy.

The model minority myth also has an effect on help-seeking attitudes and behavior among Asian Americans. Internalized expectations of being successful, achieving, strong, self-disciplined, and intelligent (Leong et al., 2011) are naturally going to impact acknowledgment of one's difficulties and need of help (Tummala-Narra et al., 2012; Tummala-Narra & Claudius, 2013b; Yoo & Castro, 2011). Students may feel that they should not have such difficulties and should be able to overcome challenges and barriers. This internalized expectation may lead to further shame over not doing well and increased denial as they continue to push forward, despite initial symptoms and difficulties, without seeking the support they need. Tummala-Narra, Alegria, and Chen (2012) argue that such conceptions of South Asians as model minorities and their success in certain areas (e.g., academically and professionally) can be harmful and potentially mask the significant problems and psychological needs of this group. Sue & Sue (2008) describe a catch-22 in which underutilization of mental health services by Asian Americans because of what they refer to as "culture-bound" factors perpetuates the model minority myth, which is internalized and in turn exacerbates cultural variables that prevent Asians from seeking help. This extreme pressure that Asian Americans have to face in relation to academics and career can create feelings of self-doubt and inadequacy, as well as the need to maintain a certain image as a successful minority in the United States. In addition, South Asians may experience discrimination from other minority and majority groups as a result of this stereotyping, leading to perceptions that South Asians are taking jobs or academic slots from other groups, or that they see themselves as better than other groups (Tummala-Narra & Claudius, 2013b). This myth can also perpetuate the pressure parents put on their children to pursue certain careers (e.g., become a physician), to meet a certain societal image or expectation, and to be accepted as successful in this country. Thus, the Indian student who internalizes this expectation may feel a sense of failure and shame, and even entertain suicidal thoughts when he or she is not living up to the expectations of parents, extended family, and society as a whole (Yoo & Castro, 2011).

Intersectionality of Identity

Assessing aspects of Indian students' identity as they intersect with environmental/college variables is critical. It is important to recognize other aspects of students' identity, including religion, gender (i.e., gender role expectations), class/SES, and sexual orientation. Different aspects of students' multiple identities may be salient at different points in their development, particularly during the college years—a time of exploration, growth, and change. Additionally, other important variables relevant to students' whole identity and college experience are their academic standing and whether they live on or off campus.

Religious identity. Hindu values tend to be pervasive and influential across subcultures and have influenced general conceptions of "Indian culture." Hinduism is not only a religion, but also a philosophical system and way of life (Almeida, 1996). Other religions among Indians include the Jain, Muslim, Buddhist, Catholic, and Sikh faiths. As with other ethnic groups, religion is strongly connected to cultural practice, and Indians are often more connected with other families within their religious faith. Among Indian students, there are considerable within-group differences across religions. In fact, Indian students may feel more connected to other students of the same religion, across ethnic groups, than to fellow Indians of different religions.

Gender. A comparison of Indian and American college students found that women in both groups had a high degree of concern related to being a good wife and mother, while males were more concerned with achievement and prestige (Raina & Vats, 1990). In Indian culture, as in many other Eastern and Middle Eastern cultures, there are very clearly defined gender role expectations (Tummala-Narra, 2013). Historically, the woman's role was traditionally that of mother and homemaker. If an Indian woman went to college, it was incompatible with those expectations and served the purpose of enrichment rather than providing for the family.

Depending on their level of acculturation, female Indian students may experience cultural conflict with regard to balancing their careers and professional aspirations with gender role expectations. For first-generation Indian students who were raised in more traditional environments in India, adapting to different gender role expectations will be more of a challenge (Tummala-Narra, 2013). On the other hand, for second-generation Indian females who were born and raised in the United States, this may be less of an issue. However, there may be divergent role expectations within the same family for male and female children, causing possible tensions within the family or between siblings (Aktar, 2011). For example, an academically driven second-generation Indian female may experience confusion, conflict, and/or frustration with regard to perceived injustice in response to the priority given to the education of her male siblings by her more traditional first-generation parents.

SES/Class. It has been suggested that there is a correlation between class level and the incidence of emotional disorders (Schwartz & Reifler, 1984). Indian students from lower-class backgrounds may have more limited resources and greater financial pressures; students from higher-class backgrounds, whose parents are more academically and professionally successful, may have other stressors to contend with, such as pressure to excel academically and major in science-related fields. For Indian students today, the history of caste dynamics may manifest more as class issues and biases among Indian subgroups. Particularly as it concerns friendships and dating, families may prefer their family friends and the student's friends to be from similar language/cultural groups (e.g., Gujrati, Punjabi, Sindhi, etc.). These within-group biases may escalate in relation to dating and marital choice. Interviews with Indian college students reveal that issues related to caste are less important than the requirement that their friends or future spouse be "from a good family," meaning from a similar family to one's own in terms of education, career, class, religion, and values (Wadhwani, 2000).

Sexual orientation. The topic of sexuality is typically taboo and not discussed openly in the Indian family (Tummala-Narra, 2013). Family image and shame may be important deterrents to Indian college students' questioning their sexuality; thus, internalized homophobia is likely to be a strong barrier to the coming-out process. In addition, feelings of betrayal to the family system, not fulfilling the ultimate goal of carrying on the family name (in traditional terms), and religious barriers (e.g., the Muslim faith) may lead the Indian LGBTQ student to present with significant internal turmoil, helplessness, and hopelessness around the coming-out process.

Often Indian students who are able to come out on campus or to friends have other lives at home, and they keep the two worlds very separate. This compartmentalization is similar to that practiced by their heterosexual Indian peers who are dating and lead two separate lives, at home and at school, but it takes place to a greater degree. Going home for the weekend (or every day for commuters) means going back into the closet of their families' heteronormative cultural world. It is when these worlds have the potential to collide that LGBTQ Indian students' internal conflict may build to a point of crisis (for example, if their parents visit them at school, or if other students from their hometown or Indian community come to the same college). For graduating seniors, whether domestic or international, the onset of senior year in relation to moving back home or getting pressure to marry can lead to feelings of depression and acute crisis, including symptoms of hopelessness, helplessness, and suicidal ideation. It is important to assess students' risks and assist them in gaining a sense of control and hope, including examining potential resources and options (e.g., possible allies and supports within and beyond the family, going to graduate school, optional practical training, etc.). It is critical for Indian students in the early stages of the coming-out process to find allies on campus, ideally from similar ethnic backgrounds, to provide hope that they can be accepted, to decrease their sense of isolation, and help them begin to see a light at the end of the tunnel. This first ally may be an advisor, professor, dean, therapist, or other resource on campus (e.g., LGBTQ Center supports).

Academic standing. Studies have found that first- and fourth-year college students display the highest level of psychological disturbance in the student population, a level that is brought on by stressors related to the transition into and out of college (Schwartz & Reifler, 1984). As with college students in general, each year comes with its own set of developmental challenges among Indian students. First-year Indian students may experience the culture shock of college as it conflicts with family life and expectations. Sophomore and junior years may bring academic challenges for Indian students struggling in their major, leading to potential emotional distress. Seniors may face additional career- or marriage-related demands upon graduation. In cases where a student has had a separate social life or significant relationship in college, the approach of graduation may trigger anxiety and crisis with the anticipation of the two worlds colliding (particularly if the student is in a significant relationship the parents would not approve of, or is gay and out on campus, but not at home). On the other hand, in open-ended interviews with Indian students, participants stated that it became easier to negotiate with parents and balance family and their own wishes as they progressed through college. However, they also stated that initial adjustment stressors were replaced with other challenges, such as academic stress, career decisions, and dating or marriage-related concerns (Wadhwani, 2000).

Residential status. Students living on campus versus commuting from home are likely to have different stressors and college experiences. Commuters may have to juggle family obligations that a student living away from home would not have to contend with. Grayson (1989) states that residential students are more likely than commuters to be caught in the traditional developmental struggles of college life, whereas commuters may be less able to engage in college life because they are still living in the family setting. Conversely, their parents could serve as a local resource when needed, and they would not have to contend with the loneliness and homesickness that often come with going far away to school.

Students who live at college have to adjust to the college setting and to the effects of living away from home on their family relationships; thus, it may be a more stressful transition for them to negotiate. Those students who continue to reside at home may not have to cope with as many changes in their lives or as many temptations from the college social environment. For some such Indian students, daily support from family may be a protective factor. A student's acculturation level and coping style are factors that could either exacerbate or buffer him or her from the stressors of living at college or at home.

Indian students may be very connected to their family and Indian culture at home, while at college they may take on a more acculturated, "Americanized" persona. Another important variable will be the type of college or university (ability and class are factors here) and how far the student is from home. If they are far away from home, in a college "bubble," they may more easily be able to juggle their two worlds. If they are closer to home or at a college with other students who live in the same hometown, striking this balance may be more challenging. Students in this situation may also have to juggle their social identity at college with their loyalty to family and expectations from self/family to attend social/cultural/religious functions at home.

Indian International Students

Indian students raised in the United States and Indian international students face different challenges. There may be significant differences in dynamics, politics, assumptions, and stereotypes between these two communities, depending on the university. There are also Indian students who may not fit into either group. They may have been raised around the world, or came to the United States at some point in their childhood or adolescence. Their transition to the United States at the time of immigration may influence their adjustment to college. Whether they were accepted or experienced racism and exclusion or bullying in their initial adjustment to the United States will likely impact their transition to college, particularly if those challenges were not addressed at the time.

International students from India potentially face their own set of challenges. In addition to experiencing similar stresses as other international students, issues of dating, marriage, coming out, or career conflict may be exacerbated for the international Indian student. Indian international students may fit in more with international students from other countries than with Indian American students. Initially, their focus may be on issues associated with adjusting to the United States (e.g., culture shock, language issues, weather, different teaching and learning styles, more discussion-oriented classes, financial challenges, worrying about family at home, coping with disappointments, not wanting to worry about family, pressure of familial expectations, loss of social supports, homesickness, adjusting to U.S. society, norms, peers, and so on) (Constantine, Kindaichi, Okazaki, Gainor, & Baden, 2005). Most likely, Indian international students (like other international students) have not seen the college campus before arriving here, unlike their domestic peers. Thus, they may be coping with disappointment and unmet expectations. It is also important to recognize that Indian international students come from an extremely wide range of settings back in India—some from urban, more "Westernized" areas where they speak English and are familiar with Western customs, others from more rural communities where they may not be as proficient in the English language or Western culture. It is important to assess their pre-migratory experience, their level of culture shock, and the particular adjustment challenges they face (Constantine et al., 2005). It should be noted that some Indian international students may have been raised in countries other than India and thus will be balancing multiple cultural, racial, and ethnic identities in their adjustment process.

Indian students who came to the United States in their pre-teens or teens face even more challenges, having come to the United States at a point when they were already influenced by the society, culture, and religion of their country of origin and brought with them a developed set of attitudes and behavior patterns (Bogardus, 1928; Sodowsky & Carey, 1988). They were adjusting to a completely discordant cultural world in their middle and high school years, a critical point in the development of identity and belonging. Depending on their immigration experience at that time, their adjustment to college may entail more cultural conflict than their Indian peers who were born in or raised in the United States from an earlier age. However, depending on the acculturation process of the student raised in the United States, there are students whose families have maintained the traditional level of culture that they took from

India decades before, while relatives in India actually westernized further because of globalization, particularly if they immigrated from a more urban part of India. There are other Indian students who may have lived in various countries throughout the world and may not feel they belong anywhere. Additionally, non-international Indian students who have more recently immigrated to the United States may be more likely to be struggling with adjustment concerns rather than experiencing the acculturation issues and cultural conflict faced by students who were raised here. This may be buffered—or in some cases complicated—by family support available to them in the United States, unlike international students.

In a qualitative study examining the cultural adjustment of Asian female international students, Constantine and colleagues (2005) found that these students may struggle to balance their degree of exposure to and internalization of American values with their cultural values of origin to ensure their ability to marry upon returning to India. They may experience conflict between maintaining more of a traditional gender role, while receiving, in the United States, alternative messages related to independence, interpersonal assertiveness, and the pursuit of personal goals (Inman, Ladany, Constantine, & Morano, 2001). The dissonance and conflict between two distinct cultural value systems could result in intense anxiety and distress, particularly when students prepare to return to India (Constantine et al., 2005).

International students who have acculturated significantly during their time in the United States may have a more well-defined, "other" life here in the United States, one that works fine for them until they face graduation and an anticipated return to India, where their parents may be preparing for their next phase of life: marriage. Some students, at the suggestion of their parents, may engage in dating or experiment with Indian marital websites. Others may be dating while simultaneously appeasing their parents about the marital process. This juggling act may take a toll on them and cause them to present with anxiety, depression, or academic concerns. In more severe cases, they may exhibit a state of crisis or even suicidality when approaching graduation, as the reality of their situation becomes unavoidable and the two worlds begin to collide. Indian international students may not see other solutions and feel stuck and heartbroken at having to end a relationship or the identity they developed in the United States. In cases where their partner in the United States is a same-sex partner and they have come out during their time here, going back home not only means ending their relationship, but going back into the closet and resuming life in a heteronormative family system. Students in this situation will need strong support in coping with their transition, feelings of loss, and anticipated change in level of independent control of their identity and life.

Supporting Asian Indian Students

Lee (1997) states that Asian Americans generally try to deal with psychological problems without seeking professional services. They have been found to make use of social support networks more than they seek professional help (Yeh & Wang, 2000), first relying on family, who often encourage self-control, trying harder, and exercising will power. Maki & Kitano (2002) argue that the stigma of mental illness is so strong among Asians that they will reach out to family and friends rather than professionals. There is a question, however, about whether they would in fact be open about their struggles with their family and friends, given the level of shame in acknowledging their difficulties to others. The concepts of self-concealment and loss of face have been identified as barriers to seeking help among Asians and Asian Americans (Liao,

Rounds, & Klein, 2005). Cramer (1999) defines "self-concealment" as a tendency to conceal personal information about oneself that is viewed as negative or distressing. Liao, Rounds, and Klein (2005) state that disclosing personal problems to someone could be experienced as a loss of face, and Asians thus tend to avoid self-disclosure, which is inconsistent with seeking mental health treatment. Maintaining a sense of control and strength (not showing emotion or weakness) are examples of self-concealment found in the Asian culture (Leong et al., 2011). Their distress may build to a point where the symptoms become too severe for them to function, leading them to eventually seek professional help (Leong et al., 2011). This acknowledgement of difficulties may be shameful and perceived as a sign of weakness and disgrace to the family name (Constantine et al., 2005; Durvasula & Mylvaganam, 1994; Lee, 1997; Prathikanti, 1997; Root, 1985; Sodowsky & Carey, 1987; Viswanathan et al., 1997). If these methods do not work, Asian individuals will then resort to other resources in the community, such as elders, spiritual healers, and physicians. Mental health services are seen as a last resort.

However, help-seeking behavior has been found to vary across immigrant generations, with later generations, who are typically more acculturated, being more open to utilizing social supports outside the family system (Frey & Roysircar, 2006). Mechanic (1975) suggests that the factor that most influences help seeking among college students is level of subjective distress. Several studies on help seeking have found women to be greater help seekers than men, who have been found to seek help only at a greater point of distress (Cook et al., 1984; Hummers & DeVolder, 1979). Among Indian college students, males who sought counseling services were found to be more distressed, indicating that Indian male students were consistent with males in other samples who wait until a more distressed or symptomatic point before seeking help (Wadhwani, 2000). Depending on the level of severity, the Indian student who does not seek mental health resources may be referred to counseling by advisors, professors, deans, residence life staff, or other concerned members of the college community.

Others have also indicated that Asians (David, 2010; Sue, Zane, & Young, 1994; Zane & Yeh, 2002), and particularly Asian Indians, underutilize mental health services (Das & Kemp, 1997; Lee, 1997; Viswanathan et al., 1997). In a study of multicultural expectations of counseling among university students, of which 29% were Asian international students (including 5% Indian, primarily graduate students), Kenney (1994) found Asian students to have less acceptance and experience with therapy than European American students. Given the skepticism of mental health care within this population, building a trusting relationship will be crucial before any other work can be done. In order to strengthen the alliance, the therapist will need to express genuine interest and willingness to learn about a student's cultural background, as well as convey respect for the student's family and culture (Prathikanti, 1997). It has been argued that traditional Western psychotherapy approaches are based on assumptions of individuation, independence, self-disclosure, and verbal expression of feelings, which may not be applicable to Asian Indians and people from Asian backgrounds in general (Lee, 1997; Viswanathan et al., 1997).

In addition, there are cultural prohibitions about revealing personal and family conflicts outside the family system, particularly since mental health problems carry significant stigma and bring shame to the family (Constantine et al., 2005; Lee, 1997). Indian students may also be concerned about issues of confidentiality. For example, they may avoid group-level therapy, since other members of the group could be from the same close-knit Indian community. Also, they may feel protective of family privacy and may consider sharing family-related problems with a professional or other member of a support group to be a betrayal of their family. Some Indian students may feel more at ease with a South Asian therapist or support provider, while others may be concerned that a South Asian therapist or provider would be more connected to their community or family. For these reasons, it is particularly important to build trust and provide psycho-education emphasizing confidentiality. Western therapy needs to be flexibly adapted when one is working with a student from a more collectivist culture (Varma, 1988), even when that person is quite acculturated or bicultural. For example, for an Asian Indian student there may be dissonance with standard therapy goals of separation-individuation due to family loyalty and cultural norms (Das & Kemp, 1997; Viswanathan et al., 1997).

Academic concerns may create a sense of legitimate distress that can lead an Indian student to seek guidance, advice, or assistance in examining options for improving academic functionality and performance. The Indian student may feel conflicted about a major or may be doing poorly in a major recommended by his or her parents and not know where to turn. Experiences of perceived discrimination can also trigger a student to feel distressed and seek support in managing adjustment difficulties or symptoms of depression that may be affecting his or her academic performance (Tummala-Narra et al., 2012). The practice of counseling centers collaborating with others, including deans, advisors, and academic departments, can increase access to support for Indian students. Consultation and training for faculty and staff can empower these potential support providers to recognize signs of distress and refer students to the counseling center or other resources in a culturally compatible, less stigmatizing manner (Mier, Boone, & Shropshire, 2009). If the student does not obtain support early on and experiences further academic distress and crisis, an escalation of psychiatric symptoms may occur and lead to a greater level of distress and concern.

Because of the cultural stigma of mental health disorders in first-generation immigrants, the Indian students' parents/family may not have an understanding of mental health factors (Tummala-Narra et al., 2012). Once the Indian student builds trust with the support provider, he or she may describe challenges related to coping with pressure from parents. Because of diverse cultural norms surrounding parenting, the therapist or other support provider may hear the Indian student's report and perceive the family to be unsupportive, pressuring, or even negligent (e.g., telling their child that he or she is lazy). It is important for the support provider to build trust and credibility by being sympathetic yet non-judgmental. Even reflecting back on negative statements that students themselves have made about their family may cause them to feel guilty for coming in and too conflicted to pursue further help. Indian students may be reluctant to question the authority structure of their families, since cultural norms may be ingrained, and they will likely have a sense of loyalty and obligation to authority figures within the family (Das & Kemp, 1997; Viswanathan et al., 1997). In fact, an Indian student may have quite mixed feelings about separating and individuating from his or her family, since there could be many perks that come with maintaining the child role within the family. It could be difficult for a student to give up such a high level of nurturance, protection, and caring. As stated by Prathikanti (1997), "the traditional family can be both a source of strength and conflict" (p. 96) as both generations adapt to the American culture. In addition, family support is a critical protective factor in the student's adjustment and psychological well-being (Masood et al., 2009; Tummala-Narra et al., 2012).

Thus, when a therapist engages in therapy with an Indian student, it is critical to meet the student at his or her point within the bicultural spectrum and assist in examining both sides of the conflict. For example, a goal might be to help the student find a balance and level of assertiveness that would be realistic for his or her particular situation. Otherwise there would be a risk of leading the student to experience potential guilt, shame, and isolation by not recognizing that the level of cultural incongruence of the therapeutic intervention could isolate the student from his or her family. Sodowsky and Carey (1988) confirm that the bicultural student can have multidimensional cultural attitudes; thus, counselors should not attempt to "Americanize" students beyond their level of readiness. In other words, they could be quite acculturated in some ways yet quite traditional in others, such that a seemingly Western action such as dating would not imply that the student feels able to individuate from family. For this reason, it is critical for the support provider to refrain from making assumptions when, in fact, the Indian student may be experiencing cultural conflict and mixed feelings about the individuation process. Across immigrant groups, it has been found that a bicultural, integrative approach to acculturation has been associated with higher mental health outcomes (Kim & Omizo, 2005; Schwartz, Unger, Zamboanga, & Szapocznik, 2010; Tummala-Narra et al., 2012), suggesting the benefit of a more integrative, bicultural, or multicultural lens when assisting Indian students in negotiating their cultural conflict-related concerns. Being transparent and making the conflict open and real, validating the conflict, and reflecting both sides of the conflict for students could help them feel understood and heard. At that point students can, with provider support, decide what are realistic goals for them in negotiating where they are now and where they want to be, and choose a realistic path along which to move forward in that process.

Given that Asian Americans tend to view psychological problems as a sign of weakness that may lead to a negative self-image and sense of shame (Root, 1998), rather than fitting these individuals into our traditional mental health service models, we may need to consider how to restructure treatment models to meet their individual needs (e.g., providing support services outside the counseling center, in academic or administrative buildings on campus, or in collaboration with other professionals or departments on campus that may be more relevant and utilized by Asian/Indian students), with the goal of increasing access to students who would not come in for psychotherapy services. In the last decade or so, an effort has been directed at increasing the cultural competence of therapists in the cross-cultural therapeutic dyad. Taking a true emic perspective means taking this one step (or, literally, several steps) further, beyond the confines of the therapy room (Mier et al., 2009).

Solberg, Ritsma, Davis, Tata, and Jolly (1994) assessed the concerns and help-seeking likelihood of 596 Asian American undergraduate and graduate students, 139 of whom were Indian American. They found that students with previous counseling experience were more willing to seek help, which led them to conclude that outreach programming targeting the Asian American student population may increase the incidence of seeking counseling to address academic, interpersonal, and substance abuse concerns. Halgin, Weaver, Edell, and Spencer (1987) reported similar results among the general college student population and therefore suggested that implementing educational interventions addressing specific target concerns might attract students to mental health settings. Kenney (1994) also recommended that counseling centers provide culturally sensitive outreach on the variety of services that are available and in such a way that makes the counseling process relevant to those who are skeptical of its potential benefit. In addition, Durvasula & Mylvaganam (1994) emphasized the importance of outreach to combat barriers to accessing the Asian Indian population and suggested using ethnically similar and/or trusted professionals to communicate available services.

Social support from peers and family has been found to play a protective role in combating acculturative stress and mental health problems across cultural backgrounds (Cho & Haslam, 2010; Smith & Silva, 2011; Tummala-Narra et al., 2012; Yoo & Lee, 2009). Constantine and fellow researchers (2005) stated that same-ethnic connection and social support networks are valued and recommended for Indian international female students. Because more informal coping practices are more familiar to these students, developmental programming and outreach to international student groups and other potential support resources to increase access by students are recommended. They also suggest framing services as workshops or seminars to increase attendance, emphasizing using non-stigmatizing language (e.g., more academically focused, possibly with a bilingual skills emphasis). Since Indian students may seek academic or career counseling because they involve less stigma, or may present with these concerns but may have underlying mental health issues, Constantine and colleagues suggest that programming in these areas could increase access to these students. Since students found that seeking counseling is akin to "talking to a stranger about my problems" and because they have been found to utilize more social supports, some specialists recommend informal support systems, developmental programming and outreach interventions, indigenous programs (yoga, meditation), outreach to campus student groups, and group formats (Mori, 2000).

Providing truly culturally competent services to Asian Indian college students requires multi-level services within the college counseling center and throughout the campus community. Such programs include:

- consultation with faculty, staff, and deans across academic and student services departments;
- ongoing outreach with the Indian student organizations, Asian Student Organization, religious student groups, and the International Student Organizations; and
- outreach and psycho-education—with a focus on decreasing mental health stigmas—to classrooms and academic departments, with an emphasis on academic majors with Asian Indian and underserved students.

In addition, programs such as Let's Talk walk-in support and consultation hours (Boone et al., 2011), Community Consultation and Intervention (Mier et al., 2009), and cultural dialogue programs on campus are recommended. Once Indian students make connections with potential support providers, they are more likely to build trust and perceive services to be of potential value in meeting their personal, academic, and professional goals.

Acknowledgments

This chapter is dedicated to my father, Mohan J. Wadhwani, M.D. (1937–1988), who motivated me to succeed; to John Kalafat, PhD (1942–2007), my academic mentor, who shaped me as a psychologist; to Mohini J. Shahani (1919–2009), my Nani and inspiration; and to Sarla M. Wadhwani, M.S., my mother and role model as a strong Indian woman. I would like to thank Gurpreet Kaur for assisting with the literature search and editing. I would also like to thank Dr. Lisa Weinberg, Dr. Jaclyn Friedman-Lombardo, Dr. Bindi Shah, and Dr. Charlie Neighbors for their guidance and feedback in the development of this chapter.

References

Ahluwalia, M.K., & Pellettiere, L. (2010). Sikh men post-9/11: Misidentification, discrimination, and coping. *Asian American Journal of Psychology, 1*(4), 303–314.

Aktar, S. (2011). *Immigration and acculturation: Mourning, adaptation, and the next generation.* New York, NY: Jason Aronson.

Almeida, R. (1996). Hindu, Christian, and Muslim families. In M. McGoldrick, J. Giordano, & J. Pearce (Eds.), *Ethnicity and family therapy* (pp. 395–423). New York, NY: Guilford Press.

American Immigration Law Foundation (AILF) American Heritage Project. (2002). *The passage from India.* Immigration Policy Center Policy Brief. Washington, DC: Author.

Basham, A.L. (1996). *The wonder that was India.* Calcutta, India: Rupa.

Berry, J.W. (1980). Acculturation as varieties of adaptation. In A.M. Padilla (Ed.), *Acculturation: Theory, models and some new findings* (pp. 9–25). Boulder, CO: Westview Press.

Bhattacharya, G., & Schoppelrey, S.L. (2004). Pre-immigration beliefs and life success, post-immigration experiences, and acculturative stress: South Asian immigrants in the U.S. *Journal of Immigrant Health, 6*(2), 83–92.

Bogardus, E.S. (1928). *Immigration and race attitudes.* Boston, MA: D.C. Heath.

Boone, M.S., Edwards, G.R., Haltom, M., Hill, J.S., Mier, S.R., Shropshire, S.Y., ... Yau, T.Y. (2011). Let's talk: Getting out of the counseling center to serve hard-to-reach students. *Journal of Multicultural Counseling and Development, 39*(4), 194–205.

Cho, Y.B., & Haslam, N. (2010). Suicidal ideation and distress among immigrant adolescents: The role of acculturation, life stress, and social support. *Journal of Youth and Adolescence, 39*(4), 370–379.

Constantine, M.G., Kindaichi, M., Okazaki, S., Gainor, K.A., & Baden, A.L. (2005). A qualitative investigation of the cultural adjustment experiences of Asian international college women. *Cultural Diversity and Ethnic Minority Psychology, 11*(2), 162–175.

Cook, E.P., Park, W., Williams, G.T., Webb, M., Nicholson, B., Schneider, D., & Bassman, S. (1984). Students' perceptions of personal problems, appropriate help sources, and general attitudes about counseling. *Journal of College Student Personnel, 25*(2), 139–145.

Cramer, K.M. (1999). Psychological antecedents to help-seeking behavior: A re-analysis using path modeling structures. *Journal of Counseling Psychology, 46*(3), 381–387.

Cross, W.E. (1971). The Negro to Black conversion experience: Toward a psychology of Black liberation. *Black World, 20*(9), 13–27.

Das, A.K., & Kemp, S.F. (1997). Between two worlds: Counseling South Asian Americans. *Journal of Multicultural Counseling and Development, 25*(1), 23–33.

David, E.R. (2010). Cultural mistrust and mental health seeking attitudes among Filipino Americans. *Asian American Journal of Psychology, 1*, 57–66.

Durvasula, R.S., & Mylvaganam, G.A. (1994). Mental health of Asian Indians: Relevant issues and community implications. *Journal of Community Psychology, 22*(2), 97–108.

Frey, L.L., & Roysircar, G. (2006). South Asian and East Asian international students' perceived prejudice, acculturation, and frequency of help resource utilization. *Journal of Multicultural Counseling and Development, 34*(4), 208–222.

Grayson, P.A. (1989). The college psychotherapy client: An overview. In P.A. Grayson & K. Cauley (Eds.), *College psychotherapy* (pp. 8–28). New York, NY: Guilford Press.

Gupta, S. (1999). Walking on the edge: Indian American women speak out on dating and marriage. In S. Gupta (Ed.), *Emerging voices: South Asian American women redefine self, family, and community* (pp. 120–145). Walnut Creek, CA: AltaMira Press.

Halgin, R.P., Weaver, D.D., Edell, W.S., & Spencer, P.G. (1987). Relation of depression and help-seeking history to attitudes toward seeking professional psychological help. *Journal of Counseling Psychology, 34*(2), 177–185.

Helms, J.E. (1995). An update on Helms' White and people of color racial identity models. In J.G. Ponterotto, J.M. Casas, L.A. Suzuki, & C.M. Alexander (Eds.), *Handbook of multicultural counseling* (pp. 181–198). Thousand Oaks, CA: Sage.

Hummers, J., & DeVolder, J.P. (1979). Comparisons of male and female students' use of a university counseling center. *Journal of College Student Personnel, 20*(3), 243–249.

Ibrahim, F., Ohnishi, H., & Sandhu, D.S. (1997). Asian American identity development: A culture specific model for South Asian Americans. *Journal of Multicultural Counseling and Development, 25*(1), 34–50.

Inman, A.G. (2006). South Asian women: Identities and conflicts. *Cultural Diversity and Ethnic Minority Psychology, 12*(2), 306–319.

Inman, A.G., Constantine, M.G., & Ladany, N. (1999). Cultural value conflict: An examination of Asian Indian women's bicultural experience. In D.S. Sandhu (Ed.), *Asian and Pacific Islander Americans: Issues and concerns for counseling and psychotherapy* (pp. 31–41). Commack, NY: Nova Science.

Inman, A.G., Ladany, N., Constantine, M.G., & Morano, C.K. (2001). Development and preliminary validation of the Cultural Values Conflict Scale for South Asian women. *Journal of Counseling Psychology, 48*(1), 17–27.

Inman, A.G., & Tummala-Narra, P. (2010). Clinical competencies in working with immigrant communities. In J. Cornish, B. Schreier, L. Nadkarni, L. Metzger, & E. Rodolfa (Eds.), *Handbook of multicultural counseling competencies* (pp. 117–152). New York, NY: Wiley.

Inman, A.G., Yeh, C.J., Madan-Bahel, A., & Nath, S. (2007). Bereavement and coping of South Asian families post 9/11. *Journal of Multicultural Counseling and Development, 35*(2), 101–115.

Kenney, G.E. (1994). Multicultural investigation of counseling expectations and preferences. *Journal of College Student Psychotherapy, 9*(1), 21–39.

Kim, B.S., & Omizo, M.M. (2005). Asian and European American cultural values, collective self-esteem, acculturative stress, cognitive flexibility, and general self-efficacy among Asian American college students. *Journal of Counseling Psychology, 52*(3), 412–419.

Kurian, G. (1986). Intergenerational integration with special reference to Indian families. *Indian Journal of Social Work, 47*(1), 39–49.

Lee, E. (1997). Overview: The assessment and treatment of Asian American families. In E. Lee (Ed.), *Working with Asian Americans: A guide for clinicians* (pp. 3–36). New York, NY: Guilford Press.

Leong, F.T., Kim, H.W., & Gupta, A. (2011). Attitudes toward professional counseling among Asian-American college students: Acculturation, conceptions of mental illness, and loss of face. *Journal of Psychology, 2*(2), 140–153.

Liao, H.Y., Rounds, J., & Klein, A.G. (2005). A test of Cramer's (1999) help-seeking model and acculturation effects with Asian and Asian American college students. *Journal of Counseling Psychology, 52*(3), 400–411.

Maki, M.T., & Kitano, H.H.L. (2002). Counseling Asian Americans. In P.B. Pedersen, J.G. Draguns, W.J. Lonner, & J.E. Trimble (Eds.), *Counseling across cultures* (5th ed., pp. 109–131). Thousand Oaks, CA: Sage.

Masood, N., Okazaki, S., & Takeuchi, D.T. (2009). Gender, family, and community correlates of mental health in South Asian Americans. *Cultural Diversity & Ethnic Minority Psychology, 15*(3), 265–274.

Mechanic, D. (1975). Sociocultural and social-psychological factors affecting personal responses to psychological disorder. *Journal of Health and Social Behavior, 16*(4), 393–404.

Mehrotra, M., & Calasanti, T.M. (2010). The family as a site for gendered ethnic identity work among Asian Indian immigrants. *Journal of Family Issues, 31*(6), 778–807.

Mehta, S. (1998). Relationship between acculturation and mental health for Asian Indian immigrants in the United States. *Genetic, Social, and General Psychology Monographs, 124*(1), 61–78.

Mier, S., Boone, M., & Shropshire, S. (2009). Community consultation and intervention: Supporting students who do not access counseling services. *Journal of College Student Psychotherapy, 23*(1), 16–29.

Mori, S. (2000). Addressing the mental health concerns of international students. *Journal of Counseling and Development, 78*(2), 137–144.

Nguyen, H.H. (2006). Acculturation in the United States. In D.L. Sam & J.W. Berry (Eds.), *Acculturation psychology* (pp. 311–330). Cambridge, UK: Cambridge University Press.

Phinney, J. (1996). When we talk about American ethnic groups, what do we mean? *American Psychologist, 51*(9), 918–927.

Prathikanti, S. (1997). East Indian American families. In E. Lee (Ed.), *Working with Asian Americans: A guide for clinicians* (pp. 79–100). New York, NY: Guilford Press.

Raina, M.K., & Vats, A. (1990). Life goals of Indian and American college students. *International Journal of Intercultural Relations, 14*(1), 57–71.

Ramisetty-Mikler, S. (1993). Asian Indian immigrants in America and sociocultural issues in counseling. *Journal of Multicultural Counseling and Development, 21*(1), 36–49.

Root, M.P. (1985). Guidelines for facilitating therapy with Asian American clients. *Psychotherapy, 22*(2S), 349–356.

Root, M.P. (1998). Facilitating psychotherapy with Asian American clients. In D.R. Atkinson, G. Morten, & D.W. Sue (Eds.), *Counseling American minorities* (pp. 214–234). Boston, MA: McGraw-Hill.

Roysircar, G., Carey, J., & Koroma, S. (2010). Asian Indian college students' science and math preferences: Influence of cultural contexts. *Journal of Career Development, 36*(4), 324–347.

Roysircar-Sodowsky, G., & Maestas, M.V. (2000). Acculturation, ethnic identity, and acculturative stress: Theory, research, and measurement. In R.H. Dana (Ed.), *Handbook of cross-cultural and multicultural assessment* (pp. 131–172). Mahwah, NJ: Lawrence Erlbaum.

Saran, P. (1985). *The Asian Indian experience in the United States*. Cambridge, MA: Schenkman.

Schwartz, A.J., & Reifler, C.B. (1984). Quantitative aspects of college mental health: Usage rates, prevalence and incidence, suicide. *Psychiatric Annals, 14*(9), 681–688.

Schwartz, A.J., Unger, J.B., Zamboanga, B.L., & Szapocznik, J. (2010). Rethinking the concept of acculturation: Implications for theory and research. *American Psychologist, 65*(4), 237–251.

Segal, U.A. (1991). Cultural variables in Asian Indian families. *Families in Society, 72*(4), 233–242.

Shon, S.P., & Ja, D.Y. (1982). Asian families. In M. McGoldrick, J.K. Pearce, & J. Giordano (Eds.), *Ethnicity and family therapy* (pp. 208–228). New York, NY: Guilford Press.

Smith, T.B., & Silva, L. (2011). Ethnic identity and personal well-being of people of color: A meta-analysis. *Journal of Counseling Psychology, 58*(1), 46–60.

Sodowsky, G.R. (1985). *MMPI manic-depressive characteristics of male Asian Indian university students.* Unpublished manuscript, Department of Educational Psychology, Texas Tech University, Lubbock.

Sodowsky, G.R., & Carey, J.C. (1987). Asian-Indian immigrants in America: Factors related to adjustment. *Journal of Multicultural Counseling and Development, 15*(3), 129–141.

Sodowsky, G.R., & Carey, J.C. (1988). Relationships between acculturation-related demographics and cultural attitudes of an Asian-Indian immigrant group. *Journal of Multicultural Counseling and Development, 16*(3), 117–137.

Solberg, V.S., Ritsma, S., Davis, B.J., Tata, S.P., & Jolly, A. (1994). Asian-American students' severity of problems and willingness to seek help from university counseling centers: Role of previous counseling experience, gender, and ethnicity. *Journal of Counseling Psychology, 41*(3), 275–279.

Steiner, G.L., & Bansil, R.K. (1989). Cultural patterns and the family system in Asian Indians: Implications for psychotherapy. *Journal of Comparative Family Studies, 20*(3), 371–375.

Sue, D.W., & Sue, D. (1990). *Counseling the culturally different* (2nd ed.). New York, NY: Wiley.

Sue, D.W., & Sue, D. (2008). *Counseling the culturally different* (5th ed.). New York, NY: Wiley.

Sue, S., Zane, N., & Young, K. (1994). Research on psychotherapy with culturally diverse populations. In A.E. Bergin & S.L. Garfield (Eds.), *Handbook of psychotherapy and behavior change* (4th ed., pp. 783–817). New York, NY: Wiley.

Tummala-Narra, P. (2009). The immigrant's real and imagined return home. *Psychoanalysis, Culture, and Society, 14*(3), 237–252.

Tummala-Narra, P. (2013). Psychotherapy with South Asian women: Dilemmas of the immigrant and first generations. *Women & Therapy, 36*(3–4), 176–197.

Tummala-Narra, P., Alegria, M., & Chen, C. (2012). Perceived discrimination, acculturative stress, and depression among South Asians: Mixed findings. *Asian American Journal of Psychology, [Special Issue: Secondary Analysis of the National Latino Asian American Study (NLAAS) Dataset-Part I], 3*(1), 3–16.

Tummala-Narra, P., & Claudius, M. (2013a). A qualitative examination of Muslim graduate international students' experiences in the United States. *International Perspectives in Psychology: Research, Practice, Consultation, 2*(2), 132–147.

Tummala-Narra, P., & Claudius, M. (2013b). Perceived discrimination and depressive symptoms among immigrant-origin adolescents. *Cultural Diversity and Ethnic Minority Psychology, 19*(3), 257–269.

Tummala-Narra, P., Inman, A.G., & Ettigi, S.P. (2011). Asian Indians' responses to discrimination: A mixed-method examination of identity, coping, and self-esteem. *Asian American Journal of Psychology, 2*(3), 205–218.

U.S. Bureau of the Census. (2007). *Census of population and housing report.* Washington, DC: U.S. Government Printing Office.

Varma, V.K. (1988). Culture, personality and psychotherapy. *International Journal of Social Psychiatry, 34*(2), 142–149.

Viswanathan, R., Shah, M.R., & Ahad, A. (1997). Asian-Indian Americans. In S. Friedman (Ed.), *Cultural issues in the treatment of anxiety* (pp. 175–195). New York, NY: Guilford Press.

Wadhwani, S.M. (2000). *An assessment of the concerns and service needs of Asian Indian college students* (Doctoral dissertation). Retrieved from ProQuest Dissertations and Theses. (Order No. 3000889)

Wakil, S.P., Siddique, C.M., & Wakil, F.A. (1981). Between two cultures: A study in socialization of children of immigrants. *Journal of Marriage and the Family, 43*(4), 929–940.

Yeh, C., & Wang, Y. (2000). Asian American coping attitudes, sources, and practices: Implications for indigenous counseling strategies. *Journal of College Student Development, 41*(1), 94–103.

Yoo, H.C., & Castro, K.S. (2011). Does nativity status matter in the relationship between perceived racism and academic performance of Asian American college students? *Journal of College Student Development, 52*(2), 234–245.

Yoo, H.C., & Lee, R.M. (2009). Does ethnic identity buffer or exacerbate the effects of frequent racial discrimination on situational well-being of Asian Americans? *Asian American Journal of Psychology, 55*(1), 70–87.

Zane, N., & Yeh, M. (2002). The use of culturally-based variables in assessment: Studies on loss of face. In K.S. Kurasaki, S. Okazaki, & S. Sue (Eds.), *Asian American mental health: Assessment theories and methods* (pp. 123–137). New York, NY: Kluwer.

SIX

Middle Eastern College Students and Their Culture

Jose M. Maldonado and Britni V. Epstein

Introduction

The 2000 U.S. Census estimated that 3.5 million individuals of Middle Eastern descent reside in the mainland United States (U.S.Census Bureau, 2000). In addition, the Center for Immigration Studies reports that Middle Easterners are the fastest-growing immigrant group in the United States (Camarota, 2002). This rapid rate of growth leads to psychological challenges that can interfere with healthy, emotional development and ethnic identity integration. The process of identifying statistical trends among Middle Eastern populations is quite complex, as many are identified as White (Haboush, 2005) and thus are rendered invisible as an ethnic identity or culture. Statistical trends are more distinct in young adult populations, which show steadily decreasing numbers of Middle Eastern university students attending U.S. colleges (Henry & Fouad, 2007). Middle Eastern identity transcends a diverse group of countries with varying cultural differences regarding traditions, language and dialect, sociopolitical structure, and their relationship with the United States.

Cultural Factors for Middle Easterners

A variety of factors contribute to the acculturation of Middle Eastern students attending colleges and universities in the United States. Social and cultural influences such as gender beliefs, family background, and religious affiliation impact the daily experience of Middle Eastern students during their transition to life in the United States (Henry & Fouad, 2007). The cultural disparity between American life and the cultural values of Middle Eastern students often causes interactions between

American and Middle Eastern students to be interrupted by "anti-Arab biases, covert and overt discrimination" and an overall isolation from the social community on college campuses (Henry & Fouad, 2007, p. 224). Attempts by Middle Eastern students to integrate into the college community are sometimes limited because small cohorts of Middle Eastern students materialize as a way of preventing the loss of cultural identity and lessening the effects of the culture shock of life in a foreign country (Alazzi & Chiodo, 2006). Many Middle Eastern students studying in the United States see their time here as temporary, so "developing social relations and understanding the American culture were low priorities" (Alazzi & Chiodo, 2006, p. 77). To support the acculturation of Middle Eastern students, it is vital that student affairs professionals have a thorough knowledge of the factors that influence the acculturation process for Middle Eastern students.

Family relationships are very influential in the acculturation process for Middle Eastern students. The family is the center of the collectivist social hierarchy in Middle Eastern countries, and Middle Eastern students' families may encourage their students "to remain interdependent and may discourage self-reliance, differentiation, and individual aspirations" (Henry & Fouad, 2007, p. 226). As family life is central to the culture of Middle Eastern individuals, Nassar-McMillan (2003) suggests involving family members in the acculturation process. Additionally, universities and colleges can find ways for student support staff to meet students and develop relationships by attending cultural events and creating a presence at international associations or student organization events. Soheilian and Inman (2009) assert the value of community relationships with Middle Easterners in countering high levels of distrust, which can hinder positive growth and communication. These ideals are in stark contrast to the American cultural ideals of individualism and the pursuit of one's own happiness. Student affairs professionals need to consider the importance of the family system to Middle Eastern students in order to help them achieve educational success without pressuring them to give up their cultural values (Henry & Fouad, 2007). Opportunities for student affairs professionals to connect positively with family members can lessen the stigma attached to seeking help and assistance as a family unit.

Religion is often central to the lives of Middle Eastern students because it dictates social and cultural beliefs that are necessary to live a good life (Henry & Fouad, 2007). Values defined by the Muslim religion differ from some cultural ideals that many Americans live by. Americans tend to believe that individuals carve out their own future by working hard toward self-defined goals, but many individuals of other cultures believe in fate, or the idea that "human beings have no control over their destiny" (Alazzi & Chiodo, 2006, p. 68). This belief in fate leads to the larger Middle Eastern need for social affiliation, which serves as a support system for dealing with the struggle of adjusting to life in a new country (Alazzi & Chiodo, 2006).

Academic problems such as language barriers, differences in study techniques, grading systems, and curriculum structure also frequently disrupt the acculturation process of Middle Eastern students (Alazzi & Chiodo, 2006). Language presents a problem for many Middle Eastern college students transitioning to life in an American institution of higher education, because an inability to communicate clearly with faculty or student affairs staff may prevent students from receiving needed academic assistance (Karabenick & Moosa, 2005). Cultural beliefs have also been shown to affect the process of knowledge acquisition (Karabenick & Moosa, 2005). Cultural styles of teaching challenge the way that students are accustomed to learning information: Middle Eastern teachers seem to focus on a straightforward memorization approach, while American students are expected to use critical thinking skills to create their own answers (Karabenick & Moosa, 2005). Karabenick and Moosa (2005) further indicate that cultural beliefs about learning influence the way in which students absorb information.

There is a cultural misunderstanding on the part of many Americans that Middle Eastern women are submissive by nature and are oppressed by Middle Eastern men and the Muslim religion (Henry & Fouad, 2007). It is important for American institutions of higher education to support Middle Eastern women studying in the United States by providing support services that promote a cultural understanding of the issues faced by this population (Ribeiro & Saleem, 2010). The wearing of a traditional Muslim hijab (head covering) can cause "acculturation and ethnic identity challenges around physical image and looking different from mainstream Americans" for Middle Eastern women (Ribeiro & Saleem, 2010, p. 234). A support group for Middle Eastern women that includes discussions about gender expectations, self-identity, and religion can be created to help deal with acculturation difficulties in the United States (Ribeiro & Saleem, 2010). For Middle Eastern women in need of support while studying in America, support groups consisting of like-minded peers from a common cultural background may provide a community similar to the family support that they had back home (Ribeiro & Saleem, 2010). Connecting with one another based on similar experiences is shown to help Middle Eastern women to develop a community of supportive relationships at college (Ribeiro & Saleem, 2010). These new cultural experiences can have a meaningful impact on the self-esteem and confidence of Middle Eastern students.

Cultural Considerations for Intervention and Support

Middle Eastern culture encompasses a diverse history in the United States. For many Middle Easterners, the transition from country of origin to a new country can significantly challenge their views on culture, decision-making, and social relationships (Ammar, 2000). For student affairs professionals, it is important to display ethnic and cultural sensitivity in addressing differences in ethnicity, cultural background, and the approaches that can maximize success in supporting these students (McGoldrick, Giordano, & Pearce, 1996).

Cultural Competency

Most important, university officials and support staff must strive to show empathy for Middle Easterners by acquiring a solid knowledge of their history and contemporary practices for use in culturally appropriate counseling and advising. To be effective in their interventions, student affairs professionals need to master relevant information about migration patterns, immigration waves to the United States, and the various psychosocial histories of Middle Eastern students (Nassar-McMillan & Hakim-Larson, 2003; Nassar-McMillan, Lambert, & Hakim-Larson, 2011). It is important to assess the current mental health of Middle Easterners and the psychological impact of uneasy relationships between U.S. and Middle Eastern countries, including dissent on religious views, cultural differences, and a vast history of military conflict (Barry, Elliot, & Evans, 2000). In addition, these experiences are exacerbated by American portrayals of Middle Easterners as terrorists and religious extremists within mainstream media and culture. The Arab American Institute (2002a, 2002b) noted alarming increases in racial profiling, reported discrimination, and anxiety regarding the self-disclosure of ethnic identity. These experiences can lead to Middle Easterners experiencing depression, isolation, and psychological distress in all facets of life. Shaheen (2001) reported the prevalence of negative stereotypes of Middle Easterners in the film industry. According to Tewari (2000), media images look to confound and blur their ethnic identity by creating rigid boundaries between "White Americans" and those identified as "Arab-Middle Eastern-Muslim." This has further fed the associated stigma in revealing one's true ethnic identity and caused fear and apprehension about participating in any activities, programs, or services.

Support-Seeking Behaviors

The act of seeking help is discouraged by the Middle Eastern cultural paradigm of collectivism and the disapproval of individualism. A submissive approach to the will of the family is highly desirable (Dwairy, 1999). In addition, there can also be overwhelming strain caused by the struggle between the Middle Eastern traditional values of parents and the modern ways of thinking of younger generations. This can foster feelings of psychological conflict, indecision, and anxiety about seeking psychological assistance or counseling for Middle Eastern university students. In addition, language problems can cause chronic difficulty in communicating and acculturation patterns for Middle Easterners studying in the United States. Keyes (2000) highlights the emotional issues associated with acculturative stress that comes from learning new laws on child abuse and domestic violence. The task of acquiring the skills to pursue an education or choose a career can be daunting for many Middle Easterners.

Since these psychological stressors are overwhelmingly present for Middle Easterners, it is essential to conceptualize mental stress from a cultural perspective. Collectively, racial and ethnic minorities such as Middle Eastern populations show a tendency to underutilize student support services (June, Curry, & Gear, 1990). Tewari (2000) specifically identifies challenges to people whose physical appearance is drastically different from that of "mainstream" Americans. In the wake of recent terrorist attacks on the United States, increasingly frequent acts of racial profiling and marginalization have left many Middle Easterners struggling with feelings of isolation and depression (Abdelkarim, 2002). However, these obstacles also engender a sense of resiliency and empowerment for some. Furthermore, Nassar-McMillan (2003) found that these racial profiling experiences led some Middle Easterners to develop initiatives for social justice and civic involvement.

Student Adjustment

Middle Eastern students face a variety of struggles during their time on American college campuses. For a large number of Middle Eastern college students, the attainment of a college education is primary to their family values. Educational goals may change, but failure to achieve those goals creates insurmountable stress and tension (Alazzi & Chiodo, 2006). The importance of education is validated by the Qur'an's teachings and is accepted by Middle Easterners and most Muslim American families (Ribeiro & Saleem, 2010). This educational development for Middle Easterners is not an easy task and engenders a type of stress that is commonly found on university campuses. Many of the students' problems involve academic struggles, communication issues, and a cultural disconnect from the majority of students on campus. For example, Muslim women are often ostracized on college campuses because of their religious clothing and the wearing of the hijab, or head covering (Ribeiro & Saleem, 2010).

These experiences can have the potential to negatively impact patterns of thinking, exhaust coping strategies, and initiate feelings of resentment. To begin, it is inevitable that many Middle Eastern students will experience significant language issues. Where these problems exist, phenomenological experiences ultimately ensue, creating a deeper level of psychological conflict. White, Brown, and Suddick (1983) assert that international students' experiences with language problems heavily impact academic performance, which in turn adds to the anxiety over educational attainment. In addition, Barber, Morgan, and Torstrick (1997) found that although international graduate students work hard, they still must grapple with the pressing issues of language and communication. This language barrier can lead to emotional instability, which is often coupled with other mental health problems. This adjustment challenge is compounded by the fact that many Middle Eastern university students must cope with being in a foreign country without access to the social and emotional supports of their home country (Hakim-Larson, Kamoo, Nassar-McMillan, & Porcerelli, 2007). Student affairs professionals should consider the individual narrative of the student's country of origin.

Attitudes About Mental Health

Kira (1999) illuminates the role of mental health practices for those individuals exposed to wartime trauma and post-traumatic stress syndrome. Related to this issue is the duality of mental illness and the issue of seeking professional help (Andrews, Issakidis, & Carter, 2001). Specific to Middle Eastern families, which are considered to be collectivist, is a strong preoccupation with appearance and family reputation. This leads to the stigmatization of mental illness and the seeking of support in the form of therapy (Sue & Sue, 2008). Because there is little empirical evidence concerning mental health practices implemented with Middle Eastern Americans (Hakim-Larson et al., 2007), professionals seek ways to understand the cultural dynamics that determine whether an individual will choose professional counseling.

Within this context, Middle Easterners will avoid seeking help for fear of bringing shame to family members (Soheilian & Inman, 2009). For instance, Al-Darmaki (2003) found that, within Arab culture, self-disclosure to outsiders is unacceptable, and issues are resolved within the family. It can be a psychological challenge for Middle Eastern university students to develop an individual, non-family identity and draw attention to their personal needs, since this approach is neither valued nor respected (Erickson & Al-Timimi, 2001). Feelings of uncertainty and doubt increase for Middle Eastern individuals when they rely on distant family members for support during times of crisis (Jackson, 1997). Research conducted by Abudabbeh (1996) further demonstrates that Middle Eastern students may harbor negative attitudes about mental illness and strongly resist seeking counseling for any type of emotional problem. To counter this, university counselors are encouraged to advocate for closer connections and support groups to help manage stress and anxiety associated with seeking help (Ribeiro & Saleem, 2010). It is important to mention that physical symptoms of emotional conflict may be present and will often be noted by health care providers for Middle Easterners (Al-Krenawi, 1999). There is a cultural norm for many Middle Eastern individuals that holds that all life's problems are God's will (Hakim-Larson et al., 2007). For student affairs professionals, these factors are critical in designing support systems and delivering culturally appropriate services.

Research recommends that counselors or student affairs professionals assume a more active and direct role in this area (Al-Krenawi & Graham, 2000); and that community leaders use education and community relations to promote a greater awareness of mental health practices (Nassar-McMillan & Hakim-Larson, 2003). Traditional modalities rooted in Western models of counseling are limited in their effectiveness; consequently, interventions should be culturally compatible with Middle Eastern values and norms. Counseling approaches that respect the importance of family and the necessity of including family members in the process are valuable at any stage of prevention or intervention (Hakim-Larson et al., 2007).

The Role of Religion

Within Middle Eastern culture, seeking help from religious and community leaders is widely accepted; so, too, is a holistic understanding of the mind and body (Hakim-Larson et al., 2007). The strength of religious values is great, and it is therefore suggested that working with spiritual leaders or imams can lend credibility and assurance to mental health services (Nassar-McMillan & Hakim-Larson, 2003). For student affairs professionals, interventions for Middle Eastern college students are instrumental in promoting effective coping skills. Almost 80% of Middle Easterners hold Islamic beliefs, so it is important to recognize this religious affiliation and understand how it can be integrated into mental health services (Zogby, 2001). Al-Krenawi (1999) asserts that interactions with Middle Eastern students should be infused with cultural rituals and an emphasis on the individual's degree of cultural connectedness to his or her respective religious affiliation. Haboush (2005) contends that familial approaches are a natural choice for collectivist cultures, since they provide a focus on solving problems rather than achieving insight or self-awareness. In addition, on college campuses it is culturally fitting for professionals to take on the role of client advocate for students who value religion and spiritual expression (Ribeiro & Saleem, 2010). With this in mind, Soheilian and Inman (2009) recommend counseling theories that embrace careful consideration of cultural values and use indigenous healing methods grounded in religious and spiritual knowledge.

It is important to make note of the religious origin of therapeutic techniques and counseling for Middle Eastern university students. As the Holy Qu'ran provides spiritual direction, it can also be utilized to advance interventions (Jackson, 1997). Badri (2007) identifies the similarities between Islamic teachings and professional counseling. Essential to supporting Middle Eastern university students are introspective abilities and examination of personal bias as the foundation of cultural competence. Further, it is imperative that student support staff have a thorough understanding of Islam and the use of such directive approaches (Al-Thani & Moore, 2012). Finally, culturally knowledgeable student support staff use such approaches to address faulty cognitive patterns while maintaining spirituality and faith as the cornerstones of daily life.

The College Campus Climate for Middle Easterners

The institutional climate of campus life is critical to the experience of Middle Eastern college students. Many of these students report feeling marginalized or being made fun of by peers who lack an understanding of Middle Eastern cultural norms and customs (University Wire, 2013). Stereotypes and presuppositions about Middle Eastern students have been an ever-present issue on college campuses, particularly since the terrorist attacks of September 11, 2001 (Fiske-Rusciano, 2008). These types of societal conditions can foster feelings of resentment and anger, which are then repressed because of the stigma associated with disclosure (Erickson & Al-Timimi, 2001). Cultural stigmas or lack of understanding of their culture by fellow students can cause Middle Eastern students to feel excluded from the campus community (University Wire, 2013). Student affairs professionals and university counselors should promote an inclusive college campus through services, programs, and awareness activities. These activities may include programming that promotes cultural sensitivity toward Middle Eastern culture while promoting advocacy and empowerment (Neider, 2010). A university-wide, open-minded, non-judgmental approach must be encouraged in order to break down stereotypes, prejudices, and biases against students of Middle Eastern heritage (Fiske-Rusciano, 2008). It is important for professionals at the university level to adhere to high standards of ethics in which self-exploration of bias is paramount in providing culturally relevant counseling.

Prior to coming to the United States, many Middle Eastern students have preconceived notions of what it will be like to live in America in a new culture, in a new place, and with a diverse population. A common notion on the part of Middle Eastern students is that of Americans as "tolerant of multicultural others and the U.S. as a melting pot, where race, ethnicity, and religion blend together in harmony" (Neider, 2010, p. 22). However, some campus climates are less tolerant than others, and the optimistic belief that Americans will generally be tolerant of diverse others is sometimes contradicted by intolerant or prejudicial behavior (Neider, 2010). Such conduct on the part of fellow students may cause isolation and social alienation for Middle Eastern college students studying in the United States (Alazzi & Chiodo, 2006). It has been found that Middle Eastern college students who engaged in "frequent positive cross-cultural contact with Americans through activities such as discussions and outings were less likely to experience loneliness and homesickness" (Alazzi & Chiodo, 2006, p. 69). A campus climate that encourages cross-cultural communication can improve the social experience of college for Middle Eastern students (Alazzi & Chiodo, 2006). This, in turn, creates new experiences based on genuineness and respect across cultures and ethnic identities.

Studies show that an open, constructive dialogue between American and Middle Eastern students can increase mutual understanding, improve relations between students of different backgrounds, and discourage negative attitudes and polarized campus communities (Fiske-Rusciano, 2008; Neider, 2010). Middle Eastern students express feelings of distress over interactions with American students who do not try to get to know them or who make assumptions about their culture, and these interactions with American peers can cause Middle Eastern students to isolate themselves or seek acceptance from other Middle Eastern students who can relate to their experience (Neider, 2010). This marginalizing behavior can only lead to a more divisive, less inclusive campus environment; however, when professionals work together to create a more inclusive environment for Middle Eastern students, there is a reinforcement of relationship-building and open dialogue between diverse student groups (Neider, 2010).

A study by Fiske-Rusciano (2008) used focused discussion to promote an exchange of ideas and increased communication between college students in the United States and college students in the Middle East. These discussions, which were designed around global topics such as international relations, terrorism, and the economy, demonstrated a change in students' attitudes toward individuals from other cultures and were proven to promote changes in behavior through deeper understanding of the opposing culture (Fiske-Rusciano, 2008). The American ideal of separation of church and state stands in direct contrast to the traditional theocracies that structure governments in many Middle Eastern countries; open discussions fostered an understanding for American students that many Middle Eastern students supported the use of religion in politics because their religious tenets shape the way in which they lead their lives (Fiske-Rusciano, 2008).

Another major point of disagreement between Middle Eastern and American students centered on women's rights and liberation; while American students tended to view Middle Eastern women as imprisoned by rules designed by men, Middle Eastern students asserted that women are influential members of their society (Fiske-Rusciano, 2008).

Such open dialogue improved understanding between American and Middle Eastern students, and students actually moved "closer to each other's positions in important and fundamental ways" (Fiske-Rusciano, 2008, p. 13). Both Middle Eastern and American students felt that they had a less biased view of the other culture and that their understanding of political, religious, and global concerns had increased through participation in the open dialogue (Fiske-Rusciano, 2008). The importance of institutional culture was reinforced by the students' opinion that it was societal prejudices and opinions in the general culture, and not individuals, that encouraged divisive views between Middle Eastern and American students (Fiske-Rusciano, 2008; Derderian-Aghajanian & Cong, 2012). Promoting an open, inclusive campus environment through dialogues and improved communication can bridge the gap between these diverse cultures and create greater unity among student populations.

Implications for Student Affairs Professionals

To begin with, it is vital for counselors to examine their own perceptions and cultural biases. In the interests of Middle Eastern students, universities can begin by collaborating with various departments on campus to promote culturally sensitive programming and inclusiveness within services (Ribeiro & Saleem, 2010). This can begin to absolve deep-rooted stigmas and initiate empowerment. Specifically, Erickson and Al-Timimi (2001) recommend psycho-educational and directive approaches. Interactions with Middle Eastern students should relay cultural appropriateness for self-disclosure in short, time-limited contexts. In addition, it is imperative to extend invitations to family members that would like to participate and thus make it an inclusive environment. Student affairs professionals should use a relational approach by establishing rapport and trust with Middle Eastern student leaders.

For American higher education institutions to continue attracting Middle Eastern students, it is essential for them to be committed to recruiting Middle Eastern students by means of appropriate outreach, marketing plans, and scholarship opportunities (Shaw, 2006). Increased competition from institutions of higher education in other parts of the world, particularly Australia and New Zealand, has caused the influx of Middle Eastern students studying in the United States to wane in recent years (Shaw, 2006). More Middle Eastern students have chosen not to study in the United States because of "difficulties in securing visas, combined with more aggressive recruiting by higher-education institutions in New Zealand and Australia" (Cohen, 2007, para. 3). In response to the increased challenges involved in recruiting Middle Eastern students, the United States has made a more concerted effort to establish educational planning centers in the Middle East, provide opportunities for virtual advising, and increase scholarship opportunities for Middle Eastern students to study in the United States (Leggett, 2013). Additional efforts that can attract Middle Eastern students to study in the United States include "a market plan that takes into consideration multiple decision makers and influencers" and frequent visits to the Middle East to meet students individually to discuss educational opportunities in the United States (Shaw, 2006, p. 5).

Many American institutions have reached the conclusion that they must provide support services for Middle Eastern students. Such support services include "lower-level English classes to help prepare them for college-level courses" and counseling services "so they can feel safe and comfortable to communicate freely and integrate with the culture" (Leggett, 2013, p. 45). Differences in cultural understanding of educational expectations often disrupt the integration of Middle Eastern students into American institutions of higher education. Some Middle Eastern cultural beliefs that are in opposition to the structure of the American educational system are "a more leisurely sense of time, an assumption that grades and deadlines can be negotiated, and a preference for face-to-face or personal communication" (Leggett, 2013, p. 45). It is crucial for student affairs professionals to work within the cultural framework of Middle Eastern students to help them understand the difference between cultural educational expectations in the Middle East and the United States.

Providing on-campus community support for Middle Eastern students is more important than ever because of the increase in animosity toward Middle Eastern individuals since the terrorist attacks of 9/11 (Henry & Fouad, 2007). In response to this cultural prejudice, many U.S. institutions of higher education have focused on creating greater support systems for Middle Eastern students on their campuses. In April 2009, the State University of New York at New Paltz opened a Center for Middle Eastern Dialogue whose mission is to "promote constructive dialogue about the Middle East that will explore ways of establishing lasting peace in the region, encouraging economic collaboration, and stimulating cultural and educational exchange" (HT Media Ltd., 2009a, para. 2). Respectful exchanges of ideas, advocacy speakers, panel discussions, and exhibitions of Middle Eastern art and food can help bridge the gap between American and Middle Eastern student populations (HT Media Ltd., 2009a). As shown in previous studies, providing greater opportunities for cross-cultural communication in a supportive environment can help Middle Eastern students feel more a part of the campus community and can increase understanding of Middle Eastern students by their American peers (Alazzi & Chiodo, 2006).

Another American institution that has put forth great effort to create a welcoming campus environment for Middle Eastern students is Queens College of the City University of New York. In 2009, the college launched an education-and-awareness program with a focus on issues that plague the Middle East (HT Media Ltd., 2009b). The 3-day event included a panel of Middle Eastern government candidates addressing the resolution of economic and political problems; lectures about "The New Muslim Anti-Semitism," "Islamic Arts of the Book and Pen," and "Myths and Realities of Jihad"; the film *Afghan Women: A History of Struggle*; and "an evening of interfaith dialogue, music and Kosher and Halal food," all of which was accompanied by an open discussion about religion and international issues (HT Media Ltd., 2009b, para. 2–8). Such an event can be beneficial to both Middle Eastern and American students by increasing awareness and communication between the two diverse populations, and by demonstrating that the well-being of Middle Eastern students is positively impacted by an increase in social interaction with American peers (Alazzi & Chiodo, 2006). Implementing similar events at other institutions of higher education could make the United States more attractive to Middle Eastern students looking to study abroad and also make the university campus more welcoming to Americans of Middle Eastern descent.

Although differences exist, there are common challenges for Middle Eastern university students. These obstacles include a cultural stigma concerning mental health, anti-Arab sentiment, and increased psychological distress in the post-9/11 era (Soheilian & Inman, 2009). Moreover, for Middle Eastern university students, it becomes increasingly difficult to cope with feelings of isolation and marginalization as they adjust to mainstream college culture. Researchers Erickson and Al-Timimi (2001) assert that for many Middle Eastern individuals, positive ethnic identity is hampered by the influence of racism, U.S. media stereotypes, and religious intolerance toward Muslims or anyone perceived to be of the Islamic faith. Consequently, these factors can lead to psychological trauma and isolation among peers. In coping with such perceptions of Middle Eastern ethnic identity, university students may also experience a significant degree of social stigma in seeking student support services. Amer (2005) notes that, in the wake of the World Trade Center attacks, there has been an increase in anxiety and depression among Arab Americans. Al-Darmaki (2003) comments further that for Middle Eastern individuals, there is a strong expectation that emotional issues will remain private, and there is considerable shame in seeking mental health counseling or other student support services. For Middle Easterners, the development of individualism runs counter to the key cultural concepts of loyalty, family cohesion, and privacy (Soheilian & Inman, 2009). Going outside of the family to resolve issues is an approach that is seen as disrespectful and suffers from a negative connotation (Soheilian & Inman, 2009). Pederson and Vogel (2007) illustrate that for Middle Eastern university students, it is likely that social stigma will overrule a willingness to seek student support services.

References

Abdelkarim, R.Z. (2002). American Muslims and 9/11: A community looks back and to the future. *Washington Report on Middle East Affairs, 21*(7), 82–84.

Abudabbeh, N. (1996). Arab families. In M. McGoldrick, J. Giordano, & J. K. Pearce (Eds.), *Ethnicity and family therapy* (2nd ed., pp. 333–346). New York, NY: Guilford Press.

Alazzi, K., & Chiodo, J.J. (2006). Uncovering problems and identifying coping strategies of Middle Eastern university students. *International Education, 35*(2), 65–105.

Al-Darmaki, F.R. (2003). Attitudes towards seeking professional psychological help: What really counts for United Arab Emirates University students? *Social Behavior and Personality, 31*(5), 497–508.

Al-Krenawi, A. (1999). Explanations of mental health symptoms by the Bedouin-Arabs of the Negev. *International Journal of Social Psychiatry, 45*(1), 56–64.

Al-Krenawi, A., & Graham, J.R. (2000). Culturally sensitive social work practice with Arab clients in mental health settings. *Health and Social Work, 25*(1), 9–22.

Al-Thani, A., & Moore, J. (2012). Nondirective counseling in Islamic culture in the Middle East explored through the work of one Muslim person-centered counselor in the State of Qatar. *Person-Centered & Experiential Psychotherapies, 11*(3), 190–204.

Amer, M. (2005). *Arab American mental health in the post September 11 era: Acculturation, stress, and coping* (Doctoral dissertation). *Dissertation Abstracts International, 66*, 4B.

Ammar, N.H. (2000). Simplistic stereotyping and complex reality of Arab-American immigrant identity: Consequences and future strategies in policing wife battery. *Islam and Christian-Muslim Relations, 11*(1), 51–70.

Andrews, G., Issakidis, C., & Carter, G. (2001). Shortfall in mental health service utilization. *British Journal of Psychiatry, 179*, 417–425.

Arab American Institute. (2002a). *Healing the nation: The Arab American experience after September 11*. Washington, DC: Arab American Institute Foundation.

Arab American Institute. (2002b). *Profiling and pride: Arab American attitudes and behavior since September 11*. Washington, DC: Arab American Institute Foundation.

Badri, M. (2007). Can the psychotherapy of Muslim patients be of real help to them without being Islamized? *Islamic World, 39*, 03925.

Barber, E.G., Morgan, R.P., & Torstrick, R.L. (1997). Foreign graduate students in U.S. engineering programs: Problems and solutions. *Engineering Education, 78*(3), 171–174.

Barry, D., Elliot, R., & Evans, E.M. (2000). Foreigners in a strange land: Self-construal and ethnic identity in male Arabic immigrants. *Journal of Immigrant Health, 2*(3), 133–144.

Camarota, S.A. (2002). *Immigrants from the Middle East: A profile of the foreign born population from Pakistan to Morocco*. Washington, DC: Center for Immigration Studies.

Cohen, D. (2007, August 17). Middle Eastern students shut out of the U.S. turn to Australia and New Zealand. *Chronicle of Higher Education, 53*(50), A37.

Derderian-Aghajanian, A., & Cong, W.C. (2012). How culture affects English language learners' (ELL's) outcomes, with Chinese and Middle Eastern immigrant students. *International Journal of Business and Social Science, 3*(5), 172–180.

Dwairy, M. (1999). Toward psycho-cultural approach in Middle Eastern societies. *Clinical Psychology Review, 19*(8), 909–916.

Erickson, C.D., & Al-Timimi, N.R. (2001). Providing mental health services to Arab Americans: Recommendations and considerations. *Cultural Diversity and Ethnic Minority Psychology, 7*(4), 308–327.

Fiske-Rusciano, R. (2008, August). *The student global village: A "global memory place" for United States and Middle Eastern students?* Paper presented at the Annual Meeting of the American Political Science Association (APSA), Boston, MA.

Haboush, K.L. (2005). Lebanese and Syrian families. In M. McGoldrick, J. Giordano, & N. Garcia-Preto (Eds.), *Ethnicity and family therapy* (3rd ed., pp. 468–486). New York, NY: Guilford Press.

Hakim-Larson, J., Kamoo, R., Nassar-McMillan, S.C., & Porcerelli, J.H. (2007). Counseling Arab and Chaldean American families. *Journal of Mental Health Counseling, 29*(4), 301–321.

Henry, C.G., & Fouad, N.A. (2007). Counseling international students from the Middle East. In H.D. Singaravelu & M. Pope (Eds.), *A handbook for counseling international students in the United States* (pp. 223–236). Alexandria, VA: American Counseling Association.

HT Media Ltd. (2009a, April 4). College to launch center for Middle Eastern dialogue to promote greater understanding of region. *U.S. Fed News Service*. Retrieved from http://bluehawk.monmouth.edu:2048/?url=/docview/470252356?accountid=12532

HT Media Ltd. (2009b, May 6). College sponsors week of Middle Eastern arts, culture. *U.S. Fed News Service*.

Jackson, M.L. (1997). Counseling Arab Americans. In C.C. Lee (Ed.), *Multicultural issues in counseling: New approaches to diversity* (2nd ed., pp. 331–352). Alexandria, VA: American Counseling Association.

June, L.N., Curry, B.P., & Gear, C.L. (1990). An 11-year analysis of Black students' experience of problems and use of services: Implications for counseling professionals. *Journal of Counseling Psychology, 37*(2), 178–184.

Karabenick, S.A., & Moosa, S. (2005). Culture and personal epistemology: U.S. and Middle Eastern students' beliefs about scientific knowledge and knowing. *Social Psychology of Education, 8*(4), 375–393.

Keyes, E.F. (2000). Mental health status in refugees: An integrative review of current research. *Issues in Mental Health Nursing, 21*(4), 397–410.

Kira, I.A. (1999, July). *Value processing and mental health.* Paper presented at the Sixth European Congress of Psychology, Rome, Italy.

Leggett, K. (2013). Influx from the Middle East. *International Educator, 22*(6), 44–47.

McGoldrick, M., Giordano, J., & Pearce, J.K. (Eds.). (1996). *Ethnicity and family therapy* (2nd ed.). New York, NY: Guilford Press.

Nassar-McMillan, S.C. (2003). *Counseling Arab-Americans: Counselors' call for advocacy and social justice.* Denver, CO: Love.

Nassar-McMillan, S.C., & Hakim-Larson, J. (2003). Counseling considerations among Arab Americans. *Journal of Counseling & Development, 81*(2), 150–159.

Nassar-McMillan, S.C., Lambert, R.G., & Hakim-Larson, J. (2011). Discrimination history, backlash fear, and ethnic identity among Arab Americans: Post-9/11 snapshots. Journal of Multicultural Counseling and Development, *39*(1), 38–47.

Neider, X.N. (2010). *"When you come here, it is still like it is their space": Exploring the experiences of students of Middle Eastern heritages in post-9/11 U.S. higher education* (Doctoral dissertation). Retrieved from ProQuest. (Accession Number ED518727)

Pederson, L., & Vogel, D.L. (2007). Male gender role conflict and willingness to seek counseling: Testing a mediation model on college-aged men. *Journal of Counseling Psychology, 54*(4), 373–384.

Ribeiro, M.D., & Saleem, S. (2010). Providing outreach services to Muslim college women. *Journal of Muslim Mental Health, 5*(2), 233–244.

Shaheen, J.G. (2001). *Reel bad Arabs: How Hollywood vilifies a people.* New York, NY: Olive Branch Press.

Shaw, S.L. (2006). Recruiting Middle Eastern students takes commitment, perseverance. *Recruitment & Retention in Higher Education, 20*(2), 5–6.

Soheilian, S.S., & Inman, A.G. (2009). Middle Eastern Americans: The effects of stigma on attitudes toward counseling. *Journal of Muslim Mental Health, 4*(2), 139–158.

Sue, D.W., & Sue, D. (2008). *Counseling the culturally diverse: Theory and practice.* Hoboken, NJ: Wiley.

Tewari, N. (2000). *Asian Indian American clients presenting at a university counseling center: An exploration of their concerns and a comparison to other groups* (Doctoral dissertation). *Dissertation Abstracts International: Section B. Sciences and Engineering, 62*(7–8), 3391.

University Wire. (2013, November 5). Middle Eastern students face differences. *Daily Trojan* (University of Southern California). Retrieved from http://dailytrojan.com/2013/11/05/students-face-differences/

U. S. Census Bureau. (2000). *Profile of selected social characteristics: Allegany County, N.Y.* Retrieved from http://factfinder2.census.gov/faces/nav/jsf/pages/index.xhtml

White, A.J., Brown, S.E., & Suddick, D. (1983). Academic performance affecting the scholastic performance of international students. *College Student Journal, 17*, 268–272.

Zogby, J. (2001). *What ethnic Americans really think: The Zogby culture polls.* Washington, DC: Zogby International.

o I never thought of all the racism they face since 9/11.

SEVEN

The Great Divides: Seven Trends That Shape the International Student Experience at U.S. Colleges and Universities

Chris R. Glass and Elizabeth J. Kociolek

International students come from hundreds of countries and cultures and represent one of the most diverse student subpopulations in American higher education. Yet it is common for higher education administrators to approach them simply as one group: international students. International students are not all the same (Choudaha, Orosz, & Chang, 2012), and there is growing evidence that the international student experience is variable and that the disparities among international students are widening (Glass & Braskamp, 2012; Glass, Buus, & Braskamp, 2013; Lee, 2013a; Lee & Rice, 2007). Although we believe that the surge in international undergraduate enrollment at U.S. universities is cause for optimism, there are also a number of cautionary trends shaping the experiences of today's international students—trends that higher education administrators ignore at their peril.

The expansion of international student enrollment is now integral to university budgets and campus internationalization plans and comes with promises of enhancing the quality of education and expanding America's global influence. Although increasing international student enrollment has become a core priority of university internationalization efforts, universities and national organizations generally maintain a numbers-oriented approach to measuring the benefits of educational exchange (Bhandari, 2013; Lee, 2013a). It is far easier to tabulate enrollment numbers, country of origin, grade point average, and TOEFL scores than the quality of the international student experience. Administrators may overlook the qualitative dimensions of the international student experience for another reason: they do not want to know (Lee, 2013b). Enrollment data present a tantalizing vision of the contribution that international students make to American higher education through tuition, fees, and the local economy; making up for skill shortages in the STEM fields; and enhancing institutional prestige. Studies of the qualitative dimensions of the international student experience highlight the fact that many students live in "separate but equal" worlds

(Gareis, 2012; Glass & Braskamp, 2012). What is most striking about these diverse qualitative studies is the consistency of the results documenting international students' encounters with ethnocentric attitudes among peers and professors (Lee & Rice, 2007), loneliness and unmet expectations (Smith & Khawaja, 2011), and even exploitation by employers (United Voice, 2013).

The doubling of international student enrollment in the last decade masks undercurrents that are cause for concern and threaten the traditional goals of academic and cultural exchange within American higher education. The authors share with other scholars a growing unease about economic rationales motivating international student mobility (Bhandari, 2013; de Wit, 2011; International Association of Universities, 2012; Lee, 2013a). International educators, disturbed by accounts of neoracism, exploitation, and isolation, are voicing deep concerns about whether the surge in international student enrollment at U.S. universities is a "false halo" (Lee, 2013a). Rajika Bhandari (2013), deputy vice president of research and evaluation at the Institute of International Education (IIE), has urged international educators to candidly assess, and then take action on, the ethical question: "An international education for what and for whose benefit?" Who benefits from the growing global mobility of students, estimated to reach 8 million by 2025 (UNESCO, 2012)? Almost weekly, new headlines such as "Many Foreign Students Find Themselves Friendless in the U.S." (Gareis, 2012) and "International Students Increasingly Ask: Is It Safe to Study in the U.S.?" (Lingzi, 2013) highlight the uneven and unequal experiences of international students. Leading scholars, educators, and advocates in international education have called for a more in-depth inquiry into the qualitative dimensions of international students' experiences (Glass & Westmont-Campbell, 2013; Lee, 2013a). In this chapter we address the question: what do we know about the lived realities of international students studying at U.S. colleges and universities?

Seven Trends That Shape the International Student Experience

In this section, seven trends that shape today's international student experience are outlined, and first-person narratives are used to illustrate how these conflicts are manifested in the lived experiences of international students. The international student experience is characterized by contradictions, and less is known regarding whether these differences result in educational disparities among international students with varying demographic characteristics. As this section will highlight, more research is needed on the extent to which these inequalities result in disparities in the long-term learning and development of international students.

Community Colleges Meet the Ivies

In 1904, the U.S. Bureau of Education reported just 2,673 international students from 74 countries attending U.S. higher education institutions. The University of California, Berkeley, had nine Chinese students that paid $20 a year for tuition; Indiana University had just one Chinese student who lived in a private house off campus (Bevis & Lucas, 2007). In the late 1900s, renowned Harvard President Charles W. Eliot questioned the benefits of international educational exchange; today, international students represent 10% of undergraduate and 27% of graduate enrollments at Harvard (Institute of International Education (IIE), 2012). America's top 100 research universities, which enroll about 40% of today's international students, have been the engine for the growth in international student enrollments (Choudaha, Chang, & Kono, 2013), attracting the world's most talented, creative, and entrepreneurial individuals.

In the last decade, community colleges have also begun to "go global," initiating efforts designed to attract, enroll, and serve international students. International students make up just under 2% of total enrollments at community colleges (IIE, 2012), which constitute the largest sector in American higher education. However, U.S. community colleges have equaled, and some institutions have surpassed, the pace of recruitment of their state flagship research university counterparts. International students, who otherwise would not qualify for admission into a U.S. research university, enroll in U.S. community colleges as a way of gaining access to a U.S. bachelor's degree and the "American dream." In 2011–2012, 87,997 international students were enrolled in community colleges, and 90,903 were enrolled in a bachelor's degree program at a college or university (IIE, 2012). The "flexible" English language admission standards, small class sizes, and low tuition have fueled this massive growth (Redden, 2010). Community colleges have been working with 4-year institutions to build transfer routes and pathways for Chinese students and other large markets of international students through 2 + 2 degree programs (Redden, 2010). The extent to which pathway programs provide access to a segment of international students who would otherwise be denied an education abroad, and the extent to which they reinforce existing disparities in outcomes among international students from more varied academic and financial backgrounds, remains an open question.

Accelerating Undergraduate Enrollments

From the 1960s to the early 1990s, international undergraduate enrollment trailed graduate enrollment (IIE, 2012). Since the 1990s, undergraduate enrollment has kept pace with graduate enrollment (Chow & Chambers, 2010). Enrollments of both undergraduates and graduates slowed following the September 11, 2001, terrorist attacks (Bevis & Lucas, 2007); however, undergraduate enrollment surpassed graduate enrollment for the first time in 2012. International student enrollments have nearly doubled in the last decade, from 59,943 in 2004–2005 to 90,903 in 2011–2012.

This sudden jump in undergraduate international student recruitment has caused concern among those who watch these trends and monitor the qualitative experiences of international students (Glass et al., 2013; Lee, 2010; Redden, 2012). Recent reports caution that the international undergraduate enrollment that today appears to be a "cash cow" for universities seeking new revenue streams is "a bubble about to pop" and that the current acceleration of enrollments "is unsustainable" (Lane & Kinser, 2013). States such as Michigan that have seen net population decreases and fewer total high school graduates have turned to international students to make up for the shortfall in enrollment. Michigan State University, for example, now receives over 8,000 applications from international students, 25% of its total applications and a jump from 5 years ago when only about 10% of its applications came from students living abroad (Howell, 2013).

While graduate education has historically focused on research, undergraduate education in America has been traditionally characterized by the "collegiate ideal," in which residential campus life is an integral part of the college experience (Chickering & Kytle, 1999). The rise in enrollments has forced universities to rethink everything from food services, housing, and residential hall programming to counseling services and advising. Whereas international graduate students were traditionally recruited as part of American diplomatic policy and in accordance with exceptionally high academic standards, today paid, commission-based agents are increasingly recruiting undergraduate students as well (Bevis & Lucas, 2007).

International students also play a key role in supporting U.S. graduate programs, as they make up a majority of enrollments in many of the STEM fields—over 70% of engineering and 63% of computer science enrollments (Lane & Kinser, 2013; National Science Board, 2012). At some universities, the percentages are significantly higher. Therefore, foreign student tuition dollars are literally supporting entire graduate programs that would otherwise be eliminated. Historically, international students enrolling in graduate programs might be fully funded by their home government or host institution as part of an academic exchange program; today, 62% of all international students get most of their funding for education from family and personal sources (IIE, 2011). This number jumps dramatically when one compares undergraduates to graduate students, with 81% of undergraduates relying primarily on family or personal sources and 44% of graduate students doing so (IIE, 2011).

Ready or Not

Universities attempting to increase their international student enrollments have increasingly offered more flexible admissions policies. International students with low English proficiency test scores are often admitted conditionally and then required to complete non-credit courses that offer a pathway to a U.S. bachelor's degree (Redden, 2010). Although the practice of conditional admissions has existed for decades, the number of institutions using conditional admissions as a mechanism to increase enrollments has vastly expanded (Redden, 2013). These more "flexible" admissions policies have helped institutions of higher education gain access to students from the growing middle classes of China, India, Vietnam, and Saudi Arabia who have adequate financial resources but not necessarily the English proficiency levels traditionally required of international students (Choudaha, 2012). Consequently, there has been lessening pressure on English proficiency requirements in university admissions policies as universities undercut one another to compete for this market segment of students (Choudaha et al., 2013). Newly admitted international students arrive with "fair" or "limited" scores for speaking, reading, writing, and listening ability (Choudaha et al., 2013). For example, demand among Saudis is high, with enrollments octupling (+800%) in 10 years; yet the mean score on the Test of English as a Foreign Language (TOEFL) for Saudi students was 61. These students' scores are significantly lower than the mean score for all international students—80 out of a possible 120 (Choudaha et al., 2013; Redden, 2010). Therefore, if institutions maintain high TOEFL score requirements, they lose out on a market of international students that opens up when these score requirements are reduced.

Institutions with reduced admissions requirements champion pathway programs as a way to help students adjust to the academic and social demands of university life. In pathway programs, students undertake intensive English language learning and academic skills preparation. However, the empirical research examining whether pathway programs fulfill these promises remains scarce. Specifically, no study has been conducted on whether the outcomes upon graduation are similar among international students who opt for pathway programs as compared with those admitted according to the typical requirements of the university. Language is strongly associated with almost every aspect of the international student experience—from academic performance to social engagement to mental health and well-being (Smith & Khawaja, 2011; Zhang & Goodson, 2011). But research needs to catch up with the practices and investigate whether or not there is any variation in the social and academic outcomes and experiences for students who opt for this alternate path to a bachelor's degree. Until the evidence is produced, the promise of pathway programs remains unsubstantiated rhetoric.

Local and Global Tensions

It is not surprising that, when highly competitive research universities lower requirements for international students, local, regional, and state students feel squeezed out of the college picture and often perceive international students as having "taken their seats" (Lewin, 2012). Universities have traditionally served their local, regional, and state communities in a manner that is fundamental to many university missions. Responding to the needs of the local economy is integral to the mission of community colleges, and land-grant institutions were created to promote the "liberal and practical education of the industrial classes" (National Archives, 1995, p. 57) to serve the economic and social needs of the state. An interesting example is the University of Wisconsin which, upon becoming a land-grant university in 1862, gave birth to the "Wisconsin Idea" in American higher education: "the boundaries of the University are the boundaries of the state" (Thelin, 2004). In 2013, however, international student enrollment at the University of Wisconsin skyrocketed from 4% to 10% of the total undergraduate population in just a year. The groundswell of new students raised concerns for the faculty senate, which questioned the impact of the administration's policy on the traditional purposes of the institution, particularly since the proportion of in-state students has declined from 64% to 56% in the last 10 years (Simmons, 2013).

Similarly, at the University of Washington, international enrollments have soared to 11% of incoming freshmen, and there are plans to increase enrollment to 20% of the university's undergraduate population (Lewin, 2012). Moreover, legislators, lured by the profit potential of enrollment growth, introduced a bill to charge international students three times the tuition in order to subsidize low-income students from the state. This created a backlash among state residents who felt that the public university was letting international students steal seats from their children. These policies are not just greeted with concern, but they result in moral outrage, as this freshman's comment illustrates:

> "Morally, I feel the university should accept in-state students first, then other American students, then international students," said Farheen Siddiqui, a freshman from Renton, Wash., just south of Seattle. "When I saw all the stories about U.W. taking more international students, I thought, 'Damn, I'm a minority now for being in-state.'" (Lewin, 2012, p. 1)

Because the international student percentage of the undergraduate population has surpassed 5–10% at many institutions, local students are taking notice and are often taking out their frustration with America's slow economic recovery on international students. Students from India are often surprised when U.S. students interpret their presence as a signal that more U.S. jobs will be sent overseas. An international student earning his bachelor's degree in engineering at a metropolitan research institution shares his plight:

> Coming to university, I had some bad experiences here. I had a conversation with one guy who said that, "You guys come here, you don't go back, we lose our jobs!" And yes, we had pretty bad experiences. It could be a fact but on my case, I don't want an H-1B visa. I've seen it for two and a half years, 29 months; I'm going back so I don't mind. Yes, I had bad experiences.

Finally, in an age of global terrorism, international students are often portrayed in the media as a security threat rather than people with their own need for security. Fears of foreign students were heightened post-9/11. These local and global tensions have been exacerbated by events such as the Boston Marathon bombing that leave international students asking whether it is safe to study in the United States (Fischer, 2013). Personal safety and security concerns have risen dramatically for international students considering study in the United States. Though only 14% of Europeans express concerns about safety, half of international students from South Asia and South Asian countries express concerns, over 40% of students from Africa express these concerns, and 27% of students from Latin America express these concerns (IIE, 2011).

The Haves and Have Nots

The net contribution of international students and their families to the U.S. economy, according to NAFSA, is over $21 billion annually (NAFSA, 2011). Tuition and fees from foreign student enrollments have grown at twice the rate of the enrollments of their U.S. peers. Federal policy subjects international students to significant work restrictions. International students are a lucrative market for universities who seek customers who will pay the full retail price for a bachelor's, master's, or doctoral degree from a U.S. college or university. International students are often prohibited from applying for many types of institutional aid. Therefore, among market segments in higher education, they offer the greatest potential for pure profit.

Since the first "academic pilgrimage" in the twelfth century, the benefits of cross-border educational exchange have been framed as an opportunity for the "cross-fertilization of ideas between the many cultures of mankind" (Caldwell, 1965, p. 65). The economic rationales and benefits for educational exchange have become more pronounced in the discourse of late, even as voiced by organizations that champion the academic and cultural benefits of cross-border exchange. In 2001, the NAFSA handbook promoting education in the United States read: "Your experience in an international setting is a marketable commodity. Your long-term career prospects can be enhanced by an experience that develops self-confidence, independence, and cross-cultural skills—attributes that are in high demand with employers world-wide" (NAFSA, 2001, p. 1). The promise of climbing the economic ladder has drawn more international students from working-class families around the world.

There is a dark side, however, to enrolling international students from more varied financial situations. Universities that enroll international students without proper financial support risk putting them in a double bind when their need to pay for their education comes into conflict with the stringent work restrictions outlined by federal law. These work restrictions drive international students in troubled financial situations into the underground workforce to generate income in support of their education, and they are then exploited by those who hire them. For example, *A Dirty Business: The Exploitation of International Students in Melbourne's Office Cleaning Industry* (United Voice, 2013) documents how international students are an invisible workforce, making up over half of the employees of Melbourne's office cleaning industry. Cleaning contractors cut costs by employing international students and underpaying them in cash. Less than 25% of these employees know about their rights as workers, and many report abuse and intimidation by employers (United Voice, 2013). Although this situation is not well covered in the U.S. media, our conversations with international students reveal that it is more common than one would infer from scant media reports.

> What I did, I'm glad that my name is not going to be on this, because as many international students have to basically do this so for the entire undergrad, I had to work 30 hours a week… so I had like 15 houses and that's what I was doing 30 hours a week. I brought my vacuum in every morning. I took all undergrad classes in the afternoon so every day I was basically during the week I was cleaning. I always managed to make enough money that semester to pay another semester. You can't take it to the bank because it's cash so what I did, I always when tuition came due, I came to register and gave them an envelope full of twenties. Once this lady, she asked me, how come you have so much cash? I didn't feel obligated to explain it so I was just quiet.

The behaviors of American colleges and universities have mimicked, in many ways, the behaviors of transnational corporations in their practices of recruiting international students by relying on agents to identify potential targets, and even paying those agents a commission. For-profit, commission-based agents—as opposed to independent governmental advising centers like EducationUSA—have proliferated. It is estimated that well over half of Chinese students use agents to assist them in applying to a U.S. college or university (Zhang & Hagedorn, 2011). Students who use agents have parents with less formal education, they score lower on the SAT/ACT, and they are ranked lower in their high schools (Zhang & Hagedorn, 2011). Although it is clear that the use of agents has buoyed total international student enrollment, what is less certain is whether the social and academic experiences of students who use agents vary significantly from their counterparts who did not use agents, and whether they come with stronger academic credentials.

The authors' research reveals that the greatest discrepancies among international students stem from their financial situation (Glass & Kociolek, 2013). Our interviews with 40 international students at research universities indicate that the quality of the faculty-student relationship is different among students with greater and lesser financial means. Virtually all international students reported predominantly positive interactions with faculty members with two important variations: students who had low financial resources and high levels of academic preparedness reflected the greatest and most widely varied types of experiences interacting with professors, and students with low financial resources and low levels of academic preparedness lacked any descriptions of positive faculty student interactions (Glass & Kociolek, 2013).

Racism, the West, and the Rest

International students arrive from an increasing number of locations, bringing with them diverse cultural foundations for learning, contrasting expectations for forming intercultural friendships, and a range of socioeconomic backgrounds (Choudaha et al., 2012; Chow & Marcus, 2009; IIE, 2012). Researchers have begun to move beyond general comparisons between international and domestic students to consider variations within the international student population that highlight subgroup differences among them (Glass & Gómez, 2013). Both quantitative and qualitative studies identify country of origin as a significant factor in the international student experience (Glass et al., 2013; Lee & Rice, 2007). As the purchasing power of middle-class families in China and Vietnam has grown, and as government-funded students from Saudi Arabia and Brazil have proliferated, international students find themselves scattered over all types of institutions across the United States—from rural community colleges to large metropolitan universities:

> [The Turkish government] sent me to Alabama, and it was terrible. I wasn't happy at all. There I was sick all the time. I always think it is because of the weather, but I think the reason was…I left my family, my friends, and I was missing them a lot. It was just hard for me. So I was sick all the time. (Anderson, 2013)

Universities become sites for ethnic conflicts—and, effectively, conflicts between nations—in students' interactions with one another. With little understanding of the cultural variation that exists within the United States, these international students soon encounter the social dynamics of race relations and perceptions of their country by American students. There is a clear difference between the experience of students from Western Europe and Canada and students from the Middle East, Africa, Latin America, and Asia (Gareis, 2012; Lee, 2010). Americans' positive attitudes toward China, for example, have turned sharply negative in the last several years, with over half of Americans expressing unfavorable opinions of China while citing concerns about job loss and other economic threats (Pew Research Center, 2013). One Chinese student found his car tagged with the words "go back home" (Redden, 2012). U.S. students post racist comments online such as "the Indian next to me at the gym smells like curry covered butthole" (Redden, 2012).

Belonging Nowhere and Everywhere

Numerous reports highlight how international students disclose having no close American friends (Gareis, 2012; Gareis, Merkin, & Goldman, 2011). Eighty percent of international students in the United States rarely or never cross-culturally interact, and 72% are somewhat worried or very worried about depression (Smith & Khawaja, 2011). Despite the potential that friendships with international students offer to broaden the outlook of their U.S. peers, this sad phenomenon endures. A theme of our research is summed up in one international student's statement: "I know American people, but we're not close friends" (Glass & Kociolek, 2013, p. 20). In our interview research, international students' top three descriptions of their relations with U.S. peers were feelings of distance, dissimilarity, and discrimination (Glass & Kociolek, 2013; Glass & Wongtrirat, 2013). Those with the most significant financial resources described more cross-cultural international student interactions and multicultural organization involvement. However, international students with more limited financial resources were more likely to report feeling distant from, ignored by, and excluded by their American peers. The resulting social isolation is palpable and visceral: "You don't want to be sitting by yourself and crying on your own by yourself" (Glass & Kociolek, 2013, p. 23).

Not all international students have an equal desire for friendships with Americans (Trice, 2004). However, a scarcity of friendships with U.S. students does not mean these students lack supportive social relationships. Many international students arrive with global aspirations and have traveled abroad extensively. Even international students who come from underprivileged backgrounds, often selected by their governments as part of national programs of academic mobility, see the social opportunities offered by a U.S. postsecondary education as an opportunity to become part of a transnational, cosmopolitan global network (Fong, 2011; Gargano, 2008). Our interviews with international students suggest that the strongest community for them is a multicultural community of international students. The networks and relationships formed as part of their experience in the United States contribute to their personal and professional aspirations, as this quote from an international student illustrates:

> I have bunch of friends from all part of the world. I have friends from Japan, Korea, I have friends from Australia, I have friends from Pakistan, Afghanistan, Bangladesh, Sri Lanka, Uzbekistan, Russia, Ukraine, and I have friends from Poland, Slovakia.

Students' identities then become more complex, more global, and more recognizably in flux. They may begin to redefine themselves—not according to their country of origin, but according to multiple dimensions of their identity and by participating in transnational migration and multicultural experiences: "Yeah, and I have been friends with almost all of the international students; and I know about their cultures and we share everything so I feel I'm an international student right now, not an Indian student." Although the lack of interaction between American and international students is a frequent concern of international educators, the opportunity for international student engagement in a global environment mitigates, if not eliminates, the potential consequences of this lack of curiosity on the part of American students.

Resilience-Based Approaches to the Acculturation Process

One might conclude from the previous discussion that what higher education leaders need to do is create new programs or services to address these issues. Moreover, it is equally simplistic to fall into the trap of focusing solely on the challenges that international students face on their path to a U.S. bachelor's, master's, or doctoral degree. Scholars compound this issue by concentrating on the problems of international students.

The discourse that emphasizes deficits that must be addressed may sound capacious and inclusive, but it may well perpetuate these issues and serve the interest of those bureaucratic elements in higher education that seek to expand administrative services. What is needed is a more complex understanding of the key features of educational experiences that have a developmental and educational impact on international students (Glass & Westmont-Campbell, 2013; Glass, 2012). This approach will require a rethinking of how we engage international students as full participants and citizens in the academic and social life of the university.

Frameworks of acculturation tend to focus on stress and coping mechanisms, with particular emphasis placed on international students' maladaptive, dysfunctional coping. Less attention has been paid to the positive coping strategies that international students engage in during their global sojourn (Pan, 2011; Pan, Wong, Chan, & Joubert, 2008). There has recently been an emphasis on resilience-based approaches to international student acculturation (Ong, Bergeman, Bisconti, & Wallace, 2006). Resilience-based frameworks are as much a shift in perspective as a shift in language: the focus is a move away from mitigating the potential risks that international students face and toward identifying the mechanisms that support international student resilience (Glass & Westmont-Campbell, 2013). International student social networks, the quality of their intimate relationships, differences in the access they have to resources, and their physical well-being—all these elements interact in shaping their experience and their capacity to remain resilient even when under duress. Traditional acculturation research has often focused on the problems and consequences of international students' experience, such as depression and anxiety, drug use, and poor social relationships (Yan & Berliner, 2011). Resilience research is a paradigm shift in health-related professions and seeks to place the strengths, resources, and competencies of individuals and groups on a par with the potential risk factors these groups may experience.

In this research, emphasis has been placed on these resilience-based frameworks and on conceptualizing them in four broad categories: risk factors, vulnerability factors, protective factors, and promoting factors (Glass & Westmont-Campbell, 2013; Gutman, Sameroff, & Cole, 2003). These models have been extended by examining the direct and indirect effects of those factors on international student academic success in cross-cultural relationships. A framework developed by Gutman and colleagues (2003) has been adapted that examines risk, vulnerability, and protective and promotive factors.

Risk factors include things such as discrimination, financial stressors, language difficulties, and immigration problems (Zhang & Goodson, 2011). Risk factors are associated with negative consequences such as poor academic performance, feelings of isolation and marginalization, and negative emotion (Smith & Khawaja, 2011). Protective factors buffer the effects of risk factors on individuals—for example, a sense of belongingness (Glass & Westmont-Campbell, 2013) and meaning in life (Pan et al., 2008) have been shown to buffer the effects of discriminatory experiences with local students. Belonging—even so-called "mere belonging" (Walton, Cohen, Cwir, & Spencer, 2012)—has profound effects on student well-being and persistence. Promotive factors influence and generate positive outcomes such as strong academic performance, positive emotion, and cross-cultural interaction. They may also fortify protective factors such as belongingness in buffering the effects of the potential risks that international students face (Glass & Westmont-Campbell, 2013). Finally, vulnerability factors reflect characteristics such as shaky financial footing or poor academic preparation. These factors have been strongly associated with undesirable outcomes.

Our research has confirmed the major risk factors cited for international students, namely, how educational stressors, discrimination, language difficulties, and visa issues impair the academic performance and social experience of international students, thus affecting both their satisfaction with life at the university (Smith & Khawaja, 2011) and their sociocultural adjustment to the United States (Zhang & Goodson, 2011). These difficulties often manifest themselves in physical symptoms of distress. In our research, we have shown that students from China, South Korea, and Saudi Arabia feel more threatened than students from the United States or Canada (Glass et al., 2013). What we have added to the research is the importance of protective and promotive factors in facilitating international student resilience (Glass et al., 2013). For example, our research indicates that belongingness, defined as "a pervasive drive to form and maintain at least a minimum quantity of lasting, positive, and significant interpersonal relationships" (Baumeister & Leary, 1995, p. 497), increases cross-cultural interaction among international and domestic students and enhances students' average grade earned, especially among international students (Glass & Westmont-Campbell, 2013). Furthermore, promotive interactions also facilitate acculturation; indeed, leadership programs, cultural events, and community service further enhance the sense of belongingness for all students by offering these protective factors in the international student experience (Strayhorn, 2012).

We have also highlighted some concerning trends: international students score perceptions of community significantly lower than their U.S. peers in almost every dimension we have measured (Glass et al., 2013). International students, in particular, rate their sense of being a part of a close and supportive community of colleagues and friends at their institution much lower than do their U.S. peers. Although international students interact with faculty as frequently as their U.S. peers, they are far less likely to believe that faculty challenge their views on a topic in class or that faculty present issues and problems in class from different cultural perspectives (Glass et al., 2013; Glass & Kociolek, 2013). This is especially true among students from the top five sending countries, including China, India, and South Korea, and is especially low among students from Saudi Arabia. Again, courses that provide opportunities for intensive dialogue or engage multicultural issues, as well as leadership programs, or discussions of current events, all have markedly strong effects on the quality of international students' interactions with faculty and other students (Glass, 2012). International students who participate in events celebrating both their own culture and other cultures are less likely to report feeling threatened than their international counterparts who do not participate in these activities.

Conclusion

Now that international students represent a significant portion of the annual budgetary planning cycles of so many U.S. institutions, and in so many sectors of U.S. higher education, it is critical that senior administrators devote more resources to this new, emerging student demographic. Universities devote significant resources to get international students "in the door," but less attention is paid to what happens once they arrive, and almost no attention is paid to what happens to them once they leave the institution and return to their home countries. The authors strongly urge institutions to match their efforts in international student recruitment with an investment in institutional capacities that better serve this large international student population. High-quality diversity experiences enhance international students' sense of community and represent the university's academic purposes, which it is believed should be at the core of campus internationalization initiatives.

References

Anderson, K. (2013). *Anthropology, globalization, and higher education* (Unpublished master's thesis). University of Wisconsin-Madison, Madison, WI.

Baumeister, R.F., & Leary, M.R. (1995). The need to belong: Desire for interpersonal attachments as a fundamental human motivation. *Psychological Bulletin, 117*(3), 497–529. doi:10.1037/0033-2909.117.3.497

Bevis, T.B., & Lucas, C.J. (2007). *International students in American colleges and universities: A history.* New York, NY: Palgrave Macmillan.

Bhandari, R. (2013). Reenvisioning internationalization: International education for what? *IIE Networker*, 49. Retrieved from http://www.iie.org/en/Blog/2013/March/Reinvisioning-Internationalization

Caldwell, O.J. (1965). Education comes of age around the world. In S. Frazer (Ed.), *Governmental policy and international education* (pp. 61–69). New York, NY: Wiley.

Chickering, A.W., & Kytle, J. (1999). The collegiate ideal in the twenty-first century. *New Directions for Higher Education, 1999*(105), 109–120.

Choudaha, R. (2012). Beyond more of the same: Top four emerging markets for international student recruitment. *World Education News & Reviews, 25*(9). Retrieved from http://wenr.wes.org/2012/10/wenr-october-2012-beyond-more-of-the-same-top-four-emerging-markets-for-international-student-recruitment/

Choudaha, R., Chang, L., & Kono, Y. (2013). International student mobility trends 2013: Towards responsive recruitment strategies. *World Education News & Reviews, 26*(2), 4–25.

Choudaha, R., Orosz, K., & Chang, L. (2012). *Not all international students are the same: Understanding segments, mapping behavior.* New York, NY: World Education Services.

Chow, P., & Chambers, J. (2010). International enrollments in the United States: 60 years of Open Doors data. *International Higher Education, 59*, 17–18. Retrieved from http://www.bc.edu/content/dam/files/research_sites/cihe/pdf/IHEpdfs/ihe59.pdf

Chow, P., & Marcus, R. (2009). International students in the United States. *International Higher Education, 55*, 13–15. Retrieved from http://www.bc.edu/bc_org/avp/soe/cihe/newsletter/Number55/p13_Chow&Marcus.htm

de Wit, H. (2011). Internationalization of higher education: Nine misconceptions. *International Higher Education, 64*, 6–7.

Fischer, K. (2013, April 23). International students increasingly ask: Is it safe to study in the U.S.? *Chronicle of Higher Education*. Retrieved from http://chronicle.com/article/International-Students-Ask-Is/138755/

Fong, V.L. (2011). The floating life: Dilemmas of education, work, and marriage abroad. In V.L. Fong, *Paradise redefined: Transnational Chinese students and the quest for flexible citizenship in the developed world* (pp. 95–141). Stanford, CA: Stanford University Press.

Gareis, E. (2012). Intercultural friendship: Effects of home and host region. *Journal of International and Intercultural Communication, 5*(4), 1–20. doi:10.1080/17513057.2012.691525

Gareis, E., Merkin, R., & Goldman, J. (2011). Intercultural friendship: Linking communication variables and friendship success. *Journal of Intercultural Communication Research, 40*(2), 153–171.

Gargano, T. (2008). (Re)conceptualizing international student mobility: The potential of transnational social fields. *Journal of Studies in International Education, 13*(3), 331–346. doi:10.1177/1028315308322060

Glass, C.R. (2012). Educational experience associated with international students' learning, development, and positive perceptions of campus climate. *Journal of Studies in International Education, 16*(3), 226–249. doi:10.1177/1028315311426783

Glass, C.R., & Braskamp, L.A. (2012). Foreign students and tolerance. *Inside Higher Ed*. Retrieved from http://www.insidehighered.com/views/2012/10/26/essay-how-colleges-should-respond-racism-against-international-students

Glass, C.R., Buus, S., & Braskamp, L.A. (2013). *Uneven experiences: What's missing and what matters for today's international students*. Chicago, IL: Global Perspective Institute.

Glass, C.R., & Gómez, E. (2013, March). International students' recreational participation, intercultural social ties, and adaptation to college in the United States: A comparison by subregion of origin. Paper presented at the annual meeting of the 57th Annual Conference of the Comparative and International Education Society, New Orleans, LA.

Glass, C.R., & Kociolek, E. (2013). *The impact of student-faculty interactions on international students' sense of belonging*. St. Louis, MO: Association of the Study of Higher Education.

Glass, C.R., & Westmont-Campbell, C. (2013). Comparative effects of belongingness on the academic success and cross-cultural interactions of domestic and international students. *International Journal of Intercultural Relations, 38*(3), 106–119.

Glass, C.R., & Wongtrirat, R. (2013, March). Understanding the educational experiences that international students identify as having a positive impact toward their development. Paper presented at the annual meeting of the 57th Annual Conference of the Comparative and International Education Society, New Orleans, LA.

Gutman, L.M., Sameroff, A.J., & Cole, R. (2003). Academic growth curve trajectories from 1st grade to 12th grade: Effects of multiple social risk factors and preschool child factors. *Developmental Psychology, 39*(4), 777–789. doi:10.1037/0012-1649.39.4.777

Howell, B. (2013, May 10). Michigan State sets application record for third straight year: Prospective international students on the rise. *MLive*. East Lansing, MI. Retrieved from http://www.mlive.com/lansing-news/index.ssf/2013/05/michigan_state_sets_applicatio.html

Institute of International Education (IIE). (2011). *International students in the U.S.* (pp. 1–30). Washington, DC: Author.

Institute of International Education (IIE). (2012). *Open Doors® 2012 Report on international educational exchange*. Washington, DC: Author.

International Association of Universities (IAU). (2012, April). *Affirming academic values in internationalization of higher education: A call for action*. Retrieved from http://www.iau-aiu.net/sites/all/files/Affirming_Academic_Values_in_Internationalization_of_Higher_Education.pdf

Lane, J., & Kinser, K. (2013, April 15). Is the international-education "bubble" about to pop? *Chronicle of Higher Education*. Retrieved from http://chronicle.com/blogs/worldwise/is-the-international-education-bubble-about-to-pop/32099

Lee, J.J. (2010). International students' experiences and attitudes at a US host institution: Self-reports and future recommendations. *Journal of Research in International Education, 9*(1), 66–84. doi:10.1177/1475240909356382

Lee, J.J. (2013a). The false halo of internationalization. *International Higher Education, 72*, 5–7.

Lee, J.J. (2013b). From here to where? *CONAHEC*. Edmonton, AB, Canada.

Lee, J.J., & Rice, C. (2007). Welcome to America? International student perceptions of discrimination. *Higher Education, 53*(3), 381–409. doi:10.1007/s10734-005-4508-3

Lewin, T. (2012, February 4). Taking more seats on campus, foreigners also pay the freight. *The New York Times*. Retrieved from http://www.nytimes.com/2012/02/05/education/international-students-pay-top-dollar-at-us-colleges.html?pagewanted=all&_r=0

Lingzi, L. (2013, May 19). U.S. campuses wrestle with safety perceptions. *The New York Times*. Retrieved from http://www.nytimes.com/2013/05/20/us/us-campuses-wrestle-with-safety-perceptions.html

NAFSA. (2001). *International student handbook*. Washington, DC: Association of International Educators.

NAFSA. (2011). *The economic benefits of international education to the United States for the 2010–2011 academic year: A statistical analysis*. Retrieved from http://www.nafsa.org/_/file/_/eis2011/usa.pdf

National Archives. (1995). *Milestone documents*. Washington, DC: Author.

National Science Board. (2012). *Science and engineering indicators 2012*. Arlington, VA: Author.

Ong, A.D., Bergeman, C.S., Bisconti, T.L., & Wallace, K. (2006). Psychological resilience, positive emotions, and successful adaptation to stress in later life. *Journal of Personality and Social Psychology, 91*(4), 730–749. doi:10.1037/0022-3514.91.4.730

Pan, J.-Y. (2011). A resilience-based and meaning-oriented model of acculturation: A sample of mainland Chinese postgraduate students in Hong Kong. *International Journal of Intercultural Relations, 35*(5), 592–603. doi:10.1016/j.ijintrel.2011.02.009

Pan, J.-Y., Wong, D.F.K., Chan, C.L.W., & Joubert, L. (2008). Meaning of life as a protective factor of positive affect in acculturation: A resilience framework and a cross-cultural comparison. *International Journal of Intercultural Relations, 32*(6), 505–514. doi:10.1016/j.ijintrel.2008.08.002

Pew Research Center. (2013). *Americans and Chinese grow more wary of each other*. Retrieved from http://www.pewresearch.org/fact-tank/2013/06/05/americans-and-chinese-grow-more-wary-of-each-other/

Redden, E. (2010, August 4). Privatized pathways for foreign sudents. *Inside Higher Ed*. Retrieved from http://www.insidehighered.com/news/2010/08/04/pathways

Redden, E. (2012, October 16). Tensions simmer between American and international students. *Inside Higher Ed*, pp. 10–12. Retrieved from http://www.insidehighered.com/news/2012/10/16/tensions-simmer-between-american-and-international-students

Redden, E. (2013, January 3). Conditionally yours. *Inside Higher Ed*. Retrieved from www.insidehighered.com/news/2013/01/03/conditional-admission-and-pathway-programs-proliferate

Simmons, D. (2013, May 9). Wisconsin students decline, international students rise as percentage of most recent UW-Madison freshman class. *Wisconsin State Journal*. Retrieved from http://host.madison.com/news/local/education/university/wisconsin-students-decline-international-students-rise-as-percentage-of-most/article_cb3e6538-2abe-5207-8aa8-a19d8145a26f.html

Smith, R.A., & Khawaja, N.G. (2011). A review of the acculturation experiences of international students. *International Journal of Intercultural Relations, 35*(6), 699–713. doi:10.1016/j.ijintrel.2011.08.004

Strayhorn, T.L. (2012). *College students' sense of belonging: A key to educational success for all students*. New York, NY: Routledge.

Thelin, J.R. (2004). *A history of American higher education*. Baltimore, MD: Johns Hopkins University Press.

Trice, A.G. (2004). Mixing it up: International graduate students' social interactions with American students. *Journal of College Student Development, 45*(6), 671–687. doi:10.1353/csd.2004.0074

UNESCO. (2012). *UNESCO Institute for Statistics glossary*. Retrieved from http://glossary.uis.unesco.org/glossary/en/term/2242/en

United Voice. (2013). *A dirty business: The exploitation of international students in Melbourne's office cleaning industry*. North Melbourne, Victoria, Australia: Author.

Walton, G.M., Cohen, G.L., Cwir, D., & Spencer, S.J. (2012). Mere belonging: The power of social connections. *Journal of Personality and Social Psychology, 102*(3), 513–532. doi:10.1037/a0025731

Yan, K., & Berliner, D.C. (2011). An examination of individual level factors in stress and coping processes: Perspectives of Chinese international students in the United States. *Journal of College Student Development, 52*(5), 523–542. doi:10.1353/csd.2011.0060

Zhang, J., & Goodson, P. (2011). Predictors of international students' psychosocial adjustment to life in the United States: A systematic review. *International Journal of Intercultural Relations, 35*(2), 139–162. doi:10.1016/j.ijintrel.2010.11.011

Zhang, Y., & Hagedorn, L.S. (2011). College application with or without assistance of an education agent. *Journal of College Admission, 212*, 6–16.

Part Two

Student Equality

EIGHT

Women in College: Environments and Identities

Paige Haber-Curran and Chris Linder

College women make up a majority of the students in American higher education and are an incredibly diverse group. They overlap with many populations covered in this book, and thus bring with them a complexity of experiences and backgrounds. There is no typical or traditional college woman; there are, however, common experiences of college women based on their gender and aspects of the campus environment that facilitate or impede their development while in college. Research demonstrates that the experiences of men and women differ on college campuses, and college impacts people of all genders in different ways (Sax, 2008).

Acknowledging that there is enough information on the topic of college women for entire books and courses, this chapter provides an overview of some key factors influencing college women. A historical context of women in college is presented. College women today are examined through Strange and Banning's (2001) campus ecology model. This chapter, along with the chapters on college men and LGBTQ students, provides an understanding of the complexity of gender in the college environment, and through this understanding, readers will be better able to serve students on their respective campuses.

In recognizing that people of all genders face many challenges on college campuses, this chapter is approached through a feminist perspective of seeking to end sexist oppression (hooks, 1984). Particularly when examining the complexity of gender intersecting with other social identities—such as race and ethnicity, socioeconomic status, sexual orientation, and disability status—there is much to be accomplished in ending sexist oppression.

Setting the Context

Historically, higher education was the privilege of a select group of men—specifically, White, economically privileged men—and whose aim was to prepare them for civil service (Allan, 2011). In 1837 Oberlin College became the first institution to admit women and began granting women degrees in 1841 (Bank, 2011a). This began a movement on the part of degree-granting institutions to begin granting women (primarily White women) admission in the mid to late 1800s (Thelin & Gasman, 2011). By 1910, women made up approximately 35% of students attending higher education institutions (Allan, 2011). Although women were attending some institutions of higher education, they were barred from many other institutions altogether. In fact, many colleges and universities prohibited women from attending until the 1970s (National Women's Law Center [NWLC], 2013); others had quotas in place for women for admission and for certain courses or majors (National Coalition for Women and Girls in Education [NCWGE], 2012).

Title IX of the Education Amendments Act of 1972 had a significant impact on women in education, prohibiting discrimination on the basis of sex for any federally funded educational activity or program (NWLC, 2013). Title IX provided increased access for women to higher education. In addition, women's participation in activities, including athletics, increased dramatically. Career education and employment opportunities also expanded for women.

The higher education landscape shifted dramatically after the passage of Title IX. Increased access to college led to a shift in student demographics. In 1970, men made up approximately 59% of student enrollment at degree-granting institutions across the United States; by 2011, women made up approximately 59% of student enrollment (National Center for Education Statistics [NCES], 2011). This changing landscape has nurtured varying perspectives on the state of gender equality and equity in higher education, including an increased focus on the state of young men in society and in college. We believe a focus on college men is warranted; however, this should not happen at the expense of college women and people of additional genders. Enrollment numbers tell only one part of the story and may not reflect the complexities of women's experiences in college today.

Although women in college have experienced great advances since the passage of Title IX, a number of issues still exist for women on college campuses today. Women's advancement in science, technology, engineering, and mathematics (STEM) fields; sexual harassment and campus safety; and educational practices and classroom environments catering to men represent a few of these challenges (NCWGE, 2012; Sax, 2008). It is vital to consider the interaction of students and campus environments.

College Women and the Campus Environment

Describing physical, human aggregate, organizational, and constructed components of an environment, Strange and Banning (2001) provide a conceptual framework for exploring campus environments, as described in Table 1. The physical environment takes into account the "place" aspect of campus; human aggregate environments describe the influence people have on the campus; organizational environments provide insight into the ways campuses operate; and constructed environments represent the interpretations of campus cultures, rituals, and social climate on a campus (Strange & Banning, 2001). In this section the four dimensions of campus environments are used to highlight issues affecting women on college campuses today.

Table 1: Overview of Campus Ecology Model and Examples for College Environments.

Environment	Description	Example
Physical	Explores campus spaces and places, including architectural design and use of space	The use of "blue lights" for safety on campus
Human Aggregate	The interaction of people and spaces to influence an environment	Male-dominated STEM majors may result in insensitive gender-related behaviors on campus
Organizational	The who, how, and why of campus operations—includes organizational charts, policies and procedures, and issues of efficiency on campus	The implementation of Title IX greatly influenced women's experiences in college by providing greater access to educational opportunities, both inside and outside the classroom
Constructed	Interpretations of campus cultures, rituals, and social climate on a campus	The concept of "effortless perfection" represents some women's interpretations of campus environments related to their need to "have it all" without showing they work too hard

Adapted from *Educating by Design: Creating Campus Learning Environments That Work*, by C.C. Strange and J.H. Banning, 2001, San Francisco, CA: Jossey-Bass.

Physical Environment

As described above, physical environment refers to the *place* aspect of campus experiences. Students are significantly influenced by the physical aspects of campus design, and great care goes into designing campus environments that promote safety, inclusion, learning, and engagement (Kenney, Dumont, & Kenney, 2005; Strange & Banning, 2001). When considering women's experiences with the physical campus environment, campus safety often comes to mind. Twenty-seven percent of women in college will experience sexual assault in their college career, and sexual violence is most often committed by someone known to the victim. Women most frequently identified boyfriends (41%), friends (29%), or acquaintances (21%) as perpetrators of sexual violence (Gross, Winslett, Roberts, & Gohm, 2006).

Although violence perpetrated by persons unknown to the victim represents a very small percentage of crime on a college campus (Gross et al., 2006), great care is taken to ensure a safe campus environment. Many aspects of this care are geared toward women. For example, "blue lights" on college campuses are highlighted as strategies to ensure safety for women walking on campus at night, and campus escort services provide trained campus security staff and volunteers to accompany students after dark. Further, staff in residence halls work to create safe environments for students by emphasizing the importance of locking doors and windows and registering guests at the front desk of the building (Turner & Torres, 2006).

Campus environments are created with the best of intentions to promote safety; yet failing to address the human aggregate, organizational, and constructed dimensions of campus environments associated with sexual violence may increase the risk of crime. Sending the message that sexual assault is primarily committed by outsiders during late-night hours perpetuates the idea that women should be cautious of strangers but comfortable with people known to them through their classes or social interactions. This message contributes to a culture that allows perpetrators of sexual violence known to the victim greater access and opportunity. Addressing sexual violence on campus must include attention to the campus culture that perpetuates notions of male privilege and shame for survivors of sexual violence (constructed), the policies and procedures influencing the reporting process for crimes of sexual violence (organizational), and the peer culture that perpetuates unhealthy expressions of power and masculinity (human aggregate).

When women do not feel safe on campus, they may not have the opportunity to engage completely in academic and additional learning opportunities. For example, if students do not feel safe walking on campus at night, they may not attend student organization meetings in the evening and may not even feel safe studying in the library at night (Turner & Torres, 2006). Jessica Valenti (2007) describes women as living under a "rape schedule," meaning that they organize their lives around keeping themselves safe from victimization by scheduling meetings and social events based on places and times that are considered "safe" for them.

In addition to physical safety, some aspects of the campus environment may unintentionally communicate exclusion to women students. For example, noting the representations of the genders of people who are highlighted in various academic buildings and athletic spaces may communicate the value of women in particular fields. If men's names and pictures dominate the hallways of the engineering and business buildings on campus, women students may feel excluded from the space and internalize the message that certain fields of study are not for them. Similarly, when the football stadium is front and center on campus, and the women's soccer field and volleyball arena are on the outskirts of campus or located in difficult-to-find places, clear messages are sent about the value of particular sports on a campus, often directly related to gender dynamics in the larger sports environment. The exclusion of women from athletic spaces contributes to inequity in resource distribution (i.e., scholarships for women athletes), reducing access to education for women. Although these aspects of campus physical environments may seem insignificant on the surface, the cumulative impact of these subtle messages increases over time, resulting in a small number of women entering careers in science, technology, engineering, and math (Allan, 2011). The physical environment of such campus contexts as athletics and STEM and business buildings is just one way of examining the under-representation of women in these arenas. As will be discussed in the next sections, there are a limited number of women coaches and faculty, as well as reports of a chilly climate for women on campus.

Human Aggregate

The human aggregate component of the campus ecology model encompasses characteristics of the people and the influence they have on the campus environment. Specifically, human aggregate environments explore the interaction of human beings and their physical environments, highlighting ways in which human characteristics influence the overall feel of a shared space. This section provides a demographic snapshot of college women today and a discussion of college women's identity and development.

Demographic snapshot of college women. As noted earlier in the chapter, women comprise a majority of college students. In 1988, women surpassed men in total number of undergraduate students, and by 2011 women made up approximately 60% of all students enrolled in higher education (57% of full-time students and 63% of part-time students) (Allan, 2011; NCES, 2011). There is a substantial gender gap for non-traditional students ages 25 and older, whereby women are enrolling and earning degrees in substantially higher numbers than men (NCES, 2011). Although women are enrolling in higher education in greater numbers than ever before, there is a notable disparity between women and men in the science, technology, engineering, and mathematics (STEM) fields. Most notably, though women made up 18% of recipients of undergraduate degrees in engineering and computer sciences in 2010, these percentages have consistently decreased over the past 10 years (National Center for Science and Engineering Statistics [NCSES], 2013). Women are also notably underrepresented in business degrees (Sax, 2008). However, they comprise the majority of students pursuing undergraduate degrees in many other fields, most notably health professions/nursing, education, and psychology (Sax, 2008).

The racial diversity of women in college has grown over the past 40 years. From 1998 to 2008, the total enrollment of African American/Black women increased by 59%, Latina/Hispanic women by 78%, Asian American/Pacific Islander by 42%, and American Indian by 33% (Kim, 2011). During this period, the total enrollment of White women increased by 14%. Although these figures demonstrate a substantial growth in the number of racially underrepresented women in college, White women still make up the majority of all students. In 1976, White women made up approximately 83% of undergraduate women attending institutions of higher education, and in 2010 White women made up approximately 62% of total women (NCES, 2011). There also exists a substantial gap in enrollment in higher education based on socioeconomic status. Among lower-income college students, though, "women account for the majority of [these] students...and across racial and ethnic groups, the gender gap in undergraduate enrollment narrows as family income rises" (Allan, 2011, p. 43).

The college student population today is more diverse than at any time in history. Student affairs educators must anticipate this diversity and approach their work in a way that recognizes those diverse backgrounds and experiences and challenges a one-size-fits-all approach to our work. College educators must recognize that "the same intervention or experience might not have the same impact for all students, but rather might differ in magnitude or even the direction of its impact for students with different characteristics or traits" (Pascarella, 2006, p. 512). College women reflect a range of identities that must be recognized and considered in our work with them on college campuses.

Women's identity development. The human aggregate environment also emphasizes the importance of identity development among women college students. Understanding women's identity development and the context in which women develop is important because college and university educators have a responsibility to facilitate the development of students. Focusing on the ways in which students develop in the context of the physical environment, among peers, and in relation to the organizational and constructed environments proves challenging for student affairs educators, as each person's developmental process is different and depends on a variety of factors.

Identity development theorists have studied developmental processes for undergraduate women students since the early 1980s (Belenkey, Clinchy, Goldberger, & Tarule, 1997;

Gilligan, 1982). Early work on identity development was criticized for focusing on the experiences of heterosexual White women in college to the exclusion of the experiences of women of color and queer women (Jones & Abes, 2013). Additionally, early models of women's identity development did not describe the importance of context on the development of women's identity. More recent identity development theorists work to address the complex nature of identity development by taking into account women's multiple identities as well as the contexts in which identity development takes place. Jones and McEwen (2000) developed the Model of Multiple Dimensions of Identity (MMDI) that explores the ways in which identity development is contextual and fluid. The model describes identity development at the intersection of three essential components of identity: the core of one's identity (identities that a person describes for herself such as personality traits and roles they play in her life); social identities (those identities that describe the social groups to which an individual belongs, such as race, gender, and sexual orientation); and context (the place in which identity development takes place). Scholars expanded the MMDI to include a meaning-making filter describing the varying degrees of complexity of the ways people make meaning of their experiences (Abes, Jones, & McEwen, 2007). Related to the concept of self-authorship, the meaning-making filter illustrates the ways in which people interpret and understand the messages they receive related to their identities. For example, a woman with a more complex filter may hear from her family that she cannot be both a lesbian and a Christian, and she may hear different messages from peers. The filter helps her to understand the context of both messages and to make sense of her experience from her own lens (Abes et al., 2007).

In addition to the MMDI, scholars have explored the intersections of women's identities in a variety of contexts, highlighting the varied experiences and developmental processes of women from diverse backgrounds. For example, one study explored the experiences of multiracial queer women in relationship to their environments, stressing similarities between the experience of not being "brown enough" and not being "gay enough" to fit into either the queer community or communities of color (King, 2011). Research focusing on the experiences of women of color activists emphasizes similar developmental issues within mainstream feminist movements on college campuses (Linder & Rodriguez, 2012). Feminist organizations claim to be welcoming and inclusive spaces, but to focus exclusively on gender issues often unintentionally marginalizes women with various additional subordinated identities (i.e., women of color, queer women, and women with disabilities). These exclusionary practices lead to exhaustion and burnout for women attempting to explore their many identities in spaces designed with a particular kind of woman in mind. Another emerging body of literature explores the developmental experiences of Black undergraduate women and the nuances of Black women's identity development that are often overlooked when too much attention is focused on the dearth of Black men in college (Patton, 2012; Winkle-Wagner, 2009). Finally, some research explores the development of dominant identities in relationship to gender for undergraduate women. Linder's (2012) model of anti-racist White feminist identity development illustrates the complexity of navigating fear, guilt, and shame as White undergraduate women seek to understand White privilege in relationship to the subordination of their gender. Research on women's identity development is complex and illustrates the importance of understanding both the person and the environment in supporting women students.

Organizational

Another key aspect of the campus environment is the organizational context in which college women study, live, and develop. This section covers organizational contexts by examining the gender makeup of faculty and staff on campus, varying institutional types, campus policies affecting college women, and women's co-curricular involvement.

Gender makeup of faculty and staff. The gender makeup of faculty and staff and its resulting dynamics are significant when considering the organizational context of higher education institutions for college women. Women faculty and staff play a crucial role in creating positive environments that are supportive of college women (Lapovsky & Slaner Larkin, 2009; Sax, 2008). Research demonstrates that "attending colleges with more female professors strengthens female students' scholarly confidence, achievement motivation, and college GPA" (Sax, 2008, p. 226). Having more women faculty on campus also positively impacts the experiences and outcomes of college men—in some cases even more so than college women (Sax, 2008).

Women make up approximately 54% of the total number of employees on college campuses, yet they hold less than one-third of high-ranking positions (Association of American Colleges & Universities [AAC&U], 2012; Association of Governing Boards of Universities and Colleges [AGB], 2010; NCES, 2011). Women fill a large number of staff roles, both professional (including student affairs positions) and nonprofessional, and lower-ranking faculty positions. But when examining higher-ranking positions that yield significant status and control, such as tenured faculty, president, and governing board members, women are substantially underrepresented. For instance, in 2012 women made up only 26% of college and university presidents (AAC&U, 2012), and in 2009 they made up only 28% of professors, the highest faculty rank (NCES, 2011). Thus, although students see and interact with a significant number of women on campus, they are much less accustomed to seeing women in substantial leadership roles, which sends a message about the value and worth of women in academia. Further, there are fewer women empowered to make substantial university decisions that can positively influence the experiences of college women on their campuses.

Beyond these worrisome figures are additional dynamics that warrant attention. Approximately three-quarters of women faculty across all ranks are White (NCES, 2011). Similarly, among staff, over three-quarters of all women professional staff are White, and 64% of nonprofessional women staff are White (NCES, 2011). This becomes particularly problematic as the racial diversity among college women continues to increase. Often women students of color feel isolated, tokenized, and out of place on college campuses. There is a need to continue to increase the number of women faculty and staff on college campuses, particularly among women of color and women in higher-ranking positions. The increased presence of women and women of color among staff and faculty provides role models and mentoring opportunities for college women. Further, it helps insure that "all voices are heard and all agendas considered" (Lapovsky & Slaner Larkin, 2009, p. 25).

Institutional types. Although this chapter discusses women on college campuses as one large entity, it is important to recognize the role that institutional type plays in women students' experiences. Women students attend a variety of institutional types, including 2-year institutions, liberal arts institutions, 4-year doctorate-granting institutions, historically Black colleges and universities (HBCUs), and women's colleges, and research suggests the experiences of women differ based on institutional type. Among co-educational institutions, women tend to make up the majority of students on campus, yet they tend to experience a "chillier" classroom climate than men (Bank, 2011a). There is evidence of professors treating women and men differently in the classroom by paying more attention to men, making more eye contact with men, allowing them to speak longer than women, and remembering their names more often than women's names (Allan, 2011; Bank, 2011a). Co-educational institutions may also create a more hostile environment for women students than for male students. The prevalence of sexual harassment at co-educational institutions from both male students and faculty "has been found to interfere with the performance of women students" (Bank, 2011a, p. 107).

Community colleges have historically provided educational access to women, low-income students, and racially underrepresented students in higher education, as well as greater access to women faculty and staff (Townsend, 2011). Community colleges are particularly conducive to non-traditionally aged women, and the presence of these colleges, offering "classes and services, combined with the low tuition, has meant that many women could afford to attend college, both financially and timewise" (Townsend, 2011, p. 111). In addition to offering associate degrees, community colleges also offer noncredit programs such as job-training and welfare-to-work programs, in which women make up a majority (Townsend, 2011).

Historically Black colleges and universities (HBCUs) were established to educate African American and Black students (Gasman, 2011). Today, Black women are academically outpacing their Black male peers at HBCUs. Historically, there have been substantial gender roles and expectations affecting women at HBCUs. Although strides have been made in breaking down gender role barriers at HBCUs, "at many campuses, an atmosphere persists that encourages women to yield to male counterparts in class discussions and in student leadership positions" (Gasman, 2011, p. 128).

Women's colleges and universities were established beginning in the 1800s. Their number has decreased substantially since the 1960s, and today they serve less than 1% of all women attending higher education institutions (Wolf-Wendel & Eason, 2011). Although women's colleges and universities serve a small number of women, they serve non-traditionally aged women and women of color in higher proportions than other institutional types, increasing access to higher education for these underrepresented populations (Wolf-Wendel & Eason, 2011). Research demonstrates that women's colleges and universities provide a more supportive environment for women students than coeducational institutions, one in which women feel empowered and taken seriously (Kinzie, Thomas, Palmer, Umbach, & Kuh, 2007; Wolf-Wendel & Eason, 2011). Further, women attending women's colleges and universities demonstrate greater levels of engagement, self-reported educational gains, support from faculty, presence of role models, participation in active and collaborative learning, student-faculty interaction, and participation in diversity-related activities than their women peers attending co-educational institutions (Kinzie et al., 2007; Wolf-Wendel & Eason, 2011). The institutional missions, the more personalized experience that stems from the small size of the institutions, the gender makeup of the student body, and the often larger percentage of female staff and faculty at women's colleges and universities are some of the organizational factors contributing to these educational gains and feelings of a supportive campus environment (Griffin & Hurtado, 2011; Wolf-Wendel & Eason, 2011). There is much to be learned about the educational environments in place at women's colleges that can inform how best to serve women attending all types of institutions.

Campus policies affecting college women. A number of policies mandated at the national, state, and institutional levels affect women on college campuses. Most prominent is Title IX, which prohibits sex discrimination in federally funded education programs (Bank, 2011b). This involves sex discrimination in admissions, enrollment in degree programs, participation in activities, participation in athletics, and career education, among other areas (NWLC, 2013). Title IX has received considerable attention and was spotlighted recently for the way in which it relates to sexual harassment and sexual violence, which are recognized as forms of sex discrimination (Paludi, 2011). To meet the requirements of Title IX, "it is necessary for educational institutions to have an explicit anti-harassment policy that complies with the provisions of Title IX" (Paludi, 2011, p. 375).

In April 2011, Russlynn Ali, U.S. Assistant Secretary for Civil Rights, issued a *Dear Colleague* letter on sexual violence that provided an overview of the obligation of institutions to respond to sexual harassment and sexual violence on campuses in accordance with Title IX (U.S. Department of Education, 2011). In addition, the letter provides guidance and suggestions on how to address and proactively prevent sexual violence on campuses. Allegations made by survivors of sexual violence across the country suggest that many campuses do not appropriately respond to reported sexual assaults on campus, resulting in few students reporting their experiences to campus officials (Sander, 2013). Sexual violence continues to be one of the most serious issues facing college women today, despite national and local policies seeking to address the problem.

It is important to note that, although a range of policies exists to improve the environment for college women, the policies are not always followed (either unintentionally or, in some cases, intentionally). Policies designed to eliminate racial and gender biases and discrimination on college campuses have faced considerable opposition (Bank, 2011b). There is a failure to enforce the policies, as well as "overt and hostile attempts to eliminate these policies altogether" (Bank, 2011b, p. 354). Some also claim that the policies are no longer relevant. As an example, evidence indicates that, in an attempt to maintain a gender balance among college students, women applying to more selective institutions are "experiencing a lower rate of admission than their male counterparts" (Allan, 2011, p. 42) despite their higher academic and co-curricular achievements. Further, there are many examples of colleges and universities not enforcing or addressing Title IX policies, particularly when they relate to issues of sexual violence.

Women's involvement in leadership organizations and groups. College women make up a majority of students involved in college organizations and groups, and they spend more time participating in student organizations and groups per week than their male counterparts (Sax, 2008). Women are also more likely than men to seek out campus involvements that "complement and enrich academic curricula" (Allan, 2011, p. 48). Research demonstrates that, although women are actively involved and hold a variety of leadership roles on campus, they are underrepresented in top leadership roles and often seek out less-visible leadership roles in organizations (Allan, 2011; Princeton University, 2011).

Women's involvement in college athletics increased substantially after the introduction of Title IX. Athletics provide a great opportunity for women to be actively engaged on campus and to develop vital leadership, teamwork, and life skills. More than 40 years after the introduction of Title IX, the playing field is still far from equitable for women. Although the number of women's athletic teams—and thus women athletes—on college campuses has increased, a vast majority of campuses (estimated at 71%–83%) are not in full compliance with Title IX in relation to women's athletics. Thus, women are underrepresented among college athletes despite their enrollment advantage in higher education (Allan, 2011; Anderson, Cheslock, & Ehrenberg, 2006). Furthermore, the number of women head coaches is quite low and has decreased substantially since the passage of Title IX; women held 43% of head coaching positions for women's teams in 2010 and 90% in 1972 (Carpenter & Acosta, 2010).

Sororities—Greek-letter organizations for college women—have existed on many college campuses since the time when women were first admitted to degree-granting institutions. Their purpose is to foster "a sense of belonging, character development, and cultural awareness through ritual, traditions, and the shared experiences of members" (Wells & Worley, 2011, p. 298). They are characterized by values and ideals of womanhood reflected in the organizations' philanthropic work, rituals, and sisterhood. Sororities have historically offered college women independence from their families and "an instrument of female agency within historically conservative, competitive, male-regulated or -centered educational institutions" (Wells & Worley, 2011, p. 301). Although sororities have historically been exclusive, serving White, economically privileged women, the scope of sororities has expanded. A number of national and local sororities have been established to support women from a variety of racial backgrounds, in addition to bisexual, and transgendered women (Wells & Worley, 2011). A number of themes related to body image, alcohol abuse, gender role expectations, and hazing emerge within the discussion of sororities, and further research is needed on the impact of sororities on women.

Constructed Environments

The constructed campus environment refers to the meaning that people make of their environments while on campus (Strange & Banning, 2001). Rituals, ceremonies, and informal norms are key components of constructed campus environments. Environmental press, the notion that behaviors and experiences are influenced by the environment in which one exists, is another important component of constructed campus environments (Strange & Banning, 2001). College women receive messages about what it means to be a woman from many segments of society, including the media, parents, religion, and peers. College women may internalize these messages to varying degrees. Often the messages include an expectation of maintaining a particular body type and size, engaging in "ladylike" behaviors to attract men's attention, and preparing to be a wife and mother (Brown, 2005). When women fall outside of these bounds because they identify as non-heterosexual or are simply uninterested in fulfilling traditionally feminine roles, they are ostracized by their peers and excluded from many aspects of campus life. Similarly, women often receive messages that label other women as their competitors for jobs and men, making relationships between and among women complex (Brown, 2005). Attempts to meet these expectations often manifest themselves in significant mental and physical health issues, including alcohol abuse, disordered eating, and anxiety-related concerns (Brown, 2005).

The pressure that college women face in relation to feminine expectations has been referred to as "effortless perfection," or the notion that college women must work to have it all, yet not let anyone know how hard they are working to achieve perfection (Duke University, 2003). Although this term was coined at Duke University in 2003, women on campuses across the country discuss the salience of this idea in their experiences. No research has explicitly explored the concept of effortless perfection on various campuses, but following the popular media and observing women students' activity on social media sites indicates that effortless perfection is likely a phenomenon on many campuses. Women feel a unique obligation to "have it all" as a result of the messages they receive about being strong and independent as well as being feminine, which is tied to being "a good wife and mother" (Spar, 2013). It is important to acknowledge that the notion of effortless perfection seems to stem from the experiences of middle-class, heterosexual, White women (Duke University, 2003) and is perpetuated through media and social relationships on campuses. In previous research, women of color described a similar burden as the result of both racism and sexism. Women of color report an additional responsibility to "hold it together" so as not to reflect poorly on their peers or the women of color who came before them and who will come after them (Winkle-Wagner, 2009).

Campus climate—that is, how people experience their level of belongingness on a campus—also falls under the category of constructed campus environments (Renn & Reason, 2013). Hall and Sandler's (1982) oft-cited study initially documented a "chilly climate" in classrooms for women undergraduate and graduate students (cf. Sandler & Hall, 1986). More recent scholarship has documented microaggressions (subtle insults directed at marginalized groups) toward women in classrooms and on the broader campus (Vaccaro, 2010b). An analysis of the comments in a campus climate survey further demonstrates the hostile gendered environment, revealing significant aggression toward diversity and inclusion efforts and highlighting the negative campus climate that exists for women and people with additional marginalized identities (e.g., people of color, LGBT people, and non-Christians) (Vaccaro, 2010b). Vaccaro (2010a) describes eight themes of gendered microaggression: sexual objectification, second-class citizenship, assumptions of inferiority, assumptions of traditional gender roles, use of sexist language, denial of sexism, men's denial of participating in sexism, and environmental microaggressions.

Women students may also experience a more overt culture of harassment and violence from their peers in classrooms and social situations (Hill & Silva, 2005). Sexual harassment includes unwanted sexual attention from peers, faculty, and staff, and it generally falls into two categories: quid pro quo and hostile environments (Hill & Silva, 2005). Quid pro quo sexual harassment refers to an exchange of sexual favors for something of value to the person with less power in the situation (e.g., grades, jobs, raises). Hostile environments are more difficult to describe and include behaviors that contribute to a "severe, persistent, or pervasive" negative environment that limits a person's ability to engage in educational opportunities (Hill & Silva, 2005, p. 7). The relationship between campus environment and the high incidence of sexual violence on campus cannot be overstated. An environment that perpetuates male privilege and entitlement, including both subtle and overt hostility toward women, contributes to conditions that encourage sexual violence (Buchwald, Fletcher, & Roth, 1993; Katz, 2006).

Some scholars argue that a "rape culture"—a set of behaviors that support and condone sexual assault—exists on college campuses today (Buchwald et al., 1993; Sweeney, 2011; Valenti, 2007). Rape-encouraging behaviors include sexual objectification and victim blaming. Sexual objectification is seen in campus rituals and norms portraying women as objects. These behaviors are often subtle and so ingrained in campus culture that they are not recognized as problematic. They include songs and chants used at campus events, memes and images highlighting women as sexual objects, and advertisements in student newspapers using women's bodies to sell items targeting men (alcohol, cars). Victim blaming occurs when women are made to feel responsible if they experience an instance of sexual violence or harassment (Buchwald et al., 1993; Valenti, 2007). By placing responsibility on women to prevent themselves from being assaulted and shaming them for what they were wearing, drinking, or doing prior to an assault, victim blaming takes away the responsibility for preventing sexual violence from the culture at large or from individual perpetrators. Self-defense programs, "rape whistles," and other violence-prevention strategies directed at women perpetuate victim-responsibility for preventing crime.

Conclusion

The sometimes bleak picture of gendered campus environments may portray women students as disempowered victims; however, women students also engage in activism and leadership to improve campus environments for themselves and the women students who will come after them. Women's activism and leadership has influenced policy and campus climate for decades on college campuses. Women were active participants in the Civil Rights Movement of the 1960s and influenced the passage of Title IX in 1972 (Allan, 2011). More recently, they have been challenging college and university responses to sexual assault (Sander, 2013).

Student affairs educators have a responsibility to be aware of the issues affecting college women and to advocate for and support women students. Recent gender-related scholarship in higher education has focused on the underrepresentation and engagement of men in college. Although these questions are important, they must not be emphasized at the expense of addressing negative campus climates for undergraduate women and transgender students. Strategies for supporting undergraduate women students include validating and supporting them as they notice and name sexism in their lives, developing women-centered spaces for students to address sexism, offering women-focused leadership and career development programs, challenging campus norms and policies that promote sexist behaviors, and creating alternative spaces for women students to explore and understand their multiple and intersecting identities.

This chapter has provided a brief overview of the challenges affecting college women. Readers are encouraged to continue to explore their role in supporting all students, including women students. Although not every professional can address every issue, understanding the complexities of identity-related concerns provides an opportunity for student affairs educators to challenge campus practices and policies that perpetuate inequitable power structures.

References

Abes, E.S., Jones, S.R., & McEwen, M.K. (2007). Reconceptualizing the model of multiple dimensions of identity: The role of meaning-making capacity in the construction of multiple identities. *Journal of College Student Development, 48*(1), 1–22.

Allan, E.J. (2011). Women's status in higher education: Equity matters. *ASHE Higher Education Report, 37*(1), 1–163.

Anderson, D.J., Cheslock, J.J., & Ehrenberg, R.G. (2006). Gender equity in intercollegiate athletics: Determinants of Title IX compliance. *Journal of Higher Education, 77*(2), 225–250.

Association of American Colleges & Universities (AAC&U). (2012). *The American college president 2012*. Retrieved from http://www.aacu.org/

Association of Governing Boards of Universities and Colleges (AGB). (2010). *Policies, practices, and composition of governing boards of public colleges and universities.* Washington, DC: Author.

Bank, B.J. (2011a). Coeducational colleges and universities. In B.J. Bank (Ed.), *Gender & higher education* (pp. 101–108). Baltimore, MD: Johns Hopkins University Press.

Bank, B.J. (2011b). *Gender & higher education.* Baltimore, MD: Johns Hopkins University Press.

Belenkey, M.F., Clinchy, B.M., Goldberger, N.R., & Tarule, J.M. (1997). *Women's ways of knowing: The development of self, voice, and mind.* New York, NY: Basic Books.

Brown, L.M. (2005). *From girlfighting to sisterhood.* New York, NY: New York University Press.

Buchwald, E., Fletcher, P., & Roth, M. (1993). *Transforming a rape culture.* Minneapolis, MN: Milkweed.

Carpenter, L.J., & Acosta, R.V. (2010). *Women in intercollegiate sport: A longitudinal national study thirty-three year update.* West Brookfield, MA: Carpenter/Acosta.

Duke University. (2003). *Women's Initiative report.* Retrieved from http://universitywomen.stanford.edu/reports/WomensInitiativeReport.pdf

Gasman, M. (2011). Historically Black colleges and universities. In B.J. Bank (Ed.), *Gender & higher education* (pp. 125–132). Baltimore, MD: Johns Hopkins University Press.

Gilligan, C. (1982). *In a different voice: Psychological theory and women's development.* Boston, MA: Harvard University Press.

Griffin, K.A., & Hurtado, S. (2011). Institutional variety in American higher education. In J.H. Schuh, S.R. Jones, & S.R. Harper (Eds.), *Student services: A handbook for the profession* (5th ed., pp. 24–42). San Francisco, CA: Jossey-Bass.

Gross, A.M., Winslett, A., Roberts, M., & Gohm, C.L. (2006). An examination of sexual violence against college women. *Violence Against Women, 12*(3), 288–300.

Hall, R.M., & Sandler, B.R. (1982). *The campus climate: A chilly one for women* (Report of the Project on the Status and Education of Women). Washington, DC: Association of American Colleges.

Hill, C., & Silva, E. (2005). *Drawing the line: Sexual harassment on campus.* Washington, DC: AAUW Educational Foundation.

hooks, b. (1984). Feminism: A movement to end sexist oppression. In b. hooks, *Feminist theory from margin to center* (pp. 17–31). Cambridge, MA: South End Press.

Jones S.R., & Abes, E.S. (2013). *Identity development of college students: Advancing frameworks for multiple dimensions of identity.* San Francisco, CA: Jossey-Bass.

Jones, S.R., & McEwen, M.K. (2000). A conceptual model of multiple dimensions of identity. *Journal of College Student Development, 41*(1), 405–414.

Katz, J. (2006). *The macho paradox: Why some men hurt women and how all men can help.* Naperville, IL: Source Books.

Kenney, D.R., Dumont, R., & Kenney, G. (2005). *Mission and place: Strengthening learning and community through campus design.* Westport, CT: Praeger.

Kim, Y.M. (2011). *Minorities in higher education: Twenty-fourth status report 2011 supplement.* Washington, DC: American Council on Education. Retrieved from http://diversity.ucsc.edu/resources/images/ace_report.pdf

King, A.R. (2011). Environmental influences on the development of female college students who identify as multiracial/biracial-bisexual/pansexual. *Journal of College Student Development, 52*(4), 440–455.

Kinzie, J., Thomas, A.D., Palmer, M.M., Umbach, P.D., & Kuh, G.D. (2007). Women students at coeducational and women's colleges: How do their experiences compare? *Journal of College Student Development, 48*(2), 145–165.

Lapovsky, L., & Slaner Larkin, D. (2009). *The White House Project report: Benchmarking women's leadership.* Retrieved from http://www.thewhitehouseproject.org/

Linder, C. (2012, March). *A conceptual model of anti-racist White feminist identity development.* Paper presented at the American College Personnel Association annual meeting, Louisville, KY.

Linder, C., & Rodriguez, K. (2012). Learning from the experiences of self-identified women of color activists. *Journal of College Student Development, 53*(3), 383–398.

National Center for Education Statistics (NCES). (2011). *Digest of education statistics.* Retrieved from http://nces.ed.gov/programs/digest/2011menu_tables.asp

National Center for Science and Engineering Statistics (NCSES). (2013). *Women, minorities, and persons with disabilities in science and engineering.* Arlington, VA: National Science Foundation. Retrieved from: http://www.nsf.gov/statistics/women/

National Coalition for Women and Girls in Education (NCWGE). (2012). *Title IX at 40: Working to ensure gender equity in education.* Retrieved from http://www.ncwge.org/PDF/TitleIXat40.pdf

National Women's Law Center (NWLC). (2013). *Title IX.* Retrieved from http://www.titleix.info

Paludi, M. (2011). Sexual harassment policies and practices. In B.J. Bank (Ed.), *Gender & higher education* (pp. 374–381). Baltimore, MD: Johns Hopkins University Press.

Pascarella, E.T. (2006). How college affects students: Ten directions for future research. *Journal of College Student Development, 47*(5), 508–520.

Patton, L.D. (2012). *Debunking the "new model minority" myth and designing a critical research agenda on Black undergraduate women.* Symposium presented at the Association for the Study of Higher Education annual meeting, Las Vegas, NV.

Princeton University. (2011). *Report of the Steering Committee on Undergraduate Student Leadership.* Retrieved from http://www.princeton.edu/reports/2011/leadership/

Renn, K.A., & Reason, R.D. (2013). *College students in the United States: Characteristics, experiences, and outcomes.* San Francisco, CA: Jossey-Bass.

Sander, L. (2013, August 12). Quiet no longer, rape survivors put pressure on colleges. *Chronicle of Higher Education.* Retrieved from http://chronicle.com/article/Quiet-No-Longer-Rape/141049/?cid=at&utm_source=at&utm_medium=en

Sandler, B.R., & Hall, R.M. (1986). *The campus climate revisited: Chilly for women faculty, administrators, and graduate students.* Washington, DC: Association of American Colleges.

Sax, L.J. (2008). *The gender gap in college: Maximizing the developmental potential of women and men.* San Francisco, CA: Jossey-Bass.

Spar, D.L. (2013). *Wonder women: Sex, power, and the quest for perfection.* New York, NY: Farrar, Straus and Giroux.

Strange, C.C., & Banning, J.H. (2001). *Educating by design: Creating campus learning environments that work.* San Francisco, CA: Jossey-Bass.

Sweeney, B.N. (2011). The allure of the freshman girl: Peers, partying, and the sexual assault of first-year college women. *Journal of College & Character, 12*(4), 1–15.

Thelin, J.R., & Gasman, M. (2011). Historical overview of American higher education. In J.H. Schuh, S.R. Jones, & S.R. Harper (Eds.), *Student services: A handbook for the profession* (5th ed., pp. 3–23). San Francisco, CA: Jossey-Bass.

Townsend, B.K. (2011). Community colleges. In B.J. Bank (Ed.), *Gender & higher education* (pp. 109–116). Baltimore, MD: Johns Hopkins University Press.

Turner, B.K., & Torres, A. (2006). Campus safety: Experiences and perceptions of women students. *Journal of College Student Development, 47*(1), 20–36.

U.S. Department of Education. (2011). *Dear colleague letter.* Office for Civil Rights. Retrieved from http://www2.ed.gov/about/offices/list/ocr/letters/colleague-201104.html

Vaccaro, A. (2010a). Still chilly in 2010: Campus climates for women. *On Campus With Women, 39*(2), 9.

Vaccaro, A. (2010b). What lies beneath seemingly positive campus climate results: Institutional sexism, racism, and male hostility toward equity initiatives and liberal bias. *Equity & Excellence in Education, 43*(2), 202–215.

Valenti, J. (2007). *Full frontal feminism.* Berkeley, CA: Seal Press.

Wells, A.E., & Worley, D. (2011). Sororities. In B.J. Bank (Ed.), *Gender & higher education* (pp. 298–304). Baltimore, MD: Johns Hopkins University Press.

Winkle-Wagner, R. (2009). *The unchosen me: Race, gender, and identity among Black women in college.* Baltimore, MD: Johns Hopkins University Press.

Wolf-Wendel, L., & Eason, B. (2011). Women's colleges and universities. In B.J. Bank (Ed.), *Gender & higher education* (pp. 156–163). Baltimore, MD: Johns Hopkins University Press.

- Female college students face a lot of potential issues with sexism, gender roles & sexual assult.
- As SA pros it is our job to support these women and provide them with proper resources when needed.

NINE

Today's College Men: Challenges, Issues, and Successes

Daniel Tillapaugh

Recent years have seen an abundance of media headlines that proclaim (and reinforce, correctly or not) a crisis of masculinity for males in the United States. With titles such as "The End of Men" (Rosin, 2010), "Men's Lib" (Romano & Dokopil, 2010), and "Is There a Crisis in Education of Males?" (Jaschik, 2008), powerful messages are being sent to readers that males are suffering and not succeeding in society. To be sure, society is changing, and, as a result, the socialization of males is shifting along with it. But is there really a crisis of masculinity, particularly in higher education? The answer is: it depends, and context matters. Certainly, we understand that the aforementioned news articles call attention to men and masculinity, but these headlines reinforce messages that are deeply entrenched in hegemonic masculinity, or those cultural practices, behaviors, and ideologies that maintain dominant power for men, particularly heterosexual men (Donaldson, 1993). Seminal works by gender studies scholars such as Michael Kimmel and Michael Messner, and higher education scholars such as Frank Harris, Shaun Harper, Tracy Davis, and Jason Laker, certainly point to challenges and issues that college males must face. But the real picture is not all doom and gloom, either.

This chapter argues that college men, like many of the other student populations discussed in this book, face particular issues and challenges, but they also have many successes within the college and university environment. The aim of the chapter is to share these issues, challenges, and successes within a framework that explores the intersectionality of gender and other social identities, aligning with Tarrant and Katz (2008), who remind us that "masculinity comes in many forms and packages and these multiple masculinities are informed, limited, and modified by race, ethnicity, class background, sexual orientation, and personal predilections" (p. 10). While much of the historical work on college men has focused on White, heterosexual males, the stories of a variety of men—including men of color, gay, bisexual, fluid, queer, and transgender—are integrated into the chapter. Understanding the breadth of what it means to be a college man in today's society (an overwhelming and difficult task) is a key consideration in illuminating the developmental experiences of this student population.

Framing the Terminology of Male and Man

While this chapter explores the issues, challenges, and successes of college men, it is important to comment at the outset on the specific terms employed herein. Throughout this chapter, specific use of the terms *male/males* and *man/men* is maintained. For the purposes of this work, male is meant as a descriptor of one's biological sex; man describes one's gender identity; and masculine and/or feminine is connected to one's gender role (Lev, 2004). Kimmel and Messner (2010) further situate this distinction in the framework of social construction: "the important fact of men's lives is not that they are biological males, but that they become men. Our sex may be male, but our identity as men is developed through a complex process of interaction with the culture..." (p. xvii). Additionally, Connell (2005) explains that gender "is social practice that constantly refers to bodies and what bodies do, it is not social practice reduced to the body" (p. 71). Evans, Forney, Guido, Patton, and Renn (2009) agree and further clarify that "*sex* and *gender* are thus very closely related, but they are not synonymous, and an individual's gender cannot be assumed in all cases to match what is expected based on his or her sex" (p. 329). Much of the literature on college *men* has largely been work on college *males*, meaning that scholars (see Kimmel, 2008; Rhoads, 2010) have often used *male* and *man* interchangeably or used the term *men* as an aggregate term without fully addressing the complexity of gender identity and expression that is represented by that term. For example, the use of *men* would suggest that transgender men or gay, bisexual, or queer men would be included in the discussion of that work; however, scholars often inadequately explore the experiences of these men and instead focus on the experiences of cisgender, heterosexual males (Harris, 2008; Tillapaugh & Nicolazzo, 2013).

Historical Implications for College Men

Colleges and universities in the United States have historically been environments designed to serve males in their ongoing education and career vocation. In their research, Harper and Harris (2010a) cite the work of Frederick Rudolph, who documented that it took 205 years (from the establishment of what is now Harvard University in 1636, to 1841, when Oberlin College graduated its first female student) for women to gain a foothold in higher education. Colleges and universities were developed to benefit males and male privilege through ideology, pedagogy, norms, and expectations (Harper & Harris, 2010a). While women were able to access higher education in the nineteenth and early twentieth centuries through women's colleges, these access issues highlight a significant disparity that reinforced a privileging of males through hegemonic ideals and gender norms (Harper & Harris, 2010a). Understanding the history of men in relation to institutions of higher education is critical to contextualizing the issues college men face today.

Who Are Today's College Men?

According to the 2010 U.S. Census, there were 151,781,326 males in the United States, or 49.2% of the total population (Howden & Meyer, 2011). Of this total, males from the ages of

15 to 24 number 12,405,142, or a little over 8% of the male population of the United States (Howden & Meyer, 2011). This is important to consider, given the emphasis on individuals within this age range who attend colleges and universities in the United States. In fact, the U.S. Department of Education's National Center for Education Statistics (2012b) indicated that "Between 2000 and 2010, the number of 18- to 24-year-olds increased from 27.3 million to 30.7 million, an increase of 12 percent" (para. 4). In addition, the percentage of males attending college immediately after high school increased from 53% in 1975 to 63% in 2010 (National Center for Education Statistics, 2012a). Furthermore, 29% of these males attend 2-year colleges (i.e., community colleges), while 34% go directly to 4-year institutions (National Center for Education Statistics, 2012a). The National Center for Education Statistics (2012c) reports that in 2010, 7,825,200 males of all ages were enrolled in undergraduate colleges and universities in the United States.

Gender Gap in College

While progress has been made over the past century in terms of women attending (as well as working in) institutions of higher education, it is important to recognize that concerns linger about the lack of gender equality on college and university campuses (Harper & Harris, 2010a). In his work, Kimmel (2006) illuminates a growing concern among educators that fewer men are attending college, with women outperforming men in terms of attendance and completion of degrees. Many college and university administrators have concerns about the declining enrollment of men within institutions and the push to provide services and outreach to that population (Kimmel, 2008). However, Kimmel also clarifies this issue, citing Cynthia Fuchs Epstein's concept of "deceptive distinction," in which differences may appear to be based on gender but, in fact, are about socioeconomic status and race or ethnicity. Indeed, Kimmel (2006) highlights the fact that racial disparity exists among college students. "Among middle-class, white, high school graduates going to college this year, half are male and half are female. But only 37 percent of black college students and 45 percent of Hispanic students are male" (Kimmel, 2006, p. 67). In adding dimensions of social class to this discussion, Reed (2011) argues that popular reports about the declining enrollment of men in colleges and universities are misleading. Instead, he finds that "SES [socio-economic status] in combination with gender appears to have the most significant influence on male student postsecondary success" (Reed, 2011, p. 116). This deeper look at the data highlights a growing concern when it comes to issues of the intersection of race, class, and gender. These intersections also provide important implications for one's identity development in college.

Identity Development of College Men

Historically, the foundational research relating to human development, particularly college student development theories, has used males as the sample population (see Chickering & Reisser, 1993; Erikson, 1980; Kohlberg, 1976; Perry, 1970). As college and university student bodies became more diversified during the mid to late 20th century, developmental theorists began to explore dimensions of identities that were underrepresented, including—but not limited to—the experiences of people of color, women, and LGBT individuals (Evans et al., 2009). Since early studies used males as their sample population, there was a widely held assumption that these works explained the experiences of males (Davis & Laker, 2004; Harper

& Harris, 2010a, 2010b). However, this assumption was troubling, as these theories were never viewed through the lens of gender (Davis & Laker, 2004). In the past decade, scholars have been particularly interested in understanding the complex question of how young men develop within the context of higher education institutions. This section includes an overview of hegemonic masculinity, a key concept that informs much of the scholarship on college men, as well as contemporary research on the identity development of college men.

Hegemonic Masculinity

The notion of hegemonic masculinity plays a central role in the socialization of young men in college. Kimmel and Davis (2011) define hegemony as "the process of influence where we learn to earnestly embrace a system of beliefs and practices that essentially harm us, while working to uphold the interests of others who have power over us" (p. 9). Through a lens of gender, specifically masculinity, hegemonic masculinity can be viewed as the reification of traditional masculine norms that damage and hurt those who uphold those notions (Kimmel & Davis, 2011). Young men, particularly those within the college environment, are influenced and affected by hegemonic masculinity every day. Through media, peers, families, and educational institutions themselves, college men (and their peers) engage in a system that perpetuates the enforcement of gender norms and expectations (Kimmel, 2008; Kimmel & Davis, 2011).

Much of the literature on college men describes negative interpersonal behaviors, with an emphasis on alcohol abuse (Capraro, 2010; Harper, Harris, & Mmeje, 2010; Harris, 2008; Harris & Struve, 2009), disciplinary actions (Harper et al., 2010), hazing behaviors (Allan & Madden, 2008; Kimmel, 2008), perpetrating sexual assaults (Harris, 2008; Stulhofer, Busko, & Landripet, 2010), online addictions, including online gambling (Kimmel, 2008), and pornography (Stulhofer et al., 2010). Often, these negative behaviors and/or experiences connect to O'Neil's (1981) concept of gender role conflict, or "a psychological state in which gender roles have negative consequences or impact on the person or others" (p. 203). Gender role conflict is a byproduct of men's fear of femininity (O'Neil, 1981), which emerges in four distinct patterns: (1) success, power, and competition; (2) restrictive emotionality; (3) restrictive associative behavior between men; and (4) conflict between work and family relations (O'Neil, Helm, Gable, David, & Wrightsman, 2010). Kimmel (2008) expands on O'Neil's work, positing that college men navigate gendered rules and expectations—in what is known as "The Guy Code"—but do so in contentious ways. Kimmel highlights the tensions these men feel in struggling "to live up to a definition of masculinity they feel they had no part in creating, and yet from which they feel powerless to escape" (p. 43). As a result, the failure these men experience in terms of measuring up to notions of hegemonic masculinity creates a culture of risk taking, restrictive posturing behaviors, and feelings of being inauthentic or fraudulent (Kimmel, 2008; O'Neil et al., 2010). Kimmel's notion of "The Guy Code" is interconnected with Butler's (1993) notion of gender performance, or the repeated (and often unexamined) self-expression of one's gender. These experiences of gender performativity play a central role in the growth and development of young men attending colleges and universities. The lessons learned from gender studies scholars such as Kimmel and O'Neil have also informed the thinking of higher education scholars who have investigated the development of college men. The next section provides an overview of these scholars' investigations of young men's experiences while attending colleges and universities in the United States.

Davis's Exploration of Gender Role Conflict on College Males

In 2002, Tracy Davis provided significant insights into the experiences of college males by building upon O'Neil's work on gender role conflict. By situating the phenomenon of gender role conflict within the confines of higher education, Davis explored the critical question of "how college men are coping with culturally defined notions of what it means to be a man" (Davis, 2002, p. 510). For his phenomenological study, Davis used 10 participants ages 18 to 21 who were all White, heterosexual, cisgender males serving in an active leadership role on campus (Davis, 2002). Five central themes emerged from Davis's study: "the importance of self-expression, code of communication caveats, fear of femininity, confusion about and distancing from masculinity, and a sense of challenge without support" (p. 514).

Elaborating on these central themes, Davis highlights how his participants discussed a growing appreciation for self-expression, something that these college males had only begun to practice in college (Davis, 2002). However, this form of self-expression had certain limitations that were often connected to others' perceptions of them and their own safety (Davis, 2002). Communication styles of these young males upheld certain gendered notions as well. The participants outlined the need for greater masculine performance such as the use of humor or put-downs in face-to-face conversations, while patterns of greater emotional vulnerability, particularly with other men, emerged in side-to-side conversations (Davis, 2002). Participants often struggled with a fear of being perceived as feminine, which is interconnected with homophobia; as a result, the males often restricted their behaviors in terms of communication patterns, apparel worn, or even the use of cologne (Davis, 2002). Finally, the males expressed a feeling of being left out on campus in terms of programs, services, and opportunities offered specifically to women. Many men perceived that faculty and administrators worked more proactively to support female students. Male students were challenged but given very little support in and out of the classroom (Davis, 2002).

Davis's work initiated an important dialogue concerning the development of young males in college. It is critical to understand that Davis's work inspired a new generation of scholars who study the complexities of one's gender in college. At the same time, a key critique of Davis's work was the absence of understanding how race and other dimensions of identity played a role in college men's development. This gap in the literature served as an impetus for emerging scholars such as Frank Harris and Keith Edwards to begin to explore how these dimensions of identity played a further role in young men's lives.

Harris's Model of College Men's Conceptualizations of Masculinities

Frank Harris III's (2008) study was conducted in an effort to understand how young men in college made meaning of masculinities and how the college environment influenced that process. His original study was conducted in two distinct phases with a total of 68 participants attending a large, private university on the West Coast (Harris, 2008; Harris & Edwards, 2010). These participants represented an array of racial, social class, and sexual orientation identities as well as different experiences related to student engagement on campus (Harris, 2008).

From Harris's grounded theory study, three main variables emerged as key factors in his (2010) model. The first variable dealt with how college men made meaning of masculinity and how their attitudes and behaviors met those ideas about masculinity (Harris, 2010). For the men in this study, masculinity was often equated with issues of being respected by others, having self-confidence, taking on responsibility, and maintaining physical prowess, including one's fitness and sexual behavior (Harris, 2010). The second variable was contextual influences within the campus environment that continued to reinforce and challenge one's meanings of masculinity. These included the influence of one's family, interactions with one's on-campus peers, and participation in masculine-affirming organizations and/or activities (Harris, 2010). Finally, gender norms and expectations that are a result of both meanings of masculinity within the context of the collegiate environment was the final variable (Harris, 2010). Activities identified by the men as those in which they participated with other men included "binge drinking, playing video games, watching and discussing sports, and sharing the details of sexual relationships" (Harris & Edwards, 2010, p. 48). This mirrors Kimmel's (2008) findings on the behaviors exhibited by college men, as well as much of the literature on the impact of fraternity life (Anderson, 2008; Rhoads, 2010) and athletics (Anderson, 2002, 2008) on college men. Harris's findings also connect with those of Keith Edwards, who similarly investigated the identity development of men in college.

Edwards's Model of College Male Identity Development

Keith Edwards's study involved 10 men, including one trans- man, all attending a large, public, 4-year university in the Middle Atlantic and represented a wide array of backgrounds and interests, including social identities—race, class, and sexual orientation—and campus involvement, such as involvement in athletics, fraternity life, residential life employees, and campus organization officers (Edwards & Jones, 2009; Harris & Edwards, 2010). Participants in this study were interviewed three times "to explore what it meant for them to be a man, how their understandings of what being a man meant changed over time, and the influences that prompted these changes" (Harris & Edwards, 2010, p. 46).

The metaphor of a mask being worn is the central organizing theme within Edwards's study (Edwards & Jones, 2009). The men described being socialized from an early age about the gender norms and expectations that were expected of them, and, consequently, they indicated a great deal of pressure to conform to those expectations by both individuals in their lives as well as institutions (Edwards & Jones, 2009; Harris & Edwards, 2010). As a result, the men indicated that they felt as though they wore different masks based upon the contexts in which they operated (Edwards & Jones, 2009). This concept of the mask was used to describe the tensions they felt when they experienced male gender role conflict in relation to the expectations of others around them (Edwards & Jones, 2009). This mask metaphor can be seen as a key ideology surrounding the performativity of gender, where men are actively attempting to perform masculinity to varying levels of success.

The subjects in Edwards's study characterized their expectations as men in college to be that of the underperforming and unprepared man, with specific behaviors including competitive heterosexual sex, alcohol and drug use and potential abuse, being unprepared for academic classes and exams, and not following policies and procedures outlined by the campus administration (Edwards & Jones, 2009; Harris & Edwards, 2010). Certainly, Edwards's findings correlate with Kimmel's (2008) discussions of college men and the aforementioned "Guy Code." Three overarching categories emerged from the study as consequences of the performance of masculinity: "misogynistic relationships and attitudes toward women, limited relationships with other men, and a loss of self" (Harris & Edwards, 2010, p. 47). Both Harris's and Edwards's studies helped advance our understanding of how young men in college develop. In addition, their work has encouraged other scholars to continue investigating the complexities of college men, particularly through an intersectional lens of gender and other social group memberships that include race, socioeconomic status, and sexual orientation.

Intersectional Approaches to Male Identity Development

While the scholarship of Frank Harris and Keith Edwards continues to provide vital information on the experiences of college men, other scholars continue to investigate issues pertaining to the intersection of gender and other social identities. This research is meant to fill a gap identified by Harris (2008), who acknowledges that "oftentimes the experiences of men of color and nonheterosexual men are not disaggregated from the larger, predominantly White, male college student population" (p. 454). Scholarship on the intersections of masculinities and social class (Reed, 2011), masculinities and race (Harper, 2005), and masculinities and sexual orientation (Tillapaugh, 2012) has continued to provide helpful insights into the development of men in college.

Shaun Harper's (2005) work with high-achieving African American males reframed the existing literature on that particular student population. Citing the fact that high-achieving African American college males are rarely discussed in the literature on college men, Harper (2005) states that typically the narratives on such a man include:

> the reasons why he is underrepresented in postsecondary education, the academic difficulty he often encounters, the racism and stereotyping that cause him grief and frustration, his incompatibility with predominantly white learning environments, the shortage of same-race faculty and staff on whom he can rely for mentoring and support, and the reasons why he is retained least often among both sexes and all racial and ethnic groups in higher education. (p. 9)

For the participants in Harper's study, involvement in student leadership positions that provide an opportunity to bring positive social change to their campuses, particularly for other students of color, became an important part of their experiences in college. Through these positions, students were able to debunk previously held assumptions of peers, faculty, and administrators about African American men (Harper, 2005). The examples of these young African American males highlight the ways in which college men act as positive role models for others on campus and provide a counter-narrative to the usual tropes attributed to African American men on campus (Harper, 2005).

Like Harper's work, Brian D. Reed's (2011) research on the intersections of socioeconomic and work identity with masculinity and college success opened up a new discussion among scholars interested in issues pertaining to college men. In Reed's (2011) review of the existing literature on socioeconomic status (SES) and masculinity, he found that males from low SES backgrounds were less likely to enroll and graduate from colleges and universities as compared to their high-SES male and low-SES female peers. "In addition, men overall are participating in fewer educationally purposeful activities associated with persistence-to-graduation and increasing their time spent on activities that actually impede their chances of success" (Reed, 2011, p. 116). Reed (2011) identified four common themes in the existing literature on the intersections of race, class, and gender on the educational journeys of low-SES males: "school as a site of lowered expectations, overtly policed behavior, curriculum tracking, and persistent disengagement" (p. 119). Young college males from low-SES backgrounds experience lower perceptions of academic success by instructors, and they are often tracked into remedial courses or programs that reinforce notions that they are unequipped to succeed academically (Reed,

2011). Additionally, parental support (or the lack thereof) also plays a central role in the academic success of these young males, particularly within postsecondary systems (Reed, 2011). Through his work, Reed provides a helpful reminder that "all men do not exact the same degree of power and privilege from patriarchy and sexism" (p. 126). This disparity between power and privilege plays out for males from low-SES backgrounds but can also connect to larger issues of racial identity or sexual orientation.

As a result of hegemonic masculinity and patriarchy, non heterosexual males often experience marginalization in terms of their masculinity (Kimmel, 2008). Tillapaugh's (2012) work investigated how gay males in college made meaning of their multiple identities, particularly the connections between their maleness and sexual orientation. The 17 males, representing a variety of races, social classes, and religions, discussed their lived experiences as gay males in college and the critical influences that either helped or hindered the meaning-making of their multiple identities. In his work, Tillapaugh outlined that these men experienced conflicting messages about masculinity. While they often rejected notions of hegemonic masculinity, they still desired to be seen as masculine by others. Those gay males who identified as "less masculine" often experienced greater issues of bullying, hostility, and alienation from other men, including their gay male peers (Tillapaugh, 2012). Participation in gay-affirming spaces such as LGBT student organizations, academic courses on gender and/or sexuality, and support networks of LGBT-identified friends provided young gay males with the opportunity to learn about their identities, make meaning of socialized messages regarding their gay male identities, and examine systems of power, privilege, and difference (Tillapaugh, 2012). For the males in the study, Tillapaugh found that the development of one's gay male identities was also deeply connected to other social and personal identities. For example, young gay males in this study who were from high-SES backgrounds often had parents who were affiliated with more conservative religious institutions and political ideologies. These young men were also more likely to have experienced mental health issues, including depression, cutting behaviors, and suicidal ideation and/or attempts, than their peers in the study because of compartmentalization of their gay identity (Tillapaugh, 2012).

Findings from studies such as these have significant implications for working with and supporting young men and their development. In addition, new research is forthcoming from other scholars, such as Chase Catalano's work on transgender men and Rachel Wagner's work on White straight men engaged in social justice work, which discusses the challenges and successes facing young men in college and promises to open new dialogues among professionals in higher education. Understanding the developmental implications for college men is essential, but the next section explores some of the environmental realities for college men today. Included in this discussion are the issues, challenges, and successes college men are experiencing today through student engagement, issues of health and well-being, and programmatic intervention.

Environmental Realities for College Men

Sociologist and gender studies scholar Michael Kimmel's book *Guyland* explores the experiences of males from the ages of 18 to 26, particularly those attending college (Kimmel, 2008). In his work, Kimmel (2008) illuminates how the college environment serves as a gendered arena for the socialization of young people. He explains that college

> becomes the arena in which young men so relentlessly seem to act out, seem to take the greatest risks, and do some of the stupidest things. Directionless and often clueless, they rely increasingly on their peers to usher them into adulthood and validate their masculinity. And their peers often have some interesting plans for what they will have to endure to prove that they are real men. (p. 43)

These plans include the abuse of alcohol and drugs, experiences of hazing, competitive sexual behavior, and upholding gender norms that are steeped in homophobia and hegemonic masculinity (Kimmel, 2008).

Health and Well-Being of College Men

There is very little question that college men are more susceptible to issues of risky behaviors, which play a role in their health and well-being (Capraro, 2010; Courtenay, 2010; Davies, Shen-Miller, & Isacco, 2010; Iwamoto, Corbin, Lejuez, & MacPherson, 2013). In fact, college men often participate in these risky behaviors, such as binge drinking (Kimmel, 2008; Wechsler & Wuethrich, 2002), competitive sexual behavior (Harris, 2008), or hazing activities (Allan & Madden, 2008), in order to prove their masculinity and acquire power and authority from their peers (Courtenay, 2010). In their research, Iwamoto and colleagues (2013) found that college men who "exhibit the norms of desiring many sexual partners at the same time (playboy), enjoying risk-taking activities regardless of potential consequences (risk taking), and focusing on the importance of winning are at heightened risk for heavy drinking" (p. 8). For the men who uphold these gender norms and performances, there is greater concern for their alcohol consumption and personal well-being (Harris, 2008; Iwamoto et al., 2013; Kimmel, 2008). At the same time, some scholars (Courtenay, 2010; Iwamoto, Cheng, Lee, Takamatsu, & Gordon, 2011) argue that some gendered norms surrounding masculinity "such as self-reliance or emotional control may protect against problematic drinking patterns because they are consistent with self-control and potentially regulate alcohol intake" (Iwamoto et al., 2011, p. 907).

Proving one's dominance and power over others, particularly other men, plays out among college men in different ways. For instance, Kimmel (2008) discusses the culture of initiation in colleges and universities where men must prove their masculinity in different contexts. Behaviors that could be considered hazing are just one example of the challenges that college men might face (Kimmel, 2008). In their nationwide study on college hazing, Allan and Madden (2008) found that 61% of male respondents had experienced a hazing incident within their organization or team. Examples of these hazing incidents include, but are not limited to, "alcohol consumption, humiliation, isolation, sleep-deprivation, and sex acts" (Allan & Madden, 2008, p. 5). For students involved in fraternities and sororities, 7 out of 10 reported experiencing acts of hazing (Allan & Madden, 2008, 2012). In terms of alcohol consumption, students reported mandatory participation in drinking games as the hazing behavior most often experienced. However, students involved in culturally based fraternities reported alcohol-related hazing experiences at a much lower rate than their peers (Allan & Madden, 2012).

Risky sexual behavior is another important phenomenon playing out among college men. In their work, LaBrie, Earleywine, Schiffman, Pedersen, and Marriot (2010) found a correlation among alcohol consumption, condom use, and one's familiarity with a sexual partner. "While 72% of casual partner sex events where no drinking occurred involved condom use, only 56% of similar events after drinking involved condom use" (LaBrie et al., 2010, p. 365).

As a result, there is a greater risk in the transmission of infection (LaBrie et al., 2010). This agrees with the findings of Tillapaugh's (2012) study of gay males in terms of their sexual experimentation with casual partners and experiences of unsafe sexual behavior fueled by alcohol and/or drug use. In addition, scholars have discussed college men's competitive sexual behavior, particularly in connection with "locker room" talk (Harris, 2008; Kimmel, 2008). Kimmel (2008) notes that for many college men, "The actual experience of sex pales in comparison to the experience of talking about sex" (p. 206). For many college males, one's report of sexual conquests and exploits serves as a means of gaining prestige, yet it is often just bluster and bravado (Kimmel, 2008).

Programming for College Men's Success & Development

There have been an increasing number of programs, initiatives, and services designed to meet the needs of college men and help them begin to explore the concept of masculinity and its influence on their lives as men. These have largely served as an opportunity for participants to be critically self-reflective in community with others around issues of gender, societal expectations of males, and how they might proactively step outside of these norms to their own benefit and that of others. For example, the Male Athletes Against Violence (MAAV) at the University of Maine is a peer education program with representatives from all men's athletic teams. They discuss issues relating to masculinity and social justice and serve as advocates for sexual assault prevention and violence against women (MAAV, n.d.).

In addition, the Masculinity Dialogues at the University of St. Thomas (Klobassa, 2009) and the Masculinity Awareness Gained through Introspection and Solidarity (MAGIS) program at Loyola University Maryland (Paquette, 2009) were two initiatives that were grounded in dialogues between college males and both professional staff and peer facilitators that worked to interrogate hegemonic masculinity and its influence on one's behaviors, perceptions, and interactions. Likewise, the Men's Group established through the University of California, San Diego's LGBT Resource Center is a peer-facilitated weekly discussion group among male-identified members of the campus's LGBT community. This group explores the intersections between sexuality and gender within the context of the UCSD community and beyond (Men's Group, n.d.). These dialogue spaces become an important place for young males to explore their larger sense of self and discuss with others the role that gender and masculinities play in their lives (Men's Group, n.d.). The four programs described here are just a few of the increasing number of initiatives, programs, and services designed specifically to help young men in their development within the college environment. As higher education professionals continue to educate themselves about the issues, challenges, and successes of college men, it is hoped that programs such as these can be adapted and implemented on campuses across the country in the name of helping young men work toward healthy masculinities.

Concluding Thoughts

Given the ever-changing dynamics of higher education, it is difficult to adequately summarize the issues, challenges, and successes of college men. It is clear that men attending colleges and universities in the United States arrive at those institutions with years of socialization about what it means to be a man, and they often feel a need to prove themselves to their peers. The college environment itself plays a major role in perpetuating those gender role expectations for them, creating "Guyland," a space where men are initiated into a culture of entitlement, silence, and protection to uphold and reproduce the concept of hegemonic masculinity (Kimmel, 2008; Kimmel & Davis, 2011). At the same time, it must be acknowledged that there are college men who proactively reject those notions of hegemonic masculinity and tap into healthy masculinities. Many men are becoming engaged as allies in developmental work such as sexual assault prevention, bystander intervention training, or taking active roles in social justice education on their campus.

While the media continue to spin the myth that there is a crisis of masculinity in our society, we need to be critical consumers of those headlines. Are college men facing issues and obstacles on their journeys through higher education? Yes, of course. Each of the student populations discussed in this book faces unique challenges because of the dynamic systems of power, privilege, and oppression of which they (and we) are a part. College men are included in this as well. Higher education professionals must continue disaggregating men as one singular monolithic identity. Instead, it must be understood that one's maleness or one's masculinity is just one part of one's larger holistic identity. By understanding the complex interconnectedness of one's holistic self, student affairs professionals are then able to gain a better understanding of the unique issues, challenges, and successes of our students, including today's college men.

References

Allan, E.J., & Madden, M. (2008). *Hazing in view: College students at risk (Initial findings from the National Study of Student Hazing).* Retrieved from http://umaine.edu/hazingresearch/files/2012/10/hazing_in_view_web.pdf

Allan, E.J., & Madden, M. (2012). The nature and extent of college student hazing. *Journal of Adolescent Medicine and Health 24*(1), 1–8. doi: 10.1515/IJAMH.2012.012

Anderson, E. (2002). Openly gay athletes: Contesting hegemonic masculinity in a homophobic environment. *Gender & Society, 16*(6), 860–877.

Anderson, E. (2008). "Being masculine is not about who you sleep with…": Heterosexual athletes contesting masculinity and the one-time rule of homosexuality. *Sex Roles, 58*(1–2), 104–115.

Butler, J. (1993). *Bodies that matter: On the discursive limits of "sex."* New York, NY: Routledge.

Capraro, R.L. (2010). Why college men drink: Alcohol, adventure, and the paradox of masculinity. In S.R. Harper & F. Harris III (Eds.), *College men and masculinities: Theory, research, and implications for practice* (pp. 239–257). San Francisco, CA: Jossey-Bass.

Chickering A. W., & Reisser, L. (1993). *Education and identity.* San Francisco, CA: Jossey-Bass.

Connell, R.W. (2005). *Masculinities* (2nd ed.). Berkeley, CA: University of California Press.

Courtenay, W. (2010). Constructions of masculinity and their influence on men's well-being: A theory of gender and health. In S.R. Harper & F. Harris III (Eds.), *College men and masculinities: Theory, research, and implications for practice* (pp. 307–336). San Francisco, CA: Jossey-Bass.

Davies, J.A., Shen-Miller, D.S., & Isacco, A. (2010). The men's center approach to addressing the health crisis of college men. *Professional Psychology: Research and Practice, 41*(4), 347–354.

Davis, T., & Laker, J. (2004). Connecting men to academic and student affairs programs and services. In G. Kellom (Ed.), *Designing effective programs and services for men in higher education* (pp. 47–57). San Francisco, CA: Jossey-Bass.

Davis, T.L. (2002). Voice of gender role conflict: The social construction of college men's identity. *Journal of College Student Development, 43*(4), 508–521.

Donaldson, M. (1993). What is hegemonic masculinity? *Theory and Society, 22*(5), 643–657.

Edwards, K.E., & Jones, S.R. (2009). "Putting my man face on": A grounded theory of college men's gender identity development. *Journal of College Student Development, 50*(2), 210–228.

Erikson, E. H. (1980). *Identity and the life cycle.* New York, NY: W. W. Norton.

Evans, N.J., Forney, D.S., Guido, F.M., Patton, L.D., & Renn, K.A. (2009). *Student development in college: Theory, research, and practice* (2nd ed.). San Francisco, CA: Jossey-Bass.

Harper, S.R. (2005). Leading the way: Inside the experiences of high-achieving African American male students. *About Campus, 10*(1), 8–15.

Harper, S.R., & Harris, F. III. (2010a). Beyond the model gender majority myth: Responding equitably to the developmental needs and challenges of college men. In S.R. Harper & F. Harris III (Eds.), *College men and masculinities: Theory, research, and implications for practice* (pp. 1–16). San Francisco, CA: Jossey-Bass.

Harper, S.R., & Harris, F. III (Eds.). (2010b). *College men and masculinities: Theory, research, and implications for practice.* San Francisco, CA: Jossey-Bass.

Harper, S.R., Harris, F. III, & Mmeje, K.C. (2010). A theoretical model to explain the overrepresentation of college men among campus judicial offenders: Implications for campus administrators. In S.R. Harper & F. Harris III (Eds.), *College men and masculinities: Theory, research, and implications for practice* (pp. 221–238). San Francisco, CA: Jossey-Bass.

Harris, F. III. (2008). Deconstructing masculinity: A qualitative study of college men's masculine conceptualizations and gender performance. *NASPA Journal, 45*(4), 453–474.

Harris, F. III. (2010). College men's conceptualizations of masculinities and contextual influences: Toward a conceptual model. Journal of College Student Development, 51(3), 297–318.

Harris, F. III, & Edwards, K.E. (2010). College men's experiences as men: Findings and implications from two grounded theory studies. *Journal of Student Affairs Research and Practice, 47*(1), 43–62.

Harris, F. III, & Struve, L.E. (2009). Gents, jerks, and jocks: What male students learn about masculinity in college. *About Campus, 14*(3), 2–9.

Howden, L.M., & Meyer, J.A. (2011). *Age and sex composition: 2010.* Retrieved from http://www.census.gov/prod/cen2010/briefs/c2010br-03.pdf

Iwamoto, D.K., Cheng, A., Lee, C.S., Takamatsu, S., & Gordon, D. (2011). "Man-ing" up and getting drunk: The role of masculine norms, alcohol intoxication, and alcohol-related problems among college men. *Addictive Behaviors, 36*(9), 906–911.

Iwamoto, D.K., Corbin, W., Lejuez, C., & MacPherson, L. (2013). College men and alcohol use: Positive alcohol expectancies as a mediator between distinct masculine norms and alcohol use. *Psychology of Men & Masculinities.* Advance online publication. doi: 10.1037/a0031594

Jaschik, S. (2008, May 21). Is there a crisis in education of males? *Inside Higher Ed.* Retrieved from http://www.insidehighered.com/news/2008/05/21/gender

Kimmel, M. (2006). A war against boys? *Dissent, 53*(4), 65–70. doi: 10.1353/dss.2006.0002

Kimmel, M. (2008). *Guyland: The perilous world where boys become men.* New York, NY: Harper.

Kimmel, M., & Davis, T. (2011). Mapping guyland in college. In J.A. Laker & T. Davis (Eds.), *Masculinities in higher education: Theoretical and practical considerations* (pp. 3–15). New York, NY: Routledge.

Kimmel, M., & Messner, M. (Eds.). (2010). *Men's lives* (8th ed.). Boston, MA: Allyn & Bacon.

Klobassa, V. (2009). *Masculinity dialogues: A theory to practice program.* ACPA Standing Committee on Men & Masculinities Briefs. Washington, DC: ACPA–College Student Educators International.

Kohlberg, L. (1976). Moral stages and moralization: The cognitive-developmental approach. In T. Lickona (Ed.), *Moral development and behavior: Theory, research, and social issues* (pp. 31–53). New York, NY: Holt, Rinehart & Winston.

LaBrie, J., Earleywine, M., Schiffman, J., Pedersen, E., & Marriot, C. (2010). Effects of alcohol, expectancies, and partner type on condom use in college males: Event-level analyses. In S.R. Harper & F. Harris III (Eds.), *College men and masculinities: Theory, research, and implications for practice* (pp. 355–369). San Francisco, CA: Jossey-Bass.

Lev, A.I. (2004). *Transgender emergence: Therapeutic guidelines for working with gender-variant people and their families.* New York, NY: Routledge.

MAAV. (n.d.). *Male athletes against violence.* Retrieved from http://umaine.edu/maav/

Men's Group. (n.d.). *UC San Diego LGBT Resource Center's Men's Group.* Retrieved from http://lgbt.ucsd.edu/community/organizations.html

O'Neil, J.M. (1981). Patterns of gender role conflict and strain: Sexism and fear of femininity in men's lives. *Personnel and Guidance Journal, 60*(4), 203–210.

O'Neil, J.M., Helm, B.J., Gable, R.K., David, L., & Wrightsman, L.S. (2010). Gender-role conflict scale: College men's fear of femininity. In S.R. Harper & F. Harris III (Eds.), *College men and masculinities: Theory, research, and implications for practice* (pp. 32–48). San Francisco, CA: Jossey-Bass.

Paquette, P. (2009). *Conduct based interventions for men: The MAGIS program.* ACPA Standing Committee on Men & Masculinities Briefs. Washington, DC: ACPA–College Student Educators International.

Perry, W.G. (1970). *Forms of intellectual and ethical development in the college years: A scheme.* New York, NY: Holt, Rinehart, and Winston.

Reed, B.D. (2011). Socio-economic and work identity intersections with masculinity and college success. In J.A. Laker & T. Davis (Eds.), *Masculinities in higher education: Theoretical and practical considerations* (pp. 111–129). New York, NY: Routledge.

Rhoads, R.A. (2010). Whales tales, dog piles and beer goggles: An ethnographic case study of fraternity life. In S.R. Harper & F. Harris III (Eds.), *College men and masculinities: Theory, research, and implications for practice* (pp. 258–275). San Francisco, CA: Jossey-Bass.

Romano, A., & Dokopil, T. (2010, September 20). Men's lib. *Newsweek*. Retrieved from http://www.thedailybeast.com/newsweek/2010/09/20/why-we-need-to-reimagine-masculinity.html

Rosin, H. (2010, June 8). The end of men. *The Atlantic*. Retrieved from http://www.theatlantic.com/magazine/archive/2010/07/the-end-of-men/308135/

Stulhofer, A., Busko, V., & Landripet, I. (2010). Pornography, sexual socialization, and satisfaction among young men. In S.R. Harper & F. Harris III (Eds.), *College men and masculinities: Theory, research, and implications for practice* (pp. 191–212). San Francisco, CA: Jossey-Bass.

Tarrant, S., & Katz, J. (2008). *Men speak out: Views on gender, sex, and power.* New York, NY: Routledge.

Tillapaugh, D.W. (2012). *Toward an integrated self: Making meaning of the multiple identities of gay men in college* (Unpublished doctoral dissertation). University of San Diego, CA.

Tillapaugh, D.W., & Nicolazzo, Z. (2013). *"It's kind of apples and oranges": Gay college males' conceptions of gender transgression as poverty.* Paper presented at the 2013 Annual Meeting of the American Educational Research Association, San Francisco, CA.

U.S. Department of Education, National Center for Education Statistics. (2012a). *The condition of education 2012* (NCES 2012-034), Indicator 34. Retrieved from http://nces.ed.gov/fastfacts/display.asp?id=51

U.S. Department of Education, National Center for Education Statistics. (2012b). *Digest of education statistics: 2011.* Retrieved from http://nces.ed.gov/programs/digest/d11/ch_3.asp

U.S. Department of Education, National Center for Education Statistics. (2012c). *Table 237: Total fall enrollment in degree-granting institutions, by level of student, sex, attendance status, and race/ethnicity: Selected years, 1976 through 2010.* Retrieved from http://nces.ed.gov/programs/digest/d11/tables/dt11_237.asp

Wechsler, H., & Wuethrich, B. (2002). *Dying to drink: Confronting binge drinking on college campuses.* Emmaus, PA: Rodale Press.

- Male students can struggle with as many issues as women.
- Masculinity expectations are huge in affecting how men see themselves.
- SA pros need to support men as well as women students on campuses.

TEN

Students With Disabilities: From Success to Significance

Karen A. Myers

Allison "Allie" Galoob is an international soccer champion. She is a member of the USA Women's Deaf Soccer Team and has won three gold medals in world competitions. Recently, she visited a Saint Louis University Disability in Higher Education and Society graduate class (she is a Saint Louis University graduate student in communication). When asked about her success as a person with a disability, she replied, "My deafness is a gift. I don't have a disability, I have a superpower. I have the power to do whatever I want, including turning off my cochlear implants when I do not want to listen!" (A. Galoob, personal communication, November 6, 2013). Applying Gibson's (2006) Disability Identity Model (described later in this chapter), Allie is in Gibson's Acceptance phase. She embraces herself, integrates into the world, and is a disability advocate. Obviously, Allie's positive attitude and sense of humor have contributed significantly to her identity development and to her athletic, academic, and personal success. In her young life, she has moved gracefully from success to significance.

What is success? According to Deepak Chopra, physician of holistic health and alternative medicine, success is what makes people happy. He advises individuals to first get in touch with the greater good inside and find happiness. Once happiness is found, the universe will provide the success (Chopra, 2013). To professionals in student affairs and higher education, achieving competencies may lead to success. National associations such as ACPA and NASPA (ACPA/NASPA, 2010) have developed professional competencies, multicultural competencies, and leadership competencies and rubrics with which to measure these competencies. Becoming proficient in competencies such as "Equity, Diversity, and Inclusion" and "Student Development and Learning," for example, will allow professionals in the field of higher education to be skilled at every level in inclusion and student development.

For the author, a woman who has low vision, success comes in all sizes—from small successes such as completing a required book for a class (I cannot see small print) and matching my jacket and pants for a job interview (I am colorblind) to large successes such as earning a PhD in higher education administration and raising a daughter (I am now the mother of twins). I am one of 20 people in my family who have a rare degenerative visual disability, which results in visual acuity of 20/200 (i.e., legal blindness) and extreme light sensitivity, making it difficult to distinguish colors, details, and at times even large objects both near and at a distance.

Although this disability had no specific name or label for most of my lifetime, members of my family have recently been diagnosed with rod/cone dystrophy and have been informed by physicians and researchers that ours is one of two families in the United States with this disability. I inherited the disability from my mother, as did my only brother and sister. In my immediate family, I was considered the child with the "good eyes." At 11, I was diagnosed with nearsightedness and wore eyeglasses. I had difficulty seeing the chalkboard in class but did not ask to sit near the front of the classroom. In high school I noticed I could not see what was displayed on the overhead projector. Because I was failing Algebra, my mother encouraged me to talk to my teacher and seek tutoring. I was able to secure a driver's license and drove until age 25.

With the assistance of the Department of Rehabilitation (a state-funded organization that provides career counseling and financial assistance to people with disabilities), I attended college and earned an Associate of Arts degree in theatre, a Bachelor of Fine Arts in speech and theatre, a Master of Arts in communication, and a PhD in higher education administration. Although my low vision began to manifest when I was in sixth grade and progressed fairly rapidly, it was not until I was in my PhD program and a professional in the field of higher education (using a white cane and wearing dark lenses) that I sought assistance from the university disability services. During my undergraduate and Master's education, I did speak to my professors individually and asked some of them for more time on exams; however, until I was a 40-year-old doctoral student, I did not navigate the system appropriately, disclose my disability, provide documentation to disability services, communicate with disability service providers, or receive reasonable accommodations.

I struggled to achieve most of my successes in college because I erroneously thought I should "do it on my own." According to Gibson's model of Disability Identity Development (defined later in this chapter), I was in the second of three phases, the Realization phase. My self-advocacy skills were restricted, and my scope was limited to my professors and my classes. I was unaware of the world beyond the classroom—the world of student services, student development, and disability education. The idea of "allies" never crossed my mind. I assumed I was alone in this situation and was responsible for finding my own way. I was *wrong*!

Disability education—or, to be more inclusive, "ability" education—is a shared responsibility. By becoming ability educators and ability allies, campus community members will open their minds and hearts to the possibilities of moving from success to significance. This chapter focuses on the lived experiences of college students with disabilities and their identity development, the importance of disability humility, and the imperative shift from success to significance.

Disability Competency and Disability Humility

As an ability educator, an ability ally, and a person with a disability, my lifetime goal has been to move from success to significance. To do so, I have recognized the importance of achieving disability humility. For persons with disabilities, allies of persons with disabilities, and ability educators, achieving disability competency is instrumental in ensuring an inclusive environment. Disability competency involves "being well-versed in all the different types of disability, varieties of accommodations and legal minutiae" (McInnes, 2008, para. 8). Knowledge and understanding of the Rehabilitation Act of 1973 (USDOE, 1973), the Americans with Disabilities Act (ADA) of 1990, and the Americans with Disabilities Act Amendments Act (ADAAA) of 2008, and upholding these legal mandates by providing reasonable accommodations for students with all types of disabilities, helps us follow the *letter of the law*. For example, according to the ADA, an individual is considered to have a disability if "s/he has a physical or mental impairment that substantially limits one or more major life activities, has a record of such an impairment, or is regarded as having such an impairment" (U.S. Department of Justice, 2002, para. 6). Possessing knowledge of and modeling these legal mandates and guidelines demonstrates disability competency. McInnes (2008) takes disability competency a step further when he describes the shift from disability competency to disability humility. Such a shift is similar to moving from cultural competency, that is, knowledge of a culture, to cultural humility in which people "reflect on the biases of their own 'cultures' and…engage in highly individualized and respectful interactions with each person—a mutually enlightening exchange, a resourceful partnership that recognizes the unique experiences, traits and perspectives" (McInnes, 2008, para. 4).

People demonstrate disability humility when they "empower and support people with and without disabilities to interact with persons with disabilities with inquisitiveness and open minds" (McInnes, 2008, para. 10). By embracing disability humility, people move from the medical and functional limitations model of disability—focusing on what is wrong with a person (i.e., a deficit that needs to be fixed)—to the social construction paradigm. That model "shifts the focus away from the individual to a society that has used normative bias to stigmatize, disenfranchise and marginalize persons with disabilities" (Higbee & Mitchell, 2009, p. 34). By embracing disability humility, all disability educators—faculty, administrators, higher education professionals, and students—welcome the shared responsibility of ensuring an equitable inclusive environment for all students, with and without disabilities.

Students With Disabilities: A Snapshot

Today, students with disabilities comprise approximately 11% of the college student population (U.S. Department of Education [USDOE], 2006), more than triple the number of college students with disabilities in 1978 (Snyder & Dillow, 2010).

> In the 2003–2004 school year, students [at three universities] reported the following disabilities: orthopedic (25.4%), mental illness/depression (21.9%), health impairment (17.3%), attention deficit disorder ([ADHD], 11%), learning disability ([LD], 7.5%), hearing impairment (5.0%), visual impairment (3.8%), speech impairment (0.4%), and other (7.8%). Females were more likely than males to report mental and physical health [disabilities], while men were more likely to report ADHD. (O'Neill, Markward, & French, 2012, p. 22)

These demographics, which are reflective of college students with disabilities throughout the United States, may shift slightly with the return of military students. According to the American Council on Education (ACE, 2008), an estimated 2 million veterans of the Iraq and Afghanistan wars will return to the United States and enroll in college. Many of these student veterans will have a range of disabilities that could impact their college experience, including post-traumatic stress disorder (PTSD) and traumatic brain injuries, in addition to physical and sensory disabilities (Madaus, Miller, & Vance, 2009).

Despite the increase in number of college students with documented disabilities and the myriad of disability types characterized by college students, nearly half (47%) of students with disabilities leave college without completing a degree, compared to approximately 36% of their counterparts without disabilities (USDOE, 2006). College degree completion and employment of people with disabilities are positively correlated. Although the employment rate of people with disabilities is low—that is, 20% of people with disabilities in the United States are employed, compared to 68.5% of people without disabilities (U.S. Department of Labor, 2013)—college graduates with disabilities do experience employment rates and salaries similar to those of college graduates without disabilities (Scott & Shaw, 2003). In keeping with the national trend, I have experienced both employment and unemployment since my college graduation. For years I worked part-time as an adjunct faculty member without benefits, even while holding a PhD; and while I have been a full-time professional in the field of higher education for over 17 years, my identity development continues.

Disability Identity Development

People with disabilities develop their identities at different times and through different periods of their lives. As in most identity development, major events and environment play a major role in the development process. To facilitate a better understanding of people with lifelong disabilities (i.e., early onset), Dr. Jennifer Gibson (2006) created the Disability Identity Development Model. Gibson, a clinical psychologist, developed this three-phase model to provide insight into behaviors, perceptions, and challenges experienced by individuals with disabilities. According to Gibson, "Persons with disabilities traditionally have experienced systematic institutional victimization from all aspects of society including, but not limited to, the medical profession, the educational system and the workforce" (Gibson, 2006, p. 6). She emphasizes the importance of realizing that disability is only a part of a person, a characteristic; it is not an individual's sole identity (Gibson, 2006). Although this approach can be useful in working with students with disabilities, as with any stage model, Gibson (2006) warns against assuming that all people with disabilities fit into a particular phase. People can move in and out of the three phases/stages—Passive Awareness, Realization, Acceptance—throughout their lifetimes, and, after reaching Phase Two or Three, they might even revert back to Phase One after experiencing a major life change or event (Gibson, 2006). Table 1 illustrates each phase/stage of the model. Phase One, Passive Awareness, may typically be in the first part of a person's life; however, it can last into adulthood for certain people (Gibson, 2006). Individuals in this phase tend not to have role models. They may be frustrated and angry about their disability, and the disability tends to be a "silent member" of the family. In Phase Two, Realization, which usually occurs in adolescence or early adulthood, people begin to see themselves as relevant individuals with disabilities. They embrace disability and are willing to disclose it. Phase Three,

Acceptance, includes a social aspect in which the individual with a disability begins to socialize with other people with disabilities and sometimes becomes a disability advocate and activist.

Table 1: Disability Identity Development Model (Gibson, 2006).

Phase/Stage:	One: Passive Awareness	Two: Realization	Three: Acceptance
Occurs:	First part of life, can continue into adulthood	Occurs in adolescence/ early adulthood	Adulthood
Interaction:	No role model of disability; deny social aspects of disability	Begins to see self as having a disability; concerned with how others perceive self	Begins to see self as relevant; involves self in disability advocacy and activism
Characteristics:	Codependency, shy away from attention	Self-hate, anger, concern with appearance	Shift focus from "being different" in a negative light to embracing self

Allie Galoob, world champion soccer player and graduate student (introduced at the beginning of this chapter) is 25 years old and has been in the Acceptance stage of her disability for most of her life. As the oldest child of parents who are deaf and the sibling of a brother and sister who are deaf, she accepted her disability early on and throughout her college career has been an advocate for people who are deaf and hard of hearing. She is a proponent of the use of cochlear implants, a spokesperson for the U.S. Women's Deaf Soccer Team, and was a sports reporter for CNN with broadcast journalist Soledad O'Brien from the 2012 World Deaf Football Championship in Turkey (A. Galoob, personal communication, November 6, 2013). According to Gibson's model, I moved from the Realization phase into the Acceptance phase of my identity when I was in my 30s. Like Allie, I had many role models and much support throughout my childhood and adolescence; however, it was not until later in life that I accepted my visual disability and became an advocate.

Voices of Students With Disabilities: The Lived Experience

When I was in graduate school, I discovered little research had been conducted from the viewpoint of students with disabilities. Most studies focused on the perceptions and behaviors of faculty, administrators, and students *without* disabilities about students *with* disabilities, and their suggestions for effective interactions—even to the point of stressing specifically what individuals with disabilities can do during the communication process to make persons without disabilities more comfortable (Crain, 2003). I continually asked myself, "What are students with disabilities saying about their own lived experiences? How do they articulate their own meaning of success?" As a result, I decided to answer those questions through my own doctoral dissertation, exploring communication styles and techniques preferred by persons who are blind and have low vision in a higher education setting. Several years later, my former student and colleague Joni Bastian and I updated my original study.

The student voices in this chapter come from two recent qualitative studies with students with disabilities: my study with Dr. Bastian (Myers & Bastian, 2010) and a study by

Garrison-Wade (2012). The first focused on understanding human behavior from the point of view of the individual with a disability. In our research, which consisted of interviews with 35 students with visual disabilities who were attending colleges and universities across the United States, three themes emerged: (1) respect and human dignity for people with disabilities; (2) comfort during interactions with people with disabilities; and (3) awareness of disability issues (i.e., disability education). The case study by Garrison-Wade (2012) focused on students' perceptions of services received in college in order to develop a clearer understanding of how to better ensure positive outcomes. Interviews with 59 students with various disabilities and six disability resource coordinators from 2- and 4-year institutions revealed three major themes: "(a) capitalizing on student self-determination skills, (b) implementing formalized planning processes, and (c) improving postsecondary support" (Garrison-Wade, 2012, p. 117).

Respect, Human Dignity, and Self-Advocacy

Most of the students in the two studies appeared to be in Gibson's Realization phase of their disability identity development. This is evidenced by their comments encouraging others to follow the Golden Rule and "treat them as you want to be treated." The dignity and respect imperative was a common thread reflected throughout: "…treat me like a human being. Treat me like you would anyone else" (Myers & Bastian, 2010, p. 277). "Don't be offended if I say that I don't need help" (p. 271). Just as the importance of self-advocacy in relation to identity development and academic success is evident in the literature (Getzel & Thoma, 2008; Gibson, 2006; Higbee & Mitchell, 2009; McCarthy, 2007), students in the studies echoed the significance of respect, human dignity, and self-advocacy as indicated in the following quote:

> I've learned that you have to rely on yourself before you learn to rely on others…. I hate it when people tell me I can't do something because then it makes me want to do it even more. It increases my motivation…. There is no shame. We're our own self-advocate. We need to go out and learn to do these things ourselves and be independent. (Garrison-Wade, 2012, p. 117)

"Just be patient with me," another student pleaded. "Sometimes, I feel people get frustrated with me…. [Teachers] forget that [I am] in their classes" (Myers & Bastian, 2010, p. 271). As one respondent so succinctly put it: "Support services should not take the lead. I should be my own advocate" (p. 271). These statements, which characterize the students' recognition of their own disabilities, thus exemplifying their transitions from the realization stage to the acceptance stage of development, encourage best practices, particularly for faculty and administrators.

Effective Communication

"So much depends on our attitude. Why make an enemy? I think it's our responsibility as people [with disabilities] to give ourselves a positive image, not a negative one" (Myers & Bastian, 2010, p. 273). Using humor was a common characteristic, as evidenced by Allie Galoob in the beginning of this chapter. Students reported laughing at themselves and their "faux pas" and trying to "make light" of their disabilities. "I have no problem making fun of myself. It can make the person more comfortable…sort of a disarming tool" (Myers & Bastian, 2010, p. 272). "I would rather build bridges than put up walls" (p. 273). My book, *The Way I See It: Bumping Into Life With Low Vision*, a first-person account of humorous anecdotes in my own life, is an example of the importance of humor in my own family.

Communicating about one's disability and articulating related accommodations may depend on the student's level of confidence and his or her level of disability identity development. Specifically, when and at what point in life students acquire their disabilities may affect their ability and willingness to disclose.

> Onset of disability often determines whether or not the student is willing or ready to disclose the disability, and onset also might determine the type of accommodation requested or needed. Despite when a student acquired a disability, a student in the realization or acceptance stage of Gibson's Disability Identity Development Model (Gibson, 2011) may be comfortable requesting large print for handouts and extended time for exams, whereas a student in the passive-awareness stage of Gibson's model might not see a need or have the confidence to request accommodations. (Myers, Lindburg, & Nied, 2013)

Students with early onset of disabilities will be more familiar and comfortable with their accommodations and knowledgeable of their requests, whereas students who acquire disabilities later in their lives may be unsure as to what they need to succeed in college and how to ask for such accommodations.

Attitudinal barriers can result in negative climates for students with disabilities (Kalivoda, 2009). Fear of stigma, judgment, and marginalizaton may lead to not disclosing a disability to peers, faculty, and college administrators (Carney et al., 2007; Gibson, 2006, 2011). These concerns were echoed by students in the studies. "I work hard to hide [my visual disability].... I try to adjust to the situation...so people do not notice" (Myers & Bastian, 2010, p. 270). Four other students shared these perceptions:

> They thought I was a freak because I wore hearing aids.... My peers were mean and called me retarded. High school was really hard. I didn't want to go and I hated it.... If people can't see your disability, they assume it's not there or that you're exaggerating.... Then there were others [teachers] who said not to bother because I wasn't going to make it. (Garrison-Wade, 2012, p. 118)

Even family members criticized students: "My step-mother and brother really teased me about the way I talk, so if I don't know you, I don't really speak up because I'm scared" (Garrison-Wade, 2012, p. 117). This student appears to be in the passive awareness phase of disability identity development because he/she seems to have no role model in the family and does not want to bring attention to his/her disability.

Language is instrumental in communication and demonstrates how a society perceives its members. Competency in appropriate disability language and its use indicates how people view their peers with disabilities. Avoiding outdated labels such as "handicapped" and replacing them with person-first language, which focuses on the person first and then the disability, creates an environment of respect and dignity (Tregoning, 2009). Being attentive to inclusive communication and using person-first language—for example, *a woman with a physical disability* rather than *a handicapped or disabled woman*—will indicate disability humility in action.

Ability Education

Social relationships with faculty and peers are essential to the success of college students as referenced by Astin (1984), Tinto (1987), and other scholars over the years. The same is true for college students with disabilities. Encouragement to pursue higher education and the support of friends, classmates, and volunteers play important roles in the success of college students with disabilities, as do mentoring and networking (Garrison-Wade, 2012; Myers & Bastian, 2010). Every respondent in Myers and Bastian's 2010 study recommended mandatory disability awareness training for faculty and staff. If such training were implemented, "College teachers and administrators would be able to relate to students with disabilities more effectively if they were even slightly aware of what it is like to have a...disability.... Teachers [do not] need to lower their standards ... they just need to understand why we need more time..." (Myers & Bastian, 2010, p. 273).

Students with disabilities report that advocacy skills are essential to their success and retention (Garrison-Wade, 2012; Getzel & Thoma, 2008); however, they also report that self-advocacy is learned by trial and error, and they recommend that identity-development efforts begin earlier in the college experience: "[S]tudents with disabilities benefit from faculty who have increased awareness and knowledge of the characteristics and needs of students with disabilities, and from faculty who incorporate concepts of universal design into their instruction and curriculum" (Garrison-Wade, 2012, p. 122). Attentiveness to the differences in readiness and development of students with disabilities and their disability onset is essential in advising, counseling, and accommodating students in higher education settings.

Supportive Frameworks: From Success to Significance

Shifting the paradigm from disability services-centered initiatives to campus-wide ability education and inclusion potentially may lead to positive practice. A disability-competent and disability-humble campus community will create a respectful, welcoming environment for all students, including students with disabilities. Disability awareness initiatives such as Allies for Inclusion: The Ability Exhibit, a national traveling exhibit developed by graduate students at Saint Louis University and promoting inclusion, might assist participants in achieving a basic competency level of ability education, which in turn might give them both the skills to move toward a higher level of competency and the potential empathy to embrace disability humility (Myers et al., 2013)

The ability education movement is gaining momentum through initiatives and resources such as those listed below (under Ability Education Resources and Initiatives). According to their descriptions and websites, these resources attempt to provide education and support regarding disability law, reasonable accommodations, effective communication, teaching and learning techniques, accessible technology, and universal design. Through the use of Universal Design (UD), Universal Instructional Design (UID), and Universal Design for Student Development (UDSD), individuals and institutions may provide accessible curricula, programs, and services to all people with limited need for accommodations (Duranczyk, Myers, Couillard, Schoen, & Higbee, 2013; Higbee & Goff, 2008).

Ability education is *for* everyone *by* everyone, and it is a shared responsibility of the entire campus community to be inclusive (Bryan & Myers, 2006; Myers, 2009). "To borrow the phrase, 'it takes a village...,' it really does take the entire higher education community to ensure the success of its students—*all* of its students—including those with disabilities" (Myers et al., 2013). Disability allies, that is, people who "see themselves as equal to those with and without disabilities [and who are] committed to eliminating negative attitudes, stereotypes, and oppressive behaviors" (Casey-Powell & Souma, 2009, p. 162), can help change negative and misguided attitudes toward students with disabilities. Educating members of the campus community to become disability allies via initiatives listed below (under Ability Education Resources and Initiatives)—such as Allies for Inclusion: The Ability Exhibit and its recently launched Ability Ally Project and Training (both of which the author is fortunate to direct), Everyone Matters, the National Service Inclusion Project, and Spread the Word to End the Word—will strengthen a community's disability competency and disability humility.

Ability educators—faculty, administrators, college student personnel, and students—may develop supportive frameworks to encourage students to shift from success to significance. Moving beyond success to significance is a holistic approach to education emphasizing that, in addition to academic success, it is self-advocacy, giving back, and paying it forward that lead to positive social change. Listening to students' voices is essential in this process. It is my opinion that student affairs professionals should talk to students with disabilities and listen to their stories. I recommend the first-person accounts penned by student affairs professionals—all former college students—in *Making Good on the Promise: Student Affairs Professionals With Disabilities* (Higbee & Mitchell, 2009). Listening to the voices of students with disabilities and understanding the important difference between *being* and *doing*—and then teaching and modeling that difference—ultimately will result in the imperative shift from success to significance.

Ability Education Resources and Initiatives

Allies for Inclusion: The Ability Exhibit and the Ability Ally Project and Training, http://www.slu.edu/theabilityexhibit

Association of Higher Education and Disability (AHEAD), http://www.ahead.org

California State University Northridge (CSUN) International Technology and Persons with Disabilities Conference, http://www.csun.edu/cod/conference

Cornell University's Employment and Disability Institute Web Accessibility Toolkit, http://www.webaccesstoolkit.org

Everyone Matters, http://everyonematters2012.com

National Service Inclusion Project, http://www.serviceandinclusion.org

Spread the Word to End the Word campaign, http://www.r-word.org

University of Minnesota's Pedagogy and Student Services for Institutional Transformation (PASS IT), http://www.cehd.umn.edu/passit

University of Washington Disabilities, Opportunities, Internetworking, and Technology (DO IT), http://www.washington.edu/doit

World Wide Web Consortium (WC3), http://www.w3.org

References

ACPA/NASPA. (2010). *Professional competency areas for student affairs practitioners.* Retrieved from http://www.naspa.org/images/uploads/main/Professional_Competencies.pdf

American Council on Education (ACE). (2008). Serving those who serve: Higher education and America's veterans. Retrieved from http://www.acenet.edu/news-room/Pages/Georgetown-Summit.aspx

Americans with Disabilities Act Amendments Act of 2008, Public Law 110–325, 42 U.S.C. § 12102. (2008). Retrieved from http://www.law.georgetown.edu/archiveada/documents/ADAAACR9.17.08.pdf

Americans with Disabilities Act of 1990, 42 U.S.C.A. § 12101 et seq. (1990). Retrieved from http://www.ada.gov/pubs/ada.htm

Astin, A.W. (1984). Student involvement: A developmental theory for higher education. *Journal of College Student Personnel, 25*(4), 297–308.

Bryan, A., & Myers, K. (2006). Students with disabilities: Doing what's right. *About Campus, 2*(4), 18–22.

Carney, K., Ginsberg, S., Lee, L., Li, A., Orr, A., Parks, L., & Schulte, K. (2007). Meeting the needs of students with disabilities in higher education: How well are we doing? Delta Kappa Gamma Bulletin, 73(4), 35–39.

Casey-Powell, D., & Souma, A. (2009). Allies in our midst. In J. Higbee & A. Mitchell (Eds.), *Making good on the promise: Student affairs professionals with disabilities* (pp. 149–170). Washington, DC: American College Personnel Association, University Press of America.

Chopra, D. (2013). *Wellbeing and visionary leadership* [Video]. Retrieved from https://www.deepakchopra.com/search/text/wellbeing%20and%20visionary

Crain, J.J. (2003). *College students with visual impairments: What they perceive as challenges and how they can succeed* (Unpublished doctoral dissertation). Michigan State University. *Dissertation Abstracts International, 64*(12), 4380.

Duranczyk, I.M., Myers, K.A., Couillard, E.K., Schoen, S., & Higbee, J.L. (2013). Enacting the spirit of the United Nations Convention on the Rights of Persons with Disabilities: The role of postsecondary faculty in ensuring access. *Journal of Diversity Management, 8*(2), 63–72.

Garrison-Wade, D.F. (2012). Listening to their voices: Factors that inhibit or enhance postsecondary outcomes for students with disabilities. *International Journal of Special Education, 27*(2), 113–125.

Getzel, E.E., & Thoma, C. (2008). Experiences of college students with disabilities and the importance of self-determination in higher education settings. *Career Development for Exceptional Individuals, 31*(2), 77–84.

Gibson, J. (2006). Disability and clinical competency: An introduction. *California Psychologist, 39*, 6–10.

Gibson, J. (2011). Advancing care to clients with disabilities through clinical competency. *California Psychologist, 44*(4), 23–26.

Higbee, J.L., & Goff, E. (Eds.). (2008). *Pedagogy and student services for institutional transformation: Implementing universal design in higher education.* Minneapolis, MN: Center for Research on Developmental Education and Urban Literacy, University of Minnesota.

Higbee, J.L., & Mitchell, A. (Eds.). (2009). *Making good on the promise: Student affairs professionals with disabilities.* Washington, DC: American College Personnel Association, University Press of America.

Kalivoda, K. (2009). Disability realities: Community, culture, and connection on college campuses. In J. Higbee & A. Mitchell (Eds.), *Making good on the promise: Student affairs professionals with disabilities* (pp. 3–25). Washington, DC: American College Personnel Association, University Press of America.

Madaus, J.W., Miller, W.K., & Vance, M.L. (2009). Veterans with disabilities in postsecondary education. *Journal of Postsecondary Education and Disability, 22*(1), 10–17.

McCarthy, D. (2007). Teaching self-advocacy to students with disabilities. *About Campus, 12*(5), 10–16.

McInnes, R. (2008, August). Disability humility for employers: A framework for training. *Diversity World.* Retrieved from http://www.diversityworld.com/Disability/DN08/DN0807.htm

Myers, K. (2009). A new vision for disability education: Moving on from the add-on. *About Campus, 14*(5), 15–21.

Myers, K., & Bastian, J. (2010, May–June). Understanding communication preferences of college students with visual disabilities. *Journal of College Student Development, 51*(3), 265–278.

Myers, K., Lindburg, J., & Nied, D. (2013). Allies for inclusion: Students with disabilities. *ASHE Higher Education Report, 39*(5), 1–132.

O'Neill, L.N.P., Markward, M.J., & French, J.P. (2012). Predictors of graduation among college students with disabilities. *Journal of Postsecondary Education and Disability, 25*(1), 21–36.

Scott, S.F., & Shaw, S.S. (2003). New directions in faculty development. *Journal of Postsecondary Education and Disability, 17*(1), 3–9.

Snyder, T., & Dillow, S. (2010). *Digest of education statistics 2009* (NCES 2010–013) (Table 231). Washington, DC: National Center for Education Statistics, Institute of Education Sciences, U.S. Department of Education.

Tinto, V. (1987). *Leaving college.* Chicago, IL: University of Chicago Press.

Tregoning, M. (2009). Being an ally in language use. In J. Higbee & A. Mitchell (Eds.), *Making good on the promise: Student affairs professionals with disabilities* (pp. 171–176). Washington, DC: American College Personnel Association, University Press of America.

U.S. Department of Education (USDOE). (1973). *Rehabilitation Act of 1973, Sec 504.* Retrieved from http://www2.ed.gov/policy/speced/reg/narrative.html

U.S. Department of Education, National Center for Education Statistics (USDOE). (2006). *Profile of undergraduates in U.S. postsecondary education institutions: 2003–2004 with a special analysis of community college students* (NCES 2006184), Section 6. Retrieved from http://nces.ed.gov/pubsearch/pubsinfo.asp?pubid=2006184

U.S. Department of Justice. (2002). *Americans with Disabilities Act: Questions and answers.* U.S. Equal Employment Opportunity Commission. Retrieved from http://www.ada.gov/q&aeng02.htm

U.S. Department of Labor, Office of Disability Employment Policy. (2013). *Current disability employment statistics.* Retrieved from http://www.dol.gov/odep/

ELEVEN

Privilege and Power: Identifying and Addressing Whiteness in the University Setting: Promoting a System of Success for All

Tina R. Paone, Krista M. Malott, and Brighid Dwyer

Introduction

This chapter seeks to identify Whiteness in the university setting by providing an examination of the ways in which policies and practices premised on dominant White cultural norms can result in biased practices toward students of color. Constructs related to Whiteness and racism will be defined. The authors will suggest actions that can be taken by student affairs professionals to develop a more inclusive campus climate. Individual and programmatic actions will be considered, along with an acknowledgment of the resiliencies and actions already in place that have ensured the success of students of color today and in the past.

The university is a unique setting in that it brings together, in both living and learning spaces, persons of diverse racial and ethnic backgrounds. Many of these students are having their first-ever, meaningful, cross-racial experience, having grown up in neighborhoods and attended primary and secondary schools that reflect the nation's de facto segregation practices (Donato & Hanson, 2012; Orfield & Eaton, 1996; Osypuk & Acevedo-Garcia, 2010; Perea, 2004; Perna, 2005; U.S. Department of Education, 2005). It should come as no surprise, therefore, that university settings are cited as spaces with high percentages of race-based incidents (Brooks & Witherspoon, 2013). Indeed, ongoing media reports and current scholarship can attest to the existence of such a situation.

It should logically follow from such a premise that faculty and administration—those who create the policies, practices, and norms in the university setting—are born of that same system of segregation, one that is premised on dominant White cultural norms that can lead inherently White individuals to act in racially biased ways. Bonilla-Silva (2012) writes of a normative structure of the very rules and ideologies of institutions and communities across the United States that promote Whiteness "as the standard for all sorts of everyday transactions rendering domination almost invisible" (p. 174). This translates into the creation of what Bonilla-Silva (2012) dubbed HWCUs (historically White colleges and universities). In such places, Whiteness is perpetuated across culture, policies, and programs at all levels, influencing every aspect, including hiring and student recruitment practices, instructional behaviors and materials of professors, menus, and recreational and academic programs offered to students. The predominance of Whiteness in such settings serves to create an educational environment that is experienced as an unwelcoming and hostile one for many students of color (Bonilla-Silva, 2012).

Bonilla-Silva (2012) acknowledged the ubiquitous presence of racist symbols at HWCUs such as the use of "Indian" mascots, as well as the more subtle symbols of White male dominance through portraits, photos, and statues of White men interspersed in campus spaces. Further, in the towns in which those universities are located, local businesses largely cater to Whites' needs and interests and, at times, practice overtly discriminatory actions against students of color (Bonilla-Silva, 2012). Turner (1994) described such spaces as those in which students of color become "guests [who] have no history in the house they occupy. There are no photographs on the wall that reflect their image. Their paraphernalia, paintings, scents, and sounds do not appear in the house" (p. 356).

Fries-Britt and Griffin (2007) asserted that students of color, facing what seems to be a racially hostile educational setting, will experience adverse impacts on academic "achievement, integration, and retention" (p. 510). Indeed, statistics have shown greater rates of dropout for students of color in comparison to Whites (Carter, 2006). Consequently, with the ever-increasing number of persons of color studying at universities (Aud, Fox, & KewalRamani, 2010; Carnevale & Fry, 2000; Hussar & Bailey, 2006), there has been increased recognition of the need for a paradigmatic shift in university policies and practices to meet the needs of all—rather than a few—students (Hurtado, Alvarez, Guillermo-Wann, Cuellar, & Arellano, 2012; Hurtado, Milem, Clayton-Pedersen, & Allen, 1999; Milem, Chang, & Antonio, 2005; Wade-Golden & Williams, 2013; Williams, 2008, 2013).

This chapter examines the impact of HWCUs on students of color. It highlights suggestions for shifting university practices and identifies ways that student affairs professionals can create a campus climate that is more welcoming and equitable for all. Solutions and relevant case studies will be presented.

Race-Related Constructs Defined

Racial terminology can be complex, particularly in light of the intersectionality of identities that can confound its meanings and manifestations (Sensoy & DiAngelo, 2011). To maintain clarity across the narrative, the term *race* will indicate a sociopolitical construction rather than a biological one, reflective of a person's external appearance such as skin color, phenotype, or hair type (Helms, Jernigan, & Mascher, 2005). Hence, when discussing students of color, *race* refers to one's external appearance, as opposed to any kind of biological indicators. Conversely, *ethnicity*, recognized by most scholars as a separate construct from race (Helms, Nicolas, & Green, 2010), reflects a person's traditions, cultural values, and, at times, use of language (Phinney, 1989). The constructs, however, do overlap. Hence, when discussing *Whiteness*, it is a discussion of race to indicate a light skin tone. Yet from the beginning, Whiteness has embedded within it ethnic values, norms, and practices that connote culture—a culture born from a history of European and British ancestry. To understand the presence and shape Whiteness takes in contemporary university settings, readers must first understand Whiteness and its complex history, its intersectionality with varied identities, and its relation to racism itself.

Racism has been variably defined by scholars who have recognized its myriad formations over time and history (Weiner & Craighead, 2010). For the purposes of this chapter, racism is defined as actions that reflect social or institutional norms that serve to systematically disadvantage persons of color. Inherent in this definition is the recognition of power differentials that enable racism, including the ability of those in the dominant White group to exercise power over persons of color. This connects individual acts of prejudice by Whites to broader societal norms (Jones, 1997), giving such acts power over others. At the systemic or structural level, racism serves to maintain power differentials, constricting the access of people of color to resources and opportunities. Related to this is cultural racism, in which dominant cultural norms serve to create standards and practices that favor Whites (Weiner & Craighead, 2010). Such norms have been identified by scholars as the culture of Whiteness.

Featherston and Ishibashi (2004) defined Whiteness as "an interlocking pattern of beliefs, values, feelings and assumptions; policies, procedures, and laws; behaviors and unwritten rules used to define and underpin a worldview. It is embedded in historic systems of oppression that sustain wealth, power, and privilege" (p.105). Whiteness as a phenomenon emerged in the formation of the United States, established by wealthy colonialists, largely of British origin, in an effort to unite a single dominant group (wealthy persons of European descent). As early as the nineteenth century, Black scholars such as W.E.B. Du Bois and Booker T. Washington were engaged in efforts to name and deconstruct the presence and effects of Whiteness in the United States (Du Bois, 1994; Washington, 1900).

Those cultural values and norms, which were largely of British origin, were an inherent part of Whiteness. Those cultural tenets were manifested as the valuing of the English language, history, music, art, and physical appearance; promotion of the Christian (specifically, Anglo-Saxon Protestant) religion; strict adherence to a linear time frame; patriarchal; future orientation; a Protestant Work ethic; rugged individualism; and an emphasis on the scientific method (Katz, 2003). Traits ascribed to Whites were viewed as predominantly positive and deeply embedded in Christianity, including wholesomeness, judiciousness, fear of God, morality, normality, and industriousness (Kivel, 1996). Those tenets have since been considered the norm in the United States—values against which all others are measured.

Historically, immigrants arriving in the United States were met with the expectation that they would assimilate into the dominant culture of Whiteness and thereby eschew their original cultures and traditions in exchange for gaining access to social, political, and economic power and privilege. Those with lighter skin tones more easily assimilated into Whiteness, while "others" with darker skin tones, although still expected to assimilate into Whiteness, were unable to gain complete acceptance and access to the same privileges as those dubbed White. They found themselves denied the many privileges and rights accorded to those who could pass for White and were discriminated against by individuals and through laws, policies, and practices enacted by Whites (Hitchcock, 2002). In this way, Whiteness, according to scholars, has become synonymous with White supremacy itself (Bonilla-Silva, 2012).

Denial of the presence of Whiteness and its related White supremacy allowed early scholars to focus predominantly on oppressed groups with a normative (White, middle-class, male, heterosexual) perspective applied to the "other," leading to pathological or deficit perspectives of people of color. In turn, Whites have maintained social, political, and economic power through assumption and promotion of certain ideologies. For instance, the myth of meritocracy, or the "American Dream," asserts that all U.S. citizens have equal access to any and *every* opportunity, provided that they work hard enough (Powell, 1997). Implied in this ideology is the message that those who fail to achieve must be inherently lazy or possess low levels of intelligence. Many Whites also assume a stance of colorblindness, defined as an attempt to minimize the presence and impact of Whiteness (Apfelbaum, Sommers, & Norton, 2008). Others have simply denied the presence of, or avoided critique of, the system of Whiteness entirely (Gomez, Allen, & Clinton, 2004).

However, a rapidly diversifying nation, one in which Whites are projected to soon become the minority (U.S. Bureau of the Census, 2012), has forced Whites to experience themselves as "other." Slowly, scholars' critiques of the system are becoming more heeded as they continually turn a critical eye toward the dominance maintained, and racial bias enacted, by Whiteness (Duster, 2001). Activists such as McIntosh (1989) have begun to make visible the ways that Whiteness norms privilege the daily existence of Whites—from easy access to grocery, health, and grooming items specific to Whites (e.g., "nude" Band-Aids and shampoos for straight-hair types), to the comfort (and advantages) gained from knowing that history, laws, and educational practices are structured to favor Whites. Scholars have cited a need for self-examination regarding Whiteness across contexts in order to identify and dismantle racially biased beliefs that can result in harmful practices toward people of color (D'Andrea, 1999; Ridley, 2005; Sue & Sue, 2008). Within university settings, Whiteness extends beyond the classroom to affect both the administrative policies as well as the campus climate in academic and social contexts.

Whiteness in University Settings

For many years the field of higher education has discussed the "chilly climate" students and faculty of color experience in predominantly White institutions (Hurtado & Carter, 1997; Hurtado & Ruiz, 2012; Moses, 1997; Myers, 2002). Only recently has Whiteness been recognized and discussed more directly as a systematic and structural force within higher education (Yeung, Spanierman, & Landrum-Brown, 2013). Centering Whiteness and discussing it as a contributing factor to the chilly climate at universities changes the conversation from identifying people of color as victims to understanding how higher education is a system that is deeply rooted in racially hierarchical practices (Hurtado et al., 1999; Law, Phillips, & Turney, 2004; Milem et al., 2005). Once colleges and universities are viewed through this lens of Whiteness and privilege, obvious manifestations of Whiteness in higher education settings become clear.

Consider, for instance, the preponderance of buildings and streets named after Whites. Academically, both the content of the library—and the classroom curriculum—are reflective of predominantly White- or European-heritage male persons and norms. From guest speakers to musical and theatrical performances, campus entertainment is predominantly organized by, and premised on, dominant cultural norms. Most important, those with the greatest power and prestige on campus—faculty members and administrators—are most often White, while lower-paid, lower-prestige positions (e.g., dining services, janitorial) tend to be disproportionately held by persons of color (Bonilla-Silva, 2012). This stratification demonstrates the dominance of Whiteness and White ideology on college campuses.

Whiteness also exists in more subtle forms and can be just as consequential for students. For instance, student resident assistants and other residence life staff, who are expected to act as mentors and role models to students in their residence halls, are most often White. Such students and professionals may be more comfortable approaching and interacting with other White residents. Because most of us feel most knowledgeable and comfortable sharing our own ethnic and cultural traditions with others, it is likely that the cultural and educational residential life programming offered will be reflective of White cultural traditions and dominant cultural norms. White ethnocentric residence hall programming could ultimately create an environment that feels alienating to students of color.

Consider also the recent proliferation of service programs across the nation's campuses whereby students are required to enter and assist nearby "communities of need," which are often communities of color (Maurrasse, 2001). These service opportunities perpetuate White positions of superiority and solidify students' stereotypes of persons of color as victims. Ultimately, they work to maintain the status quo (Sperling, 2007).

Beyond stepping into a culture premised on dominant White cultural norms, students of color must also interact, and at times live with, Whites who are steeped in these norms of Whiteness, or what bell hooks (2004) calls a White supremacy ideology. As previously noted, students from all racial backgrounds often experience their first interaction with diverse others upon entering college (Frankenberg, Lee, & Orfield, 2003; Osypuk & Acevedo-Garcia, 2010). Moreover, precollege living environments are key in determining collegiate cross-racial interactions (Eaton & Orfield, 2003; Orfield & Eaton, 1996; Orfield & Lee, 2006). Students who have had experience engaging in cross-racial interactions prior to college bring a sense of ease and comfort to such interactions in college (Hurtado et al., 1999; Milem et al., 2005). Conversely, because of their inexperience and lack of knowledge of cultures other than their own, less experienced students may hesitate to engage with others of different backgrounds (Dwyer, 2012). This is particularly problematic at HWCUs because students—White students in particular—would be unlikely to challenge themselves to overcome their fear of engaging with students from backgrounds different from their own.

Even more problematic, however, are the troubling exchanges between those White students and students of color. When students do interact cross-racially, White students may default to the norms of Whiteness by unconsciously expecting non-Whites to uphold White cultural norms and values, and pathologizing or criticizing those who fail to do so (Yosso, Smith, Ceja, & Solórzano, 2009). White students may also (consciously or unconsciously) communicate a lack of understanding and empathy for the experiences of discrimination that can negatively affect their peers of color. This lack of understanding can be experienced by students of color as a microaggression, causing them to feel disconnected, and even leading to conflict in cross-racial interactions (Sue & Constantine, 2007).

Racism at universities also profoundly impacts White college students. For instance, Todd, Spanierman, & Poteat (2011) discuss the psychosocial costs of racism to Whites across the college experience and find that there is a great need for increased interaction between Whites and students of color. This includes attending diversity events and participating in diversity courses. Because of a lifetime of limited interaction with persons of color, White students often lack core diversity competencies that many employers seek when hiring recent college graduates (Bikson & Law; 1994; Business-Higher Education Forum, 2002). These issues reveal a need for college officials to incorporate diversity and dialogue around racism and Whiteness across university settings.

Microaggressions and the Campus Setting

Modern-day racism has been described as something that is often more subtle than it was in the past. In considering racist acts by individuals, scholars have coined the term *microaggressions,* defined as "subtle, innocuous, preconscious, or unconscious degradations, and putdowns.... [T]he cumulative burden of a lifetime of microaggressions can theoretically contribute to diminished mortality, augmented morbidity, and flattened confidence" (Pierce, 1995, p. 281). Myriad scholars give voice to specific examples of racism and racial tension experienced by students of color on college campuses (Minikel-Lacocque, 2013; Solórzano, Ceja, & Yosso, 2000). For instance, researchers have found that African American and Latino students experience racial microaggressions in both academic and non-academic university spaces, and that those acts of racism negatively influence the campus climate (Solórzano et al., 2000; Yosso et al., 2009). Notably, researchers found that such racism negatively affected students' confidence levels and academic performance (Solórzano et al., 2000; Yosso et al., 2009), resulting in what Yosso and colleagues (2009) have described as "a negative, and even hostile, campus racial climate in which they endure incessant covert, yet shocking, racial assaults" (p. 679).

Scholars have conducted extensive research on racial microaggressions made by both White students and faculty members in university settings (Sue, Capodilupo, Nadal, & Torino, 2008; Sue & Constantine 2007). Findings include the reluctance of White faculty members to address race at all, even when it is identified as an essential topic for the curriculum and professional training of students. The reason for such reluctance was reported by faculty members as fear of appearing racist or of losing "control" of the classroom setting (Sue et al., 2008). Sue and Constantine (2007) also found that, in classroom settings, White students engaged in unconscious racial microaggressions cited as hurtful by students of color, potentially nullifying the experiences of people of color. Minikel-Lacocque (2013) aptly described the damage enacted by such racism, noting that "the insidious, slippery, sometimes hard-to-name nature of microaggressions is precisely where their power lies to cause damage" (p. 459). She asserted that such attacks should not be considered small and insignificant, as connoted by the term "micro," suggesting, rather, that they be more accurately renamed as "racialized aggressions" (Minikel-Lacocque, 2013, p. 459).

When people of color repeatedly experience microaggressions across co-curricular, social, and classroom settings, they develop negative psychological and physical symptoms. The exhaustion associated with combating those assaults has been named *racial battle fatigue* (Smith, Allen, & Danley, 2007). Racial battle fatigue is rooted in studies that document the psychological and physiological effects of racism and the coping strategies that individuals utilize to manage racism-induced stress (Feagin & McKinney, 2003; Steele, 1997). Responses associated with racial battle fatigue include a range of emotional and coping strategies that may include avoidance, aggravation, resentment, fatigue, emotional withdrawal, hostility, and combative behavior (Smith et al., 2007). In turn, the time, energy, and effort required to sustain emotional and psychological well-being in this way will reduce the amount of energy available for academic, social, and career-related activities.

Once it is understood that the time and energy of students of color has been diverted from their academic and co-curricular pursuits, it must be considered that the issue is a contextual and systemic one. Furthermore, the onus for change is on those in power positions—Whites in particular—who must redress policies and practices at the university level in order to create a more inclusive space for all. Finally, we must transform our understanding of students of color as victims in order to recognize their ongoing resilience in overcoming current discriminatory systems and to draw upon their knowledge and skills in transforming the university landscape.

Resilience and Solutions

Despite the dire picture we have painted for students of color who are attempting to exist and thrive within the dominant system of Whiteness, there are survival mechanisms applied by persons of color that allow them to succeed in educational and social spaces across the United States. Successful historical and contemporary practices for persons of color must be understood by professionals working in the university system. These can be drawn upon in developing policies and practices to support such groups, yet always with the understanding that such findings cannot be applied in a stereotypical or blanket manner. There are vast individual and contextual differences that warrant dialogue with, and response to, each context and student group.

It is proposed that actions by professionals to make the university system a more fair and equitable experience for students of color should first and foremost be guided by the empirical and theoretical literature that identifies student resilience and current best practices. In reviewing the literature, one discovers a disproportionate focus on Black males, as this population has been cited as experiencing the greatest number of stressors related to discrimination, accompanied by the lowest rate of college attainment and highest dropout rate from college (Harper, 2012). However, attempts to broaden such findings, to be more inclusive, or to consider the needs of varied ethnic and racial groups, including immigrants from non-European nations, are seldom included.

Student tactics and skills in responding to racism. A study by Fries-Britt & Griffin (2007) found that Black students cope with racism in university settings in various ways. Such behaviors were deemed to be simultaneously helpful and exhausting to the individuals. Those actions included attempts at dispelling myths and stereotypes with overtly nonstereotypical behaviors and teaching others about the Black experience (Fries-Britt & Griffin, 2007). The authors also noted the importance of support from Black faculty members, who could identify with the racism experienced by the students (Fries-Britt & Griffin, 2007).

Same-group spaces, programs, mentoring, and organizations. In one study, Harper (2012) examined the experiences of successful Black college males across the nation. Those males overwhelmingly attributed their success to exposure to "people or culturally relevant experiences that motivated them to be engaged, strive for academic success, and persist through baccalaureate degree attainment" (p. 15). Leaders in the university system can seek to provide such influential persons and experiences. Indeed, the literature is replete with findings indicating the success born from spaces, activities, programs, and support groups for students of color in university settings (Dwyer, 2012; Guiffrida, 2003; Harper, 2012; Museus, 2008). Such academic and social counterspaces (Solórzano et al., 2000) can be created in collaboration with faculty members or by student groups themselves, such as cultural organizations. Specific examples of counterspaces include rooms or buildings reserved for particular student groups of color, academic support or same-group mentoring programs, political or social groups facilitated by students of color who seek to promote their voices and effect change in policies and campus climate (Harper, 2012).

The intent of such spaces can vary from academic, to career, to social support. For instance, with the dominant presence of Whiteness on college and university campuses, non-White students often have to find their own spaces on campus where their identity can be affirmed, and such programs or spaces allow for this. As such, these programs or spaces offer a positive racial climate (Dwyer, 2012), wherein "deficit notions of people of color can be challenged and where a positive collegiate racial climate can be established and maintained" (Solórzano, et al., 2000, p. 70).

In creating same-group supports or programs, there are complexities and nuances related to student identities (and the intersectionality of identities) that should be considered. Black immigrants will differ vastly from Black Americans, for instance. Those educated in wealthier school districts will seek different supports than those who came from underfunded schools. In addition, students attending HWCUs in rural settings may require different services, supports, or programs than those attending universities in more racially diverse urban settings (Bonilla-Silva, 2012). Within-group differences may be considered according to sexual identity or religion, such as the need for each group to access same-group-and-trait spaces of respite and support. In addition, racial or ethnic groups that may appear "similar" to some may actually differ culturally or politically. For instance, those who appear "Middle Eastern" may differ vastly according to cultural, political, or religious beliefs (Erikson & Al-Timimi, 2001), and students who fall within the umbrella description of "Latino" will often present vast differences from other Latinos according to family origins, religious practices, language, and immigrant experiences (Malott, 2009).

Hence, a program or space designed to support varied student groups must be created with those differences in mind, as well as whole academic programs (minors and majors) dedicated to highlighting the history, contribution, and scholarship of varied groups (Hernandez, 2009). In turn, when bringing many groups together in one setting, staff members should be proficient in engaging members in intergroup dialogue and in facilitating conflict if it arises (Dessel & Rogge, 2008; Gurin, Nagda, & Zúñiga, 2013). Considering the complexity of human identities, the creation of programming and spaces for students of color would ideally be undertaken by professionals from those particular groups, with ongoing input and rotating leadership from all members involved (Reason, Scales, & Roosa Millar, 2005).

Finally, in designing such programs and spaces, particular effort must be directed at outreach to the students most vulnerable to college attrition—those who are unable to live on campus because of financial difficulties or family responsibilities. Commuter students, a group that is growing in number, are often the least likely to receive supports (such as same-group mentoring) that can facilitate adjustment to campus climate and foster academic and career success (Alford, 2000). Those students can be asked to contribute to the design and scheduling of same-group programming so as to meet their unique needs and scheduling challenges.

Designing such programming and spaces begs the question of where the onus of responsibility is placed on agency in regard to student engagement. Traditionally, as noted by Harper (2012),

> In a self-directed fashion, [the student] is expected to seek out resources, engagement opportunities, and enriching educational experiences that will best prepare him for post-college success. It is unreasonable and unrealistic to expect that the majority of students (Black, male, or otherwise) will engage themselves in this way. (p. 22)

Harper (2012) proposed that professionals and administration avoid a deficit-based approach (e.g., asking "What's wrong with these students, why aren't they engaged in classroom settings and campus events?") and instead critically examine university practices, policies, and actions that impede the success and participation of students of color. The students themselves must be given voice in that effort, and university professionals must be assigned the responsibility for outreach to encourage student involvement in programs born from such systematic assessment (Harper, 2012).

Systemic change. Limited space prohibits an extended discussion of systemic solutions such as altering racially biased policies or practices in the university system. Those in power can, with the support of racially diverse members of the campus community, seek to critically review and alter major university policies and practices formed on dominant cultural norms. Examples of areas for critical examination include: student recruitment practices; admissions standards and policies; curricular decisions (content, requirements, and the training of White faculty in regard to how their biases are played out in the classroom with students of color); student programming (Which events, artists, and scholars are brought to the campus? To whom do they appeal, to whose issues do they speak?); campus safety policies (Is there a transparent way for people to report and address racism? Are students of color racially profiled regularly by campus safety officers?); campus climate decisions (spaces of respite where students of color can come together to escape racism; decorations, music in the dining hall, food being served—Which groups are represented?); hiring practices and policies (e.g., resident assistants, faculty, student leadership positions both paid and unpaid, graduate assistantships, deans, etc.).

Applying Solutions to Cases

There are myriad ways of finding solutions to the problems outlined in this chapter. The following is a set of cases based on actual—and common—experiences in university settings. The authors suggest that best solutions are derived from collaboration among professionals, and we encourage consultations with others in the discussion of solutions for the following cases. Where possible, it is suggested that one consider solutions that foster systemic change (changes to policies, for instance) to minimize the chances of a recurrence of such issues.

Case #1: Linda, a graduate student, complains of being the only student of color in her entire department (all faculty, staff, and students are White). During class, her peers sometimes make offensive comments directed at various racial and cultural groups and are never challenged by faculty members. She finds that students completely ignore her in most classes, or may occasionally make comments about her "beautiful skin" and "interesting hair" (she wears it natural, as an afro, and every day someone asks to touch it, to her great offense). Faculty members present a curriculum that is reflective of White, middle-class culture and that is, at times, offensive in its representation of those outside the dominant White group.

Faculty members have singled her out, making her highly uncomfortable, saying such things as, "Linda, you're Black, what do you think about this?" Linda is thinking about dropping out. What do you think Linda should do?

Case #2: Imagine you are a consultant who is asked to work with a science department to increase the hiring of "diverse" faculty members. The department is populated with older White men who have recently hired new faculty members (women, one of whom was Asian, another, Latina), who have all left within a year of being appointed. They cannot understand what they are doing wrong. What do you think some possible causes of faculty departure might be?

Case #3: Swastikas and racist epithets are spray-painted anonymously on the walls of a dormitory in the center of the campus. Students, staff, and faculty alike express discomfort but remain silent and inactive. You are asked to create a forum to discuss the topic, as well as to bring about some kind of action or strategy for addressing the silent tension around the issue. How do you create this forum? What are the essential components of it? What are some possible solutions?

Case #4: You work at a university that has provided little or no voice to students of color on campus. Nearly every position of power (including student government positions and graduate assistantships) and every event seems to promote White students' norms, interests, and leadership. You've been asked to develop venues for student activities to "bring more diversity" to campus. How do you first broach the topic of the lack of inclusiveness in past events? Next, how do you suggest more events that are inclusive of diverse perspectives and people? Imagine your campus has a large Asian and Latino population. How do you establish ideas for diversifying events? What is the process?

Case #5: You've been asked to develop a training program for the all-White resident assistants who responded to a recent report of racism from students of color with admonishments about "being too sensitive." The students of color are demanding that some kind of action be taken regarding the racism exhibited both by peers in the dorms and the RAs. How do you address this?

Case #6: You work in residence life, and room assignments have been made. The most common issue is a White parent calling to explain that college is hard enough, and that asking his White son to room with two Black roommates will just be too "different" for him to deal with. He is not being racist, he explains, noting that "some of my best friends are Black," but he is only being realistic because his son has "never really been around Blacks." You do know there can be racial tension, misunderstandings, and clashes when students are asked to room across cultures or races. First directly address the issue of how to respond to the parent. Second, create a program that facilitates greater positive connectivity for students as they attempt to live in new settings and with new roommates.

Case #7: You have been asked to improve the racial climate of the campus by developing a range of programs and initiatives. How do you do this? List the steps for assessing needs and program development. [As a suggestion to course instructors, consider making this a semester-long, research-based case study that involves consulting literature, research, interviewing key campus experts, and one that students can best accomplish in a group.]

Conclusion

This chapter has sought to identify Whiteness in the university setting in order to increase understanding of the ways in which policies and practices premised on dominant White cultural norms can create a hostile campus climate for students of color. An essential challenge for student affairs professionals as they enter into this type of work is to focus inward, to engage in continual self-development as a means for greater impact in efforts at racial equity in work spaces. Questions to consider, many which are meaningful for both Whites and persons of color, include: How can you work to continually increase understanding and awareness of the presence and impact of Whiteness on yourself and the surrounding environments? In what ways do you act that uphold, or reify, Whiteness, and in what ways can you seek to notice, and mitigate, the harm it does to you and others? How do you make positive and negative meaning of your race, and how are you also harmed by racism toward you or others? How do you make meaning of your intersecting identities such as gender, ethnicity, nationality, religion, and sexual orientation, and how do those identities impact your insights and ability to empathize with others? What are some ways in which you can create supportive networks to continually work on such topics and effect greater change?

Strategies for addressing this topic further include ongoing education through involvement in courses, training, and support. Training that instills action-based skills to address and eradicate inequities is essential, as general awareness of injustices is not the same as skillfully addressing and changing those injustices. Finally, the authors assert that personal and professional growth in this area is a never-ending process or journey (Malott, Paone, Schaefle, & Cates, 2013). One must allow for mistakes and missteps along the way, as it is difficult and complex work. What is essential is not doing it perfectly but making the commitment to do it consistently and to share that journey and related challenges with supportive persons and communities.

References

Alford, S.M. (2000). A qualitative study of the college social adjustment of Black students from lower socioeconomic communities. *Journal of Multicultural Counseling and Development, 28*(1), 2–15.

Apfelbaum, E.P., Sommers, S.R., & Norton, M.I. (2008). Seeing race and seeming racist? Evaluating strategic colorblindness in social interaction. *Journal of Personality and Social Psychology, 95*(4), 918–932. doi: 10.1037/a0011990

Aud, S., Fox, M., & KewalRamani, A. (2010). *Status and trends in the education of racial and ethnic groups* (NCES 2010-015). U.S. Department of Education, National Center for Education Statistics. Washington, DC: U.S. Government Printing Office.

Bikson, T.K., & Law, S.A. (1994). *Global preparedness and human resources: College and corporate perspectives.* Santa Monica, CA: Rand Institute of Education and Training.

Bonilla-Silva, E. (2012). The invisible weight of Whiteness: The racial grammar of everyday life in contemporary America. *Ethnic and Racial Studies, 35*(2), 173–194. doi: 10.1080/01419870.2011.613997

Brooks, J.S., & Witherspoon, N. (2013). *Confronting racism in higher education: Problems and possibilities for fighting ignorance, bigotry and isolation.* Charlotte, NC: Information Age.

Business-Higher Education Forum. (2002). *Public accountability for student learning in higher education: Issues and options.* Washington, DC: American Council on Education.

Carnevale, A.P., & Fry, R.A. (2000). *Crossing the great divide: Can we achieve equality when generation Y goes to college?* Princeton, NJ: Educational Testing Service.

Carter, D.F. (2006). Key issues in the persistence of underrepresented minority students. *New Directions for Institutional Research, 2006*(130), 33–46. doi: 10.1002/ir.178

D'Andrea, M. (1999). The evolution and transformation of a White racist: A personal narrative. *Journal of Counseling & Development, 77*(1), 38–42.

Dessel, A., & Rogge, M.E. (2008). Evaluation of intergroup dialogue: A review of the empirical literature. *Conflict Resolution Quarterly, 26*(2), 199–238. doi: http://dx.doi.org/10.1002/crq.230

Donato, R., & Hanson, J.S. (2012). The politics of de jure and de facto school segregation in the American Southwest. *Harvard Educational Review, 82*(2), 224–326.

Du Bois, W.E.B. (1994). *The souls of Black folk.* Mineola, NY: Dover.

Duster, T. (2001). The "morphing" properties of Whiteness. In B.B. Rasmussen, E. Klinenberg, I.J. Nexica, & M. Wray (Eds.), *The making and unmaking of Whiteness* (pp. 113–137). Durham, NC: Duke University Press.

Dwyer, B. (2012). *Students' cross-racial interactions at an emerging Hispanic-serving institution* (Unpublished doctoral dissertation). University of Michigan, Ann Arbor.

Eaton, S.E., & Orfield, G. (2003). Rededication not celebration: *Brown* at fifty. *College Board Review, 200*, 28–33.

Erikson, C.D., & Al-Timimi, N.R. (2001). Providing mental health services to Arab Americans: Recommendations and considerations. *Cultural Diversity and Ethnic Minority Psychology, 7*(4), 308–327.

Feagin, J.R., & McKinney, K.D. (2003). *The many costs of racism.* Lanham, MD: Rowman & Littlefield.

Featherston, E., & Ishibashi, J. (2004). Oreos and bananas: Conversations on Whiteness. In V. Lea & J. Helfand (Eds.), *Identifying race and transforming Whiteness in the classroom* (pp. 87–105). New York, NY: Peter Lang.

Frankenberg, E., Lee, C., & Orfield, G. (2003). *A multiracial society with segregated schools: Are we losing the dream?* Cambridge, MA: Harvard University Civil Rights Project. Retrieved from http://www.civilrightsproject.harvard.edu

Fries-Britt, S., & Griffin, K. (2007). The Black box: How high-achieving Blacks resist stereotypes about Black Americans. *Journal of College Student Development, 48*(5), 509–524. doi: 10.1353/csd.2007.0048

Gomez, M.L., Allen, A.-R., & Clinton, K. (2004). Cultural models of care in teaching: A case study of one preservice secondary teacher. *Teaching & Teacher Education, 20*(5), 473–488. doi: 10.1016/j.tate.2004.04.005

Guiffrida, D.A. (2003). African American student organizations as agents of social integration. *Journal of College Student Development, 44*(3), 304–319. doi: 10.1353/csd.2003.0024

Gurin, P., Nagda, B.A., & Zúñiga, X. (Eds.). (2013). *Dialogue across difference: Practice, theory, and research on intergroup dialogue.* New York, NY: Russell Sage Foundation.

Harper, S.R. (2012). *Black male student success in higher education: A report from the National Black Male College Achievement Study.* Philadelphia, PA: University of Pennsylvania, Center for the Study of Race and Equity in Education. Retrieved from www.works.bepress.com/sharper/43

Helms, J.E., Jernigan, M., & Mascher, J. (2005). The meaning of race in psychology and how to change it: A methodological perspective. *American Psychologist, 60*(1), 27–36.

Helms, J.E., Nicolas, G., & Green, C.E. (2010). Racism and ethnoviolence as trauma: Enhancing professional training. *Traumatology, 16*(4), 53–62. doi: 10.1177/1534765610389595

Hernandez, A. (2009). The re-education of a Pocha-Rican: How Latina/o studies Latinized me. *Harvard Educational Review, 79*(4), 601–609.

Hitchcock, J. (2002). *Lifting the White veil: An exploration of White American culture in a multiracial context.* Roselle, NJ: Crandall, Dostie & Douglass Books.

Hooks, b. (2004). Overcoming White supremacy: A comment. In L. Heldke & P. O'Connor (Eds.), *Oppression, privilege, & resistance: Theoretical perspectives on racism, sexism, and heterosexism* (pp. 69–75). New York, NY: McGraw-Hill.

Hurtado, S., Alvarez, C.L., Guillermo-Wann, C., Cuellar, M., & Arellano, L. (2012). A model for diverse learning environments: The scholarship on creating and assessing conditions for student success. In J.C. Smart & M.B. Paulsen (Eds.), *Higher education: Handbook of theory and research* (pp. 41–122). New York, NY: Springer.

Hurtado, S., & Carter, D.F. (1997). Effects of college transition and perceptions of the campus racial climate on Latino college students' sense of belonging. *Sociology of Education, 70*(4), 324–345. doi: 10.2307/2673270

Hurtado, S., Milem, J., Clayton-Pedersen, A., & Allen, W. (1999). *Enacting diverse learning environments: Improving the climate for racial/ethnic diversity in higher education* (Report No. 26). Washington, DC: George Washington University.

Hurtado, S., & Ruiz, A. (2012). *The climate for underrepresented groups and diversity on campus.* Los Angeles, CA: Higher Education Research Institute.

Hussar, W.J., & Bailey, T.M. (2006). *Projections of education statistics to 2015* (NCES 2006-084). Washington, DC: U.S. Government Printing Office.

Jones, J.M. (1997). *Prejudice and racism* (2nd ed.). New York, NY: McGraw-Hill.

Katz, J. (2003). *White culture and racism: Working for organizational change in the United States.* The Whiteness Papers, No. 3. Roselle, NJ: Center for the Study of White American Culture.

Kivel, P. (1996). *Uprooting racism: How White people can work for racial justice.* Philadelphia, PA: New Society.

Law, I., Phillips, D., & Turney, L. (Eds.). (2004). *Institutional racism in higher education.* Oakhill, VA: Trentham Books.

Malott, K.M. (2009). Investigation of ethnic self-labeling in the Latina population: Implications for counselors and counselor educators. *Journal of Counseling & Development, 87*(2), 179–186.

Malott, K.M., Paone, T.R., Schaefle, S., & Cates, J. (2013). Examining White racial identity: An exploratory study. In C. Behar & A. Chung (Eds.), *Image of Whiteness* (pp. 181–191). Retrieved from https://www.interdisciplinarypress.net/online-store/ebooks/diversity-and-recognition/images-of-Whiteness

Maurrasse, D.J. (2001). *Beyond the campus: How colleges and universities form partnerships with their communities.* New York, NY: Routledge.

McIntosh, P. (1989). *White privilege: Unpacking the invisible knapsack.* New York, NY: McGraw-Hill.

Milem, J.F., Chang, M.J., & Antonio, A.L. (2005). *Making diversity work on campus: A research-based perspective.* Washington, DC: Association of American Colleges and Universities.

Minikel-Lacocque, J. (2013). Racism, college, and the power of words: Racial microaggressions reconsidered. *American Educational Research Journal, 50*(3), 432–465. doi: 10.3102/0002831212468048

Moses, Y.T. (1997). Black women in academe. In L. Benjamin (Ed.), *Black women in the academy* (pp. 23–38). Gainesville, FL: University of Florida Press.

Museus, S.D. (2008). The role of ethnic student organizations in fostering African American and Asian American students' cultural adjustment and membership at predominantly White institutions. *Journal of College Student Development, 49*(6), 568–586. doi: 10.1353/csd.0.0039

Myers, L.W. (2002). *A broken silence: Voices of African American women in the academy.* Westport, CT: Bergin & Garvey.

Orfield, G., & Eaton, S. (1996). *Dismantling desegregation: The quiet reversal of Brown v. Board of Education.* New York, NY: New Press.

Orfield, G., & Lee, C. (2006). *Racial transformation and the changing nature of segregation.* Cambridge, MA: Civil Rights Project at Harvard University.

Osypuk, T.L., & Acevedo-Garcia, D. (2010). Support for smoke-free policies: A nationwide analysis of immigrants, US-born, and other demographic groups, 1995–2002. *American Journal of Public Health, 100*(1), 171–181.

Perea, J.F. (2004). Buscando America: Why integration and equal protection fail to protect Latinos. *Harvard Law Review, 117*(5), 1420–1469. doi: 10.2307/4093258

Perna, L.W. (2005). The key to college access: Rigorous academic preparation. In W. Tierney, Z.B. Corwin, & J.E. Colyar (Eds.), *Preparing for college: Nine elements of effective outreach* (pp. 113–134). Albany, NY: State University of New York Press.

Phinney, J.S. (1989). Stages of ethnic identity development in minority group adolescents. *Journal of Early Adolescence, 9*(1–2), 34–49. doi: 10.1177/0272431689091004

Pierce, C.M. (1995). Stress analogs of racism and sexism: Terrorism, torture, and disaster. In C.V. Willie, P.P. Rieker, B.M. Kramer, & B.S. Brown (Eds.), *Mental health, racism, and sexism* (pp. 277–293). Pittsburgh, PA: University of Pittsburgh Press.

Powell, L.C. (1997). The achievement (k)not: Whiteness and Black underachievement. In M. Fine, L. Weis, L.C. Powell, & L. Mun Wong (Eds.), *Off White: Readings on race, power, and society* (pp. 2–13). New York, NY: Routledge.

Reason, R.D., Scales, T.C., & Roosa Millar, E.A. (2005). Encouraging the development of racial justice allies. *New Directions for Student Services, 2005*(110), 55–66.

Ridley, C.R. (2005). *Overcoming unintentional racism in counseling and therapy: A practitioner's guide to intentional intervention* (2nd ed.). Thousand Oaks, CA: Sage.

Sensoy, Ö., & DiAngelo, R. (2011). *Is everyone really equal? An introduction to key concepts in social justice education.* New York, NY: Teachers College Press.

Smith, W.A., Allen, W.R., & Danley, L.L. (2007). "Assume the position.... You fit the description": Psychosocial experiences and racial battle fatigue among African American male college students. *American Behavioral Scientist, 51*(4), 551–578. doi: 10.1177/0002764207307742

Solórzano, D., Ceja, M., & Yosso, T. (2000). Critical race theory, racial microaggressions, and campus racial climate: The experiences of African American college students. *Journal of Negro Education, 69*(1–2), 60–73.

Sperling, R. (2007). Service-learning as a method of teaching multiculturalism to White college students. *Journal of Latinos and Education, 6*(4), 309–322. doi: 10.1080/15348430701473454

Steele, C.M. (1997). A threat in the air: How stereotypes shape intellectual identity and performance. *American Psychologist, 52*(6), 613–629. doi: 10.1037/0003-066X.52.6.613

Sue, D.W., Capodilupo, C.M., Nadal, K.L., & Torino, G.C. (2008). Racial microaggressions and the power to define reality. *American Psychologist, 63*(4), 277–279. doi: 10.1037/0003-066X.63.4.277

Sue, D.W., & Constantine, M.G. (2007). Racial microaggressions as instigators of difficult dialogues on race: Implications for student affairs educators and students. *College Student Affairs Journal, 26*(2), 136–143. doi: 10.1037/a0014191

Sue, D.W., & Sue, D. (2008). *Counseling the culturally diverse: Theory and practice* (5th ed.). Hoboken, NJ: John Wiley.

Todd, N.R., Spanierman, L.B., & Poteat, V.P. (2011). Longitudinal examination of the psychosocial costs of racism to Whites across the college experience. *Journal of Counseling Psychology, 58*(4), 508–521. doi: 10.1037/a0025066

Turner, C.S. (1994). Guests in someone else's house: Students of color. *Review of Higher Education, 17*(4), 350–370.

U.S. Bureau of the Census. (2012). *Most children younger than age 1 are minorities.* Retrieved from http://www.census.gov/newsroom/releases/archives/population/cb12-90.html

U.S. Department of Education. (2005). *Postsecondary participation rates by sex and race/ethnicity, 1974–2003.* Washington, DC: National Center for Education Statistics.

Wade-Golden, K.C., & Williams, D.A. (2013). *The chief diversity officer: Strategy, structure, and change management.* Sterling, VA: Stylus.

Washington, B.T. (1900). *Up from slavery.* Garden City, NY: Country Life Press.

Weiner, I.B., & Craighead, W.E. (Eds.). (2010). *The Corsini of psychology.* Hoboken, NJ: John Wiley.

Williams, D.A. (2008). Beyond the diversity crisis model: Decentralized diversity planning and implementation. *Planning for Higher Education, 36*(2), 27–41.

Williams, D.A. (2013). *Strategic diversity leadership: Activating change and transformation in higher education.* Sterling, VA: Stylus.

Yeung, J.G., Spanierman, L.B., & Landrum-Brown, J. (2013). "Being White in a multicultural society": Critical Whiteness pedagogy in a dialogue course. *Journal of Diversity in Higher Education, 6*(1), 17–32. doi: 10.1037/a0031632

Yosso, T.J., Smith, W.A., Ceja, M., & Solórzano, D.G. (2009). Critical race theory, racial microaggressions, and campus racial climate for Latina/o undergraduates. *Harvard Educational Review, 79*(4), 659–690.

TWELVE

LGBTQIAA: From Invisibility to Visibility: Queer-Spectrum and Trans-Spectrum College Students

Susan Rankin, Genevieve Weber, and Jason Garvey

Perhaps nowhere is the expression "the only constant is change" more evident than in higher education. The experiences of college students are ever changing, which means that faculty and staff members have to recognize and act on these changes or they will quickly find themselves left behind. Those of us who work with students who identify within the queer-spectrum[1] (bisexual, gay, lesbian, queer, pansexual, same-gender loving, etc.) and/or the trans-spectrum (androgynous, gender nonconforming, genderqueer, transfeminine, transmasculine, transgender, etc.) can attest to the extensive changes that members of these groups have experienced just in the last decade.

One of the biggest changes has been the age at which students disclose their sexual identity. From the 1970s through the 1990s, it was commonplace for queer-spectrum individuals who were planning to attend college, especially if the college was away from home, to wait until they were on campus and had developed new friends before they disclosed their identity. This disclosure is colloquially known as "coming out" (Chauncey, 1994). In some cases, the students were not delaying disclosure, but simply did not recognize themselves as lesbian, gay, bisexual, or queer (LGBQ) until they met others like themselves and were in a more supportive environment. Today, with a growing number of gay–straight alliances in middle and high schools and the availability of online resources, students more readily understand themselves to be attracted to others of the same sex/gender and often come out in high school and, increasingly, in middle school (Kosciw, Greytak, Diaz, & Bartkiewicz, 2010; Macgillivray, 2007).

Trans-spectrum youth in the twenty-first century are also more frequently acknowledging their gender identities to themselves and others. Twenty years ago, the predominant pattern for individuals who felt themselves to be a gender different from the one assigned to them at birth, especially for male-bodied individuals who recognized themselves as female, was to "come out" in middle age. Typically, transsexual people feel gender different from a young age. Recent research (Beemyn &

Rankin, 2011) indicates that most of those who grew up from the 1950s through the 1980s faced severe social stigma and, as a result, often spent decades repressing their gender identities. Not until they reached a point where they could no longer deny their "true" selves—which was often during a midlife crisis—did they begin to accept themselves and, in many instances, seek to transition. In contrast, trans-spectrum youth growing up today are much less likely to feel compelled to hide their identities (Beemyn & Rankin, 2011). Even if their immediate families and friends are unsupportive, they may be able to gain validation and find a community online. As a result, this is the first generation of trans-spectrum teens who can actually be transgender teens.

In a recent review of LGBTQ research in higher education, Renn (2010) identified three strands of LGBTQ scholarship: visibility, campus climate, and identity and experiences. This chapter will offer an overview of developmental models for queer and trans-spectrum youth and a review of the literature that examines their experiences on college campuses. Given the fluid and evolving sexual and gender identities of individuals, the terms queer-spectrum and trans-spectrum are used to value how individuals choose to identify themselves, as opposed to placing them into socially constructed, fixed categories of sexuality and gender. That said, in the majority of the literature examining sexual identity and gender identity, researchers use the acronym "LGBT" to reference sexual and gender minorities. The authors feel that it is important to value individual identities rather than place people into fixed, socially constructed categories of sexuality or gender (Rankin, Weber, Blumenfeld, & Frazer, 2010a). In the summary of the literature offered here, the terminology that the authors have used in their own studies will be used (e.g., LGB, LGBT, LGBQ, etc.), while any synthesis and discussion will adopt the queer- and trans-spectrum language.

Queer-Spectrum Identity Development

Theoretical stage models emerged in the 1970s to describe the development of homosexual identity among young adults. These theoretical models centered on the process of coming out, or resolving an internal conflict related to identifying as lesbian or gay (Cass, 1979, 1984; Fassinger, 1991; Savin-Williams & Demo, 1984; Troiden, 1989).

Martin (1991) outlined key features shared by many of these coming out models: coming out is a developmental journey that spans many years; the process usually begins in childhood with feelings of being different; a person coming out goes through various stages; and the process ends in consolidation when a person no longer views him/her/hirself primarily in terms of sexual orientation. Gonsiorek (1995) similarly described the coming out process through developmental theories: individuals block recognition of same-sex feelings; a gradual recognition of same-sex attraction emerges; adolescents experiment both emotionally and behaviorally with homosexuality and develop a stronger sense of normalcy; and, as the individual develops an acceptance of same-sex feelings, a gay or lesbian identity is successfully integrated and accepted as a positive dimension of self. Though designated as having stages, most of these theoretical models are generally seen as fluid and allow for stops, starts, and regression (Bilodeau & Renn, 2005). Among the stage models of lesbian and gay identity development, the most prominent examples come from Cass (1979), Fassinger (1991), and D'Augelli (1994). The following paragraphs describe key tenets of each example.

Cass's Model of Sexual Orientation Identity Formation

Originally called the model for homosexual identity formation, Cass's (1979) model of sexual orientation identity formation examines "how an individual acquires a homosexual identity" (p. 219). The original six stages consist of identity confusion, identity comparison, identity tolerance, identity acceptance, identity pride, and identity synthesis (Cass, 1979). Cass later added a pre-stage, which is characterized as an individual identifying as heterosexual (Cass, 1984). During the development of a sexual orientation identity, a person moves from minimal awareness of a gay or lesbian identity to a final stage in which that person's public and private selves integrate into one. Cass's (1979, 1984) stages describe both cognitive and affective dimensions, and she notes the importance of an individual's perspective and others' perception of the individual. Several factors influence the development of a homosexual identity, including biological components and contextual variables.

Fassinger's Model of Gay and Lesbian Identity Development

McCarn and Fassinger (1996) constructed a model of lesbian identity development that was followed by a similar study validating identity development among gay men (Fassinger & Miller, 1997). These models attempted to integrate psychological and sociological dimensions of identity development to account for individual sexual identity formation and group membership identity (Fassinger & Miller, 1997; McCarn & Fassinger, 1996). These processes take place parallel to one another and describe a four-phase sequence to include awareness, exploration, deepening/commitment, and internalization/synthesis (Fassinger, 1998). A person can be in different phases of development for individual and group membership identity processes, and development of one process can influence the development of the other (Fassinger & Miller, 1997). Especially in new environmental contexts, individuals may repeat or recycle through phases. Unlike Cass's 1979 or 1984 model, coming out to others is not required for identity integration (Fassinger, 1998).

D'Augelli's Model of Lesbian, Gay, and Bisexual Development

In their review of identity development models, Bilodeau and Renn (2005) noted that as more scholars describe the development of sexual identity as fluid and complex, stage models become less relevant to describe the process. Furthermore, bisexual and transgender experiences were not historically included in lesbian and gay stage models of development. D'Augelli (1994) introduced the lifespan model of lesbian, gay, and bisexual (LGB) identity development to take into account social contexts and varied experiences. In contrast to previous models, D'Augelli's (1994) model recognizes that development evolves in fluid and multiple directions and is influenced by a person's understanding of self, family, and community connections. Identity formation, according to D'Augelli (1994), involves three sets of interrelated variables: personal actions and subjectivities, interactive intimacies, and sociohistorical connections.

D'Augelli's (1994) model describes six interactive processes that function independently of one another: exiting heterosexuality, developing a personal LGB identity, developing an LGB social identity, becoming an LGB offspring, developing an LGB intimacy status, and entering an LGB community. Identity may evolve differently across the processes and may be experienced at a greater magnitude depending on a person's social contexts and experiences.

Trans-Spectrum Identity Development

There is a scarcity of research examining transgender identity development. Recent studies of transgender identity development take a human development approach, emphasizing the relationship between an individual and the environment. Two of these studies are described below.

Bilodeau's Transgender Identity Development

Bilodeau (2005) adapted the six processes from D'Augelli's (1994) model of LGB development to describe the development of a transgender identity. This model, based on college students, includes the following processes: exiting a traditionally gendered identity, developing a personal transgender identity, developing a transgender social identity, becoming transgender offspring, developing a transgender intimacy status, and entering a transgender community (Bilodeau, 2005). Like that of D'Augelli, Bilodeau's model of transgender identity development is a lifespan process, allowing for a multidimensional, fluid understanding of how a person's identity is influenced by experiences and specific contexts (Bilodeau, 2005).

Beemyn and Rankin's The Lives of Transgender People

More recently, Beemyn and Rankin (2011) described developmental milestones in the process of individuals identifying across the trans-spectrum. Using data from over 5,000 survey respondents and 400 follow-up interviews, the authors identified eight "milestones" or significant life moments that many of the respondents in each group shared as they came to recognize and accept themselves as transgender (Beemyn & Rankin, 2011). These milestones are: feeling gender different from a young age; seeking to present as a gender different from the one assigned to them at birth; repressing or hiding their identity in the face of hostility and/or isolation; initially misidentifying their identity; learning about and meeting other trans people; changing their outward appearance in order to look more like their self-image; establishing new relationships with family, partners, friends, and coworkers; and developing a sense of wholeness within a gender normative society (Beemyn & Rankin, 2011).

Outcomes Related to Identity Development

Healthy identity development is related to positive contact with the LGBT community, other LGBT individuals, and affirmative heterosexual individuals (Hogan & Rentz, 1996). Because the early stages of sexual minority identity development often occur during collegiate years (D'Augelli & Rose, 1990; Hogan & Rentz, 1996), the campus climate could pose a substantial threat to the willingness of an LGBT individual to disclose his or her sexual identity to the campus community and to his or her personal development as an LGBT individual (Evans & Broido, 1999). According to Wolf-Wendel, Toma, and Morphew (2001), gay men contemplate suicide, experience depression and anxiety, feel isolated, and fear for their own safety when they are part of a hostile environment. It is logical and sensible to generalize these results to lesbians, bisexuals, and transgender people who are also exposed to a hostile campus climate.

In their qualitative study, Evans and Broido (1999) examined the "coming out" process of 20 LGB students living in the residence halls of a major research institution. Findings from this study underscored the strong influence of one's environment, particularly the campus climate. Being around supportive people, perceiving the campus climate as supportive, and having visible LGB role models were identified as factors that encouraged LGB individuals to disclose their sexual identity (Evans & Broido, 1999). On the other hand, lack of support and active hostility were described as factors that discouraged "coming out."

Minority stress theory contends that LGBT individuals may experience mental and physical health problems as a result of negative social environments created by anti-gay attitudes, prejudice, and discrimination (DiPlacido, 1998; Silverschanz, Cortina, Konik, & Magley, 2007). LGBT students who function in a negative campus climate are at increased risk of psychological, vocational, and physical health concerns; an unwelcoming campus environment might also act as a barrier to supportive resources for LGB students who experience such concerns (D'Augelli & Rose, 1990).

Silverschanz and colleagues (2007), in exploring the prevalence of heterosexist harassment on campus, examined correlates such as psychological health and academic well-being. Findings suggested that respondents who experienced both ambient and personal heterosexist harassment had the lowest overall well-being compared to respondents who experienced only ambient heterosexist harassment and those who did not experience any heterosexist harassment (Silverschanz et al., 2007). The researchers also explored whether sexual minorities were more negatively impacted than heterosexual students, but no differences in overall well-being were found. This finding was explained by bystander stress such that heterosexual students experienced stress as a result of hearing and experiencing heterosexism in their campus environments. Silverschanz and fellow researchers (2007) contend that "an institutional environment in which anti-LGB remarks and jokes are present may have negative implications for the whole campus community, regardless of sex or sexual orientation.... [T]his suggests the harms of heterosexist victimization...may have a troublesome influence far beyond harm to any direct targets" (p. 180).

Because of the pervasive nature of homophobia and heterosexism on college and university campuses, psychosocial tasks such as choosing a major and committing to a vocational path may be more daunting for the LGBT student (Tomlinson & Fassinger, 2003). To explore this concept, Tomlinson and Fassinger (2003) conducted a study that examined the relationships among lesbian identity development, perceptions of campus climate, and vocational development. Although both lesbian identity development and perceptions of campus climate were indicated as important to consider in predicting the career path of lesbian college students, campus climate explained more of the variance of vocational development (Tomlinson & Fassinger, 2003). The researchers suggested that a negative campus climate could make a lesbian's same-sex identity more salient, which might lead her to be fearful of using campus resources such as academic advisement or career counseling. More positive perceptions of campus climate might lead her to take advantage of campus resources, which, in turn, would augment her vocational development. Thus, the findings from this study underscore the "campus climate as capable of either facilitating or inhibiting lesbian students' vocational development" (Tomlinson & Fassinger, 2003, p. 857).

Campus Climate for Queer-Spectrum and Trans-Spectrum Students

Given the importance of a positive campus climate for healthy identity development noted in the previous section, it is imperative to examine the experiences of queer-spectrum and trans-spectrum students on campus. According to researchers (Hurtado & Carter, 1997; Pascarella & Terenzini, 2005), involvement, engagement, and affiliation are central to students' development and progress in college. Furthermore, students' educational success is strongly influenced by the "context of and attitude toward their education…including their sense of school and social 'inclusion' and 'exclusion'" (Silverschanz et al., 2007, p. 181). Since development associated with the college years has far-reaching implications for students' lives, it is imperative that barriers to personal development are addressed for LGBT college students (Sorgen, 2011).

Great strides have been made since the establishment of the preeminent Student Homophile League at Columbia University in 1967. Before such campus organizing and officially recognized groups, furtive underground networks existed where fear and mistrust prevailed.[2] Today, literally thousands of campus groups composed of many thousand students organize events and support groups (Turkowitz, 2012). Despite these resources, challenges remain for queer-spectrum and trans-spectrum students on campuses, as they are not immune to the homophobic and heterosexist attitudes, environments, and behaviors perpetuated by society.

The thread of heterosexism is woven throughout the everyday experiences of LGB individuals. This context is one that has proliferated within the educational environment of middle and high schools and has spread into the college and university setting (Rankin, 2003; Rankin et al., 2010a). According to Hill and Grace (2009), the U.S. academic environment promulgates a dominant heteronormative culture. Within higher education research, the majority of findings related to campus climate are from survey-based college climate studies (Brown, Clarke, Gortmaker, & Robinson-Keilig, 2004; Malaney, Williams, & Geller, 1997; McRee & Cooper, 1998; Rankin, 2003; Rhoads, 1995; Waldo, 1999).

One of the first national studies of campus climate (Rankin et al., 2010a)—one that involved more than 5,000 LGBTQ students, staff, and faculty—found that one-quarter of LGBQ respondents and one-third of trans-identified respondents had experienced harassment or violence on their college campus because of their sexual or gender identity. Most of the rest—from 44% of gay male students, to 52% of bisexual and lesbian students, to 55% of transfeminine students, to 65% of transmasculine students—did not come out at times because of a fear of mistreatment. Some of the students who had been out in high school even went back into the closet when they entered college because they did not have the benefit of the support networks that they had before (Rankin et al., 2010a). Thus, generally speaking, if a student was out as LGBTQ, he/she/ze had likely been subjected to harassment. Given these circumstances, it is not surprising that one-third of LGBTQ students seriously considered transferring to another college or university.

Pusch (2005) asserts that many transgender students experience isolation and rejection from their family and friends. Unfortunately, these behaviors are not limited to experiences with their immediate social support network, but rather extend to experiences on campus as college students. According to Beemyn and Rankin (2011), people who are perceived as transgender often face a hostile social climate that includes behaviors ranging "from verbal harassment, to threats of violence, to acts of discrimination, to the destruction of property, to assaults and murder" (p. 24).

Campus Climate Within Athletics and Greek Systems

A number of specific student constituent groups on college or university campuses—such as athletic programs and the Greek system—might be sources of specific concern for queer-spectrum and trans-spectrum students. Wolf-Wendel and fellow researchers (2001) find the heterosexist and homophobic attitudes held by student athletes, coaches, and athletic administrators "striking," considering the differences in race, ethnicity, socioeconomic status, and gender found among the athletic community (p. 466). In their research study, they explored how sports teams respond to diversity, including race, gender, socioeconomic level, geographic region, and sexual orientation on the campuses of five Division I institutions (Wolf-Wendel et al., 2001). The authors noted that "questions about sexual orientation brought about the most highly charged responses" (Wolf-Wendel et al., 2001, p. 467). Many also denied that LGBT individuals were members of their teams or expressed a negative reaction to the idea of having LGBT team members. The overall message from the findings was that hostility toward gay men and lesbians exists on nearly all teams and at all the case study sites.

In one of the first studies to comprehensively explore the perceptions and experiences of student-athletes with regard to campus climate, Rankin and colleagues developed and tested a comprehensive model (Rankin, Merson, Sorgen, McHale, Loya, & Oseguera, 2011). This framework, the Student-Athlete Climate Conceptual Frame, suggests that individual and institutional characteristics directly influence both how student-athletes experience climate and a variety of educational outcomes unique to student-athletes (Rankin et al., 2011). At the same time, student-athletes' experiences of climate can also influence these educational outcomes. A secondary analysis of this data examining the experiences of 401 self-identified LGBTQ student-athletes was conducted by Rankin and Merson (2012). Since there were only seven student-athletes who identified as transgender, those athletes were not included in the final analysis. It was noted by the authors that most of the transgender student-athletes who identified as LGBQ competed in non-featured sports and were in Division III. The findings suggested that climate significantly affects LGBQ student-athletes' academic and athletic outcomes. LGBQ student-athletes generally perceive and experience a more negative climate than their heterosexual peers. Although sexual identity is not a direct predictor of academic success or athletic identity, the way LGBQ student-athletes experience the climate significantly influences their academic success as well as their athletic identity.

A study by Rankin (2007) explored the experiences of LGBT people who were members of fraternities and sororities between 1960 and 2007. Particular emphasis was placed on exposure to harassment as part of the students' overall perceptions and experiences with the campus and their fraternity or sorority climate. Twenty-two percent of undergraduate students indicated they were victims of harassment because of their sexual orientation, gender identity, or gender expression (Rankin, 2007). The most common forms of harassment for students were derogatory remarks and direct or indirect verbal harassment (Rankin, 2007). The perpetrators of harassment were most often another chapter member or an undergraduate student. A follow-up analysis by Rankin, Weber, and Hesp (2013) that was limited to male respondents by cohort (i.e., members who joined their chapters in the year 2000 or after, between the years 1990 and 1999, and in the year 1989 or before) revealed similar findings. Respondents who identified as gay or bisexual and who joined in the year 2000 or after reported more positive experiences overall as fraternity members than participants who joined in the year 1989 or before or between the years of 1990 and 1999. Although this finding highlighted progress for LGBT members of fraternities and sororities over the last few decades, it was suggested that hostile campus climates still exist for LGBT students.

Classroom Climate for Queer-Spectrum and Trans-Spectrum Students

The impact of diversity on the educational experience is an area that is more thoroughly explored with racial minority college students, where the "educational benefits of diversity" have been appropriately coined and substantiated through research (Hurtado, Cuellar, Alvarez, & Colin, 2009). The theoretical link between increased diversity and positive educational outcomes continues to strengthen, supporting the idea that all college students benefit from substantial encounters with diversity (Harper & Hurtado, 2007). However, these studies have predominantly focused on interactions between White, Black, and Latino students. In a review of the current landscape of LGBT research in higher education, Renn (2010) found that there has been no recent attempt to synthesize information on the place of LGBT studies within higher education curricula, academic programs, or courses.

Multiple climate studies of LGB college students reveal a theme of students feeling "invisible" and "silenced," since they do not see their experiences reflected in coursework, classroom dialogue, or through faculty relationships (Ellsworth, 1989; Evans, 2000; Gortmaker & Brown, 2006; Lopez & Chims, 1993; Rankin, 2003; Renn, 2000). In line with these findings, LGB students have been expressing the need for more courses addressing gay topics and content in the college classroom since campus climate studies began to proliferate in the 1990s (Brown et al., 2004; Rankin, 2003).

Despite the documented need in climate studies for more courses and content on gay subjects, classrooms appear to be lacking in information or dialogue that addresses the LGB experience. In one study, 43% of gay students felt that the curriculum at their institution did not represent gay issues or perspectives (Rankin, 2003). To homosexual students especially, an incomplete curriculum implies that they are to see themselves as deviant, psychologically abnormal, invisible, or, at best, barely tolerated (Crumpacker & Vander Haegen, 1987).

An analysis of the LGBT classroom experience by DeSurra and Church (1994), as identified in Connolly (2000), describes four ways in which gay students may experience homophobic messages in the classroom setting. The first type of message is *explicit marginalization*, defined as overt homophobic messages. An example is a classroom where a faculty member explicitly states that gay health-related issues will not be addressed in a public health course, as they are not relevant. The second type of message is *implicit marginalization*, which is defined as a classroom that includes subtle and indirect homophobic messages. For example, a faculty member in a public health course might state that all gay health-related concerns will be addressed by a review of the AIDS epidemic. The third type is *implicit centralization*, or a message that includes explicit and implicit messages about the experiences and perspectives of gay individuals. An example would be a public health course that has multiple classes that address LGB health issues, and within each class a new area of focus is highlighted. The last message described is an *explicit centralization* that informs students about the marginalized experiences of gay individuals, and this framework is actively integrated within the course (DeSurra & Church, 1994). A course that exemplifies *explicit centralization* would be a public health course that focuses entirely on the history of gay health in the United States in the 1900s.

Based upon the available LGB research, it appears that classrooms described as *explicitly centralized* are rare (Evans, 2000). When gay students do find classes that have gay subject matter, they seek them out as "safe spaces" to learn more about issues that often remain unexplored.

Therefore, "gay courses" can be a fertile learning ground for all students (Evans, 2000). Based on an assessment of the research in this field, most classroom experiences would be best depicted by the idea of *implicit marginalization*. Although gay students are not experiencing overt discrimination, they are subject to heterosexist language and ideology within the course, as well as a lack of classroom discussion on sexual orientation. This situation may contribute to feelings of being silenced and invalidated, which can lead to mentally and cognitively disengaging from the course. The result is a less-than-optimal learning experience (Evans, 2000).

With a focus on overall climate concerns, there has been limited research on the experience of LGB students inside the classroom at the college level, and even less in graduate school (Schueler, Hoffman, & Peterson, 2008; Turkowitz, 2012). With its entrenched tendency to replace heteronormativity, fighting back has proven an arduous task requiring the courage and persistence of queer adult educators and graduate students (Hill & Grace, 2009). A recent study of over 8,000 college students across 130 colleges that examined student perceptions of the learning environment found that over two-thirds of students observed discrimination directed toward LGB students (Cress, 2008). In fact, LGB students received the highest level of reported discrimination directed at any group on campus as compared to racial minorities and individuals with disabilities (Renn, 2010).

Overall, there has been slow progress among colleges in implementing practices to improve the learning environment of LGB students (Brown et al., 2004; Rankin, 2003). Within college campus studies, there is also preliminary data to suggest that LGB students have negative experiences in the college classroom connected to their sexual identity (Gortmaker & Brown, 2006; Hill & Grace, 2009; McRee & Cooper, 1998; Rankin, 2003) and that this negative climate may lead to LGB students feeling silenced and disengaged from classroom dynamics (Evans, 2000; Lucozzi, 1998).

According to Sanlo (2004), there is a need to identify the stressors faced by LGB college students and how those stressors affect students' academic achievement and success in college. It is rare to witness classroom conversations among students related to issues of sexual orientation (Evans, 2001). Although this suggests a more subtle type of discrimination against LGB college students, this situation may contribute to feelings of being silenced and invalidated that can lead to cognitive disengagement from the course (Sue, 2010). For example, in the classroom, LGB students can be subject to heterosexist language and prevailing ideas in the course content that are exclusionary of the perspective and experiences of LGB individuals. Overall, a less inclusive classroom setting can cause gay students to have an inferior learning experience (Evans, 2000).

Findings specific to the classroom climate for LGBTQ students are similar to reports of overall campus climate. In the earliest climate studies conducted on the basis of gender, the expression "chilly classroom" was coined to signify that a classroom climate does not have to be overtly hostile to affect learning; even neglect of LGBT issues can result in a "chilly" or unwelcoming environment (Ambrose, Bridges, DiPietro, Lovett, & Norman, 2010; Hall & Sandler, 1984). In fact, an accumulation of subtle forms of marginalization or "micro-inequities" can have a profound negative impact on learning (Ambrose et al., 2010; Hall & Sandler, 1984).

Numerous scholars have documented the negative experiences of LGBTQ college students in the classroom (Gortmaker & Brown, 2006; Rankin, 2003). Lovaas, Baroudi, and Collins (2002) found that "issues dealing with gender and sexuality present special challenges for teachers and students, both when these subjects are the clearly marked focus of a course and when they arise in the midst of seemingly unrelated classroom discussions" (p. 178). Furthermore, Lopez & Chims (1993) offered that students did not believe that LGB topics were adequately discussed in class or academic programs and "were afraid to disclose their identity in situations in which they felt the instructor might retaliate by grading them lower, might make them 'an object' in class, or might patronize them by giving them special treatment" (Lopez & Chims, 1993, p. 98).

There has been no recent attempt to synthesize information on LGBT studies within the higher education curriculum, academic program, or courses (Renn, 2000; Renn, 2010). Rankin (2003) noted: "A heterosexist climate has not only inhibited the acknowledgment and expression of GLBT perspectives, it has also limited curricular initiatives and research efforts, as seen in the lack of GLBT content in the university course offerings" (p. 3).

Research on trans-spectrum students, though limited, yields similar findings (Bilodeau, 2005, 2009; Hart & Lester, 2011). The National Center for Transgender Equality (NCTE) released its 2011 report on national transgender discrimination, documenting oppression against transgender and gender non-conforming Americans. Regarding discrimination in education, the report revealed that harassment among transgender and gender non-conforming students was so severe that it led almost one-sixth of respondents to leave their schools (Grant, Mottet, & Tanis, 2011). This study examined classroom climate for queer-spectrum and trans-spectrum students. Earlier researchers demonstrated a hostile campus and classroom climate for LGBTQ students, yet they oftentimes conflated sexuality and gender. Research among trans-spectrum individuals, though limited, has documented significantly higher rates of harassment and chillier climates than queer-spectrum students. Garvey and Rankin (in review) found that among LGBTQ students, trans-spectrum students have more negative perceptions of classroom climate than queer-spectrum students, with a strong correlation between campus climate and classroom climate for LGBTQ undergraduate students.

Influence of Climate on Queer-Spectrum and Trans-Spectrum Students' Well-Being

Thirty years of research chronicle the disproportionately higher rates of depressive symptoms, substance use/abuse, suicidal ideation, and suicide attempts among queer-spectrum and trans-spectrum youth (Almeida, Johnson, Corliss, Molnar, & Azrael, 2009; Cabaj, 2000; Diamond et al., 2012; Fergusson, Horwood, Ridder, & Beautrais, 2005; Hughes & Eliason, 2002; Poteat, Espelage, & Koenig, 2009; Weber, 2008; Zhao, Montoro, Igartua, & Thombs, 2010). Many of these studies, particularly those that are older, were based on clinical samples, and none focused exclusively on college students. Although there is a growing body of literature on the campus climate for trans-spectrum and queer-spectrum students, few studies have examined the influence of campus climate on health outcomes (Reed, Prado, Matsumoto, & Amaro, 2010; Silverschanz et al., 2007; Waldo, Hessen-McInnis, & D'Augelli, 1998; Woodford, Krentzman, & Gattis, 2012). There are no studies that have specifically examined the relationship between suicidality and campus climate among these students.

Alcohol and Drug Use/Abuse

Experiences with harassment place queer-spectrum and trans-spectrum individuals at high risk for alcohol and drug use/abuse (Cabaj, 2000; Flowers & Buston, 2001; Weber, 2008). Previous studies noted that binge drinking is more prevalent among LGB college students than their heterosexual counterparts and that there is a relationship between psychological distress and alcohol use for LGB college students (DeBord, Wood, Sher, & Good, 1998). Using minority stress as a conceptual framework, Woodford, Howell, Silverschanz, and Yu (2012) found that sexual minority college students were more likely to experience and witness incivility (disrespectful behaviors) and hostility (overt violence), and that personal incivility and witnessing hostility were associated with greater odds of problematic drinking. McCabe, Bostwick, Hughes, West, and Boyd (2010) reported similar findings when they examined the relationship between discrimination and alcohol and drug use among LGB adults, concluding that LGB adults who experienced discrimination were four times more likely to use alcohol and drugs than LGB adults who did not (McCabe et al., 2010). Findings by Weber (2008) further substantiate the role of minority stress in the mental health and behavioral problems for LGB adults. Weber (2008) found that LGB individuals who experienced heterosexist events were more likely to have an alcohol or drug use disorder. These studies and others generally conclude that experiences with minority stress place LGB individuals at high risk for adverse mental health outcomes, including alcohol and drug use/abuse.

Depression and Suicide

Over the past decade, an increasing number of researchers have agreed that the social stigma and discrimination associated with LGBTQI identities are contributing factors to elevated rates of depression and suicide (Haas et al., 2010). Discrimination at the individual level (hostility, harassment, bullying, and physical violence) and institutional level (laws and public policies) has been identified as a risk factor for depression, social isolation, and hopelessness which, in turn, place LGBTQ people at risk for contemplating suicide (Diamond et al., 2012; Haas et al., 2010).

Based on analyses by the National Longitudinal Study of Adolescent Health (NLSAH), LGB adolescents were at increased risk for depressive symptoms and suicidality compared to their heterosexual peers (Galliher, Rostosky, & Hughes, 2004; Russell & Joyner, 2001; Silenzio, Pena, Duberstein, Cerel, & Knox, 2007). In particular, LGB youths were more than two times more likely to attempt suicide (Galliher et al., 2004). Furthermore, using data from the NLSAH, problem alcohol use and depression were identified as risk factors for suicidal ideation among LGB respondents (Silenzio et al., 2007). Victimization was found to be associated with suicidality for all LGB youth who participated in the NLSAH (Russell & Joyner, 2001).

Among college students, existing studies also indicate that sexual minorities are at increased risk for poorer mental health, including suicide attempts (Kisch, Leino, & Silverman, 2005). LGB students have been found to be more depressed and lonely, and had fewer reasons for living compared to heterosexual students (Westefeld, Maples, Buford, & Taylor, 2001). Similarly, using data from the 1999–2000 National College Health Assessment Survey, Kisch and colleagues (2005) found that being non-heterosexual was a risk factor for seriously considering suicide at least once in the past school year. In terms of rates of suicide among LGBTQ individuals, it is difficult to determine prevalence rates because sexual identity/gender identity information is not recorded in death records; however, over a one-month period in 2010, seven LGBTQI youth and young adult suicides received national media attention.

Institutional Policies and Resources

In response to the victimization of LGBTQI students, many colleges and universities have developed more inclusive policies and/or created resources to assist LGBTQI students (Biegel

& Kuehl, 2010; Rankin et al., 2010a; Zemsky & Sanlo, 2005). Some policy and resource responses have included equal opportunity statements, extending same-sex benefits to partners, creating or supporting LGBT centers, and providing health care for transitioning transgender students (Sanlo, 2004; Zemsky & Sanlo, 2005). The Campus Pride's LGBT-Friendly Campus Climate Index, a tool for measuring campus LGBTQI policies, programs, and practices, notes the importance of inclusive institutional policies and resources in creating a more welcoming climate for LGBTQI students.[3] Only one study has examined the influence of LGBT campus resources on substance use, specifically binge drinking among LGB students (Eisenberg & Wechsler, 2003). In addition to not exploring other health outcomes, Eisenberg and Wechsler's study did not include transgender students.

Beyond the Rainbow

The previous review indicates that, in addition to the normative challenges of college, queer-spectrum and trans-spectrum youth are often exposed to stressors related to their identity, including harassment, discrimination, and violence (Beemyn & Rankin, 2011; Marine, 2011). Internalized stigma related to LGBTQI identity and exposure to discrimination can contribute to negative outcomes among queer-spectrum and trans-spectrum students (Halpin & Allen, 2004; Meyer, 2003; Rankin et al., 2010a; Sorgen, 2011; Weber, 2008). These stressors may aggravate health disparities among these students, including substance use/abuse (Kisch et al., 2005; Oswalt & Wyatt, 2011), depression, and suicide ideation/attempts (Galliher et al., 2004; Russell & Joyner, 2001), and increase risks for leaving their college/university (Reason, 2009). Research provides insights into the challenges and negative behavioral responses of queer-spectrum and trans-spectrum students, but the findings and generalizability are limited, as they are often single-institution studies with small sample sizes (Rankin et al., 2010a; Silverschanz et al., 2007; Woodford, Howell, et al., 2012; Woodford, Krentzman, et al., 2012), thereby preventing sub-group analysis (e.g., gay men as compared to pansexual). Also, researchers have not considered internalized stigma, and very few have examined potential protective factors such as spirituality and institutional resources (Byrd & McKinney, 2012). Finally, no study has examined these factors among transgender students, the role of intersecting identities (e.g., gender, sexuality, race, class), or the relationship between psychological health risks and academic outcomes among LGBTQI college students (Sanlo, 2004; Silverschanz et al., 2007). Research suggests that institutional policies and non-discrimination statements augmented by supportive services are fundamental to creating positive changes in the campus climate for LGBT community members (McRee & Cooper, 1998). Based on the recent Campus Climate Index[4] and information from the Consortium[5] since 2003, many institutions have developed more inclusive policies (e.g., added sexual orientation and/or gender identity to their non-discrimination clause; added domestic partner benefits, etc.). In addition, there has been an increase in the number of campuses with LGBT Resource Centers and both curricular and co-curricular programs.

Despite the persistence of anti-LGBTQ harassment on college campuses, heterosexual and cisgender (non-transgender) students have become more supportive of their queer- and trans-spectrum peers over the last two decades. One indication of this growing support is the findings of the annual national survey of first-year students conducted by the Cooperative Institutional Research Program (CIRP). Since 1973, CIRP has asked incoming students their opinion on same-sex marriage, and the level of support has grown to the point that today about two-thirds of respondents indicate their approval (Higher Education Research Institute, 2011). At more "progressive" colleges, the percentage of entering students in favor of same-sex marriage is often greater than three-fourths (Higher Education Research Institute, 2011). In 2010, CIRP introduced a question on attitudes toward lesbians and gay men adopting children, and more than three-fourths of the respondents agreed that they should have the legal right to do so. Even more than half the students who self-identified as "conservative" or "far right" supported lesbians and gay men adopting (Higher Education Research Institute, 2011). Further, experimentation with one's sexual orientation and gender identity, once decried by college administrators as "immoral" and "perverse" (Paley, 2002a, 2002b) is now unremarked upon at all but the most conservative campuses.

The parents of queer-spectrum and trans-spectrum students have likewise become more supportive overall of their children in recent years. In the 1990s, when the authors began working with queer-spectrum and trans-spectrum college students, a frequent narrative was for students to report that they had been financially cut off by their parents, if not thrown out of the house, when they came out to them. Sadly, this scenario is by no means an anachronism. However, the opposite trend has emerged and, seemingly, has become more common in the last decade: parents who fully embrace their children's gender and sexual identity and who help them look for an LGBTQ-friendly college. It has been a tremendous sea change, from being asked for support by students who are afraid to come out to their parents, to working with parents who want an institution to be as supportive of their queer-spectrum and trans-spectrum children as they can. It is hoped that the high expectations of students and parents will push campuses to be more LGBTQ inclusive.

In response to the negative experiences of the campus climate on the part of queer-spectrum and trans-spectrum students, many colleges and universities have implemented structural changes on their campuses. The individuals who sought change and initiated change were usually LGBT faculty members, staff members, and students or heterosexual allies (Messinger, 2009). Such changes include forming committees that are charged with the task of improving the quality of life for LGBT students and employees; creating LGBT resource centers and safe space programs; offering at least one course on gay and lesbian topics; offering a formal academic program in gay and lesbian studies; offering domestic partner health benefits; offering gay and lesbian residential areas; encouraging preferential hiring for LGB individuals; providing new staff orientation programs inclusive of LGBT issues; and instituting nondiscrimination policies inclusive of sexual identity (Malaney et al., 1997). Findings from a study by Sears (2002) underscore the positive outcomes of implementing structural changes. LGB faculty respondents from Sears's (2002) study who work at a college or university with a non-discrimination statement that includes sexual orientation, a curriculum that offers courses in LGB studies, or one that provides partner benefits are more likely to perceive their campus climate as positive as compared to those who do not report such structural changes.

With the positive results shown by including sexual orientation and gender identity in a non-discrimination policy, one might wonder how many institutions have implemented such policies. Self-reported data provided to the Human Rights Campaign identified 823 (19%) of U.S. colleges/universities that currently offer protection against discrimination on the basis of sexual identity, with 632 (15%) protecting on the basis of gender identity.[6]

Recommendations for future research and promising best practices have been offered in recent studies by Beemyn and Rankin (2011), Marine (2011), and Rankin and fellow researchers (2011). Other recommended resources include the Campus Pride Friendly Campus Index,[7] Promising Practices for Inclusion of Gender Identity/Gender Expression in Higher Education,[8] and the Consortium for LGBT Professionals in Higher Education Architect.[9]

Notes

1. Given the fluid and evolving sexual and gender identities of individuals, we use the terms queer-spectrum and trans-spectrum to value how individuals chose to identify themselves as opposed to placing them into socially constructed, fixed categories of sexuality and gender. That said, in the majority of the literature examining sexual identity and gender identity, researchers use the acronym "LGBT" to reference sexual and gender minorities. Our paradigm suggests that sexual identities and gender identities are fluid. We feel it is important to value individual identities, as opposed to placing people into fixed, socially constructed categories of sexuality or gender (Rankin, Weber, Blumenfeld, & Frazer, 2010b). In our summary of the literature offered here we will use the terminology that the authors have used in their own studies (e.g., LGB, LGBT, LGBQ, etc.), while any synthesis and discussion will adopt the queer-spectrum and trans-spectrum language.
2. For a more comprehensive review of the LGBTQ student history on college campuses, the reader is referred to Susan Marine's 2011 work, "Stonewall's Legacy: Bisexual, Gay, Lesbian, and Transgender Students in Higher Education." *ASHE Higher Education Report, 37*(4).
3. http://www.campusprideindex.org/
4. http://www.campusclimateindex.org
5. http://www.lgbtcampus.org
6. http://www.hrc.org/issues/workplace.asp; http://www.transgenderlaw.org/college/index.htm#policies
7. http://www.campusprideindex.org/
8. http://www.campuspride.org/tools/promising-practices-for-inclusion-of-gender-identitygender-expression-in-higher-education/
9. http://www.lgbtcampus.org/architect

References

Almeida, J., Johnson, R.M., Corliss, H.L., Molnar, B.E., & Azrael, D. (2009). Emotional distress among LGBT youth: The influence of perceived discrimination based on sexual orientation. *Journal of Youth and Adolescence, 38*(7), 1001–1014.

Ambrose, S.A., Bridges, M.W., DiPietro, M., Lovett, M.C., & Norman, M.K. (2010). *How learning works: Seven research-based principles for smart teaching.* Hoboken, NJ: John Wiley.

Beemyn, G., & Rankin, S. (2011). *The lives of transgender people.* New York, NY: Columbia University Press.

Biegel, S., & Kuehl, S.J. (2010). *Safe at school: Addressing the school environment and LGBT safety through policy and legislation.* Boulder, CO: National Education Policy Center.

Bilodeau, B. (2005). Beyond the gender binary: A case study of two transgender students at a midwestern research university. *Journal of Gay and Lesbian Issues in Education, 3*(1), 29–44.

Bilodeau, B. (2009). *Genderism: Transgender students, binary systems and higher education.* Saarbrücken, Germany: Verlag Dr. Müller.

Bilodeau, B., & Renn, K.A. (2005). Analysis of LGBT identity development models and implications for practice. In R.L. Sanlo (Ed.), *Sexual orientation and gender identity: New directions for student services* (Vol. 111, pp. 25–40). San Francisco, CA: Jossey-Bass.

Brown, R.D., Clarke, B., Gortmaker, V., & Robinson-Keilig, R. (2004). Assessing the campus climate for gay, lesbian, bisexual, and transgender (GLBT) students using a multiple perspectives approach. *Journal of College Student Development, 45*(1), 8–26.

Byrd, D.R., & McKinney, K.J. (2012). Individual, interpersonal, and institutional level factors associated with the mental health of college students. *Journal of American College Health, 60*(3), 185–193.

Cabaj, R.P. (2000). Substance abuse, internalized homophobia, and gay men and lesbians: Psychodynamic issues and clinical implications. *Journal of Gay & Lesbian Psychotherapy, 3*(3–4), 5–24.

Cass, V.C. (1979). Homosexual identity formation: A theoretical model. *Journal of Homosexuality, 4*(3), 219–235.

Cass, V.C. (1984). Homosexual identity formation: Testing a theoretical model. *Journal of Sex Research, 20*(2), 143–167.

Chauncey, G. (1994). *Gay New York: Gender, urban culture, and the makings of the gay male world, 1890–1940.* New York, NY: Basic Books.

Connolly, M. (2000). Issues for lesbian, gay, and bisexual students in traditional college classrooms. In V.A. Wall & N.J. Evans (Eds.), *Toward acceptance: Sexual orientation issues on campus* (pp. 109–130). Lanham, MD: University Press of America.

Cress, C.M. (2008). Creating inclusive learning communities: The role of student-faculty relationships in mitigating negative campus climate. *Learning Inquiry, 2*(2), 95–111.

Crumpacker, L., & Vander Haegen, E.M. (1987). Pedagogy and prejudice: Strategies for confronting homophobia in the classroom. *Women's Studies Quarterly, 15*(3–4), 65–73.

D'Augelli, A.R. (1994). Identity development and sexual orientation: Toward a model of lesbian, gay, and bisexual development. In E.J. Trickett, R.J. Watts, & D. Birman (Eds.), *Human diversity: Perspectives on people in context* (pp. 312–333). San Francisco, CA: Jossey-Bass.

D'Augelli, A.R., & Rose, M.L. (1990). Homophobia in a university community: Attitudes and experiences of heterosexual freshmen. *Journal of College Student Development, 31*(6), 484–491.

DeBord, K.A., Wood, P.K., Sher, K.J., & Good, G.E. (1998). The relevance of sexual orientation to substance abuse and psychological distress among college students. *Journal of College Student Development, 39*(2), 157–168.

DeSurra, C.J., & Church, K.A. (1994, November). *Unlocking the classroom closet: Privileging the marginalized voices of gay/lesbian college students.* Paper presented at the Annual Meeting of the Speech Communication Association, New Orleans, LA.

Diamond, G.M., Diamond, G.S., Levy, S., Closs, C., Ladipo, T., & Siqueland, L. (2012). Attachment-based family therapy for suicidal lesbian, gay, and bisexual adolescents: A treatment development study and open trial with preliminary findings. *Psychotherapy, 49*(1), 62–71.

DiPlacido, J. (1998). Minority stress among lesbians, gay men, and bisexuals: A consequence of heterosexism, homophobia, and stigmatization. In G. Herek (Ed.), *Stigma and sexual orientation* (pp. 138–159). Thousand Oaks, CA: Sage.

Eisenberg, M., & Wechsler, H. (2003). Social influences on substance-use behaviors of gay, lesbian, and bisexual college students: Findings from a national study. *Social Science & Medicine, 57*(10), 1913–1923. doi: 10.1016/S0277-9536(03)00057-1

Ellsworth, E. (1989). Why doesn't this feel empowering? Working through the repressive myths of critical pedagogy. *Harvard Educational Review, 59*(3), 297–324.

Evans, N.J. (2000). Creating a positive learning environment for gay, lesbian, and bisexual students. *New Directions for Teaching and Learning, 2000*(82), 81–87.

Evans, N.J. (2001). The experiences of lesbian, gay, and bisexual youths in university communities. In A.R. D'Augelli & C.J. Patterson (Eds.), *Lesbian, gay, and bisexual identities and youth: Psychological perspectives* (pp. 181–198). Oxford, UK: Oxford University Press.

Evans, N.J., & Broido, E. (1999). Coming out in college residence halls: Negotiation, meaning making, challenges, supports. *Journal of College Student Development, 40*(6), 658-668.

Fassinger, R. (1991). The hidden minority: Issues and challenges in working with lesbian women and gay men. *Counseling Psychologist, 19*(2), 157–176.

Fassinger, R. (1998). Lesbian, gay, and bisexual identity and student development theory. In R. L. Sanlo (Ed.), *Working with lesbian, gay, bisexual, and transgender college students* (pp. 13–22). Westport, CT. Greenwood Press.

Fassinger, R., & Miller, B. (1997). Validation of an inclusive model of sexual minority identity formation on a sample of gay men. *Journal of Homosexuality, 32*(2), 53–78.

Fergusson, D.M., Horwood, L.J., Ridder, E.M., & Beautrais, A.L. (2005). Subthreshold depression in adolescence and mental health outcomes in adulthood. *Archives of General Psychiatry, 62*(1), 66–72.

Flowers, P., & Buston, K. (2001). "I was terrified of being different": Exploring gay men's accounts of growing-up in a heterosexist society. *Journal of Adolescence, 24*(1), 51–65.

Galliher, R.V., Rostosky, S.S., & Hughes, H.K. (2004). School belonging, self-esteem, and depressive symptoms in adolescents: An examination of sex, sexual attraction status, and urbanicity. *Journal of Youth and Adolescence, 33*(3), 235–245.

Garvey, J., & Rankin, S. (In review). Making the grade? Examining the classroom climate for queer spectrum and trans-spectrum students. *Journal of Diversity in Higher Education.*

Gonsiorek, J. (1995). Gay male identities: Concepts and issues. In A.R. D'Augelli & C.J. Patterson (Eds.), *Lesbian, gay, and bisexual identities over the lifespan: Psychological perspectives.* New York, NY: Oxford University Press.

Gortmaker, V., & Brown, R. (2006). Out of the closet: Differences in perceptions and experiences among out lesbian and gay students. *College Student Journal, 40*, 606–619.

Grant, J., Mottet, L., & Tanis, D. (2011). *Injustice at every turn: A report of the National Transgender Discrimination Survey.* Washington, DC: National Gay and Lesbian Task Force.

Haas, A.P., Eliason, M., Mays, V.M., Mathy, R.M., Cochran, S.D., D'Augelli, A.R. … Rosario, M. (2010). Suicide and suicide risk in lesbian, gay, bisexual, and transgender populations: Review and recommendations. *Journal of Homosexuality, 58*(1), 10–51.

Hall, R., & Sandler, R. (1984). *Out of the classroom: A chilly campus climate for women?* Washington, DC: Association of American Colleges.

Halpin, S.A., & Allen, M.W. (2004). Changes in psychosocial well-being during stages of gay identity development. *Journal of Homosexuality, 47*(2), 109–126.

Harper, S.R., & Hurtado, S. (2007). Nine themes in campus racial climates and implications for institutional transformation. *New Directions for Student Services, 2007*(120), 7–24. doi: doi.org/10.1002/ss.254

Hart, J., & Lester, J. (2011). Starring students: Gender performance at a women's college. *NASPA Journal About Women in Higher Education, 4*(2), 193–217.

Higher Education Research Institute. (2011). *Diverse learning environments: Assessing and creating conditions for student success.* Retrieved from http://heri.ucla.edu/dle/index.php

Hill, R.J., & Grace, A.P. (2009). *Adult and higher education in queer contexts: Power, politics, and pedagogy.* Chicago, IL: Discovery Association.

Hogan, T.L., & Rentz, A.L. (1996). Homophobia in the academy. *Journal of College Student Development, 37*(3), 309–314.

Hughes, T.L., & Eliason, M. (2002). Substance use and abuse in lesbian, gay, bisexual and transgender populations. *Journal of Primary Prevention, 22*(3), 263–298.

Hurtado, S., & Carter, D.F. (1997). Effects of college transition and perceptions of the campus racial climate on Latino college students' sense of belonging. *Sociology of Education, 70*(4), 324–345.

Hurtado, S., Cuellar, M., Alvarez, C.L., & Colin, L. (2009, May). *Assessing diverse learning environments: Integrating assessments of campus climate, practices, and outcomes.* Paper presented at the NCORE, San Diego, CA.

Kisch, J., Leino, E.V., & Silverman, M.M. (2005). Aspects of suicidal behavior, depression, and treatment in college students: Results from the Spring 2000 national college health assessment survey. *Suicide and Life-Threatening Behavior, 35*(1), 3–13.

Kosciw, J., Greytak, E., Diaz, E., & Bartkiewicz, M. (2010). *The 2009 national school climate survey: The experiences of lesbian, gay, bisexual and transgender youth in our nation's schools.* New York, NY: Gay, Lesbian and Straight Education Network.

Lopez, G., & Chims, N. (1993). Classroom concerns of gay and lesbian students: The invisible minority. *College Teaching, 41*(3), 97–103.

Lovaas, K.E., Baroudi, L., & Collins, S. (2002). Transcending heteronormativity in the classroom: Using queer and critical pedagogies to alleviate trans-anxieties. *Journal of Lesbian Studies, 6*(3–4), 177–189.

Lucozzi, E. (1998). A far better place: Institutions as allies. In R.L. Sanlo (Ed.), *Working with lesbian, gay, bisexual, and transgender college students: A handbook for faculty and administrators* (pp. 47–52). Westport, CT: Greenwood Press.

Macgillivray, I.K. (2007). *Gay-straight alliances: A handbook for students, educators, and parents.* New York, NY: Harrington Park Press.

Malaney, G., Williams, E., & Geller, W. (1997). Assessing campus climate for gays, lesbians, and bisexuals at two institutions. *Journal of College Student Development, 38*(4), 365–375.

Marine, S.B. (2011). Stonewall's legacy: Bisexual, gay, lesbian, and transgender students in higher education. *ASHE Higher Education Report, 37*(4), 1–145.

Martin, H.P. (1991). The coming-out process for homosexuals. *Hospital & Community Psychiatry, 42*(2), 158–162.

McCabe, S.E., Bostwick, W.B., Hughes, T.L., West, B.T., & Boyd, C.J. (2010). The relationship between discrimination and substance use disorders among lesbian, gay, and bisexual adults in the United States. *American Journal of Public Health, 100*(10), 1946–1952.

McCarn, S., & Fassinger, R. (1996). Revisioning sexual minority identity formation: A new model of lesbian identity and its implications for counseling and research. *Counseling Psychologist, 24*(3), 508–534. doi: 10.1177/0011000096243011

McRee, T.K., & Cooper, D.L. (1998). Campus environments for gay, lesbian, and bisexual students at southeastern institutions of higher education. *Journal of Student Affairs Research and Practice, 36*(1), 1–13.

Messinger, L. (2009). Creating LGBTQ-friendly campuses. *Academe, 95*(5), 39–42.

Meyer, I.H. (2003). Prejudice, social stress, and mental health in lesbian, gay, and bisexual populations: Conceptual issues and research evidence. *Psychological Bulletin, 129*(5), 674–697.

Oswalt, S.B., & Wyatt, T.J. (2011). Sexual orientation and differences in mental health, stress, and academic performance in a national sample of U.S. college students. *Journal of Homosexuality, 58*(9), 1255–1280.

Paley, A. (2002a). The secret court of 1920, Part I. *Harvard Crimson*. Retrieved from http://www.thecrimson.harvard.edu/article/2002/11/21/the-secret-court-of-1920-at/

Paley, A. (2002b). The secret court of 1920, Part II. *Harvard Crimson*. Retrieved from http://www.thecrimson.com/article/2002/11/21/the-secret-court-of-1920

Pascarella, E.T., & Terenzini, P.T. (2005). *How college affects students: A third decade of research* (Vol. 2). San Francisco, CA: Jossey-Bass.

Poteat, V.P., Espelage, D.L., & Koenig, B.W. (2009). Willingness to remain friends and attend school with lesbian and gay peers: Relational expressions of prejudice among heterosexual youth. *Journal of Youth and Adolescence, 38*(7), 952–962.

Pusch, R.S. (2005). Transgender college students' perceptions of the reactions of others. *Journal of Gay and Lesbian Issues in Education, 3*(1), 45–61.

Rankin, S. (2003). *Campus climate for gay, lesbian, bisexual, and transgendered people: A national perspective*. New York, NY: National Gay and Lesbian Task Force Policy Institute.

Rankin, S. (2007). *Experiences of gay men in fraternities: From 1960 to 2007*. Charlotte, NC: Lambda 10 Project.

Rankin, S., & Merson, D. (2012). *LGBTQ college athlete national report*. Charlotte, NC: Campus Pride.

Rankin, S., Merson, D., Sorgen, C., McHale, I., Loya, K., & Oseguera, L. (2011). *Student-Athlete Climate Study (SACS) final report*. University Park, PA: Pennsylvania State University.

Rankin, S., Weber, G., Blumenfeld, W., & Frazer, S. (2010a). *2010 state of higher education for lesbian, gay, bisexual & transgender people*. Charlotte, NC: Campus Pride.

Rankin, S., Weber, G., Blumenfeld, W., & Frazer, M.S. (2010b). *2010 state of higher education for LGBT people*. Charlotte, NC: Campus Pride.

Rankin, S., Weber, G., & Hesp, G. (2013). Experiences and perceptions of gay and bisexual fraternity members from 1960 to 2007: A cohort analysis. *Journal of College Student Development, 14*(5), 12–27.

Reason, R. (2009). An examination of persistence research through the lens of a comprehensive conceptual framework. *Journal of College Student Development, 50*(6), 659–682.

Reed, E., Prado, G., Matsumoto, A., & Amaro, H. (2010). Alcohol and drug use and related consequences among gay, lesbian and bisexual college students: Role of experiencing violence, feeling safe on campus, and perceived stress. *Addictive Behaviors, 35*(2), 168–171.

Renn, K.A. (2000). Including all voices in the classroom: Teaching lesbian, gay, and bisexual students. *College Teaching, 48*(4), 129–135.

Renn, K.A. (2010). LGBT and queer research in higher education: The state and status of the field. *Educational Researcher, 39*(2), 132–141. doi:10.3102/0013189X10362579

Rhoads, R.A. (1995). Learning from the coming-out experiences of college males. *Journal of College Student Development, 36*(1), 67–74.

Russell, S.T., & Joyner, K. (2001). Adolescent sexual orientation and suicide risk: Evidence from a national study. *American Journal of Public Health, 91*(8), 1276–1281.

Sanlo, R.L. (2004). Lesbian, gay, and bisexual college students: Risk, resiliency, and retention. *Journal of College Student Retention, 6*(1), 97–110.

Savin-Williams, R.C., & Demo, D.H. (1984). Developmental change and stability in adolescent self-concept. *Developmental Psychology, 20*(6), 1100–1110.

Schueler, L., Hoffman, J., & Peterson, E. (2008). Fostering safe, engaging campuses for lesbian, gay, bisexual, transgender, and questioning students' engagement in higher education. In S.J. Quaye & S.R. Harper (Eds.), *Student engagement in higher education: Theoretical perspectives and practical approaches for diverse populations* (pp. 61–79). New York, NY: Routledge.

Sears, J.T. (2002). The institutional climate for lesbian, gay and bisexual education faculty. *Journal of Homosexuality, 43*(1), 11–37. doi: 10.1300/J082v43n01_02

Silenzio, V.M., Pena, J.B., Duberstein, P.R., Cerel, J., & Knox, K.L. (2007). Sexual orientation and risk factors for suicidal ideation and suicide attempts among adolescents and young adults. *American Journal of Public Health, 97*(11), 217–219.

Silverschanz, P., Cortina, L., Konik, J., & Magley, V. (2007). Slurs, snubs, and queer jokes: Incidence and impact of heterosexist harassment in academia. *Sex Roles, 58*(3–4), 179–191. doi: 10.1007/s11199-007-9329-7

Sorgen, C.H. (2011). *The influence of sexual identity on higher education outcomes* (Unpublished doctoral dissertation). The Pennsylvania State University, University Park.

Sue, D. (2010). *Microaggressions in everyday life: Race, gender and sexual orientation*. Hoboken, NJ: John Wiley.

Tomlinson, M.J., & Fassinger, R.E. (2003). Career development, lesbian identity development, and campus climate among lesbian college students. *Journal of College Student Development, 44*(6), 845–860.

Troiden, R.R. (1989). The formation of homosexual identities. *Journal of Homosexuality, 17*(1–2), 43–73.

Turkowitz, A. (2012). *Navigating the nuances: The experiences of lesbian, gay and bisexual students in the graduate classroom* (Unpublished doctoral dissertation). Teachers College, Columbia University, New York, NY.

Waldo, C. (1999). Out on campus: Sexual orientation and academic climate in a university context. *American Journal of Community Psychology, 26*(4), 745–774. doi: 10.1023/A:1022110031745

Waldo, C., Hessen-McInnis, M., & D'Augelli, A.R. (1998). Antecedents and consequences of victimization of lesbian, gay, and bisexual young people: A structural model comparing rural university and urban samples. *American Journal of Community Psychology, 26*(2), 307–334.

Weber, G.N. (2008). Using to numb the pain: Substance use and abuse among lesbian, gay, and bisexual individuals. *Journal of Mental Health Counseling, 30*(1), 31–48.

Westefeld, J.S., Maples, M.R., Buford, B., & Taylor, S. (2001). Gay, lesbian, and bisexual college students: The relationship between sexual orientation and depression, loneliness, and suicide. *Journal of College Student Psychotherapy, 15*(3), 71–82.

Wolf-Wendel, L., Toma, J.D., & Morphew, C. (2001). How much difference is too much difference? Perceptions of gay men and lesbians in intercollegiate athletics. *Journal of College Student Development, 42*(5), 465–479.

Woodford, M.R., Howell, M.L., Silverschanz, P., & Yu, L. (2012). "That's so gay!": Examining the covariates of hearing this expression among gay, lesbian, and bisexual college students. *Journal of American College Health, 60*(6), 429–434.

Woodford, M.R., Krentzman, A.R., & Gattis, M.N. (2012). Alcohol and drug use among sexual minority college students and their heterosexual counterparts: The effects of experiencing and witnessing incivility and hostility on campus. *Substance Abuse and Rehabilitation, 3*, 11–23.

Zemsky, B., & Sanlo, R.L. (2005). Do policies matter? *New Directions for Student Services, 2005*(111), 7–15.

Zhao, Y., Montoro, R., Igartua, K., & Thombs, B.D. (2010). Suicidal ideation and attempt among adolescents reporting "unsure" sexual identity or heterosexual identity plus same-sex attraction or behavior: Forgotten groups? *Journal of the American Academy of Child & Adolescent Psychiatry, 49*(2), 104–113.

THIRTEEN

First-Generation Students

William Arnold and Will Barratt

Why are first-generation students a current topic of interest in higher education? The answer depends on who is asking the question. For some the answer is the sheer number of new students entering 2- or 4-year colleges and universities each year who share this demographic characteristic. According to Berkner and Choy (2008), just over one-third of all new students are first generation by some definition. *The Chronicle of Higher Education Almanac* (2013a) reports that 53.0% of students had a father with a college degree or higher, 56.2% had a mother with a college degree or higher, and 19.5% report being first-generation students.

The number of first-generation students on any campus depends on institution type, with twice as many first-generation students at community colleges and open admissions state universities than can be found at highly selective, high-prestige private colleges (Berkner & Choy, 2008). The number of students in any demographic category affects the campus human aggregate and campus climate (Holland, 1973). For example, a campus with 70% women will have a different environment than a campus with 30% women.

For others, the answer relates to the fact that this population of students consistently demonstrates high rates of attrition after the first year, slower rates of progress toward degree attainment, and low rates of degree completion (Berkner & Choy, 2008; Chen, 2005; U.S. Department of Education, National Center for Education Statistics [NCES], 2001a, 2001b). As retention and graduation become paramount measures of institutional success, the presence of any group with historically low retention and graduation rates presents a challenge to campus administrators.

Beyond this, there are others whose answer is tied to the close connection between first-generation status and other demographic characteristics such as race or socioeconomic status: roughly 36% of first-generation students are racial/ethnic minorities, and 50% come from low-income households (Chen, 2005). The Higher Education Research Institute (2007) reports data on first-generation students by ethnicity, demonstrating important differences between ethnic groups in first-generation status. The intersections between demographic characteristics such as ethnicity, gender, social class, and generational status make this a complex issue.

Regardless of the basis for interest in first-generation students, the fact remains that a large number of today's college students are first generation and, as a result, all university administrators share a need to better understand how to define first-generation students and, perhaps more important, to understand what it means to be a first-generation student.

The orientation of the authors toward the study of this student population is aligned most closely with the tenets of critical theory. As a result, the authors are somewhat suspect of the assumptions that often lead to the classification of students as first generation, as well as the subsequent analyses that result in their depiction as an at-risk student population. The predominant approaches to assessing, evaluating, and supporting first-generation students sustain a system that inevitably reinforces social stratification and continues to position these students as "academic outsiders" (Oldfield, 2007, p. 3). In an effort to counteract this influence, the authors adopt the following four principles taken from Rice's *6 Steps to Gender Equality* (2013) as a starting point in understanding first-generation students:

1. First-generation students are as academically capable as any college student.
2. First-generation students have exhibited the desire to be successful in college by applying to and enrolling in college.
3. First-generation students come to campus with a set of academic, social, and cultural skills and needs that are often different than the established norm.
4. There are structural and interpersonal impediments on campus that prevent first-generation students from being successful.

Multiple Definitions of First-Generation Students

There is a lack of consensus among researchers as to what denotes someone as being a first-generation student. One definition states that neither of the students' parents has attained a 4-year degree (Engle & Tinto, 2008). Another definition holds that neither parent has any experience in a 4-year, degree-granting institution (U.S. Department of Education, NCES, 2001a). Yet another definition states that neither parent has any experience in post-secondary education of any sort (Chen, 2005). Couture (2010) added another degree of complexity when he wrote about college students whose grandparents had gone to college but whose parents had not. But this inconsistency in establishing the parameters of who should be considered a first-generation student is of little relevance if one considers that the term "first-generation college student," like so many other demographic categorizations, is multifaceted and is contextually situated. In this regard, first generation signifies more than a simple acknowledgment of the amount of formal education acquired by one or both of one's parents. The meaning of first generation is critical and depends very much on how first generation is understood.

Of prime importance in establishing the meaning of this label is to acknowledge that identifying someone as a first-generation college student implies the existence of another population of individuals who are second-, third-, or perhaps fourth-generation college students. It would be fair to say that the delineation of this first-generation group, and the majority of current literature pertaining to them, is based on an *other* orientation that identifies *them* as different from *us*. This is not dissimilar to the approach that has been used with other populations of students over the years, including women, African Americans, Native Americans, Latinos, Asian Americans, gays, lesbians, non-Christians, and members of other non-majority groups. In the case of first-generation students, this tendency to define them relative to others—which seemingly speaks only to previous family educational experience—is ultimately about socioeconomic grouping, given the strong correlation between level of education achieved and family income (U.S. Department of Labor, 2013). And as Barratt (2011b) reminds us, socioeconomic groups are always defined relative to other groups because of the inherent hierarchical nature of social class.

Of equal—if not greater—importance in understanding the meaning of first generation is the awareness that the concept of the first-generation student is completely context-dependent; individuals only take on this status or identity if they elect to enroll as students at a college or university. In addition, the implications of what it means to be first generation pertain solely to this context. In this way a first generation definition is different from other aspects of students' identities—for example, ethnicity and gender—that they bring with them to campus and that they continue to possess after they leave. While it is certain that students who are the first in their family to attend college are quite aware of this fact prior to enrolling in their first set of classes, few of these students refer to themselves as first-generation students or comprehend the extent to which this moniker may situate them differently than their classmates who are *legacy* or second-or-more-generation students.

Considered in these terms, what it means to be first generation may have less to do with what we know about the individuals who can be placed into this demographic and more to do with examining the contexts that make it necessary to identify students in this way. How we classify students makes a difference in how we interact with them.

First-Generation Students

How would one know whether someone is a first-generation college student? Few, if any, individuals refer to themselves in this fashion, or even know that this is a demographic category of interest, like gender and ethnicity. Most first-generation students simply know that their parents did not, either out of choice or necessity, attend college or earn a college degree. In this regard, many are unaware that this aspect of their family profile places them in a category of students who, research tells us, have only a one-in-three chance of earning a college degree.

While having practical value in terms of record-keeping and tracking purposes, lumping all students whose parents did not earn a college degree into one category is an oversimplification. Attempting to understand this population of students as a singular monolithic population serves only to further disenfranchise these students from a system that is at best foreign and at worst openly discriminatory toward them. In an effort to avoid devaluing the unique contributions of those who comprise this broad population of students, attention is focused on those aspects of the college experience that inherently place these students at a disadvantage.

An economic deficit model of first-generation students will lead to an economic intervention; a social deficit model of first-generation students will lead to social interventions; an academic deficit model of first-generation students will lead to academic interventions; and so on. While this demographically defined group has been identified as having lower-than-average graduation rates—hence the cause for concern—exploring the causes of the lower graduation rates and how those might be related to being first generation is critical to a more complete understanding and consequent complete programming on campus for all students.

It is worth noting that, given the demographics of the larger U.S. population, those who comprise the current population of first-generation students possess a number of attributes that result in them diverging qualitatively from their non-first-generation peers (Engle, Bermeo, & O'Brien, 2006; Nomi, 2005). The fact that these attributes tend to be aspects of individual identity that are particularly salient for most people cannot be overlooked, and it thus draws attention to the value of utilizing recent research and literature in the areas of identity intersectionality as a lens through which to view the first-generation student experience. In this regard, higher education professionals cannot think of these students solely in terms of their first-generation status. It is likely that the majority of these students are unaware that the way in which they are experiencing the college environment is a result of their first-generation status. Rather, they are more likely to attribute it to aspects of their identity that are more salient at that particular time—for example, gender, race, ethnicity, and socioeconomic status (Coffman, 2011; Kim & Sax, 2009). It is these aspects of their identity that tend to literally and figuratively place these individuals at the margins of their academic communities.

What Is Known About First-Generation Students

What is known about first-generation students is a function of the kinds of questions that have been asked. (Whether or not these are the most appropriate questions is a matter of discussion.) A survey of the literature and research regarding first-generation students reveals that there has been no shortage of efforts to understand their pre-college characteristics, their transition to college, and their progress toward degree completion, but there exists little in terms of understanding these students beyond the aggregate (Pascarella, Pierson, Wolniak, & Terenzini, 2004). Existing studies suggest that if someone is a first-generation college student, he or she will likely

- have lower college entrance exam scores;
- have completed a less academically rigorous high school curriculum;
- have to take remedial coursework;
- have a greater need for financial assistance to cover the cost of college;
- have difficulty transitioning into college;
- have a higher need to work while enrolled;
- have a lower GPA at the end of the first year;
- have lower academic aspirations, have a higher attrition rate; and
- have only a one-in-three chance of ever earning a college degree. (U.S. Department of Education, NCES, 2001a, 2001b)

While all of these are valid interpretations of existing data regarding the aggregate population of first-generation students, most of the characteristics used in establishing this profile are based on a comparison group: students whose parents have obtained at least a bachelor's degree.

The comparison with students who are the product of the baccalaureate-earning population as the de facto normative standard makes the profile for first-generation students often that of a deficit orientation, one that reflects how much less or lower first-generation students rate and rank on various measures than the normative or exemplar college student (Pascarella et al., 2004). In this regard, first-generation students are seen as a deviation from the norm.

Another perspective is that these individuals are being assessed based on a comparative standard, one in which the norm is skewed in the direction of a privileged group rather than a true population norm. More important, should the norm be a campus norm or a U.S. population norm? In this scenario, rather than presenting first-generation students as being deficient, we would acknowledge students of college-educated parents as members of a privileged class that finds greater levels of opportunity and success because of their privileged position. The use of children of college-educated parents as the normative group seems particularly questionable when one considers the reality that less than one-third, or 30.4%, of Americans above the age of 25 have a bachelor's degree or higher (Snyder & Dillow, 2011).

In addition to the above-mentioned comparative analyses, other studies have brought to light what appears to be a ubiquitous challenge for first-generation students: the felt need to straddle two worlds, one of which encompasses their life as a college student and the other their daily home life outside of the college experience (London, 1992; Pardon, 1992; Rendon, 1992). This unique aspect of first-generation students' college experience was aptly described by Oldfield (2007) as "…a cultural journey to a very different land than the one they knew as youngsters" (p. 3).

This dichotomy between worlds, while acknowledged as an inherent aspect of the first-generation student experience, is one of the root causes of the persistent struggle to increase the retention and completion rates of first-generation students (Engle & Tinto, 2008). However, there are distinct ways in which to interpret this struggle. For those leading the academy, the predominant line of thinking generally characterizes the student's life outside college as a deficit in the equation and a distraction from the ideal identity that the student should be striving to acquire. Historically, the only way for students to balance this imbalanced equation was to let go of or distance themselves from their existing life and accommodate/adopt the preferences of the academy (Tinto, 1993). From the students' perspective, there is intrinsic value and a sense of identity associated with both worlds and a need to construct an appropriate balance between the two (Davis, 2010; Hsiao, 1992).

Forms of Capital and First-Generation Students

Underpinning the first-generation students' perception of inhabiting two distinct worlds is the reality that the entire experience of going to college, from admission to graduation, involves an exercise of multiple forms of capital (Bourdieu, 1986)—for example, economic, cultural, social, and academic capital to which, by virtue of simply growing up in a family without a legacy of college attendance, these students find they have limited access. Economic capital can be understood as the economic resources a student has available to cover the cost of attending college. In this instance, we know that the ability to pay for college continually appears as a key factor influencing the likelihood of applying, enrolling, and persisting in college (Boulard, 2004; King, 1996; Long & Riley, 2007).

Economic Capital

If we think of economic capital strictly in terms of family income, it is not surprising that many first-generation students tend to find themselves wanting in this area, given the correlation between educational attainment and income. National data clearly corroborate the link between the two, with only 3% of families where parents have a high school diploma or less earning more than $75,000 per year, compared to 35% for those where the parents have a bachelor's degree or higher (U.S. Department of Education, NCES, 2001a).

In the context of college costs, economic capital—defined by Bourdieu (1986) as money and things immediately convertible into money—includes access to scholarships, loans, grants, and gifts. In this regard, economic capital becomes interrelated with academic capital in that the greater a student's academic capital, the more likely she/he is to reduce the cost of college attendance by earning scholarships, grants, or other forms of merit-based aid. Yet evidence supports the theory that the strongest predictor of student academic capital is parental education level and income (Sackett, Kuncel, Arneson, Cooper, & Waters, 2009; Strage & Brandt, 1999).

In some ways, federal, state, and institutional-level efforts have served to reduce the inevitable scarcity of economic and academic capital experienced by first-generation students. The Federal Pell Grant program provides "need-based grants to low-income undergraduate and certain postbaccalaureate students to promote access to postsecondary education" (U.S. Department of Education, 2012). The federally funded TRIO program consists of a variety of initiatives to support low-income, first-generation, and other disadvantaged students with their educational pursuits (U.S. Department of Education, 2013a). Numerous states have initiated need-based as well as merit-based forms of college financial assistance. Many colleges and universities offer their own forms of need-based financial aid as well as college preparation, transition support, and developmental education programs (National Center for Education Statistics (NCES), 2013).

For many first-generation students, the combination of these efforts enables them to pursue a college degree. However, economic capital is not simply a matter of access; it is also clearly tied to the type of college experience students will have. The nature of their experience is likely to be qualitatively different, depending on the type of institution they attend. A quick look at enrollment data of Pell Grant-eligible students (99% of Pell Grant awards in 2011–2012 went to families earning $80,000 per year or less) offers a glimpse at the likely distribution of first-generation students within the spectrum of higher educational institutions (i.e., community colleges, public 4-year, private 4-year, and highly selective 4-year colleges; see Table 1). Although Pell Grants are not a measure of first-generation student status, they can serve as an approximate measure because of the association between family income and parental educational attainment (Romano & Millard, 2005).

Table 1: Percent receiving Pell Grant aid at selected colleges and universities.

College or university	Percentage of all undergraduate students receiving Pell Grant aid	Percentage of full-time, first-time students who completed their program within 150% of "normal time"
Mid Michigan Community College	58%	10%
Eastern Iowa Community College District	47%	23%
Indiana State University	43%	61%
Sonoma State University	37%	55%

College or university	Percentage of all undergraduate students receiving Pell Grant aid	Percentage of full-time, first-time students who completed their program within 150% of "normal time"
Michigan State University	25%	79%
The University of Iowa	19%	70%
Dartmouth College	15%	96%
Harvard University	11%	97%

Note: Data are from College Navigator (NCES, 2013; http://nces.ed.gov/collegenavigator/)

Clearly, the enrollment patterns of Pell Grant recipients indicate that first-generation students are not as likely to be admitted to the same institutions as their more privileged peers and as a result are likely to find the path to achieving their degree even more complicated. Pascarella and colleagues (2004) conclude that differences in social capital function as a handicap for first-generation students in terms of their ability to successfully navigate a system that favors the dominant or prestige culture in our society.

> Our findings are also quite consistent with the expectation that family cultural capital plays a significant role in informing the choices students make about the types of institutions they attend and the kinds of experiences they have once enrolled. Such family cultural capital and the attendant understandings and expectations of a college education that it engenders are likely to be relatively more modest for first-generation students than similar students whose parents are highly educated to make the kinds of informed choices about institutions and involvements during college that potentially maximize educational progress and benefits. (p. 277)

The economic capital is often the primary mental model that people use in thinking about first-generation students, and this leads to solution strategies involving economic capital. While money is certainly a requirement for education, especially in terms of addressing issues of access, money is not sufficient to help all students succeed in college (Engle & Tinto, 2008).

Cultural Capital

Cultural capital refers to the knowledge base and skill set of the prestige social class. For example, dress, etiquette, style of speech, and which utensil to use at which stage of dinner are general cultural knowledge. The accumulation of cultural capital begins at home and continues through education. For students growing up with college- or even graduate-level-educated parents, prestige cultural capital is accumulated at the dinner table, in conversations, and on trips to museums and art galleries. A student from a home with the knowledge and skills of the prestige class who accumulates this capital before going to college is at a clear advantage in a college environment where faculty, staff, and students value that knowledge base and skill set (Bourdieu, 1986). Cultural capital is the outcome of interest in many campuses' cultural, music, and art events, as well as the outcome of interest in general education. Events such as etiquette dinners, dress-for-success training, and social networking lessons are designed to build cultural capital, and the presence of these events is one way to measure the aggregate social class of any campus community (Barratt, 2013). Fraternities and sororities in particular are active in transmitting prestige cultural capital on campus by way of leadership programs, social skill-building programs, and etiquette dinners.

This culturally privileged world is normalized on campuses where knowledge of prestige art, music, politics, and history are highly valued. Unfortunately, many first-generation students are unaware of the value of prestige cultural capital and do not seek to accumulate it. While all knowledge and skills constitute some form of cultural capital, the knowledge of NASCAR standings is not as prestigious in terms of cultural capital as knowing the outcome of the America's Cup. There is a difference in cultural capital between the student who has been to World War II historic sites and one who cannot find Normandy on a world map.

Social Capital

Social capital refers to the network of personal relationships that can be used to find and organize resources, and it has been described as the collection of personal relationships, family ties, networks, and lived experiences that give one a sense of familiarity and confidence relative to the environment in which he/she is immersed (Oldfield, 2007). It requires a certain skill set to accumulate this network of relationships, so there is a skill component to social capital. According to McClenaghan (2000), although social capital serves as an asset for an individual, it is not something that one possesses. Rather, it exists in the relationships between individuals and results in the ability of those individuals to improve their performance in a variety of areas, including education. In this context, social capital has direct implications for knowing how to perform the student role (Stanton-Salazar, 1997).

One feature of social capital—collective action—is recognized by the World Bank:

> Social Capital refers to the norms and networks that enable collective action. It encompasses institutions, relationships, and customs that shape the quality and quantity of a society's social interactions. Increasing evidence shows that social capital is critical for societies to prosper economically and for development to be sustainable. Social capital, when enhanced in a positive manner, can improve project effectiveness and sustainability by building the community's capacity to work together to address their common needs, fostering greater inclusion and cohesion, and increasing transparency and accountability. (World Bank, 2013, para. 1)

This idea of collective action is extremely important. Having a network of friends is one thing, and being able to bring friends together for action is commendable. Not all actions are equivalent. Assembling friends to attend a sporting event is one thing; assembling them to create a campus organization and attain funding is another. Creating and maintaining relationships with people who have access to material as well as knowledge resources is central to having high social capital (Bourdieu, 1986).

Personal learning networks are an example of social capital. These informal collections of people with whom we purposefully interact and learn are a particular form of social capital that is gaining popularity. While these networks have always existed, personal learning networks are emerging as a normal part of the college experience. Students who bring to campus an awareness of these social networks and who have the skills to build and maintain them will have access to more resources than other students (Barratt, 2011b). Further, in their post-college work experience, individuals who can build and maintain personal learning networks will be at an advantage.

When it comes to college, first-generation students face the challenge of entering an environment in which it appears that everyone understands how to perform the student role. In general, new-student orientation programs operate under the assumption that entering students share a baseline of knowledge about coming to college as a result of having successfully navigated the application process (Davis, 2010; Sacks, 2007). However, for first-generation students, this is far from the case. A small percentage of each year's entering first-generation student population has the benefit of participating in college preparatory programs intended to enhance their readiness in terms of the academic and social capital that is expected when they arrive on campus in the fall in bridge programs like those publicized on the websites of Winston-Salem University, Hampton University, Berkeley College, and Indiana State University. Programs such as the federally funded Upward Bound (U.S. Department of Education, 2013d) and Talent Search (U.S. Department of Education, 2013b), as well as campus-specific bridge programs, have proven to be successful in easing the culture shock for those who are fortunate enough to be selected and are able to participate. In spite of the success of these types of programs, too few of them exist, and too few families and students anticipate the extent of their capital deficit that would warrant the investment of time, money, and energy associated with participating in such programs.

In 2012, there were a total of 826 Upward Bound programs across the country serving just over 62,500 students (U.S. Department of Education, 2013c), as compared to the estimated 4 million first-generation students who enrolled in 2- or 4-year institutions in the same year. Without the support of federal grant dollars, individual campus-based programs targeting first-generation students considered to be at "higher risk" are often viewed as too expensive (Sacks, 2007). The intersection of economic and social capital is seen here once again: not only are first-generation students in need of social capital-boosting programs; they also tend to have a greater need of financial assistance. The combination of these two factors makes this population a less desirable pool of students in terms of the institutional bottom line.

Academic Capital

Academic capital refers to the academic preparation that students have engaged in prior to college. In short, academic capital is the knowledge base and skill set that produces a successful student. In particular, it speaks to the rigor of the high school curriculum in terms of the content, quantity, and quality of the courses taken; grades earned in high school; and performance on college entrance exams (U.S. Department of Education, NCES, 2001b). Existing studies show a direct correlation between the factors that comprise academic capital and college attendance, performance, and completion (U.S. Department of Education, NCES, 2001a, 2001b).

Given what is known about college and university environments (Boyer, 1987; Delbanco, 2012), it is fair to say that, regardless of the institution in question, one is likely to encounter a culture unlike that which exists outside of the campus boundaries and thus would only be familiar to those whose cultural capital intersects with this cultural milieu. Members of the campus culture normalize certain kinds of capital, thus marginalizing students who do not have sufficient capital or who have low-prestige forms of cultural capital (Barratt, 2011a; Sacks, 2007; Davis, 2010).

Consequences of Being First Generation

According to the U.S. Department of Education, approximately 36% of all students entering postsecondary education each year are first-generation students (Berkner & Choy, 2008). This represented 6.7 million students enrolled in Spring 2013 (*Chronicle of Higher Education*,

2013c). Seen in another way, 64% of college students come from 30% of the U.S. population, based on the 30% of the U.S. adult population who hold a college degree (U.S. Bureau of the Census, 2013a, 2013b). In fact, though it is presented in a different way, research supports the latter position.

Studies show that first-generation students are at a distinct disadvantage when it comes to postsecondary access—a disadvantage that persists even after controlling for other important factors such as educational expectations, academic preparation, support from parents and schools in planning and preparing for college, and family income (Sacks, 2007; U.S. Department of Education, NCES, 2001a, 2001b). These same studies indicate that among those who overcome the barriers to access and enroll in postsecondary education, students whose parents did not attend college remain at a disadvantage with respect to staying enrolled and completing a degree program (referred to as persistence and attainment throughout this essay), again controlling for other related factors. Economic, social, cultural, and academic capital is one of many ways to conceptualize the differences between first- and second- generation students.

While the research demarcates "parents' education—specifically, having a parent with a bachelor's degree" (Choy, 2001, p. 8) as the key indicator related to entrance and persistence in college, what is seldom discussed is what this indicator ultimately represents—privilege. And, as was noted above, colleges and universities, particularly 4-year institutions, utilize this privileged existence as the norm in determining their standards.

The concept of privilege is widely referenced but seldom defined (Barratt, 2012). Social privilege, based on interpersonal transactions (social capital), is one way in which second-, third-, and fourth-generation students have cultural norm-based social privilege; group membership is based on social privilege (Barratt, 2011a; Bourdieu, 1986). They also have economic privilege. Being normative, or being in the majority, is recognized in social interactions. Social class is inherent in every interpersonal interaction through language, gesture, dress, semiotics, and signals. Individuals quickly recognize other peoples' gender, social class, and ethnicity and make assumptions based on these quick judgments. Non-normative students—in this case, first-generation students—will respond to these interactions in various ways, perhaps to accentuate their differences by proudly exhibiting their first-generation status, or perhaps by class passing, or trying to fit in (Barratt, 2011a).

The Campus Context for First Generation

On most college campuses, the majority group is made up of second-generation (or more) students, which becomes the standard of comparison (Barratt, 2011b; Davis, 2010). Exacerbating this tendency to normalize the non-first-generation student is the socialization process for faculty and administrators that emphasizes membership in a culturally and socially elite group in the United States (Tierney & Rhoads, 1993). In the United States, the default standard for students, faculty, and staff more often than not reflects the existing heterosexual, European American, and Christian majority in U.S. society in general (Center for Sexual Health Promotion, 2010; *Chronicle of Higher Education*, 2013a, 2013b; U.S. Bureau of the Census, 2012, 2013b). While women students constitute a numerical majority on many campuses, men continue to constitute the majority of faculty and administrators (*Chronicle of Higher Education*, 2013a). Within this environment, members of minority groups become marginal men and women at best and, at worst, the *stranger*. They are segregated according to their difference, which becomes their primary identity—for example, the gay students, the Jewish students, or the first-generation students.

The fact is that, in spite of what could clearly be considered an un-level playing field that favors the lived experiences of privileged students, first-generation college students who persist demonstrate that they can achieve the same educational and learning outcomes as their privileged counterparts (Pascarella et al., 2004; Pike & Kuh, 2005). The reader will recall the previous assumptions of the author about the abilities and determination of first-generation students. This reality reinforces the need to stop considering first-generation students to be of low ability and to begin to consider them as any other student, albeit one with unique needs. The next step would logically be to identify the interpersonal and structural barriers that make their lives difficult. Such findings also shed light on the notion that if educators truly want to understand the first-generation student experience and the conditions that can inhibit those students' success, it may be more productive to focus on social structures and class bias rather than individual qualities (Jarvis, 1985; Jung & Cervero, 2002; McClenaghan, 2000).

The unspoken truth is that the academy is an elitist system. Barratt (2012) refers to faculty and administrators on campus as the *ruling class* because they make and enforce the rules, typically to the advantage of the economically, culturally, socially, and academically wealthy. The label of social capital is a simple way of acknowledging cultural bias and institutional classism that exists within the traditional higher education environment (Bourdieu, 1986). This is not to overlook the existence of those institutions whose mission is to create opportunity and provide access to all individuals within our society and who excel at supporting first-generation students. It is simply to shed light on the reality that as an overall system, the academy is inherently biased against those who have no prior family experience with the system.

Research has helped us bring to light the existence of many types of institutionalized "isms" such as racism, sexism, and ageism. This line of research clearly demonstrate that organizations reflect the biases of those who make up the organization and that these biases preserve, in legacy fashion, the policies, practices, and procedures that serve—knowingly or unknowingly—to perpetuate the advantaging of some while simultaneously disadvantaging others. Research has repeatedly shown that the most successful way to combat such institutional-level biases is to work on re-culturating the institution. In spite of these findings, recommendations put forth on how to support the success of more first-generation students continually focus on assimilating or correcting the student rather than adapting the system to the needs of all students.

Inevitably, the recommendations call for providing more access to college preparatory coursework; increased academic support and tutoring; increased financial aid information, counseling, and access; and more developmental math and language courses in the curriculum (Davis, 2010; Sacks, 2007). The just recommendation would be for all students to participate in structured coursework to enhance their academic capital.

The Campus Social Class Culture

The terms first-generation, second-generation, and third-generation college student are not part of a common language for referencing social class. But generational status is a social class indicator, given the correlation between educational attainment and nearly all indices used to differentiate social class—particularly income, parental education, and residence (National Center for Education Statistics (NCES), 2012). One needs to look no further than the distribution of Pell Grant dollars to see this portrayed in stark clarity. The National Center for Education Statistics College Navigator (2013) provides comparative data, shown below in Table 2. The environment will be different for each college campus based on the human aggregate of students. That is, more first-generation, poor, Pell Grant students can be found at some colleges than at others (NCES, College Navigator, 2013).

Table 2: Percentage of students receiving Pell Grant aid at selected colleges and universities.

College or university	Percentage of all undergraduate students receiving Pell Grant aid
Mid Michigan Community College	58%
Eastern Iowa Community College District	47%
Indiana State University	43%
Sonoma State University	37%
Michigan State University	25%
The University of Iowa	19%
Dartmouth College	15%
Harvard University	11%

Note: Data are from College Navigator (NCES, 2013; http://nces.ed.gov/collegenavigator/)

Being a first-generation student at Harvard will be quite a different experience from being a first-generation student at Indiana State University or at a community college. The contrast within the student body between first-generation students and the majority student human aggregate on a highly selective campus will be a source of stress for the first-generation student, much like being an African American student on a predominantly White campus (Watson et al., 2002).

Although it is possible for first-, second-, and third-generation students to claim middle-class status (Pew Research Center, 2008), these students come from different social class subcultures. The differentiation between social class cultures can be demarcated in terms of level of income, but when it comes to differentiating between subcultures, the element that appears to play an even greater role is cultural capital (Barratt, 2011a; Bourdieu, 1986). On campus, the prestige or valued cultural capital comes from the knowledge and skills of the prestige classes, and the acquisition of prestige cultural capital begins at home for those whose families have a history of college completion.

Cultural capital relates to a particular culture. Shared worldviews, values, perceptions, practices, manners, food preferences, norms, and fashion of the majority campus culture become the norms of the campus (Kuh, Kinzie, Schuh, & Whitt, 2010). Knowing these norms makes campus life comfortable; not knowing these norms makes it difficult. Faculty, students, and administrators reproduce culture by reinforcing certain normative behaviors and attitudes. Non-natives to that culture struggle with learning these hidden and unspoken campus and academic norms (Barratt, 2011a; Davis, 2010; Sacks, 2007). Second-, third-, and fourth-generation students are privileged to have learned these campus and academic norms at home before college and have relatives who can provide mentoring (Bourdieu, 1986).

Examples

First-generation students come to campus with notable academic, social, and cultural pre-college characteristics that affect their persistence on campus (U.S. Department of Education, NCES, 2001b). These students interact with a campus system designed for second-, third-, and fourth-generation students.

Two examples are in order. Mark is a third-generation college student. His parents, grandparents, aunts, and uncles helped him select a college, talked with him about their college experiences, and gave him suggestions about how to be successful in college by getting involved and talking with professors. His family members sent him care packages during his first semester during midterm and final exam times. Larry is a first-generation student. His father went to college on the GI Bill but only completed two semesters. He has an uncle who went to college but who now lives far away. He has no stories from family members about college; he has only a simple basis for selecting a college, and while he has the moral support of his family, that is about all he has. His family drops him off at college and doesn't send him care packages. When he calls and is upset, they encourage him to come home, where they know he will be fine. In Mark's case and in Larry's case, members of the campus community make no effort to help them select a campus, enroll, or fit in. One idea is that privilege is not seeing something as a problem because you don't have it as a problem. The transition to college life is not seen as a problem for Mark, who is in the majority, so members of the community don't do anything. Larry's problem is seen as his problem, and the members of the college community think they are respecting his autonomy by not helping.

On some campuses, students who are deemed underprepared are placed in pre-college bridge programs, remedial classes, academic opportunity programs, and TRIO programs that may or may not help but which certainly lead to a higher likelihood of stigmatizing students (Watson et al., 2002). On a few campuses—for example, Knox and Union Colleges—all students enroll in a transition-to-college course whose content and instruction are based on data collected and refined over the years. Examples abound of systemic inequities on campus, which make life difficult for first-generation students who don't have the academic and cultural capital to be successful (Barratt, 2011a; Sacks, 2007).

Social Status and First-Generation Students

Given the structure of the current socioeconomic stratification in the United States, the large majority of first-generation students are classified as lower-class, working-class, or lower-middle-class on the socioeconomic scale (Davis, 2010). While intended to be simply an index of one's level of income, these classifications also bring with them an established set of assumptions and presumed limitations. The implications associated with the level of disposable income available for those who find themselves in lower- to middle-class socioeconomic classifications are certainly worth noting in terms of the first-generation student experience: greater reliance on loans to finance the cost of attending college, increased likelihood of having to work part-time or full-time while attending college, less likely to reside on campus, and more likely to attend college part-time (Richardson & Skinner, 1992). Each of these factors has been shown to increase the likelihood of attrition and decrease the chances of degree completion. But if it were merely a financial issue, the difficulty would be easy to resolve; simply providing these students with more money would solve the problem. But even in those situations in which the issue of cost is negated, first-generation students still encounter a greater chance of "failure" than do their peers who are from multi-generation college-going families (Engle & Tinto, 2008).

First-Generation Students as Academic Outsiders

Oldfield (2007)] refers to first-generation students as academic outsiders:

> With proper nurturing, certain so-called disadvantages can be reinterpreted as differences rather than shortcomings. In sum, the ultimate goal should be reforming the campus culture so that it better reflects the lives of all who go there, irrespective of their socioeconomic background. (p. 3)

Assuming that all first-generation students are alike is a poor place to start. The within-group variance for first-generation students is much larger than the between-group variance for first- and second-generation students—much like gender, where differences within gender groups are greater than differences between gender groups. The idea of academic outsiders implies the idea of academic insiders (in this case the children of the college educated) against whom the outsiders are measured and found wanting.

Conclusion

"All first-generation students are below average." This negative adaptation of the Lake Woebegone epithet reflects the reality of how first-generation students are often perceived, and it summarizes the underlying assumptions behind programs for first-generation students. "First-generation students are…" is an equally ineffective way of thinking about and working with any group of students. The variations among first-generation students as a group are much larger than the variations between first-generation students and second-generation students. The effects of being first generation across a large population are known, but this does not inform educators about what it is like to be a first-generation student. The difficulties that first-generation students face on their pathways to success are the interpersonal interactions and organizational structures that the ruling class on campus has created. Chances are good that if you are reading this, you are being socialized to become one of the ruling class—someone on campus who makes and enforces the written and unwritten rules. The authors challenge you to question the written and unwritten rules about students from multiple perspectives.

References

Barratt, W. (2011a). *Social class hierarchy and inequity: How social class is different than gender and ethnicity.* Retrieved from http://socialclassoncampus.blogspot.com/2011/08/social-class-hierarchy-and-inequity-how.html

Barratt, W. (2011b). *Social class on campus.* Sterling, VA: Stylus.

Barratt, W.R. (2012). *Unpacking social class privilege.* Retrieved from http://socialclassoncampus.blogspot.com/2012/03/unpacking-social-class-privilege.html

Barratt, W.R. (2013, May 24). *Etiquette and campus* [Web log entry]. Retrieved from http://socialclassoncampus.blogspot.com/2013/05/etiquette-and-campus.html

Berkner, L., & Choy, S. (2008). *Descriptive summary of 2003–04 beginning postsecondary students: Three years later* (NCES 2008-174). Washington, DC: National Center for Education Statistics, Institute of Education Sciences, U.S. Department of Education.

Boulard, G. (2004). College access still tied to income, report says. *Diverse Issues in Higher Education.* Retrieved from http://diverseeducation.com/article/3688/#

Bourdieu, P. (1986). The forms of capital. In J. Richardson (Ed.), *Handbook of theory and research for the sociology of education* (pp. 241–258). Westport, CT: Greenwood Press.

Boyer, E. (1987). *College: The undergraduate experience in America.* New York, NY: Harper & Row.

Center for Sexual Health Promotion. (2010). *National survey of sexual health and behavior.* Bloomington, IN: Indiana University School of Health, Physical Education and Recreation. Retrieved from http://www.nationalsexstudy.indiana.edu/

Chen, X. (2005). *First generation students in postsecondary education: A look at their college transcripts* (NCES 2005–171). Washington, DC: U.S. Department of Education, National Center for Education Statistics.

Choy, S. P. (2001). *Students whose parents did not go to college: Postsecondary access, persistence, and attainment* (NCES 2001-126). Washington, DC: U.S. Department of Education, National Center for Education Statistics.

Chronicle of Higher Education. (2013a). *Almanac of higher education.* Retrieved from http://chronicle.com

Chronicle of Higher Education. (2013b). *A profile of freshmen at 4-year colleges, Fall 2012.* Retrieved from http://chronicle.com/article/A-Profile-of-Freshmen-at/140387/

Chronicle of Higher Education. (2013c). *Enrollment in Title IV degree-granting institutions, by sector and region, Spring 2013.* Retrieved from http://chronicle.com/article/Enrollment-in-Title-IV/140621/

Coffman, S. (2011). A social construction view of issues confronting first-generation college students. *New Directions for Teaching and Learning, 2011*(127), 81–90. doi: 10.1002/tl.459

Couture, R. (2010). *The first-again generation: A qualitative study of first-generation college student siblings whose grandparents attended college* (Unpublished doctoral dissertation). University of Northern Colorado, Greeley. Retrieved from http://digitalunc.coalliance.org/fedora/repository/cogru:323/Couture_unco_0161N_10034.pdf

Davis, J. (2010). *The first-generation student experience: Implications for campus practice, and strategies for improving persistence and success.* Sterling, VA: Stylus.

Delbanco, A. (2012). *College: What it was, is, and should be.* Princeton, NJ: Princeton University Press.

Engle, J., Bermeo, A., & O'Brien, C. (2006). *Straight from the source: What works for first-generation college students.* Washington, DC: Pell Institute for the Study of Opportunity in Higher Education. Retrieved from www.pellinstitute.org

Engle, J., & Tinto, V. (2008). *Moving beyond access: College success for low-income, first-generation students.* Washington, DC: Pell Institute for the Study of Opportunity in Higher Education.

Higher Education Research Institute. (2007). *First in my family: A profile of first-generation college students at four-year institutions since 1971.* Retrieved from http://www.heri.ucla.edu/pdfs/pubs/briefs/firstgenresearchbrief.pdf

Holland, J. (1973). *Making vocational choices: A theory of careers.* Englewood Cliffs, NJ: Prentice-Hall.

Hsiao, K.P. (1992). *First-generation college students. ERIC Digest.* Los Angeles, CA: ERIC Clearinghouse for Junior Colleges. Retrieved from http://eric.ed.gov.proxy1.cl.msu.edu/?id=ED351079

Jarvis, P. (1985). Thinking critically in an information society: A sociological analysis. *Lifelong Learning, 8*(6), 11–14.

Jung J.-C. & Cervero R.M. (2002). The social, economic and political contexts of adults' participation in undergraduate programmes: A state-level analysis. *International Journal of Lifelong Education, 21*(4), 305–320.

Kim, Y.K., & Sax, L.J. (2009). Student-faculty interaction in research universities: Differences by student gender, race, social class, and first-generation status. *Research in Higher Education, 50*(5), 437–459. doi: 10.1007/s11162-009-9127-x

King, J.E. (1996). *The decision to go to college: Attitudes and experiences associated with college attendance among low-income students.* Washington, DC: The College Board.

Kuh, G.D., Kinzie, J., Schuh, J.H., & Whitt, E.J. (2010). *Student success in college: Creating conditions that matter.* San Francisco, CA: Jossey-Bass.

London, H.B. (1992). Transformations: Cultural challenges faced by first-generation college students. In L.S. Zwerling & H.B. London (Eds.), *First generation students: Confronting the cultural issues issues* (pp. 5–11). New Directions for Community Colleges Series No. 80. San Francisco, CA: Jossey-Bass.

Long, B.T., & Riley, E. (2007). Financial aid: A broken bridge to college access? *Harvard Educational Review, 77*(1), 39–63.

McClenaghan, P. (2000). Social capital: Exploring the theoretical foundations of community development education. *British Educational Research Journal, 26*(5), 565–582.

National Center for Educational Statistics (NCES). (2012). *Improving the measurement of socioeconomic status for the national assessment of educational progress: A theoretical foundation.* Retrieved from http://nces.ed.gov/nationsreportcard/researchcenter/socioeconomic_factors.aspx

National Center for Education Statistics (NCES). (2013). *National postsecondary student aid study.* Retrieved from http://nces.ed.gov/surveys/npsas/

National Center for Education Statistics (NCES). College Navigator. (2013). Retrieved from http://nces.ed.gov/collegenavigator/

Nomi, T. (2005). *Faces of the future: A portrait of first-generation community college students.* Washington, DC: American Association of Community Colleges.

Oldfield, K. (2007). Humble and hopeful: Welcoming first-generation poor and working-class students to college. *About Campus, 11*(6), 2–12.

Pardon, E.J. (1992). The challenge of first-generation college students: A Miami-Dade perspective. In L.S. Zwerling & H.B. London (Eds.), *First generation students: Confronting the cultural issues* (pp. 71–80). New Directions for Community Colleges, No. 80. San Francisco, CA: Jossey-Bass.

Pascarella, E.T., Pierson, C.T., Wolniak, G.C., & Terenzini, P.T. (2004). First-generation college students: Additional evidence on college experiences and outcomes. *Journal of Higher Education, 75*(3), 249–284.

Pew Research Center. (2008). *Inside the middle class: Bad times hit the good life.* Retrieved from http://www.pewsocialtrends.org

Pike, G. R., & Kuh, G. D. (2005b). First- and second-generation college students: A comparison of their engagement and intellectual development. *Journal of Higher Education, 76*(3), 276–300.

Rendon, L. I. (1992). From the barrio to the academy: Revelations of a Mexican American "scholarship girl." In L.S. Zwerling & H.B. London (Eds.), *First generation students: Confronting the cultural issues* (pp. 55–64). New Directions for Community Colleges, No. 80. San Francisco, CA: Jossey-Bass.

Rice, C. (2013). *6 steps to gender equality: And more essays about how every university gets more women to the top and why they should.* Retrieved from http://curt-rice.com/wp-content/uploads/2012/11/6-Steps-to-Gender-Equality1.pdf

Richardson, R.C., & Skinner, E.F. (1992). Helping first-generation minority students achieve degrees. In S.L. Zwerling & H.B. London (Eds.), *First generation students: Confronting the cultural issues* (pp. 29–43). New Directions for Community Colleges, No. 80. San Francisco, CA: Jossey-Bass.

Romano, R.M., & Millard, T. (2005). *If community college students are so poor why do only 16.9% of them receive Pell Grants?* Ithaca, NY: Cornell Higher Education Research Institute. Retrieved from http://digitalcommons.ilr.cornell.edu

Sackett, P.R., Kuncel, N.R., Arneson, J.J., Cooper, S.R., & Waters, S.D. (2009). Does socioeconomic status explain the relationship between admissions tests and post-secondary academic performance? *Psychological Bulletin, 135*(1), 1–22.

Sacks, P. (2007). *Tearing down the gates.* Berkeley, CA: University of California Press.

Snyder, T.D., & Dillow, S.A. (2011). *Digest of education statistics, 2010.* NCES 2011–015. Jessup, MD: National Center for Education Statistics. Retrieved from http://search.proquest.com/docview/870286935?accountid=12598

Stanton-Salazar, R. D. (1997). A social capital framework for understanding the socialization of racial minority children and youth. *Harvard Educational Review, 67*(1), 1–40.

Strage, A., & Brandt, T.S. (1999). Authoritative parenting and college students' academic adjustment and success. *Journal of Educational Psychology, 91*(1), 146–156.

Tierney, W.G., & Rhoads, R.A. (1993). *Enhancing promotion, tenure and beyond: Faculty socialization as a cultural process.* ASHE-ERIC Higher Education Report No. 6. Washington, DC: George Washington University.

Tinto, V. (1993). *Leaving college: Rethinking the causes and cures of student attrition.* (2nd ed.). Chicago, IL: University of Chicago Press.

U.S. Bureau of the Census. (2012). *The 2012 statistical abstract: Population: Religion.* Retrieved from http://www.census.gov/compendia/statab/cats/population/religion.html

U.S. Bureau of the Census. (2013a). *Educational attainment: CPS historical time series tables.* Retrieved from http://www.census.gov/hhes/socdemo/education/data/cps/historical/fig2.jpg

U.S. Bureau of the Census. (2013b). *People and households—data by subject.* Retrieved from http://www.census.gov/people/

U.S. Department of Education. (2012). *Federal Pell Grant program.* Retrieved from http://www2.ed.gov/programs/fpg/index.html

U.S. Department of Education. (2013a). *Federal trio programs—Home page.* Retrieved from http://www2.ed.gov/about/offices/list/ope/trio/index.html

U.S. Department of Education. (2013b). *Talent Search program.* Retrieved from http://www2.ed.gov/programs/triotalent/index.html

U.S. Department of Education. (2013c). *Upward Bound funding status.* Retrieved from http://www2.ed.gov/programs/trioupbound/funding.html

U. S. Department of Education. (2013d). *Upward Bound program.* Retrieved from http://www2.ed.gov/programs/trioupbound/index.html

U.S. Department of Education. National Center for Education Statistics (NCES). (2001a). *Bridging the gap: Academic preparation and postsecondary success of first-generation students* (NCES 2001–153). Retrieved from http://nces.ed.gov/das/epubs/pdf/2001153_es.pdf

U.S. Department of Education. National Center for Education Statistics (NCES). (2001b). *Students whose parents did not go to college: Postsecondary access, persistence, and attainment* (NCES 2001–126). Retrieved from http://nces.ed.gov/pubsearch/pubsinfo.asp?pubid=2001126

U.S. Department of Labor. (2013). *Employment projections: Earnings and unemployment rates by educational attainment.* Retrieved from http://www.bls.gov/emp/ep_chart_001.htm

Watson, L.W., Terrell, M.C., Wright, D.J., Bonner, F.A., Cuyjet, M.J., Gold, J.A.,... Person, D.R. (2002). *How minority students experience college: Implications for planning and policy.* Sterling, VA: Stylus.

World Bank. (2013). *Overview: Social capital.* Retrieved from http://web.worldbank.org

FOURTEEN

Privileged Access: Higher Education's Unfulfilled Promise

Dafina-Lazarus Stewart and Keenan Y. Colquitt, Jr.

The role of higher education as a public good has been increasingly debated as colleges and universities have responded to more utilitarian demands and assumed a more corporate character (Gumport, 2000; Kezar, 2004). Scholars typically argue that serving the public good was part of higher education's historic mission (Gumport, 2000; Kezar, 2004). However, when examined against the historical record of U.S. higher education, such arguments ring hollow. Founded to serve the wealthy elite in the colonies in what would become the United States, the colonial colleges did not seek to serve farmers' sons (Thelin, 2011). Moreover, financial aid was often based on merit or affiliation, rather than need, and government-sponsored aid did not exist until the passage of the GI Bill in the mid-twentieth century (Thelin, 2011). Indeed, it would seem more accurate to say that whatever consciousness U.S. higher education developed to serve the public good evolved over time, as democratic and populist activists made demands on colleges and universities (Thelin, 2011).

According to Ross (2003b), universities "have been powerful agents of socialization…established, organized and supported at different periods to either initiate and sustain social change or to substantiate social inertia" (p. 22). As such, higher education is not inherently devoted to ideals of liberation and societal transformation. From a sociological perspective, the educational enterprise, inclusive of higher education, "has always been centrally positioned within sociological theories of class re/production, playing an important role in ensuring either reproduction of (middle class) privileges or (working class) disadvantages" (Archer, 2003, p. 5).

It is within this context, then, that higher education must be understood. Although providing greater access to working-class students than at its inception, higher education is not yet an inclusive and welcoming environment for poor and working-class students. Access to higher education for working-class students has been uneven and tenuous (Hurst, 2009). Moreover, once on campus, their participation and engagement in the community is not assured. Recent scholarship has argued that the presence alone of marginalized student groups produces neither engagement nor a sense of belonging in the college environment for those students (Harper & Quaye, 2009; Strayhorn, 2012). Consequently, it is important to examine the character of higher education environments and whether they have defaulted on the heritage of higher education as a public good.

The Hope for Social Mobility

For people from marginalized groups, particularly racial and ethnic minoritized people, a college degree has represented a way out and a means of both individual and community uplift. These ideas inspired the founding of Howard University by the Freedmen's Bureau in the aftermath of the Civil War, as well as other colleges and universities whose missions were to educate African Americans to take their rightful place as full-fledged citizens and contributing members of the United States (Anderson, 1988). As El Hajj Malik El-Shabazz (better known as Malcolm X) would say in 1964:

> Education is an important element in the struggle for human rights. It is the means to help our children and our people rediscover their identity and thereby increase their self respect. Education is our passport to the future, for tomorrow belongs only to the people who prepare for it today. (X, 1970/2011, para. 30).

His words echoed sentiments expressed by other African Americans for over a century that education was a requisite tool for liberation and full citizenship in a democratic society.

From W.E.B. Du Bois (1903/1989) to Carter G. Woodson (1933/2006) to bell hooks (1994) and others, higher education was sought after by African Americans who were caught in the intersection of racism and social class oppression to achieve the freedom granted to them through constitutional amendments and congressional legislation. Research by Bowen and Bok (1998) evidenced that African American graduates of elite universities not only secured better socioeconomic status for themselves, but for their children as well. The bachelor's degree became a generational legacy, ensuring the continued upward mobility of these typically first-generation and working-class African Americans, as well as other students across race and ethnicity who were first-generation college students and/or from the working class (Pascarella & Terenzini, 2005).

Higher education is still seen as the ticket to a better life for students from the working class (Hurst, 2009). Despite the lack of social class capital that these students bring to their educational encounters (Lareau, 1989), families and students still regard attaining a college degree as a worthy aspiration. For those in the working class who matriculate to higher education, the stakes are clear, and the system appears to be amenable. Cabrera and La Nasa (2000) characterized higher education as a "meritocratic system in which socioeconomic factors play a secondary role to such factors as academic ability, preparation for college, and educational expectations" (p. 13).

However, a critical perspective of the cultural production of schooling might view with cynicism the hope of trading on a college degree to attain middle-class status for those in the working class, while such degrees merely affirm the class status of those already in the middle and upper classes. As Archer (2003) wrote, "young people from different social classes do not attend the same types of educational institutions, nor do they gain similar levels of qualifications and results" (p. 5). Because institutions do not have equal status or resources, cultural (re)production in higher education reflects existing structures of social class privilege and marginalization. Consequently, Archer (2003) suggested that education may not be a reliable path to upward mobility.

Social Class Effects in U.S. Higher Education History

Difficult admissions requirements, high tuition rates, religious restrictions, room and board fees, and lack of prior college preparation made attending college for the working class in the colonial United States an impossibility. Harvard, William and Mary, Yale, Princeton, Columbia, Brown, Dartmouth, Rutgers, and Pennsylvania are the nine institutions founded before 1781, and they have influenced the development of the educational system in America (Thelin, 2011). These institutions, in turn, were greatly influenced by Oxford and Cambridge, not only in their attempt to integrate academic and character development through residential colleges (Thelin, 2011), but also in their elitism and social exclusivity.

The colonial colleges were founded to educate "a relatively privileged group of young men who were expected to be serious about their studies and their religion" (Thelin, 2011, p. 24). Higher education was a place for the wealthy "to impart to their privileged sons a sense of responsibility and public service" (Thelin, 2011, p. 26). The admissions requirements at colonial colleges ensured a homogeneous student population of young men from wealthy, upper-class families:

> When any Scholar is able to read Tully or such like classical Latin Author *ex tempore*, and make and speak true Latin in verse and prose *suo (ut aiunt) Marte*, and decline perfectly the paradigms of Nouns and verbs in Greek tongue, then may he be admitted into the College, nor shall any claim admission before such qualifications. (*Statutes of Harvard, ca. 1646*, 1646/1961)

In the absence of an existing primary or secondary school system in the United States, education in Latin and Greek came by way of private tutors hired by wealthy colonial families for their children (Rudolph, 1990). This was also inherited from the British, where

> [e]xclusion was, and remained, built into the system. Catholics were excluded by statute, but others were excluded more subtly. Until the early twentieth century, the assumption that Latin and Greek were necessary for university admission meant that only those who had attended a particular, and small, set of schools could be considered for entry. (Ross, 2003b, p. 23)

Such an education was for the elite and reflected lives of leisure and ease. Families who were not privileged to be members of the landed gentry could afford neither the luxury of such private tutors nor the time to spare their sons' help in the fields.

Though there were disingenuous experiments with educating Native Americans, designed as they were for religious indoctrination instead of educational enlightenment, early higher education in the United States was exclusively for free, wealthy, Christian, White men. This description of English higher education also characterizes early colleges in the North American colonies:

> [C]ollege was seen as: "A finishing school for people with wealth and standing.... As many of the students who came were already prosperous, their teachers were little inclined to provide a training for particular professions and consequently presented a view of education which emphasized that diligent study in the older disciplines produced better men [*sic*] with alert minds who would be able eventually to fulfil their proper calling within a governing elite." (Gordon, Aldrich, & Dean, 1991, p. 233, as cited in Ross, 2003b, p. 24)

These ideas, already well established in England, would also come to characterize early higher education institutions in the United States. However, the United States would eventually experience a radical shift in the character of its colleges and universities as they were affected by national events during the first century of the new nation (Rudolph, 1990).

Democracy, Populism, and a New Era in Higher Education

The Revolutionary War, the Civil War and Emancipation Proclamation, and the western expansion of the new nation, along with the passage of the Morrill Acts, transformed the purpose, funding models, and student demographics for colleges and universities in the United States (Thelin, 2011). The wars exacted a significant toll on the colonial colleges: their lands were sometimes commandeered for military forts, and their students either volunteered or were drafted into the military. Finances were strained and recovery was slow (Rudolph, 1990). Between the wars, the legal conflict between Dartmouth and its state regents in 1818 served to clarify the heretofore blurry lines between state-controlled institutions and those under private control (Thelin, 2011). New funding models for higher education were another implication of this decision, with state legislatures having a more defined role in financially supporting—and therefore controlling—colleges and universities (Rudolph, 1990).

The next decade saw another development in U.S. higher education. The distinction between what forms of education were appropriate for whom was first formally expressed by a faculty committee at Yale in 1828 (*The Yale Report of 1828*, 1828/1961). Through this report, commissioned less than 50 years after the Revolutionary War at a time of declining enrollment and increasing competition for students, the faculty at Yale was responding to pressures to offer a more practical curriculum of use to the burgeoning mercantile classes. The report's authors argued against lowering admission standards to increase student enrollment or adding professional studies to the curriculum. Instead, Yale's faculty saw the emergence of new types of institutions as an opportunity for Yale and other institutions like it to further refine and concentrate on what they did best—teach a classic liberal arts education appropriate for the new republic—while other institutions provided a mercantile education (Lane, 1987). However, the Yale faculty did not presume that a classical liberal arts curriculum should be restricted based on one's background (*The Yale Report of 1828*, 1828/1961). *The Yale Report of 1828* states:

> Our republican form of government renders it highly important, that great numbers should enjoy the advantage of a thorough education. On the Eastern continent, the *few* who are destined to particular departments in political life, may be educated for the purpose; while the mass of people are left in comparative ignorance. But in this country, where offices are accessible to all who are qualified for them, superior intellectual attainments ought not to be confined to any description of persons. (p. 289)

The report affirmed that those from the working class should have access to higher education, but it disputed the legitimacy of combining professional studies with a classical liberal arts curriculum. Such an education was most suitably provided by other institutions. The authors of the report were attempting to define a place for a focus on civic virtue. This was the ultimate goal of a classical curriculum—in the face of increasing emphasis on the virtues of private enterprise.

Despite Lane's (1987) assertion that the report should not be seen as reactionary, elitist, and authoritarian, the implications of the report's philosophical orientation cannot be ignored. The report did not include any reconsideration of the college's admissions requirements, which had not changed much from what Harvard had been requiring in the mid-seventeenth century (*Statutes of Harvard, ca. 1646*, 1646/1961), and primary and secondary education was still not publicly available. Consequently, access to the classical liberal arts curriculum at an institution like Yale was still restricted to the wealthy. The Yale faculty's attempt to craft a neorepublican compromise between civic virtue and private enterprise (Lane, 1987) belies the report's prominence as a foundational philosophical treatise in support of higher education's role in social (re)production.

Attending college required that an individual be a person of means. Thelin (2011), despite seeking to underplay the "pejorative modern connotations of *elitism*" (p. 26; emphasis in original), does concede that "the colonial colleges ratified and perpetuated an elite that would inherit positions of influence in communities" (p. 26). This purpose and character of higher education carried over into the new national period (Fuhrmann, 1997). Enrollment meant that your family had the means to pay tuition, lodging, and board while being able to maintain their homes during your absence. This manifestation of class privilege was diffused throughout higher education in the United States and Europe. In the United States specifically, this took the form of literary societies and exclusive fraternal organizations in which one's wealth and social standing were the primary membership criteria.

The secession of the Confederate states and the outbreak of the U.S. Civil War in 1861 brought more upheaval to fledgling colleges and those universities still recovering from the Revolution (Rudolph, 1990). The war pitted states' rights against federalism against the backdrop of the question of slavery. As reflected in Thelin's (2011) history, U.S. higher education came to be identified more clearly with public control and financial support. This is best illustrated by the Morrill Land Grant Act of 1862. Passed by Congress to punish the South for seceding from the Union, the Morrill Act of 1862 granted federal funds to the Union states for use in creating institutions of higher education that would be primarily invested in agricultural innovations, mechanical and engineering education, and military advancement. These institutions were also intended to educate the sons and daughters of the middle class. After the Civil War, another Morrill Act was passed in 1890, which extended the same opportunity to the states of the former Confederacy. The initial purpose of the 1862 Morrill Act was reiterated in 1890: to support education in agricultural, mechanical, and military science. However, the 1890 legislation also provided the means for establishing racially segregated, dual university systems for the higher education of African Americans, newly freed from chattel slavery and in need of training for skilled labor and professional roles and education for citizenship. These institutions, known as land-grants, reflected populist ideals and used admission standards that reflected a more utilitarian and practical curriculum.

Other colleges also reflected this evolving philosophical shift in the role of higher education. The meaning of attaining a college degree expanded from merely securing and affirming the social elitism of the wealthy, who were mostly White and male, to extending those class privileges and opportunities to others who were becoming more racially diverse and included increasing numbers of women. Denominational colleges in the Midwest, although influenced by the more established Eastern universities, were clearly distinguished from them (Rudolph, 1990; Thelin, 2011). These colleges sought to "offer new avenues of mobility to poor young men into a rapidly expanding middle class" (Findlay, 2000, p. 125) largely by educating young adults to be teachers and preachers. Identifying and maintaining social class elitism was subsumed in "the evangelical effort to Christianize America in the nineteenth century" (Findlay, 2000, p. 125).

Further Expansion, Contradictory Access

From the late nineteenth to the twentieth century, access to higher education in the United States increased to include a more diverse student body (Gumport, Iannozzi, Shaman, & Zemsky, 1997). Several forces came together to produce this outcome. The continued strengthening of both public and private historically Black colleges and universities (HBCUs), the emergence of the community college sector, and greater federal involvement in myriad policymaking activities all combined to make higher education both more democratic and more stratified.

The central argument of the Yale Report, that certain schools (like Yale) should be devoted to the classics while others engaged in practical education for those not sufficiently equipped for such pursuits, was repurposed for a new era. Proponents of education for the masses of newly freed African Americans debated what form such education should take (Anderson, 1988; Du Bois, 1903/1989; Dunn, 1993; Thelin, 2011). Some, like Booker T. Washington, argued for an industrial education suitable for skilled laborers and domestics; others, like W.E.B. Du Bois, asserted a greater need to make available a classical liberal arts foundation necessary for civic leadership to those intellectually equipped to handle it (Anderson, 1988; Du Bois, 1903/1989; Dunn, 1993). White philanthropists tended to favor Washington's philosophy and supported colleges for African Americans that promised to emphasize an industrial education (Anderson, 1988). Although access to a college education had been made available to African Americans, access to a liberal education was either restricted or outright denied due to continued racial segregation in colleges and universities throughout both the North and the South.

Even without racist, eugenics-inspired arguments about the presumed intellectual inferiority of African Americans, debates about the utility of a classical liberal arts education for the masses informed the development of other sectors of higher education as well. Community colleges are unique to the United States, and their origins in the early twentieth century positioned them to be gateways to 4-year institutions (Cohen & Brawer, 2008; Thelin, 2011). Four-year institutions were beginning to divorce themselves from the remedial mission that had been necessary prior to the emergence and wide-scale availability of publicly funded primary and secondary education (Thelin, 2011). Community colleges stepped in and filled the void, opening up higher education to students who otherwise would not have been admitted to college.

In time, however, the academic emphasis would be "supplemented—and sometimes eclipsed—by the inclusion of a technical or vocational curriculum" (Thelin, 2011, p. 250). As

Dougherty (1994) argued, the vocationalization of the community college reflected the interests of local leaders, state and federal government officials, and corporations looking to train their own skilled workers. Eventually, community college students who aspired to transfer to a 4-year institution to earn a bachelor's degree would find their hopes dampened and their efforts blocked (Dougherty, 1994; Pascarella & Terenzini, 2005).

The federal government also became more involved in higher education, attempting to promote greater access and equity for broader segments of the U.S. population. After the Morrill Acts, the Servicemen's Readjustment Act—commonly known as the GI Bill—made the most significant impact on U.S. higher education. Passed by Congress in anticipation of the need to reintegrate military personnel serving in World War II without flooding the labor market, the GI Bill is regularly hailed as the single greatest instrument in democratizing higher education in U.S. history (Gumport et al., 1997; Thelin, 2011) because of its role in making higher education affordable to returning soldiers, who often came from working- and middle-class families. However, as Maher and Tetreault (2007) point out, access to the GI Bill's provisions—which only incidentally included tuition benefits—was not equitable. Women and African Americans were disenfranchised from the law's benefits by structural inequities reflected in their military status and conditions of service (Maher & Tetreault, 2007). The GI Bill thereby reproduced social inequity in higher education based on race and gender.

Another piece of federal legislation that was intended to dramatically change the landscape of higher education access was the Basic Educational Opportunity Grant created in 1972, known popularly since 1980 as the Pell Grant Program (Pell Institute, 2013). As described by the Pell Institute for the Study of Opportunity in Higher Education (2013), Pell Grants are based on the expected family contribution (EFC) to a student's college education as reported on the Federal Application for Student Financial Aid (FAFSA) form and awarded to low-income students. Pell Grants are not loans that have to be repaid. Congress sets the maximum award. Despite the evidence supporting the effectiveness of Pell Grants in facilitating the academic progress and completion of low-income students (Wei & Horn, 2002), congressional battles over the maximum value of the grant are regularly debated (Shapiro, 2012; Spetrini, 2013; Timmeney, 2011). Moreover, the purchasing power of the Pell Grant has declined over time (Brown, Rocha, & Sharkey, 2005).

Over time, through institutional innovation and government intervention, financial accessibility to higher education has increased, though some would argue that there are still large gaps in college accessibility for the poorest of the poor due to myriad factors, including affordability, the persistent role of standardized tests in admissions, and self-selection (Radford, 2013; Rooks, 2013; Ross, 2003a, 2003b; Webley, 2013). In addition, in a race to attract students from wealthier families who can afford most of the cost of their tuition, more colleges are reducing need-based aid and considering an applicant's ability to pay in admissions decisions (Burd, 2013). Nevertheless, significant progress has been made since the colonial era in getting poor and working-class students to college.

Yet paying for college is not the only hurdle to college access and completion for low-income students; it may not even be the primary barrier (Radford, 2013). As found by Engle and O'Brien (2007), low-income students often could not take advantage of retention programs at their institutions that were either fee-based or offered during hours inconvenient for working students. It is necessary to consider the ways in which college itself is a classed environment that disincentivizes poor and working-class students' persistence and undermines their success.

Social Class on Campus: Environments of Exclusion

Defining what is meant by *social class* is necessary at this point in the discussion. Despite the presumed classlessness of U.S. society (Barratt, 2011), people in the United States think they know what social class is. Sometimes social class is used synonymously with *socioeconomic status*, defined as "the social standing or class of an individual or group…often measured as a combination of education, income and occupation" (American Psychological Association (APA), 2013). However, as Barratt (2011) discussed, social class is a complex construct defined as much by what it is *not* as by what it *is*.

Barratt (2011) defines social class as something more than money but inclusive of income and wealth. It is a multifaceted construct that is simultaneously subject to individual perceptions and an intercultural experience, a tool and an identity, and something reflected in social capital, education, occupation, and prestige. Examinations of social class or socioeconomic status involve issues related to "privilege, power, and control" (APA, 2013, para. 2; Barratt, 2011). Barratt's (2011) portrayal of social class as a culture that can be performed through norms and habits and worn like a style of dress requires an understanding of the dominant social class of higher education and the way it privileges students from familiar class backgrounds, while marginalizing those from divergent social class backgrounds. As Ross (2003a) illustrated, attending college and attaining a college education in the United Kingdom does not by itself guarantee one's entrance into a higher social class status.

For many poor students in the United States, however, even applying to elite colleges seems out of reach (Radford, 2013). Despite having the high grades required for admission, many of these students have "difficulty envisioning themselves at prestigious universities" (Radford, 2013, para. 12). Part of the reason for this may be that these poor and working-class students do not reflect the *majority class culture* of the college they attend (Barratt, 2011). Majority social class culture students have a hard time articulating the social class distinctions present in their environment because they are immersed in it, according to Barratt (2011). He asks students to ask themselves the following question: "In what ways are your attitudes, behaviors, and fashion, food, and music preferences different from those of people in the majority social class on your campus?" (Barratt, 2011, p. 100). The possible answers to this question can reveal the ways in which majority social class culture, typically reflecting middle- and upper-middle-class norms and values, is apparent throughout the campus: the food served in the dining hall, the music played on the campus radio station, the stories and perspectives covered in the student newspaper, the art that decorates the academic buildings and residence halls, the classes taught in the curriculum, and the activities and events planned by campus programming boards. Moreover, "lower class students' speech patterns, writing, and classroom behavior are different, nonnormative, and deviant" (Barratt, 2011, p. 67). Archer (2003) asserted that the working class "are often the subject of discourses that blame them, rather than social inequalities, for their inability to access higher education" (p. 16) and that despite social class inequality, working-class students are more likely to blame themselves for that inequality.

Conclusion

The barriers that working-class students face in comparison to their more economically privileged peers are numerous and pervasive. The legacies of elitist admissions policies and restrictive philosophies about occupationally appropriate education have combined to withhold full access to the working class in U.S. colleges and universities. Efforts to redress social class inequity in accessing higher education have not been entirely successful; they are unfulfilled promises of education's ability to promote upward social mobility. By seeking only to give lower-income students more money to attend college, policymakers and legislators have merely scratched the surface of college accessibility for these students. Left unaddressed has been the palpable force of an unquestioned and unchecked majority class culture (Barratt, 2011) that leaves poor and working-class students isolated, disenfranchised, and at risk of attrition.

Fulfilling the transformative and liberating promise of higher education will require more than just adding on to the existing system, which has characterized the evolution of U.S. higher education's philosophies and aims up to this point (Fuhrmann, 1997). Rather, substantive and systemic transformational change is required. Calls to reform higher education abound from governmental, institutional, and private stakeholders (for the most recent federal proposals, see White House, 2013). However, past history and current evidence suggest that these reforms will also fall short.

Truly transformative higher education reforms must first be linked to K–12 educational reforms. Although higher education in the United States predates public primary and secondary education by nearly 2 centuries (Thelin, 2011), it can ill afford to act as though their fortunes are not linked. Sufficient numbers of students from diverse backgrounds who are adequately prepared for the rigors of a college curriculum will come only from well-funded, well-equipped, and fully staffed public primary and secondary schools. Moreover, discussions about standards and educational quality are best initiated by collaboration among K–16+ educators, not policymakers and legislators.

Successful reforms must also challenge the dominant class values and beliefs reflected in such documents as the *Yale Report*. These tacit assumptions include the belief that education should be a commodity bought by families primarily to confirm their child's station in life. This assumption restricts access to our nation's most elite colleges, effectively shutting out the poor and working class. Another limiting and privileged assumption is that technical occupations and liberal arts education are mutually exclusive. A plumber or automotive mechanic may not need to read Toni Morrison's novel *Beloved* or understand China's Cultural Revolution in order to fix a leaky faucet or a busted carburetor. However, such workers do need the critical thinking and other intellectual skills that come from discussing *Beloved* and the Cultural Revolution in their social, cultural, and historical contexts and considering their present-day implications. These cognitive skills could prompt the plumber or automotive technician to investigate whether there is an underlying issue causing a persistent leaky faucet or repeated mechanical breakdowns. Just as important, though, given the democratic character of our government as noted by the authors of the *Yale Report*, these skills are essential for effective citizenship in a democratic nation. As a democracy, the United States cannot afford to limit access to high-quality liberal arts education to those who can pay for it. If this is done, the "government of the people, by the people, for the people" may in fact perish from the earth (Lincoln, 1863).

References

American Psychological Association (APA). (2013). *Socioeconomic status*. Retrieved from http://www.apa.org/topics/socio economic-status/

Anderson, J. (1988). *The education of Blacks in the South, 1860–1935*. Chapel Hill, NC: University of North Carolina Press.

Archer, L. (2003). Social class and higher education. In L. Archer, M. Hutchings, & A. Ross (Eds.), *Higher education and social class: Issues of exclusion and inclusion* (pp. 5–20). London, UK: RoutledgeFalmer.

Barratt, W. (2011). *Social class on campus: Theories and manifestations.* Sterling, VA: Stylus.

Bowen, W.G., & Bok, D. (1998). *The shape of the river: Long-term consequences of considering race in college and university admissions.* Princeton, NJ: Princeton University Press.

Brown, C.G., Rocha, E., & Sharkey, A. (2005). *Getting smarter, becoming fairer: A progressive education agenda for a stronger nation.* A Joint Initiative of the Center for American Progress and the Institute for America's Future. Retrieved from http://www.americanprogress.org/issues/education/news/2005/08/23/1611/getting-smarter-becoming-fairer/

Burd, S. (2013, September–October). Merit aid madness. *Washington Monthly* [online]. Retrieved from http://www.washingtonmonthly.com/magazine/september_october_2013/features/merit_aid_madness046459.php

Cabrera, A.F., & La Nasa, S.M. (2000). Understanding the college-choice process. In A.F. Cabrera & S.M. La Nasa (Eds.), *Understanding the college choice of disadvantaged students* (pp. 5–22). San Francisco, CA: Jossey-Bass.

Cohen, A.M., & Brawer, F.B. (2008). *The American community college* (5th ed.). San Francisco, CA: Jossey-Bass.

Dougherty, K.J. (1994). *The contradictory college: The conflicting origins, impacts, and futures of the community college.* Albany, NY: State University of New York Press.

Du Bois, W.E.B. (1989). *The souls of Black folk.* New York, NY: Bantam Books.

Dunn, F. (1993). The educational philosophies of Washington, Du Bois, and Houston: Laying the foundations for Afrocentrism and multiculturalism. *Journal of Negro Education, 62*(1), 24–34.

Engle, J., & O'Brien, C. (2007). *Demography is not destiny: Increasing the graduation rates of low-income college students at large public universities.* Washington, DC: The Pell Institute for the Study of Opportunity in Higher Education. Retrieved from http://www.pellinstitute.org/publications-Demography_Is_Not_Destiny.shtml

Findlay, J. (2000). Agency, denominations, and the western colleges, 1830–1860: Some connections between evangelicalism and American higher education. In R. Geiger (Ed.), *The American college in the nineteenth century* (pp. 115–126). Nashville, TN: Vanderbilt University Press.

Fuhrmann, B.S. (1997). Philosophies and aims. In J.G. Gaff, J.L. Ratcliff, & Associates (Eds.), *Handbook of the undergraduate curriculum* (pp. 86–99). San Francisco, CA: Jossey-Bass.

Gordon, P., Aldrich, R., & Dean, D. (1991). *Education and policy in England in the twentieth century.* London, UK: Woburn.

Gumport, P.J. (2000). Academic restructuring: Organizational change and institutional imperatives. *Higher Education, 39*(1), 67–91.

Gumport, P.J., Iannozzi, M., Shaman, S., & Zemsky, R. (1997). *Trends in United States higher education from massification to post massification.* Stanford, CA: National Center for Postsecondary Improvement.

Harper, S.R., & Quaye, S.J. (2009). Beyond sameness, with engagement and outcomes for all: An introduction. In S.R. Harper & S.J. Quaye (Eds.), *Student engagement in higher education: Theoretical perspectives and practical approaches for diverse populations* (pp. 1–16). New York, NY: Routledge.

hooks, b. (1994). *Teaching to transgress: Education as the practice of freedom.* New York, NY: Routledge.

Hurst, A. (2009). The path to college: Stories of students from the working class. *Race, Gender, & Class, 16*(1–2), 257–281.

Kezar, A. (2004). Obtaining integrity: Reviewing and examining the charter between higher education and society. *Review of Higher Education, 27*(4), 429–459.

Lane, J.C. (1987). The Yale report of 1828 and liberal education: A neorepublican manifesto. *History of Education Quarterly, 27*(3), 325–338.

Lareau, A. (1989). Social class differences in family-school relationships: The importance of cultural capital. *Sociology of Education, 69*(2), 73–85.

Lincoln, A. (1863, November 19). *The Gettysburg address.* Abraham Lincoln Online: Speeches and writings. Retrieved from http://www.abrahamlincolnonline.org/lincoln/speeches/gettysburg.htm

Maher, F.A., & Tetreault, M.K.T. (2007). *Privilege and diversity in the academy.* New York, NY: Routledge.

Pascarella, E., & Terenzini, P. (2005). *How college impacts students: A third decade of research* (Vol. 2). San Francisco, CA: Jossey-Bass.

Pell Institute. (2013). *Pell Grants.* Washington, DC: Author. Retrieved from http://www.pellinstitute.org/pell_grants.shtml

Radford, A.W. (2013, September 16). "No point in applying": Why poor students are missing at top colleges. *The Atlantic* [online]. Retrieved from http://www.theatlantic.com/education/archive/2013/09/no-point-in-applying-why-poor-students-are-missing-at-top-colleges/279699/

Rooks, N.M. (2013, February 27). The biggest barrier to elite education isn't affordability; it's accessibility. *Time Magazine* [online]. Retrieved from http://ideas.time.com/2013/02/27/the-biggest-barrier-to-elite-education-isnt-affordability-its-accessibility/

Ross, A. (2003a). Access to higher education: Inclusion for the masses? In L. Archer, M. Hutchings, & A. Ross (Eds.), *Higher education and social class: Issues of exclusion and inclusion* (pp. 45–74). London, UK: Routledge-Falmer.

Ross, A. (2003b). Higher education and social access: To the Robbins Report. In L. Archer, M. Hutchings, & A. Ross (Eds.), *Higher education and social class: Issues of exclusion and inclusion* (pp. 21–44). London, UK: RoutledgeFalmer.

Rudolph, F. (1990). *The American college and university: A history*. Athens, GA: University of Georgia Press.

Shapiro, G. (2012, May 31). Both sides fail in student loan debate. *The Daily Caller*. Retrieved from http://dailycaller.com/2012/05/31/both-sides-fail-in-student-loan-debate/

Spetrini, P.J. (2013, February 12). RI congressional delegation pledge to fight for Pell Grant funding. *GoLocalProv*. Retrieved from http://www.golocalprov.com/news/ri-congressional-delegation-pledge-to-fight-for-pell-grant-funding/

Statutes of Harvard, ca. 1646. (1961). Reprinted in R. Hofstadter & W. Smith (Eds.), *American higher education: A documentary history, Vol. 1* (pp. 8–9). Chicago, IL: University of Chicago Press.

Strayhorn, T.L. (2012). *College students' sense of belonging: A key to educational success for all students*. New York, NY: Routledge.

Thelin, J.R. (2011). *A history of American higher education* (2nd ed.). Baltimore, MD: Johns Hopkins University Press.

Timmeney, B. (2011, May 6). The growing debate over Pell Grants [Web log message]. *The Upjohn Institute blog*. Retrieved from http://www.upjohn.org/node/518

Webley, K. (2013, May 9). We're doing a lousy job of getting poor kids to college. *Time Magazine* [online]. Retrieved from http://nation.time.com/2013/05/09/were-doing-a-lousy-job-of-getting-poor-kids-to-college/

Wei, C.C., & Horn, L. (2002). *Persistence and attainment of beginning students with Pell Grants* (NCES 2002-169). Washington, DC: U.S. Department of Education, National Center for Education Statistics.

White House. (2013). *Education*. Retrieved from http://www.whitehouse.gov/issues/education

Woodson, C.G. (2006). *The mis-education of the Negro*. San Diego, CA: Book Tree.

X, M. [El-Hajj Malik El-Shabazz]. (2011). [Malcolm X's speech at the founding rally of the Organization for Afro-American Unity, 28 June 1964.] Reprinted in *By any means necessary: Speeches, interviews, and a letter by Malcolm X* (pp. 35–67). New York, NY: Pathfinder Press. Retrieved from http://www.blackpast.org/1964-malcolm-x-s-speech-founding-rally-organization-afro-american-unity#sthash.t59rOWsh.dpuf

The Yale Report of 1828. (1961). Reprinted in R. Hofstadter & W. Smith (Eds.), *American higher education: A documentary history* (Vol. 1, pp. 279–289). Chicago, IL: University of Chicago Press.

Part Three

Student Life

FIFTEEN

The Typology and Needs of American Transfer Students

Karen L. Archambault

Introduction

At its core, the question "What is a transfer student?" is a simple one. A transfer student is any student who arrives at an institution of higher education with previously accumulated college credits. But accurate though it may be, that definition betrays a complex issue that continues to perplex practitioners and policymakers alike. Transfer students used to be easier to ignore, as they were not included in retention and graduation numbers designed to measure the comparative quality of institutions and which focused on first-time, full-time students (National Student Clearinghouse Research Center, 2013). But with fully one-third of college students attending at least two institutions during their college careers (not including those who achieve college credits during high school), the sheer number of transfer students has become impossible to ignore (National Student Clearinghouse Research Center, 2013). A better understanding of the experiences of transfer students benefits not only the students, but also the institutions from which they transfer and into which they are received. Institutions can develop programs and supports to greater benefit these students and improve transfer agreements with partner institutions. Perhaps most important, individual practitioners can more effectively work with these students to overcome the challenges that they may face.

Thus, in order to understand the newer, multifaceted transfer student, we must consider a number of factors that contribute to this complexity. First, practitioners must understand that transfer student enrollment is not a monolith. While several common "types" of transfer students and transfer patterns exist, even these have multiple variables within them; transfer student experiences are as unique as the students themselves. First, practitioners must understand the various motivations for transfer, particularly because transfers are planned and unplanned, expected and unexpected, and these components affect the supports they require. Second, those who will work with these students must understand the ways in which they differ demographically from mainstream college students. The institution that prepares only for its first-time, full-time students will often find that its transfers represent a demographic anomaly. Finally, this chapter will review the common needs and challenges students have when planning for their transfer or arriving on a new campus.

Types of Transfer Students

Years ago, transfer students were assumed to be those who had attended a community college, usually because of academic or financial under-preparedness, and then transitioned to a senior institution.[1] In recent years, however, the types of transfer students have become much more numerous and complex.

Traditional transfers, also referred to as "vertical transfers," move from the community college to the senior institution (Borst, Jones, & Cohen, 2012). With 45% of undergraduate students enrolled at the community college level for coursework, the population is too large to be ignored (American Association of Community Colleges, 2013). With the increasing costs of financing an education, the lower cost of the community college is certainly one attraction, especially for those who are eligible for federal grants. But students also pursue education at community colleges in order to gain academic preparedness prior to pursuing the baccalaureate degree, or to develop personally or professionally prior to advancing (American Association of Community Colleges, 2013; College Board, 2007). Other students use the community college for exploration prior to the personal and financial commitment of pursuing the baccalaureate.

Grites and McDonald (2012) rightly refer to student enrollment and mobility as increasingly "dynamic" (p. 21). Just as students transfer from community colleges to senior institutions, they also move between institutions within the same sector. This is known as "lateral transfer" (Borst et al., 2012). In fact, lateral transfer is second only to vertical transfer in size and scope (Bahr, 2009). As is true for students' initial reasons for enrolling in community colleges, they move laterally between institutions within the same sector for academic, financial, and personal reasons. A new institution might offer different academic programs or a more affordable financial profile, or it might be closer to home.

"Reverse transfer" has two distinct meanings, both of which are relevant to understanding transfer student patterns. In some research, the term is used to describe a student who previously attended a senior institution but has moved to a community college (Borst et al., 2012). These students might do so because the first institution was a poor fit for the student's academic goals, because its financial costs were too high, or for personal reasons, including geography or family needs. The second use of the term is to refer to the transfer of senior-institution credit to the community college to achieve the requirement for the associate's degree while continuing to pursue the bachelor's degree (National Student Clearinghouse Research Center, 2012b). While the first definition is still routinely used, the second is becoming increasingly common, particularly when used in the framework of agreements between partner institutions for the awarding of the associate's degree.[2] With the push for college completion, students who are close to attaining the associate's degree prior to transfer are encouraged to transfer from their senior institution back to the community college in order to complete the last requirements of the degree. This is an attractive option for those who might be looking to ensure documentation of their efforts, especially those who are enrolled part-time while simultaneously pursuing professional goals, or those who might be anxious about personal and financial obstacles to degree completion and might therefore desire documented degree completion. The recognition of the associate's degree as a valuable credential has increased the likelihood that students will pursue this avenue of transfer (American Association of Community Colleges, n.d.).

The final significant enrollment pattern for transfer students is often called "swirling," and it refers to enrollment patterns in which students move between multiple institutions, often between various institutional types (McCormick, 2003). While transcripts may suggest that this enrollment is haphazard or disorganized, it is often rather an intentional action comprised of concurrent enrollments, summer and online courses, and attendance at institutions of various type, location, and cost, pieced together in an attempt to build an academic profile that meets educational goals despite an unconventional path. McCormick (2013) argues that students engage in swirling behavior for a number of reasons including, but not limited to, trial enrollment, in which they fail to commit to a given institution but consider transfer; special program enrollment, such as study-abroad programs; supplemental enrollment, such as through summer programs; consolidated enrollment, in which students choose programs that require enrollment in two institutions, such as for dual-degree programs; or independent enrollment, in which students pursue education and credentials separate from their degree program with no intention of officially transferring the credit for degree attainment. This swirling pattern of enrollment perhaps most clearly demonstrates the complexity of transfer students and their experiences.

Other, less commonly discussed transfer patterns shape the landscape of enrollment. Dual enrollment programs in which students complete college credits while in high school, including through more coordinated programs such as early college high school, are on the rise (Hoffman & Bayerl, 2006). Professionals must also consider the challenges of "thwarted" transfer students, who may enter a new institution without credits, having assumed that those credits acquired at an unaccredited institution were transferrable (Marklein, 2010).

The Impact of Demographics

As if the challenges of effective transfer enrollment alone were not enough to overcome, these potential hurdles are compounded by transfer student demographics. While transfer students are certainly individuals with individual academic, financial, and personal needs, when looked upon collectively, they share certain characteristics that differentiate them from the larger college student population. Racial and ethnic minorities, first-generation students, students with disabilities, and part-time students exist in all colleges, but their increased numbers among transfer students make working with these students more challenging within institutions where native[3] students are much more homogeneous.

Though there is a growing variety in transfer student enrollment patterns, most of these students remain vertical community college transfers from public community colleges to senior institutions (National Student Clearinghouse Research Center, 2012c). Because of the diversity of the community college population as compared to that of senior institutions, transfers are likely to be more racially and ethnically diverse than their native counterparts, more likely to be the first in their families to attend college, more likely to come from lower socioeconomic backgrounds, to enroll part-time, and to commute (Clery, 2009; Cohen, Brawer, & Lombardi, 2008). These characteristics make transfer students more likely to face challenges of assimilation and engagement with their new institutions. Though it may seem counterintuitive, these students may actually suffer at the point of transfer because community college staff and faculty are particularly conscious of the challenges these demographics create and therefore provide a higher level of care (Dougherty & Kienzl, 2006). Faculty and administrators at senior institutions may find it easier to ignore or overlook the differences between native and transfer students and assume that, because they have chosen the same institution, they have the same needs. The National Survey of Student Engagement (NSSE) (2011) demonstrates a lower level of engagement for transfer students as compared to their native peers, especially in terms of connection to faculty. This may reflect the need for greater attention to the differences between these students.

First-generation students are particularly vulnerable to these transfer risks. Because they do not have the social capital needed to navigate educational environments, they may erroneously believe that all institutions operate as their community college did and therefore become overwhelmed by the increased complexity of the senior institution (Cushman, 2006). This challenge is compounded for first-generation students of ethnic and racial minorities, who often do not have the role models to shepherd them through the conflicting information, complex processes, and potential lack of compatibility with a new campus (Ornelas & Solorzano, 2004). These multiple challenges create self-doubt, which can be the greatest hurdle for students, and which often results in their avoiding asking for assistance for fear of being found to be deficient (Ornelas & Solorzano, 2004).

Like ethnic and racial minorities and first-generation students, students with disabilities are also significantly more likely to begin their academic careers by attending community colleges (National Center for Education Statistics, 2000). These students have particular needs, especially for navigating a new institution's disability support, and may not be aware of the resources available on a new campus. Special attention must be paid to the unique needs of this subset of transfer students (Ponticelli & Russ-Eft, 2009).

Enrollment patterns and the need to work also create greater complexity for transfer students. While 62% of community college students attended part-time in 2005 (usually because of work or familial obligations), only 21% of their public senior institution counterparts did the same (Handel, 2009). This distinction in opportunity to pursue education as a full-time endeavor makes transfer students particularly vulnerable at institutions where registration options are guided by the expectation that students are able to organize their lives around the college's schedule. This difference in ability to engage full-time may result in a disconnect between the student and his or her commitment to degree attainment (Chen & Carroll, 2007). The results of this financial challenge will be discussed in greater detail below.

A crucial part of comprehending transfer demographics is to appreciate that identification as a transfer student is but one part of the student profile. Transfer students are complex individuals and are more than the sum of their prior credit. They are transfers/athletes; transfers/veterans; transfers/undocumented persons; or transfers/honors—just to name a few—as well as transfers/parents, transfers/workers, and so on. When considering their needs, therefore, those new to the field should remain alert to these complexities and identify interventions that recognize the holistic needs of the student whenever possible.

Needs of Transfer Students

Despite this caveat, transfer students are distinct from their native peers and so, in spite of their diversity, they do have transfer-specific needs. Institutions must recognize these academic, financial, and personal challenges that affect transfer students in order to provide an environment that is most conducive to their learning and that rewards their persistence in seeking a degree.

Academic Needs

For many years, assumptions were made about the ability of transfer students to succeed academically upon transfer. Certainly, academic adjustment can challenge students moving between institutions. Laanan (2007) identified five reactions by students that suggest such difficulty. These are: (1) difficulty in meeting academic standards, (2) dip in grades or grade point average, (3) identified increase in stress related to academics, (4) difficulty in adjusting to changes in academic policies such as term length, and (5) a sense of competition between students that was not present at the 2-year college. With all these challenges, it is no surprise that students often face "transfer shock," a term coined by Hills (1965) and commonly used to describe the downturn in GPA that often occurs after transfer from community college to senior institution (Carlan & Byxbe, 2000; Cejda & Kaylor, 1997; Davies & Casey, 1999).

In one study, the effect of transfer shock was so significant that results showed that more than half of students experienced a decrease of at least one-half point in grade point average (Jones, 1994). Though usually temporary, the dip in GPA suggests that students struggle with the transfer process itself. In her seminal work *Counseling Adults in Transition*, Schlossberg (1984) argued that the support one can identify and receive during a transition can make the difference between success and failure. This is perhaps most true with transfer students.

Financial Needs

As stated above, many students make their decisions about higher education based on their financial situation. As funding sources have dried up, the burden of paying for college has increasingly rested on the student (Heller, 2006; Weerts & Ronca, 2006). For transfer students with multiple responsibilities, the pressure to meet all of those responsibilities simply increases their need for financial support. However, many transfer students are hesitant to seek the needed financial assistance and often complain of overly complicated forms, fears of debt, and beliefs that they do not qualify for aid (Handel, 2008). Some students who may not have needed aid at their first institution may mistakenly believe that their education should be "pay as you go," rather than viewing it as an investment, or they may view debt as too great a risk (Handel, 2008; Long, 2007). Understandably, financial aid packages differ from institution to institution, but the irony of the funding model for transfers is that while many choose their first institutions based on financial considerations, many institutions (more than one-quarter) do not provide scholarships specific to entering transfers, reserving the majority of their funding for freshman students (Dowd, Cheslock, & Melguizo, 2008; National Association for College Admissions Counseling, 2010). Students who are challenged financially may find that on-campus employment can connect them to the institution (Astin, 1997). However, these financial challenges can also create a greater push for the off-campus employment and part-time enrollment that disconnect the transfer student from the campus community.

Psychological and Personal Needs

Many students struggle with their arrival on a new campus because of the assumptions that they (and campus officials) carry with them. The students assume that, because they have been college students before, they are already familiar with how to be successful and therefore do not seek out the supports and services on campus. Campus officials assume, for the same reason, that supports specific to the needs of transfer students are unnecessary. It is often only when students face obstacles that they realize that the distinctions between campuses may be significant (Archambault, Forbes, & Schlosberg, 2012). In order to help students overcome these challenges, campuses should not only identify resources that can assist students in making a smooth transition but also identify contact people familiar with the needs of transfers, develop transfer orientations specific to their needs, and—perhaps most important—develop community among transfer students to ensure not only that students become familiar and comfortable with their surroundings, but that they know that they are not alone (Archambault, Forbes, & Schlosberg, 2012).

Davies and Casey (1999) coined the term "campus culture shock" to describe the disconnect many transfer students experience at a new campus. This shock goes beyond the academic and results from the psychological, emotional, and institutional upheaval students undergo in the move from institution to institution. While all those in transition may suffer from this kind of shock, vertical transfers are more likely to face challenges than those trying to navigate a horizontal transfer (Keeley & House, 1993). Community colleges are designed to be easy to navigate and rarely include the complex hierarchies of the senior institution (Corkery, Ingram, & Davis, 2007). These challenges are even greater for those transferring from community colleges to selective institutions that they may find to be polar opposites. Handel (2009) argues that this comes from the core differences in culture between institutions that prize access and those that prize academic commitment. Cohen and colleagues (2008) suggest that community college faculty members are viewed by students as distinctly committed to their success, resulting in students who, upon transfer, are challenged to seek out less visible resources on the new campus.

In his seminal study *Leaving College: Rethinking the Causes and Cures of Student Attrition*, Tinto (1993) argued that student involvement was vital to the success and persistence of college students. Because of the aforementioned challenges in campus integration, transfer students are less likely than their native counterparts to be involved on campus, though it is perhaps even more important that transfer students become engaged in student organizations (Laanan, 2007; NSSE, 2008, 2009). This engagement, though, does not some easily; transfer students' demographic differences, family responsibilities, and part-time enrollment often make a "traditional" college experience a challenge (NSSE, 2011). Tinto (1993) also argued for the clear communication of community norms to students, something that is especially important for potential transfer students so that they can select institutions that are compatible with their needs, interests, and future plans.

Conclusion

Transfer students are a growing part of the higher education landscape, both in raw numbers and in their importance to institutional strength, and the debate continues about how to "count" transfer students and to document their ease or difficulty in achieving degree completion (Fain, 2012). For many institutions, counting these transfer students is to their benefit: the National Student Clearinghouse reported increases in 6-year degree completion of 4% to 13% when full-time transfer students were included, and increases of up to 15% for those who did not enroll full-time but instead had the freedom to choose both full- and part-time status over their peers for time to degree completion (National Student Clearinghouse Research Center, 2012a). Increasing these numbers, however, requires that higher education professionals—and new practitioners in particular—take steps to identify and address the potential roadblocks that keep students from attaining a degree. The increasing demand for accountability will mandate that the success of these students—personally, professionally, academically, and socially—will become one of the measures by which our success is evaluated.

Notes

1. For the purposes of this chapter, the term "community college" will be used to refer to those institutions that primarily award the associate's degree, while "senior institution" will be used to refer to those that award bachelor's degrees and higher. These are more accurate than the terms "2-year" and "4-year" institutions, which do not reflect the actual experience of most students.
2. See, for example, the websites of the University of Michigan at Dearborn (http://www.umd.umich.edu/rr_reversetransfer/) and Macomb Community College (www.macomb.edu) for their formal agreements to accept this reverse credit.
3. "Native" refers to those students who began their career at the institution in which they are enrolled and is used throughout this chapter as a counter to "transfer" students, who began their education elsewhere and are, essentially, immigrants to the receiving institution.

References

American Association of Community Colleges. (n.d.). *The college completion challenge fact sheet.* Washington, DC: Author. Retrieved from http://www.aacc.nche.edu/About/completionchallenge/Documents/Completion_Toolkit_Complete.pdf

American Association of Community Colleges. (2013). *2013 Community college fact sheet.* Washington, DC: Author. Retrieved from http://www.aacc.nche.edu/AboutCC/Documents/2013facts_fold_revised.pdf

Archambault, K.L., Forbes, M., & Schlosberg, S. (2012). Challenges in the transfer transition. In T.J. Grites & C. Duncan (Eds.), *Advising transfer students: Strategies for today's realities and tomorrow's challenges* (pp. 105–118). Manhattan, KS: NACADA.

Astin, A.W. (1997). *What matters in college: Four critical years revisited.* San Francisco, CA: Jossey-Bass.

Bahr, P.R. (2009). College hopping: Exploring the occurrences, frequency, and consequences of lateral transfer. *Community College Review, 36*(4), 271–298.

Borst, M.E., Jones, K.J., & Cohen, B.E. (2012). Classifying transfer students from the 2-year college perspective. In T.J. Grites & C. Duncan (Eds.), *Advising transfer students: Strategies for today's realities and tomorrow's challenges* (pp. 50–57). Manhattan, KS: NACADA.

Carlan, P.E., & Byxbe, F.R. (2000). Community colleges under the microscope: An analysis of performance predictors for native and transfer students. *Community College Review, 28*(2), 27–42.

Cejda, B.D., & Kaylor, A.J. (1997). Academic performance of community college transfer students at private liberal arts colleges. *Community College Journal of Research and Practice, 21*(7), 651–659.

Chen, X., & Carroll, C.D. (2007). *Part-time undergraduates in postsecondary education: 2003–2004.* NCES 2007-165. Washington, DC: U.S. Department of Education.

Clery, S. (2009). Academic outcomes of high risk students. *Data Notes, 4*(4), 1–3. Retrieved from http://www.achievingthedream.org/Portal/Modules/ ad91771c-1578-450a-a4fd-4381285f15ce.asset?

Cohen, A.M., Brawer, F.B., & Lombardi, J.R. (2008). *The American community college.* San Francisco, CA: Jossey-Bass.

College Board. (2007). *Trends in college pricing.* Washington, DC: Author. Retrieved from http://www.collegeboard.com/prod_downloads/about/news_info/trends/trends_pricing_07.pdf

Corkery, B.J., Ingram, L., & Davis, M. (2007, October). *Navigating the transfer experience: A classroom initiative for new transfer students.* Paper presented at the meeting of the National Academic Advising Association, Baltimore, MD.

Cushman, K. (2006). *First in the family: Advice about college from first-generation students.* Providence, RI: Next Generation Press.

Davies, T.G., & Casey, K. (1999). Transfer student experiences: Comparing their academic and social lives at the community college and university. *College Student Journal, 33*(1), 60–71.

Dougherty, K.J., & Kienzl, G.S. (2006). It's not enough to get through the open door: Inequalities by social background in transfer from community colleges to four-year colleges. *Teachers College Record, 108*(3), 452–487.

Dowd, A.C., Cheslock, J.J, & Melguizo, T. (2008). Transfer access from community colleges and the distribution of elite higher education. *Journal of Higher Education, 79*(4), 442–472.

Fain, P. (2012, November 15). Getting more complete. *Inside Higher Ed.* Retrieved from http://www.insidehighered.com/news/2012/11/15/national-student-clearinghouse-releases-broad-deep-data-college-completion

Grites, T.J., & McDonald, N.L. (2012). General influences on the transfer landscape. In T.J. Grites & C. Duncan (Eds.), *Advising transfer students: Strategies for today's realities and tomorrow's challenges* (pp. 21–28). Manhattan, KS: NACADA.

Handel, S.J. (2008). Aid and advocacy: Why community college transfer students do not apply for financial aid and how counselors can help them get in the game. *Journal of College Admission, 201*, 8–16.

Handel, S.J. (2009). Transfer and the part time student. *Change, 41*(4), 48–53.

Heller, D.E. (2006). State support of higher education: Past, present, future. In D.M. Priest & E.P. St. John (Eds.), *Privatization and public universities* (pp. 11–37). Bloomington, IN: Indiana University Press.

Hills, J.R. (1965). Transfer shock: The academic performance of the junior college transfer. *Journal of Experimental Education, 33*(3), 201–215.

Hoffman, N., & Bayerl, K. (2006). *Accelerated learning for all.* Boston, MA: Early College High School Initiative. Retrieved from http://www.earlycolleges.org/Downloads/accelerated%20learning.pdf

Jones, A.E. (1994). *Academic performance of Northwest Arkansas Community College transfer students at the University of Arkansas* (Doctoral dissertation). *Dissertation Abstracts International, 56*(1). (UMI No. 9514273.)

Keeley, E.J. III, & House, J.D. (1993, May). *Transfer shock revisited: A longitudinal study of transfer academic performance.* Paper presented at the annual forum of the Association for Institutional Research, Chicago, IL.

Laanan, F.S. (2007). Studying transfer students, Part II: Dimensions of transfer students' adjustment. *Community College Journal of Research and Practice, 31*(1), 37–59.

Long, B.T. (2007). The contributions of economics to the study of college access and success. *Teachers College Record, 109*(10), 2367–2443.

Marklein, M.B. (2010, September 29). For profit colleges under fire over value, accreditation. *USA Today.* Retrieved from http://www.usatoday.com/news/education/2010-09-29-1Aforprofit29_CV_N.htm

McCormick, A.C. (2003). Swirling and double-dipping: New patterns of student attendance and their implications in higher education. In J.E. King, E.I. Anderson, & M.E. Corrigan (Eds.), *Changing student attendance patterns: Challenges for policy and practice* (pp. 13–24). New Directions for Higher Education, No. 12. San Francisco, CA: Jossey-Bass.

McCormick, A.C. (2013). Why do students attend multiple institutions? *Electronic Educational Environment, University of California, Irvine* (Fall 2013). Retrieved from https://eee.uci.edu/news/articles/0507multiple.php

National Association for College Admissions Counseling (NACAC). (2010). *Special report on the transfer admission process.* Arlington, VA: Author. Retrieved from http://www.nacacnet.org/PublicationsResources/Research/Documents/TransferFactSheet.pdf

National Center for Education Statistics (NCES). (2000). *Students with disabilities in postsecondary education: A profile of preparation, participation, and outcomes, 1999.* Washington, DC: U.S. Department of Transportation.

National Student Clearinghouse Research Center. (2012a). *Completing college: A national view of student attainment rates.* Herndon, VA: Author. Retrieved from http://www.nscresearchcenter.org/signaturereport4

National Student Clearinghouse Research Center. (2012b). *Reverse transfer: A national view of student mobility from four-year to two-year institutions.* Herndon, VA: Author. Retrieved from http://www.nscresearchcenter.org/signaturereport3

National Student Clearinghouse Research Center. (2012c). *Transfer & mobility: A national view of pre-degree student movement in postsecondary institutions.* Herndon, VA: Author. Retrieved from http://www.nscresearchcenter.org/signaturereport2

National Student Clearinghouse Research Center. (2013). *Baccalaureate attainment: A national view of the postsecondary outcomes of students who transfer from two-year to four-year institutions.* Herndon, VA: Author. Retrieved from http://www.nscresearchcenter.org/signaturereport5

National Survey of Student Engagement (NSSE). (2008). *Promoting engagement for all students: The imperative to look within—2008 results.* Bloomington, IN: Indiana University Center for Postsecondary Research.

National Survey of Student Engagement (NSSE). (2009). *Assessing for improvement: Tracking student engagement over time—Annual results 2009.* Bloomington, IN: Indiana University Center for Postsecondary Research.

National Survey of Student Engagement (NSSE). (2011). *Fostering student engagement campuswide—Annual results 2011.* Bloomington, IN: Indiana University Center for Postsecondary Research.

Ornelas, A., & Solorzano, D.G. (2004). Transfer conditions of Latina/o community college students: A single institution case study. *Community College Journal of Research and Practice, 28*(3), 233–248.

Ponticelli, J.E., & Russ-Eft, D. (2009). Community college students with disabilities and transfer to a four-year college. *Exceptionality, 17*(3), 164–176.

Schlossberg, N.K. (1984). *Counseling adults in transition.* New York, NY: Springer.

Tinto, V. (1993). *Leaving college: Rethinking the causes and cures of student attrition* (2nd ed.). Chicago, IL: University of Chicago Press.

Weerts, D.J., & Ronca, J.M. (2006). Examining differences in state support for higher education: A comparative study of state appropriations for research I universities. *Journal of Higher Education, 77*(6), 935–967.

SIXTEEN

The History of Student Life in American Higher Education

Amy E. Wells Dolan and Sara R. Kaiser

Introduction

Student life encompasses the preoccupations and activities of students apart from the formal curriculum in American colleges and universities. It emerged from student rebellion and resistance in colonial and early nineteenth-century colleges (Geiger, 2000; Horowitz, 1987) and exists now as a thriving co-curriculum and social enterprise that largely defines the college experience for first-time college students of traditional age (18–24) enrolled in predominantly residential 4-year colleges and universities. Over time, college life has embodied a confluence of forces defining late adolescence and emerging adulthood in American society co-opted by the developing organization and administration of American higher education.

Student life steered a course of adaptation characterized by an increasing secularity, institutional size, complexity (Fenske, 1980), and heterogeneity as old institutions admitted new student populations and new institutions emerged with diverse missions. These include large state-supported and small liberal arts colleges, women's colleges, normal schools, historically Black institutions, online (versus brick-and-mortar) institutions, rural or urban, all of which carved out a niche to enroll students and educate accordingly. Despite ever-evolving campus demography and new technologies, student life has maintained a remarkable fidelity to an old ideal, namely the "collegiate way" and "an adherence to the residential scheme of things…respectful of quiet rural settings, dependent on dormitories, committed to dining halls, permeated by paternalism" (Rudolph, 1990, p. 87).

Although student life brought much progress to campus culture over time and pushed the boundaries of decorum related to gender expectations and sexual freedom, it also exacted a conservative quality, preserving patriarchal values and the sociopolitical power of elites. A powerful counterbalance to the preoccupations of faculty, student life often opposed intellectual pursuits, preventing them from being taken too seriously by the institution or the public at large (Rudolph, 1990). Furthermore, it imbued the college experience with a mythical allure that enhanced the "social motivation for college-going" among the middle class (Levine, 1986, p. 115) and endeared college as home to alumni who provide future resources for institutional improvement and expansion.

At times, student life also steered a course that needed correction by management. The faculty used to perform this function. Now, a trained class of professional administrators works closely with students to set the boundaries of permissible behavior in the collegiate environment. Thus, student life also refers to the professional field of student affairs and the student services that support students and/or their activities such as campus recreation, student clubs and organizations, new student orientation, or student financial aid, to name a few. As a profession, the field of student affairs is "largely an American higher education invention" (Rhatigan, 2000, p. 5) and a requisite partner of the collegiate way—each legitimizing the other and enabling the other to grow. In this way, the term "student life" also signifies the work of educators who ostensibly teach the co-curriculum from a theory base designed to promote students' development and help them make sense of the learning provided from the out-of-classroom experiences of college, both planned and accidental.

Student life has evolved to meet the changing needs of students and higher education institutions, and has been characterized by greater emphasis on student learning outcomes over time. This chapter provides a brief history of student life beginning with the colonial period and the founding of the first U.S. institutions of higher learning. Further, it examines the role of student life in the diversification of American higher education through the founding of new institutions and the importance of educating a responsible citizenry. In addition, the chapter examines the role of deans of women, deans of men, and the rise of the student personnel movement in American higher education for the management and legitimization of student life. Finally, this chapter reviews the impact of the Servicemen's Readjustment Act (GI Bill) and post-World War II influences, including student activism, the Civil Rights Movement, and the role of technology and changing social dynamics in shaping student life today.

The First American College Students

The first colonial colleges, founded in the United States in the mid-1600s, were modeled after Oxford and Cambridge in England. Rudolph (1990) argued that mastery of a subject was not the only purpose of Harvard College in the 1600s, or any of the other colonial colleges founded in the Northeast in the late 1600s and early 1700s. Religious undertones were present in the colonial colleges, and religion was often mentioned as a central part of the mission for colonial colleges. However, colonial colleges offered no divinity degrees (Thelin, 2012) and primarily educated society's "leaders disciplined by knowledge and learning" (Rudolph, 1990, p. 7). Although colonial colleges ostensibly educated prospective clergy, no single denomination dominated any colony, and "no college found it possible to impose a religious test for admission or doctrinal requirements for graduation" (Lucas, 2006, p. 107). The result was a mild religious tolerance among students and faculty.

Low student enrollment characterized the colonial colleges in the mid-1700s (Lucas, 2006), and institutions often expanded their curricula to include grammar school (Thelin, 2004). The type of student who was educated in the 1700s and the limited type of curriculum offered further explains low student enrollment. As Thelin (2004) argued, education at the primary and secondary level in the colonial era was unreliable; thus, preparatory curriculum helped to build and maintain enrollment as well as keep doors open. College faculty and the president assumed responsibility for all major aspects of student life during the colonial period (Thelin, 2004). The faculty (often few) and the president assumed responsibility for the enrollment of new students, course selection, registration, and bill collection (Thelin, 2004). Institutions struggled financially due, in part, to low enrollment. The College of William and Mary founded a grammar school to ensure that Latin and Greek were taught. Not only were students at the College of William and Mary educated in classical languages, but student morality was also a central focus, especially at the grammar school (Hofstadter & Smith, 1961). It is important to remember that, since only a small proportion of the American population attended college in the 1700s and 1800s, and grammar schools and primary education were often provided at colonial colleges, these factors tailored student life as a gendered phenomenon, especially rooted in the concerns of adolescent males and the colleges' authoritative stance toward them (Geiger, 2000; Lowery, 2011).

Of particular importance is the fact that colonial colleges only educated young *men* and acknowledged them on class lists by family rank rather than alphabetically or by academic achievement—a reminder of the importance of hierarchy and social status in early American higher education (Geiger, 2000; Thelin, 2004, 2012). Furthermore, the founders of the colonial colleges, most of whom were educated at Oxford and Cambridge in England, used this ideal to establish the foundation of the colonial colleges, thus resulting in a more residential, often rural, educational schema for American higher education (Rudolph, 1990; Thelin, 1982). Although the educational institutions of Oxford and Cambridge influenced American higher education, differences included governance structure, wherein the president of the college reported to an external governing board, not the faculty (Thelin, 1982).

Handling student disagreements and controlling student behavior were a dominant concern of student life in early American higher education. Student discipline and student academic welfare issues fell on the shoulders of the president and faculty, who served dual roles as educators in the classroom and mentors to the young men in their care (Rudolph, 1990). As Thelin and Gasman (2011) described, this approach to student discipline and accountability often strained faculty-student relationships. As no separate residential life department existed, faculty often lived with the students in the main campus building (Lucas, 2006) and played a central role in controlling daily activities. During the colonial college period, most students lived in a "residential dormitory" (Lucas, 2006, p. 111) where "the aim was to foster among all students a common social, moral, and intellectual life" (p. 111). Perhaps this concern over social, moral, and intellectual development is an early example of colleges developing students as informed and responsible citizens rather than simply persons with a mastery of subject material.

In a campus environment marked by rigid discipline and limited curriculum, students sought more opportunities than their academic study could provide. Chapel, communal meals, and evening study were not enough to satisfy the students. As students attended college in an evolving and increasingly more democratic society, the need and desire for increased freedom and extracurricular opportunities flourished. One of the earliest extracurricular opportunities for college students was the campus literary society or debate team, and athletics soon followed (Geiger, 2000; Rudolph, 1990; Thelin, 2004, 2012). The first literary societies at the College of William and Mary and Yale appeared as early as 1770 and "supplemented the formal course of study" (Horowitz, 1987, p. 24), giving students increased freedom and responsibility for their own activities. Other groups continued to form and created "the collegiate way," an emerging cultural ethos that college offered its own special secular social experience beyond academic study (Rudolph, 1990, pp. 86–87).

During the 1800s, American higher education experienced a period of growth that brought variety and important shades of innovation to college student life. In this period of transition, old modes of discipline lost sway, and students carved out new freedoms in their environs. For example, many institutions in the South were founded at this time and began to handle student behavior through the use of student conduct codes. These codes varied, but they often established rules relating to dress codes, academic honesty, and prohibitions on drinking and gambling—affording insight into the out-of-classroom activities and preoccupations of students. Other student codes of conduct compelled students to develop and uphold honor, as was the case at the University of South Carolina, an institution founded in 1801. Other institutions moved further away from a religious emphasis. One example is the University of Virginia, which did not hold mandatory chapel services for students. In addition, students there were charged with developing their own honor code and enforcing that code, a significant break from the authoritarian order of the colonial colleges in an earlier era (Geiger, 2000; Thelin, 2004, 2012).

In time, the earliest institutions of higher education exhibited increased diversity by enrolling a variety of students, from merchants' sons to the sons of wealthy planters. These nuances in student background and dynamics of interpersonal interactions within the collegiate environment enforced new modes of discipline, new standards for student behavior, and, eventually, a new curriculum for a changing economy and society. These shifts also enhanced the immediate value of student life, as the collegiate environment became a new, shared ground apart from family for enforcing social values, proving masculinity, and pursuing passions outside of the classic curriculum and recitation pedagogy. In this new era, literary and oratorical societies or debate clubs with Greek names and Greek letters arose for the reading of literature or discussion of current events to help students make sense of the times and, ostensibly, the future (Geiger, 2000; Glover, 2003; Moore, 1976; Rudolph, 1990).

Beginning around the 1870s, new monies became available for support of higher education (Veysey, 1965). The possibilities for graduate education inspired by European models and research took hold, and a more complex university ideal and structure began to compete with the old-time college and its preoccupation with discipline and piety (Veysey, 1965). In this emerging institution, new administrative positions were created to handle the tasks once performed by the faculty and/or president (Nidiffer & Cain, 2004). Consequently, students' needs and motivations for enrolling in college became further diversified. Eventually institutions adapted to accommodate students' pastimes and interests through new legislation and the increasing enrollment of women in higher education.

Diverse Institutions Created Diverse Student Needs

Influences on student life in American higher education often involved wartime and new legislation from the federal government. In 1862, the American higher education landscape changed dramatically with the passage of the Morrill Land Grant Act. The Morrill Act established land-grant education with an agricultural and mechanical focus in every state in the country (Lucas, 2006; Rhatigan, 2000; Rudolph, 1990; Thelin, 2004). The newly established institutions, as well as institutions that added new program areas, now had a more diverse mission and, eventually, a more diverse student population to serve. The institutions that were founded as a result of the Morrill Act facilitated access to higher education for students in every state and prompted an increase in graduate-level education with an emphasis on new research (Johnson, 1981). These new land-grant colleges provided agricultural and mechanical education to students (Rudolph, 1990; Thelin, 2004) and further leveraged increased state support for higher education (Rasmussen, 1989; Thelin & Gasman, 2011). Applied research and agricultural extension services that began addressing the states' needs further justified state involvement in higher education (Dennis, 2001).

Although the newly created institutions provided increased access to higher education for students across the country, students did not enroll in large numbers, and institutions thus became creative in their efforts to increase enrollment (Johnson, 1981). Today the recruitment of college students is an important aspect of higher education. Colleges promote their academic curriculum, campus grounds, and student events in a variety of ways. In the late 1800s, land-grant institutions created catalogs to advertise themselves, financial support for students was offered as a way to increase enrollment, and faculty worked to encourage new students to enroll (Johnson, 1981). Eventually the Morrill Act did see a surge in student enrollment in American universities, especially for those students who had often been left out of higher education in the 1700s and early 1800s, but the enrollment was not as rapid as hoped (Thelin, 2004). Johnson (1981) argued that the institutional missions created through the Morrill Act fueled the academic trilogy of teaching, research, and service that acts as an organizing principle for faculty work and institutions of higher education today.

Other institutions were established to educate previously marginalized sections of the population, and older institutions grafted on new courses, programs, and departments to attract new enrollees. For example, Georgetown College was founded in 1789 to educate Catholics, and more than ten Catholic-serving institutions had opened by 1860 (Goodchild, 2007). Women gained access to higher education in the 1800s when Troy Female Seminary opened in 1822 (Goodchild, 2007). Also in this period, the implicit goal of teacher training as a function of higher education became explicit when "growing numbers of colleges and academies offered teacher training as a specific course of study or curricular track" (Ogren, 2005, p. 17). Soon state normal schools opened to train teachers for common schools, further leveraging and legitimizing the states' role in higher education, as well as expanding educational opportunity to women and non-elites, the culture of college-going, and multi-faceted missions for American colleges and universities (Ogren, 2005).

Outside of teacher training institutes, most women who pursued higher education in the 1800s attended private, women-only institutions such as Mount Holyoke Seminary (later College), Vassar College, Wellesley College, and Bryn Mawr College in the Northeast, or Georgia's Wesleyan Female College or Sophie Newcomb in the South (McCandless, 1999). Institutions in the Midwest were the first to operate coeducational private colleges, including Oberlin College in Ohio, which became the first coeducational institution in the United States in 1837 (McCandless, 1999; Thelin, 2004). The first public institution to open as coeducational was the State University of Iowa (University of Iowa), which began admitting both men and women in 1865 (McCandless, 1999). By 1900, more than 70% of institutions accepted both men and women (McCandless, 1999).

Although women gained admission to coeducational institutions, they were held back by limited curricular and living opportunities, and habitually suffered the "hostilities of a gender-biased education" (Faragher & Howe, 1988, p. 4) and a male-dominated student life. Increasingly preoccupied with football, hazing, class rushes, secret societies, and eating clubs, college student life—especially in its more benign iterations such as student government, college newspapers, and academic honor societies—prohibited women's full participation. Due to the often hostile classroom experience for women in many early coeducational institutions, the emerging field of student affairs became more important in providing young women students with opportunities for learning and growth outside of the classroom. It helped them to negotiate student life as well.

Negotiate is a key word, however, as the presence of or participation by women did not radically alter the main currents of student life, which were quite "agreeable to affluent male adolescents" (Horowitz, 1987, p. 11). Quite definitively, student life became significantly stylized in the late 1800s and early 1900s as an alluring, competitive world dominated by "college men" who were "subjected to" (and opposed to) the "seemingly arbitrary authority of their faculty" (Horowitz, 1987, p. 12). Horowitz explained the prevailing attitude that united students across institutions in an intra-campus struggle for power among insiders, outsiders, and rebels:

> In the competitive world of peers, college men could fight for position on the playing field and in the newsroom and learn the manly arts of capitalism. As they did so, they indulged their love of rowdiness and good times in ritualized violence and sanctioned drinking. Classes and books existed as the price one had to pay for college life, but no right-thinking college man worried about marks beyond the minimum needed to stay in the games. Faculty and students faced each other across the trenches. If cheating was needed to win the battle, no shame inhered in the act. No real college man ever expected to learn in the classroom, not at least the kind of knowledge that bore any relation to his future life in the world. No, college life taught the real lessons; and from it came the true rewards. (Horowitz, 1987, p. 12)

Rather than sit on the sidelines and be excluded from campus activities, women joined in the fun. Their participation through sororities, dances, clubs, and campus beauty contests and the like reinforced instead of challenged women's traditional gender roles, models of femininity and White patriarchy. That is why student life activities in different types of institutions, such as state normal schools, women's colleges, and later Historically Black Colleges and Universities, show an overwhelming similarity to some of the same activities and adolescent "peer consciousness" (Horowitz, 1987, p. 11) that emerged at the turn of the twentieth century.

In addition to the increase in public institutions across the country partly as a result of the Morrill Land Grant Act, the establishment of more women's colleges in the 1800s, the arrival of coeducation, the newly formed elective system in higher education, and the "view of higher education as a social status phenomenon…" (Rhatigan, 2000, p. 6) helped to create the student personnel movement and the field of student affairs in American higher education. Student life was born not only out of a need to handle student discipline and problems of late adolescent peer culture and dynamics, but also out of a need to occupy student time outside of the classroom learning environment. It was during the late 1800s and early 1900s that the president's focus shifted from student challenges and discipline to fundraising efforts, the development of new academic curricula at the institution, and campus building expansion (Rhatigan, 2000). Furthermore, faculty became attentive to research and service activities, further distancing their work from out-of-classroom activities. New models of student leadership and distinction promoted in the elective system helped institutional leaders fill the vacancies in responsibility left as the structure of paternalism shifted. Essentially, they "empowered college men as the official student leaders." As a result, the historic tenet of "antagonism" changed into a stance of camaraderie and "support of the administration" among college men (Horowitz, 1987, p. 13).

While the federal oversight role in American higher education increased through the report requirements of the Morrill Act and other land-grant legislation, higher education also adhered strongly to a tradition of internal or institutional regulation, a notable custom and practice of the medieval university (Thelin, 1982). In American higher education, voluntary peer association and review emerged as a primary vehicle for promoting quality and conformity to mutually beneficial standards of business, thereby staving off negative consequences such as institutional or government regulation (O'Brien, 2009). In terms of college student life, major reforms to student life occurred as voluntary associations emerged to help regulate the excesses of sororities, intercollegiate athletics, and fraternities, giving rise, for example, to the organizations known today as the National Panhellenic Conference (NPC), the National Collegiate Athletic Association (NCAA), the North-American Interfraternity Conference (NIC), and the National Panhellenic Council, Inc. (NPHC) (Thelin, 1994; Wells & Thelin, 2002).

In the period of expansion in American higher education, some of the excesses of student life came to light. Specifically, student injuries and deaths in college football compelled President Theodore Roosevelt to meet with institutional leaders regarding his concerns about football (Rudolph, 1990; Thelin, 1994). As a result of the meeting, colleges and universities formed the organization now known as the National Collegiate Athletic Association (NCAA) in 1905 to address these issues (Thelin, 1994). Likewise, institutional leaders began to question the integrity and viability of college sororities and fraternities in a democratic society, and the NPC was established in 1902, the NIC in 1909, and the NPHC in 1930 to regulate among member groups standards for conduct of business and practices related to recruitment and membership, among other issues (Wells & Thelin, 2002; Wells & Worley, 2011). So instead of being shut down or out, student life became co-opted and forever reconciled to slowly increasing levels of self-management by higher education institutions. This came about by way of a changing mindset and advocacy from a new type of student life administrator who championed the essential role of student life and student leaders within the collegiate experience and campus environment.

Deans of Women, Deans of Men, and Student Personnel Work

By the 1890s, the student life field as a profession began to emerge, in part through the work of a few deans of women. Before the 1890s, most midwestern universities did not provide, or permit, housing for women students; therefore, there was no need for a dean of women to supervise their activities (Nidiffer, 2001a). Later on, however, institutions began hiring deans of women to protect and supervise women students—mainly women living on college campuses. The deans of women also provided guidance to women students to further develop their morality (Nidiffer, 1995, 2001a, 2001b; Schwartz, 1997a, 1997b).

Historians Bashaw (1999) and Nidiffer (2000) credit Alice Freeman Palmer and Marion Talbot, two early deans of women, with making an impact on women's education and the development of the role of a dean of women as a profession. Both women were deans at the University of Chicago and were great friends. Nidiffer (2001a) suggests that Talbot, as the dean of women, gave women a voice at the University of Chicago and advocated on their behalf to create separate spaces on campus that enabled a safe and nurturing learning environment. The need for student space for activities outside of the classroom was a major contribution to American collegiate student life. Having separate spaces from those of men on college coeducational campuses ensured that women students were safe on campus and were able to maintain propriety. Although women students had separate spaces on campus for congregating and enjoying clubs and other activities, they were still required to conform to set campus behavioral standards, including using proper manners and wearing appropriate attire (Nidiffer, 2000).

According to Herron (2004) and Schwartz (1997a), finding faculty roles for women in higher education was often difficult and resulted in many deans of women serving in dual roles as both the dean of women and a member of the teaching faculty. Herron (2004) argued that being a dean of women was a "back door" to a faculty position; however, the faculty position usually received secondary consideration and focus. As an example, Lois Mathews was hired as a faculty member in the history department at the University of Wisconsin and served as the dean of women from 1911 to 1918 (Nidiffer, 1995, 2001a). However, most of her time was devoted to administrative work in her role as dean of women (Nidiffer, 1995, 2001a).

Nidiffer (2001a, 2002) argued that in the Progressive Era (1880–1915), deans of women did two things: first, they improved the college environment and advocated for opportunity for women students; second, they created a new professional identity for their careers as deans of women. The deans of women of the Progressive Era were, in most cases, the first women administrators on coeducational campuses (Nidiffer, 2001a, 2002) and thus some of the earliest working professionals dedicated to student life in American higher education. Deans of women continued to work to change the educational experience of women students and advocated for access to facilities and opportunities for women students. Because college campuses were dominated by male students and faculty, being a dean of women was difficult. Often these women were forced to balance their on-campus commitments as they conducted research on student guidance and student support. Many deans of women collaborated with other deans on different college campuses. These new relationships helped forge professional associations and propelled the profession in a new direction (Nidiffer, 2000, 2001a, 2002).

Women students were not the only students on the college campus that were assigned a dean to address social, moral, and sometimes academic challenges that faced them. Deans of men were also hired on college campuses to address the needs of male students (Schwartz, 1997a). According to Schwartz (1997a), deans of men were first hired to address disciplinary matters involving male students, and their professional meetings were more social outings than forums for professional development of good practice and research.

Schwartz (1997a) argued that deans of men were much more reluctant to engage in professional research than deans of women. By the 1930s, many deans recognized the shift to a student personnel model and understood the possibility that both deans of men and deans of women positions might be combined or eliminated (Schwartz, 1997a). Schwartz (1997a) found that by the 1940s and 1950s, most deans of women positions disappeared, in part because of the Servicemen's Readjustment Act (GI Bill), which led to a dramatic rise in the number of males on college campuses and reshaped the character of campus life.

The Student Personnel Point of View

Two major works had a significant effect on student personnel in U.S. higher education: *The Student Personnel Point of View* of 1937 and *The Student Personnel Point of View* of 1949, both written by the American Council on Education (ACE). In 1937, a group of educational professionals met in Washington, D.C., and drafted *The Student Personnel Point of View* (American Council on Education, 1937). The group identified and articulated the experiences and goals that college students should strive to achieve. These professionals wished to promote the "betterment of society" (American Council on Education, 1937, p. 39) through college education. In support of this goal, the group developed a philosophy focused on the importance of educating the whole student (American Council on Education, 1937). Eight specific areas for student development were identified in the report: intellectual, emotional, physical, social, vocational, moral and religious, economic, and aesthetic growth and education (American Council on Education, 1937).

Administrators of colleges and universities believed it would be difficult for faculty to provide education for the whole student, so a new type of educator was hired. Many of these educators' original duties concerned student discipline, but their responsibilities grew to include "educational counseling, vocational counseling, the administration of loans and scholarship funds, part-time employment, graduate placement, student health, extracurricular activities, social programs, and a number of others" (American Council on Education, 1937, p. 40).

The report by the ACE (1937) described how these job duties evolved into student services on college campuses. Areas encompassed by student services identified in the document included orientation, career assessments, placement, family and parent programs, student development, student health and wellness, residence life, food service, student activities, campus ministry, development of curriculum electives, financial aid, student records, discipline and conduct, advertising of services, and assessment of programs (American Council on Education, 1937). The group believed that, for the student personnel division to be successful, the administration had to view it as vital. Coordination of these services was important so as not to duplicate work by various personnel and departments. In addition, academic divisions must be aware of the services available to students.

The American Council on Education (1937) connected high schools to higher education. As high school seniors made plans for continuing their education, it was important that they be linked to resources to help them make informed choices (American Council on Education, 1937). As a result, communication and coordination with high schools became important, since high school grades and test scores affect admission into college. Furthermore, career and vocational goals identified from high school shaped student success in college. Connecting high school students with information about college and providing an action plan was the beginning of cooperative admission efforts (American Council on Education, 1937).

The Student Personnel Point of View of 1937 (American Council on Education, 1937) highlighted the impact the division of student personnel can have on students even after they complete their higher education. Career programs during college, professional development opportunities, and alumni relations were all part of student personnel programs (American Council on Education, 1937). These various programs helped keep graduates connected to the institution even after they had left the campus. Finally, the group adopted six research areas important to the work and success of student personnel: aptitude testing, social development, diagnostic techniques, scholastic aptitude test scale, occupational information, and traits necessary for specific occupations (American Council on Education, 1937).

As a follow-up to the 1937 document, *The Student Personnel Point of View* of 1949 recommended new goals to further the education of the whole student. *The Student Personnel Point of View* of 1949 (American Council on Education, 1949) recognized that students were responsible for their own development. The student personnel movement grew after World War I as more students enrolled in colleges and extracurricular activities became more important in the collegiate experience (Thelin, 2004). Education was no longer viewed as being confined to the classroom. The American Council on Education (1949) believed that educating each student as an individual and supporting individual needs was important. It deemed it important that students develop cultural values and understanding, adapt to changing school conditions, develop emotional control, cultivate moral and ethical values, foster physical well-being, and develop a vocational goal that can contribute to society (American Council on Education, 1949).

The American Council on Education (1949) stressed in *The Student Personnel Point of View* of 1949 that personal growth is the responsibility of the individual student, but that colleges have an obligation to influence experiences and attitudes to foster student development. The college can support this growth by providing orientation programs to help students transition to their new environment (American Council on Education, 1949). Furthermore, by providing proper admissions guidance and developing standards in the institutional admissions criteria, institutions can nurture student development and success.

The Student Personnel Point of View of 1949 identified retention and graduation concerns among students because students "lacked proficiency or personal motivation" (American Council on Education, 1949, p. 22). Other factors contributing to low student retention included lack of maturity, lack of an emotional ability to deal with the stress of college, and failure to choose a curriculum path suitable to their goals (American Council on Education, 1949). To help students achieve success, colleges can provide services such as study skills development opportunities and time management development strategies, counseling services, remedial support in reading and speech, develop opportunities for students to meet other students, activities, diverse social programming, collaboration with community colleges, proper academic advising, financial aid guidance, career guidance and placement, and even marriage counseling (American Council on Education, 1949). With a plethora of services offered to support them, it was the responsibility of students to be in control of their actions (American Council on Education, 1949). *The Student Personnel Point of View* of 1949 maintained that living with others prepares students for social obligations outside of college and further develops their leadership abilities (American Council on Education, 1949).

Trained professionals should provide these skills, and institutions should tap into these services to meet their particular needs. Defining what department is responsible for each of the student development areas "should be clearly established" (American Council on Education, 1949, p. 30) among employees to avoid duplication of duties and to ensure the best possible service for students. *The Student Personnel Point of View* of 1949 argued that students should have input and be involved in the development of programs and services, and that assessments should take place on a regular basis.

The Student Personnel Point of View of 1937 and *The Student Personnel Point of View* of 1949 outlined the student experience and student success initiatives. Deans of women were responsible for the safety, well-being, and educational opportunities for women students. After deans of women were hired, faculty and administrators saw the usefulness of the position; thus, deans of men emerged on college campuses. The two reports published by the American Council on Education urged college administrators to review services provided to students and changed the student life division in higher education (American Council on Education, 1937, 1949; Roberts, 2012).

Student Life—Post-World War II

Many professional organizations developed during a 30-year span that steered the profession into what Schwartz (1997a) described as the "personnel movement." Schwartz (1997b) argued that by the 1950s, the role of the dean of women had faded out on college campuses, in part because of the emergence of the dean of students position, which often went to the dean of men. Furthermore, institutions began placing emphasis on creating a well-rounded student experience in light of the student personnel movement—and this coalesced nicely with the collegiate way, legitimizing it as a key component of the American college experience (Kerr, 2001; Roberts, 2012). Furthermore, the role of *in loco parentis* began to diminish, furthering the student personnel movement (Bashaw, 2001; Tuttle, 1996) and the collegiate co-curriculum.

As Sartorius (2010) illustrated, women made great strides in attending institutions of higher education before World War II, but the end of the war brought a dramatic increase in the number of male students attending college on the GI Bill. This increase in enrollment further masculinized the campus in many ways and attracted men to programs such as engineering and business (Thelin, 2004). By the 1960s, the role of the dean of women was no longer that of a high-ranking administrator, and as a result the position lost influence and power. Sartorius (2010) explained that, with the demise of the position of the dean of women, women administrators were often excluded from policy decisions until the 1980s.

Other policy decisions at the federal level had an impact on American college student life. The Civil Rights Act of 1965 and the Higher Education Acts of 1965 and 1972 increased access to higher education across the country (Lucas, 2006; Rhatigan, 2000; Thelin, 2004). As a result of the GI Bill, the Civil Rights Act of 1965, and the Higher Education Act of 1965, institutions adapted to the new type of student emerging on college campuses. Institutions changed and became "multiversities" (Kerr, 2001, p. 5) in part to meet the needs of the changing student demographic. With federal support through grant aid and student loans, a new demographic of students arrived on college campuses (Levine, 1986; Thelin & Gasman, 2011). With access to higher education reaching new student populations, college became available to every man, not just White, heterosexual males from more affluent family backgrounds—although, of course, this brought new challenges (Clark, 1998; Thelin & Gasman, 2011). However, the tradition of student life in the 1960s did not change to meet the needs of the new students; rather, the new students on college campuses were to conform to the campus traditions and histories of the past.

In the realm of student life, the 1960s and 1970s were a period of student activism and protest.

> At first centered in large, prestigious, highly selective institutions, it [campus unrest] gradually diffused to colleges and universities of all types. At the same time, the scope of campus unrest enlarged to cover broad social problems rather than single campus issues, and its direction changed. (Astin, Astin, Bayer, & Bisconti, 1997, p. 727)

Astin and colleagues (1997) argued that many campuses, especially those that increased their recruitment of Black students, were unprepared to handle the student challenges of a more diverse student population. Likewise, Black students struggled to fit in on predominately White campuses, and especially to participate equally in the tradition of college student life.

Student Life—2000 and Beyond

Today's population of college students is more diverse than in any previous generation. Howe and Strauss (2000) attributed to millennial college students (students born between 1982 and 2002) seven traits that distinguished them from other generations. Millennial students are: special, sheltered, confident, team-oriented, achieving, pressured, and conventional (Howe & Strauss, 2000, pp. 43–44).

Furthermore, the millennial college student is more likely to be biracial or multiracial (Broido, 2004). More students entering colleges across the country are children of immigrants who speak another language at home (Broido, 2004). But race and ethnicity are only one way in which students are more diverse today. Today's college students arrive on campus with varied socioeconomic backgrounds (Broido, 2004). Because of the diversity of the millennial generation, students are entering college with a better grasp of political and social justice issues than ever before. Broido (2004) argued that the millennial generation is more polarized in its political identity and viewpoint, and that the millennial generation "is likely to engage in behaviors that relate to social justice issues (including voting, community service, protest and demonstrations, and discussion of social and political issues) differently from their predecessors" (p. 80).

College campuses have experienced a rise in the number of students with mental health challenges. Kitzrow (2003) argued that "students with emotional and behavior problems have the potential to affect many other people on campus, including roommates, classmates, faculty, and staff, in terms of disruptive, disturbing or even dangerous behavior" (p. 173). The increased needs of students with mental health problems impact student affairs professionals, "who are on the front lines of dealing with student behavioral problems" (Kitzrow, 2003, p. 173). Hunt and Eisenberg (2010) argued that colleges and universities are faced with a unique challenge due to the prevalence of students with mental health issues, as well as the perceived increase in students with mental health issues that are more severe. The awareness of mental health issues among today's college students provides an opportunity for students to receive support and services during a critical time in their development (Hunt & Eisenberg, 2010). Improving campus safety is a popular and multi-faceted topic among college administrators, faculty, staff, and students.

In 1990, due partly to the efforts of Howard and Connie Clery, President George H.W. Bush signed landmark legislation mandating the reporting of campus crime. The Clerys' daughter, Jeanne, was brutally raped and murdered in 1986 in her dorm room at Lehigh University (Lipka, 2009; Security on Campus, Inc., 2008). The Clery Act mandates that all universities receiving federal funding "file annual reports with the U.S. Department of Education about criminal activity on their campuses" (Roberts, Fossey, & DeMitchell, 2005, p. 195).

The tragic events at Virginia Polytechnic Institute and State University (Virginia Tech) in 2007, when a student killed 33 people on campus including himself (Hauser & O'Connor, 2007; Hsu & Heron, 2007), once again pushed campus safety into the spotlight and made it a leading concern among student affairs professionals. College administrators are faced with the difficult and often expensive task of creating and implementing security procedures to provide a safe learning environment for students, faculty, and staff.

As a more diverse group of students enrolls on college campuses across the country, the needs and methods of supporting students have changed in a variety of ways. College students today use technology—especially social media—to connect to one another, and student affairs professionals and other campus administrators take advantage of technological advances to better support students. According to Schneider (2010), mass notification systems use multiple technology devices to deliver a customized message to alert students, faculty, staff, and administrators of a campus threat or danger. "Phone, email, instant messaging, text messaging, fax, BlackBerry®, PDAs, and pagers" (n.p.) are all technologies available to universities to reach their constituents. Technology is changing so rapidly that it is often hard for faculty and student affairs professionals to stay abreast of the latest means of communication. Rubin (2013) described the declining use of e-mail communication among college students as newer technologies have emerged. Students today are able to form their own connections to campus, departments, and people without leaving their residence hall rooms. Gemmill and Peterson (2006) found that female college students used technology more than male students to communicate with family and friends. However, there are challenges for college students who rely heavily on technology. For example, using technology can cause difficulties for students in completing coursework (Gemmill & Peterson, 2006).

Although technology increases student access to resources and people, student life traditions and normative collegiate behavior have been slow to change, especially for first-time college-going students of traditional age who enroll in 4-year, degree-granting institutions immediately after high school. In many ways, student life has remained idyllic, often centering on intercollegiate athletics, ritualized drinking, and a period of sexual exploration (e.g., Holland & Eisenhart, 1990; Horowitz, 1987; Moffatt, 1989; Peril, 2006). Newcomers to campuses are taught the traditions of student life within the particular collegiate environment, ostensibly partaking in its indulgences rather than re-creating or transforming it. Those students who do not participate in this traditional full-time, residence-based student life experience often miss much of what we know as student life or the traditional collegiate experience on American college campuses. For example, students of a non-traditional age, online learners, and students who are working full-time or caring for dependents often miss out on campus traditions, student activities, and the behavioral rituals of college student life. Although institutions have shaped their more traditional academic services and functions around teaching and learning to meet the needs of many "new" types of student learners and an increasingly diverse body of college students, the model of student life has maintained an abiding fidelity to the model of student life forged in the 1800s by White, affluent, male adolescents and described by Rudolph (1990) as the "collegiate way" (p. 86).

Despite the increasing secularity of American colleges and universities, many changes in student diversity, and an overall tolerance of permissiveness toward lifestyle freedoms, student life—and the dominant perceptions of it held by faculty, staff, students, and the public at large—caters to the old ideal of the early American college student and the prototype of the college man and college woman (Horowitz, 1987). However, as student life is indelibly linked to the profession of student affairs, student affairs professionals play a unique role within the campus setting, as they are called to customize their work to meet the needs of new students and the student environments provided through technology and social media (Martínez Alemán & Wartman, 2011). In addition, student affairs professionals hold the key to addressing many other urgent concerns that have emerged in the twenty-first century, including student mental and physical health, wellness, and overall campus safety. Although student personnel professionals typically work to include all new students in campus life through orientation programs and courses to support students' successful transition into the college environment, they are also capable of supporting students and student leaders in creating new models of student life that take on new forms in a new age and within new political power structures. The extent to which student affairs professionals, faculty, other administrators, and students are able to break the mold is key to determining whether American higher education will conserve student life as more deeply rooted in the past than poised for a radically different future.

References

American Council on Education. (1937). *The student personnel point of view.* Retrieved from http://www.myacpa.org/pub/documents/1937.pdf

American Council on Education. (1949). *The student personnel point of view.* Retrieved from http://www.myacpa.org/pub/documents/1949.pdf

Astin, A.W., Astin, H.S., Bayer, A.E., & Bisconti, A.S. (1997). Overview of the unrest era. In L. Goodchild & H. Weschsler (Eds.), *The history of higher education* (2nd ed., pp. 724–738). Needham Heights, MA: Simon & Schuster.

Bashaw, C.T. (1999). *Stalwart women: A historical analysis of deans of women in the South.* New York, NY: Teachers College Press.

Bashaw, C.T. (2001). "To serve the needs of women": The AAUW, NAWDC, and persistence of academic women's support networks. In J. Nidiffer & C.T. Bashaw (Eds.), *Women administrators in higher education: Historical and contemporary perspectives* (pp. 13–34). Albany, NY: State University of New York Press.

Broido, E.M. (2004). Understanding diversity in millennial students. *New Directions for Student Services, 2004*(106), 73–85.

Clark, D.A. (1998). The two Joes meet. Joe College, Joe Veteran. *History of Education Quarterly, 38*(2), 165–189.

Dennis, M. (2001). *Lessons in progress: State universities and progressivism in the New South, 1880–1920.* Urbana, IL: University of Illinois Press.

Faragher, J.M., & Howe, F. (1988). *Women and higher education in American history: Essays from the Mount Holyoke College Sesquicentennial Symposia.* New York, NY: W.W. Norton .

Fenske, R.H. (1980). Historical foundations. In E. Delworth, G.R. Hanson, & Associates (Eds.), *Student services: A handbook for the profession* (pp. 3–24). San Francisco, CA: Jossey-Bass.

Geiger, R. (Ed.). (2000). *The American college in the nineteenth century.* Nashville, TN: Vanderbilt University Press.

Gemmill, E., & Peterson, M. (2006). Technology use among college students: Implications for student affairs professionals. *NASPA Journal, 43*(2), 280–300.

Glover, L. (2003). An education in southern masculinity: The Ball family of South Carolina in the new republic. *Journal of Southern History, 69*(1), 49–70.

Goodchild, L. (2007). History of higher education in the United States. In H.S. Weschsler, L.F. Goodchild, & L. Eisenmann (Eds.), *The history of higher education* (pp. 36–47). Boston, MA: Pearson.

Hauser, C., & O'Connor, A. (2007, April 16). Virginia Tech shooting leaves 33 dead. *The New York Times.* Retrieved from http://www.nytimes.com/2007/04/16/us/16cnd-shooting.html
Herron, R.I. (2004). *True spirit of pioneer traditions: An historical analysis of the University of Florida's dean of women, Marna Brady* (Unpublished doctoral dissertation). Florida State University, Tallahassee.
Hofstadter, R., & Smith, W. (1961). *American higher education: A documentary history* (Vol. I). Chicago, IL: University of Chicago Press.
Holland, D.C., & Eisenhart, M.A. (1990). *Educated in romance: Women, achievement, and college culture.* Chicago, IL: University of Chicago Press.
Horowitz, H.L. (1987). *Campus life: Undergraduate cultures from the end of the eighteenth century to the present.* Chicago, IL: University of Chicago Press.
Howe, N., & Strauss, W. (2000). *Millennials rising: The next great generation.* New York, NY: Vintage.
Hsu, N., & Heron, L. (2007). Virginia Tech shootings: The sequence of events. *The Washington Post.* Retrieved from http://www.washingtonpost.com/wp-srv/metro/interactives/vatechshootings/shootings_timeline.html
Hunt, J., & Eisenberg, D. (2010). Mental health problems and help-seeking behavior among college students. *Journal of Adolescent Health, 46*(1), 3–10.
Johnson, E.L. (1981). Misconceptions about the early land-grant colleges. *Journal of Higher Education, 52*(4), 333–351.
Kerr, C. (2001). *The uses of the university* (5th ed.). Cambridge, MA: Harvard University Press.
Kitzrow, M.A. (2003). The mental health needs of today's college students: Challenges and recommendations. *NASPA Journal, 41*(1), 167–181.
Levine, D.O. (1986). *The American college and the culture of aspiration, 1915–1940.* Ithaca, NY: Cornell University Press.
Lipka, S. (2009, January 30). In campus-crime reports, there's little safety in the numbers. *Chronicle of Higher Education.* Retrieved from http://0-chronicle.com.umiss.lib.olemiss.edu/article/In-Campus-Crime-Reports/30058/
Lowery, J.W. (2011). Students' rights. In B.J. Bank (Ed.), *Gender and higher education* (pp. 382–389). Baltimore, MD: Johns Hopkins University Press.
Lucas, C.J. (2006). *American higher education: A history* (2nd ed.). New York, NY: Palgrave Macmillan.
Martínez Alemán, A.M., & Wartman, K.L. (2011). Student technology use and student affairs practice. In. M.J. Barr, M.K. Desler, & Associates (Eds.), *The handbook of student affairs administration* (2nd ed., pp. 515–533). San Francisco, CA: Jossey-Bass.
McCandless, A.T. (1999). *The past in the present: Women's higher education in the twentieth-century American South.* Tuscaloosa, AL: University of Alabama Press.
Moffatt, M. (1989). *Coming of age in New Jersey: College and American culture.* New Brunswick, NJ: Rutgers University Press.
Moore, K.M. (1976). Freedom and constraint in eighteenth century Harvard. *Journal of Higher Education, 47*(6), 649–659.
Nidiffer, J. (1995). From matron to maven: A new role and new professional identity for deans of women, 1892–1918. *Mid-Western Educational Researcher, 8*(4), 17–24.
Nidiffer, J. (2000). *Pioneering deans of women: More than wise and pious matrons.* New York, NY: Teachers College Press.
Nidiffer, J. (2001a). Advocates on campus: Deans of women create a new profession. In J. Nidiffer & C.T. Bashaw (Eds.), *Women administrators in higher education: Historical and contemporary perspectives* (pp. 135–156). Albany, NY: State University of New York Press.
Nidiffer, J. (2001b). Crumbs from the boy's table: The first century of coeducation. In J. Nidiffer & C.T. Bashaw (Eds.), *Women administrators in higher education: Historical and contemporary perspectives* (pp. 13–34). Albany, NY: State University of New York Press.
Nidiffer, J. (2002). The first deans of women: What we can learn from them. *About Campus, 6*(6), 10–16.
Nidiffer, J., & Cain, T.R. (2004). Elder brothers of the university: Early vice presidents in the late nineteenth century universities. *History of Education Quarterly, 44*(4), 487–523.
O'Brien, P.M. (Ed.). (2009). *Accreditation: Assuring and enhancing quality.* New Directions for Student Services, 145. San Francisco, CA: Jossey-Bass.
Ogren, C.A. (2005). *The American state normal school: "An instrument of great good."* New York, NY: Palgrave Macmillan.
Peril, L. (2006). *College girls: Bluestockings, sex kittens, and coeds, then and now.* New York, NY: W.W. Norton .
Rasmussen, W.D. (1989). *Taking the university to the people: Seventy-five years of cooperative extension.* Ames, IA: Iowa State University Press.
Rhatigan, J. (2000). The history and philosophy of student affairs. In. M.J. Barr, M.K. Desler, & Associates (Eds.), *The handbook of student affairs administration* (2nd ed., pp. 3–24). San Francisco, CA: Jossey-Bass.

Roberts, D.C. (2012). *The Student Personnel Point of View* as a catalyst for dialogue: 75 years and beyond. *Journal of College Student Development, 53*(1), 2–18.

Roberts, N., Fossey, R., & DeMitchell, T. (2005). Tort liability. In J. Beckham & D. Dagley (Eds.), *Contemporary issues in higher education law* (pp. 183–207). Dayton, OH: Education Law Association.

Rubin, C. (2013, September 27). Technology and the college generation. *The New York Times.* Retrieved from http://www.nytimes.com/2013/09/29/fashion/technology-and-the-college-generation.html?pagewanted=1&_r=0

Rudolph, F. (1990). *The American college and university: A history.* Athens, GA: University of Georgia Press.

Sartorius, K.C. (2010). Experimental autonomy: Dean Emily Taylor and the women's movement at the University of Kansas. *Kansas History: A Journal of the Central Plains, 33*(1), 2–21.

Schneider, T. (2010, July). Mass notification for higher education. *National Clearinghouse for Educational Facilities.* Retrieved from http://www.ncef.org/pubs/notification.pdf

Schwartz, R.A. (1997a). How deans of women became men. *Review of Higher Education, 20*(4), 419–436.

Schwartz, R.A. (1997b). Reconceptualizing the leadership roles of women in higher education: A brief history on the importance of deans of women. *Journal of Higher Education, 68*(5), 502–522.

Security on Campus, Inc. (2008). *Summary of the Jeanne Clery Act.* Retrieved from http://www.securityoncampus.org/index.php?option=com_content&view=article&id=297%3Aclerysummary&catid=64%3Acleryact&Itemid=60

Thelin, J.R. (1982). *Higher education and its useful past.* Cambridge, MA: Schenkman.

Thelin, J.R. (1994). *Games colleges play: Scandal and reform in intercollegiate athletics.* Baltimore, MD: Johns Hopkins University Press.

Thelin, J.R. (2004). *A history of American higher education.* Baltimore, MD: Johns Hopkins University Press.

Thelin, J.R. (2012). *A history of American higher education* (2nd ed.). Baltimore, MD: Johns Hopkins University Press.

Thelin, J.R., & Gasman, M. (2011). Historical overview of American higher education. In J.H. Schuh, S.R. Jones, S.R. Harper, & Associates (Eds.), *Student services: A handbook for the profession* (pp. 3–23). San Francisco, CA: Jossey-Bass.

Tuttle, K.N. (1996). *What became of the dean of women? Changing roles for women administrators in American higher education, 1940–1980* (Unpublished doctoral dissertation). University of Kansas, Lawrence.

Veysey, L.R. (1965). *The emergence of the American university.* Chicago, IL: University of Chicago Press.

Wells, A.E., & Thelin, J. (2002). Greek life. In J.F. Forest & K. Kinser (Eds.), *Encyclopedia of higher education in the United States* (Vol. I, pp. 295–297). Santa Barbara, CA: ABC-CLIO.

Wells, A.E., & Worley, D. (2011). Sororities. In B.J. Bank (Ed.), *Gender and higher education* (pp. 298–304). Baltimore, MD: Johns Hopkins University Press.

SEVENTEEN

Fraternities and Sororities: Developing a Compelling Case for Relevance in Higher Education

James P. Barber, Michelle M. Espino, and Daniel Bureau

A Case for Relevance

With over 60 collective years of serving the fraternal movement as fraternity/sorority members, chapter[1] advisors, fraternity/sorority life advisors, and (inter)national fraternal leaders, we approached writing about the experiences of college students who participate in fraternities and sororities from an affirming and positive perspective. We believe these distinctive and intergenerational organizations can provide a forum for college students to create meaningful, well-rounded, and learning-oriented experiences. Deep and long-standing challenges continue to exist, but the juxtaposition of the best and worst actions of today's college students make fraternities and sororities among the most complex organizations on college campuses. In addition, there is a high level of interaction between and among students, the campus community, administrators, faculty, alumni, and external stakeholders such as parents and (inter)national fraternity/sorority headquarters. Such dynamic experiences can create shared and distinctive realities for students that are integral to student development. This chapter provides insight into the historical and modern-day complexities that affect students' experiences in fraternities and sororities and offers a framework for working with this population across contexts.

The Complexities of Involvement in Fraternities and Sororities

Today's members supersede conventional notions of what it means to be part of fraternities and sororities.[2] This student population faces challenges and experiences that reflect concerns about values, inclusivity, and the institutional expectations of fraternity/sorority life (Asel, Seifert, & Pascarella, 2009). In addition, as most collegiate members are of traditional age, these students are exploring and developing their personal identities (Abes, Jones, & McEwen, 2007). Their individual understandings of their race, ethnicity, social class, gender, spirituality, and sexual orientation, among other characteristics, are emerging while they are also managing being a "fraternity/sorority member." Identity is socially constructed, and what it means to be a member differs based on particular campus contexts, the values of a particular organization, and the historical legacy embedded within that organization. As suggested by Abes and colleagues' (2007) Model of Multiple Dimensions of Identity, each individual has a core identity surrounded by these multiple social identities, with certain dimensions of identity becoming more salient in certain situations. For example, a student's identity as a woman may be less important in interacting as a member of an all-female sorority than it is in her engineering course. However, the individual's identity is one element of a larger and more complex system.

As members of fraternities and sororities, college students move within individual, organizational, community, and institutional contexts. The role of student affairs practitioners is to understand how the fraternal experience affects student learning and development at various levels and to dismantle practices and behaviors at the individual, institutional, and system levels that inhibit student engagement and learning. For fraternities and sororities to remain relevant, meaningful, contributory, and trusted, those who work on college campuses must not only understand the issues but know how to manage and address the complexities found within these unique organizations and among members. This chapter aims to increase that understanding.

We begin with a brief history of the fraternal movement and the extent to which traditions developed through the years continue to affect long-standing opportunities and challenges that are part and parcel of the organizations. Following an overview of the fraternal community, we offer a case study to illustrate the complexities of the fraternity/sorority experience through the perspectives of fraternity/sorority chapter presidents who are attending a leadership retreat. Although the student participants are the presidents of their organizations and share similar identities as leaders, their priorities for change differ based on their personal and organizational experiences. The case study reveals the diverse experiences students have as individuals, as members of their organizations, and as part of the larger fraternity/sorority community and campus.

We conclude with recommendations for college educators working with fraternal organizations. To frame our recommendations, an interpretation of Bronfenbrenner's (1977, 1986, 1994, 2005) ecological systems model is presented as a framework for examining how issues, opportunities, and challenges present themselves at different levels within fraternity/sorority experiences: the individual student, organization/chapter, fraternity/sorority community, campus, and the (inter)national organization.

Overview of the Fraternal Movement

The first Greek-letter organization, Phi Beta Kappa, was founded at the College of William and Mary on December 5, 1776. Phi Beta Kappa was the first college student organization to incorporate many of the hallmarks of present-day fraternities and sororities, including a secret handshake or grip, motto, password, oath of obligation, initiation ritual, and a public membership badge. In 1779, the William and Mary chapter authorized the establishment of two additional chapters at Harvard and Yale (Anson & Marchesani, 1991). Few Greek-letter organizations that formed in the next 40 years took hold on college campuses. It was not until the Kappa Alpha Society was founded in 1825 at Union College in New York, followed by Sigma Phi and Delta Phi in 1827 (the three are often referred to as the "Union Triad"), that the fraternity system as we know it began to take shape (Anson & Marchesani, 1991). Thirty years later, women's fraternities were established when Alpha Delta Pi (1851) and Phi Mu (1852) were founded at Wesleyan Female College in Macon, Georgia.

As fraternities and sororities began to flourish on college campuses, secrecy and exclusivity were especially significant to the fraternal experience. Faculty members and administrators were particularly skeptical of secret societies, and many institutions prohibited student participation in fraternal organizations. For example, the "Fraternity War" instigated by faculty members at the University of Michigan during the 1840s and 1850s called for the expulsion of any men who did not renounce their fraternity membership (Tobin, 2008). Fraternal organizations were viewed as exclusionary, elitist, and anti-democratic—criticisms that linger today.

Such claims were not unfounded. During this era, college fraternities were frankly discriminatory in terms of race and religion and in some cases remain so today (Grasgreen, 2013). Early fraternities and sororities limited membership to White, Protestant students. Zeta Beta Tau fraternity, the first Jewish fraternity, was founded in 1903 in direct response to discrimination and sectarianism against Jewish students (Schreck, 1976). As Black students began to enter predominantly White colleges and universities, they were generally excluded from the existing fraternity and sorority chapters and began organizing their own fraternal organizations. The first Black fraternity to take root and establish chapters on multiple campuses was Alpha Phi Alpha, founded in 1906 at Cornell University. Alpha Kappa Alpha Sorority, founded in 1908 at Howard University, was the first Greek-letter organization established by African American women. Other culturally based fraternities and sororities soon followed, including the first Asian American interest sorority, Chi Alpha Delta, founded at the University of California, Los Angeles, in 1928 and the first organization for Latino men, Phi Iota Alpha, established in 1931 at Rensselaer Polytechnic Institute (Kimbrough, 2003).[3]

Greek-letter organizations soon began to form (inter)national governing councils with those fraternities/sororities that shared similar membership demographics and historical roots. The Inter-Sorority Conference, which is now known as the National Panhellenic Conference (NPC), was established in 1902 by historically White sororities that wanted to "advance their organizations in the face of restrictive social customs, unequal status under the law…[and faced] the same challenges as their male counterparts [such as] hostile college administrations and the threat of being outlawed by state legislatures" (National Panhellenic Conference, 2012, p. 4). The North-American Interfraternity Conference (NIC, 1909) was formed by 26 traditionally White men's organizations. Historically Black fraternities and sororities formed the National Pan-Hellenic Council (NPHC) in 1930. With the proliferation of Latina/o-based and multicultural fraternities and sororities in the 1990s, the National Association of Latina/o Fraternal Organizations (NALFO) and the National Multicultural Greek Council (NMGC) were both founded in 1998. The National Asian Pacific Islander American Panhellenic Association (NAPA) was created in 2004.

Dismantling the Vestiges of Discrimination and Elitism

Despite efforts to eliminate fraternities and sororities in the late nineteenth century, the majority of American colleges and universities host fraternal groups today. Unfortunately, criticisms of the fraternity/sorority community as elitist and exclusionary persist and are rooted in institutions of higher education that also contend with elitist and exclusionary traditions and practices.

There are a number of perspectives to consider in terms of exclusivity, diversity, history, and identity, all of which are embedded in larger systems and structures that affect student behavior and development. For example, single-sex membership remains a defining characteristic of college fraternal organizations. Some coeducational groups exist and thrive, but the majority of organizations remain all male or all female. Single-sex as well as culturally based organizations can provide important contexts for college student identity development and exploration. Particularly for marginalized populations, fraternal organizations can become "counter spaces" where students can express themselves and socialize in groups apart from the dominant cultural spaces on campus (Cuyjet, Howard-Hamilton, & Cooper, 2011). As evidenced by the proliferation of culturally based organizations, some students seek groups that value and promote various cultural backgrounds and identities, something that is not consistently available through traditionally White fraternities and sororities. Racial/ethnic integration across chapters poses a significant issue that is difficult to resolve, because student affairs practitioners have limited input in decisions about who is invited to join each chapter, even if they empower fraternity/sorority members to have conversations about race and racism and other issues of difference. In addition, the fraternity/sorority life infrastructure on most college campuses offers separate options for membership, but not always equal access to resources and support such as a dedicated student affairs staff member, leadership development opportunities, or programming that focuses on unlearning issues of oppression.

Barriers to membership such as social class, gender expression, and sexual orientation also remain in place across fraternal organizations (Asel et al., 2009; Ryan, 2009). All fraternities and sororities have removed membership restrictions based on race and religion (although what results in practice may differ), and a growing number have established anti-discrimination policies regarding sexual orientation. Unfortunately, these policy changes at the (inter)national level may not reflect campus realities and practices. In addition, despite changes in membership restrictions, campus-specific governing council structures have remained relatively intact, grouping organizations by historical mission. There are limited interventions on the part of student affairs administrators and fraternity/sorority alumni/ae to shift undergraduate membership within individual chapters to more accurately reflect changing demographics as well as to develop specific policy implementation strategies based on (inter)national policy changes.

Although challenges remain, fraternity/sorority advisors can create significant opportunities for members and those seeking membership in fraternities and sororities to focus on the core values that served as the basis for the founding of these unique organizations. Members are selected for and expected to demonstrate espoused organizational values, and higher education institutions are holding organizations and members accountable to these values.

A Focus on Values and Values Congruence

A primary goal of colleges and universities is to help students develop the skills and competencies to enter into a global society, with specific consideration of personal value systems. Fraternities and sororities are one context in which a student can solidify, modify, and strengthen values (Matthews et al., 2009). According to Scott (1965), values clarification is a cyclical and dynamic process, with individual students determining whether the values they hold are congruent with the values espoused by an organization. "[Members'] desire [to devote time and effort to an organization] will presumably be increased if they find colleagues who share their own values...and whom they can therefore admire and work for willingly" (Scott, 1965, p. 95). In turn, the organization reinforces or challenges those values, causing the individual student to decide whether to modify or strengthen his/her value system in accordance with the values of the organization.

Many have offered that the aspiration of developing and living one's values as a positive contribution to the betterment of a student and those around her/him has been a long-standing attribute of the fraternity/sorority experience (Clegg, 2010; Scott, 1965; Shalka, 2008). Although this may be true, it is also plausible that values, as a distinctive and vital niche within the fraternal movement, have been a point of emphasis, particularly over the last 25 years.[4] Two changes within the higher education landscape led to this focus. First, the promulgation of diverse activities on college campuses increased the perception that value-added student involvement and engagement did not occur only through membership in a fraternity/sorority (i.e., increased competition for members with other campus and community organizations). Second, increased concerns with risk management and hazing in the 1980s and 1990s led to a concerted effort by administrators, including university presidents, to challenge social fraternities and sororities to return to their values and promote more positive behavior (Shalka, 2008). These efforts have resulted in an increased emphasis on values development and alignment as primary outcomes of fraternity/sorority membership.

In 2002, a group of college presidents, executive directors from fraternity and sorority (inter)national headquarters, and the presidents of the American Association of State Colleges and Universities, the National Association of Independent Colleges and Universities, and the National Association of State Universities and Land Grant Colleges met in Washington, D.C., to discuss the need to focus on values congruence (Franklin Square Group, 2003; Grund, 2005). Called the Franklin Square Group, this body ushered in a galvanizing moment in the fraternal movement: focusing on values in order to remain relevant on today's college campuses (Clegg, 2010).

Rather than focusing solely on the consequences of negative behavior and discriminatory practices, the Franklin Square Group and leadership across the fraternal community argued for analyzing their root causes. Fraternity/sorority members would need to be challenged to uncover their own personal beliefs and values, determine if their values were congruent with the values espoused by social Greek-letter organizations, and then act in accordance with those internalized and espoused values (Clegg, 2010; Shalka, 2008). The process may seem reasonable, but helping students to identify their personal values and then contrast them to an organization's values is a tremendous and arduous challenge (Martin & Bureau, 2008). Maintaining values congruence from recruitment through one's life is the responsibility of individuals, chapters, the fraternity/sorority community, the university, and the (inter)national headquarters.

The Presidents' Retreat: A Case Study

West Coast University is a large, public state university located in a metropolitan area. The fraternity/sorority community is comprised of 45 chapters, four governing councils, and represents 15% of the total undergraduate student population. Every year, the Fraternity/Sorority

Life Office sponsors a Presidents' Retreat for all of the chapters and trains chapter advisors to serve as retreat facilitators. The theme for this year is "Managing Change."

As part of the retreat curriculum, Lisa, the Fraternity/Sorority Life Coordinator, has divided the presidents into nine groups of five participants with a trained facilitator for each group. The groups are randomly assigned, although Lisa has ensured that there is representation from each council in each group. Prior to a break-out session, she asks the students to answer the following questions as a small group: "What are the most important aspects of the fraternity/sorority experience to preserve? What are the most important to change?" After the group completes a few activities to learn more about each other, Thomas, the group facilitator, asks the students to share their thoughts on the questions provided.

Luis, a senior, is a member of an international Latino fraternity that was chartered on campus 3 years ago and is the first to break the silence. His fraternity, which is the largest of the culturally based fraternities, has 15 members and recently secured membership in the newly formed Multicultural Greek Council.[5] Luis's father is a member of a predominantly White fraternity, and his mother, who left college after her sophomore year, was active in a Latina/o-based student organization but did not join a sorority. Luis considered joining one of the Interfraternity Council (IFC)[6] chapters during his first year but declined the invitation and became involved in the Residence Hall Association. During his sophomore year his fraternity established a chapter on campus, and he crossed[7] in the founding line (i.e., the first group of new members). Luis offers a suggestion to the group: "I think we need to have more interaction across the four councils. Although I knew many of the guys in IFC during my freshman year, now that I'm in my fraternity, it seems that our chapters stay separated from each other."

Sara, a sophomore, is a first-generation college student. She was significantly involved in her synagogue during high school and has tried to maintain connections to her religion. As a result, Sara has struggled with the components of her sorority's ritual that have Christian overtones, including swearing on a Bible during initiation. Because she believed that the values of her Panhellenic[8] sorority matched her own, she was happy to become a member. Now, as chapter president, she is concerned that the most recent new member class is more interested in gaining popularity with one of the larger fraternities than enacting the organization's values. Sara wants the chapter to be run well, but she has encountered resistance from senior members who do not respect her as the chapter president. She is already feeling challenged to make any changes in the chapter, and many are making it hard for her to lead. "For me," Sara says, "the thing we need to change is helping our members understand the values and goals of the organization. If they only thought about how their actions reflect on the principles we say we believe in, maybe these new members would contribute more to the well-being of the chapter."

Krystal is an African American junior who joined a predominantly White sorority because she knew many of the women in the chapter. In high school, she interacted with a range of students from diverse backgrounds, particularly through her involvement on the volleyball and tennis teams. During sorority recruitment, she experienced two racist interactions at one chapter, but she still felt welcomed by many in the Panhellenic community. Krystal is the first woman of color in recent history to serve as chapter president. Her relationship with the alumnae advisor is very strong, but she has had experiences with the housing corporation president[9] who, from Krystal's perspective, does not know how to interact with people of color. "I'm not sure our fraternity and sorority community is a welcoming place for people of all backgrounds," she says. "We need to help our alumni understand how our chapters are different now because we're not all 'girls' majoring in an MRS. Degree and our sisters aren't all going to look alike—no matter what the stereotypes say. We're smart, sophisticated, hard-working, goal-oriented women from different backgrounds and experiences and people need to get used to that."

Michael is also a junior. Serving as president of a popular fraternity on the campus with over 70 members, he joined during his first year for the parties and the drinking. The fraternity allowed him the rules-free environment that he sought. During the second semester of his first year, the chapter was placed on probation by the Office of Fraternity/Sorority Life because of hazing issues. After a membership review, the national headquarters removed 30 members. Nearing the end of probation, the chapter has made some progress, including revising a new member education program that had numerous components of hazing. While having to lead some of these changes, Michael also revealed to his brothers that he is gay, an identity he has yet to resolve for himself. Most members of the chapter have been very supportive; however, a few have not. Michael says, "Look, I agree with all that's been said so far—we need to collaborate more, we need to be more focused on our values, and we need to be more welcoming." He goes on to add, "But let me play Devil's advocate here. Things don't have to be so serious. I joined my chapter because being in a fraternity is fun. And I wish there was a way to keep having fun but in a safe manner so we don't get in trouble. Every time there's a hazing case, fraternities are blamed, but no one does anything about what's happening with the band or in athletics. I think there's a double standard here on campus in terms of who gets in trouble and who doesn't and that needs to change."

Clarice pauses before it is her turn to speak, continuing to collect her thoughts. She joined her National Pan-Hellenic Council[10] sorority last year as a junior, following in the footsteps of her mother and aunt. At first, she had no interest in sororities because she believed that they focused too much on underground pledging processes incorporating hazing. She preferred to demonstrate her leadership skills through involvement in the Black Student Union. However, a conversation with a graduate member of her sorority, who was returning to campus after a 3-year hiatus, changed her mind. Now, as president of the six-woman chapter, she is concerned about declining numbers. There are only about 90 members within the eight NPHC groups on campus, although the undergraduate student population is 20% African American. "Fun isn't enough, Michael," she says. "I'm worried that we won't have a place on this campus in the near future. Do we really add anything? My national organization is one big lawsuit away from closing because of all that 'fun,' and I wonder if my daughter will someday be able to also be my Soror.[11] I want to do something to help us be meaningful. I want to do something to help the chapter exist for another 100 years, but I'm lost. I'm a student. I have things to do other than my sorority. How can I make the difference I need to make while also doing well in school?" As the presidents continue to share, Thomas wonders how he will help the students address these various and complicated concerns.

Recommendations for Practice

Environmental contexts are important to consider when supporting the development of college students who are members of fraternities and sororities. Ecological systems theory is a useful framework to employ in considering the complexities of fraternity/sorority experiences because it identifies five levels embedded within and external to the college environment that affect a person's development: microsystems, mesosystems, exosystems, macrosystems, and chronosystems (See Figure 1; Bronfenbrenner, 1977, 1986, 1994, 2005). These levels illustrate the interrelated effect of social contexts and processes on individuals over time. To demonstrate the utility of this framework, we draw from the case study to provide recommendations for practitioners like Thomas as they support student and organizational learning as well as development across the levels of ecological systems theory.

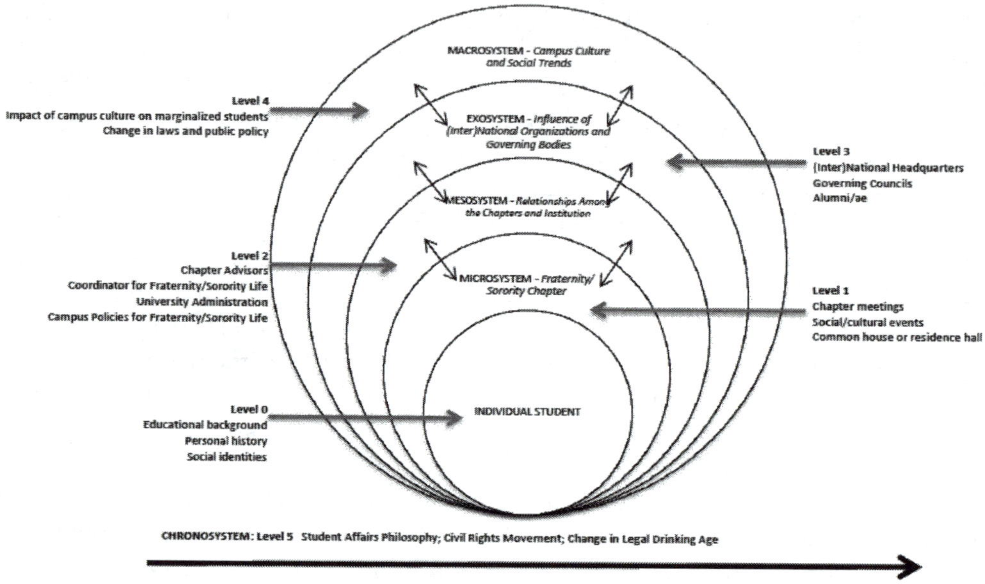

Figure 1. Use of Bronfenbrenner's framework in working with members of fraternities and sororities.

The individual is situated at the center of the model and is surrounded by the microsystem, which is the relationship between the person and his/her environment within a particular setting (e.g., the relationship between a fraternity member and his/her family, chapter, university, or neighborhood). Mesosystems include the relationships between these settings (e.g., the relationship among the campus chapters and the institution), and the exosystem is an extension of the mesosystem, including events and processes that indirectly affect the student (e.g., inter/national organization events, governing body policies, national economic trends, and changes in state/federal law). The macrosystem describes the attitudes or ideologies of a culture in which an individual lives (e.g., campus culture, patriarchy, White culture, Western culture). Across these systems, the chronosystem accounts for the change that occurs in the environment over time (Bronfenbrenner, 1986, 1994). All of the systems are interrelated, affecting one another and the individual; this interaction is represented by the arrows bridging the levels in Figure 1.

Level 0: Individual Student

At the core of fraternity/sorority experiences are individuals who are selected for membership and choose to accept. Each of these students comes to the institution and fraternal organization with a distinct educational background, personal history, and ways of seeing the world. The majority of those joining fraternities and sororities are 18–22 years old. Theories of college student development based on empirical research document that individuals in this stage of life are at a formative period in cognitive approach, identity, and key relationships. For example, Baxter Magolda's (2001) work on self-authorship illustrates that many younger college students are heavily reliant on external authorities and are only beginning the journey toward a more internally driven orientation. Identity is a key domain of individual development, and students in college are at a critical point in the formation of personal values and self-awareness. This exploration can have interesting implications when played out in the context of an organization in which dependence on others is so pervasively promoted.

Practitioners should consider working with fraternity and sorority members on an individual basis, much as they would when approaching other students. Because of the size, scope, and typically large-group activities of fraternal groups, it may be difficult to see beyond the organizational facade. However, approaching members as individuals with unique histories, aspirations, and developmental trajectories allows for a greater implementation of student development theory as a framework for promoting personal learning and growth. In the case study, for example, Sara experiences her sorority as president, as a Jewish woman, and as a first-generation college student. Michael is leading a chapter in reform while addressing challenges as a gay man.

The individual frame and developmental journey of the student is important to consider in determining the most effective ways to connect with members of fraternities and sororities. The challenge at this level is that helping the individual student move through various developmental processes takes time and continues after college. Members of fraternities and sororities are contending with understanding their own identities and ways of seeing the world and also interacting with individuals who may or may not share the same values within the chapter, in the classroom, and in the larger environment. Practitioners must strike a balance between creating interventions that lead to higher-order critical thinking (i.e., values congruence) and simultaneously helping students manage their first stages of development as young adults (Martin & Bureau, 2008).

Level 1: Microsystem—Fraternity/Sorority Chapter

The individual members of a fraternity/sorority on a particular campus form the microsystem, or chapter. Members of the chapter hold regular meetings at least once per week and work in concert to recruit new members, plan social/cultural events, support one another academically, and volunteer in the community. On many campuses, chapter members may live together in a common house or residence hall, which may affect the quality of interactions among members and may silo members from interacting with informal groups and campus organizations external to the fraternity/sorority community. The chapter is a very fluid group, with membership turning over each academic year as students graduate and new members join. Alumni advisors are in frequent contact with the student leaders and may or may not support initiatives, goals, and interventions crafted by the campus fraternity/sorority life advisor. Because they are dedicated to the success of the individual chapter, they are a part of the chapter microsystem, along with the undergraduate members. In the case study, as a woman of color in a predominately White sorority, Krystal feels that she belongs, but her interactions with the House Corporation President, who seems to be uncomfortable with working with someone of a different race, become a frequent source of concern. By contrast, Michael experiences a mostly supportive chapter environment as he works through his identity as a gay man.

Scott (1965) explained that a chapter can be a stronger organization if it attracts members who already espouse the founding values of the organization. From a different perspective, an individual can be vulnerable to changing his/her values if he/she is seeking external approval from chapter members. The chapter as a whole has a responsibility to cultivate the development of individual students while also enacting the values that it espouses. Practitioners need to become familiar with the chapter structures and environments on college campuses, regardless of whether one is formally involved in working with this student population. Understanding how often and where chapter meetings take place can provide additional context for developing policies, curricula, and programming that chapters will find useful and relevant as student organizations. Attending chapter meetings to meet members provides an opportunity to see a chapter meeting in action and build rapport with the organization and its membership. Visiting chapter residential space, if applicable, or attending a cultural event is another excellent opportunity to learn about the chapter's culture, organizational limitations, and level of diversity awareness. Training chapter leaders, new members, and alumni advisors on values congruence is an important part of helping students to thrive within their chapters. The case study described earlier is a good example of practitioners providing opportunities to connect with students and for students to connect among themselves in an effort to examine these structures and identify areas to retain, modify, and dismantle.

Level 2: Mesosystem—Relationships Among the Chapters and Within the Institution

In applying Bronfenbrenner's (1977, 1994) ecological systems model to fraternity/sorority communities, the mesosystem is comprised of the relationships among the individual chapters on a campus, and with the institution. The greater campus culture also figures prominently in the mesosystem. The practitioner responsible for oversight of fraternity/sorority affairs is generally at the nexus of the mesosystem, facilitating and negotiating interactions between chapters (often through advising local governing councils) and serving as the administration's representative to the students. Luis comments on this dynamic in the case study, pointing out that chapters are often divided along racial, cultural, and gender lines; these divisions are reinforced by the governing structures of the fraternity/sorority system and, perhaps unintentionally, supported through fraternity/sorority campus advisors. Practitioners must recognize meaningful opportunities to correct division (perceived and real) between the fraternity and sorority community and the greater campus community.

The mesosystem is also the area where conflict is most visible in the ecological system, especially with regard to adhering to regulations and implementing campus-specific policies that affect all chapters. The needs of a five-member Latino fraternity and a 150-woman Panhellenic sorority are quite different, although the chapters may be seen as the same by campus policymakers. Collaboration among key stakeholders and effective, timely, and transparent communication are ways to mitigate conflict, especially with regard to recruitment, new member education, and social activities that occur on or off campus.

The challenge that practitioners face at this level is the tension between managing and enforcing policies while also serving as advisors and advocates for these organizations. A balance between these two positions is crucial for ensuring that policies are followed and students are gaining meaningful educational experiences as members of fraternities and sororities. Although campus crises are unpredictable and require immediate intervention, working to establish more robust relationships between chapters and the institution is valuable, necessary, and an ongoing process. Creating regular opportunities for fraternity/sorority members to meet with campus fraternity/sorority advisors and upper-level administrators (preferably in student spaces) is one way to institutionalize this relationship. Too often, interactions are limited to beginning-of-the-year welcome speeches at community-wide events and interventions in times of crisis. Likewise, opportunities for members to interact with others in different chapters are often limited to governing councils in which chapters are organized with other groups that are historically and demographically similar. Returning to the case study, Luis wanted interaction across chapters. Implementing fraternity/sorority community-wide educational and social programs, such as new member retreats or the NIC's campus-based Impact Weekend program, as well as smaller intergroup dialogues that tackle lingering discriminatory practices can assist in building better relationships across fraternity/sorority communities.

Level 3: Exosystem—Influence of (Inter)National Organizations and Governing Bodies

The exosystem is an extension of the mesosystem, with the distinction that the mesosystem directly includes the individual member, and the exosystem indirectly affects the individual. In our framework for understanding fraternity/sorority experiences, the (inter)national headquarters, governing councils, and alumni comprise the exosystem. Although most organizations have student representation on their (inter)national boards of directors and allow undergraduate representatives to legislate policy at (bi)annual conventions, these positions of authority are rare for students, and much of the political and day-to-day decision making among (inter)national organizations is carried out at the level of professional headquarters staff, elected alumni leadership, and/or alumni volunteers.

Since most chapters are part of a much larger organization, the actions of members on one campus can have implications for members across the nation. For example, an incident of hazing, such as the one that occurred in Michael's chapter, could result in policy changes within the institution and the larger organization. Decisions made by a governing body can have even more far-reaching implications. For example, policy changes implemented by the National Pan-Hellenic Council in 1990 in response to campus hazing incidents changed the way that the member organizations recruited new members (Kimbrough, 2003). Referred to as the Membership Intake Process, this legislation has helped eliminate the traditional pledging model in favor of a more formal application and interview process.

Changes at the (inter)national level have direct consequences for how students lead and manage their chapters at the local level, even if they did not directly participate in developing those changes. In most situations, campus-based practitioners are also not included directly in the (inter)national or governing councils' decisions. There are limited opportunities to interact with headquarters staff members and volunteers at annual professional association meetings such as those held by the Association of Fraternity/Sorority Advisors, which can be a valuable in-person time to build relationships. The ties among practitioners, (inter)national headquarters, and governing councils should focus on outcomes that serve campus chapters, as well as those that promote student learning, improve the undergraduate experience, and increase retention and graduation rates.

Level 4: Macrosystem—Campus Culture and Social Trends

The macrosystem is more complex and abstract than the exosystem. It includes the underlying culture, values, and social norms of the environment. Bronfenbrenner (1977) describes macrosystems as "carriers of information and ideology that, both explicitly and implicitly, endow meaning and motivation to particular agencies, social networks, roles, activities, and their interrelations" (p. 515). Macrosystems are often difficult to identify because they are part of the fabric of daily life; as such, they often become invisible in context.

A prime example of a macrosystem is how the campus culture relates to student demographics and dominant/marginalized groups. The campus culture will be different at Historically Black Colleges and Universities (HBCUs), Predominantly White Institutions (PWIs), and Hispanic Serving Institutions (HSIs), and the fraternity/sorority community will likely reflect those differing cultures. Likewise, broader national attitudes and societal norms influence the macrosystem such as systemic oppression and privilege.

For example, the societal shift toward favoring LGBT rights over the past 20 years has seen more openly gay and lesbian students join fraternity/sorority chapters on a number of campuses, as well as the establishment of Delta Lambda Phi, a fraternity affiliated with the NIC that is dedicated to supporting gay, bisexual, and progressive men. Michael's story at West Coast University in our case study is an example of the modern-day reality for most out gay members: many of their fellow members are supportive, but some are not. The issue becomes more complex when one considers the intergenerational ties of these organizations: approaches to how individuals with diverse backgrounds are to support the common values and goals of the organization often vary and can create conflict within the hierarchies of these organizations. Consider two other students from the case study: Sara, a Jewish woman, and Krystal, an African American woman, both presidents of their respective Panhellenic sororities. Shifting social attitudes toward inclusion have provided opportunities for these women to join and lead organizations that once would have excluded them, but they still may experience Christian privilege and racism within their organizations.

Practitioners are surrounded by cultural values and move through the campus environment in similar ways as students and may not always believe that they can influence the macrosystem. However, practitioners have valuable opportunities to raise awareness of cultural elements that may be difficult for others to see and can play an important role in drawing attention to larger institutional patterns of culture, privilege, and oppression. Practitioners should become aware of the prevailing campus cultures, beliefs, and values in order to better educate students about them. In some cases, practitioners may have a chance to influence culture through policy and procedure. Strategies for effecting cultural shifts on a campus include revising the campus alcohol policy to include all students rather than focusing solely on the fraternity/sorority community, updating governance structures to eliminate divisions between organizations, and promoting anti-hazing strategies across student organizations and athletics.

Practitioners should consider whether there is values congruence between fraternal values espoused within a particular campus context and prevailing cultural attitudes across the campus community. They should also interrogate the social structures they support by virtue of being part of the macrosystem that may unintentionally lead to values incongruence across the ecosystem. Frameworks for addressing these challenges and attending to vital aspects of learning and development that occur through membership are provided by the Association of Fraternity/Sorority Advisors' (2013) *Core Competencies*, the Council for the Advancement of Standards (2012), and other professional associations.

Level 5: Chronosystem—Era of Undergraduate Experience

The chronosystem was added to the ecological systems theory by Bronfenbrenner in 1986 to include the changes and continuities over time in the environment; it is represented by a horizontal line at the bottom of Figure 1 to represent the progression of time in sociohistorical context. Some students join fraternities and sororities during times of great change; others join in times of relative stability.

Regulation of fraternities/sororities has shifted based on our philosophical stance as student affairs practitioners on the student as an adolescent, as an adult, and as a learner. Women, in particular, experienced greater degrees of freedom with changing times, moving away from curfew restrictions and "house mothers." The legal drinking age was changed from 18 to 21, which added a new set of concerns regarding serving alcohol to minors, binge drinking, and increased sexual assaults while under the influence. In the case study, Clarice highlights a few elements of the contemporary chronosystem: the increase in state and federal litigation against hazing in the 2000s and beyond, as well as the growing diversity of the student body. These two characteristics of college life in the mid-2010s affect the experiences of fraternity and sorority members and have a strong impact on chapter leaders as well as higher education administrators.

The growing prevalence of social media is another element of the chronosystem in the early twenty-first century. The increase in various social media outlets has been a good recruiting tool for promoting positive aspects of the fraternal movement, as well as the challenges that remain in holding students accountable for actions related to race and racism, misogyny, and hazing. Further research should examine whether social media are serving as a deterrent or as a means for pushing these issues further underground.

The chronosystem is the most abstract and long-ranging element of Bronfenbrenner's ecological systems model. Due to the relatively short time of an individual's undergraduate experience (traditionally 4 to 5 years), major shifts in sociohistorical context are not often perceived in the moment. For example, Luis, Krystal, Michael, and the other chapter presidents may not see social media, a litigious environment, or the legal drinking age of 21 as notable to their experiences, because they have known nothing else. Campus administrators, chapter advisors, faculty members, and others who are involved in the fraternal movement across generations will have a broader view of the chronosystem than undergraduate members and, through the sharing of stories and experience through the years, can help students understand where they fit in the greater context across time and ecosystem level.

Conclusion

Since its inception in 1776, the fraternal movement has been a critical gauge for understanding the experiences of college students. Fraternities and sororities offer opportunities for student learning, engagement, and development. Members of fraternities and sororities should be considered as individuals who navigate multiple contexts and systems while also interacting within a unique organization that is rooted in leadership, service, culture, and scholarship. Fraternities and sororities are learning organizations that still contend with antisocial behavior, discrimination, and elitism. Bronfenbrenner's ecological systems theory is a useful framework for illustrating the complex, interrelated levels in which the individual student lives his or her daily life.

Student affairs practitioners play an invaluable role in providing learning opportunities and resources to cultivate greater understanding about issues of difference while also understanding the complexities with which individuals enter their fraternal organizations. Our role as student affairs practitioners, regardless of our personal or professional involvement in the fraternal movement, is to first see these students as individuals who have similar needs and challenges as other students on college campuses, and then as members of organizations that have the potential to disrupt stereotypes and uphold their values. In order to best serve this population of students, we need to understand the intricate systems in which the individuals live and learn (see also Strange & Banning, 2001). Fraternity/sorority membership should be complementary to their lived experiences and development and enhance the student learning experience. We all have a responsibility across contexts and systems to help these students succeed.

Notes

1. A chapter is a local group that is connected to an (inter)national fraternity or sorority.
2. For the purposes of this chapter, we employ the terms *fraternity* and *sorority* rather than the phrase *Greek Letter Organizations.* Not all fraternities and sororities have Greek letters connected to their names—for example, the Farmhouse and Triangle fraternities.
3. Although many chapters have developed national headquarters structures and joined (inter)national umbrella organizations, there are fraternities and sororities that are "local," or found only on a single campus.
4. For a comprehensive review of empirical research on the fraternity/sorority experience between 1996 and 2013, see Biddix, Matney, Norman, & Martin 2014.
5. Multicultural Greek Councils are campus-specific governing bodies generally comprised of culturally based fraternities and sororities that are not (inter)national members of the North American Interfraternity Conference, the National Panhellenic Conference, or the National Pan-Hellenic Council.
6. Interfraternity Councils are generally comprised of men's fraternities whose (inter)national headquarters are members of the North-American Interfraternity Conference, a trade organization with 75 members (www.nicindy.org).
7. A common phrase used in culturally based fraternities and sororities: *to cross* is akin to *initiation* into a fraternity/sorority.
8. The National Panhellenic Conference is comprised of 26 women's fraternities and sororities (www.npcwomen.org).
9. Depending on the campus, some fraternity and sorority (inter)national headquarters own houses and have housing corporations that maintain the facilities.
10. The National Pan-Hellenic Council, Inc., is comprised of nine historically Black international fraternities and sororities (http://www.nphchq.org).
11. The term *soror* is Latin for *sister* and is commonly used by culturally based sororities.

References

Abes, E.S., Jones, S.R., & McEwen, M.K. (2007). Reconceptualizing the model of multiple dimensions of identity: The role of meaning-making capacity in the construction of multiple identities. *Journal of College Student Development, 48*(1), 1–22. doi: 10.1353/csd.2007.0000

Anson, J. L., & Marchesani, R. F. Jr. (Eds.). (1991). *Baird's manual of American college fraternities, 20th edition.* Indianapolis, IN: Baird's Manual Foundation.

Asel, A.M., Seifert, T.A., & Pascarella, E.T. (2009). The effects of fraternity/sorority membership on college experiences and outcomes: A portrait of complexity. *Oracle: The Research Journal of the Association of Fraternity/Sorority Advisors, 4*(2), 56–70.

Association of Fraternity/Sorority Advisors. (2013). *Core competencies for excellence in the profession.* Retrieved from http://www.afa1976.org/AssociationBusiness/CoreCompetenciesforExcellenceintheProfession.aspx

Baxter Magolda, M. B. (2001). *Making their own way: Narratives for transforming higher education to promote self-development.* Sterling, VA: Stylus.

Biddix, J.P., Matney, M., Norman, E., & Martin, G. (2014). *The influence of fraternity and sorority involvement: A critical analysis of research (1996–2013).* ASHE Higher Education Report Series. San Francisco, CA: Jossey-Bass.

Bronfenbrenner, U. (1977). Toward an experimental ecology of human development. *American Psychologist, 32*(7), 513–531. doi: 10.1037/0003-066X.32.7.513

Bronfenbrenner, U. (1986). Ecology of the family as a context for human development: Research perspectives. *Developmental Psychology, 22*(6), 723–742. doi: 10.1037//0012-1649.22.6.723

Bronfenbrenner, U. (1994). Ecological models of human development. In *International encyclopedia of education* (2nd ed., Vol. 3, pp. 1643–1647). Oxford, UK: Elsevier.

Bronfenbrenner, U. (2005). *Making human beings human: Bioecological perspectives on human development.* Thousand Oaks, CA: Sage.

Clegg, K.S. (2010). *In search of belongingness: Perceptions, expectations, and values congruence within sorority new members* (Unpublished master's thesis). Oregon State University, Corvallis.

Council for the Advancement of Standards. (2012). *CAS professional standards for higher education* (8th ed.). Washington, DC: Author.

Cuyjet, M.J., Howard-Hamilton, M.F., & Cooper, D.L. (Eds.). (2011). *Multiculturalism on campus: Theory, models, and practices for understanding diversity and creating inclusion.* Sterling, VA: Stylus.

Franklin Square Group. (2003). *A call for values congruence.* Retrieved from http://afa1976.org/Portals/0/documents/CallForValuesCongruence.pdf

Grasgreen, A. (2013, September 19). It's not just Alabama. *Inside Higher Ed.* Retrieved from http://www.insidehighered.com/news/2013/09/19/segregated-sororities-not-limited-alabama-experts-say

Grund, N.E. (2005). Returning to core values: Changing behavior in sororities and fraternities. *Leadership Exchange, 3*(3), 5–11.

Kimbrough, W.M. (2003). *Black Greek 101: The culture, customs, and challenges of Black fraternities and sororities.* Madison, NJ: Fairleigh Dickinson University Press.

Martin, G., & Bureau, D. (2008, Winter). Student development theory and implications for the values movement. *Association of Fraternity Advisors Perspectives*, 20–22.

Matthews, H., Featherstone, L., Bluder, L., Gerling, A.J., Loge, S., & Messenger, R.B. (2009). Living in your letters: Assessing congruence between espoused and enacted values of one fraternity/sorority community. *Oracle: The Research Journal of the Association of Fraternity/Sorority Advisors, 4*(1), 29–41.

National Panhellenic Conference. (2012). *Adventure in friendship: A history of the National Panhellenic Conference.* Indianapolis, IN: Author.

Ryan, H.G. (2009). *Class matters: The experience of female college students in a Greek-letter organization* (Unpublished doctoral dissertation). Indiana University, Bloomington.

Schreck, T.C. (1976). *Fraternity for the year 2000.* Commission on the American College Fraternity. Bloomington, IN: Center for the Study of the College Fraternity.

Scott, W. A. (1965). *Values and organizations: A study of fraternities and sororities.* Chicago, IL: Rand McNally.

Shalka, T.R. (2008). *An exploration into differences in consciousness of self and congruence among culturally based fraternity, social fraternity, and non-affiliated college men* (Unpublished master's thesis). University of Maryland, College Park.

Strange, C.C., & Banning, J.H. (2001). *Educating by design: Creating campus learning environments that work.* San Francisco, CA: Jossey-Bass.

Tobin, J. (2008, March 11). Fraternity war. *Michigan Today.* Retrieved from http://michigantoday.umich.edu/2008/mar/fratwar.php

EIGHTEEN

The Future of Spirituality in Higher Education: Becoming More Inclusive

Kathleen M. Goodman

In the past decade, higher education has returned to its holistic roots by providing more opportunities for students to focus on spirituality. In colleges and universities throughout the United States, spirituality has been incorporated into courses and the co-curriculum. Many of these practices were described in *A Guidebook of Promising Practices: Facilitating College Students' Spiritual Development* (Lindholm, Millora, Schwartz, & Spinosa, 2011). A growing body of literature has encouraged and supported this focus on spirituality through books such as *Encouraging Authenticity and Spirituality in Higher Education* (Chickering, Dalton, & Stamm, 2006) and *Exploring Spirituality and Culture in Adult and Higher Education* (Tisdell, 2003). Likewise, research has supported the focus on spirituality in colleges and universities. The Higher Education Research Institute (HERI) conducted an extensive national survey about the spiritual lives of college students. An often quoted statistic from that research, used to support many of the efforts described above, suggests that 80% of the students surveyed are interested in matters related to spirituality (HERI, 2005). What that finding also suggests is that a full 20% of students are not interested in matters of spirituality. A major premise of this textbook is that higher education must redefine student development paradigms in order to meet the diverse needs of the current student population. Higher education's response to the HERI statistic is a telling example of how higher education has focused on traditional students to the detriment of others. While the renewed efforts to attend to the inner lives of college students should be celebrated, it is time to become more inclusive in order to meet the holistic needs of all students, including those who are not representative of dominant identities—those students who may very likely fall into the 20%.

Spiritual and Religious Diversity Among Today's College Students

A recent study of college students revealed that college-age Americans are about equally divided among three existential (relating to human existence) worldviews: religious, spiritual, and secular (Kosmin & Keysar, 2013). Among those who identify as secular, 77% do not believe in God or don't know whether there is a God. Among those that identify as religious, the majority are Christian. Those who predominately identify as spiritual represent a variety of perspectives, including those who do not identify as religious (one-third of the group) and those that identify with Eastern religions, Judaism, or other religious traditions. Kosmin and Keysar (2013) point out that "each of the three worldviews is attached to a distinct outlook on theological, philosophical, scientific, public-policy, and political issues" (p. 1). In order to appropriately meet the holistic developmental needs of all students, educators and administrators need to understand the "distinct outlook" associated with these three existential worldviews and develop programming that is relevant to the diversity of perspectives.

While there has been considerable progress in understanding college student spirituality and developing relevant programming, the focus has been on a one-size-fits-all model of spirituality with Christian undertones. Far less has been achieved when it comes to understanding secular students and non-Christian religious groups. A notable exception is the *New Directions for Student Services* volume focused on intersections of religious privilege (Watt, Fairchild, & Goodman, 2009). The editors of the volume suggest that educators must be attentive to the inequities that exist between dominant and marginalized religions and between religious and non-religious individuals. The volume provides suggestions for how to "engage students in dialogue that will move them beyond debates about good and evil on this topic and toward more nuanced understandings and appreciation of difference" (Watt et al., 2009, p. 2). In order to move toward nuanced understanding, it is important to recognize that privilege exists and that word choices matter.

Christian and Religious Privilege

Focusing on the needs of the majority, which is common in higher education, makes sense from an "efficiency" perspective. It allows educators and administrators to meet the needs of many with limited resources. However, focusing on the majority perpetuates privilege while further marginalizing non-dominant populations. Within the realm of spirituality, Christian privilege is the norm (Fairchild, 2009; Seifert, 2007). For example, many college calendars are set up to accommodate Christian holidays such as Christmas, which falls between semesters at most institutions. Many college food services provide vegetarian options on Fridays during Lent but do not provide Kosher or Halal options, which may be daily dietary needs for Jewish and Islamic students. "Non-denominational" prayers offered at ceremonies such as commencement are typically Christian.

However, Christian privilege is only one form of privilege inherent in spirituality. The concept of spirituality includes a belief in a higher power for many people (Ellison, 1983; Love & Talbot, 1999), creating a form of religious privilege that marginalizes individuals who do not believe in God. The belief that spiritual development is an outcome of college is an example of religious privilege. Certainly student affairs practitioners must focus their attention on holistic development, including students' "inner lives" and existential worldview; however, to suggest that values, meaning, and life purpose equate to spirituality for all students is a form of privilege that must be dismantled.

Becoming More Inclusive

In order to address the spiritual, religious, and secular needs of all students while limiting the impact of privilege and providing inclusive opportunities for today's diverse students, student affairs educators must rethink how they approach spirituality work. Four major tasks for the future of spirituality in higher education are discussed in the remainder of this chapter.

Use Inclusive Language in "Spirituality" Education and Initiatives

Spirituality, religion, and secularity are three distinct pathways to values, meaning, and life purpose. Secular pathways can include science, reason, humanism, and other non-spiritual, non-religious ways that individuals use to make meaning. The pathways are not mutually exclusive—certainly many recognize the strong link between spirituality and religion. However, those students who identify with secular pathways to purpose—typically atheists, agnostics, and freethinkers—often do not relate to the spiritual and religious pathways. To try to force "spiritual development" on these students and to insist that spirituality is an inclusive term further marginalizes a group that already exists on the periphery of society (Goodman & Mueller, 2009). Therefore, developing values, meaning, and life purpose are outcomes of college, and spirituality is one means for developing those outcomes. Once spiritualty is thought of as a means rather than an end, truly inclusive environments can be created.

In order to avoid the privilege associated with the term spirituality, student affairs professionals should focus on existential worldview—the many ways that students find purpose and meaning in life—and not define that as spirituality. Students should be able to position themselves in the conversation in ways that apply to them. For some students, that will include talking about the influence of religion in their lives; for others it will entail spirituality; and still others will identify reason, science, or humanism as their source of purpose and meaning. This can be visualized as differing pathways, which can be distinct or overlap, that lead to meaning and purpose (Figure 1).

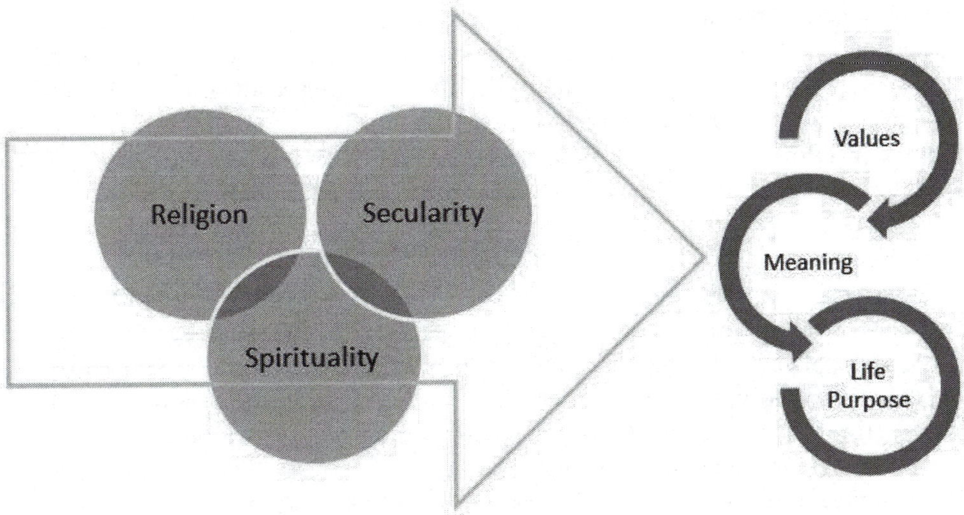

Figure 1. Multiple Pathways to Values, Meaning, and Life Purpose.

The key to being inclusive, is to use terminology that invites multiple perspectives, such as "purpose and meaning," "existential worldview," or "religious, spiritual, and secular traditions" to frame conversations that have typically been identified as "spiritual." Some students will still identify these topics as spiritual, but it will also open up space for those who identify as secular or religious to discuss their perspectives. By broadening language in this way, students can be more precise about the influences in their life, which could be humanism, Islam, evangelical Christianity, or any number of secular or religious perspectives that the student may or may not identify as spiritual. Furthermore, discussing the differences and similarities among spirituality, religion, and secularity with students will help dispel misconceptions and reduce privilege.

Develop an "Interfaith" Approach

Students need opportunities to deepen their understanding of their existential worldview, but they also need opportunities for interpersonal engagement focused on spiritual, religious, and secular perspectives. Engaging students in conversations about differing existential worldviews is highly beneficial to learning, personal development, and interpersonal abilities. Students who are exposed to other perspectives and provided the opportunity to reflect on their own beliefs will gain in their own development and self-knowledge, whether their beliefs are reinforced by encounters with religious, spiritual, or secular difference or changed because of them. By providing opportunities for students to reflect on the purpose and meaning of life, practitioners can help them begin to articulate and make explicit the values that guide their behaviors as well as the forces that provide meaning and purpose in their lives. Furthermore, when given the opportunity to engage with religious difference, students can learn to respect difference and gain greater skills for living in the diverse world. These types of conversations can be held as part of the learning curriculum in residence life, within career services in relation to understanding one's vocation, or coordinated with student activities where existing student groups are already focused on issues related to spirituality, religion, and secularity. Courses in interfaith dialogue for undergraduates and in student affairs preparation programs also provide a location for such dialogue.

For resources and ideas related to interfaith initiatives, student affairs educators can turn to the Interfaith Youth Core (IFYC), an organization dedicated to "making interfaith cooperation a social norm" (Patel, 2012, p. 86). Although "interfaith" is a problematic word in that it implies a religious perspective, the work of the IFYC focuses broadly on creating understanding among college students with differing spiritual, religious, and secular beliefs. IFYC reaches college students directly through its Better Together interfaith action campaign and annual Interfaith Leadership Institutes. Interested faculty members, student affairs educators, and other administrators can also partner with IFYC to create campus environments that are committed to religious diversity and interfaith cooperation.

Educators can also draw on the body of knowledge related to Intergroup Dialogue (IGD), which focuses on creating structured dialogues across difference in order to "illuminate intellectual and experiential similarities and differences" (Nagda, Gurin, Sorensen, & Zuniga, 2009, p. 4). Many individuals who facilitate IGD have been trained to "create an inclusive and involved learning environment, use structured activities to promote reflection and integration of academic content, and model dialogic communication and collaboration" (Nagda et al., 2009, p. 5). Educators use IGD to prepare students to live in a diverse world and learn to live/work with those who are different from themselves; however, it also provides the opportunity for students to gain greater understanding of themselves (Nagda, 2006). While much of the scholarship and practice of IGD focuses on race, it could also be an effective tool for discussing spirituality, religion, and secularity.

In order for IGD to be successful, it must create structured opportunities for students from different backgrounds to engage in respectful dialogue guided by a skilled facilitator (Nagda et al., 2009). These criteria should also be adhered to for dialogue about existential worldview in order to limit inadvertent reinforcement of Christian or religious privilege. Therefore, it is essential to include individuals of dominant and non-dominant religions (which will vary depending on the environment) as well as individuals from atheist, agnostic, or secular perspectives. Group leaders should have training in facilitating difficult dialogues and be knowledgeable about multiple existential worldviews. The leader should be prepared to work with the group to set guidelines for the discussion and provide structured opportunities for multiple perspectives to be represented.

Chris Stedman, author of *Faitheist: How an Atheist Found Common Ground With the Religious* (2012), provides a compelling case for the importance of including individuals of both religious and non-religious perspectives in these types of dialogues. He explains that we live in a time when individuals readily proclaim and abide by stereotypes, which prevents reaching common goals such as improving the world (Stedman, 2012). While it may be true that some atheists believe that all religion must be dismantled, and some religious folks believe that atheists are evil and destined for hell, structured dialogue can provide the opportunity to understand one another better and see that a multiplicity of perspectives exists among atheists and religious individuals. Once students find some common ground, they can work together to make the world a better place (Stedman, 2012).

Create an Infrastructure Focused on Spirituality, Religion, and Secularity

Most institutions of higher education have some office, program, or personnel focused on racial diversity on campus. Many institutions also have some office, program, or personnel focused on LGBT diversity on campus. Yet few institutions have an office, program, or personnel dedicated to the diversity of existential worldviews of their students. Eboo Patel (2012) describes the situation this way:

> Higher Education officials have spent years reading widely and deeply in the literature of multiculturalism, and so feel equipped to deal with the normal culture conflicts that emerge during those conversations. They have little or no fluency in interfaith matters. This is a solvable problem. Consider the fact that race, gender, class, and sexuality are equally complex issues. The reason we have a more robust movement devoted to these issues is because people within the academy decided they were important enough to soldier through all the challenges and address. Religious diversity requires the same time, effort, and purpose. (p. 126)

In order to address the spiritual, religious, and secular worldviews of all students, existential worldview must become part of the infrastructure of colleges and universities. Having dedicated resources such as staff, space, and money for programming will send the message that institutions are concerned with these matters. Furthermore, it will normalize the process of exploring existential worldviews with college students. Once resources are in place, the institution can create inclusive spaces and programs for students of all perspectives. Staff dedicated to the diversity of existential worldviews of students can contribute more than programming for students. They can assess the campus climate for religious/non-religious diversity and provide training and resources for other faculty and administrators.

Many institutions could benefit from a formal assessment to see how students of existential worldviews are faring at the institution. IFYC administers a Campus Religious and Spiritual Climate Survey that could be used for the formal assessment. Institutions must also be willing to informally assess their climate to see whether religious privilege (privileging of a particular religion over others, or privileging religion over non-religion) or Christian privilege prevails. Data gathered from these efforts can guide institutions as they work to create a campus environment that is welcoming to students of all religious, spiritual, and secular backgrounds. Yet without dedicated staff, endeavors of this type rarely take place.

Attending to the individualized approaches necessary for different groups to make the most of their existential development may seem overwhelming to student affairs practitioners and faculty. Indeed, simply learning about the many religious traditions and secular avenues related to spiritual development can be a daunting task. Without an entity that has the mission of training and personnel to arrange training and educational opportunities, it is common for many faculty and administrators to disguise their lack of knowledge by avoiding conversations about religious, spiritual, and secular perspectives.

Building an infrastructure to carry out the work of existential development and interfaith understanding is imperative if those in higher education want to create inclusive opportunities and environments for students of many spiritual, religious, and secular perspectives. An office or program with staff and resources within the division or office of diversity would provide a solid foundation for the future of this work.

Use a Developmental Model to Guide Campus Practice

The revised Developmental Model of Intercultural Sensitivity (DMIS) (Bennett, 2004; Hammer, 2011) provides a good tool for guiding educators in helping students reflect on their own existential worldview and become more open to perspectives that differ from their own. Since existential worldview is often tied to one's culture, the model is applicable to this topic. The DMIS reflects a continuum from a monocultural mindset to an intercultural/global mindset. Individuals typically move sequentially through five stages in thinking about cultural differences: Denial, Polarization/Defense, Minimization, Acceptance, and Adaptation (Hammer, 2011). See Table 1 for a description of the mindsets and how they relate to existential worldviews of college students.

Table 1: Application of Intercultural Development Continuum to Existential Worldview of Students.

	Denial	Polarization/ Defense	Minimization	Acceptance	Adaptation
Personal Mindset	Not aware of differing religious, spiritual, and secular perspectives. Avoids or ignores those with different beliefs.	Acknowledgment of differing religious, spiritual, and secular perspectives but has little to no interaction with those whose beliefs differ from own. Often expressed as an "us vs. them" attitude or animosity.	Acknowledgment of differing religious, spiritual, and secular perspectives. Interactions with those whose beliefs differ from own focus on similarities and "universal truths" (e.g., love, compassion, community service).	Acknowledgment of differing religious, spiritual, and secular perspectives. Interactions focus on understanding similarities and differences.	Individuals are capable of shifting cultural perspectives and changing behavior in culturally appropriate ways while still being true to one's own beliefs.
Developmental Task Necessary to Move Toward More Intercultural Mindset	Become aware of differing religious, spiritual, and secular perspectives. Willingness to learn about those perspectives.	Become aware that one shares commonalities with those of differing religious, spiritual, and secular perspectives. Willingness to see commonalities as good.	Become aware that there are both commonalities and differences between those of differing religious, spiritual, and secular perspectives. Willingness to see that it is ok for differences to exist.	Willingness to change cultural behavior depending on context and recognize that adapting behavior doesn't mean abandoning one's own beliefs and culture.	N.A.
Activities to Move Toward More Intercultural Mindset*	Structured exposure to those of different beliefs. This can be knowledge awareness, as opposed to interpersonal interactions.	Structured interactions between groups that focus on commonalities.	Structured interactions between groups that recognize that differences exist.	Ongoing structured interactions between groups and sharing information about ways to adapt behaviors in various cultural situations.	N.A.

*In addition to structured group activities at each level of intercultural understanding, individuals also need ongoing opportunities to explore and reflect on their own existential worldview, either alone or in groups of individuals with similar perspectives.

To use this model to guide campus practice, educators must understand each mindset and the developmental tasks required to help an individual move to the next, more intercultural, mindset. As explained in Table 1 and the paragraphs below, the activities that help students become more intercultural are structured engagement with ideas and people of differing worldviews. It must also be noted that in order to become more aware of the similarities and differences one shares with those who have an existential worldview different from one's own, opportunities for personal reflection on one's own worldview are also necessary. Learning to articulate one's perspective and understanding the sociocultural influences on that perspective make it easier to understand others. Therefore, educators should provide students with ongoing opportunities to explore and reflect on their own existential worldview, either alone or in groups of individuals with similar perspectives.

Applying DMIS to an existential worldview. In the most monocultural mindset, called denial, individuals are not aware of differing religious, spiritual, and secular perspectives. They tend to avoid or ignore those who have different beliefs. The developmental task necessary for students in this mindset is to become aware of differing religious, spiritual, and secular perspectives and become willing to learn about those perspectives. Educators can provide structured exposure to different beliefs in the form of knowledge (as opposed to intercultural interaction). Workshops and classes that provide information about multiple spiritual, religious, and secular worldviews in a non-threatening (i.e., non-interactive) way can help students move to the next mindset (polarization/defense). Once students have accepted that multiple perspectives exist, it is quite common for that to lead to an "us/them" attitude characterized by lack of interaction with those who are different, and even animosity. Therefore, the developmental task they must achieve to reach a more intercultural mindset is to become aware that one shares commonalities with those of differing religious, spiritual, and secular perspectives. Structured interactions between groups that focuses on commonalities can help achieve this task. For example, in a class or program, one could ask students of differing existential worldviews to talk about the similarities that exist between them. You could even make it a contest to see which group can come up with the greatest number of similarities in a given amount of time. This keeps their focus on similarities and can help them move beyond an "us/them" attitude. Achievement of this developmental task leads to the next, more intercultural mindset: minimization.

Minimization is a common mindset among college students, who often have a strong desire to get along with others without encountering potential upset or problems. This mindset straddles monocultural thinking and intercultural thinking because individuals recognize that there are differences but only focus on similarities. Educators must help students become aware that there are both commonalities and differences between those of differing religious, spiritual, and secular perspectives and help them recognize that the existence of differences is not a problem. One way to get them to recognize differences in a non-threatening way is through multicultural and arts programming such as a lecture from the Dali Llama, a Diwali Festival (a Hindu celebration of light), a National Darwin Day conference (a secular celebration of science and reason), or a multicultural fair that focuses on foods, symbols, clothing, and rituals of multiple groups. This would also be an appropriate time to introduce a structured interfaith dialogue that helps students learn about both similarities and differences among various existential worldviews. Ideally these activities will lead students to the next intercultural mindset: acceptance.

Helping students achieve an acceptance mindset is an appropriate goal for colleges and universities. This mindset is characterized by acknowledgment of differing religious, spiritual, and secular perspectives and interactions that focus on understanding both similarities and differences. The developmental task that must be accomplished to reach adaptation—the most intercultural mindset—is a willingness to change cultural behavior depending on context and recognize that adapting behavior does not mean abandoning one's own beliefs and culture. This can be achieved by ongoing structured interactions among individuals of multiple perspectives. Part of those dialogues should provide information about ways to adapt behaviors in various cultural situations. While institutions can strive to help students reach the adaptation mindset, the reality is that helping most students achieve the minimization and acceptance mindsets would be a significant accomplishment.

Conclusions

In the past decade, higher education has provided students opportunities for spiritual development. While it is laudable that attention has been paid to this aspect of personal development, religious and Christian privilege have prevented efforts from being inclusive for students of diverse perspectives. The task for the next decade is to take a more inclusive approach to meet the needs of today's students—students who come from a variety of religious, spiritual, and secular backgrounds. Four actions will contribute to a more inclusive approach. First, language and educational initiatives must reflect the diversity of students' perspectives by replacing the word "spiritual" with a phrase such as "spiritual, religious, and secular," "existential worldview," or "life purpose and meaning." Second, in addition to providing opportunities for personal reflection and exposure to groups of people with similar perspectives, students need opportunities for structured, facilitated, "interfaith" discussions that include individuals with a range of religious, spiritual, and secular perspectives. Third, institutions must build an infrastructure of people, places, and resources specifically focused on existential worldview. Finally, using the DMIS to guide programming and services related to spiritual, religious, and secular perspectives will help students deepen their understanding of themselves and develop an intercultural mindset for understanding those with perspectives different from their own. Implementing these four tasks will allow practitioners to begin to meet the diverse existential needs of today's college student.

References

Bennett, M.J. (2004). Becoming interculturally competent. In J. Wurzel (Ed.), *Toward multiculturalism: A reader in multicultural education* (2nd ed., pp. 62–77). Newton, MA: Intercultural Resource Corporation.

Chickering, A.W., Dalton, J.C., & Stamm, L. (Eds.). (2006). *Encouraging authenticity and spirituality in higher education.* San Francisco, CA: Jossey-Bass.

Ellison, C.W. (1983). Spiritual well-being: Conceptualization and measurement. *Journal of Psychology and Theology, 11,* 330–340.

Fairchild, E.E. (2009). Christian privilege, history, and trends in U.S. religion. *New Directions for Student Services, 2009*(125), 5–11.

Goodman, K.M., & Mueller, J.A. (2009). Invisible, marginalized, and stigmatized: Understanding and addressing the needs of atheist students. *New Directions for Student Services, 2009*(125), 55–63.

Hammer, M.R. (2011). Additional cross-cultural validity testing of the Intercultural Development Inventory. *International Journal of Intercultural Relations, 35*(4), 474–487. doi: 10.1016/j.ijintrel.2011.02.014

Higher Education Research Institute (HERI). (2005). *The spiritual life of college students: A national study of college students' search for meaning and purpose.* Los Angeles, CA: University of California, HERI.

Kosmin, B.A., & Keysar, A. (2013). *Religious, spiritual and secular: The emergence of three distinct worldviews among American college students.* Retrieved from http://www.trincoll.edu/Academics/centers/isssc/Documents/ARIS_2013_College%20Students_Sept_25_final_draft.pdf

Lindholm, J.A., Millora, M.L., Schwartz, L.M., & Spinosa, H.S. (2011). *A guidebook of promising practices: Facilitating college students' spiritual development.* Los Angeles, CA: Regents of the University of California.

Love, P., & Talbot, D. (1999). Defining spiritual development: A missing consideration for student affairs. *NASPA Journal, 37*(1), 361–375.

Nagda, B.A. (2006). Breaking barriers, crossing borders, building bridges: Communication processes in intergroup dialogues. *Journal of Social Issues, 62*(3), 553–576. doi: 10.1111/j.1540-4560.2006.00473.x

Nagda, B.A., Gurin, P., Sorensen, N., & Zuniga, X. (2009). Evaluating intergroup dialogue: Engaging diversity for personal and social responsibility. *Diversity & Democracy, 12*(1), 4–6.

Patel, E. (2012). *Sacred ground: Pluralism, prejudice, and the promise of America.* Boston, MA: Beacon Press.

Seifert, T.A. (2007). Understanding Christian privilege: Managing the tensions of spiritual plurality. *About Campus, 12*(2), 10–17.

Stedman, C.D. (2012). *Faitheist: How an atheist found common ground with the religious.* Boston, MA: Beacon Press.

Tisdell, E.J. (2003). *Exploring spirituality and culture in adult and higher education.* San Francisco, CA: Jossey-Bass.

Watt, S., Fairchild, E., & Goodman, K. (Eds.). (2009). Religious privilege and student affairs practice: Intersections of difficult dialogues. *New Directions for Student Services, 2009*(125).

NINETEEN

Nontraditional Students: The New Traditional

Jeannette M. Passmore

Conversations about college or university typically bring to mind an image of 18–24-year-old students living in residence halls, fraternity houses, or off-campus apartments. The tradition of parents dropping off their first-year students, who then attend football games, celebrate homecoming, and hold part-time jobs to earn spending money is part of the American perception of higher education. Institutions of higher education are steeped in tradition, including serving the student who is right out of high school and living on, or near, campus. The reality is that in the 1999–2000 academic year, 73% of all undergraduate students had one or more characteristics that made them nontraditional (Choy, 2002). This was the last time a comprehensive study of nontraditional students was completed. *The Digest of Education Statistics* states that the percentage of adult students age 25 and older enrolling in higher education is expected to outpace the enrollment of traditional-age students (18–24) by 9% (Snyder & Dillow, 2012).

The National Center for Education Statistics (NCES) (Choy, 2002) identifies seven characteristics that distinguish a student as nontraditional:

- works more than 35 hours per week;
- delayed postsecondary education for a year or more after completing high school;
- earned a GED;
- is considered independent for the purposes of federal financial aid;
- has dependents other than a spouse;
- is a single parent; and
- attends college part-time for at least part of the academic year.

A student with one or two of these characteristics is minimally nontraditional; the more such characteristics a student has, the more nontraditional he or she becomes (Horn, 1996). The nontraditional student population is continuing to grow. For nontraditional students by age alone, the number of students over the age of 25 is projected to grow 37% by 2018 (Hussar & Bailey, 2009). The continuing growth of nontraditional students in higher education can be linked to a decline in the number of high school graduates (which is expected to continue), the loss of blue collar jobs combined with the outsourcing of low- and middle-skills jobs, and the need for increased technical skills and retooling for new middle-skills jobs (Compton, Cox, & Laanan, 2006). A study by Mbilinyi (2006) found that more than half of adults ages 25–60 would like additional education and training. With President Barack Obama's call for more degrees for those 70 million, adults become an impressive pool of potential students (Obama, 2009).

The diversity of the nontraditional student population goes beyond race and ethnicity as well as socioeconomic status (Home, 1998). This population experiences a variety of life roles and combinations of life roles that can cause stress when the role of postsecondary student is added. Their educational preparedness, past experiences with education, age, career experiences and paths, military service, and the support systems available to them all play a part in adding to the stress of their education or mitigating their perceptions of the stress (Home, 1998). Nontraditional students also enter college with a variety of motivations for attending, as well as widely diverse expectations of the services student affairs provides (Compton et al., 2006). Throughout this chapter we will share students' stories to illustrate the barriers they face and how we, as professionals, can support them.

Barriers

Nontraditional students face many barriers to participating in higher education. These barriers fall into three categories: dispositional, situational, and institutional. Dispositional barriers stem from a student's attitude and may be the result of previous educational experiences (Malhotra, Shapero, Sizoo, & Munro, 2007) that include attitudes about his or her ability to succeed or perceived lack of support. Situational barriers come from the various roles a student has, for example, being a parent, caregiver, employee, or being active in the community (Malhotra et al., 2007). Institutional barriers stem from the policies, schedules, and practices of the college and include timing of services that are offered and physical issues such as parking and access (Malhotra et al., 2007).

Dispositional Barriers

Dispositional barriers arise from a student's attitudes, beliefs, ability to deal with role demands, level of social and family support, and prior educational experiences (Fairchild, 2003; Malhotra et al., 2007). These barriers are personal and may be difficult to identify or define for students and student affairs professionals. Students who did not enroll directly out of high school or who have negative educational experiences may lack interest in pursuing further education or may experience a negative self-perception about their learning abilities (Advisory Committee on Student Financial Assistance, 2012).

Dispositional barriers are experienced by traditional students as well, but are often more ingrained for nontraditional students. A case study demonstrating dispositional barriers follows:

Sue did not have positive experiences in high school, which led to her leaving school and later earning her GED; she is also over the age of 25 and working two part-time jobs. When she experienced problems enrolling in college for the first time, the feelings of frustration she experienced led to negative self-talk about her ability to be a college student, and she was tempted to quit before she even began her college journey.

Social and family supports are extremely important to nontraditional students and have a strong positive correlation with goal attainment and student success (Lundberg, 2003; Wormus, 2009). For example, Bob is experiencing pressure from his wife to forget about going to college and to continue searching for a job. Her comments are contributing to Bob's self-doubt about being able to be successful at his age. How a student perceives the intensity of the demands on his or her time and attention is the "strongest predictor of conflict" (Wormus, 2009). For example, Amy and Chris are experiencing the demands on their time very differently. Whereas Chris experiences role strain from trying to balance parenting, working, and school, Amy makes a smooth transition between being a parent and a student. Amy's family is very supportive and encouraging. This does not mean that Amy isn't facing challenges, but she is able to approach them differently because of her perceptions.

Situational Barriers

Situational barriers are also a product of role conflict. The conflicts may come in the form of finances, working full- or part-time, parenting or caregiving, and civic duties (Fairchild, 2003). Family issues are often cited as a primary factor when nontraditional students stop out of post-secondary education. Over 4 million students self-identify as parents, and half of those identify as single parents (Arnold & Hickman, 2012). Students with some type of family responsibility experience stress in their role as students and in their family role. This role conflict impacts a student's performance and retention. Here is a case study that exemplifies this:

Chris is a single parent who is employed full-time. He has a tight schedule in dropping off and picking up his daughter from school, attending to her, his coursework, and class time, along with working the third shift. Chris's roles as parent, student, and third-shift employee are in conflict on a daily basis.

How a student regards the intensity of the demands on his or her time and attention is the "strongest predictor of [role] conflict" (Wormus, 2009). Acknowledgment of, and planning for, the various roles students play need to be part of all student affairs programming.

Finances also play a large role in the life of a nontraditional student. One-third of all nontraditional students do not receive federal or state grants (Turner et al., 2007). Nontraditional students often enroll part-time or less than part-time, which prevents them from applying for student loans and scholarships. They are often unable to participate in other financial benefits such as assistantships or internships that come with tuition waivers (Taniguchi & Kaufman, 2005). Almost one-third of nontraditional students do not apply for financial aid under the assumption that they would be turned down based on their income or nontraditional status (Turner et al., 2007). Some relief from the financial burden may come from employer incentives, which average about $1,200 per year (Berker, Horn, & Carroll, 2003).

Another case study of the impact of financial struggles on a student concerns Sue:

Sue is working two jobs and wants to enroll in school at least part-time. Unfortunately, her work schedule prevented her from completing the placement testing and registering in a timely manner. It *is now a week before classes begin, and she is trying to register for a developmental math course and a college-level English course. Because of the late date, all of the English sections that fit her work schedule are full. Her choice is to enroll less than part-time and take the developmental math course or wait until next term. The tuition rate at the local community college is $150 per credit hour, and the math course is four credit hours. Sue is not going to be able to afford the tuition, fees, and books on her own. She decides to delay registration until the following term. There is a strong chance that Sue may not return to the college.*

Chris and Sue have something in common. They are among the two-thirds of nontraditional students who would say they are employees first and students second (also known as employees who study). Traditional students are more likely to describe themselves as students who work (Berker et al., 2003). Chartrand (1992) found that working can have a positive effect on a nontraditional student's mental and emotional state because it helps mitigate role strain by increasing academic self-efficacy and time management skills. Even with these increased skills, employees who study and attend school part-time are still less likely to achieve their academic goals. The U.S. Department of Education (Berker et al., 2003) found that "68 percent of working adults who identified themselves as employees who study in 1999–2000 carried a substantial risk of not completing their postsecondary program: they were both employed full time and attended part time" (p. ix). The situational barriers that both Chris and Sue experience as employees who study mean that it is likely one of them will not complete the degree program. In this instance it would be difficult to tell who is more likely to graduate—Chris, who is in a slightly better situation with a full-time job that has regular hours, or Sue, who is already refining her time management skills by balancing two part-time jobs.

Institutional Barriers

Institutional barriers are part of what defines how welcome a campus feels to nontraditional students (Spanard, 1990) and are outside a student's control. Navigating institutional barriers requires time and effort from the student (Knight, Steinbach, & Hop, 2012). They go beyond inconvenient service hours and instructor office hours and include situations such as class times or course sequencing that prevents nontraditional students from progressing, programming that does not meet the needs of a nontraditional student's schedule or interests, policies and procedures that inadvertently exclude nontraditional students, and class requirements that include group work or out-of-class, on-campus time that is challenging for students with multiple roles to fulfill (Brown & Nichols, 2013; Fairchild, 2003; Malhotra et al., 2007). If an institution does not provide sufficient guidance on navigating its system or culture, nontraditional students, with their limited time and energy, may move on to an institution that does provide assistance (Knight et al., 2012). Academic advising is an example of an institutional trait that may be a barrier to nontraditional students. A student who works from 8:00 a.m. to 5:00 p.m. may not be able to communicate with his or her advisor if the advising office is only open during those hours. Electronic communication and phone calls are not always a sufficient solution. When a nontraditional student is able to connect and the advisor does not understand the roles and barriers the student is navigating, the extended office hours or electronic communication does little to mitigate the challenges. Good academic advising has a strong influence on nontraditional student retention rates (Flint & Frey, 2003).

Supports

Nontraditional students experience role strain brought on by their multiple responsibilities. They battle dispositional barriers that make them feel isolated. They confront institutional barriers on a regular basis. Tackling all of these challenges is indeed difficult. It is impressive that, in 1994, highly nontraditional students with bachelor's degree goals had completed at a rate of 11% after five years, and 27% had earned their associate's degree (Choy, 2002). This is a testament to their resourcefulness and determination, and many of them would admit that they could not have done it without the support of a mentor, faculty member, or a student affairs practitioner. Support for nontraditional students takes as many forms as the barriers they face, and research into how to help them succeed is horribly scant. In a study examining seven peer-reviewed journals published from 1999 to 2003, 1.29% of the articles addressed adult or nontraditional undergraduate students (Donaldson & Townsend, 2007). This section will discuss how we can best assist this growing population of eager and dedicated students.

Helping students navigate dispositional barriers can be approached in several different ways. It is important for these students to hear positive messages about their place within higher education as well as their ability to succeed. Marketing materials are one of the first things a nontraditional student encounters when considering entering an institution of higher education. Materials that feature age-diverse students and students with families are good primers for helping nontraditional students begin to envision their own success (Arnold & Hickman, 2012). Having students participate in adult orientation, bridge, or first-year experience courses to continue the positive messaging will also help address the institutional barriers (Schlossberg, Lynch, & Chickering, 1989). These programs will provide students with a way to ease into what can be a very intimidating environment, and they also provide a time and place to begin developing the various academic skills and support systems that will help them find success.

Dispositional Supports

Two theories that are applicable in helping students conquer dispositional barriers are self-efficacy theory (Bandura, 1994) and transition theory (Schlossberg et al., 1989).

Self-efficacy theory. Self-efficacy is how one evaluates his or her ability to achieve a desired outcome. In working with nontraditional students, the focus should be on academic self-efficacy, which has been shown to increase retention and success (Carney-Crompton & Tan, 2002; Zajacova, Lynch, & Espenshade, 2005). Academic self-efficacy applies specifically to a student's belief in his or her ability to achieve goals within the higher education setting (Zajacova et al., 2005). Because students may not have a positive self-efficacy viewpoint when they join us on campus, higher education professionals can help them develop these skills by providing places for them to discuss their education and network with other students. Nontraditional student organizations, lounges, and the previously mentioned orientations and courses are good ways to provide these experiences. Wellness programs, particularly those that address stress, are also helpful (Lundberg, 2003). Self-efficacy helps reduce role strain and presents academic issues as challenges rather than as threats (Zajacova et al., 2005). Transition theory will also assist students in developing self-efficacy.

Transition theory. Transition theory provides a framework for helping students assess and use the resources they have available to them. The resources are divided into four types:

situational, self, supports, and strategies (Schlossberg, Waters, & Goodman, 1995). Student affairs professionals can promote self-efficacy by helping students focus on self, supports, and strategies. Situation resources relate to where in the transition a person is and how the transition is viewed. Is this a planned positive change that is almost complete, or an unexpected negative change that the student is just beginning? Self supports examine what strengths and inner resources students possess. Have they experienced this type of transition before? Do they have skills from other transitions that could be used in this setting? Are they positive and able to cope with the challenges? Supports refer to external supports that students have access to, such as family, friends, and mentors—and sometimes supports are surprising.

Sue's case is an example of the implementation of situational, self, supports, and strategies. During a workshop, Sue revealed that her support came from her landlord, who always had a positive word for her and inquired about her academic progress. The landlord was the only friend or family member that attended Sue's graduation. It is important to help students think beyond their immediate circle when considering what supports are available. Strategies are a way to help students use their transferable skills. Perhaps a nontraditional student has not experienced trouble with an instructor before. Working with the student to discuss conflicts that have occurred in other venues and the strategies he or she used to resolve those conflicts helps introduce him or her to the transferability of prior experience. Working with students to identify transitional resources in self, support, and strategies provides them with a foundation to continue their personal and academic growth.

Situational Supports

Situational barriers are rooted in the various roles that nontraditional students play. The role of professionals is not to help students make role adjustments, but to help them mitigate the stress that arises from role strain. In addressing situational barriers, student affairs professionals are also addressing institutional barriers. Support from friends and family is integral to students' success. They are more likely to receive support at the beginning of their academic journey and have it fade as they progress through what can sometimes be a long path (Lundberg, McIntire, & Creasman, 2008). Student affairs professionals can assist in eliciting and maintaining family support through programming. A family orientation is one option. Providing the student's family and friends with information about what their student should expect and how they can support him or her can begin to alleviate some of the role strain (Gold, 2006). A family orientation should contain the pertinent information that is presented in a new student orientation, including details about financial aid, what to expect in the transition to college, key institutional resources and personnel, and any additional resources that may be useful to the family, such as childcare or nontraditional student services offices (Jarnot, 2009). Beyond the standard orientation information, it is important to share with the family that they should express genuine interest in the student's education and experiences (Lundberg et al., 2008). A family orientation is also a good opportunity to stress the need for support during the entire academic journey and to provide a guide to family-friendly services on campus (Brown & Nichols, 2013).

Employees who study often struggle to maintain a balance between work, school, and home. Studies have shown that the most effective employer supports for students are instrumental in nature (Lundberg et al., 2008). By providing employees with access to data or equipment, flexible schedules, and a positive understanding of their role as students, employers can improve a student's self-efficacy and reduce role strain (Home, 1998; Lundberg et al., 2008).

The role of student affairs professionals is not to educate employers on how to support their employees who are students; rather, it is to educate employees who study on how to best use the resources provided and to ask for support as needed. Many student affairs professionals and students have experienced this type of support through assistantships and internships.

Online education may be a viable option for some students who are facing institutional barriers related to the times at which courses meet (Hardin, 2008). It is important to remember that online education is not a panacea. It requires technical skills, Internet access on a daily basis, and a dedicated student. Even nontraditional students who are able to meet these criteria may not be interested in the online delivery method. It is important to guide students to programs that are right for them and to help them choose programs for reasons other than convenience. When technology is used to provide academic content at a reduced cost, students need to be encouraged to look for institutions and programs that use the savings to provide enhanced or additional support services that will have a positive impact on retention and completion (Chao, DeRocco, & Flynn, 2008).

Institutional Supports

Institutional barriers are often the first to be addressed when colleges and universities begin recruiting and enrolling nontraditional students. Extending the hours of campus services such as academic advising, financial aid, and the registrar are the quick fixes (Knowles, Holton, & Swanson, 2012). These adjustments are important, but it is also important to realize that, beyond the structural changes, there is a need for social and academic support changes. The campus must work to foster a climate that is friendly to nontraditional students. Examining and confronting issues of ageism and sexism are just as important as married student housing, daycare, meal plans, and family spaces (Bandura, 1994; Schlossberg et al., 1989). Faculty and staff trained to work with nontraditional students are an important institutional support. They can help students build a sense of community and are more willing to work outside of the traditional classroom and calendar constraints. Professionals providing career or academic advising can assist students in developing a sense of mastery and competency that is a significant part of nontraditional student success. When students feel trapped by a lack of options, it becomes imperative that faculty and staff work with them to review what is available to them and to think creatively about scheduling, locations, and courses (Schlossberg et al., 1989).

Andragogy. Knowles (1970) developed the theory of andragogy to guide how adult students are taught in a classroom setting. Andragogy does translate well to developing programs for nontraditional students on campus. The process would include establishing a climate that is conducive to nontraditional student learning, creating a structure that allows them to participate in the planning process, and the ability to provide feedback while remembering that the students are the experts on what services they need and are able to assist in identifying learning objectives (Knowles, 1970). Allow them to be partners in the development and implementation of programs, and make adjustments based on the evaluations provided (Knowles, 1970). Activities that encourage nontraditional students to engage in campus activities and spend more time on campus will increase their chances of completion. To engage nontraditional students on campus, faculty and staff must understand how the theory of andragogy applies to nontraditional students (Wyatt, 2011). Designing campus experiences that acknowledge the various time commitments the students have and that engage nontraditional students in marketing and communication campaigns creates a welcoming campus environment (Wyatt, 2011).

Conclusion

Alfred Whitehead, as quoted in Knowles (1970), stated in 1931: "For the first time we are in an era where culture and knowledge change during a lifespan" (p. 41). Consider the implications of the intervening eight decades and the pace at which education and work continue to change. If culture and knowledge are changing within a lifespan, then every person needs to become a lifelong learner. The expectation that the number of students over the age of 25 will increase 37% by 2018 (Hussar & Bailey, 2009) may be a conservative one, and our campuses need to prepare to serve this nontraditional population.

The top support services that nontraditional students report being likely to use include career services, stress management education, financial aid seminars, orientations for nontraditional students, time management education, study skills education, personal counseling, childcare, and nontraditional student organizations (Bauman et al., 2004). They will need to be educated in these areas as well as in self-efficacy, distance education options, homework loads, and library use (Bye, Pushkar, & Conway, 2007). Students must be provided with peer support, family education, and opportunities to connect on campus (Wormus, 2009). It is important for student affairs professionals to have a basic understanding of the experiences and needs of nontraditional students, and it is just as important for each higher education institution to have an understanding of the nontraditional students on their particular campus. Be flexible and innovative in serving this diverse population.

For further information on working with nontraditional students, consult the Council for Adult and Experiential Learning (CAEL), the Association for Nontraditional Students in Higher Education (ANTSHE), and the American Association for Adult and Continuing Education (AAACE).

References

Advisory Committee on Student Financial Assistance. (2012). *Pathways to success: Integrating learning with life and work to increase national college completion.* Washington, DC: U.S. Department of Education. Retrieved from http://www2.ed.gov/about/bdscomm/list/acsfa/ptsreport2.pdf

Arnold, S., & Hickman, L.N. (2012). Student parent success: A piece of the reform puzzle. *Colleagues, 9*(1), Article 8. Retrieved from http://scholarworks.gvsu.edu/colleagues/vol9/iss1/8

Bandura, A. (1994). Self-efficacy. In V. S. Ramachandran (Ed.), *Encyclopedia of human behavior* (Vol. 4, pp. 71–81). New York, NY: Academic Press. (Reprinted in H. Friedman [Ed.], *Encyclopedia of mental health*. San Diego, CA: Academic Press, 1998)

Bauman, S.S.M., Wang, N., DeLeon, C.W., Kafentzis, J., Zavala-Lopez, M., & Lindsey, M.S. (2004). Nontraditional students' service needs and social support resources: A pilot study. *Journal of College Counseling, 7*(1), 13–17.

Berker, A., Horn, L., & Carroll, C.D. (2003). *Work first, study second: Adult undergraduates who combine employment and postsecondary enrollment.* Postsecondary educational descriptive analysis reports (NCES 96-155). Washington, DC: U.S. Department of Education, National Center for Education Statistics.

Brown, V., & Nichols, T.R. (2013). Pregnant and parenting students on campus policy and program implications for a growing population. *Educational Policy, 27*(3), 499–530.

Bye, D., Pushkar, D., & Conway, M. (2007). Motivation, interest, and positive affect in traditional and nontraditional undergraduate students. *Adult Education Quarterly, 57*(2), 141–158.

Carney-Crompton, S., & Tan, J. (2002). Support systems, psychological functioning, and academic performance of nontraditional female students. *Adult Education Quarterly, 52*(2), 140–154.

Chao, E.L., DeRocco, E.S., & Flynn, M.K. (2008). *Adult learners in higher education: Barriers to success and strategies to improve results.* Washington, DC: Employment and Training Administration. Retrieved from http://wdr.doleta.gov/research/FullText_Documents/ Adult%20Learners%20in%20Higher%20Education.pdf

Chartrand, J.M. (1992). An empirical test of a model of nontraditional student adjustment. *Journal of Counseling Psychology, 39*(2), 193–202.

Choy, S. (2002). *Nontraditional undergraduates* (NCES 2002-012). Washington, DC: U.S. Department of Education, National Center for Education Statistics.

Compton, J.I., Cox, E., & Laanan, F.S. (2006). Adult learners in transition. *New Directions for Student Services, 2006*(114), 73–80.

Donaldson, J.F., & Townsend, B.K. (2007). Higher education journals' discourse about adult undergraduate students. *Journal of Higher Education, 78*(1), 27–50.

Fairchild, E.E. (2003). Multiple roles of adult learners. *New Directions for Student Services, 2003*(102), 11–16.

Flint, T.A., & Frey, R. (2003). Alternative programming for adults. *New Directions for Student Services, 2003*(102), 69–80.

Gold, J.M. (2006). Exploring marital satisfaction among graduate students: Implications for service delivery. *Family Journal, 14*(4), 417–419.

Hardin, C.J. (2008). Adult students in higher education: A portrait of transitions. *New Directions for Higher Education, 2008*(144), 49–57.

Home, A.M. (1998). Predicting role conflict, overload and contagion in adult women university students with families and jobs. *Adult Education Quarterly, 48*(2), 85–97.

Horn, L. (1996). *Nontraditional undergraduates, trends in enrollment from 1986 to 1992 and persistence and attainment among 1989–90 beginning postsecondary students* (NCES 97-578). Washington, DC: U.S. Department of Education, NCES.

Hussar, W.J., & Bailey, T.M. (2009). *Projections of education statistics to 2018* (NCES 2009-062). Washington, DC: U.S. Department of Education, NCES.

Jarnot, K.C. (2009). Parent and family institutional philosophy and on-campus partners. *Journal of Student Affairs, 18*, 40–50. Retrieved from http://digitool.library.colostate.edu///exlibris/dtl/d3_1/apache_media/L2V4bGlicml zL2R0bC9kM18xL2FwYWNoZV9tZWRpYS80MDYyOQ==.pdf

Knight, L.V., Steinbach, T.A., & Hop, J. (2012). Informing science and andragogy: A conceptual scheme of client-side barriers to informing university students. *Informing Science: The International Journal of an Emerging Transdiscipline, 15*, 121–145.

Knowles, M.M.S. (1970). *The modern practice of adult education.* New York, NY: Association Press.

Knowles, M.S., Holton III, E.F., & Swanson, R.A. (2012). *The adult learner.* New York, NY: Routledge.

Lundberg, C.A. (2003). The influence of time-limitations, faculty, and peer relationships on adult student learning: A causal model. *Journal of Higher Education, 74*(6), 665–688.

Lundberg, C.A., McIntire, D.D., & Creasman, C.T. (2008). Sources of social support and self-efficacy for adult students. *Journal of College Counseling, 11*(1), 58–72.

Malhotra, N.K., Shapero, M., Sizoo, S., & Munro, T. (2007). Factor structure of deterrents to adult participation in higher education. *Journal of College Teaching & Learning, 4*(12), 81–90.

Mbilinyi, L. (2006). *Degrees of opportunity: Adults' views on the value and feasibility of returning to school.* A Study Conducted for Capella University by TNSNFO. Retrieved from http://www.degreesofopportunity.org/inc/degrees_opportunity_report.pdf

Obama, B. (2009, July 12). Rebuilding something better. *The Washington Post.* Retrieved from http://www.washingtonpost.com/wp-dyn/content/article/2009/07/11/AR2009071100647.html

Schlossberg, N., Lynch, A., & Chickering, A. (1989). *Improving higher education for adults: Response programs and services from entry to departure.* San Francisco, CA: Jossey-Bass.

Schlossberg, N.K., Waters, E.B., & Goodman, J. (1995). *Counseling adults in transition* (2nd ed.). New York, NY: Springer.

Snyder, T.D., & Dillow, S.A. (2012). *Digest of education statistics 2011* (NCES 2012-001). Washington, DC: National Center for Education Statistics, Institute of Education Sciences, U.S. Department of Education.

Spanard, J.A. (1990). Beyond intent: Reentering college to complete the degree. *Review of Educational Research, 60*(3), 309–344.

Taniguchi, H., & Kaufman, G. (2005). Degree completion among nontraditional college students. *Social Science Quarterly, 86*(4), 912–927.

Turner, S.E., Breneman, D.W., Milam, J.H., Levin, J.S., Kohl, K., Gansneder, B.M., & Pusser, B. (2007). *Returning to learning: Adults' success in college is key to America's future.* Indianapolis, IN: Lumina Foundation for Education.

Wormus, K. (2009). Considering students with families in higher education. *Journal of Student Affairs, 18*, 19–26.

Wyatt, L.G. (2011). Nontraditional student engagement: Increasing adult student success and retention. *Journal of Continuing Education, 59*(1), 10–20.

Zajacova, A., Lynch, S.M., & Espenshade, T.J. (2005). Self-efficacy, stress, and academic success in college. *Research in Higher Education, 46*(6), 677–706.

TWENTY

The Residential Experience

Matthew Varga and Jeannie Hopper

"Moving into the residence halls was an exciting time for me. I was able to find a lot of students who I wanted to hang out with. Immediately, I knew me and my roommate were going to be friends because we had a lot in common. We both came from great neighborhoods, great high schools, and our parents went here too."

—*Alex, a third-generation, White, affluent college student*

"When I moved in, the first couple of weeks were weird to me. A lot of the people I met talked about how much their parents helped them move in and helped prepare them for school. It was difficult for me because my parents never attended college and couldn't help answer any of my questions. I had to figure everything out on my own. Living with other students really helped me feel like I belonged and always had someone to turn to when I had questions."

—*Lewis, a first-generation college student*

"I could barely afford to attend school, let alone live in housing, but I knew I wanted to live on campus so I made it work. I was hardly ever in my room because I was either working, studying, or sleeping. I couldn't afford to go to parties and let my grades slip because if I did, I would lose my scholarships and financial aid. My parents couldn't afford to send me to school and I was really alone. It was sad for me to see everyone having fun and going out. I didn't have that luxury because I had to work if I wanted to survive."

—*Michael, a low-income, first-generation college student*

"I was petrified when I moved in and lived in the dorms. I had not yet come out to my family or friends, but I knew everyone assumed I was gay. It was hard for me to relate to the other students because they all acted like something was wrong with me. I spent a lot of my time in my room by myself because it was where I felt the safest. If it wasn't for my RA who really helped me feel good about myself, I don't think I would have stayed in college. She really helped others see that I wasn't any different than them."

—*Lisa, an LGBTQ student*

"Living on campus was really hard for me. There was like 10 Black students in my building and everyone else was White. It was like a sea of Whiteness. We always felt like they were staring at us, judging us, or didn't want us there. In fact, when I moved in I saw racial slurs carved into the doors on my hall. I was never comfortable in my room and really ended up living with friends off campus where I felt included and safe."

—*Xavier, an African American male student*

These quotes depict a very different residential experience for various types of students. The residential experience can be a quintessential component for student persistence and overall success in college (Billson & Terry, 1982; Milem & Berger, 1997; Pascarella & Terenzini, 2005; Tinto, 1993). However, the residential experience can also be a time of turmoil, hardship, racism, isolation, and overall stress for many students, particularly those who identify with oppressed or marginalized populations (Hawkins & Larabee, 2009). In an effort to explicate the residential experience in relation to minority students, Tinto's (1993) Theory of Student Departure and Astin's (1999) Theory of Involvement help explain the relationship between the characteristics and challenges of minority students and their residential experience. After a brief explanation of these theories, a review of various minority students and their challenges in relation to the residential experience follows, and includes students who identify as first generation, low income, LGBTQ, and racial and ethnic minority.

Theoretical Framework

According to Astin's (1999) Theory of Involvement, the level of involvement, both psychological and physical, ultimately impacts a student's commitment to an institution and subsequently affects her development. The more committed a student is to her surroundings and education, the more likely she is to experience growth, development, and educational attainment (Astin, 1999). This is also true for the residential experience. An on-campus experience is only as beneficial as the student makes it for herself. While Astin postulated five components to student involvement, this chapter focuses only on the last two: (a) the greater the student commitment to and involvement in an institutional program, the greater the impact of said program, and (b) the overall effectiveness of a program is dependent upon its policies and overall ability to involve students in it. In other words, a positive residential experience is one that not only has intentional policies to involve and engage students, but is also only effective when students altruistically want to be involved in their residential experience.

Understanding the relationship between the student and residential program is only part of the equation for defining the relationship between minority students and the residential experience. Tinto's (1993) Theory of Student Departure contributes to an understanding of the residential experience by affirming the importance of students' feelings connected to their residential experience, one component of the social system of college. Tinto theorizes that a student is more likely to persist if she connects to the academic and social systems of college. The more committed and engaged a student is to either of the systems, the better her chances of graduating. Alex is an example of a student immediately feeling connected to an institution, as he found other students with whom he immediately related and felt connected to the residential experience. Thus, the goal of student affairs professionals is to help students feel connected to the social system of an institution who are less likely to feel an immediate connection to campus. Students that fail to find others with whom to relate or join extracurricular activities often experience a negative attitude toward an institution (Tinto, 1993). Tinto notes that the more negative experiences or attitudes a student encounters, the greater the likelihood it will affect his desire to depart.

The positive or negative experience and commitment to an institution connects Astin's (1999) and Tinto's (1993) theories to the effectiveness of the residential experience for all types of students. Astin concluded, as did Tinto, that the more positively perceived interactions a student experiences, the more likely it is that he will be involved and committed to the residential experience, whereas a negatively perceived environment or experience will likely result in disengagement and possibly departure. Once again, using Alex as an example, students who face few challenges connecting to an institution, friends, or finding positive activities in which to participate on campus are much more likely to succeed in college. Alex, being a White, third-generation student, encounters little opposition at a predominantly White institution. He finds his experience to be positive, accepting, and inclusive, which is critical for a student to be connected to the overall social system of college. Therefore, it is not unreasonable to assume that students who identify with a marginalized or oppressed population, as compared to students who identify with the dominant culture, may often experience negative feelings living on campus due to the difficulty of finding students with whom to relate and the perception of discrimination, racism, or exclusivity (Milem & Berger, 1997). The residential experience becomes an environment that can either encourage and support marginalized and oppressed students' involvement or exacerbate feelings of exclusion, oppression, racism, and separation (Hawkins & Larabee, 2009).

Residential Experience

It is known that the residential experience plays an important role in students' persistence, development, and overall success (Astin, 1999; Billson & Terry, 1982; Pascarella & Terenzini, 2005; Tinto, 1993). However, the overall educational effectiveness of a residential program is dependent upon its ability to involve students (Astin, 1999; Tinto, 1993). Specifically, a strong and intentional residential experience has the ability to promote an environment that is inclusive and developmental to all types of students, regardless of how they may self-identify (Pascarella & Terenzini, 2005). According to Pascarella and Terenzini (2005), a residential experience affects students' "aesthetic, cultural, and intellectual values" but also has the ability to diversify students' experiences and liberalize their "social, political, and religious values and attitudes" (p. 605). The liberalization of students' views is more likely to occur when the residential experience is specifically structured to intentionally engage students who are racially, politically, sexually, and religiously different (Pascarella & Terenzini, 2005). Living on campus provides students with the opportunity to interact with all types of students. Students retreat to their living quarters subsequently resulting in indirect interactions with different students (Pascarella & Terenzini, 2005).

The diversity of students living on campus makes it distinct from other traditional college programs (Pascarella & Terenzini, 2005). Therefore, it is important to recognize the impact a residential experience has on a variety of students. The aforementioned stories are of students who recounted their impressions of the residential community. These stories are going to be referenced throughout the chapter, and first-generation students, low-income students, minority students, and students who identify as LGBTQ are discussed. Each group of students confronts different challenges, resulting in a unique residential experience that can either facilitate their college success or exacerbate their desire to leave. The first group of students that will be discussed is first-generation students, who often come to college not knowing what to expect or feel a lack of support from their parents (Lohfink & Paulsen, 2005).

First-Generation Students

First-generation students are students whose parents did not attend college (Gupton, Castelo-Rodriguez, Martínez, & Quintanar, 2009; Pascarella, Pierson, Wolniak, & Terenzini, 2004; Strayhorn, 2006). It has been documented that first-generation students also identify as low-income students (Corrigan, 2003) and are from disadvantaged backgrounds (Strayhorn, 2006). However, in an effort not to present first-generation students as a homogenous group, low-income and disadvantaged students will be discussed separately.

First-generation students are at a variety of disadvantages compared to their second- and third-generation counterparts. First-generation students are less likely to become involved in extracurricular activities or the residential experience, as they may not understand the significance of their involvement (Pascarella et al., 2004; Pike & Kuh, 2005), and this subsequently affects their ability to connect to the social aspects of college (Terenzini, Springer, Yaeger, Pascarella, & Nora, 1996; Tinto, 1993). What's more, first-generation students experience some form of discrimination and receive less support from peers and family; they are also less likely to engage with faculty or to study, and they typically spend more time working than their second- and third-generation counterparts (Billson & Terry, 1982; Pike & Kuh, 2005; Terenzini et al., 1996). These students tend to experience fewer positive out-of-classroom experiences (Billson & Terry, 1982; Strayhorn, 2006), which significantly impacts their ability to connect socially to an institution (Terenzini et al., 1996; Tinto, 1993). The unique and negative nature of these characteristics provides a challenge for administrators and the residential experience.

Revisiting Lewis's and Alex's stories, the different struggles a first-generation and a third-generation student may encounter become evident. Lewis's sense of connection to other students, or finding those with whom he can relate, was difficult and possibly intimidating. This affected his ability to interact and feel connected to other students. In order for the residential experience to benefit first-generation students, it should intentionally develop an environment that helps them overcome the challenges of being a first-generation student—such as not becoming involved, working part-time, or feeling disconnected from peers (Billson & Terry, 1982). Fortunately, first-generation students who live on campus are at a significant advantage compared to their off-campus counterparts (Pascarella et al., 2004; Pike & Kuh, 2005). First-generation students like Lewis are able to encounter students who may be different, but they understand the nuances of the college experience (information normally obtained from parents). Despite feeling different, students exposed to the collegiate lifestyle prior to attending college may serve as an important resource for Lewis. The residential experience also encourages students to become engaged in other aspects of the social and academic system that will affect their connection to the campus (Astin, 1999; Pike, 1999; Tinto, 1993). However, the residential experience will only benefit first-generation students if they become physically and psychologically involved. Students who remain disconnected and aloof are less likely to feel a connection to the institution or their residential experience (Astin, 1999).

Within the residence halls themselves, there are many things departments and staffs can do to help ensure that all students feel comfortable, safe, and connected to the community. For first-generation college students, this begins by connecting the student with a solid mentor. Peer mentors such as RAs or upper-division students are beneficial, but it is the professional or para-professional in the hall that can provide the best support for first-generation students by assisting them in developing the physical and physiological investment needed to become involved (Astin, 1999). Hall Directors or Resident Coordinators should actively seek out these students to engage them in dialog about the college experience, an important piece of college preparation they may have been unable to secure on their own. A mentorship experience is important to any student (Crisp & Cruz, 2009), but for those who lack a parental figure who can provide those conversations at home, a professional in the hall is the best possible stand-in once the student arrives on campus looking for resources.

Similarly, first-generation students may arrive at college with a less-informed notion of what "college life" means, and therefore may not know what to expect in both academic and social settings (Pike & Kuh, 2005). Social norming programs are excellent ways to combat the many myths students are exposed to through media outlets like television and movies (Perkins, 2002). Ideally, these programs would begin at new student orientation, but it is important to continue the message within the residence halls, where a free night of pizza provides a captive audience. Taking the time to show students firsthand that perceptions and reality differ quite a bit when it comes to time spent in study, alcohol consumption, and sexual activity could prevent high-risk behaviors by first-generation students who simply did not know the social norm (Perkins, 2002).

Programming and community building activities in the halls should always be tailored to the needs of the students who reside on the floor or hall. RAs should take the time to get to know their residents in the first few weeks and provide the resources and opportunities they need. By doing so, hall staffs can identify which students may need specific skill-building programming, like Laundry 101, campus tours, course recommendations, and so on. First-generation students may not want to be specifically identified, but by offering programs to an entire group, the staff can provide what is needed without isolating any one particular group of students.

Living and Learning Communities (LLC) are an extremely effective way to engage students with faculty and hall staff, and first-generation students would benefit more than most in these settings (Tinto, 2003). The very foundation of an LLC is to provide on-site academic and social support for students in common programs in a residence hall (Pike, 1999). All the help they need is there: faculty and staff mentors, peers with similar interests, and an automatic community that the student is immediately a member of, both on the residential floor and in the classroom.

Low-Income Students

Similar to first-generation students, low-income students (i.e., students from families living at or below the national poverty line) have difficulty adjusting and connecting to the social and academic aspects of college (Gupton et al., 2009). Part of this may be because low-income students rarely live on campus or become involved, since they spend most of their time working (Bozick, 2007). The National Center for Education Statistics (2003) supports this claim by noting that 10.5% of students enrolling in 4-year institutions and living on campus come from families with an annual income of $20,000 or less. However, once these students are enrolled and living on campus, they are confronted with the critical challenges of finance, time management, and general disengagement (Corrigan, 2003).

Low-income students often do battle with educational, familial, social, and other challenges that traditional, affluent students do not encounter (Corrigan, 2003). These students often earn lower grades, which affects their connection to the academic social system, but they are also less likely to be involved on campus because they work part- or full-time (Bozick, 2007). Despite these challenges, low-income students are more likely to work for either personal money reasons, to pay for school, or to support their family (Bozick, 2007). This causes a burden on these students when academic and social demands increase. Students must choose among reducing their work schedules, increasing their academic and social commitments, or dropping out altogether (Bozick, 2007). Unfortunately, the lack of involvement on campus and an overall lack of connection to college typically result in a feeling that the benefits of working outweigh the benefits of college (Bozick, 2007). Therefore, it becomes critical that residence life staff provide an experience that is supportive of and encouraging to low-income students.

Low-income students are often less engaged in their residential experience because of their need to work either part- or full-time (Bozick, 2007). This was true for Michael as well. He was forced to manage his time much more closely than other students. He could not afford to engage in the traditional college experience, as he had to work and maintain his grades. His priorities were significantly different from Alex's. Students such as Michael are also more likely to remain close to home and family, and this affects their ability to separate and transition to college (Bozick, 2007). The residential experience provides students a time to separate from their families and to begin to explore and engage in new values, traditions, and customs (Tinto, 1993). Therefore, a residential experience needs to be intentional and educational to engage students like Michael. In fact, low-income students who live at home are 41% more likely to drop out as compared to low-income students living on campus (Bozick, 2007). It thus becomes critical that residential programs are employed to assist students who are working excessively or are considered low-income students.

Reaching out to students rather than waiting for them to ask for help is the key to making these connections (Gupton et al., 2009). RAs are equipped with resource and referral information to help most any student, but the students who need that help the most rarely, if ever, ask for it (Arboleda, Wang, Shelley, & Whalen, 2003). Particularly when finances are an issue, students can be extremely reticent with peers about their concerns. One way for RAs to avoid this reluctance is to be diligent about offering programs and activities at a variety of times. If every hall event is on Tuesday at 7:00 p.m., someone who works a shift during that time will never be able to attend and will therefore remain disconnected from the community through absolutely no fault of his own. A good RA is one who can actively engage all residents on the floor, so knowing the students and offering activities around work and involvement schedules is paramount (Bierman & Carpenter, 1994).

After times are selected that work for all students, ensuring that those activities and programs have helpful content is the next step in supporting low-income students (Gupton et al., 2009). Hall staff should be versed in the best resources on campus when it comes to financial support. Be it the registrar's office, financial aid, the bursar, or a "one-stop" set-up, RAs should know their campus and be able to get students where they need to go without taking extra time to look up information or request and wait for assistance from a supervisor. Again, if students are too busy to make it to free pizza night on the floor where they live, how can we expect them to have time to bounce around campus from office to office as they search for exactly what they need? Training for residence hall staff should focus on these very concerns to equip RAs and desk staff appropriately.

One of the best ways that residence halls are equipped to support and assist students who need to work, though, is by offering them employment where they live, something that may help them feel connected to their residence hall while providing additional income. Residence halls offer some of the most numerous, convenient jobs on any given college campus. Almost every hall has RAs, and most have a front desk of some sort, a post office, and even security opportunities for student employment. This not only helps students who need money to create income and is convenient for those who do not own a vehicle, but it also immediately connects students to a community through a campus leadership position, which is a key factor in creating a sense of belonging (Astin, 1999; Tinto, 1993).

Offering a variety of housing options at a range of prices is also an important policy for residence hall administrators to consider when assisting with student engagement, and aligns with Astin's (1999) fifth postulate. Not all students can afford to live on campus, as noted above, but they are definitely more likely to succeed if they do. And not all students are coming in with the same needs or wants, so their housing options should reflect these differences. Assigning students to live based on socioeconomic status is not the intention or goal, but offering enough options that could appeal to a variety of student backgrounds is essential.

Minority Students

Compared to Caucasian students on predominantly White campuses, minority students are often confronted with different challenges (Attinasi, 1989; Eimers & Pike, 1997; Feagin & Sikes, 1995; Lagdameo et al., 2002). For instance, minority students often struggle to find students with whom they identify (Bourassa, 1991). This creates a unique struggle wherein they may feel they have to negotiate an environment that is "foreign, socially exclusive, culturally irresponsive, and wrought with contradictions" (Hawkins & Larabee, 2009, p. 180). Minority students at predominately White institutions may feel pressured to relinquish their racial identity and feel forced to assimilate into the dominant culture (Feagin & Sikes, 1995). When confronted with such dilemmas, minority students may retreat to safe havens where they do not feel forced to assimilate into the dominant culture or experience racism, discrimination, or other exclusive contradictions (Feagin & Sikes, 1995). College residence halls in predominantly White institutions present a similar dilemma of forcing a student to choose between the dominant culture and his own, resulting in a student feeling forced to leave his primary living quarters in an effort to feel safe.

This adjustment to a residential experience can be even more difficult when minority students are confronted with a racial or discriminatory environment, as was the experience of Xavier (Eimers & Pike, 1997).The negative perception of such a residential experience can result in a lack of involvement and, ultimately, the departure of the students from an institution (Astin, 1999; Tinto, 1993). More important, the feeling on the part of students that they do not belong in their rooms may force them to find alternative housing. Minority students need to feel connected to the residential experience in a way that encourages and supports their growth and sense of connection to the institution (Watson & Kuh, 1996). As it is their home away from home, the residential experience provides a unique environment for students. In Xavier's case, he already felt a negative racial environment on campus, and for him to feel judged in his living space as well makes it extremely less likely that he will continue at his institution. He will probably neither feel committed and connected, nor have the physical or psychological energy needed to invest in a collegiate experience that is not supportive of him (Astin, 1999; Feagin & Sikes, 1995; Tinto, 1993). In addition, exacerbating the disconnect from the social system and residential experience is the feeling that campus administrators fail to provide minority students with the same attention as Caucasian students on a predominantly White campus (Hawkins & Larabee, 2009).

The focus on the dominant culture by administrators presents a unique problem for minority students. Xavier felt that his environment was unforgiving to minority students, and he was forced to either (a) accept the dominant culture, resulting in one-way assimilation, or (b) reject the mainstream culture and be subjected to further persecution and judgment (Allen, 1992; Ancis, Sedlacek, & Mohr, 2000; Feagin & Sikes, 1995). Xavier chose to remove himself from the environment. Despite feeling safe and supported, his new environment distanced him from the institution and created feelings of resentment. This choice is presented to many minorities across the United States attending a predominately White institution and creates a negative campus and residential environment that affects students' ability to build relationships or connect on a social level (Hawkins & Larabee, 2009). It therefore becomes critical for residential staff to create an environment and experience that is inclusive and supportive, and that incorporates the cultural values of all kinds of students, not just those of the dominant culture.

Unlike socioeconomic or generational status, cultural diversity is a visible and therefore quite obvious indicator of student identity. A student can hide or deny his or her income or family background, but he cannot as easily conceal his race, nationality, or, oftentimes, religion. This is not to suggest that students should hide their diversity markers, but rather to illustrate that when it comes to these issues, what students can see plainly outweighs what they are told, taught, or read in the campus life brochure. As such, it is important that the staffing structures of the residence halls accurately represent the residential population being served. Students connect with people to whom they can relate (Hawkins & Larabee, 2009), so if the staff responsible for building the community and planning all events is one with which students do not identify, they may be less likely to take advantage of the opportunities presented. RA staffs, desk staffs, and Hall Association executive boards should consist of unique and diverse students who bring different strengths and skills to their teams and, if at all possible, should embody racial, cultural, and religious diversity.

Marketing campaigns and deliberate hiring strategies can be used to connect to all student populations, but a one-on-one approach is often most effective in connecting students who might not normally apply for these positions to think about how they can relate to the team. Again, knowing the students who live in the halls is the single most important thing any residential staff member can do to promote and encourage diversity. Only when positive and responsible students are known can they be urged to apply and take on leadership roles on a campus, and there is no staff member better suited to getting to know students on a personal level than the RA.

Social justice programming is also important in making all students feel accepted and comfortable in the hall (Hawkins & Larabee, 2009; Nicols & Quaye, 2009). There are numerous examples of this type of programming that educate students on social issues and behaviors, but leading by example can be the most impactful (Hawkins & Larabee, 2009). Tunnels of Oppression and Privilege Houses are two examples of programs that increase students' awareness and help them empathize with marginalized populations. In addition, these programs help educate and inform students, particularly racially and financially privileged students, on their privilege. Christmas decorations are popular and common sights in residence halls in the month of December. However, including decorations for Hanukkah, Kwanzaa, and other religious and cultural events around the same time, or even promoting religious holidays that do not align with mainstream holidays, can go a long way to showing students that their beliefs are respected and accepted in the building.

Residential staff members can make strides in creating comfortable atmospheres with staff and programs, but the effect that other residents can have on the community can help or harm these efforts immensely. Immediate and serious documentation and follow-up needs to occur if any act of bias takes place in the hall (Hawkins & Larabee, 2009). Having bias training and a strict protocol can assist in damage control when an incident does occur, either major or minor in nature. In our experience, proper bias protocol should ideally be a collaborative effort among residence life staff, the dean of students' office, judicial affairs, and campus police. Students need to see that acts of discrimination are not tolerated in the residence halls and that there will be repercussions for those who choose to harm the community.

LGBTQ Students

The fourth population reviewed includes students who self-identify as lesbian, gay, bisexual, transgender, or are questioning their sexuality (LGBTQ). This population confronts a unique residential experience, especially for those who feel they are incorrectly grouped with other students based on their biological gender. Students who identify as LGBTQ may also face ridicule from roommates that leads to a stressful, hostile environment. Tyler Clementi, a student at Rutgers University, is one example of the negative and hostile environment that LGBTQ students may encounter living on campus. Tyler committed suicide after discovering that his college roommate had secretly recorded him kissing another man (*The New York Times*, 2012). Tyler's experience is one that many LGBTQ students fear in a residential community—namely, being ridiculed for their sexual identity (Evans & Broido, 1999).

College is often a time for students to disclose to others how they identify sexually (Evans & D'Augelli, 1996). This is surprising, considering that research suggests the campus environment may be hostile and unsupportive to students identifying as LGBTQ (Draughn, Elkins, & Roy, 2002; Engstrom & Sedlacek, 1997; Renn, 2000; Rhoads, 1995). However, for students who live on campus, disclosing their sexual identity may present additional difficulties. The residential experience for students who identify as LGBTQ often includes being greeted with harassment, discrimination, and fear (Evans & Broido, 2002). In fact, the residential environment can vary from supportive to depressing.

A residential experience that is supportive is typically one in which the building staff—such as the residence director and resident assistants—are supportive of LGBTQ students and immediately confront homophobic and discriminatory behavior (Evans & Broido, 1999). Lisa's story reiterates the impact that staff can have on developing a positive residential experience for students who identify as LGBTQ. Lisa felt that the institution was supportive and encouraging of her lifestyle based on the roles of her building staff. The staff's commitment to her will likely contribute to her ability to feel connected to the institution and lead to her overall success and development, and is an example of the importance of inclusive policies to a residential experience. Therefore, it is important for residence life staff to understand their role in the residential experience of students who identify as LGBTQ.

In order to create a supportive environment, students need to be surrounded by people who are informed and are willing to accept them for themselves. Safe Zone training, which is an LGBTQ and ally program offered at most college campuses, is one nationally recognized way to provide diversity and inclusion education for staff members (Schueler, Hoffman, & Peterson, 2009). This type of training cannot be forced on an individual, but can be encouraged and made available to all who live and work in the residence halls. Once a student or staff member is Safe Zone certified, he and his office or room become public places of "safety" or acceptance and support on campus (Schueler et al., 2009). One integral piece of the Safe Zone training is to ensure that all participants are aware of the best referral offices on campus for students who are struggling with identity issues or discrimination (Schueler et al., 2009).

Once staff members are comfortable and educated properly on these issues, they can begin providing programs to encourage a celebration and understanding of all student lifestyles. Once again, simple and seamless immersion into everyday activities can be the best way to make students feel naturally accepted (Sanlo, Rankin, & Schoenberg, 2002). Recognizing LGBTQ-related events such as Pride Month, Day of Silence, National Coming Out Day, and so forth can help create a sense of community awareness as students learn more about certain issues (Sanlo et al., 2002). More traditional awareness-type programming, such as Spread the Word to End the Word, a program directed toward ending the use of slang words like "gay" and "retarded," are excellent ways to educate students about how even their casual conversations and actions can be unintentionally harming others (Joseph P. Kennedy Jr. Foundation, n.d.).

Recent strides in making LGBTQ students feel more accepted on college campuses have led to an influx of gender-neutral housing and restroom options in residence halls. Gender-neutral housing allows students to live with one another without any gender qualifications, meaning that men and women can live together as roommates or apartment-mates (Schueler et al., 2009). Gender-neutral restrooms are more prevalent at the present time and offer a safe space for students who do not identify with a traditional gender assignment. Similarly, residence hall administrators can make students feel more accepted through simple changes to the contracting process by allowing students to identify as a gender other than male or female when signing up for a residential space, as well as in any demographic data areas of departmental, campus, hall, or floor surveys and assessments (Schueler et al., 2009).

In our experience, bias protocol and training—as outlined in a previous section of this chapter—is also an important factor in making LGBTQ students feel comfortable in the halls. Discriminatory behaviors cannot be tolerated, and students need to seek immediate redress if they do occur (Gupton et al., 2009; Hawkins & Larabee, 2009). Even minor incidents such as derogatory words written on a dry erase board outside a student's door can have a major effect on floor community. A proper bias protocol would handle both minor and major issues with the same degree of professionalism and appropriate investigation and sanctioning. Only when students know they are safe and advocated for will they truly feel that they belong to a community.

Conclusion

We shared narratives of several different students who identify with a marginalized or oppressed group. Their stories offer only a brief glimpse into the diversity of students entering college campuses. The residential experience has multiple purposes not only for these students but for all students. It helps to develop, educate, support, and connect students to their institution (Pascarella & Terenzini, 2005). Feeling connected to an institution is easier for some than for others. For example, Alex, who is a White, affluent, third-generation college student, may feel it is easier to find other students with whom he relates on a predominately White campus. His likelihood of experiencing a nonthreatening and positive residential experience is very high. However, once students begin to identify with characteristics different from the dominant culture, they begin to experience new and challenging pressures. The support that students receive from their institution to overcome those new challenges and pressures will ultimately determine their success.

The residential experience becomes the quintessential piece in supporting students who do not identify with the dominant culture and who must function in the midst of an environment that can be one of racism and oppression. The student residential experience will ultimately determine a student's success in college. Using Astin's (1999) Theory of Involvement and Tinto's (1993) Theory of Student Departure to connect students to a positive and supportive residential experience is only part of the solution. Residential programs and staff must recognize and understand the importance of developing an inclusive and supportive environment for all types of students, no matter how they identify. It becomes equally important to understand the challenges that marginalized and oppressed students confront regularly. If the residential experience is one that is positive, supportive, and encouraging, then marginalized students may be more inclined to invest their personal and psychological energy in an institution (Alvarez, 2002; Attinasi, 1989; Evans & Broido, 2002; Feagin & Sikes, 1995). The increase in energy and commitment will significantly improve their sense of institutional commitment to the social aspect of college (Tinto, 1993). Residence life programs and residence life staff can be the source for developing a positive, inclusive, and supportive environment that will help students feel connected and supported in college.

References

Allen, W. (1992). The color of success: African-American college student outcomes at predominantly White and historically Black public colleges and universities. *Harvard Educational Review, 62*(1), 26–45.

Alvarez, A.N. (2002). Racial identity and Asian Americans: Support and challenges. *New Directions for Student Services, 2002*(97), 33–44. doi: 10.1002/ss.37

Ancis, J.R., Sedlacek, W.E., & Mohr, J.J. (2000). Student perceptions of campus cultural climate by race. *Journal of Counseling & Development, 78*(2), 180–185.

Arboleda, A., Wang, Y., Shelley, M.C., & Whalen, D.F. (2003). Predictors of residence hall involvement. *Journal of College Student Development, 44*(4), 517–531.

Astin, A. (1999). Student involvement: A developmental theory for higher education. *Journal of College Student Development, 40*(5), 518–529.

Attinasi, L.C., Jr. (1989). Getting in: Mexican Americans' perceptions of university attendance and the implications for freshman year persistence. *Journal of Higher Education, 60*(3), 247–277. doi: 10.2307/1982250

Bierman, S.E., & Carpenter, D.S. (1994). An analysis of resident assistant work motivation. *Journal of College Student Development, 35*(6), 467–474.

Billson, J.M., & Terry, M.B. (1982). In search of the silken purse: Factors in attrition among first-generation students. *College and University, 58*(1), 57–75.

Bourassa, D.M. (1991). How White students and students of color organize and interact on campus. *New Directions for Student Services, 1991*(56), 13–23. doi: 10.1002/ss.37119915604

Bozick, R. (2007). Making it through the first year of college: The role of students' economic resources, employment, and living arrangements. *Sociology of Education, 80*(3), 261–285.

Corrigan, M.E. (2003). Beyond access: Persistence challenges and the diversity of low-income students. *New Directions for Higher Education, 2003*(121), 25–34.

Crisp, G., & Cruz, I. (2009). Mentoring college students: A critical review of the literature between 1990 and 2007. *Research in Higher Education, 50*(6), 525–545.

Draughn, T., Elkins, B., & Roy, R. (2002). Allies in the struggle: Eradicating homophobia and heterosexism on campus. *Journal of Lesbian Studies, 6*(3–4), 9–20.

Eimers, M.T., & Pike, G.R. (1997). Minority and nonminority adjustment to college: Differences or similarities? *Research in Higher Education, 38*(1), 77–97. doi: 10.2307/40196235

Engstrom, C.M., & Sedlacek, W. (1997). Attitudes of heterosexual students toward their gay male and lesbian peers. *Journal of College Student Development, 38*(6), 565–576.

Evans, N.J., & Broido, E.M. (1999). Coming out in college residence halls: Negotiation, meaning making, challenges, supports. *Journal of College Student Development, 40*(6), 658–668.

Evans, N.J., & Broido, E.M. (2002). The experiences of lesbian and bisexual women in college residence halls. *Journal of Lesbian Studies, 6*(3–4), 29–42. doi: 10.1300/J155v06n03_04

Evans, N.J., & D'Augelli, A. (1996). Lesbians, gay men, and bisexual people in college. In R.C. Savin-Williams & K.M. Cohen (Eds.), *The lives of lesbians, gays, and bisexuals: Children to adults* (pp. 201–226). Fort Worth, TX: Harcourt Brace College.

Feagin, J.R., & Sikes, M.P. (1995). How Black students cope with racism on White campuses. *Journal of Blacks in Higher Education,* (8), 91–97.

Gupton, J., Castelo-Rodriguez, C., Martínez, D., & Quintanar, I. (2009). Creating a pipeline to engage low-income, first-generation college students. In S.R. Harper & S.J. Quaye (Eds.), *Student engagement in higher education.* New York, NY: Routledge.

Hawkins, V.M., & Larabee, H.J. (2009). Engaging racial/ethnic minority students in out-of-class activities on predominantly White campuses. In S.R. Harper & S.J. Quaye (Eds.), *Student engagement in higher education* (pp. 179–198). New York, NY: Routledge.

Joseph P. Kennedy Jr. Foundation. (n.d.). *Spread the word to end the word.* Retrieved from http://www.r-word.org/

Lagdameo, A., Lee, S., Nguyen, B., Liang, C.T.H., Lee, S., Maekawa Kodama, C., & McEwen, M.K. (2002). Voices of Asian American students. *New Directions for Student Services, 2002*(97), 5–10. doi: 10.1002/ss.34

Lohfink, M.M., & Paulsen, M.B. (2005). Comparing the determinants of persistence for first-generation and continuing-generation students. *Journal of College Student Development, 46*(4), 409–428.

Milem, J.F., & Berger, J.B. (1997). A modified model of college student persistence: Exploring the relationship between Astin's Theory of Involvement and Tinto's Theory of Student Departure. *Journal of College Student Development, 38*(4), 387–400.

National Center for Education Statistics. (2003). *Beginning postsecondary students longitudinal study: 2003–04.* Washington, DC: U.S. Department of Education.

The New York Times. (2012, March 16). Tyler Clementi. Retrieved from http://www.nytimes.com/top/reference/timestopics/people/c/tyler_clementi/index.html

Nicols, A., & Quaye, S.J. (2009). Beyond accommodation: Removing barriers to academic and social engagement for students with disabilities. In S.R. Harper & S.J. Quaye (Eds.), *Student engagement in higher education.* New York, NY: Routledge.

Pascarella, E.T., Pierson, C.T., Wolniak, G.C., & Terenzini, P.T. (2004). First-generation college students: Additional evidence on college experiences and outcomes. *Journal of Higher Education, 75*(3), 249–284.

Pascarella, E.T., & Terenzini, P.T. (2005). *How college affects students: A third decade of research* (Vol. 2). San Francisco, CA: Jossey-Bass.

Perkins, H. (2002). Social norms and the prevention of alcohol misuse in collegiate contexts. *Journal of Studies on Alcohol and Drugs, 14,* 164–172.

Pike, G.R. (1999). The effects of residential learning communities and traditional residential living arrangements on educational gains during the first year of college. *Journal of College Student Development, 40*(3), 269–284.

Pike, G.R., & Kuh, G.D. (2005). First- and second-generation college students: A comparison of their engagement and intellectual development. *Journal of Higher Education, 76*(3), 276–300.

Renn, K.A. (2000). Including all voices in the classroom: Teaching lesbian, gay, and bisexual students. *College Teaching, 48*(4), 129–135. doi: 10.1080/87567550009595829

Rhoads, R.A. (1995). Learning from the coming-out experiences of college males. *Journal of College Student Development, 36*(1), 67–74.

Sanlo, R.L., Rankin, S., & Schoenberg, R. (Eds.). (2002). *Our place on campus: Lesbian, gay, bisexual, transgender services and programs in higher education.* Westport, CT: Greenwood Press.

Schueler, L.A., Hoffman, J.A., & Peterson, E. (2009). Fostering safe, engaging campuses for lesbian, gay, bisexual, transgender, and questioning students. In S.R. Harper & S.J. Quaye (Eds.), *Student engagement in higher education.* New York, NY: Routledge.

Strayhorn, T.L. (2006). Factors influencing the academic achievement of first-generation college students. *NASPA Journal, 43*(4), 82–111.

Terenzini, P.T., Springer, L., Yaeger, P.M., Pascarella, E.T., & Nora, A. (1996). First-generation college students: Characteristics, experiences, and cognitive development. *Research in Higher Education, 37*(1), 1–22.

Tinto, V. (1993). *Leaving college: Rethinking the causes and cures of student attrition* (2nd ed.). Chicago, IL: University of Chicago Press.

Tinto, V. (2003). Learning better together: The impact of learning communities on student success. *Higher Education Monograph Series,* 1–8.

Watson, L., & Kuh, G.D. (1996). The influence of dominant race environments on student involvement, perceptions, and educational gains: A look at historically Black and predominantly White liberal arts institutions. *Journal of College Student Development, 37*(4), 415–424.

TWENTY ONE

The Student-Veteran Experience

Mark Bauman, Denise L. Davidson, and Daniel Roesch

Introduction

> *I've seen some of the worst possible things I think a human could see; I've done some of the worst things I think a person could do in their life in situations; I'm glad most people don't have to see. I lost people who were very good at what they did—very nice people who were just there for money for college or there cause they had a kid that was born unexpectedly and this was the only way they could get a job cause where they are from there's no economy and they just go out and they try to do their job every day and they end up not* (pausing) *being able to come home.* (Bauman, 2009 p. 129)

Randy was a 23-year-old college sophomore when he provided the passage above. His reflection on his 18 months in Iraq was mature and thoughtful, qualities that many student-veterans exhibit. And Randy is similar to student-veterans in another respect: He is one of several hundred thousand who are currently enrolled and attending classes on our nation's campuses. Research related to this group has been slow to materialize; similarly, efforts to serve this population on our campuses have been mixed. What is clear, however, is that student-veteran enrollment in higher education is likely to increase with the passage of time and the continual draw down of our armed forces in the Middle East. How, then, can we best understand these students? How might this understanding translate into effective and helpful campus services—services that focus on academic and personal success and that engage the student-veteran in campus life?

The purpose of this chapter is to highlight key areas related to the student-veteran population that is currently (or will soon be) on campus. Examined first is the Post-9/11 GI Bill, under which more than 700,000 military personnel have already enrolled in college. The chapter then reviews selected and contemporary findings related to student-veteran transition into higher education. While many readers of this study may not necessarily be GI Bill administrators, many will work with student-veterans in other capacities. And it is this transition into and through higher education that presents the best opportunity to work with student-veterans over a period of time. This review is coupled with implications for student development, an area that is particularly thin with regard to understanding this population. The chapter ends with some notes about the importance of language and ideas for moving forward, framed in part by President Barack Obama's recent declaration concerning military student and family success on campus. Readers should note that writing of this kind presents a snapshot of sorts. To that end, continued renewal of information, review of resources, and efforts to remain current with various laws and benefits are imperative.

Post-9/11 GI Bill

Though veterans and other military personnel have enrolled in college for generations, their numbers skyrocketed with the passage of the Servicemen's Readjustment Act in 1944 (Nam, 1964). This law, also known as the GI Bill, provided educational benefits to millions of service personnel returning from the Second World War (Mettler, 2005). In the decade following its passage, some 2.2 million veterans attended college or received postsecondary education or training (Mettler, 2005), some of whom would likely not have followed such a path without these newly created educational benefits (Nam, 1964). The GI Bill has experienced many adjustments and modifications since its initial passage, resulting in alternating declines and improvements in benefits over the last 70 years (Humes, 2006). But what has remained consistent is the educational opportunity afforded to service personnel who are either active-duty military, reserve or National Guard, or otherwise honorably discharged from military service.

Many present-day service personnel have access to a more fortified GI Bill than their historical counterparts, and this has resulted in a substantial increase in active-duty military and veteran enrollment (McBain, Kim, Cook, & Snead, 2012). Eligibility criteria for the Post-9/11 GI Bill include "at least 90 aggregate days on active duty after September 10, 2001, or [an] honorabl[e] discharge[] from active duty for a service-connected disability after serving 30 continuous days following September 10, 2001" (Department of Veterans Affairs, 2012). As a service member accrues active duty time, the educational benefit increases accordingly (Department of Veterans Affairs, 2012). Many college and university personnel are familiar with the basic GI Bill benefit insofar as it covers tuition costs, either partially or fully. But the Post-9/11 GI Bill benefit goes beyond tuition, providing financial support related to housing, books, and supplies (Department of Veterans Affairs, 2012). As generous as these provisions are, costs at many private 4-year institutions would still exceed what the new GI Bill covers. In an effort to address this shortfall, more than 1,770 colleges and universities have agreed to work with the federal government to make their institutions more accessible to veterans (Department of Veterans Affairs, n.d.[a]). With this effort, which is called the Yellow Ribbon Program, "approved institutions of higher learning and the VA [can] partially or fully fund tuition and fee expenses that exceed the established thresholds under the Post-9/11 GI Bill" (Department of Veterans Affairs, n.d.[a]). Given this robust package of benefits, colleges and universities have seen a collective increase in veteran enrollment. McBain and colleagues (2012) noted that "more than 500,000 veterans and their families have utilized Post-9/11 GI

Bill benefits since the law's enactment in 2008" (p. 7). Data provided more recently revealed that 773,000 military members, veterans, and eligible family have used these Post-9/11 GI Bill benefits (Department of Veterans Affairs, n.d.[b]).

Information regarding the Post-9/11 GI Bill benefits—as well as all other educational programs—is highly detailed and nuanced. Given that veteran enrollment is slated to continue its upward trend (Gayheart, 2009), we cannot overemphasize the importance of becoming familiar with these programs. Much in the way that well-rounded practitioners apprise themselves of many or most of their campus offerings and programs, greater knowledge of the various educational opportunities and their associated components for student-veterans will allow for more informative and focused conversations with this group. Further, scores of information packets, brochures, handouts, and other publications are readily available through the Veterans Affairs website, making regular visits a requirement for any practitioner working with this population (see, e.g., benefits.va.gov/gibill/handouts_forms.asp).

Transition to Higher Education: Understanding the Population

Providing educational benefits in the form of financial support is certainly a critical variable with regard to veterans' access to higher education. However, this financial piece is only one aspect of the whole picture. Once on campus, some student-veterans may require more than financial assistance to ensure a successful experience. DiRamio, Ackerman, and Mitchell (2008) were the first researchers to publish an empirical work describing the transition experiences and subsequent challenges faced by today's student-veterans (Bauman & Davidson, 2012). In this landmark study, the authors chronicled the experiences of 25 student-veterans as they transitioned from the military to higher education. Participants in the study discussed their accelerated maturity relative to their civilian, college-going peers, their interest in establishing relationships with other college student-veterans, their desire to downplay or otherwise understate their military experience on the campus, and the arduous paperwork and administrative hurdles related to tapping into one's educational benefits (DiRamio et al., 2008).

Though the DiRamio paper was the first study of its kind, subsequent research has reinforced its findings. Bauman's (2009) study of 24 stopped-out student-veterans showed that they arrive on campus with some very real (but often hidden) struggles, including a change in one's status (from "hero" to unknown college student, sometimes unemployed or underemployed), muscle memory responses in the civilian world that were ingrained during deployment (reacting to loud noises, reaching for a weapon), an absent or largely moved-on social network, and difficulty fitting in with the remaining, often more youthful and less mature peer group. One participant summed up the overall experience in this way: "you hope that someone pushed pause when you left and hit play when you return" (Bauman, 2009, p. 164). Findings from Rumann and Hamrick's (2010) study echoed many of these results. Their research revealed conflicts in the various roles and settings that student-veterans occupy (college student, military member, campus culture, military culture), lingering stress and anxiety following active duty, advanced maturity, and difficulty connecting with new civilian peers once back on campus (Rumann & Hamrick, 2010).

Livingston, Havice, Cawthon, and Fleming's (2011) study of 15 student-veterans corresponded with this growing understanding. The researchers found returning veterans to be largely invisible, a concept that Livingston, Scott, Havice, and Cawthon (2012) later referred to as "social camouflage." This sense of invisibility—indeed this sense of "social camouflage"—is at times intentional, since student-veterans often seek to blend in so as to avoid being "called out" as representatives of the war or the military, and they rarely use their military status for special consideration or treatment (Livingston et al., 2011). While in some ways aligning with their military values, the Livingston research team (2011) noted the bidirectional consequences of this social camouflage. On the one hand, these student-veterans generally did not seek academic support; on the other, campus practitioners found it difficult to reach a population that wished to remain off the radar (Livingston et al., 2011).

The selected research mentioned above provides a foundation for understanding the transition to higher education experienced by some student-veterans. While this footing is important, readers should also be familiar with more nuanced research that highlights issues faced by military personnel in general, as well as those returning to college more specifically. Mental health issues represent some of these challenges faced by some military personnel—including activated reservists and National Guard members—which is often a significant portion of the campus veteran population. Since World War II, contemporary researchers have indicated the broad presence of mental health challenges in soldiers who participated in major American military campaigns, including the Korean War (Sutker, Winstead, Galina, & Allain, 1991), the Vietnam War (Kaylor, King, & King, 1987), and Operation Desert Storm (Bell et al., 2000).

Still other researchers have focused on the psychological illnesses themselves, with many scholars, particularly since the early 1980s, concentrating on the presence—or absence—of post-traumatic stress disorder, or PTSD (Parker-Konkle, Parker, & Reeves, 2005). The Vietnam War was the first military campaign to truly bring mental health issues to the attention of the American public, due in large part to the creation of the diagnosis of PTSD. In 1980, PTSD as a diagnosis was codified in the American Psychiatric Association's *Diagnostic and Statistical Manual Version III* (Lasiuk & Hegadoren, 2006). Research examining today's veterans of Iraq and Afghanistan shows that PTSD is clearly a concern. Many service personnel deployed to Iraq and Afghanistan are experiencing the types of stressors linked to the development of PTSD (Hoge et al., 2004). However, as with other mental health studies, reports on the actual prevalence of PTSD in current veterans vary. Auchterlonie, Hoge, and Milliken's (2006) initial study of Army and Marine personnel revealed that almost 18% of participants returning from Iraq screened positive for PTSD; a subsequent study found 30–35% percent of returning veterans screening positive for PTSD (Auchterlonie, Hoge, & Milliken, 2007).

While PTSD seems to be the most frequently examined mental health challenge, others are equally deserving of practitioners' attention. For example, in one of the more comprehensive studies, several thousand service personnel were tested before and after their deployment. Results from this study by Hoge and fellow researchers (2004) noted that mental health disorders in veterans covered four main areas: depression, anxiety, PTSD, and alcohol misuse. Similarly, Gaylord's examination (2006) outlined a number of common challenges experienced by returning service personnel, including major depression, substance abuse, adjustment disorders, and anger and violence issues. Rudd, Goulding, and Bryan's (2011) national study of student-veterans revealed that "the 'average' student veteran participant reported experiencing moderate anxiety, moderately severe depression, significant symptoms of PTSD, and evidencing at least some noticeable suicide risk" (p. 358). And a report from the RAND Corporation (2008) demonstrated that "about one third of returning servicemembers report symptoms of a mental health or cognitive condition" (p. 2). These conditions, which include traumatic brain injury, can "affect mood, thoughts, and behavior and often remain invisible to other servicemembers, family, and society" (RAND, 2008, p. 1).

At times this research presents a challenging picture. However, as practitioners we know that effective engagement and effective student development with this population begins with understanding—and this understanding must be comprehensive in nature, including a firm grasp of those difficult findings. To be clear, these findings *do not* apply to all returning service personnel nor do they apply to all students. In fact, Bauman (2009) and others (e.g., Rumann & Hamrick, 2010) indicated that some student-veterans were indifferent to or unaffected by their return. Either way, the key component for the practitioner is a sense of readiness, which is particularly important given the lack of clarity regarding the overall readiness of colleges and universities. Rudd and colleagues (2011) commented that "little discussion has emerged about how these issues are, or will be, handled on college and university campuses, not to mention the expected frequency, severity, and potentially unique nature of problems" (p. 354). O'Herrin (2011) concurred with this assessment, stating that postsecondary institutions welcome student-veteran enrollees but lack a clear sense of how best to assist this population. What is clear, however, is that our understanding of this population is still growing. Certainly the discussions revolving around student-veterans have increased in the last few years, but, much remains to be learned. And while colleges and universities must ready themselves as institutions, so too must individual practitioners, for the second "veteran bulge" of college enrollment has clearly begun (Bauman & Davidson, 2012).

Implications for Student Development

Present-day student development theory has grown to address a wide range of individuals and groups on campus and includes an emphasis on co-curricular engagement and involvement (Astin, 1999; Dannells & Stage, 2000). Although theory is an important building block for the field of student affairs, the current base provides scant attention to the development of students who are also members of the military, the main exception being with transition theory. Alternately, trying to make a theory fit this population may also lead practitioners astray. For example, Evans, Forney, Guido, Patton, and Renn, (2010) state that Chickering's theory is based on the notion that identity development in college, and the environmental and external influences of this development, is at the center of the college years. There is no provision, however, for one's military experience or involvement in this model. Given the seemingly transformative nature of the military experience, it seems reasonable that a student who is also a military member could develop in a manner either partially or entirely separate from Chickering's scheme. Similarly, theories of student engagement that consider military involvement are also absent. For example, Astin (1999) posited that the right type and amount of involvement in one's college can increase one's connectedness to that institution, thereby increasing overall satisfaction and success. But what of those students whose "involvement" takes them away from the campus? What if the student is very involved in the military and that involvement subsequently impacts his or her overall satisfaction or identity development? Consider, too, the ROTC cadet who is very involved in his or her ROTC community. This involvement might look and function quite differently than an undergraduate who is engaged in student government, residence life, student activities, or other such areas. Like developmental theories, theories of student involvement or engagement also miss the military student group.

In light of the start-stop-start enrollment patterns exhibited by some student-veterans, coupled with the often advanced maturation of this population, it is easy to see why theories of student development and/or student engagement are not readily applicable. What does seem clear, however, is the importance of the collective. That is, rather than placing their focus solely on *individual* student development, practitioners would be wise to consider the meaningful and important relationships shared between student-veterans, resulting in *collective* identity development. Brenner and colleagues (2008) found that returning veterans were highly bonded with other veterans. Similarly, Wong, Kolditz, Millen, and Potter (2003), in trying to understand what motivated military personnel in times of war, found that the presence of one's "buddies" was the critical variable. This collective experience, which results in a collective identity, occurs between military members in general, and during and after deployment more specifically, and is readily apparent on most campuses with a student-veteran population. Given this proclivity for collective identity development, it is thus no surprise that much emphasis has been placed on the formation of student-veteran organizations. Summerlot, Green, and Parker (2009) noted that:

> Veterans are interested in connecting with fellow students who have similar experiences. Student organizations provide a vehicle through which veterans can express a collective voice of advocacy while also supplying a setting for learning, reflection, and participation beyond the traditional classroom. It is important to note that a student veterans organization can provide an environment to support transition from the military to the campus. (p. 74)

If your campus has not already established such an organization, moving in this direction is an excellent first step, as these groups can facilitate important relational connectivity, spawn collective identity development, and seek to establish that sometimes-missing component of veteran engagement with the campus. Pragmatically, forming such an organization requires minimal expense while potentially providing positive returns.

Once identity development is understood *collectively*, identity formation during college within the *individual* student-veteran can be considered because, for these individuals, group identity may be at least equal to—if not greater than—individual identity. How then might individual identity development be influenced by: (a) being a member of the military and (b) being deployed for an extended period? To date, the most commonly applied theoretical lens is adult transition theory, advanced by Goodman, Schlossberg, and Anderson (2006). DiRamio, Ackerman, and Mitchell's (2008) article used this theoretical model to understand the study's participants, as did Rumann and Hamrick (2010) and others (e.g., Livingston et al., 2011). Certainly application of adult transition theory—particularly the ideas of moving in, moving through, and moving out, along with consideration of the 4S's—is entirely reasonable. But to advance our collective understanding—and our collective ability to meet the needs of this population—empirical work must move beyond this theoretical lens. Indeed, although any theoretical model has its limitations, future research should at least consider new student development constructs so as to adequately understand the student-veterans on our campuses.

Importance of Language

At this point, readers of this chapter may have noticed that a number of terms are used to refer to this population (student-veterans, service members, military-students, military personnel, etc.). Though many categorize this group as "student-veterans," it is clear that this term is not accurate in all cases. As defined by the federal government:

> *U.S. Code, Title 38, Part 1, Chapter 1, Section 101*, the term "veteran" means a person who served in the active military, naval, or air service, and who was discharged or released therefrom under conditions other than dishonorable.

Note, too, that the definitions used by one's state may also encompass certain details, exclusions, or inclusions with which practitioners should be familiar. Add to this the notion that not all veteran benefits have identical eligibility requirements, and it becomes clear that each "student-veteran" should be regarded individually and not automatically grouped with the larger population simply by virtue of his or her military affiliation. Consider the following examples:

- A member of ROTC.
- A member of ROTC who is also enlisted in the Army reserves.
- An enlisted individual who finished basic training the summer between high school graduation and college enrollment and is currently "drilling" once per month.
- An enlisted individual in the Naval reserve who served two tours of active duty in Iraq and is now a student on your campus, but still in the Naval reserve.
- An enlisted individual who is now in the "inactive ready reserve."
- A Marine officer who retired after 20 years of service and is now enrolled as a graduate student at your university.

Who meets the federal definition of "veteran?" Who meets your state's definition of "veteran?" Who is eligible for Post-9/11 benefits? Who is eligible for tuition assistance or other educational benefits? The point is to demonstrate the great diversity that is present in the "student-veteran" population on your campus. Certainly these individuals may feel a kinship to one another and, as a result, demonstrate the collective identity that was noted earlier. But from a practitioner's perspective, it is crucial to understand each individual's background, history, and current status, after which the ability to serve the student is greatly increased. Care should also be given to the term(s) used to refer to this population; as with other groups, language that is the most inclusive is preferred.

Pushing on a bit further with language, consider the campus that wishes to hold an event on Veteran's Day. A well-intentioned program flyer might say something like this: "*Come Recognize Our Soldiers as We Celebrate Veteran's Day.*" Recognizing military students on Veteran's Day is of course an excellent gesture and one that any campus could reasonably adopt at little or no cost. Unfortunately, however, the statement on this imaginary flyer reveals the campus' limited knowledge of the military. The term "soldier" refers specifically to a member of the Army—and *only* a member of the Army (or Army National Guard, or Army Reserves, to be clear). As a result, this sign unintentionally excludes personnel from the Marines, Air Force, Navy, and Coast Guard. This population can already feel marginalized; small oversights like these can amplify that marginalization.

These two brief examples are offered as evidence of the nuances and intricacies that are present within this population. To us as practitioners, it is entirely understandable that a full grasp of this group's language, culture, and traditions is lacking. However, on any given campus there are current and former military personnel—some of whom likely work alongside you—who would generally be quite pleased to provide guidance in this area. Consider tapping into this already existing campus network as you design programs and services. This will lessen the burden on the practitioner for knowing all the nuances, and it will contribute to the discussion with those members of your campus who are resident experts.

Moving Forward

Although the conflicts in the Middle East began more than 10 years ago, our understanding of the student-veteran population—past, present, and future—is limited. While the conversation surrounding these students has clearly intensified, more work is yet to be done. Often the emphasis is on administrative assistance, processing of the GI Bill, and other related paperwork. Bauman (2012) argued that, while such efforts were indeed critical, little attention was being paid to these students once they arrived on campus. But in 2013, President Obama made an aggressive effort to address this void. Recognizing that this void was more than administrative support, the President presented *8 Keys to Success: Supporting Veterans, Military and Military Families on Campus* (U.S. Department of Education, 2013). These guidelines' emphasis is on creating an atmosphere of inclusion and engagement, providing comprehensive support, training of faculty and staff related to this population, tracking and monitoring of student progress, and consolidating campus efforts for all military students and their families. Practitioners—especially those in the process of developing programs for their military student population—could easily use this as a guide. For those programs that are well underway, assessing oneself in relation to these eight keys to success provides an excellent benchmark for progress. Further, it provides a tool by which military students themselves can assess individual colleges and universities in terms of their readiness to assist service personnel and their families as they transition into higher education and move through their academic careers. Though stated early in the implementation of this initiative the president's remarks created goals that colleges and universities across the country can seek to achieve and that military personnel and their families can use to make enrollment choices.

More specifically, institutions should make student-veterans a *genuine* priority. Much as colleges and universities seek to serve distinct populations, so too should efforts be made to serve this group. To that end, a review of federal guidelines, efforts, and recommendations, coupled with an analysis of best practices from around the country, would certainly make an excellent start. However, in that each campus has its own personality, its own nuances, and its own culture, truly effective programmatic efforts may use these ideas as guides but should tailor efforts locally. In concert with one's existing student-veteran population, and with collaboration from veterans within the faculty and staff ranks, campuses can endeavor to serve those who have served us so well.

References

Astin, A. (1999). Student involvement: A developmental theory for higher education. *Journal of College Student Development, 40*(5), 518–529.

Auchterlonie, J.L., Hoge, C.W., & Milliken, C.S. (2006). Mental health problems, use of mental health services, and attrition from military service after returning from deployment to Iraq or Afghanistan. *Journal of the American Medical Association, 295*(9), 1023–1032.

Auchterlonie, J.L., Hoge, C.W., & Milliken, C.S. (2007). Longitudinal assessment of mental health problems among active and reserve component soldiers returning from the Iraq War. *Journal of the American Medical Association, 298*(18), 2141–2148.

Bauman, M. (2009). *Called to serve: The military mobilization of undergraduates* (Unpublished doctoral dissertation). Pennsylvania State University, State College.

Bauman, M. (2012). From the box to the pasture: Student-veterans returning to campus. *College Student Affairs Journal, 31*(1), 41–53.

Bauman, M., & Davidson, D.L. (2012). We've been here before: Meeting the needs of student-veterans. *CSPA-NYS Journal of Student Affairs, 12*(2), 3–22.

Bell, N.S., Amoroso, P.J., Williams, J.O., Yore, M.M., Engle Jr., C.C., Senier, L., ... Wegman, D.H. (2000). Demographic, physical, and mental health factors associated with deployment of U.S. army soldiers to the Persian Gulf. *Military Medicine, 165*(10), 762–772.

Brenner, L.A., Gutierrez, P.M., Cornette, M.M., Betthauser, L.M., Bahraini, N., & Staves, P.J. (2008). A qualitative study of potential suicide risk factors in returning combat veterans. *Journal of Mental Health Counseling, 30*(3), 211–225.

Dannells, M., & Stage, F.K. (2000). *Linking theory to practice*. New York, NY: Routledge.

Department of Veterans Affairs. (n.d.[a]). *Post-9/11 GI Bill Yellow Ribbon FAQs*. Retrieved from http://www.benefits.va.gov/gibill/docs/factsheets/2012_Yellow_Ribbon_Student_FAQs.pdf

Department of Veterans Affairs. (n.d.[b]). *VA and the post 9/11 GI Bill*. Retrieved from http://www.va.gov/opa/issues/post_911_gibill.asp

Department of Veterans Affairs. (2012). *Post 9/11 GI Bill: It's your future*. Retrieved from http://www.benefits.va.gov/gibill/docs/pamphlets/ch33_pamphlet.pdf

DiRamio, D., Ackerman, R., & Mitchell, R.L. (2008). From combat to campus: Voices of student-veterans. *NASPA Journal, 45*(1), 73–102.

Evans, N.J., Forney, D.S., Guido, F.M., Patton, L.D., & Renn, K.A. (2010). *Student development in college: Theory, research, and practice* (2nd ed.). San Francisco, CA: Jossey-Bass.

Gayheart, J. (2009). Increasing veteran enrollment on college campuses: Implementation of consumer behavior strategies. *Gatton Student Research Publication, 1*(2), 1–19. Retrieved from http://gatton.uky.edu/GSRP/Downloads/Issues/Fall2009/Increasing%20Veteran%20Enrollment%20on%20College%20Campuses.pdf

Gaylord, K.M. (2006). The psychosocial effects of combat: The frequently unseen injury. *Critical Care Nursing Clinics of North America, 18*(3), 349–357.

Goodman, J., Schlossberg, N.K., & Anderson, M.L. (2006). *Counseling adults in transition: Linking practice with theory*. New York, NY: Springer.

Hoge, C.W., Castro, C.A., Messer, S.C., McGurk, D., Cotting, D.I., & Koffman, R.L. (2004). Combat duty in Iraq and Afghanistan, mental health problems, and barriers to care. *New England Journal of Medicine, 351*(1), 13–22.

Humes, E. (2006). *Over here: How the GI Bill transformed the American dream*. Orlando, FL: Harcourt.

Kaylor, J.A., King, D.W., & King, L.A. (1987). Psychological effects of military service in Vietnam: A meta-analysis. *Psychological Bulletin, 102*(2), 257–271.

Lasiuk, G.C., & Hegadoren, K.M. (2006). Posttraumatic stress disorder part I: Historical development of the concept. *Perspectives in Psychiatric Care, 42*(1), 13–20.

Livingston, W.G., Havice, P.A., Cawthon, T.W., & Fleming, D.S. (2011). Coming home: Student veterans' articulation of college re-enrollment. *Journal of Student Affairs Research and Practice, 48*(3), 315–331.

Livingston, W.G., Scott, D.A., Havice, P.A., & Cawthon, T.W. (2012). Social camouflage: Interpreting male student veterans' behavior for residence life professionals. *Journal of College and University Student Housing, 39*(1), 176–185.

McBain, L., Kim, Y.M., Cook, B.J., & Snead, K.M. (2012, July). *From soldier to student II: Assessing campus programs for veterans and service members*. Washington, DC: American Council on Education. Retrieved from: http://www.acenet.edu/news-room/Documents/From-Soldier-to-Student-II-Assessing-Campus-Programs.pdf

Mettler, S. (2005). *Soldiers to citizens: The GI Bill and the making of the greatest generation*. Oxford, UK: Oxford University Press.

Nam, C.B. (1964). Impact of the "GI Bills" on the educational level of the male population. *Social Forces, 43*(1), 26–32.

O'Herrin, E. (2011). Enhancing veteran success in higher education. *Peer Review, 13*(1). Retrieved from http://www.aacu.org/peerreview/pr-wi11/prwi11_oherrin.cfm

Parker-Konkle, D.J., Parker, J.D., & Reeves, R.R. (2005). War-related mental health problems of today's veterans. *Psychiatric Annals, 35*(11), 930–942.

RAND Center for Military Health Policy Research (2008, April). *Invisible wounds: Mental health and cognitive care needs of America's returning veterans.* Retrieved from http://www.rand.org/pubs/research_briefs/RB9336

Rudd, M.D., Goulding, J., & Bryan, C.J. (2011). Student veterans: A national survey exploring psychological symptoms and suicide risk. *Professional Psychology: Research and Practice, 42*(5), 354–360.

Rumann, C.B., & Hamrick, F.A. (2010). Student veterans in transition: Re-enrolling after war zone deployments. *Journal of Higher Education, 81*(4), 431–458.

Summerlot, J., Green, S.-M., & Parker, D. (2009). Student veterans organizations. In R. Ackerman & D. DiRamio (Eds.), Creating a veteran-friendly campus: Strategies for transition and success. *New Directions for Student Services, 126* (pp. 71–79). San Francisco, CA: Jossey-Bass.

Sutker, P.B., Winstead, D.K., Galina, Z.H., & Allain, A.N. (1991). Cognitive deficits and psychopathology among former prisoners of war and combat veterans of the Korean conflict. *American Journal of Psychiatry, 148*(1), 67–72.

U.S. Department of Education. (2013). *8 keys to success: Supporting veterans, military and military families on campus.* Retrieved from http://www.ed.gov/blog/2013/08/8-keys-to-success-supporting-veterans-military-and-military-families-on-campus/

Wong, L., Kolditz, T.A., Millen, R.A., & Potter, T.M. (2003). *Why they fight: Combat motivation in the Iraq war.* Carlisle Barracks, PA: Strategic Studies Institute, U.S. Army War College.

TWENTY TWO

Distance Learners: Their Challenges and Successes

Andy Casiello, Richard Overbaugh, Heather Huling, and Mitsue Blythe

Introduction

Understanding Distance Education

Distance education encompasses a broad range of instructional approaches and technologies driven by the assumption that faculty and students are not co-located but are connected through technology. Roblyer and Edwards (2000) define distance learning as "the acquisition of knowledge and skills through mediated information and instruction, encompassing all technologies and other forms of learning at a distance" (p. 192). The history of this modality of education in the United States can be traced to the generation of Pennsylvania State University's correspondence study in 1892. Much change has taken place since its formulation from early modalities of correspondence via postal mail (Prewitt, 1998) to broadcast systems and recorded media. The development and marketization of the Internet enhanced distance learning, and modern approaches are now entirely dominated by the use of mediated instruction through this medium (Nagel, Maniam, & Leavell, 2011). Because of the ever-changing enhancements to technology and the resulting societal impact, among other factors, distance education as a mode of learning has become mainstream in recent years.

The use of distance learning modalities, in which teacher and student are likely separated through geographic and even temporal distance, has been expanding at a tremendous rate over the past decade. According to a study conducted in 2002, "less than one-half of all higher education institutions reported online education was critical to their long term strategy" (Allen & Seaman, 2013, p. 16). This number has increased substantially in the last decade and stood at 70% in 2013.

Enrollment in online education in the United States has grown from 9.6% of the total enrollment in higher education institutions in 2002 to over 30% in 2011 (Allen & Seaman, 2013, p. 17), and that number is growing by 3–4% each year. In the United States alone, over 6.7 million students took at least one online course during the Fall 2011 semester. The growth of distance learners is partially due to the issue of access to higher education. Lei and Gupta (2010) note: "Initially, distance learning was created for students who were unable to attend school" (p. 616). According to Caruth and Caruth (2013), distance education "is thriving internationally, particularly in higher education, and shows no signs of slowing down. The ease of learning via the Internet has made it viable to reach students that were previously unserved." Domestically and internationally, distance learning is accelerating, with an increase in student enrollment fueled by the increase in student access.

Online Learning Is Not Just About Geographical Distance

Despite distance learning's common association with access to education for those who either reside in geographically remote areas or have time or career considerations that limit their ability to attend traditional daytime classes, this educational modality continues to move into the mainstream of higher education. According to Lei and Gupta (2010), "Presently, distance education has never been so popular. A large, diverse group of students comprise the target audience of Distance Education. Regardless of their demographic backgrounds and academic disciplines, students all over the globe are embracing these educational resources" (p. 617). Online learning is here to stay, and it is an increasingly important component of most higher education institutions' strategic plan for the future.

A plethora of attractions exists for both institutions and students in regard to online education. First, distance education increases the number of courses an institution can offer and provides a larger audience without the necessity of expanding physical classroom space (Lei & Gupta, 2010). For students, online education solves time and location problems. Students are able to schedule courses around busy work and life schedules, can often work at their own pace, and have the convenience of working from home or office, all the while avoiding travel time and the related transportation costs (Lei & Gupta, 2010). Given the flexibility in time and place of asynchronous online education, students can plan around busy work schedules and, for students with children, around their soccer practice, dinnertime, and bedtime activities (Nagel et al., 2011). The benefits of distance education for institutions and students alike contribute to the growth of this modality.

Growing Significance of Distance and Online Learning

As noted above, distance education systems, though not a new educational phenomenon, have grown significantly over the past 15 years. Faced with declining state-funded support and growing competition from private online colleges, public institutions that were considered fairly traditional academic research institutions have begun to offer distance education programs. Many of these institutions have added distance education broadly within their offerings as more students, many of them of traditional age, have been enrolling in such record numbers. As computer systems have become a common and central component of our lives, education delivered by way of these systems has followed suit. In years past, distance education students were older, already a part of the professional workforce, and returning to extend their educational credentials to enhance their careers. Today's distance education is attracting increased numbers of graduating high school students who are already proficient, ready, and accepting of technology-based education. Thus it is imperative that higher education's administrators, faculty, and staff understand who today's distance learning students are, what needs they bring to the education process, what successes and challenges are the hallmarks of this demographic, and how best to support their increasing numbers in the future.

Profile of Distance Learners

Historical Demographics of Distance Learners

For years, higher education has maintained a clear depiction of distance learners. They were adults between the ages of 25 and 45, largely female, with familial obligations and time constraints. They were unable to leave their communities and homes to complete a degree program on-campus in a traditional academic setting. Motivated to pursue a degree primarily for the purpose of gaining employment or advancing their careers, these students were focused, results oriented, and uninterested in the traditions and social dynamics of a campus community. Access, cost, and convenience were the driving factors in deciding whether or not to complete a degree program, and distance learning degree programs were often the only option for distance learners.

Contemporary Demographics of Distance Learners

Distance education, even in its earliest forms, made higher education accessible to these place- and time-bound learners. Broadly defined, distance learning is the delivery of instruction to students who are not physically present in a traditional, face-to-face classroom environment. This instruction can occur when faculty and students meet through the use of technology at the same time (synchronously), or when instructional materials are provided through the use of technology and are available at any time (asynchronously). The synchronous delivery systems used to provide simultaneous instruction at multiple remote locations met the needs of adult learners in the past. Today, however, with the broad reach and acceptance of the Internet, the growth of online learning has resulted in a more diverse student population spanning multiple strata. On-campus students, traditional-age students, and the traditionally defined distance learners are now taking online courses to complete their degrees. At Old Dominion University, a public doctoral research institution located in Norfolk, Virginia, student demographics reflect that trend. While still predominantly female (63.4%), 48% of enrolled students in technology-delivered courses are full-time students. Further, 41% are under the age of 26, 67% are in undergraduate courses, and 59% are located either on campus or within 50 miles of the campus.

Availability of Distance and Online Learning

According to the Babson Survey Research Group and College Board 2012 Survey of Online Learning (Allen & Seaman, 2013), online offerings of complete degree programs have increased from 48.9% in 2002 to 70.6% in 2012. Nearly one-third of the 21 million American college students have taken at least one online course, and approximately 3 million are estimated to be enrolled in fully online programs. This trend is mirrored in the K–12 environment. In the Evergreen Education Group's report entitled *Keeping Pace With K–12 Online and Blended Learning: An Annual Review of Policy and Practice* (Watson, Murin, Vashaw, Gemin, & Rapp, 2013), it is reported that 27 states have virtual schools in place offering online courses, with over 600,000 total course enrollments as of Fall 2012. Thirty-one states have at least one full-time online school operating statewide. In 2012, approximately 275,000 students attended a full-time online school. In Virginia, for example, the state virtual school, Virtual Virginia, which serves middle and high school student populations, has been in operation since 2005. In the 2012–2013 school year, course enrollment reached 13,026, an increase of 102% over the prior year. Legislation is largely driving that increase. In 2012, the Commonwealth of Virginia instituted legislation modifying graduation requirements to include the successful completion of one virtual course. Other states with similar requirements include Alabama, Idaho, Florida, and Michigan.

As more students become familiar and comfortable with online learning at an earlier age, and as more colleges and universities leverage the power of online learning to enrich the learning experience and improve the efficiency of providing instruction for all student populations, clearly defining a distance learner will become even more challenging. Technology-delivered instruction will continue to serve a variety of student types, from on-campus freshmen, to in-region traditional-age students and adult learners, to international students. Their needs will vary, and their expectations regarding on-demand quality student services available online will continue to rise.

Accessing Student Services Online

Meeting the need for improved on-demand, online, central services, including admission, registration, student accounts, financial aid, schedule of classes, and so on, is critically important. In an environment where competition for highly qualified students is strong, providing high-quality, easy-to-use administrative service support online can determine whether or not a prospective student becomes newly admitted or a current student is retained. In a recent study of online learning, it was determined that student support services and university connection are important aspects of online learner retention (Heyman, 2010). Student interactions with all types of student support specialists can be as important to student persistence as are the academic courses and experiences they are engaged in (M. Moore & Kearsley, 2012).

Given the number of high-quality web conferencing resources available, many of the face-to-face interactions occurring on campus in these areas can easily be transferred to the online environment. Implementing such practices would require departments to modify business practices and train staff.

The limitations in these areas are no longer a result of limited quality communication options. There are now numerous online solutions available for servicing student-to-student, faculty-to-student, and institution-to-student communications. It is imperative that institutions committed to online learning invest in the creation of high-quality and responsive student services, just as they have invested in the development of high-quality online courses. As noted in the LAAP partnership grant program activity sponsored by the U.S. Department of Education in the late 1990s—and still relevant today—institutions should focus on implementing online student service solutions that best serve all students in an online environment, beginning with the core services and moving to more specialized service areas.

Students who participate in distance education systems are expected to become proficient in the use of these tools, to be able to manage their own computing and communications devices and resources, and to embrace the use of these technologies as a significant part of the educational experience. As digital natives have entered higher education, this is less of an impediment than it was in the past. Many of today's traditional-age college students grew up around these devices and tools—for example, Skype and FaceTime—and already use them in their everyday interactions with family and friends. While it is likely that students already have access to these devices and knowledge of their operation, the use of such ubiquitous Internet-based tools poses new challenges to institutions, faculty, and students.

Importance of Financial Aid

Financial aid is perhaps the leading determinant in the decision-making process of a distance learner. Providing online assistance with the financial aid process from start to finish can be one of the most important resources available online. Academic support services available to all students, but especially the distance learner, can have a significant impact on continuance and retention goals. These services include academic advising, accessibility services, tutoring, library services, bookstore services, technical support, and others.

Courses That Work for Today's Learner

As already noted, today's students have sought more flexible course delivery modes, and universities have responded by investing in the development of high-quality, engaging courses in online learning environments to attract and retain these online learners. Teams consisting of instructional designers, technologists, multimedia developers, and video production specialists, in partnership with faculty subject-matter experts, follow proven instructional design techniques to ensure that course content is rich and aligns with the objectives of the course and overall program. This front-end investment has been identified as being important to student satisfaction and persistence, since well-designed courses that motivate students through the use of relevant content and transferable knowledge positively influence those students' online learning experience (Park & Choi, 2009).

Training faculty to become competent online course facilitators is critical to the creation of online learning experiences that promote student engagement. Student-to-student, faculty-to-student, and student-to-interface interactions have been identified as important aspects of successful online student learning (Pentina & Neeley, 2007). The quality of faculty engagement with students has been established as a relevant aspect of student retention (Heyman, 2010). Both the delivery of instructional materials through a content management system and the interactions referenced above are necessary for transforming information into personally relevant knowledge and for keeping students engaged and motivated to complete a program (Boston, Ice, & Buress, 2012; M. Moore & Kearsley, 2012).

While to some extent student success can be attributed to all of the aspects of online learning discussed thus far, individual student characteristics and circumstances can be attributed to student success and satisfaction as well (Tinto, 1975). A student's age has been identified as a factor influencing student success in both on-campus and online environments (Patterson & McFadden, 2009). Transfer credit, maintaining a sufficient GPA, and making progress toward program completion have also been identified as being relevant to student retention (Boston et al., 2012). While more traditional distance learners are inclined to be more self-directed and disciplined, these student characteristics may not be as prevalent in traditional-aged students, and this can impact their success (Pentina & Neeley, 2007). Providing students with the opportunity to complete a self-assessment of their readiness for online learning or to explore their learning styles is one way to mitigate inappropriate student expectations and inadequate preparedness.

Given the nature and diversity of individual student circumstances, be they personal characteristics or external circumstances, accessible and timely university support in all relevant areas—from the registration process to academic advising—is critical to retaining distance learners (Heyman, 2010).

Challenges

Historical Characteristics of Distance Education

Distance education systems rely on technology to enable the connection between faculty and student, and often from student to student. The earliest systems of distance education involved distribution of printed books, instructions, and tests. The early days of radio and television saw the introduction of broadcast systems of education; later, larger colleges and universities set up their own such systems using broadcast television, Instructional Television Fixed Service (ITFS) microwave delivery, satellite broadcasting, and similar broadband communications systems. Most of these earlier systems utilized very expensive infrastructures located at both the central (teacher) location and the remote (student) locations. Such systems were expensive, but quite reliable, as qualified staffs of engineers and technicians could manage the entire infrastructure from end to end. With these systems, students were not required to purchase and manage the distance hardware, but would travel to nearby locations arranged for by the educational institution. These early solutions provided regional access but left potential students with the challenges of traveling to the nearest regional location and finding the time flexibility, family, and financial support systems necessary to take on the educational opportunities available through distance. Relatively modest communications systems, typically involving telephone communication, had the potential to leave students feeling isolated and removed from the on-campus students who might also be participating in the same course offerings.

Contemporary Characteristics of Distance Education

Today's infrastructure is quite different. Almost all current systems utilize Internet-based delivery wherein the actual connection occurs through the commodity Internet, and the technology on the student end is usually owned and maintained by the individual student. This introduces a variety of complexities and challenges to maintaining the infrastructure and to establishing and maintaining reliable communications connections. It also places challenges on the students in cases where they must purchase the necessary computer equipment, become competent in utilizing the related software, manage their own technology, and purchase and manage their own Internet connections.

Cost and financial implications. The cost of the equipment, often borne by the student either directly or indirectly through additional fees included with tuition, can be a barrier to entry for some. Reliability issues introduced by bottlenecks in broadband network bandwidth, network congestion, software version conflicts, and myriad other technical issues can cause interruption or delay in the time both faculty and students spend on the actual educational experience. Individuals may tolerate slow connections or disruptions of this type while using the tools for everyday communication or information gathering in their daily lives, but interruptions to live course lectures or interaction is the cause of much greater distress. While these technical problems plagued early adopters of Internet-based educational systems, advances in technology, bandwidth, computing power, technical support systems and procedures, and adoption and comfort with the technology have all aided in smoothing out many of these issues within mature educational environments, at least for those who can afford to purchase and manage the equipment.

Challenges for today's distance learner are numerous. They include the above-mentioned technical concerns and issues with the cost of the equipment, as well as concerns over access to broadband connectivity, cost of tuition, and any technology fees related to the distance delivery, understanding, and navigating of distance-related software and student support systems. They also include issues concerning the motivation and discipline necessary to be successful as a distance student.

Need for Self-Motivation and Discipline

Traditional "bricks and mortar" classes, held with faculty and fellow students at a regularly scheduled interval and particular time and place, afford students a structure and time parameter that can help them stay in sync with the course and coursework. However, the "asynchronous" nature of many online courses, whereby students work when/where their schedule allows, creates both additional flexibility and challenges related to the need for self-motivation. In such an environment it is easy to procrastinate, and students may find themselves overwhelmed when all assignments are required to be turned in. It is important for potential distance students to understand this concern and to create—and stick with—a time structure that works with their schedule. In their 2013 update to the annual Babson survey of online learning, Allen and Seaman (2013) found that students' need for additional discipline beyond what they would require to be successful in a standard face-to-face course is a major concern for institutions supporting online learners. They also noted the lower retention rates found with students who take exclusively online courses, versus those in face-to-face classes. This concern has increased in the past five years of that survey.

Incorrect Assumptions About Course Rigor

There may also be an (incorrect) assumption on the part of a potential distance student that online courses might be "easier" than an on-campus version of the same course. While there are examples of poorly created online courses (just as there are examples of poorly created and managed on-campus courses), most institutions and faculty work hard to create courses of the same rigor, with the same level of effort demanded, and the same learning outcomes as the on-campus counterparts. Unless the student stays connected, completes all reading and work in a timely manner, and expects to expend (at least) the same amount of energy with an online class, the student may fall behind or do poorly in an online course.

Access to Comprehensive Support Services

As institutions create student success centers full of services deemed necessary for today's student, and the population of distance education comes increasingly into alignment with the demographic of the traditional student, institutions are challenged to provide the same support services, tools, and approaches in an online format as they are providing to their on-campus populations. Institutions also must find ways of supporting the additional needs of the distance student, such as counseling them on self-discipline and self-motivation techniques, assisting with the selection of appropriate computer technology, and providing easy-to-follow pathways to student support systems for those who cannot simply roam the halls of the student center looking for help.

Connecting With Faculty and Students

A significant challenge to distance learning during its first two Internet-based decades was communication among faculty and students, especially when distance instruction meant asynchronous communication between the instructor and students, as well as between students. Earlier systems of distance education tended to be largely broadcast mode and followed fairly didactic, lecture-based approaches to education. Large pipes, such as broadcast television, connected faculty to students in one direction, but the return path from students to faculty—such as telephone or email connection—was often much more restricted. A great deal of research was conducted from the 1990s into the 2000s about the advantages and disadvantages of "slow motion" discourse; however, no matter how effective asynchronous discourse might be in certain situations and with particular learners, it was rarely efficient. In fact, asynchronous discourse is considered by many educators to be simply not suitable for seminar-type learning and is a deterrent to building advanced programs via distance. Thus, asynchronous communication, even within groups by way of tools such as discussion boards, wikis, blogs, and shared documents, remains inefficient. Many instructional situations with today's distance students demand synchronous communications, including the sharing of audio, video, and various media. Depending on students' level of self-efficacy and their own personalities, as well as their comfort with the material and with their colleagues and the faculty in the course, students may prefer to communicate asynchronously or synchronously.

Asynchronous communication, usually using the written word but now often using video and/or audio recording tools, allows students to gather their thoughts and put together a cogent argument, comment, or answer. Synchronous tools, such as live video and audio, allow a highly interactive give-and-take among participants. Each mode suits a different type of individual. As previously noted, however, often the decision on which tools to utilize is not made by an institution based on student preference, but rather on availability of tools and efficiency of the process. Student preference should be a consideration when developing online course and program structures; an optimal solution for the students might well be to find ways of including both types of communication.

Perceived Value of Online Education

In addition to the costs involved, not only with tuition but with the purchase, management, and maintenance of any necessary computer technology, potential concerns about feelings of isolation or lack of sense of community (especially with poorly managed or entirely asynchronous educational environments), and the need for additional discipline and self-motivation, there remains a concern among many in higher education that the perceived value of an "online degree" may lead to a lack of acceptance of online education by potential employers. Allen and Seaman (2013) found that 40% of surveyed academic leaders saw this "as an '*Important or a Very Important*' barrier" (p. 31) that has remained consistent over the years during which their survey has been conducted.

Successes

Increased Access to Higher Education

As mentioned above, in the United States over 6 million students participated in online education during the Fall 2011 semester alone. This widespread use of distance education has allowed many individuals who may have faced barriers to traditional on-campus education to advance their educations and their careers. As the United States has turned toward a knowledge economy, distance education has broadened access to the education necessary to prepare people for the jobs of today.

At Old Dominion University (ODU), a partnership generated in 1994 with the Virginia Community College System (VCCS) allows Virginia citizens to obtain a 2-year associates-level degree at their local community college campus, and then continue on with ODU at that same local campus by participating in upper-division courses, delivered through technology, toward a bachelor's degree, master's degree, or even a PhD. Today ODU and the VCCS have incorporated online delivery into many of the articulated programs, allowing students to participate in the entire educational experience by way of the Internet and freeing up individuals with time and place commitments to make the same investments in their future as their on-campus colleagues. Many of the students within this program have commented that without the flexibility of the distance connection, they simply would not have been able to work toward an advanced degree while working, raising a family, and so forth.

Improvements to Pedagogy and Interaction

Distance Learning is not simply about access to education, however. Instructional technologies are often used to enable interactions among participants that would be difficult to facilitate in a live classroom setting. Learning Management Systems (LMS), first used in distance education environments but now commonly used in campus-based learning, include asynchronous tools for communication such as threaded discussion functions. These tools allow students to read and consider one another's comments and reflect on each other's contributions, opinions, and input, while comparing and contrasting them with their own thinking. As stated above, students may not be inclined to speak up or contribute in other ways during live classroom sessions, as they are often more comfortable communicating in writing. Communication and interaction, initially difficult to conduct using early distance learning environments, are now often touted as advantages of modern LMSs.

In their recent study, Nagel and colleagues (2011) found that 74% of the higher education students in their survey felt that they understood the subject matter of the courses better with technology-delivered education. In addition, 87% of those surveyed indicated that the technology-delivered courses were more interesting, and 94% of the students indicated that they preferred to communicate with their professors electronically versus face-to-face. However, in general, both professors and students in this study felt that communications was an "issue" with online courses.

Academic Community in Online Learning

Education requires the transfer of information, combined with instructional approaches that enable critical thinking and learning. The process involves interaction and collaboration among participants and is emphasized by Garrison (2009), who asserts: "online learning approaches have been less about bridging distances and more about engaging learners in discourse and collaborative learning activities" (p. 94). Advances in LMSs such as Blackboard, along with educational communications tools such as Adobe Connect, provide significant horsepower for collaboration within these educational environments.

The Distance Experience

Why Many Students Choose Distributed Courses Over Campus-Based Courses

As highlighted in the introduction to this chapter, one of the purported advantages of distance learning is that students can attend when and where they want, which can be considered a lifestyle or convenience factor. Overbaugh, Nickel, and Brown (2006) validated this by surveying students who had a choice of taking the same course face-to-face or online. Students who chose online did so for convenience, whereas those who chose face-to-face did so because they believed they learned better by being in a traditional classroom with the instructor and fellow students—a metacognitive reason. Notably, both online and face-to-face sections used all the same web-based materials and projects. To see whether students in 2013 still choose course format for the same reasons, a similar survey was deployed by ODU to the same population of social science students as part of ongoing efforts to learn more about current and potential student preferences. This 2013 survey reflects essentially the same preferences and decisions by the students, with 76% of the students who elected to take the online version of the course indicating that they did so for convenience's sake, while 61.5% indicated that they also prefer to take courses in the online mode. Further, 75% of the students who selected the face-to-face version of the course did so because of preference, whereas the other 25% were unaware that there was an online section or the online section was full before they registered for the course. While there are certainly two camps of students—those who prefer face-to-face courses and those who prefer online—at many schools there is an increasing interest in online courses that is outpacing face-to-face growth. The reasons are likely to be changing attitudes and greater availability of the online courses for those already committed to online instruction, because it is their only option (because of work, family, etc.).

Academic Community and Today's Distributed Students

While the "distance" in distance education is often assumed to be geographical in scope, the more critical concept of "distance" with regard to the quality of the educational experience is "transactional distance." Moore (as cited in Saba, 2012) noted that "distance in education is a social and psychological phenomenon in contrast to the idea of distance in terms of physical separation between learner and instructor" (p. 32). The notion that learning can be more effective when there is a high level of communication is certainly not new. In 1938 John Dewey offered that "education is essentially a social process" (ch. 4, para. 15), and significant traditional theorists such as Vygotsky, Bandura, Pajares, and Jonassen based their work on the view that learners become better educated through interaction with others. However, the advent of asynchronous online learning in the 1990s led to a concerted effort to design instruction to build "classroom community" or, using our preferred term, "academic community." Today, institutions heavily involved in distance education work hard to reduce this "transactional distance" while at the same time embracing the geographical and temporal distance that is such an enabling feature for the enrolled student population. Often the goal is to provide the distance learner something as close to a transactional experience as possible, tightly linking all participants to allow a sense of academic community to prosper. The existence of academic community engenders a high level of trust and interaction among participants, regardless of the geographical or temporal distances between them and, perhaps more important, differences in cultures, socioeconomic status, life experience, academic expectations, and so on.

Why Reducing Transactional Distance Is Important

Today's students are aware that, as a result of global education and technology, discipline-specific knowledge is not enough. Students recognize the need to develop what are termed "soft skills": the ability to think critically, communicate effectively, work in teams, and use contemporary electronics. However, soft skills are nothing new; these types of skills have been important for many decades. But the reference changes periodically, with the latest term being "21st-century skills." It should be pointed out, however, that the emphasis on the importance of soft skills has changed because of the shift from the industrial age to the information age (Levy & Murnane, 2004).

Integrating and Engaging Students

Distributed students, as noted elsewhere in this chapter, often choose online courses to meet lifestyle needs, preferring the anytime/anywhere freedom of asynchronous courses. (This is a point that universities need to keep in mind, now that incorporating synchronous components with tools like Adobe Connect is easy.) Because academic community is based on the perspective that social processes are vital to the learning experience (Rovai, Baker, & Ponton, 2013), what are the ways instruction can be designed to engage students in active learning with each other or with their larger academic community or communities of practice? Students expect learning to be meaningful, relevant, and directly related to employment and, when applicable, professional standards and certifications.

Training of Faculty in the Use of Technology for Education

"Instructional technology" refers to any technology that either enhances the instructional process in some way or enables a new strategy. This term and the notion of "online education" are widely used in higher education vernacular to denote the idea of technology-delivered education as a pedagogical concept, no matter the geographical distance between faculty and students. Successful technology integration is predicated on the ability of instructors and students to use the technology without having to devote excessive brain power to the tool itself and thus getting in the way of the intended learning. Successful technology integration enhances the effectiveness, efficiency, and/or attractiveness of the instruction. Unfortunately, many professional development efforts focus strictly on the former, not the latter, and can result in less-than-ideal student and faculty satisfaction with the environment. This is especially true when a technology is imposed on faculty by an institution without sufficient input from users and training for users. Examples run the gamut from simple tools such as smart boards to complex tools such as classroom management systems. In order to effectively support the needs of today's distance learner, the faculty must be provided with appropriate tools for educational communications and instruction and then must be trained on the pedagogical applications of those tools, not just the technological and operational aspects.

Preparing Faculty to Meet the Needs of Today's Online Student

No treatise on contemporary distance students would be complete without at least a mention of the infrastructure, staff, and faculty who design, develop, and deliver meaningful instruction. Successful institutions commit to helping faculty use solid instructional designs and strategies from individual courses to whole programs. Typically, they also provide dedicated centers staffed by specialists that offer assistance, guidance, and development of distributed courses and programs, including media development. These centers work with instructors and administrators to build instruction based on best practices, research, and theory—not just technology itself.

Development of successful technology-delivered education begins with the creation of matrices that map content across the curriculum, including applicable national and state standards from accreditation and "add-on" certificates or programs, such as National Board Certification for Teachers. Just as important is the question of context, or what Reigeluth (2009) describes as "situationalities," which includes identifying values and conditions. Values refer to core values of the instructor, such as preferred instructional strategies (e.g., problem-based learning, direct instruction, or seminar-type learning), what kinds of instructional outcomes beyond content-specific outcomes, such as cognitive strategies or affective objectives they want to incorporate into their teaching. Conditions include a number of things that have an influence on the instructional strategies chosen, including learner characteristics (e.g., Do students want synchronous sessions? Are they older adults or traditionally aged, or a mix? Are they full- or part-time students?), and the learning environment (e.g., What instructional tools are available, and do the students have the resources and ability to use them?), and even the nature of the content (e.g., Is the content skills-based, such as auto mechanics, which might mean that direct instruction with group problem solving may be appropriate, or is it theoretical and elusive, so that a seminar-type discussion approach is called for?). Overbaugh and Casiello (2008) found that having access to faculty and fellow students through these practices and through reliable and easy-to-use rich media tools were important factors in student satisfaction with distance learning.

Today higher education is a competitive environment, leaving students in what is essentially a buyers' market. Students can look for the type of education that suits their needs and preferences. Institutions of higher education must analyze these factors and be sure to clearly communicate their instructional offerings to students so that today's students can make informed choices about where to pursue their education.

Conclusion

Over the past several decades, the use of distance education in higher education has moved from a peripheral form of education meant primarily to address access needs within the domain of the working adult to an increasingly popular and broadly utilized form of higher education at all levels and disciplines. During this same time period, the demographics, environment, and needs of the students involved in distance education have broadened and deepened. In the past, distance education focused almost solely on the dedicated, highly motivated adult learner, who was not necessarily looking for a broad range of support services. Early distance systems were end-to-end broadcast delivery systems where reliability could be effectively built into the infrastructure. Many of today's students are younger, perhaps more technologically savvy, but almost certainly in greater need of a wide variety of support services and systems that are now universally found on college campuses. Students are demanding that these same approaches make their way into the provisions established by the education providers, or they will look elsewhere for the assistance and services they need to achieve their educational goals. (For further reading, see Hansen, 2013; J.C. Moore, 2002; M.G. Moore, 1983.)

References

Allen, I.E., & Seaman, J. (2013). *Changing course: Ten years of tracking online education in the United States.* Wellesley, MA: Babson College/Quahog Research.

Boston, W., Ice, P., & Buress, M. (2012). Assessing student retention in online learning environments: A longitudinal study. *Online Journal of Distance Learning Administration, 15*(2).

Caruth, G.D., & Caruth, D.L. (2013). Distance education in the United States: From correspondence courses to the Internet. *Turkish Online Journal of Distance Education (TOJDE), 14*(2), 141–149. Retrieved from https://tojde.anadolu.edu.tr/tojde51/articles/article_8.htm

Dewey, J. (1938). *Experience and education.* New York, NY: Collier Books.

Garrison, R. (2009). Implications of online learning for the conceptual development and practice of distance education. *Journal of Distance Education, 23*(2), 93–103.

Hansen, R.S. (2013). *Distance learning pros and cons.* Retrieved from http://www.quintcareers.com/distance_learning_pros-cons.html

Heyman, E. (2010). Overcoming student retention issues in higher education online programs. *Online Journal of Distance Learning Administration, 13*(4).

Lei, S.A., & Gupta, R.K. (2010). College distance education courses: Evaluating benefits and costs from institutional, faculty and students' perspectives. *Education, 130*(4), 616–631.

Levy, F., & Murnane, R. J. (2004). *The new division of labor: How computers are creating the next job market.* Princeton, NJ: Princeton University Press.

Moore, J.C. (2002). *Elements of quality: The Sloan-C framework.* Needham, MA: Sloan Consortium.

Moore, M., & Kearsley, G. (2012). *Distance education: A systems view of online learning* (3rd ed.). Independence, KY: Wadsworth.

Moore, M.G. (1983). The individual adult learner. In M. Tight (Ed.), *Adult learning and education* (pp. 153–168). London, UK: Croom Helm.

Nagel, S.L., Maniam, B., & Leavell, H. (2011). Pros and cons of online education for educators and students. *International Journal of Business Research, 11*(6), 136–142.

Overbaugh, R.C., & Casiello, A.R. (2008). Distributed collaborative problem-based graduate-level learning: Students' perspectives on communication tool selection and efficacy. *Computers in Human Behavior, 24*(2), 497–515.

Overbaugh, R.C., Nickel, C.E., & Brown, H.M. (2006, February). *Student characteristics in a university-level foundations course: An examination of orientation toward learning and the role of academic community.* Paper presented at the Eastern Educational Research Association Annual Conference, Hilton Head, SC.

Park, J., & Choi, H. (2009). Factors influencing adult learners' decision to drop out or persist in online learning. *Educational Technology & Society, 12*(4), 207–217.

Patterson, B., & McFadden, C. (2009). Attrition in online and campus degree programs. *Online Journal of Distance Learning Administration, 12*(2).

Pentina, I., & Neeley, C. (2007). Differences in characteristics of online versus traditional students: Implications for target marketing. *Journal of Marketing for Higher Education, 17*(1), 49–65.

Prewitt, T. (1998). The development of distance learning delivery systems. *Higher Education in Europe, 23*(2), 187–194.

Reigeluth, C.M. (2009). *Instructional-design theories and models.* Hillsdale, NJ: Lawrence Erlbaum.

Roblyer, M.D., & Edwards, J. (2000). *Integrating educational technology into teaching* (2nd ed.). Upper Saddle River, NJ: Merrill.

Rovai, A. P., Baker, J. D., & Ponton, M. K. (2013). *Social science research design and statistics: A practitioner's guide to research methods and IBM SPSS analysis* (2nd ed.). Virginia Beach, VA: Watertree Press.

Saba, F. (2012). A systems approach to the future of distance education in colleges and universities: Research, development, and implementation. *Continuing Higher Education Review, 76*, 30–37.

Tinto, V. (1975). Dropouts from higher education: A theoretical synthesis of recent research. *Review of Educational Research, 45*(1), 89–125.

Watson, J., Murin, A., Vashaw, L., Gemin, B., & Rapp, C. (2013). *Keeping pace with K–12 online and blended learning: An annual review of policy and practice.* Evergreen Education Group. Retrieved from http://kpk12.com/cms/wp-content/uploads/EEG_KP2013-lr.pdf

TWENTY THREE

A Generation Divided: An In-Depth View of Millennial Students

Pietro A. Sasso, Blair Dayton, and Stephanie Rosseter

Introduction

As mentioned in the Introduction to this work and in Chapter 19, which highlighted nontraditional students, higher education is increasingly serving a diverse cross-section of students. This chapter will frame the population of traditional college students known as "millennials" and discuss their challenges, the practices that support them, and the echo generation succeeding them. It will also provide an historical overview and critical discourse about the so-called millennials—and the myths and misconceptions surrounding the very construction of that notion.

Defining Millennial Students

Millennials as a Student Culture

Millennial students are a symbolic artifact of a continuing historical narrative. They are part of an historical trend, namely, the emergence of a new class of student that is professional in nature and is attending college for a very narrow, specific reason. The *purpose* of college was to discover what specifically that *purpose* truly was, but a consumer culture arose instead with the arrival of the millennial generation of students. Helen Lefkowitz Horowitz (1987) has described the dominant student cultures that have existed since the 1700s and their impact on campus life and community. She defines four cultures that have thrived throughout collegiate history and can still be found on American college campuses: (a) collegians, (b) rebels, (c) outsiders, and (d) new outsiders.

Although many institutions reflect more than one culture, Horowitz argues that most campuses are dominated by only one of the four cultures.

This spectrum of student cultures also reflects the maturation of the traditional student from one invested in the collegiate experience to one purchasing its commodity value with fixed expectations. These four student types reflect a spectrum of undergraduate culture, including an involved student leader (collegian), rebel (socially conscious, intellectual), outsider (commuter, day-student), or new outsider (professional student). The collegians, outsiders, and rebels continue to exist across specific, more diverse populations within higher education. These four cultures serve as the basis for the emergence of the professional students, who currently predominate on the contemporary college campus. The new outsider dominates the traditional undergraduate population and is representative of the millennial student. Moreover, traditional college students can be typified as the "new outsiders," or the professional students. They were the first to evolve with technology and a consumer mentality which provides for a series of challenges and characteristics.

Professional students as consumers believe that college is a right and not a privilege (Horowitz, 1987). However, they are supported by a federal government that has recently limited increases for Pell Grants and embraced a trend toward low-interest loans for college students. Traditional students have also realized that the same lucrative job opportunities afforded their older siblings or previous generations would be less available to them. This evolution has transformed traditional student expectations and perceptions about the college experience: it is no longer considered to be necessarily a transformational, value-added, and immersion learning opportunity. Instead, students have brought a consumer mindset to their college experience, beginning with the application process and ending with their determination to gain the credentials that will allow them to succeed in a world of more limited opportunities. Thus, they come to higher education with expectations and attitudes that prior generations did not have (Horowitz, 1987).

Horowitz (1987) described professional students, or millennials, this way: they "lack…the sparks of intellectual life that were the saving grace of many earlier outsiders" (p. 268). Professional students have sought high grades, recommendations, and resume items. Moreover, they have been reluctant to engage in garnering genuine respect from mentors or in more meaningful, time-consuming activities. They expect classes to be offered in the evening; further, they increasingly expect services—such as luxurious residence halls with single rooms and private bathrooms—to be available to them on campus. They have come to campus with different expectations and a strong consumer mentality.

Whereas earlier students were in awe of the institutions they entered, professional students tend to exhibit an almost anti-institutional attitude (Horowitz, 1987; Thelin, 2004). Earlier students could be transformed into the students that academia ideally sought; professional students have come mainly to acquire credentials. These professional students primarily value grades, which are perceived as the mark leading to the credential. They have become intensely competitive to the point of sabotaging the efforts of others. They perceive the faculty, fairly or unfairly, as the gatekeepers of high grades. These students either "play" the faculty or compete with the faculty to obtain them. Millennials have transformed the academe from an insular ivory tower to one that is more malleable and willing to offer services to meet consumer demand.

Horowitz (1987) profiles the early millennial student as an anti-establishment consumer transforming traditional academia. Numerous authors (Boyer, 1987; Coomes & DeBard, 2004; Horowitz, 1987; Howe & Strauss, 1993, 2000, 2003; Levine, 1980; Levine & Cureton, 1998; Light, 2001; Loeb, 1994; Moffatt, 1989; Strauss & Howe, 1991) have discussed the various college student generations in terms of their similarities, differences, and characteristics. Specifically, Howe and Strauss (1993, 2000, 2003), Levine and Cureton (1998) and Coomes and DeBard (2004) approached college students largely from the vantage point of generational differences, depicting their experiences and similarities as shaped by historical and societal events. However, this generational approach fails to truly address particular features of the millennial student.

Millennials as a Student Generation

The overall profile of millennial students suggests that they are comparable to previous generations in terms of an overall increase in the numbers of college-going students and an increase in diversity. Millennial students began entering college in 2000 and have been identified both as millennials or the "Y generation" (Coomes & DeBard, 2004; Howe & Strauss 2000, 2003), named for the beginning of the new millennium. Millennials are those students who were born between 1982 and 2002. However, other researchers posit the range to be between 1984 or 1986 to 2002 (Twenge, 2006). In addition, they are projected to attend college as traditional freshmen between 2000 and 2021 and to attend undergraduate institutions until 2027 (Howe & Strauss, 2000). It is anticipated that there will be 6.9 million college attendees within this generation. They are expected to be extremely diverse; 35.5% of them will be non-White students (Coomes & DeBard, 2004). The estimated time that they will spend in college, both as entering traditional freshmen and in subsequent years of enrollment, is up to 6 years beyond initial enrollment. With their large estimated enrollment numbers, this presents a numerical profile of a large and diverse student generation. However, upon examination of the characteristics of this generation, one can discern a stark difference from previous generations in that millennials comprise the dominant student population on current college campuses.

Today, college student populations are principally comprised of students from the millennial or Y generation, combined with a significant number of "generation X" students and many returning baby boomers. However, millennials stand in marked contrast to their prior student generational counterparts. Howe and Strauss (2000) found that seven key characteristics define today's millennial college students. These traits are:

1. Special: These students come from smaller families with fewer siblings. It is hypothesized that because of the decreased size of the nuclear family, "helicopter parents" emerged, providing wrap-around support for their children. Their increased hovering and attention facilitates millennial students' feelings that they are unique and "special," even among their peers.
2. Sheltered: The use of technology by millennial students facilitated the outcome of the extension of the umbilical cord. Parents kept their children within hearing distance and closer to home. Therefore, millennials were protected, or "sheltered," by their parents from the realities of the external world.
3. Confident: Consistent praise and support from adults provides for an inflated sense of self-worth. This adulation is reflected in the projection of a high level of confidence.

4. Team oriented: Diversity has increased with every succeeding American generation, and millennials are the most diverse generation to date. Millennials were raised to become civically engaged and less individually focused. They experience group and team-oriented environments at younger ages than previous generations.
5. Conventional: Millennials have been described as highly pragmatic and focused on immediate and threatening issues. This notion has been used to explain why they are so environmentally conscious.
6. Pressured: A specific cross-section of millennials has been over-scheduled and mentored to succeed among peers. The goal for this group was to attend college, and the assumption was that this would guarantee success in life.
7. High achieving: Millennials were projected to be future oriented as planners and focused on long-term success.

According to Howe and Strauss (2000), millennials were born with technological luxuries such as cell phones and more than one color television per household. Culturally, they always experienced MTV as a significant influence. They do not remember the Reagan assassination attempt, but their generational-shaping moments include Columbine, the 9/11 terrorist attacks, and the Virginia Tech shootings. The expectation that technology and its capacity to connect would be a significant influence on this group was met through social media, Smartphones, and the umbilical cord with parents or guardians as "helicopter parents." This would connect the notion of family ties with their emergence into adulthood.

Building on the research of Howe and Strauss (2000), Twenge (2006) painted a much more negative portrait of the millennial generation and characterized them as the "me" generation. Twenge found that millennials engage in higher levels of socially desirable behaviors. Crowne and Marlowe (1960) defined social desirability as "the need to obtain approval by responding in a culturally appropriate and acceptable manner" (p. 352). Johnson and Fendrich (2002) defined social desirability as the tendency for individuals to project favorable images of themselves while interacting socially. Social desirability is of particular concern when social norms identify a specific attitude as desirable, when in fact numerous individuals hold a different attitude (DeLamater, 1982).

Millennial students are part of a larger trend against conformity and have demonstrated lower levels of need for social approval. Although overall social desirability levels have declined steadily among contemporary college students, millennials strive to present themselves in a favorable manner when interacting with others. Their behaviors are strongly influenced by the need to obtain recognition—not approval—from others. In a meta-analysis of 241 studies comprised of a total sample of 40,745 college students, it was determined that social desirability has decreased since the concept was first articulated by Crowne and Marlowe in 1958 (Twenge, 2006). The average student in 2001 scored 62% lower on the inventory than his counterpart in 1958, which means that millennials have a 38% lower need for social approval (Twenge, 2006). It was concluded that this is representative of a larger societal trend toward self-recognition and individualism among members of the millennial generation (Twenge, 2006).

However, societal trends such as individualism and the seven core traits of millennials provide researchers and educators with only a portion of the picture. The label "millennial" has come to describe a narrow profile of traditional students. The label has typically applied to White, affluent students who grow up in the suburbs, apply to selective schools, and move through life with their helicopter parents always hovering overhead (Hoover, 2009). The initial sample collected by Howe and Strauss (2000), from which they created their profile of the current generation, was drawn from primarily wealthy, White Anglo-Saxon Protestant (WASP) school districts within Fairfax County in Northern Virginia, which is nestled in the Washington, D.C., suburbs. The area traditionally has one of the highest median family incomes in the United States, in the range of $90,000–$120,000.

Thus, the term "millennial" is not inclusive, nor is it representative. It does not refer to minority students, students from poor families, students who struggle through high school and college, or students whose parents are not involved in their education and extracurricular activities. Reflective of this profile of the millennials is that 83% of undergraduate minority students have plans to attend college and believe they will be successful (Nagaoka, Roderick, & Coca, 2009). However, this conceptual projection of millennials is not applicable, since once minorities attend college, less than 20% of African American and Hispanic students persist to graduation within 6 years (American Council on Education [ACE], 2012). Further, a majority remain underemployed if they do graduate (ACE, 2013), as they do not have the same support, helicopter parenting, and so forth as their White peers.

The problem with the lack of research on the aforementioned students from non-dominant groups is that colleges and universities are becoming much more diverse, and there are no guidelines regarding how to support these students from the millennial generation. It is also not indicative of their consumer nature as anecdotally reported by student affairs professionals and so adeptly described by Horowitz (1987). Even though Howe and Strauss's (2000) portrayal of millennials has been met with some debate, there is a framework from which to work in regard to the millennial student population that they studied. This framework is based on the use of technology such as social media and other devices in their academic pursuits and their personal lives.

Millennials as Two Distinct Groups: 1980s vs. 1990s

Impact of Technology

Advances in technology, including the immense popularity of social media, have certainly become a way of life for all millennials. The adoption of technology has shaped the narrative of this generation of students in a way that distinguishes them from their predecessors. There are those students born *before* the proliferation of the Internet during the 1990s and those born *afterward*, thus marking two distinct groups within this generation. Individuals born in the 1980s experienced the emergence of technology, whereas those of the 1990s were born into it. Figure 1 helps the reader to conceptualize the emergence of technology over time and how it may have impacted millennials.

Figure 1. The Emergence of Technology and Its Impact on Millenials.

Even though this chapter proposes a division of the generation into two decades, there is a clear overlap in terms of technological influence on all millennials. As advances in technology have steadily taken place, the gap between early and later millennials has narrowed. Early millennials did not grow up with a strong presence of technology, but as exposure and popularity increased, they learned to embrace it. However, early millennials may still be more reluctant to document their entire lives online or share pictures and opinions instantly. Twitter and Instagram allow for such use, and these sites seem to be more popular with the younger members of this generation. The conveniences are undeniable, but the preferences between the two groups may differ. For example, early millennials may prefer e-mail or phone calls as their forms of communication with friends, whereas later millennials may favor online postings or tweeting. However, text-messaging is the common denominator. This form of instant communication is desirable across all segments of the millennial generation.

These types of communication are also finding their way into higher education practices. Today the best approach to reaching out to current college students is through online marketing. Institutions have their own Facebook pages or Twitter accounts, which allow for faster postings of events and a better chance of achieving widespread outreach. Higher education has also embraced technology for distance learning purposes as well as for student engagement in the form of virtual classrooms, meetings, and workshops. This is not to say that technology has not enabled great advances, but the basis for all these advances is the effort of the individual and the human experience. One of the most essential experiences during college is social interaction. We strive in higher education, especially within student affairs, to aid in the development of the student as a whole. It has been argued that technology potentially reduces our ability to reach students on a deeper level by inhibiting face-to-face interactions. Future generations may not have the same opportunity to develop social skills; if we continue to exist strictly behind a glowing screen, there may be a much more daunting task facing the profession of student affairs.

If we are unable to assist students wholly, then we are doing them a disservice. However, incoming generations will not understand or embrace this notion. They want instant results—something they have grown accustomed to through the immediacy of technology. With more and more online classes, training, workshops, and meetings, future graduates will be able to say they *virtually* attended college. It is this generation that most centrally witnessed the rise of technology, along with the subsequent developmental schism that the currently accepted paradigm by Howe and Strauss (2000) and Twenge (2006) does not acknowledge. Moreover, it is the opinion of the authors that, on college campuses, there is perhaps no simple way to characterize millennial students other than to conceptualize them as being split between two distinct groups. This delineates two groups with different ambitions, attitudes, and different developmental experiences that have shaped, and are forming, their future.

Higher education research accepts the categorization of millennials as a whole generation, but the framing of them over a 20-year period cannot be ignored. It is important to identify what behaviors and attitudes are specific to students born earlier within the generation (early millennials), and to those born in later years (later millennials). Splitting up the generation into two 10-year periods provides a more accurate picture of the similarities and differences between millennials as college students.

Drawn from the professional experiences of the authors, the two case studies that follow illustrate an obvious differential gap between early and later millennials and serve to defend the argument that sweeping generalizations cannot be made about a very large group of individuals. Howe and Strauss (2000) attributed to millennials the seven characteristics of (a) special, (b) sheltered, (c) confident, (d) team oriented, (e) conventional, (f) pressured, and (g) high achieving. These case studies address some of the commonalities ascribed to millennial students as a way of drawing a comparison between early and later millennials.

Early Millennials (born in the 1980s)

Student A was born in 1982 and grew up in a White, middle-class household with three siblings. The student's main goal for attending college was to further her education. She was brought up with the notion that going to college was the next step after high school. It was expected. In the year 2000, the student entered college, where she obtained her first cell phone. Student A's only form of online socializing was through AOL Instant Messenger (AIM), a quick way to chat with friends on the computer. This early millennial's parents were not overly involved in her education or her extracurricular activities. They were mostly present during the application process, but their involvement ceased once the student was accepted into college. Without a strong technological presence, Student A relied on the college's textbooks and library resources in order to do research and complete her coursework. Prior to the popularity of e-mailing or the invention of Facebook, this student learned about events, workshops, or programs from bulletin board postings, flyers, and word-of-mouth. If she needed to make an appointment with her professor or advisor, making a phone call was the best option.

Student A was in high school at the time of the Columbine shootings. She remembers her parents being more concerned about it than she. By the time 9/11 occurred, Student A was a sophomore in college. She felt the impact of this event and knew a friend's older sibling who was lost in the tragedy. This early millennial was more aware of her surroundings and concerned with public safety after this event.

Student A entered graduate school in 2012. The differences between her undergraduate and graduate experiences were evident in terms of how she completed her coursework and the types of online resources she used (including online classes). This early millennial primarily used e-mail when communicating with professors or her advisor. In addition to text-messaging and Facebook, it was a convenient tool for getting in touch with peers regarding assignments. She used much more social media, in fact, to learn about events or workshops at her institution. Student A now had an abundance of online resources to choose from when working on assignments. However, she still preferred using traditional materials such as books, printed articles, and so forth. When taking notes in class, Student A put pen to paper rather than typing on a laptop or tablet, like some of her peers. This early millennial used a balance of old and new in her current college experience.

Later Millennials (born in the 1990s)

Student B was born in 1995 to a small, middle-class family from a suburban neighborhood. Her parents were very involved in her extracurricular activities and in her education. Student B's parents paid her college tuition and thus had a say in what classes she took and where she lived on campus. Student B defined her main purpose in going to college as earning a degree and also learning more about her specific area of interest. While in college, Student B's main forms of communication were online. Research for papers was done through her library's online databases; events were marketed to her through Facebook and e-mails; and advising appointments or faculty meetings were scheduled through her university e-mail. Student B used Facebook, Twitter, and Instagram daily. Her technology use started when she was given a cell phone in the seventh grade. In regard to the defining events of Columbine and the Virginia Tech shootings, Student B was too young to be affected by those events. (She was around 5 years old and 11 years old at the time of those events, respectively.) However, 9/11 impacted Student B despite her young age, because she felt the fear instilled in her by her parents after the tragedy occurred.

The Generation Divided: Professional Students vs. Consumers

As illustrated in the case of student A, early millennials do not necessarily meet the definition of the Y generation. When considering Howe and Strauss's seven key characteristics, these particular students seem to be excluded. Those born in the earlier years of the 20-year time span typically come from larger families and do not live sheltered lives with overly involved parents. Instead they exhibit more independence. These individuals understand the need for a college degree, but they maintain a focus on the meaning behind it. It is considered a privilege and an educational *reward*, rather than an *award*. They do not necessarily share the same ideals as later millennials, whose focus is on high-paying jobs and long-term financial success. The early millennial reflects the professional student (new outsider), and the later millennial mirrors the consumer student based on the typology provided by Horowitz (1987).

Student B truly exemplifies the typical young, White, middle-class later millennial student, fully immersed in technology and coddled and controlled by helicopter parents. Her small family size provides every opportunity to feel special and exude confidence. Later millennials are often sheltered but are also future oriented, with long-term plans for success. Their goals are centered on obtaining the right credentials to be successful after graduation, which mirrors the notion of the professional student that was mentioned earlier in this chapter. For the majority of their young lives, they have had cell phones, the Internet, and a growing number of social media sites. Later millennials live a life of instant gratification and constant communication.

By contrast, early millennials evolved with technology, and many of them did not even acquire a cell phone until they were in college. These students did not have as many online resources available to them for the majority of the time they were enrolled in college. Therefore, they are more capable of reverting back to traditional methods and exhibiting patience; in fact, they might prefer it. They can appreciate the need for a slower pace. However, as previously discussed, later millennials are more privy to immediate results and having answers within reach. We may be able to see this when comparing traditional- and non-traditional-aged students, or even when earlier millennials are entering graduate school.

Early millennials entering college or graduate school today are faced with more options when it comes to their higher education experience. Advances in technology allow for online courses and resources that were not available even 10 years ago. This earlier group can certainly appreciate the ease and convenience of these new additions to the college experience while still holding on to the conventional methods they grew up with. The notion of consumerism is where the transformation occurs. With higher costs and the need to take out loans to afford college, students are becoming more invested in how their institution's education and services are delivered. There is a new mentality on the part of the professional student as a consumer: "Here's my money, now what can you do for me?" Students today have the expectations of consumers. They demand the best: the most up-to-date technology, resources, and facilities.

And if these are not available, students can and will take their money to another institution that better meets the needs of their generation. However, later millennials are faced with this dilemma more so than early millennials. Those born during the first half of this generation are still capable of adapting and appreciating colleges' bottom line: education.

As stated earlier, millennials born in the 1990s are less likely to adapt and sometimes have a difficult time with adjustment. College is a time of transition, when students deal with stress, anxiety, and new learning styles. Later millennials often struggle with all of these areas because they never learned coping skills from their helicopter parents. Parents are often too afraid to let their children experience these natural emotions and handle the consequences on their own. This is why higher education professionals continue to hear from parents even though college students are adults.

According to research from Howe and Strauss (2000) and Twenge (2006), later millennials suffer from a form of narcissism typical of the era of social media. Facebook statuses, Tweets, and Instagrams are posted daily, if not hourly, and this generation feels exceedingly comfortable divulging almost everything about themselves on these sites. The increasing addiction to and desire for technology also have ramifications for college campuses and higher education administrators. Students research colleges extensively before applying and often seek out the schools with the most cutting-edge technology. They have become consumers and hope to buy the best educational package available to them. If an institution with an excellent academic reputation has lackluster fitness centers, outdated residence halls, and a lack of online classes and resources, the consumer student may pass on an acceptance offer because another college could offer the whole spectrum of amenities. In attempting to remain competitive, colleges and universities have adopted the mentality of "the customer is always right" and work tirelessly to keep students interested in their institutions.

Student affairs professionals and faculty members are met with the predicament of whether to cater to the demands of the late-wave millennial generation or ask them to adapt to older means of teaching and learning, such as physical textbooks and printed syllabi. Many professors and administrators have decided to "meet students where they are" and utilize social media sites and other technologies in their courses, marketing efforts, and on-campus events. Some advisors accept texts from students who want to schedule an appointment. Offices use Facebook and Twitter to advertise events and create fewer printed flyers for bulletin boards. The majority of later millennial students do not use the library to check out books for reports; they use the library's online databases to do research from their laptops or iPads. Many courses are online or hybrid; most utilize a web-based learning portal to post assignments and syllabi, receive student work, provide access to quizzes and tests, and facilitate discussion in forums. As early millennials graduate and the professional student has disappeared, universities have evolved into institutions meeting the needs of the consumerist, later millennial student. Universities feel the need to keep pace with the demands of later millennials in order to stay competitive in a market of student-consumers.

Colleges and universities have embraced technology to meet the marketplace demands of the later millennial student and, in doing so, have reinforced a generation dependent upon its very existence. The later millennials are merely a precursor to the echo generation that has cast a shadow over their emergence. Technology, like students as consumers, has become ubiquitous and assumed a heightened status in higher education. The next wave of college students—those born after 9/11—will only further emphasize this notion.

The Next Student Generation: Tech Gens

Researchers have shifted their focus from millennials to the next generation of individuals who were born after 9/11 and have debated their ascribed generational name (Horovitz, 2012). They have dubbed them the "homelanders" (Horovitz, 2012; Howe & Strauss, 2003). This name derives from the assumption that this generation will be a group of homebodies, sitting behind their tablets, interacting through text and touch screens, and smothered by overprotecting, helicopter parents. Other names have also been proposed, such as the "pluralist generation" (a reference to its tolerance of diversity), or the "re-generation," a reference to its projected commitment to the environment. However, all of the names miss the single most important characteristic of the generation: the ubiquitous use of technology among its members. They have often been referred to as the first generation of "digital natives" entering a world where technology has always existed (Palfrey & Gasser, 2008). Therefore, the "tech generation" ("tech gens") would more accurately describe the entire group.

Tech gens have not yet been extensively researched, so not much is known about how members of this generation will act once they enter college. However, most people in higher education believe that this next generation will probably resemble millennials to some degree, but will also be distinct from them in a few important ways. For example, in today's society people do not think twice about having electricity in their homes, at work, or at school. That is how the next student generation feels about technology. It just exists, in various forms, for multiple purposes. Unlike some millennials who transitioned into technology, tech gens will not have known a time without it, therefore making it completely essential to a normal life.

According to Straz (2013), the tech generation will also be characterized as comfortable about being monitored. This generation is used to surveillance in a multitude of forms, from government-mandated acts to crib cameras. Facebook, Twitter, and Instagram provide platforms for individuals to be watched and scrutinized by countless numbers of people every day, and this next generation has grown up being documented from birth. Helicopter parents hold a tighter grip and extend their locus of control over this generation even more than the parents of millennials. Fear of terrorism since 9/11 has caused parents to keep their children closer to home. Straz (2013) also speculates that tech gens will be a silent generation that does not produce many leaders, but instead carries out the grand ideas of the millennials.

As seen with later millennials, tech gens will struggle with adjustment and lack the adaptability needed to work with different populations. Toggling between traditional methods and advanced technology will be an arduous task met with resistance, confusion, and apathy. Tech generation students will scoff at the idea of reading a physical book when they could use their Kindle. Texting will be their main form of communication, not unlike both early and later millennials, but many tech gens will lack the social ability to converse effectively with others. Social awkwardness may even become the rule rather than the exception.

These assumptions paint the picture of a mindless, tech-centered generation, which may be slightly unfair to tech gens. This generation was born into the Great Recession and has learned the value of doing more with less. They are environmentally conscious and have more of a sense of collectiveness than the millennials. This, however, may not necessarily mean that the tech gens will not rise to the challenge of leadership and innovation. Like the millennials, they will receive excessive attention from their parents and other adults, boosting their confidence and making them feel special. Couple those traits with their extensive knowledge of technology, resourcefulness, and egalitarian mindset, and the tech generation may surprise its critics.

Tech generation members will undoubtedly further influence how higher education is structured. Being mindful of trends is important, but there is also a need to balance tradition with technology. Higher education should embrace new ideas while preserving conventional methods of student learning. Higher education needs to ensure that its ethos for the traditional student remains the face-to-face learning format and that it facilitates the development of the whole student.

Conclusion

This chapter has detailed the evolution of the traditional college student, both through the typology presented by Horowitz (1987) and through the use of generational theory. Generational theory was applied using the benchmark and foundational research by Twenge (2006) and Howe and Strauss (2000) regarding the millennial student. The millennial student was identified as the majority traditional college student within the contemporary context. The use of generational theory was also critiqued in its application to this majority.

The millennial student was disaggregated into the two distinct subgroups of early and later millennials. It was argued that the earlier models and profiles of these college students did not truly acknowledge the impact of technology. The distinguishing characteristic between the generations was that early millennials had to transition into the use and adoption of technology, and later millennials were born into the use of the new or recent technologies that proliferated during the 1990s. This dividing line is apparent in the developmental narratives provided in the case studies. In addition, implications for future practice have been provided, as was a projected profile of the echo student generation often referred to as "homelanders."

This chapter reflects a continued evolutionary narrative regarding the traditional contemporary college student. Though no longer the majority of college students, this subpopulation continues to be the dominant culture as discussed by Horowitz (1987). However, this student population of millennials has evolved from the professional students with specific expectations as it has become more consumer oriented. Coupled with technology, the millennial student as a consumer is the most consistent narrative that has thus far emerged from the development of that generation.

1. Also, one should remember to acknowledge the inconsistencies of the definition of the millennial generation as discussed within this chapter. It is therefore necessary to reframe how generational study is conducted in order to address and minimize potential limitations. It is suggested that additional factors should be considered when studying future generations. These include:
2. Diversity: Ensure that the participants in the study represent diverse backgrounds, including demographics, socioeconomic status, race, ethnicity, disability, orientation, and gender.
3. Time Span: A generation should be limited to one decade.
4. Technological Trends and Advances: These change rapidly and can significantly impact experiences, behaviors, attitudes, and beliefs of an entire generation.

5. Adjustment/Adaptability: With a smaller time span, these issues will not be as prevalent as with the millennial generation.
6. Generalizations: The biggest concern is that generational study stereotypes an entire population of people.

Generations of students came before the millennials and will continue to succeed them. Today's college students as millennial students will continue to populate our campuses until 2027. Therefore, if we are to frame students through a generational, or time-span cultural lens, some of these suggestions should be considered. It is the duty of educators to ensure that our students have the capacity to appreciate the value-added experience of higher education and that they enjoy the necessary academic support. This means that it is imperative that the student voice is actively listened to and that the student experience is readily understood. Millennial students, with their associated social and developmental issues that previous generations did not present, constitute a very challenging population that student affairs practitioners must address. If we do not understand the specific developmental needs of this generation, we will effectively cede the university and alma mater to consumerism.

References

American Council on Education (ACE). (2012). *The education gap: Understanding African American and Hispanic attainment disparities in higher education.* Washington, DC: Author.

American Council on Education (ACE). (2013). *With college degree in hand: Analysis of racial minority graduates and their lives after college.* Washington, DC: Author.

Boyer, E.L. (1987). *College, the undergraduate experience in America.* New York, NY: Harper & Row.

Coomes, M.D., & DeBard, R. (2004). Serving the millennial generation. *New Directions for Student Services*, (106), 73–85.

Crowne, D.P., & Marlowe, D. (1960). A new scale of social desirability independent of psychopathology. *Journal of Consulting Psychology, 24*(4), 349–354.

DeLamater, J. (1982). Response-effects of question content. In W. Dijkstra & J. van der Zouwen (Eds.), *Response behaviour in the survey-interview* (pp. 13–48). London, UK: Academic Press.

Hoover, E. (2009, October 11). The millennial muddle: How stereotyping students became a thriving industry and a bundle of contradictions. *Chronicle of Higher Education.* Retrieved from http://chronicle.com/article/The-Millennial-Muddle-How/48772/

Horovitz, B. (2012, May 5). After Gen X, millennials, what should next generation be? *USA Today*. Retrieved from http://usatoday30.usatoday.com/money/advertising/story/2012-05-03/naming-the-next-generation/54737518/1

Horowitz, H.L. (1987). *Campus life: Undergraduate cultures from the end of the eighteenth century to the present.* New York, NY: Knopf.

Howe, N., & Strauss, W. (1993). *13th gen: Abort, retry, ignore, fail?* New York, NY: Vintage Books.

Howe, N., & Strauss, W. (2000). *Millennials rising: The next great generation.* New York, NY: Vintage Books.

Howe, N., & Strauss, W. (2003). *Millennials go to college.* Great Falls, VA: American Association of Registrars and Admissions Officers and Life Course Associates.

Johnson, T., and Fendrich, M. (2002). A validation of the Crowne-Marlowe social desirability scale. Paper presented at the American Association for Public Opinion Research, St Petersburg, FL.

Levine, A. (1980). *When dreams and heroes died.* San Francisco, CA: Jossey-Bass.

Levine, A., & Cureton, J.S. (1998). *When hope and fear collide.* San Francisco, CA: Jossey-Bass.

Light, R.J. (2001). *Making the most of college.* Cambridge, MA: Harvard University Press.

Loeb, P.R. (1994). *Generation at the crossroads.* New Brunswick, NJ: Rutgers University Press.

Moffatt, M. (1989). *Coming of age in New Jersey.* New Brunswick, NJ: Rutgers University Press.

Nagaoka, J., Roderick, M., & Coca, V. (2009). *Barriers to college attainment, lessons from Chicago.* Washington, DC: Center for American Progress.

Palfrey, J., & Gasser, U. (2008). *Born digital: Understanding the first generation of digital natives.* New York, NY: Basic Books.

Strauss, W., & Howe, N. (1991). *Generations: The history of America's future, 1584 to 2069.* New York, NY: William Morrow.

Straz, M. (2013, October 21). *Generation next: Here come the homelanders.* Retrieved from http://www.mediapost.com/publications/article/211686/generation-next-here-come-the-homelanders.html

Thelin, J.R. (2004). *A history of American higher education.* Baltimore, MD: Johns Hopkins University Press.

Twenge, J.M. (2006). *Generation me: Why today's young Americans are more confident, assertive, entitled—And more miserable than ever before.* New York, NY: Free Press.

- I am a millennial (late)
- I think you can change from your gen.
- The tech gen. sounds exciting, yet challenge.
- How do we, as millennials, help steer higher ed. in the right direction?

Part Four

Student Development

TWENTY FOUR

Student Mental Health Issues on Today's Campuses

Alan M. Schwitzer and Brian Van Brunt

Although college counseling professionals "tend to be more visible during crises" such as the April 16, 2007, Virginia Tech tragedy in Blacksburg, "they serve student mental health needs every day" (Schwitzer, 2007a, p. 99). Further, today's mental health concerns often seem increasingly disruptive for the learners who experience them, for their peers, and for the campus educators who work with them (Van Brunt, 2012). In fact, based on his comparison of college counseling trends and the mental health trends of adolescents and young adults in off-campus settings, Rudd (2004) concluded that during the past decade, college counseling centers and university psychological services have essentially become community mental health clinics in a specialized institutional context. As a result, higher education professionals in every corner of the campus confront students in need—from individuals in acute crisis to those struggling with the common adjustment and developmental issues that affect college academic and social success (Reynolds, 2011). Correspondingly, this chapter is designed to inform higher education professionals' knowledge and practice regarding current student mental health needs. First, the college student mental health domain is defined. Next, contemporary college student mental health trends and several specific student mental health issues are presented. Then, the continuum of disruption that student mental health problems can cause for campus constituencies is discussed. Finally, some conclusions are drawn about the future.

The College Student Mental Health Domain

Educators and professionals working in U.S. higher education settings attend to the "needs of the whole student...actively [assisting learners] with the emotional and academic demands of college life and [promoting] their personal development" (Reynolds, 2011, p. 399). Student affairs practitioners are highly visible, accessible, and approachable to learners with a wide range of personal concerns (Pope, Reynolds, & Mueller, 2004). However, only some of these concerns fall within the student mental health domain. Specifically, college counseling professionals characterize a student problem as a mental health need when:

- the student's thinking, emotions, behaviors, and/or physiology are disrupted or have the potential to be disrupted; and
- the student experiences, or has the potential to experience, significant distress or disability in important life areas like academics and social activities. (American Psychiatric Association (APA), 2013)

Disruption in functioning and distress or disability in important life areas are the key factors distinguishing mental health needs from general college student concerns. The importance of addressing problems that meet these criteria on college and university campuses is well documented. In fact, according to a National Survey of College Counseling Center Directors report, 10.4% of U. S. students—an estimated 2.2 million learners—utilized counseling services in a recent year (Gallagher, 2012). Many of these students would be unable or unlikely to remain in, or succeed in, college without effective institutional supports (Gallagher, 2012; Rudd, 2004).

How Students Access Mental Health Support on Campus: The College Counseling Professional Specialty

Student counseling centers and psychological services are specialized offices providing professional mental health services within a specific institutional context (Council for the Advancement of Standards in Higher Education, 2011; May, 1988). The counseling center's purpose is to support the institution's mission by "helping students work through psychological and emotional issues that may affect their academic success and personal development" (Dungy, 2003, p. 345). This is accomplished through counseling and other mental health interventions, as well as prevention, education, and outreach services provided in natural campus settings such as residence halls, Greek organization sites, and student commons (AUCCCD, 2012). Similarly, college health centers provide learners with public health services, often including psychiatric and mental health services, in the special context of the college or university community (Reifler, Liptzin, & Fox, 2006). Students with psychological issues visit these centers to facilitate their ability to become successful learners and ultimately to graduate by addressing the mental health needs that—as defined earlier—disrupt their functioning, cause them distress, or disable their academic or social functioning (Boyd et al., 2003; Schwitzer, 1997, 2002). College counseling professionals assess the student's (a) current level of need, (b) perceived sense of urgency, and (c) motivation for change. On the basis of this assessment, college counseling professionals may offer the following: prevention services to "forestall the onset of problems or personal-emotional needs" (Schwitzer, 2012, p. 229); limited intermediate interventions when the student's need is "emerging or clearly present" but currently falls short of severe impairment (Schwitzer, 2012, p. 230); or crisis and psychotherapeutic interventions when the student presents recurrent psychological difficulties or entrenched dysfunctional problems that are highly or fully disruptive, distressing, or disabling (Drum & Lawler, 1988; Schwitzer, 2012).

Mental Health on Today's Campuses: Increased Demand and Greater Complexity

In the mental health domain, there is a high overall demand on today's campuses for counseling and psychological services, pressure to serve students with increasingly complex concerns, and the challenge of working with highly diverse campus populations and constituencies (Bishop, 2006; Hodges, 2001; Lippincott & Lippincott, 2007; Stone & Archer, 1990). On the one hand, large numbers of students seek counseling services for modest mental health needs arising from typically expected adjustment, developmental, and other personal concerns (Gallagher, 2012). In the adjustment area, learners present difficulties with the following:

- academic adjustment to college- and university-level educational pressures;
- social adjustment to faculty, peer, and other interpersonal relationships at the institution, along with changing relationships with family, peers, and others outside of school;
- institutional adjustment, requiring commitments to age-appropriate college pursuits, educational goals, and career plans; and
- personal-emotional adjustment, which is the ability to manage one's emotional and physical well-being over the long trek of one's college experience. (Baker & Siryk, 1999; Schwitzer, 2012; Schwitzer, Ancis, & Brown, 2001).

Likewise, students commonly present difficulties they encounter as they tackle late adolescent, young adult, or adult developmental tasks—such as concerns related to psychosocial development, cognitive development, career development, gender identity, racial identity, or sexual identity (Evans, Forney, Guido, Patton, & Renn, 2010; Lippincott & Lippincott, 2007; Schwitzer, 2012; Sharkin, 2012). Disruptions in any of these adjustment and developmental areas potentially can lead to distress or impairment in academic performance or social functioning.

On the other hand, the presence on campuses of moderate mental health concerns as well as highly demanding student personal and psychological needs is also well documented (Gallagher, 2009, 2012; Lippincott & Lippincott, 2007). Moderate personal problems can range from pressing time-management or career problems, to threshold-level depression or problematic anxiety, to experiencing brief moments of suicidal ideation or transient periods of bizarre thinking (Bishop, 2006; Gallagher, 2009).

Beyond these moderate needs, about half of the students seen by college counseling professionals present "severe psychological problems," including clinical depression and suicidality, anxiety disorders and panic attacks, and other psychological problems (Gallagher, 2009, p. 3). In fact, for roughly the past 20 years, college and university counseling center directors have consistently reported a trend toward greater numbers of students with more severe needs (AUCCCD, 2012; Gallagher, 2012; Sharkin, 2012). Counseling center directors recently reported that almost 40% of their clients have severe mental health problems requiring treatment in order to remain in, and be successful at, college (Gallagher, 2012). Counseling center staff reported perceptions of increases in a variety of mental health problems, including crises requiring immediate responses; psychiatric medication issues; alcohol abuse, as well as problems with illicit drug use other than alcohol; self-injury (e.g., non-suicidal cutting of oneself); on-campus sexual assault concerns, as well as problems related to pre-college sexual abuse; and eating disorders (Gallagher, 2012). In addition, counseling staff reported extensive work evaluating and treating student depressive disorders and suicidality (Gallagher, 2012). The college counseling domain also includes students with severe psychiatric disorders such as schizophrenia and the bipolar disorders (Lippincott & Lippincott, 2007). Likewise, an increasing number of students arrive on campus already on psychiatric medication, and this can present special challenges during college (Gallagher, 2012; Sharkin, 2012). Altogether, in the United States, a combination of increased effectiveness of early mental health support services for K–12 learners (including better psychological care and psychiatric medication, along with heightened use of Individual Educational Plans in schools), plus widened access via the American Disabilities Act, has made higher education more attainable for students with mental health needs (Van Brunt, 2012; Van Brunt & Lewis, 2013). While there is some internal debate in the college counseling specialty about the exact degree to which the severity of student psychological concerns has increased (Jenks Kettmann et al., 2007; Schwartz, 2006; Sharkin, 1997, 2012), there is agreement that students' mental health needs have become increasingly complex and demanding (Archer & Cooper, 1998; Davis & Humphrey, 2000; Rudd, 2004).

A Closer Look at Student Mental Health Issues

There are several different, interacting sources of student mental health difficulties (Rosenberg & Kosslyn, 2011). First, the individual may arrive on campus predisposed to experience certain psychological disorders. This type of *predisposition* may be a *biological factor* (a physiological or genetic vulnerability to certain mental health problems), or it may be a *psychological factor*, stemming from the student's pre-college social and developmental experiences with family; peers, school, or neighborhood; or traumas inside or outside the home. Biological factors matter because for some mental disorders, such as schizophrenia and bipolar disorder, genetic and neurological factors are by far the strongest contributor (Rosenberg & Kosslyn, 2011). In fact, of special importance to professionals who work with traditional-age college students, the mental disorder symptoms of these types of highly *biologically predisposed disorders* most often are first experienced by the individual during late adolescence or young adulthood—the traditional college years—and can be notably disruptive for the student and those around him or her. *Pre-college psychological factors* (pre-college social, family, and trauma factors) matter because students who arrive on campus with existing concerns or psychologically problematic backgrounds often experience recurring episodes of crisis during the college years (Lippincott & Lippincott, 2007)—which, once again, may result in disruptive or disturbing behavior, potentially affecting not only the student but also roommates, classmates, and other peers, as well as faculty and student affairs and other professionals (Kitzrow, 2003).

Second, stressful circumstances during the college years can lead to psychological concerns. Turning from predispositions to *stressful circumstances*, the individual may encounter *intrapersonal or interpersonal stresses, problematic experiences, or traumas* during their college years, which can lead to mental health needs. Such stresses can include discomfort from overwhelming developmental issues; academic overwork, homesickness, and transition to college issues, peer social demands, and other college adjustment pressures; social and interpersonal difficulties arising because of ethnicity, culture, race, sexual identity, and other individual differences; being the victim of a crime, hazing, interpersonal harassment, or sexual trauma; relationship abuse; family or other off-campus concerns; finances or poverty; surviving a large-scale traumatic event; and the like (Lippincott & Lippincott, 2007; Rosenberg & Kosslyn, 2011; Schwitzer, 2003; Van Brunt, 2012). When *stress factors* contribute to a student's mental health problems, it is not only the *objective circumstance*, but also the *individual's perception and experience* of the circumstance that matters. In other words, different people might experience the same negative event with different reactions—some having only mild responses, but others having stronger reactions that fall within the mental health domain. This *interaction or combination* of (a) the individual's predispositions and (b) the level of stress in the circumstance provides an indicator of whether a mental health problem will arise. Psychologists refer to this roadmap of student mental health as the *diasthesis-stress model* (Rosenberg & Kosslyn, 2011).

Among the various mental health issues that can arise from biological predispositions, psychological predispositions, stressful circumstances, or some combination or interaction of these within a student, college counseling professionals generally agree that the most pressing issues on today's campuses—due to their prevalence among contemporary student populations, their complexity and demandingness, or their potential for disruption—are alcohol and other substance use; anxiety and depression; dating, relationships, and sexual violence; eating disorders; learning disabilities and attention-deficit hyperactivity disorder (ADHD); non-suicidal self-injury; and severe psychological issues (bipolar disorder and schizophrenia) (Gallagher, 2012; Lippincott & Lippincott, 2007; Schwitzer & Burnett, 2011).

Alcohol and Other Substance Use

Misuse of alcohol and other drugs and substances is a well-established college counseling and health concern (Archer & Cooper, 1998; Sharkin, 2012). In particular, mental health problems developing from problematic alcohol consumption continue to be especially prominent (Buettner, Andrews, & Glassman, 2009; Epler, Sher, Loomis, & O'Malley, 2009). In fact, 36% of counseling center directors reported recent increases in alcohol-related student difficulties (Gallagher, 2012). The use of alcohol and other substances evolves into a mental health concern for students when one of the following takes place: it becomes a "problematic pattern" leading to significant impairment in daily function (such as in academics or social functioning) or distress (emotional problems); the student repeatedly finds himself or herself drinking or using larger amounts, or for a longer time period, than planned; the individual engages in repeated failed attempts to cut down use; he or she continues drinking or using "despite having persistent or recurrent social or interpersonal problems" due to use; and recurrent use results in failure to meet major school, work, or social obligations, or to fulfill other major role obligations on or off campus (APA, 2013, pp. 490–491).

Anxiety and Depression

Anxiety disorders and depressive disorders are among the most common mental health problems in U.S. populations, with anxiety disorders generally being more prevalent among late adolescents and young adults than among later adults, and depression being three times more prevalent among 18–29-year-olds than among older individuals (APA, 2013). As a consequence, they are prevalent issues for college and university students (Archer & Cooper, 1998; Sharkin, 2012). Counseling centers regularly address difficulties stemming from anxiety, stress, depression, and coping (Ashby, Noble, & Gnilka, 2012; Chao, 2012). In fact, counseling centers on 52% of campuses offer depression screening days, and 69% provide stress reduction programs (Gallagher, 2012).

With anxiety disorders, the student may experience one or more of the following: excessive fear, which is an "emotional response to real or perceived imminent threat"; anxiety, which is excessive worry about a future threat; and possible panic, avoidance, and physical problems (APA, 2013, p. 189). Anxiety disorders can be disabling, impairing, and distressing. They differ from normal, everyday student anxieties, stresses, and worries because they are excessive, persistent, and cause dysfunction. With depressive disorders, the student experiences very low, empty, or irritable moods accompanied by physical symptoms (trouble with sleep, appetite, energy, etc.) and cognitive changes (hopeless thoughts, etc.) that have a very negative effect on his or her ability to function. Depressive disorders differ from everyday sadness or grief because they are characterized by emotional and cognitive suffering that causes severe symptoms and can be long-lasting or become entrenched. Although certainly not all depression leads to suicide, suicidal thoughts and behaviors are a risk that campus personnel must consider, as counseling center directors reported more than 100 completed student suicides in 2012 (Gallagher, 2012).

Dating and Relationship Violence and Sexual Violence

The need to address gender-related health and mental health problems on campus is well documented (Arnstein, 1995; Choate, 2008; Lippincott & Lippincott, 2007; Sharkin, 2012). Although the negative effects of dating violence, relationship violence, and sexual violence are certainly experienced by males and females, they are more commonly presented by college girls and women (White, Trippany, & Nolan, 2003). Rape, physical assault, stalking, and related abuses and violent behaviors all fall into this category—whether perpetrated by a person known intimately, known socially, or unknown to the student (Aspy, 2007). Difficulties resulting from physical abuse or sexual victimization within dating and romantic relationships (Aspy, 2007) and from physical violence, sexual assault or abuse, or rape (Kress, Williams, & Hoffman, 2007) are critical student mental health problems. Almost one-third of counseling center directors recently reported a perceived increase in clients arriving on campus with existing psychological difficulties from pre-college traumas, and about one-third reported increases in clients confronted by these negative situations or events during their college years (Gallagher, 2012). Students experiencing this type of traumatic background, recent traumatic event, or ongoing traumatic relationship or circumstance may develop mental symptoms that include severe fear or anxiety, impairing depression or suicidal ideation, impairing anger, feelings of worthlessness, and declines in self-esteem and sexual self-esteem (APA, 2013; Kress, Williams, et al., 2007). In more advanced situations, the student might develop the diagnosable mental disorder Post-Traumatic Stress Disorder (PTSD), which is characterized by any or all of these elements of psychological stress, as well as intrusive dreams, nightmares, or flashbacks; avoidance of people or places; certain memory problems; or other very debilitating reactions (APA, 2013).

Eating Disorders

Eating disorders are another gender-related college mental health concern. Although boys and men also experience eating-related problems (Ousley, Cordero, & White, 2008), they are far outnumbered by females with eating-related disorders (Choate, 2010, 2013; Schwitzer et al., 2008). From 25% to 40% of college girls and women (of various ethnicities, including African American, Latina, and European American students) experience moderate eating-related symptoms, including body image worries, problems brought about by unhealthy weight management, and out-of-control eating (Choate, 2010; Rich & Thomas, 2008; Schwitzer et al., 2008), and about one-fourth of college counseling center directors reported recent increases in clients with eating disorders (Gallagher, 2012). Eating disorders differ from normally expected dieting and weight concerns because they are persistent, overwhelming, distressing, and cause health or mental health impairment. Eating concerns evolve into a mental health need when the student develops an entrenched pattern characterized by refusing to maintain a normal body weight or to accept their normal body weight; engaging in recurrent unhealthy weight management behaviors such as purging through vomiting or laxative use, or excessive exercise; binge eating or lacking control over eating; misperception of body size; and cognitive-emotional problems of perfectionism and self-evaluation that is overly based on body shape and weight.

Learning Disabilities and ADHD

Learning disabilities and attention-deficit hyperactivity disorder (ADHD) are both important student counseling issues (Gallagher, 2012; Schwitzer & Burnett, 2011) that share a potential to disrupt learners' academic adjustment and possibly their social adjustment to college (Bergin & Bergin, 2007; Sharkin, 2012). Learning disabilities, or "learning disorders," are neurodevelopmental disorders that are usually documented prior to age 17 (APA, 2013, p. 66). Diagnosable learning disorders are characterized by "difficulties learning and using academic skills" (APA, 2013, p. 67), leading to measurable impairment in reading, written expression, or math. Most young adults with learning disorders are able to succeed academically in higher education. However, they may encounter hurdles that include educational disruption, language skill troubles, and pragmatic thinking difficulties (Bergin & Bergin, 2004; Henderson, 2001). They also may experience challenges such as problematic impulsiveness, poor judgment, disorganization, poor social perceptions, self-esteem problems, developmental immaturity, and social difficulties making and maintaining friendships (Bergin & Bergin, 2007; Sharkin, 2012).

ADHD also is a neurodevelopmental disorder usually emerging before young adulthood, although ADHD is sometimes first assessed during the college years (Ramsay & Rostain, 2006; Reilley, 2005). Students with ADHD experience "a persistent pattern of inattention and/or hyperactivity that interferes with functioning or development" (APA, 2013, p. 59). They confront impairment in academic or social adjustment brought about by problems focusing on the details needed to be successful in academics, work, or other campus roles; difficulty sustaining attention to school, work, or social role tasks; difficulty organizing tasks and activities, or finishing tasks; poor time management, or failing to meet normal deadlines; and other signs of inattention (APA, 2013). Likewise, they might confront difficulties associated with feeling overly restless; feeling compelled to be "on the go"; or being overly interruptive, intrusive, or impatient with others (APA, 2013). Diagnosable learning disorders and ADHD are measurable psychological disorders that are distressing and potentially impairing patterns of thought and behavior—and therefore differ from the everyday academic and personal-emotional adjustments typical of the college experience.

Non-Suicidal Self-Injury

Non-suicidal self-injury (NSSI) is an increasingly urgent college and university mental health concern (Gallagher, 2012; Kress, Trepal, Petuch, & Ilko-Hancock, 2007; Wester & Trepal, 2010). NSSI refers to "an intentional physical act, against oneself, which causes immediate tissue damage, with no intention to die from the self-harming behavior" (Nock & Prinstein, 2004; Wester & Trepal, 2010, p. 141). On U.S. campuses, examples of NSSI include cutting one's skin, scratching oneself, burning one's skin, pulling out one's hair or body hair, hitting oneself, or head banging (Nock & Prinstein, 2004; Wester & Trepal, 2010). With NSSI, the acts and gestures are non-suicidal, that is, not intended to take one's life; individuals may engage in NSSI for emotional self-regulation, for emotional control, to relieve feelings of emptiness or numbness, or to cope with histories of family discord or sexual abuse (Kress, Trepal, et al., 2007; Simeon & Favazza, 2001; Wester & Trepal, 2010). Adolescence and young adulthood are especially high-risk life phases for developing NSSI behaviors (Kress, Trepal, et al., 2007; Wester & Trepal, 2010). Learners may arrive on campus with NSSI behaviors already established or may develop them while in college (Brumberg, 2006). NSSI is a salient mental health issue because at least 7% of students actively engage in NSSI during their college years (Murray, Wester, & Paladino, 2008), and as many as 35% of college students self-injure while in college or have a previous history of NSSI (Gratz, 2001). These issues are also associated with additional academic and social adjustment problems (Kelly, Kendrick, Newgent, & Lucas, 2007).

Severe Psychological Issues: Bipolar Disorder and Schizophrenia

Although any mental health need can be or become severe, today's college students increasingly present two especially complex psychiatric conditions: bipolar disorder and schizophrenia (Federman & Thomson, 2010; Gallagher, 2012; Lippincott & Lippincott, 2007). While these are two different, very distinct disorders, they have several elements in common (Becker, Martin, Wajeeh, Ward, & Shern, 2002; Collins & Mowbray, 2005; Federman & Thomson, 2010; Lippincott & Lippincott, 2007):

- they are especially challenging mental disorders that have potentially severe negative influences on college adjustment;
- they can include acute symptoms that negatively disrupt others on campus beyond the student himself or herself (roommates, faculty, staff);
- the medications used to treat these two disorders are increasingly successful, and therefore learners with bipolar disorder or schizophrenia are more able to successfully pursue college careers; and
- these disorders, which have strong biological or genetic predisposing factors, usually first appear during late adolescence or young adulthood (the traditional college years)—and therefore commonly require attention from campus professionals (and can require a combination of counseling, medication, hospitalization, and crisis intervention).

With bipolar disorder, the student experiences one or more manic episodes. A manic episode is "a distinct period of abnormally and persistently elevated, expansive, or irritable mood and abnormally and persistently increased goal-directed activity" for a week or more at a time, in which the episode is severe enough to cause mood disturbance, social and academic or occupation impairment, or psychotic features (hallucinations or delusional thinking)—and usually is severe enough to require crisis intervention, hospitalization, and/or medication (APA, 2013, p. 124). At other times, the student might also experience episodes of depression or additional mood problems.

The schizophrenic disorders are a spectrum of disorders wherein the student experiences one or more of the following: delusions, hallucinations, disorganized thinking or speech, disorganized or abnormal behavior, and deteriorated adjustment (APA, 2013). Delusions are strong, irrational beliefs that may be implausible or not understandable to others—such as the belief that one is being persecuted by others (when this is not the case), one has special abilities or powers, one is being controlled by others, and so on. Hallucinations are perceptions that one is hearing, seeing, feeling, or otherwise sensing voices or sounds, visions, tactile stimuli, or other sensations that do not exist. Disorganized thinking, disorganized behavior, and deteriorated adjustment (clinicians call these negative symptoms) all share a reduced ability to respond appropriately to the physical and social world around oneself (APA, 2013).

Continuum of Individual and Campus Disruption

Given the wide variety of mental health problems and environmental stressors they encounter, it should come as no surprise that students often find themselves overwhelmed and struggling to achieve balance in their academic studies, personal relationships, and emotional wellness. These hurdles are exacerbated by the developmental challenges and myriad adjustments now facing students in their transition to college (Kadison, 2004). Both the individuals experiencing such concerns firsthand, as well as the higher educators who are charged with assisting these students, are impacted.

Individual difficulties increase and decrease with the ebb and flow of the academic semester. For example, the most common reason students seek services from the college counseling center is anxiety (AUCCCD, 2012; CCMH, 2012). These learners have a particularly challenging time adjusting to the numerous syllabi and instructor expectations set during the first week of classes. Traditional-age students realize that college requires more balancing and management than they experienced in high school—while non-traditional students struggle with the additional stress of balancing family, work, technology gaps, and feelings of isolation and difference from other students. Approximately one-quarter of those seeking counseling on campus experience the further strain of being a first-generation college student, while over 70% worry over financial stress (CCMH, 2012).

Students rate depression as the second-highest reason for seeking counseling services (AUCCCD, 2012; CCMH, 2012). They encounter increasing hurdles in the face of being far from home or the ennui and the struggle involved in finding meaning and purpose as they choose a major or career path. Turning to life-threatening behavior, over 25% of those seeking counseling have seriously considered suicide, with 8% having attempted suicide (AUCCCD, 2012). As the cumulative stress of the semester builds with numerous assignments, financial anxieties, and relationship complications, depression symptoms worsen. These symptoms often affect the surrounding community and professional staff as well as the student.

Sexual assault and violence also are increased risks for students as they transition to the university campus. The Association of University and College Counseling Center Directors found that 12–15% of students who seek care at the university counseling center do so as a consequence of sexual assault or rape (AUCCCD, 2012). In an environment with greater control of their personal schedule, access to alcohol and other substances, and the pressure to conform and define oneself, the risk of sexual assault increases. In addition, over one-third of students who seek services at college counseling centers do so because of relationship problems (AUCCCD, 2012). Students may lack experience with forming dating relationships or experience challenges given the increased freedom and choices available at college. In this environment, the risk increases for unclear communication, frustration, abuse, and assault.

Those students struggling with more severe mental health disorders such as bipolar disorder, schizophrenia, or ADD/ADHD may begin to question the effectiveness of their medication or ongoing psychotherapy as they explore their future with a chronic mental illness. About 50% of those seeking therapy at the counseling center report a history of treatment, with 35% reporting taking medication for mental health reasons (CCMH, 2012). Some students may attempt to be successful at college by discontinuing their medication. They may try to manage their problems on their own or become disenchanted and frustrated by being tethered to potential life-long treatment, while those around them seem to be living a carefree life of fun. Spikes in suicide attempts and inpatient admissions may occur, causing further difficulty for students already experiencing serious mental health concerns. What was once demanding becomes intolerable as they try to manage time away from school for inpatient care, assignments piling up, and the strain of feeling increasingly different from those around them.

Beyond the disruption to the individual, professional staff, administrators, and faculty also experience significant challenges with students experiencing mental health problems. These disruptions include responding to crises such as substance overdose, suicide attempts, and rape, as well as managing more chronic concerns such as odd or eccentric behavior from students with autism spectrum disorder and assisting those students with learning disorders to access services through the ADA office on campus (Van Brunt & Lewis, 2013; Kadison, 2004).

Extreme crisis events such as suicide attempts, alcohol intoxication, out-of-control manic behavior, and threats of violence create anxiety for front-line professionals such as residence hall staff, conduct officers, campus law enforcement, and student activities staff. Student affairs administrators such as Deans of Students and Vice Presidents of Student Affairs are then asked to strike a balance between the needs of the individual student and his or her family, and the safety needs of the larger community (Van Brunt, 2012; Van Brunt & Lewis, 2013). Recent changes in Office of Civil Rights (OCR) standards regarding forced medical leaves and withdrawals for students with mental health issues further complicate the administrative and legal challenges that arise from trying to manage these students (Lewis, Schuster, & Sokolow, 2012).

Following the tragedies at Virginia Tech and Northern Illinois University, staff and faculty are increasingly concerned with identifying, assessing, and intervening with students who present a threat to themselves or others on campus (Leavit, Spellings, & Gonzales, 2007; Sander, 2008). This rise of campus Behavioral Intervention Teams (BIT) requires faculty and staff to attend weekly meetings, increase their attention and focus toward at-risk student behavior, and complete wellness checks and follow-up interventions for students. In a recent study surveying over 400 institutions, the National Behavioral Intervention Team Association (NaBITA) found that 68% of behaviors handled by the team are mental health in nature (Van Brunt, Sokolow, Lewis, & Schuster, 2012).

More chronic mental health management problems take their toll on faculty and staff as well. Issues related to bullying and cyber-bullying behavior may occur with students who are seen as different or odd. A student who engages in non-suicidal self-injury in the residence hall may create cascading ripple effects that impact roommates, hallmates, instructors, parents, and the larger campus community. Staff may worry about not being vigilant enough as they attend to warning signs of violence, or struggle with the implications of reporting a student to the BIT and transforming their role from advocate to police officer.

While students struggle with their mental health problems, faculty and staff also experience a wide range of disruptions subsequent to each student's experience. Training and education can assist staff and faculty in better managing the potential stress and burnout associated with these events. Supervision and collaboration with campus mental health officials can also help mitigate this stress and frustration and ensure that staff are able to assist those struggling with mental health problems on a college campus.

Future Trend: Student Mental Health at 2-Year Colleges

Finally, today's 2-year community colleges and non-residential colleges are experiencing special challenges in providing care and managing students with mental health disorders on campus. When compared to their 4-year residential counterparts, community and 2-year colleges have fewer mental health resources and are less likely to provide on-campus psychological services (Community College Task Force [CCTF], 2013).

Further, mental health professionals at community colleges often have additional job duties and a limited ability to provide counseling treatment or offer medication management for students with more serious mental health disorders. It is common for mental health practitioners to be asked to provide academic support services or practice below their clinical abilities due to limitations in the ways community and 2-year colleges define the scope of practice for these professionals. In fact, more than 57% of counseling staff time is spent on academic issues, despite the growth in mental health concerns at these institutions (CCTF, 2013). While 73% of community colleges provide some kind of mental health services, only 51% of those staff members are licensed professionals, and only 14% offer psychiatric services (CCTF, 2013).

These service limitations are of particular concern given the non-traditional populations at 2-year institutions. Students who attend 2-year community colleges often come back to school later in life when additional stressors such as marriage, children, balancing work and school, transportation, returning from active duty in the military, and multiple financial responsibilities increase the challenge for the learner as he or she tries to manage school responsibilities as well. When mental health problems are added to the equation, the stress and potential for an acute crisis rise considerably. Naturally, these difficulties impact both the student and those professional staff who are expected to offer advocacy and care in order to promote these learners' academic success: staff can become frustrated and overwhelmed in the face of enormous need and limited resources. Coming from their perspective, community college student services professionals perceive that student problems and difficulties are identified, but services and resources to mitigate the risk are insufficient.

At the same time, among the most salient future trends in the area of college student mental health is the growing attention these issues are receiving on 2-year campuses. In the post-Virginia Tech era, community colleges are increasing the resources devoted to mental health needs on their campuses, relying more heavily on BITs, adding more formal counseling and mental health services to their array of student supports, and hiring more licensed counseling professionals. Nationally, leading 2-year institutions already have engaged in this process, and this trend will continue (Schwitzer, 2007b; Van Brunt, 2012; Virginia Tech Review Panel, 2007).

Conclusion

In many ways, today's mental health climate in higher education is the product of the success of modern interventions with students in the K–12 arena. With better early access to assessment, individualized educational plans, medication review, psychotherapy, and family support services, the United States has seen an increase in traditional-age students coming to college. For many of these matriculants, the transition to college while managing mental health difficulties creates unique challenges and worries as they adjust to new expectations and overcome acute crises.

Beyond their personal struggles, these students may generate some challenges for the professional staff that are charged with accommodating their illness, responding to crisis events, and mitigating ongoing emotional, academic, and personality struggles (see also Waple, 2006). The key to better managing the stress and difficulty that can impact administrators, staff, and faculty who encounter students struggling with mental health disorders is a better understanding of the nature of the various disorders and consulting with counseling services and mental health experts in order to choose the correct intervention. Self-care is also essential for student affairs staff. Understanding what to do when responding to mental health problems is trumped only by understanding the importance of establishing boundaries and limits, and the ability to refer students for the specialized additional support and help that college mental health experts can provide.

References

American Psychiatric Association (APA). (2013). *Diagnostic and statistical manual of mental disorders* (5th ed., DSM-5). Washington, DC: Author.

Archer, J. Jr., & Cooper, S. (1998). *Counseling and mental health services on campus: A handbook of contemporary practices and challenges.* San Francisco, CA: Jossey-Bass.

Arnstein, R.L. (1995). Mental health on the campus revisited. *Journal of American College Health, 43*(6), 248–251.

Ashby, J.S., Noble, C.L., & Gnilka, P.B. (2012). Multidimensional perfectionism, depression, and satisfaction with life: Differences among perfectionists and tests of a stress-mediation model. *Journal of College Counseling, 15*(2), 130–143.

Aspy, C.B. (2007). When dating relationships go bad: Counseling students involved in relationship violence. In J.A. Lippincott & R.B. Lippincott (Eds.), *Special populations in college counseling: A handbook for mental health professionals* (pp. 117–128). Alexandria, VA: American Counseling Association.

Association of University and College Counseling Center Directors (AUCCCD). (2012). *Survey of counseling center directors.* Retrieved from www.aucccd.org

Baker, R.W., & Siryk, B. (1999). *SACQ: Student adaptation to college questionnaire: Manual.* Los Angeles, CA: Western Psychological Services.

Becker, M., Martin, L., Wajeeh, E., Ward, J., & Shern, D. (2002). Students with mental illness in a university setting: Faculty and student attitudes, beliefs, and experiences. *Psychiatric Rehabilitation Journal, 25*(4), 359–368.

Bergin, J.W., & Bergin, J.J. (2004). The forgotten student. *ASCA School Counselor, 41*(6), 38–41.

Bergin, J.W., & Bergin, J.J.. (2007). The hidden disabilities: Counseling students with learning disabilities. In J.A. Lippincott & R.B. Lippincott (Eds.), *Special populations in college counseling: A handbook for mental health professionals* (pp. 259–272). Alexandria, VA: American Counseling Association.

Bishop, J.B. (2006). College and university counseling centers: Questions in search of answers. *Journal of College Counseling, 9*(1), 6–19.

Boyd, V., Hattauer, E., Brandel, I.W., Buckles, N., Davidshofer, C., Deakin, S., … Steel. C.M. (2003). Accreditation standards for university and college counseling centers. *Journal of Counseling & Development, 81*(2), 168–177.

Brumberg, J.J. (2006). Are we facing an epidemic of self-injury? *Chronicle of Higher Education, 53*, p. B6.

Buettner, C.K., Andrews, D.W., & Glassman, M. (2009). Development of a student engagement approach to alcohol prevention: The pragmatics project. *Journal of American College Health, 58*(1), 33–38.

Center for Collegiate Mental Health (CCMH). (2012). *2012 annual report.* Pennsylvania State University. Retrieved from http://ccmh.squarespace.com/storage/CCMH_Annual_Report_2012.pdf

Chao, R.C.-L. (2012). Managing perceived stress among college students: The roles of social support and dysfunctional coping. *Journal of College Counseling, 15*(1), 5–21.

Choate, L.H. (2008). *Girls' and women's wellness: Contemporary counseling issues and interventions.* Alexandria, VA: American Counseling Association.

Choate, L.H. (2010). Counseling college women experiencing eating disorder not otherwise specified: A cognitive behavior therapy model. *Journal of College Counseling, 13*(1), 73–86.

Choate, L.H. (Ed.). (2013). *Eating disorders and obesity: A counselor's guide to prevention and treatment.* Alexandria, VA: American Counseling Association.

Collins, M.E., & Mowbray, C.T. (2005). Higher education and psychiatric disabilities: National survey of campus disability services. *American Journal of Orthopsychiatry, 75*(2), 304–315.

Community College Task Force. (2013). *Community College Task Force survey.* Alexandria, VA: American College Counseling Association.

Council for the Advancement of Standards in Higher Education. (2011). *Counseling services: CAS standards and guidelines.* Retrieved from http://www.collegecounseling.org/cas-counseling-standards

Davis, D.C., & Humphrey, K.M. (2000). *College counseling: Issues and strategies for a new millennium.* Alexandria, VA: American Counseling Association.

Drum, D., & Lawler, A. (1988). Developmental interventions: Theories, principles, and practice. Columbus, OH: Merrill.

Dungy, G.J. (2003).Organization and functions of student affairs. In S.R. Komives, D.B. Woodard, Jr., & Associates (Eds.), *Student services: A handbook for the profession* (4th ed., pp. 339–357). San Francisco, CA: Jossey-Bass.

Epler, A.J., Sher, K.J., Loomis, T.B., & O'Malley, S.S. (2009). College student receptiveness to various alcohol treatment options. *Journal of American College Health, 58*(1), 26–32.

Evans, N.J., Forney, D.S., Guido, F.M., Patton, L.D., & Renn, K.A. (2010). *Student development in college: Theory, research, and practice* (2nd ed.). San Francisco, CA: Jossey-Bass.

Federman, R., & Thomson, J.A. Jr. (2010). *Facing bipolar: The young adult's guide to dealing with bipolar disorder.* Oakland, CA: New Harbinger.

Gallagher, R.P. (2009, Spring). Highlights of the 2008 national survey of counseling center directors. *Visions*, 3–6. Alexandria, VA: American College Counseling Association.

Gallagher, R.P. (2012). *National survey of college counseling 2012.* American College Counseling Association, Monograph Series Number 9T. Retrieved from http://www.collegecounseling.org/wpcontent/uploads/NSCCD_Survey_2012.pdf

Gratz, K.L. (2001). Measurement of deliberate self-harm: Preliminary data on the Deliberate Self-Harm Inventory. *Journal of Psychopathology and Behavioral Assessment, 23*(4), 253–263.

Henderson, C. (2001). *College freshmen with disabilities: A biennial statistical profile.* Washington, DC: American Council on Education.

Hodges, S. (2001). University counseling centers at the twenty-first century: Looking forward, looking back. *Journal of College Counseling, 4*(2), 161–173.

Jenks Kettmann, J. D., Schoen, E. G., Moel, J. E., Cochran, S. V., Greenberg, S. T., & Corkery, J. M. (2007). Increasing severity of psychopathology at counseling centers: A new look. *Professional Psychology: Research and Practice, 38*(5), 523–529.

Kadison, R. (2004). *College of the overwhelmed: The campus mental health crisis and what to do about it.* San Francisco, CA: Jossey-Bass.

Kelly, J.T., Kendrick, M.M., Newgent, .A., & Lucas, C.J. (2007). Strategies for student transition to college: A proactive approach. *College Student Journal, 41*(1), 1021–1035.

Kitzrow, M.A. (2003). The mental health needs of today's college students: Challenges and recommendations. *NASPA Journal, 41*(1), 167–181.

Kress, V.E., Trepal, H., Petuch, A., & Ilko-Hancock, S. (2007). Self-injurious behavior: Counseling students who self-injure. In J.A. Lippincott & R.B. Lippincott (Eds.), *Special populations in college counseling: A handbook for mental health professionals* (pp. 297–308). Alexandria, VA: American Counseling Association.

Kress, V.E., Williams, R.L., & Hoffman, R. (2007). Counseling college students who have been sexually assaulted. In J.A. Lippincott & R.B. Lippincott (Eds.), *Special populations in college counseling: A handbook for mental health professionals* (pp. 129–142). Alexandria, VA: American Counseling Association.

Leavit, M., Spellings, M., & Gonzales, A. (2007). *The report to the president on issues raised by the Virginia Tech tragedy.* Retrieved from http://www.hhs.gov/vtreport.pdf

Lewis, W., Schuster S., & Sokolow, B. (2012). *Suicidal students, BITs and the direct threat standard.* Retrieved from www.nabita.org

Lippincott, J.A., & Lippincott, R.B. (Eds.). (2007). *Special populations in college counseling: A handbook for mental health professionals.* Alexandria, VA: American Counseling Association.

May, R. (1988). Boundaries and voices in college psychotherapy. In R. May (Ed.), *Psychoanalytic psychotherapy in a college context.* New York, NY: Praeger.

Murray, C., Wester, K.L., & Paladino, D. (2008). Dating violence and self-injury among undergraduate college students: Attitudes and experiences. *Journal of College Counseling, 11*(1), 42–57.

Nock, M.K., & Prinstein, M.J. (2004). A functional approach to the assessment of self-mutilative behavior. *Journal of Consulting and Clinical Psychology, 72*(5), 885–890.

Ousley, L., Cordero, E.D., & White, S. (2008). Eating disorders and body image of undergraduate men. *Journal of American College Health, 56*(6), 617–621.

Pope, R.L., Reynolds, A.L., & Mueller, J.A. (2004). *Multicultural competencies in student affairs.* San Francisco, CA: Jossey-Bass.

Ramsay, J.R., & Rostain, A.L. (2006). Cognitive behavior therapy for college students with attention-deficit/hyperactivity disorder. *Journal of College Counseling, 21*(1), 3–20.

Reifler, C.B., Liptzin, M.B., & Fox, J.T. (2006). College psychiatry as public health psychiatry. *Journal of American College Health, 54*(6), 317–325.

Reilley, S.P. (2005). Empirically informed attention-deficit/hyperactivity disorder evaluation with college students. *Journal of College Counseling, 8*(2), 153–164.

Reynolds, A. L. (2011). Counseling and helping skills. In J. Schuh, S. Jones, & S. Harper (Eds.), *Student services: A handbook for the profession* (5th ed.) (pp. 399–412). San Francisco, CA: Jossey-Bass.

Rich, S.S., & Thomas, C.R. (2008). Body mass index, disordered eating behavior, and acquisition of health information: Examining ethnicity and weight-related issues in a college population. *Journal of American College Health, 56*(6), 623–628.

Rosenberg, R.S., & Kosslyn, S.M. (2011). *Abnormal psychology.* New York, NY: Worth.

Rudd, M.D. (2004). University counseling centers: Looking more and more like community clinics. *Professional Psychology: Research & Practice, 35*(3), 316–317.

Sander, L. (2008). At Northern Illinois U., leaders grapple with a tragedy. *Chronicle of Higher Education, 54*(25), A26.

Schwartz, A. J. (2006). Are college students more disturbed today? Stability in the acuity and qualitative character of psychopathology of college counseling center clients: 1992–1993 through 2001–2002. *Journal of American College Health, 54*(6), 327–337.

Schwitzer, A.M. (1997). Utilization-focused evaluation: Proposing a useful method of program evaluation for college counselors and student development professionals. *Measurement and Evaluation in Counseling and Development, 30*(1), 50–61.

Schwitzer, A.M. (2002). Using a chain-of-effects framework to meet institutional accountability demands. *Journal of American College Health, 50*(4), 183–186.

Schwitzer, A. M. (2003). A framework for college counseling responses to large scale traumatic incidents. *Journal of College Student Psychotherapy, 18*(2), 49–66.

Schwitzer, A.M. (2007a). In memoriam. *Journal of College Counseling, 10,* 97.

Schwitzer, A.M. (2007b, March). *Psychological difficulties: Beyond the characteristics.* Conference address, Annual Conference of the Association for Higher Education and Disability (AHEAD), in Norfolk, VA.

Schwitzer, A.M. (2012). Humanism in college and university counseling. In M.B. Scholl, A.S. McGowan, & J.T. Hansen (Eds.), *Humanistic perspectives on contemporary counseling issues* (pp. 227–254). New York, NY: Routledge.

Schwitzer, A.M., Ancis, J.R., & Brown, N. (2001). *Promoting student learning and student development at a distance: Student affairs concepts and practices for televised instruction and other forms of distance learning.* Washington, DC: American College Personnel Association.

Schwitzer, A.M, & Burnett, D. (2011, March). *College counseling and psychological services: Summarizing ten years of literature.* Presentation at the annual meeting of the convention of the American College Personnel Association, Baltimore, MD.

Schwitzer, A.M., Hatfield, T., Jones, A.R., Duggan, M.H., Jurgens, J., & Winninger, A. (2008). Diagnosing, conceptualizing, and treating eating disorders not otherwise specified. *Journal of American College Health, 90*(3), 281–289.

Sharkin, B. S. (1997). Increasing severity of presenting problems in college counseling centers: A closer look. *Journal of Counseling and Development, 75*(4), 275–281.

Sharkin, B.S. (2012). *Being a college counselor on today's campus: Roles, contributions, and special challenges.* New York, NY: Routledge.

Simeon, D., & Favazza, V.R. (2001). Self-injurious behaviors: Phenomenology and assessment. In D. Simeon & E. Hollander (Eds.), *Self-injurious behaviors: Assessment and treatment* (pp. 1–28). Washington, DC: American Psychiatric Press.

Stone, G.L., & Archer, J. Jr. (1990). College and university counseling centers in the 1990s: Challenges and limits. *Counseling Psychologist, 18*(4), 539–607.

Van Brunt, B. (2012). *Ending campus violence: New approaches to prevention.* New York, NY: Routledge.

Van Brunt, B., & Lewis, W.S. (2013). *A faculty guide to disruptive and dangerous behavior.* New York, NY: Routledge.

Van Brunt, B., Sokolow, B., Lewis, W., & Schuster, S. (2012). *NaBITA team survey.* Retrieved from www.nabita.org

Virginia Tech Review Panel. (2007). *Mass shootings at Virginia Tech, April 16, 2007: Report of the review panel.* Richmond, VA: Author.

Waple, J.N. (2006). An assessment of skills and competencies necessary for entry-level student affairs work. *NASPA Journal, 43*(1), 1–18.

Wester, K.L., & Trepal, H.C. (2010). Coping behaviors, abuse history, and counseling: Differentiating college students who self-injure. *Journal of College Counseling, 13*(2), 141–154.

White, V.E., Trippany, R.L., & Nolan, J. (2003). Responding to sexual assault victims: A primer for college counselors. *Journal of College Counseling, 6*, 124–133.

TWENTY FIVE

Undergraduate College Drinking: A Brief Review of the Literature

Jason R. Kilmer and Véronique S. Grazioli

College entrance for an undergraduate student represents a critical period associated with a significant increase in alcohol use (Hartzler & Fromme, 2003). In fact, college students are at greater risk regarding alcohol use than their peers not enrolled in college (Johnston, O'Malley, Bachman, & Schulenberg, 2010; Substance Abuse and Mental Health Services Administration, 2012). In response, tremendous research efforts have been made to better understand this phenomenon and to develop specific alcohol-related prevention and intervention efforts tailored to this population. These efforts have revealed the uniqueness of college drinking and related factors (Ham & Hope, 2003). Although students in technical and community colleges (i.e., 2-year schools) and graduate schools (i.e., following completion of an undergraduate degree) clearly face challenges related to health, mental health, and substance abuse, the majority of the research on "college student drinking" has focused on undergraduates at 4-year institutions.

The purpose of this chapter is to briefly review the general trends from college campuses, focus on specific factors associated with alcohol use among undergraduate college students, explore the co-occurring issues shared by this population, review prevention and intervention efforts made to reduce alcohol-related harm, and explore future directions and implications for those working directly with college students.

General Trends in College Student Drinking

Prevalence of Alcohol Use in the College Population

Alcohol consumption is common on college campuses. Almost 80% of college students report that they have consumed alcohol at least once in the past year, and approximately two-thirds report drinking in the past 30 days (Johnston, O'Malley, Bachman, & Schulenberg, 2013). College students may engage in heavy episodic drinking (HED), which is defined as having five or more drinks in a row for men and four or more for women (Wechsler, Dowdall, Davenport, & Castillo, 1995). Prevalence rates of HED in the last 30 days for the college population are known to be high and have remained quite stable over the past several decades (i.e., 44% and 37% in 1980 and 2012, respectively) (Johnston et al., 2013). Further, among heavy drinkers, many drink well beyond the heavy drinking threshold: 14% of college students report having 10 or more drinks in a row, and 5% report having 15 or more drinks in a row on at least one occasion in the past 2 weeks (Johnston et al., 2013).

This pattern of alcohol use increases the risk of developing an alcohol-use disorder (AUD) (Jennison, 2004; Knight et al., 2002). Although approximately one in five college students meets past-year criteria for an alcohol use disorder, only 3.9% of full-time students with an AUD receive services of any kind (Wu, Pilowsky, Schlenger, & Hasin, 2007). Further, while some students "mature out" of problematic drinking after college, some maintain AUDs upon college completion (i.e., about half of college students diagnosed with an AUD still exhibit it at age 25) (Sher & Gotham, 1999).

Most research on college drinking has been conducted in the United States. There is, however, empirical evidence of a generally similar pattern of college drinking in many other countries (Karam, Kypri, & Salamoun, 2007; Kypri et al., 2009). With one study of Swedish college students showing more risky drinking (Stahlbrandt et al., 2008) and others highlighting the lack of research in many regions of the world (Karam et al., 2007), further research is needed worldwide.

Alcohol-Related Consequences

Many harmful outcomes are associated with alcohol use, particularly heavy drinking among college students (Perkins, 2002). We review a sample of such outcomes here.

Impaired Academic Performance

Although there is some inconsistency among findings, alcohol use has been most often associated with impaired academic performance (Perkins, 2002). In particular, heavy episodic college drinkers are more likely to report that drinking made them miss a class, fall behind in their schoolwork, or perform poorly on a task or a project (Presley & Pimentel, 2006; Singleton & Wolfson, 2009; Wechsler, Lee, Kuo, & Lee, 2000). Further, a negative association has been found between alcohol use and grade-point average (Singleton, 2007; Wolaver, 2002). Yet when accounting for precollege factors likely to explain this relationship (e.g., high school academic aptitudes), this relationship was found to be either modest (Singleton, 2007) or no longer significant (Wood, Sher, Erickson, & DeBord, 1997).

Other factors could play a part in how alcohol use affects academic success. Alcohol use was found to be related to a later sleep-wake schedule, which was in turn associated with more daily sleepiness and lower academic performance (Singleton & Wolfson, 2009). In addition, heavy drinking episodes have been associated with impaired verbal declarative memory (i.e., ability to recall everyday events and factual knowledge) (Eichenbaum, 2000; Parada et al., 2011) and poorer performance of certain executive functions (i.e., lower capacity to retain and manipulate information in verbal working memory) (Parada et al., 2012). Ongoing research is needed to evaluate the relationship between alcohol use and cognitive factors and to examine its impact on academic performance over time (Parada et al., 2011).

Physical Illness Caused by Alcohol Consumption and Blackouts

Many college students experience short-term, health-related consequences brought on by alcohol consumption, including nausea, vomiting, and hangovers (Perkins, 2002). For instance, 30% of male and 52% of female students report having experienced hangovers/sickness in the past 2 months (Read, Wood, Lejuez, Palfai, & Slack, 2004). Heavy drinking episodes can also induce a type of memory impairment referred to as a "blackout." A blackout involves amnesia for events that occurred under the influence of alcohol, without the subject's being unconscious (White, Jamieson-Drake, & Swartzwelder, 2002). Experiencing blackouts is quite common among the college population, with 34% of undergraduates who drink reporting having forgotten where they were or what they did while drinking at least once in the past year (American College Health Association, 2012).

Unintended/Unprotected Sexual Activity, Interpersonal Violence, and Sexual Assault

There is evidence that alcohol use in college increases the risk of engaging in unintended sexual activity as well as not protecting against pregnancy or sexually transmitted diseases (Perkins, 2002). Among undergraduate college drinkers, 20.3% report having had unprotected sex while under the influence of alcohol in the past year (American College Health Association, 2012). Further, alcohol can have consequences related to anger and violence. Almost one in four (22.9%) college drinkers reported arguing with friends while drinking at least once in the past year (Wechsler et al., 2002). It has been estimated that over 696,000 U.S. college students were hit or assaulted by a drinking college student, with 97,000 having been victims of alcohol-related sexual assaults or date rapes (Hingson, Heeren, Winter, & Wechsler, 2003). Sexual assault refers to forced touching or kissing, verbally coerced intercourse, and/or forced vaginal or anal penetration; it is unfortunately quite common on campus (Abbey, 2002). Research reveals that alcohol use increases the risk of such occurrence (Abbey, 2002; Palmer, McMahon, Rounsaville, & Ball, 2010), with 50–75% of sexual assaults involving alcohol use by the perpetrator and/or the victim (Abbey, 2002; Abbey, Thomson Ross, McDuffie, & McAuslan, 1996). This highlights the importance of campus efforts to provide support services for and education about sexual assault and relationship violence.

Impaired Driving

Approximately 2.7 million U.S. college students drove after drinking last year (Hingson & White, 2012). Among undergraduates who drive and report alcohol use, 2.8% report having driven after five or more drinks in the past month, and 21.4% after any alcohol in the past month (American College Health Association, 2012).

Injuries and Deaths

Among undergraduates who drink, 16.7% report physically injuring themselves while drinking in the last 12 months (American College Health Association, 2012). Of 1,870 deaths from alcohol-related, unintentional injuries among 18–24 year-old U.S. college students in 2007, most (1,395) were caused by traffic accidents that involved alcohol or were a result of alcohol poisoning (262) (Hingson & White, 2012).

Risk Factors

Efforts have also been underway to identify subgroups of drinkers who might be at greater risk of experiencing harm, and a selection of these are reviewed here.

Demographics: Ethnicity and Gender

Research has consistently identified different patterns of drinking across ethnic groups. In particular, White students report the most HED, followed by Hispanics/Latinos, whereas Asian-Pacific Islander Americans and African Americans typically report less drinking and HED than other ethnic groups (Del Boca, Darkes, Greenbaum, & Goldman, 2004; O'Malley & Johnston, 2002; Wechsler et al., 2002). Further, research has indicated that male students drink more often, in larger quantity, and engage in higher-risk drinking than female students (O'Malley & Johnston, 2002). Although this trend appears to be quite stable over time, there is evidence that high-risk drinking practices, such as engaging in heavy drinking episodes, is escalating among female students (Kelly-Weeder, 2008; O'Malley & Johnston, 2002). Further, even though male students report more drinking, male and female students report similar levels of alcohol-related sequelae (Perkins, 2002).

College-Specific Social Contexts and Activities

Certain living arrangements and/or involvement in organizations, for example residence hall living and Greek organizations, are known to place students at higher risk of problem drinking (Larimer et al., 2001; Wechsler et al., 2002). Similarly, student-athletes report more alcohol use, heavy episodic drinking, and alcohol-related consequences than non-athletes (Hildebrand, Johnson, & Bogle, 2001; Leichliter, Meilman, Presley, & Cashin, 1998; Nelson & Wechsler, 2003).

Drinking Motives and Alcohol Expectancies

Drinking motives refer to reasons why students consume alcohol, including to be social, to conform, to cope with negative affect, and to enhance experience (Cooper, Frone, Russell, & Mudar, 1995). Drinking enhancement and coping motives have been associated with heavy drinking and alcohol-related consequences, respectively (Carey, 1993; Kassel, Jackson, & Unrod, 2000).

Very close to the concept of drinking motives are alcohol expectancies. Expectancies are beliefs endorsed by students about the effects of alcohol, which can be positive (e.g., "I feel more social when I drink") or negative (e.g., "alcohol makes me aggressive"). In general, research has revealed that students who engage in problem drinking have more positive alcohol expectancies than non-problem drinker students (Del Boca et al., 2004; Greenbaum, Del Boca, Darkes, Wang, & Goldman, 2005; Lewis & O'Neill, 2000), and this is particularly true for men (Read et al., 2004; Thompson et al., 2009).

Personality: Impulsivity Traits

Certain impulsive traits have been consistently associated with alcohol use in college. For instance, higher levels of sensation seeking (i.e., a tendency to prefer and enjoy physiological arousal and novel experiences, even if they might be risky) (Adams, Kaiser, Lynam, Charnigo, & Milich, 2012) have been associated with alcohol use and heavy drinking (Curcio & George, 2011; Del Boca et al., 2004; White, Kraus, & Swartzwelder, 2006), whereas lack of premeditation (i.e., a tendency to behave without planning and considering potential consequences) and negative urgency (i.e., impulsive behaviors under conditions of negative affects) have been associated with problem drinking (Adams et al., 2012).

First Age of Onset

Early initiation into drinking tends to be associated with increased risks and problems. The literature has established that students who report having first been drunk prior to age 19 are more likely to (a) meet criteria of alcohol dependence, (b) report frequent heavy drinking, (c) report driving after drinking, (d) report riding with a driver who was intoxicated, and (e) report being injured (Hingson, Heeren, Zakocs, Winter, & Wechsler, 2003). Further, another study has revealed that college drinkers who report having first been drunk before age 13 are more likely to report unplanned and/or unprotected sex because of drinking than those who never drank until age 19 (Hingson, Heeren, Winter, et al., 2003).

Event- and Context-Specific Drinking

Given the pattern of college drinking (i.e., fluctuation throughout the year and high prevalence of heavy drinking occasions), researchers have worked to identify events and contexts that might be associated with an increase in problematic drinking.

Event-Specific Drinking

Spring Break and 21st birthdays are two events that have been associated with increased alcohol consumption (Beets et al., 2009; Lee, Lewis, & Neighbors, 2009; Lewis, Lindgren, Fossos, Neighbors, & Oster-Aaland, 2009). For instance, research shows that compared to typical weekly consumption, students consume significantly more alcohol and experience more negative consequences—44% of students report hangovers, 26% report vomiting, and 31% report blackouts during the week of their 21st birthday (Lewis et al., 2009). Other events have been found to be associated with increased rates of drinking as well as reaching higher blood alcohol content, including New Year's Eve, New Year's Day, Independence Day, and graduation (Neighbors et al., 2011).

Research has also found that students who are most likely to experience negative consequences related to HED during the week of their 21st birthday (Lewis et al., 2009) and Spring Break (Lee et al., 2009) are those who do not typically report drinking excessively. Students who have little or no drinking experience thus appear to be at high risk when drinking heavily on a "special occasion" (Lee et al., 2009; Lewis et al., 2009).

Drinking Games Participation

Drinking games are common on college campuses, with 47–62% of college students reporting participation in activities with various rules and skills that have the apparent goal of getting the participant intoxicated quickly (Borsari, Bergen-Cico, & Carey, 2003). Research has demonstrated that drinking games are associated with greater frequency and quantity of alcohol use, as well as alcohol-related consequences (Johnson & Cropsey, 2000; Zamboanga, Leitkowski, Rodriguez, & Cascio, 2006).

Prepartying

Prepartying (also referred to as "pregaming") refers to drinking alcohol prior to departing for an event (e.g., party, bar, concert, sporting event) where more alcohol may or may not be consumed (LaBrie & Pedersen, 2008), and this could include drinking games (described above). Research reveals that up to 85% of college drinkers engage at least once a month in prepartying (LaBrie & Pedersen, 2008; Pedersen & LaBrie, 2007). Prepartying has been associated with further heavy drinking post-partying (Pedersen & LaBrie, 2007) and increased levels of BACs (Borsari, Boyle, et al., 2007); this might be particularly true for women (LaBrie & Pedersen, 2008). Research has consistently found prepartying to be associated with more alcohol-related problems such as blackouts and passing out (LaBrie & Pedersen, 2008; Pedersen & LaBrie, 2007).

Energy Drinks

Energy drinks are beverages that are designed to provide a burst of energy through a range of ingredients (e.g., ginseng) (Brache & Stockwell, 2011). About one in four college drinkers reports consumption of alcohol mixed with energy drinks (AmED) in the last month (Brache & Stockwell, 2011; Miller, 2008; O'Brien, McCoy, Rhodes, Wagoner, & Wolfson, 2008). In general, research has found AmED to be more prevalent among males, Whites, athletes, fraternity or sorority members, and younger students (O'Brien et al., 2008). College students who consume AmED tend to drink alcohol in larger quantities and more frequently than students who do not mix alcohol with energy drinks, and this behavior has also been associated with an increased risk of experiencing alcohol-related consequences (Brache & Stockwell, 2011; O'Brien et al., 2008; Thombs et al., 2010).

Peer Influence: Norm Perceptions

The indirect influence of peers on college drinking through perceived norms has received considerable research attention (Borsari & Carey, 2001). Perceived norms include beliefs about peers' drinking behaviors (i.e., descriptive norms) and the degree to which peers approve of these behaviors (i.e., injunctive norms) (Borsari & Carey, 2001). Students consistently overestimate the prevalence and rates of drinking as well as the acceptability of excessive behavior (Borsari et al., 2003; Neighbors, Lee, Lewis, Fossos, & Larimer, 2007). Perceived descriptive norms are among the strongest predictors of drinking behaviors in the college population (Borsari et al., 2003; Borsari & Carey, 2001; Larimer, Turner, Mallett, & Geisner, 2004; Lewis & Neighbors, 2004; Neighbors et al., 2007). Literature has established that perceived descriptive norms are even stronger predictors of problematic drinking when they are gender-specific (i.e., they are perceptions of same-sex drinking), and that perceived same-sex drinking norms are more strongly associated with drinking among female students than among male students (Lewis & Neighbors, 2004).

Overall, research on perceived injunctive norms has also revealed their predictive role on drinking behaviors in the college population (Larimer et al., 2004; Neighbors et al., 2007), with perceived approval of important others (i.e., close friends, parents) specifically predicting drinking behaviors (Neighbors et al., 2008). Further, students tend to overestimate peers' approval of driving after drinking, which has been found to predict this risky behavior over time (LaBrie, Napper, & Ghaidarov, 2012).

Protective Factors

An extensive body of work has documented the use of protective behavioral strategies (PBS) aimed at mitigating the harmful consequences of heavy drinking among college students (Benton et al., 2004; Martens et al., 2005). PBSs refer to cognitive and behavioral strategies that can be used to limit alcohol use and related consequences when students choose to drink (Martens, Pedersen, LaBrie, Ferrier, & Cimini, 2007), including using a designated driver, staying with the same group of friends during the entire drinking occasion, eating before and/or during drinking, and keeping track of how many drinks have been consumed. College students' PBS use has been associated with reduced alcohol use and related harm (Araas & Adams, 2008; Benton et al., 2004; Martens et al., 2007).

A few other protective factors have been documented in the literature, including parental influences (Borsari, Murphy, & Barnett, 2007). For instance, quality of parent-child relationships (Turner, Larimer, & Sarason, 2000), parental monitoring (e.g., knowing where their children go and what they do when they go out), and disapproval of alcohol use have been found to be negatively associated with alcohol-related consequences among college students (Wood, Read, Mitchell, & Brand, 2004). Finally, living at home with parents or family (i.e., not with peers) has been found to be a predictor of less drinking among college students (Gfroerer, Greenblatt, & Wright, 1997; Wechsler et al., 1995).

Evidence also shows that religion appears to act as a buffer against problematic drinking (Kitsantas, Kitsantas, & Anagnostopoulou, 2008). Specifically, there is an association between intrinsic religiosity (i.e., internalized and meaningful integration of religious beliefs in one's life) and less alcohol use in college (Galen & Rogers, 2004).

Co-Occurring Issues

College campuses typically provide counseling and additional support for students struggling with mental health issues, and these often co-occur with the use of alcohol and other substances. Associations have been demonstrated between problematic drinking and problematic eating (e.g., bulimia symptoms) (Anderson, Simmons, Martens, Ferrier, & Sheehy, 2006), mood disorders (e.g., depression, anxiety, and social phobia) (Dawson, Grant, Stinson, & Chou, 2005), and attention deficit/hyperactivity disorder (ADHD) (Blase et al., 2009; Glass & Flory, 2012). Additional research is needed to address etiology, prevention, and appropriate intervention for these co-occurring issues.

Prevention/Intervention Efforts

As early as the 1970s and 1980s, prevention efforts emerged and grew on college campuses, yet most of what was being implemented had no demonstrated effectiveness (Gadaleto & Anderson, 1986). This changed with the emergence of the Alcohol Skills Training Program (ASTP), a group-based intervention using motivational enhancement strategies and emphasizing strategies for reducing the harms associated with drinking (much like the PBS described above) for those who choose to drink (Fromme, Kivlahan, & Marlatt, 1986; Kivlahan, Marlatt, Fromme, Coppel, & Williams, 1990). Subsequent research compared the ASTP to single-session interventions and eventually led to the development of the Brief Alcohol Screening and Intervention for College Students (BASICS), a personalized feedback intervention in which the impacts of drinking are presented to a student by a facilitator who utilizes motivational interviewing strategies to elicit personally relevant reasons to change (Dimeff, Baer, Kivlahan, & Marlatt, 1999). A full 4 years after the intervention, BASICS participants reported significant reductions in drinking and related consequences (Baer, Kivlahan, Blume, McKnight, & Marlatt, 2001). In later years, subsequent research demonstrated the impact of extensions of in-person, personalized feedback interventions to feedback delivered through other outlets—including the mail, computers, and the Internet (Cronce & Larimer, 2011; Larimer & Cronce, 2007).

Additional research established other opportunities for prevention. As the field began to understand the impact of misperceptions of drinking norms (see above), efforts to correct those misperceptions were incorporated into programs like ASTP and BASICS. They were the focus of social norms mass-marketing campaigns (advertising on campus what "most" students do, for example) and eventually became stand-alone personalized normative feedback interventions.

The impact of expectancies (also described above) provided another opportunity. Research utilizing the balanced-placebo design demonstrated that students who are told they are receiving alcohol, yet who receive a placebo, nevertheless demonstrate the social effects typically attributed to alcohol. These findings served to advance expectancy challenge research and the implications for the college setting (Kilmer, Cronce, & Larimer, 2014).

In 2002, the National Institute on Alcohol Abuse and Alcoholism (NIAAA) released the "Call to Action" Task Force report and provided suggestions for responding to college student alcohol use that were organized by tiers of effectiveness. Approaches with demonstrated effectiveness in reducing alcohol use, consequences, or both ("Tier One") were: (a) combining cognitive behavioral skills with norms clarification and motivation enhancement strategies (the only program mentioned by name as an example was the ASTP), (b) offering brief motivational enhancement interventions (the only example offered was BASICS), and (c) challenging alcohol expectancies. Additional efforts, including environmental strategies, policies (and their enforcement), and campus-based practices were highlighted as well, yet it was noted that these approaches needed to be further researched for their impact in the college setting (National Institute on Alcohol Abuse and Alcoholism, 2002). Subsequent updates from NIAAA in 2007 and 2011 highlight the many empirically supported and evidence-based approaches available to address this issue (National Institute on Alcohol Abuse and Alcoholism, 2007, 2011).

Future Directions

Undergraduates report several challenges and struggles, and this is certainly being sensed on college campuses as student affairs and student life staff and administrators consider how to best meet students' needs. Briefly, future directions may include:

- *Early identification of students who may be struggling.* In an effort to reduce the likelihood of students "slipping through the cracks," more campuses are screening and referring to (or providing) brief interventions in counseling and health center settings independent of the reason that prompted a student's clinical visit. In fact, the efficacy of this has been so well established that it has been stated that if more campuses implemented screening, it would ultimately have a population-wide benefit because it would connect more students to empirically supported intervention approaches (Hingson, 2010). On other campuses, proactive efforts to reach out to students following medical transports provide a way to check in separate from student conduct or judicial affairs to see what the needs of the student might be (Kilmer & Bailie, 2012).

- *Other substances.* It is clear that alcohol use does not occur in a vacuum, and more research is needed to determine how to best approach other substances (e.g., marijuana, prescription drugs used for non-medical reasons, etc.) as well as use of more than one substance at the same time.
- *Bystander interventions.* Tragically, the alcohol-related death of a college student occurs far too often. In addition to programs tailored for those who engage in high-risk drinking, other programs emphasize the role bystanders can play in getting help for a classmate. Such programs (e.g., the "Red Watch Band") (Stony Brook University, 2009) teach participants the signs of alcohol poisoning and review steps to take when an emergency occurs. Additional research can examine how to bring such programs to scale and under what circumstances (and for whom) they work most effectively.
- *Collaborations within and across campuses.* As early as the NIAAA Task Force report, the value of getting key stakeholders to the same table on campus was highlighted. Increased collaboration across campus can help to bring staff from multiple offices onto the same page and to address trends and approach a strategic plan in a multi-faceted way. Recently, national efforts have emphasized collaboration across campuses so that institutions of higher education can learn from one another's successes and challenges while improving the quality of prevention and intervention in the college setting (e.g., the National College Health Improvement Project) (Dartmouth College, 2011). Future efforts can continue to expand such collaborations within regions and/or nationally.
- *Community colleges.* Much of the research on college student drinking has tended to focus on 4-year institutions, and more research is needed on trends within community colleges as well as best practices for prevention and intervention programs for and with these students.

The start of each academic year brings an entirely new segment to the campus community; this turnover, and the ever-changing make-up of the campus community, underlines the fact that responding to college student alcohol use is an ongoing effort. As a field, we can continue to work together to understand factors that contribute to drinking and ways to best meet the needs of our students.

References

Abbey, A. (2002). Alcohol-related sexual assault: A common problem among college students. *Journal of Studies on Alcohol, Supplement 14*, 118–128.

Abbey, A., Thomson Ross, L., McDuffie, D., & McAuslan, P. (1996). Alcohol and dating risk factors for sexual assault among college women. *Psychology of Women Quarterly, 20*(1), 147–169.

Adams, Z.W., Kaiser, A.J., Lynam, D.R., Charnigo, R.J., & Milich, R. (2012). Drinking motives as mediators of the impulsivity-substance use relation: Pathways for negative urgency, lack of premeditation, and sensation seeking. *Addictive Behaviors, 37*(7), 848–855. doi: 10.1016/j.addbeh.2012.03.016

American College Health Association. (2012). *National College Health Assessment II: Reference group executive summary Fall 2012.* Hanover, MD: American College Health Association.

Anderson, D.A., Simmons, A.M., Martens, M.P., Ferrier, A.G., & Sheehy, M.J. (2006). The relationship between disordered eating behavior and drinking motives in college-age women. *Eating Behaviors, 7*(4), 419–422. doi: 10.1016/j.eatbeh.2005.12.001

Araas, T.E., & Adams, T.B. (2008). Protective behavioral strategies and negative alcohol-related consequences in college students. *Journal of Drug Education, 38*(3), 211–224.

Baer, J.S., Kivlahan, D.R., Blume, A.W., McKnight, P., & Marlatt, G.A. (2001). Brief intervention for heavy-drinking college students: 4-year follow-up and natural history. *American Journal of Public Health, 91*(8), 1310–1316.

Beets, M.W., Flay, B.R., Vuchinich, S., Li, K.K., Acock, A., & Snyder, F.J. (2009). Longitudinal patterns of binge drinking among first year college students with a history of tobacco use. *Drug and Alcohol Dependence, 103*(1–2), 1–8. doi: 10.1016/j.drugalcdep.2008.12.017

Benton, S.L., Schmidt, J.L., Newton, F.B., Shin, K., Benton, S.A., & Newton, D.W. (2004). College student protective strategies and drinking consequences. *Journal of Studies on Alcohol, 65*(1), 115–121.

Blase, S.L., Gilbert, A.N., Anastopoulos, A.D., Costello, E.J., Hoyle, R.H., Swartzwelder, H.S., & Rabiner, D.L. (2009). Self-reported ADHD and adjustment in college: Cross-sectional and longitudinal findings. *Journal of Attention Disorders, 13*(3), 297–309. doi: 10.1177/1087054709334446

Borsari, B., Bergen-Cico, D., & Carey, K.B. (2003). Self-reported drinking-game participation of incoming college students. *Journal of American College Health, 51*(4), 149–154. doi: 10.1080/07448480309596343

Borsari, B., Boyle, K.E., Hustad, J.T., Barnett, N.P., O'Leary Tevyaw, T., & Kahler, C.W. (2007). Drinking before drinking: Pregaming and drinking games in mandated students. *Addictive Behaviors, 32*(11), 2694–2705. doi: 10.1016/j.addbeh.2007.05.003

Borsari, B., & Carey, K.B. (2001). Peer influences on college drinking: A review of the research. *Journal of Substance Abuse, 13*(4), 391–424.

Borsari, B., Murphy, J.G., & Barnett, N.P. (2007). Predictors of alcohol use during the first year of college: Implications for prevention. *Addictive Behaviors, 32*(10), 2062–2086. doi: 10.1016/j.addbeh.2007.01.017

Brache, K., & Stockwell, T. (2011). Drinking patterns and risk behaviors associated with combined alcohol and energy drink consumption in college drinkers. *Addictive Behaviors, 36*(12), 1133–1140. doi: 10.1016/j.addbeh.2011.07.003

Carey, K.B. (1993). Situational determinants of heavy drinking among college students. *Journal of Counseling Psychology, 40*(2), 217–220.

Cooper, M.L., Frone, M.R., Russell, M., & Mudar, P. (1995). Drinking to regulate positive and negative emotions: A motivational model of alcohol use. *Journal of Personality and Social Psychology, 69*(5), 990–1005.

Cronce, J.M., & Larimer, M.E. (2011). Individual-focused approaches to the prevention of college student drinking. *Alcohol Research & Health: Journal of the National Institute on Alcohol Abuse and Alcoholism, 34*(2), 210–221. doi: SPS-AR&H-33

Curcio, A. L., & George, A.M. (2011). Selected impulsivity facets with alcohol use/problems: The mediating role of drinking motives. *Addictive Behaviors, 36*(10), 959–964. doi: 10.1016/j.addbeh.2011.05.007

Dartmouth College. (2011). National College Health Improvement Project. Retrieved from http://www.nchip.org/

Dawson, D.A., Grant, B.F., Stinson, F.S., & Chou, P.S. (2005). Psychopathology associated with drinking and alcohol use disorders in the college and general adult populations. *Drug and Alcohol Dependence, 77*(2), 139–150. doi: 10.1016/j.drugalcdep.2004.07.012

Del Boca, F.K., Darkes, J., Greenbaum, P.E., & Goldman, M.S. (2004). Up close and personal: Temporal variability in the drinking of individual college students during their first year. *Journal of Consulting and Clinical Psychology, 72*(2), 155–164. doi: 10.1037/0022-006X.72.2.155

Dimeff, L.A., Baer, J.S., Kivlahan, D.R., & Marlatt, G.A. (1999). *Brief alcohol screening and intervention for college students (BASICS): A harm reduction approach.* New York, NY: Guilford Press.

Eichenbaum, H. (2000). A cortical-hippocampal system for declarative memory. *Nature Reviews Neuroscience, 1*(1), 41–50. doi: 10.1038/35036213

Fromme, K., Kivlahan, D.R., & Marlatt, G.A. (1986). Alcohol expectancies, risk identification, and secondary prevention with problem drinkers. *Advances in Behavior Research and Therapy, 8*(4), 237–251.

Gadaleto, A.F., & Anderson, D.S. (1986). Continued progress: The 1979, 1982, and 1985 college alcohol surveys. *Journal of College Student Personnel, 27*(6), 499–509.

Galen, L.W., & Rogers, W.M. (2004). Religiosity, alcohol expectancies, drinking motives and their interaction in the prediction of drinking among college students. *Journal of Studies on Alcohol, 65*(4), 469–476.

Gfroerer, J.C., Greenblatt, J.C., & Wright, D.A. (1997). Substance use in the US college-age population: Differences according to educational status and living arrangement. *American Journal of Public Health, 87*(1), 62–65.

Glass, K., & Flory, K. (2012). Are symptoms of ADHD related to substance use among college students? *Psychology of Addictive Behaviors, 26*(1), 124–132. doi: 10.1037/a0024215

Greenbaum, P.E., Del Boca, F.K., Darkes, J., Wang, C.P., & Goldman, M.S. (2005). Variation in the drinking trajectories of freshmen college students. *Journal of Consulting and Clinical Psychology, 73*(2), 229–238. doi: 10.1037/0022-006X.73.2.229

Ham, L.S., & Hope, D.A. (2003). College students and problematic drinking: A review of the literature. *Clinical Psychology Review, 23*(5), 719–759.

Hartzler, B., & Fromme, K. (2003). Heavy episodic drinking and college entrance. *Journal of Drug Education, 33*(3), 259–274.

Hildebrand, K.M., Johnson, D.J., & Bogle, K. (2001). Comparison of patterns of alcohol use between high school and college athletes and non-athletes. *College Student Journal, 35*(3), 358–365.

Hingson, R., Heeren, T., Winter, M.R., & Wechsler, H. (2003). Early age of first drunkenness as a factor in college students' unplanned and unprotected sex attributable to drinking. *Pediatrics, 111*(1), 34–41.

Hingson, R., Heeren, T., Zakocs, R., Winter, M., & Wechsler, H. (2003). Age of first intoxication, heavy drinking, driving after drinking and risk of unintentional injury among U.S. college students. *Journal of Studies on Alcohol, 64*(1), 23–31.

Hingson, R.W. (2010). Focus on: College drinking and related problems: Magnitude and prevention of college drinking and related problems. *Alcohol Research & Health: The Journal of the National Institute on Alcohol Abuse and Alcoholism, 33*(1), 45–54.

Hingson, R.W., & White, A.M. (2012). Prevalence and consequences of college student alcohol use. In C.J. Correia, J.G. Murphy, & N.P. Barnett (Eds.), *College student alcohol abuse: A guide to assessment, intervention, and prevention* (pp. 3–24). Hoboken, NJ: John Wiley.

Jennison, K.M. (2004). The short-term effects and unintended long-term consequences of binge drinking in college: A 10-year follow-up study. *American Journal of Drug and Alcohol Abuse, 30*(3), 659–684.

Johnson, T.J., & Cropsey, K.L. (2000). Sensation seeking and drinking game participation in heavy-drinking college students. *Addictive Behaviors, 25*(1), 109–116.

Johnston, L.D., O'Malley, P.M., Bachman, J.G., & Schulenberg, J.E. (2010). *Monitoring the Future national survey results on drug use, 1975–2009: Volume I, secondary school students* (NIH Publication No. 10-7585). Bethesda, MD: National Institute on Drug Abuse.

Johnston, L.D., O'Malley, P.M., Bachman, J.G., & Schulenberg, J.E. (2013). *Monitoring the Future national survey results on drug use, 1975–2012: Volume 2, college students and adults ages 19–50.* Ann Arbor, MI: Institute for Social Research, The University of Michigan.

Karam, E., Kypri, K., & Salamoun, M. (2007). Alcohol use among college students: An international perspective. *Current Opinion in Psychiatry, 20*(3), 213–221. doi: 10.1097/YCO.0b013e3280fa836c

Kassel, J.D., Jackson, S.I., & Unrod, M. (2000). Generalized expectancies for negative mood regulation and problem drinking among college students. *Journal of Studies on Alcohol, 61*(2), 332–340.

Kelly-Weeder, S. (2008). Binge drinking in college-aged women: Framing a gender-specific prevention strategy. *Journal of the American Academy of Nurse Practitioners, 20*(12), 577–584. doi: 10.1111/j.1745-7599.2008.00357.x

Kilmer, J.R., & Bailie, S.K. (2012). The impact of college student substance use: Working with students on campus. In H.E. White & D.L. Rabiner (Eds.), *Substance use in college students.* New York, NY: Guilford Press.

Kilmer, J.R., Cronce, J.M., & Larimer, M.E. (2014). College student drinking research from the 40s to the future: Where we have been and where we are going. *Journal of Studies on Alcohol and Drugs, 75*(17), 26–35.

Kitsantas, P., Kitsantas, A., & Anagnostopoulou, T. (2008). A cross-cultural investigation of college student alcohol consumption: A classification tree analysis. *Journal of Psychology, 142*(1), 5–20. doi: 10.3200/JRLP.142.1.5-20

Kivlahan, D.R., Marlatt, G.A., Fromme, K., Coppel, D.B., & Williams, E. (1990). Secondary prevention with college drinkers: Evaluation of an alcohol skills training program. *Journal of Consulting and Clinical Psychology, 58*(6), 805–810.

Knight, J.R., Wechsler, H., Kuo, M., Seibring, M., Weitzman, E.R., & Schuckit, M.A. (2002). Alcohol abuse and dependence among U.S. college students. *Journal of Studies on Alcohol, 63*(3), 263–270.

Kypri, K., Paschall, M.J., Langley, J., Baxter, J., Cashell-Smith, M., & Bourdeau, B. (2009). Drinking and alcohol-related harm among New Zealand university students: Findings from a national Web-based survey. *Alcoholism, Clinical and Experimental Research, 33*(2), 307–314. doi: 10.1111/j.1530-0277.2008.00834.x

LaBrie, J.W., Napper, L.E., & Ghaidarov, T.M. (2012). Predicting driving after drinking over time among college students: The emerging role of injunctive normative perceptions. *Journal of Studies on Alcohol and Drugs, 73*(5), 726–730.

LaBrie, J.W., & Pedersen, E.R. (2008). Prepartying promotes heightened risk in the college environment: An event-level report. *Addictive Behaviors, 33*(7), 955–959. doi: 10.1016/j.addbeh.2008.02.011

Larimer, M.E., & Cronce, J.M. (2007). Identification, prevention, and treatment revisited: Individual-focused college drinking prevention strategies 1999–2006. *Addictive Behaviors, 32*(11), 2439–2468. doi: 10.1016/j.addbeh.2007.05.006

Larimer, M.E., Turner, A.P., Anderson, B.K., Fader, J.S., Kilmer, J.R., Palmer, R.S., & Cronce, J.M. (2001). Evaluating a brief alcohol intervention with fraternities. *Journal of Studies on Alcohol, 62*(3), 370–380.

Larimer, M.E., Turner, A.P., Mallett, K.A., & Geisner, I.M. (2004). Predicting drinking behavior and alcohol-related problems among fraternity and sorority members: Examining the role of descriptive and injunctive norms. *Psychology of Addictive Behaviors, 18*(3), 203–212. doi: 10.1037/0893-164X.18.3.203

Lee, C.M., Lewis, M.A., & Neighbors, C. (2009). Preliminary examination of spring break alcohol use and related consequences. *Psychology of Addictive Behaviors, 23*(4), 689–694. doi: 10.1037/a0016482

Leichliter, J.S., Meilman, P.W., Presley, C.A., & Cashin, J.R. (1998). Alcohol use and related consequences among students with varying levels of involvment in college athletics. *Journal of American College Health, 46*(6), 257–262.

Lewis, B.A., & O'Neill, H.K. (2000). Alcohol expectancies and social deficits relating to problem drinking among college students. *Addictive Behaviors, 25*(2), 295–299.

Lewis, M.A., Lindgren, K.P., Fossos, N., Neighbors, C., & Oster-Aaland, L. (2009). Examining the relationship between typical drinking behavior and 21st birthday drinking behavior among college students: Implications for event-specific prevention. *Addiction, 104*(5), 760–767. doi: 10.1111/j.1360-0443.2009.02518.x

Lewis, M.A., & Neighbors, C. (2004). Gender-specific misperceptions of college student drinking norms. *Psychology of Addictive Behaviors, 18*(4), 334–339. doi: 10.1037/0893-164X.18.4.334

Martens, M.P., Ferrier, A.G., Sheehy, M.J., Corbett, K., Anderson, D.A., & Simmons, A. (2005). Development of the Protective Behavioral Strategies Survey. *Journal of Studies on Alcohol, 66*(5), 698–705.

Martens, M.P., Pedersen, E.R., LaBrie, J.W., Ferrier, A.G., & Cimini, M.D. (2007). Measuring alcohol-related protective behavioral strategies among college students: Further examination of the Protective Behavioral Strategies Scale. *Psychology of Addictive Behaviors, 21*(3), 307–315. doi: 10.1037/0893-164X.21.3.307

Miller, K.E. (2008). Wired: Energy drinks, jock identity, masculine norms, and risk taking. *Journal of American College Health, 56*(5), 481–489. doi: 10.3200/JACH.56.5.481–490

National Institute on Alcohol Abuse and Alcoholism. (2002). *A call to action: Changing the culture of drinking at U.S. colleges*. Bethesda, MD: National Advisory Council on Alcohol Abuse and Alcoholism Task Force on College Drinking.

National Institute on Alcohol Abuse and Alcoholism. (2007). *What colleges need to know now, an update on college drinking research*. Bethesda, MD: National Advisory Council on Alcohol Abuse and Alcoholism Task Force on College Drinking.

National Institute on Alcohol Abuse and Alcoholism. (2011). Preventing alcohol abuse and alcoholism: An update [Special issue]. *Alcohol Research & Health: The Journal of the National Institute on Alcohol Abuse and Alcoholism, 34*(2).

Neighbors, C., Atkins, D.C., Lewis, M.A., Lee, C.M., Kaysen, D., Mittmann, A., … Rodriguez, L.M. (2011). Event-specific drinking among college students. *Psychology of Addictive Behaviors, 25*(4), 702–707. doi: 10.1037/a0024051

Neighbors, C., Lee, C.M., Lewis, M.A., Fossos, N., & Larimer, M.E. (2007). Are social norms the best predictor of outcomes among heavy-drinking college students? *Journal of Studies on Alcohol and Drugs, 68*(4), 556–565.

Neighbors, C., O'Connor, R.M., Lewis, M.A., Chawla, N., Lee, C.M., & Fossos, N. (2008). The relative impact of injunctive norms on college student drinking: The role of reference group. *Psychology of Addictive Behaviors, 22*(4), 576–581. doi: 10.1037/a0013043

Nelson, T.F., & Wechsler, H. (2003). School spirits: Alcohol and collegiate sports fans. *Addictive Behaviors, 28*(1), 1–11.

O'Brien, M.C., McCoy, T.P., Rhodes, S.D., Wagoner, A., & Wolfson, M. (2008). Caffeinated cocktails: Energy drink consumption, high-risk drinking, and alcohol-related consequences among college students. *Academic Emergency Medicine, 15*(5), 453–460. doi: 10.1111/j.1553-2712.2008.00085.x

O'Malley, P.M., & Johnston, L.D. (2002). Epidemiology of alcohol and other drug use among American college students. *Journal of Studies on Alcohol, Supplement 14*, 23–39.

Palmer, R.S., McMahon, T.J., Rounsaville, B.J., & Ball, S.A. (2010). Coercive sexual experiences, protective behavioral strategies, alcohol expectancies and consumption among male and female college students. *Journal of Interpersonal Violence, 25*(9), 1563–1578. doi: 10.1177/0886260509354581

Parada, M., Corral, M., Caamano-Isorna, F., Mota, N., Crego, A., Holguin, S.R., & Cadaveira, F. (2011). Binge drinking and declarative memory in university students. *Alcoholism, Clinical and Experimental Research, 35*(8), 1475–1484. doi: 10.1111/j.1530-0277.2011.01484.x

Parada, M., Corral, M., Mota, N., Crego, A., Rodriguez Holguin, S., & Cadaveira, F. (2012). Executive functioning and alcohol binge drinking in university students. *Addictive Behaviors, 37*(2), 167–172. doi: 10.1016/j.addbeh.2011.09.015

Pedersen, E.R., & LaBrie, J. (2007). Partying before the party: Examining prepartying behavior among college students. *Journal of American College Health, 56*(3), 237–245. doi: 10.3200/JACH.56.3.237-246

Perkins, H.W. (2002). Social norms and the prevention of alcohol misuse in collegiate contexts. *Journal of Studies on Alcohol, Supplement 14*, 164–172.

Presley, C.A., & Pimentel, E.R. (2006). The introduction of the heavy and frequent drinker: A proposed classification to increase accuracy of alcohol assessments in postsecondary educational settings. *Journal of Studies on Alcohol, 67*(2), 324–331.

Read, J.P., Wood, M.D., Lejuez, C.W., Palfai, T.P., & Slack, M. (2004). Gender, alcohol consumption, and differing alcohol expectancy dimensions in college drinkers. *Experimental and Clinical Psychopharmacology, 12*(4), 298–308. doi: 10.1037/1064-1297.12.4.298

Sher, K.J., & Gotham, H.J. (1999). Pathological alcohol involvement: A developmental disorder of young adulthood. *Development and Psychopathology, 11*(4), 933–956.

Singleton, R.A. (2007). Collegiate alcohol consumption and academic performance. *Journal of Studies on Alcohol and Drugs, 68*(4), 548–555.

Singleton, R.A. Jr., & Wolfson, A.R. (2009). Alcohol consumption, sleep, and academic performance among college students. *Journal of Studies on Alcohol and Drugs, 70*(3), 355–363.

Stahlbrandt, H., Andersson, C., Johnsson, K.O., Tollison, S.J., Berglund, M., & Larimer, M.E. (2008). Cross-cultural patterns in college student drinking and its consequences: A comparison between the USA and Sweden. *Alcohol and Alcoholism, 43*(6), 698–705. doi: 10.1093/alcalc/agn055

Stony Brook University. (2009). *Red Watch Band Project.* Retrieved from http://www.stonybrook.edu/sb/redwatchband/mission.html

Substance Abuse and Mental Health Services Administration. (2012). *Results from the 2011 National Survey on Drug Use and Health: Summary of national findings.* Rockville, MD: Author.

Thombs, D.L., O'Mara, R.J., Tsukamoto, M., Rossheim, M.E., Weiler, R.M., Merves, M.L., & Goldberger, B.A. (2010). Event-level analyses of energy drink consumption and alcohol intoxication in bar patrons. *Addictive Behaviors, 35*(4), 325–330. doi: 10.1016/j.addbeh.2009.11.004

Thompson, M.P., Spitler, H., McCoy, T.P., Marra, L., Sutfin, E.L., Rhodes, S.D., & Brown, C. (2009). The moderating role of gender in the prospective associations between expectancies and alcohol-related negative consequences among college students. *Substance Use & Misuse, 44*(7), 934–942. doi: 10.1080/10826080802490659

Turner, A.P., Larimer, M.E., & Sarason, I.G. (2000). Family risk factors for alcohol-related consequences and poor adjustment in fraternity and sorority members: Exploring the role of parent-child conflict. *Journal of Studies on Alcohol, 61*(6), 818–826.

Wechsler, H., Dowdall, G.W., Davenport, A., & Castillo, S. (1995). Correlates of college student binge drinking. *American Journal of Public Health, 85*(7), 921–926.

Wechsler, H., Lee, J.E., Kuo, M., & Lee, H. (2000). College binge drinking in the 1990s: A continuing problem. Results of the Harvard School of Public Health 1999 College Alcohol Study. *Journal of American College Health, 48*(5), 199–210. doi: 10.1080/07448480009599305

Wechsler, H., Lee, J.E., Kuo, M., Seibring, M., Nelson, T.F., & Lee, H. (2002). Trends in college binge drinking during a period of increased prevention efforts. Findings from 4 Harvard School of Public Health College Alcohol Study surveys: 1993–2001. *Journal of American College Health, 50*(5), 203–217. doi: 10.1080/07448480209595713

White, A.M., Jamieson-Drake, D.W., & Swartzwelder, H.S. (2002). Prevalence and correlates of alcohol-induced blackouts among college students: Results of an e-mail survey. *Journal of American College Health, 51*(3), 117–119, 122–131. doi: 10.1080/07448480209596339

White, A.M., Kraus, C.L., & Swartzwelder, H. (2006). Many college freshmen drink at levels far beyond the binge threshold. *Alcoholism, Clinical and Experimental Research, 30*(6), 1006–1010. doi: 10.1111/j.1530-0277.2006.00122.x

Wolaver, A.M. (2002). Effects of heavy drinking in college on study effort, grade point average, and major choice. *Contemporary Economic Policy, 20*(4), 415–428.

Wood, M.D., Read, J.P., Mitchell, R.E., & Brand, N.H. (2004). Do parents still matter? Parent and peer influences on alcohol involvement among recent high school graduates. *Psychology of Addictive Behaviors, 18*(1), 19–30. doi: 10.1037/0893-164X.18.1.19

Wood, P.K., Sher, K.J., Erickson, D.J., & DeBord, K.A. (1997). Predicting academic problems in college from freshman alcohol involvement. *Journal of Studies on Alcohol, 58*(2), 200–210.

Wu, L.T., Pilowsky, D.J., Schlenger, W.E., & Hasin, D. (2007). Alcohol use disorders and the use of treatment services among college-age young adults. *Psychiatric Services, 58*(2), 192–200. doi: 10.1176/appi.ps.58.2.192

Zamboanga, B.L., Leitkowski, L.K., Rodriguez, L., & Cascio, K.A. (2006). Drinking games in female college students: More than just a game? *Addictive Behaviors, 31*(8), 1485–1489. doi: 10.1016/j.addbeh.2005.10.010

TWENTY SIX

Student Rights and Responsibilities: Duty to Care and the Pendulum of *In Loco Parentis*

Dennis E. Gregory

Introduction

The legal concept of *in loco parentis* has been identified as being part of the law of American education for many years and, in fact, was adopted in the United States from English common law. Until 1961 it was perceived as the primary legal principle by which cases regarding the student–institutional relationship within higher education were judged. The impact of this concept has continued to be important within elementary and secondary education to this day, because students in elementary and high schools are largely minors and thus are legally under the control of their parents.

In loco parentis is defined as "A Latin term meaning 'in [the] place of a parent' or 'instead of a parent.' It refers to the legal responsibility of some person or organization to perform some of the functions or responsibilities of a parent" (*In Loco Parentis*, n.d.). In a higher education context, this means that the college or university in which the student is enrolled controls the behavior of the student and provides the student with guidelines related to how he or she should or should not act.

Because of this legal principle, there was very little litigation in the early years of U.S. higher education regarding the student–institutional relationship. From the founding of Harvard in 1636 until after the Civil War and the Morrill Land Grant Act of 1862, and virtually up to the 20th century, college students were often the age of today's older high school students, were male, and were largely from wealthy families. After 1865, more women and older men began to attend colleges and study for a broader range of careers.

According to Cohen (1998):

> College life was designed as a system for controlling the often exuberant youth and for inculcating within them discipline, morals and character. Each student was to attend the lectures and tutorials, obey the rules, and avoid the company of base people. Yale issued a set of rules describing the rigor with which the college expected its students to attend to a way of life.... (p. 23)

Cohen goes on to write: "There were no provisions for grievance proceedings" (p. 23), and "The family that sent its youngster to the college expected that the institution would take charge of the boy's life" (p. 23).

While admitting this to be the case, Rudolph (1990) notes:

> The system of discipline used in many colleges, however, thoroughly failed to achieve either its purpose or the larger purposes it intended to serve. For while discipline was an aspect of paternalism, the strict, authoritarian, patriarchal family was making no headway in American life, and for the colleges to insist upon it was for them to fight the course of history. (p. 104)

According to President F.L. Patton of Princeton (1889), as cited in Vesey (1965):

> When common fame (i.e., heresay) accuses a man of exerting a corrupting influence in the college, I want no maxims from the common law to stand in the way of college purity.... Do not tell me that a man is innocent until he is found to be guilty, or suppose that the provisions of the criminal suit will apply to college procedure. There are times when a man should be held guilty until he is found innocent, and when it is for him to vindicate himself and not for us to convict him. (p. 34)

Thus, while colleges sought to control the behavior of their students, they were often unable to do so. What this meant was that when the institution used the concept of *in loco parentis* to enforce its strict and often draconian rules against students and was unable to do so consistently or even benignly, rules and enforcement were upheld, and very few challenges of rules found receptive audiences on campus or in the courts. In fact, two cases are often cited as demonstrating the court's perception of *in loco parentis*. These cases largely reflect the attitude taken by the courts prior to 1961.

The Legal Concept of *In Loco Parentis*

In *Gott v. Berea College* (1913), a Kentucky court for the first time explicitly cited *in loco parentis* as a legal theory under which colleges could act. Here a local restaurant had been ruled off-limits to Berea College students, and the owner of the restaurant sued to ask that the rule be abrogated since it had the purpose of ruining his business, which catered primarily to Berea students. He claimed that the college had conspired against him and that the limitation placed on student behavior was specifically intended to ruin his business. The court ruled that Berea College had no duty to the restaurant owner and had every right to control the behavior of its students. According to the court:

> College authorities stand *in loco parentis* concerning the physical and moral welfare, and mental training of the pupils, and we are unable to see why to that end they may not make any rule or regulation for the government, or betterment of their pupils that a parent could for the same purpose. Whether the rules or regulations are wise or their aims worthy, is a matter left solely to the discretion of the authorities or parents as the case may be, and in the exercise of that discretion, the courts are not disposed to interfere, unless the rules and aims are unlawful, or against public policy. (p. 206)

In *Anthony v. Syracuse* (1928), a student was dismissed from the university because campus authorities had heard rumors about her behavior and that she was not "a typical Syracuse girl." In fact, the student had been accused of smoking and sitting on the lap of a male student in public and causing disruptions in her residence. She had signed a card that indicated that she would follow the rules and that, if violations were found, she could be removed without cause. She sued for breach of contract. In its ruling the court noted:

> The university may only dismiss a student for reasons falling within two classes, one, in connection with safeguarding the university's ideals of scholarship, and the other in connection with safeguarding the university's moral atmosphere. When dismissing a student, no reason for dismissing need be given. The university must, however, have a reason and that reason must fall within one of the two classes mentioned above. Of course the university authorities have wide discretion in determining what situation does and what does not fall within the classes mentioned and the courts would be slow indeed in disturbing any decision of the university authorities in this respect. (p. 491)

While these cases clearly display the mood of the courts of the time, there were some judges who, at least in dicta, gave lip service to the concept that students had rights (Wright, 1969). There was also one obscure case from 1887 (*Commonwealth*, 1887) in which the court indicated that students likely did have due process rights.

As late as 1959, in *Steier v. New York State Education Commissioner*, the Second Circuit ruled that dismissals from state institutions were the responsibility of state courts, and that

> For a Federal District Court to take jurisdiction of a case such as this would lead to confusion and chaos in the entire field of jurisprudence in the states and in the United States. The judgment dismissing the complaint is affirmed on the ground that the United States District Court lacked jurisdiction over this matter. (p. 16)

Thus, as late as 1959, a federal court dismissed the idea that students had constitutional rights as they related to the student–institutional relationship. As noted below, it was only 2 years later that this began to change.

The End of *In Loco Parentis* as a Legal Concept in Higher Education

It was not until 1961, in *Dixon v. Alabama State Board of Education*, that a federal court indicated that students had constitutional rights to their education and that a level of due process must be provided. Here the Fifth Circuit, ruling in a case where students' participation in civil rights protests resulted in their being removed from Alabama State University without notice or hearing, opened the floodgates for constitutional rights for college students at public institutions. In this case, a group of students from Alabama State University engaged in a civil rights demonstration off campus and were later notified that they were expelled from the university. They had received no notice of the charges filed against them and had no opportunity to be heard regarding the charges (*Dixon*, 1961). This was true despite the fact that the university had procedures in place for hearings. The students sued the university, alleging that their Fourteenth Amendment right to due process had been abridged. They lost in the federal district court and appealed to the Fifth Circuit. In his opinion, Judge Rives wrote for the court:

> It is shocking that the officials of a state educational institution, which can function properly only if our freedoms are preserved, should not understand the elementary principles of fair play. It is equally shocking to find that a court supports them in denying to a student the protection given to a pickpocket. Dismissal of Students: "Due Process," Warren A. Seavey, 70 Harvard Law Review 1406, 1407. We are confident that precedent as well as a most fundamental constitutional principle support our holding that due process requires notice and some opportunity for hearing before a student at a tax-supported college is expelled for misconduct. (*Dixon*, 1961, p. 158, citation in original text)

With this opinion, the fabric of *in loco parentis* was torn asunder. Following this decision, a torrent of cases were brought to the federal courts on all manner of constitutional issues. While in this chapter Fourteenth Amendment due process rulings are those with which we are most concerned, these cases in the federal courts dealt with a variety of First, Fourth, and Fourteenth Amendment cases that were filed by students over the next 15 years, and continue to come apace. While many of the precedents around this issue have now been settled, nuances of individual cases still occasionally make the news.

In any case, *in loco parentis* as a legal concept in the relations between public institutions of higher education and their students has been eclipsed. According to Alexander and Alexander (2011), "The old legal theory of in loco parentis that places the school in a parental role appears to have little relevance in modern society" (p. 155). In place of *in loco parentis* came a virtual opening of the floodgates to and from federal courts that shaped a new direction in the student and institutional relationship and the beginning of the "Constitutional Period" (Bickel & Lake, 1999), which saw extensive challenges to the once-unfettered power of the institution. In fact, there were so many constitutional challenges to institutional policies during this period that the entire fabric of student affairs was torn asunder and rebuilt.

Bickel and Lake (1999) have noted:

> With the fall of *in loco parentis*, the American College was no longer insular: it entered a new era of accountability in the courts. The fall of *in loco parentis* and the new role of the legal system on campus facilitated important developments in legal relations between students and administrators (and others) on campus. (p. 8)

Bickel and Lake (1999) convincingly argue that this new relationship was one of constitutionalism (and thus a bystander mentality on campus), followed by a more contractual and consumer-based approach in recent years. While one may disagree with them regarding some of the trends in case law they predicted (and which did not come to pass), their facilitator model is an excellent one.

Is There Still a Parenting Function in Higher Education?

Even though the legal concept of *in loco parentis* has fallen by the wayside at public institutions, it can be argued that the quasi-parental role endures at many private institutions and is still particularly strong at many private historically Black colleges and universities (HBCUs). This is not based on the legal theory but more on the basis that the purpose of the institution is to fill in and support all of the gaps in pre-college education and to prepare students for society. In fact, Bickel and Lake (1999) argue that some demand for such a role has evolved as tuition costs have risen and parents desire, as consumers, to get more parental types of service provided even at public institutions, which for many years acted as bystanders to student life.

A number of theorists and scholars, going as far back as the late 1970s, have posited that some sort of quasi-parental role still exists within higher education. Recent writing about expectations of "helicopter parents" who expect a high level of service for and protection of their children seems to suggest that parents expect institutions, as noted above, to serve in this role, and that millennial students expect this as well.

Gregory and Ballou (1986) coined the term *in loco parentis reinventis* to describe this redefined quasi-parental role. They noted:

> While the strict, 1950s-type of interpretation of *in loco parentis* may be dead, what has arisen from its ashes, like a phoenix from ancient lore, is a new form and meaning for the term. This new definition, almost an *in loco parentis* reinvented, includes both a broader legal responsibility (as noted by Bickel and Lake, 1999—added to original citation) and a new nurturing and developmental function only vaguely called for in the past. (p. 30)

Gregory and Ballou (1986) argued that the focus on student development theory and the rise in consumerism, along with a growing alliance with faculty to support the academic focus of the institution and the engagement with students of all aspects of the university community, were in fact somewhat quasi-parental. This article seems to serve as a backdrop for subsequent documents such as *Learning Reconsidered* (Keeling, 2004) and *Learning Reconsidered 2* (Keeling, 2006), both of which argued for these growing connections.

Gregory and Ballou (1986) also cited two other articles in which the authors coined their own terms related to *in loco parentis*. Parr and Buchanan (1979) offered *in loco uteri*, which they argued placed an even heavier demand on institutions in several legal areas and service provision. Pitts (1980) offered *in loco parentis indulgentis*, which placed an even broader responsibility on institutions than did Parr and Buchanan, and indicated that institutions had used *in loco parentis* as a means to foster student development and that colleges are still in the nurturing business.

Szablewicz and Gibbs (1987) posited the idea that cases that they cited were creating a return to *in loco parentis* by providing an additional liability for institutions that required them to supervise students more closely. Bickel and Lake (1999) take these authors to task for that statement and note that this perception "was fueled by the legal political dynamics of university law" (pp. 91–92).

In his 1994 work entitled *Campus Rules and Moral Community: In Place of In Loco Parentis*, Hoekema suggested that "there is a place for colleges and universities in the moral and social, as well as intellectual lives of students. Both students and institutions suffer when that place is left vacant" (p. 19). He, too, indicated that colleges and universities should not give up their nurturing roles.

Bickel and Lake (1999) examine the movement away from *in loco parentis* through a tort liability lens. They propose, from a liability perspective, that "students have a responsibility not to be negligent in their conduct and must be willing to share or bear the consequences of their own voluntary, informed choices. Safety on campus depends on shared responsibility" (p. 116) They propose the concept of the "facilitator university" as a model for this proposition for shared responsibility. This is an excellent model and one that makes perfect sense. This is true because it enhances the relationship between the student and the institution and places responsibility on the shoulders of the students as part of the learning process. It is of benefit to institutions in that it makes students a part of the resolution of such issues and enhances their ability to work with students to help them be safer and understand the risks of their behaviors.

In any case, Bickel and Lake (1999) note that "*In loco parentis* was once the key paradigm for university law but is dead, should be dead, and should not 'return'" (p. 106). This is a commonly held belief on the part of higher education legal scholars and is considered general knowledge in the field of higher education law.

What Describes the Current Student (Parent)-Institutional Relationship?

The question then becomes: What replaced *in loco parentis* as a guiding legal and ideological focus for the student–institutional relationship? While Bickel and Lake (1999) focus on tort responsibility, the legal relationship is broader than that. They argue that the relationship should be based on contracts voluntarily entered into by both parties and rooted in a consumer mentality and focus and that, as consumers, college students (and their parents) demand a higher level of service and oversight. This would seem to be a logical conclusion. Further, this change applies to more than tort liability and extends to contracts (using that term in a non-legal sense) that are imposed on institutions by federal legislation, court decisions, and circumstances that would not normally be imposed on an entity or agency outside of higher education.

This relationship is also certainly enhanced by the characteristics of the current generation of traditional-age students. While it is beyond the scope of this chapter to describe the current "millennial generation" of students (Howe & Strauss, 2000; Strauss & Howe, 2007; Twenge, 2006) (see Chapter 23 above for a fuller discussion) and "Helicopter Parents" (Coburn, 2006; Howe & Strauss, 2000; Hunt, 2008), suffice it to say that the characteristics of this generation and their parents have hastened the movement toward a requirement of service by universities to their students (and parents).

It appears that the federal government—and, to a lesser degree, state governments—has created a web of laws and regulations that focus undue scrutiny on higher education and that force institutions to spend untold dollars and untold personnel hours enforcing unfunded mandates that appear to be needless and are of limited benefit to students, parents, or institutions (Gregory & Janosik, 2002). While these laws and regulations are well intentioned, they appear to be the work of lobbying by advocacy groups, the pandering of politicians who seek ways to get votes without investing much thought or focus, and an overreach by federal agencies. They are being implemented by administrators who rightly fear retribution by politicians and parents and the loss of a positive public image and federal funds.

Clearly, tragedies have occurred on campus. The murders at Virginia Tech in 2007 and other campuses made headlines across the country and have rightfully raised concerns about the safety of college campuses. While murders, robberies, sexual assaults, and other crimes certainly occur on college campuses, and while universities should do everything in their power to prevent these horrific crimes, the questions raised are these: Are the efforts made by the federal government and others having any effect? Are the crime statistics on college and university campuses higher or lower than those in the communities that surround the campuses? Why have colleges and universities become a primary focus of efforts to eliminate crime, perhaps even more so than public schools?

The Jeanne Clery Campus Safety Act (n.d.), the Family Educational Rights and Privacy Act (n.d.), Title IX of the Education Amendments of 1972 (n.d.), and *Dear Colleague Letters* (2011, 2013) regarding the enforcement of this act, President Barack Obama's desire to reform and make higher education more affordable and available (*Education: Knowledge and Skills for the Jobs of the Future*, n.d.), and any number of other federal laws have set the stage for parents to take aim at the university if they perceive some action—or failure to act—as problematic. Institutions, because of the fear of litigation, concerns about their reputations and their ability to recruit and retain students, and fear of losing federal aid and research dollars must abide by these laws.

In addition, students choose to leave an institution rather than challenge rules and policies with which they disagree. If they and their parents feel that they are not being taken care of properly, are not getting proper attention, or are not safe in and around campus, they have no compunction about transferring to another institution. Students demand high-quality, single residence hall rooms with all of the amenities; faculty members who provide exciting and interesting classes; guaranteed internship and job opportunities after graduation; and other services. Parents wish to be deeply involved with their traditional-age students and wish to participate in governance and to have direct access to faculty (Howe & Strauss, 2000). They do not hesitate to call the office of the president of the institution to demand satisfaction.

If students or parents feel they have not been treated properly, another option is to sue for services they feel are proper or damages they believe they are owed as a result of paying tuition. While these suits have largely been decided in favor of the institutions, this author believes that the concept of educational malpractice and breach of contract hang over the heads of administrators like the sword of Damocles. This is not surprising, since tuition costs have skyrocketed, financial burdens have increased for students, millennial students are attached to their parents in both physical and electronic ways, and serious crimes on and around campus, such as at Virginia Tech (though clearly at lower rates than in the communities that surround them) are trumpeted by the media. The value of college, while still quite high, has failed to increase, and the financial crisis of 2008 served to erode the faith that a degree assures a well-paying job.

Discussion

All of the elements discussed above conspire to maintain the quasi-parental role of campuses. This is demanded by traditional-age students and their parents and supported by federal law, if not by court decisions. While *in loco parentis* is dead as a legal concept, the parental role remains. In fact, it can be argued that the massive presence of millennial students has exacerbated and extended this role.

This is, however, not universally true. The growing number of college students who gain their degrees through distance education and who may never set foot on a brick-and-mortar campus, the growth of community colleges as a viable form of education for both traditional and non-traditional-age students (and from which 4-year institutions receive large numbers of transfers), and the increasing number of current and former military personnel who are taking advantage of the Post-9/11 GI Bill (Post-9/11 GI Bill, n.d.) all make the higher education environment more diverse than ever. While these older and more mature students, as well as those who matriculate through distance education, may not have the same demands as traditional-age residential students, institutions still must provide expansive services and programs and face legal threats.

In terms of a legal conception that controls the student–institutional relationship, the constitutional era as described by Bickel and Lake (1999), the contractual and consumer-based culture that has spawned significant federal legislation, and enhanced tort law responsibility and contractual disputes now serve as a legal background, if not a universal concept like *in loco parentis*.

Higher education law is a complex web of tort law, contract law, constitutional law, administrative law, tax law, and many other types of law. The role of the college and university legal counsel is key in seeking to provide a preventive legal approach while dealing with a growing and increasingly complex set of statutes, regulations, and case law at every level.

College and university administrators must also study higher education law because they need to be careful not to step on legal landmines, need to understand the legal concepts that apply to their work, need to be able to do basic legal research, and need to be able to ask attorneys the right questions to achieve educational outcomes. Faculty must also increase their understanding of basic legal concepts as they work with students with disabilities, examine their employment contracts, deal with privacy issues related to FERPA, and serve in administrative roles.

The legal landscape within higher education is an ever-evolving one. Issues concerning affirmative action, whether interns are actually employees, liability related to study-abroad programs, campus safety, and many other legal concerns are changing as new issues come to the foreground. As millennial students move out of the traditional higher education age group, as baby boomers retire, and as a new generation with needs still unimagined enter higher education, this legal landscape will continue to evolve.

However, the *in loco parentis* pendulum has made its final swing. While it is dead, parenting in higher education continues apace with new directions, new reasons, and new parents.

References

Alexander, K.W., & Alexander, K. (2011). *Higher education law: Policy and perspectives.* New York, NY: Routledge.

Anthony v. Syracuse. (1928). 224 A.D. 487; 231 N.Y.S. 435 (N.Y. App. Div. 1928).

Bickel, R.D., & Lake, P.F. (1999). *The rights and responsibilities of the modern university: Who assumes the risks of college life?* Durham, NC: Carolina Academic Press.

Coburn, K.L. (2006, July/August). Organizing a ground crew for today's helicopter parents. *About Campus, 11*(3), 9–16.

Cohen, A.M. (1998). *The shaping of American higher education: Emergence and growth of the contemporary system.* San Francisco, CA: Jossey-Bass.
Commonwealth ex. Rel. Hill v. McCauley. (1887). 3 Pa. C.C. Rep. 77 (C.P. Cumberland Cy).
Dear colleague letter, April 2011. Retrieved from www2.ed.gov/about/offices/list/ocr/letters/colleague-2011104.html
Dear colleague letter, June 2013. Retrieved from www2.ed.gov/about/offices/list/ocr/letters/colleague-201306-tittle-ix.pdf
Dixon v. Alabama State Board of Education. (1961). 294 F.2d 150.
Education: Knowledge and skills for the jobs of the future—Higher education. (n.d.). Retrieved from www.whitehouse.gov/issues/education/higher-education
Family Educational Rights and Privacy Act (FERPA). (n.d.). 20 USC § 1232g; 34 CFR Part 99.
Gott v. Berea College. (1913). 156 Ky. 376, 161 S.W. 204.
Gregory, D.E., & Ballou, R.A. (1986). *In loco parentis* reinventis: Is there still a parenting function in higher education? *NASPA Journal, 24*(2), 28–31.
Gregory, D.E., & Janosik, S.M. (2002). The *Clery Act*: How effective is it? Perceptions from the field—The current state of the research and recommendations for improvement. *Stetson Law Review, 32*, 61–89.
Hoekema, D.A. (1994). *Campus rules and moral community: In place of in loco parentis.* Lanham, MD: Rowman and Littlefield.
Howe, N., & Strauss W. (2000). *Millennials rising: The next great generation.* New York, NY: Vintage Books.
Hunt, J. (2008, Spring). Make room for daddy…and mommy: Helicopter parents are here. *Journal of Academic Administration in Higher Education, 4*(1), 13–18.
In Loco Parentis. (n.d.). Legal Information Institute. Retrieved from www.law.cornell.edu/wex/in-loco-parentis
Jeanne Clery Disclosure of Campus Security Policy and Campus Crime Statistics Act. (n.d.). 20 USC § 1092 (f).
Keeling, R.P. (Ed.). (2004). *Learning reconsidered: A campus-wide focus on the student experience.* Washington, DC: National Association of Student Personnel Administrators (NASPA) and American College Personnel Association (ACPA).
Keeling, R.P. (Ed.). (2006). *Learning reconsidered 2: Implementing a campus-wide focus on the student experience.* Washington, DC: National Association of Student Personnel Administrators (NASPA), American College Personnel Association (ACPA), Association of College and University Housing Officers-International (ACUHO-I), Association of College Unions International (ACUI), National Academic Advising Association (NACADA), National Association for Campus Activities (NACA), and National Intramural-Recreation Sports Association (NIRSA).
Morrill Land Grant Act of 1862. 7 U.S.C. § 301 et seq.
Parr, P., & Buchanan, E. (1979). Responses to the law: A word of caution. *NASPA Journal, 17*(2), 12–15.
Patton, F.L. (1889). *Religion in college.* Princeton, NJ: Princeton University Press.
Pitts, J. (1980). In loco parentis indulgentis? *NASPA Journal, 17*(4), 20–25.
Post-9/11 GI Bill. (n.d.). Retrieved from www.gibill.va.gov/benefits/post_911_gibill/
Rudolph, F.R. (1990). *The American college & university: A history.* Athens, GA: University of Georgia Press.
Steier v. New York State Education Commissioner. (1959). 271 F.2d 13 (2d Cir. 1959).
Strauss, W., & Howe, N. (2007). *Millennials go to college: Strategies for a new generation on campus* (2nd ed.). Great Falls, VA: LifeCourse.
Szablewicz, J.J., & Gibbs, A.D. (1987, Fall). College's increasing exposure to liability: The new *in loco parentis. Journal of Law and Education, 16*(4), 453–465.
Title IX of the Education Amendments of 1972. (n.d.). 20 USC §1681.
Twenge, J.M. (2006). *Generation me.* New York, NY: Free Press.
Vesey, L.R. (1965). *The emergence of the American university.* Chicago, IL: University of Chicago Press.
Wright, C.A. (1969). The Constitution on the campus. *Vanderbilt Law Review, 22*(5), 1027–1088.

TWENTY SEVEN

Service-Learning and Student Learning

S. Mei-Yen Ireland and Susan R. Jones

Service-learning, since its inception, has been viewed as a particularly efficacious strategy for promoting student learning. Grounded in the philosophy and practice of experiential learning, effective service-learning enjoys the benefits of learning through active practice, reflection, and analysis (Stanton, Giles, & Cruz, 1999). In their groundbreaking study, *Where's the Learning in Service-Learning?* (1999), Janet Eyler and Dwight Giles, Jr., identified the outcomes most often associated with service-learning as well as the program characteristics likely to produce these outcomes. Service-learning initiatives have become so prevalent in higher education that such learning outcomes are simply expected and transformative results presumed. As King and Baxter Magolda (2011) pointed out:

> Student learning in postsecondary education involves more than the acquisition of knowledge and skills; it also includes developing a frame of mind that allows students to put their knowledge in perspective; to understand the sources of their beliefs and values; and to establish a sense of self that enables them to participate effectively in a variety of personal, occupational, and community contexts. It is in such contexts that students apply their knowledge, skills, and capacities for deeper understanding to responsibilities that span work, family, and civic contexts. (p. 207)

In this chapter we explore service-learning as such a context for student learning. We begin by discussing definitions of service-learning and the competing discourses of intended outcomes. We also place these definitions within discussions of desired learning in higher education. We then explore what is known about contemporary college students and their interest and participation in service-learning. Next we turn to student learning outcomes associated with service-learning and examine students' perceptions of their learning in service-learning contexts. Finally, we address issues that may emerge when student learning is placed at the center of service-learning.

Purpose and Goals of Service-Learning

Civic engagement and civic leadership have long been educational goals of higher education institutions in the United States (Campus Compact, 2007; Eyler & Giles, 1999; Jacoby, 2009). Initiatives designed to promote civic engagement such as service-learning are recognized for the educational, social, and developmental benefits accrued to students who participate in them (Jacoby, 2009). Further, recent reports from leading professional organizations (Association of American Colleges and Universities [AAC&U], 2005, 2007; Keeling [ACPA & NASPA], 2004) highlight the centrality of learning outcomes such as civic knowledge and engagement as fundamental to student success in a global century (AAC&U, 2007) and identify service-learning as a learning strategy for accomplishing such outcomes (Keeling, 2004). In another national study completed by Dey, Ott, Antonaros, Barnhardt, and Holsapple (2009) as part of AAC&U's Core Commitments project, perspective taking was examined as crucial to a key learning outcome: the development of students' personal and social responsibility. In this study, researchers investigated whether and which educational environments promote students' abilities to understand and be informed by perspectives that differ from their own. What they found was that among a diverse group of responders (faculty, administrators, and students) the majority in all groups agreed that campuses should be focusing on personal and social responsibility; however, far fewer strongly agreed that their campuses were actually making these outcomes a major focus. Further, Dey and colleagues (2009) reported that greater numbers of students who participated in community service (45% of all students surveyed reported they spent at least 1–2 hours per week in community service) strongly agreed that they had developed an enhanced ability to understand the perspectives of others and that their campuses promoted the connection between appreciating diverse perspectives and being a well-informed citizen. These reports and the data used to write them set up the foundation for suggesting that service-learning is an educational strategy that promotes the development of important and central learning outcomes for college students as they encounter a quickly changing global society. But how is it that service-learning accomplishes such outcomes? To respond to this question, we turn to definitions of service-learning.

Defining Service-Learning

For many years, Barbara Jacoby's definition (1996) has served as the standard for the field of service-learning. Drawing upon the work of early scholars and practitioners in service-learning, Jacoby (1996) articulated the definition of service-learning as "a form of experiential education in which students engage in activities that address human and community needs together with structured opportunities intentionally designed to promote student learning and development" (p. 5). Others have emphasized the necessity of curricular integration to effective service-learning (Bringle & Hatcher, 1996), or the importance of deepening students' understandings of themselves, the community, and complex social issues through service-learning (Council for the Advancement of Standards, 2005). Still others have delineated service-learning initiatives by their emphasis on charity and the individual or social change and ameliorating social injustices (Kahne & Westheimer, 1999; Mitchell, 2008; Morton, 1995). Butin (2010) suggested that many service-learning educators rely on definitions of service-learning that privilege "(a) volunteer activities done by (b) individual students with high cultural capital for the sake of (c) individuals with low cultural capital (d) within the context of an academic class (e) with ameliorative consequences" (p. 6). These definitions of service-learning are then operationalized in the many popular service-learning initiatives seen on college campuses today, including large-scale community service projects, short-term immersion programs such as alternative breaks, campus responses to natural disasters, faculty development, and service-learning classes, all presumably connecting to intended learning outcomes.

College Students and Service

Before we turn to a discussion of learning outcomes associated with service-learning, we introduce some data about contemporary college students and their participation in service as a backdrop. Results from the annual Freshman Survey conducted by UCLA's Higher Education Research Institute provide intriguing contextual information that relates to the intended learning outcomes for participants engaged in service-learning. Consider that in 2006, first-year students indicated that their top reasons for going to college were, in this order: (a) to learn about things that interest me; (b) to get a better job; and (c) to be able to make more money. Since 2009, results consistently indicate that the number one reason for attending college is to be able to get a better job. In 2012, 87.9% of first-year students reported this as their primary reason for attending college (Pryor et al., 2012, p. 4). Levine and Dean (2012) developed a student profile based on their survey results from over 5,000 college students and emphasized the utilitarian goals held by them. They reported that "two out of three undergraduates (67 percent) say the chief benefit of a college education is that it increases one's earning power" (p. 38). What implications might these trends have for the learning outcomes associated with service-learning?

Another contextual trend is the enormous growth in online education. According to the National Center for Education Statistics (2011), 20% of all undergraduate students take at least one course through distance education. Over 1.5 million students are enrolled in Phoenix-type programs, with the number of degrees conferred by for-profit institutions outpacing those conferred by public and private non-profit universities. Further, much attention has recently been directed to the rapid growth in the number of MOOCs—massive open online courses. In the fall of 2012, edX, coming out of Harvard and MIT, enrolled 370,000 students, and Coursera, begun by a Stanford professor as a for-profit enterprise, had an enrollment of over 1.7 million students. What do service-learning outcomes look like when it is projected that, in 2014, 50% of students will engage in online education rather than solely a brick-and-mortar experience (Christensen, Horn, Caldera, & Soares, 2011)? What does engagement look like in a virtual environment? What about community impact if one's service takes place online? Where is the community in a virtual reality? How do we design and facilitate service-learning programs to include the well-established program characteristics that promote positive outcomes associated with service-learning? These are important questions to ponder when considering learning outcomes in our contemporary educational context.

Looking more specifically at college students and community service, Levine and Dean (2012) found that 65% of students reported that they were engaged in service. Levine and Dean (2012) went on to suggest that contemporary college students think of themselves as global citizens, but they know little about the world. Many reported feeling more comfortable addressing local issues through direct service such as tutoring, neighborhood clean-ups, and fundraising, with the most popular service activities identified as "church and religious activities, work for charity organizations such as United Way, and child and youth work" (Levine & Dean, 2012, p. 142). According to Levine and Dean (2012), direct service provided students with a tangible activity and a perceived ability to make a measurable difference in people's lives, which they referred to as "white collar voluntarism"—as opposed to activities that get "their hands dirty," such as efforts related to homelessness (p. 141). Despite claims by researchers that service-learning can lead to a greater appreciation of diversity (e.g., Eyler & Giles, 1999; Jones & Abes, 2003; Jones & Hill, 2001), Levine and Dean (2012) found that the least popular activities were those that explicitly involved issues of race. The main reason that 97% of students gave for participating in service activities was that it was "important to them to do good and help people" (Levine & Dean, 2012, p. 145). Most of the students indicated they would perform more service if they were compensated (which some service-learning scholars would suggest is not service), though their interest drops when the service involves teaching in urban or low-income schools or military service (Levine & Dean, 2012).

Further, Levine and Dean (2012) reported that this generation of college students is characterized by digital dominance, which led them to assert that "today's undergraduates are weak in interpersonal skills, face-to-face communication skills, and problem-solving skills" (p. xiii). This result appears to run counter to many of the intended outcomes associated with participation in higher education and related to the outcomes associated with service-learning. What we know about the outcomes of service-learning suggests that it is an important pedagogical approach for preparing students for the twenty-first century. We now turn to a discussion of these outcomes.

Learning Outcomes Associated With Service-Learning

For nearly two decades, student affairs professionals have been encouraged to frame the student learning process in terms of simultaneous cognitive and affective learning (King & Baxter Magolda, 1996). King and Baxter Magolda's integrated view of learning and personal development emphasizes the connections between individually and culturally contextualized relationships and constructing knowledge, making meaning, and cultivating self-awareness. The results of much research on service-learning affirms such a view of learning and emphasizes positive outcomes associated with students' participation in service-learning, including civic, cognitive, moral, interpersonal, social justice, and personal outcomes (e.g., Astin & Sax, 1998; Bowman, Brandenberger, Mick, & Toms Smedley, 2010; Einfield & Collins, 2008; Eyler & Giles, 1999; Holsapple, 2012; Jones & Abes, 2004; Mayhew & Engberg, 2011; Pascarella & Terenzini, 2005; Steinberg, Hatcher, & Bringle, 2011; Vogelgesang, 2005; Warren, 2012).

In their landmark book, *Where's the Learning in Service-Learning?* (1999), Eyler and Giles published the results of their mixed methods research on the impact of curricular-based service-learning on undergraduate students. They argued that service-learning relies on students making personal connections and is necessary to cultivate citizenship; their findings highlighted that service-learning participation promotes tolerance and personal development and decreases stereotyping. Students reported greater self-knowledge and spiritual growth, as well as an augmented sense of personal efficacy. Interpersonally, participation in service-learning was found to help students develop skills in working effectively in groups while also fostering leadership skill development. Student participation in service-learning brings about authentic connections with and increased understanding of the community, often resulting in the development of meaningful relationships. Eyler and Giles (1999) also found that students worked harder, learned more, and understood subject matter in more profound ways when participating in curricular service-learning throughout a semester.

In their meta-analysis that synthesized the research on the impact of college on students, Pascarella and Terenzini (2005) noted conclusively that "community service in general, and service-learning in particular, has statistically significant and positive net effects on students' sociopolitical attitudes and beliefs" (p. 304). Pascarella and Terenzini (2005) discussed service-learning's impact on students in terms of eight categories: sociopolitical attitudes and beliefs, civic values and activities, civic attitudes and orientations, cognitive skills and intellectual growth, awareness and attitudes toward other groups, acquisition of subject matter knowledge, moral development, and psychosocial change. Given that service-learning work frequently brings students into contact with people who are different from themselves in terms of race, culture, class, and age, research also suggests that these encounters lead to increased awareness of diversity and changes in attitudes toward others (Pascarella & Terenzini, 2005). These encounters have important implications for students' identity development and understanding of social justice and diversity, which has become a burgeoning area of service-learning research in recent years.

Identity Development

Identity development is an integral part of college student development and learning (Jones & Abes, 2013). In a study investigating the enduring influences of service-learning on college students' identity development, Jones and Abes (2004) interviewed students 2 to 4 years after their service-learning course and found that service-learning led to the construction of a more integrated identity, which was evident through complexity of thinking about self and others, openness to new ideas, and shifts in future commitments. Providing a clear conceptualization of the outcomes associated with service-learning, Steinberg, Hatcher, and Bringle (2011) developed a framework of measures of civic learning outcomes from service-learning programs. The key measures include identity (self-understanding, self-awareness, self-concept), educational experiences (academic knowledge, skills), and civic experiences (community, advocacy, leadership, and political involvement).

Chesbrough (2011) studied the motivations and learning outcomes of undergraduate students who participated in at least 25 hours of service. The type of service project and use of reflection were important determinants of learning outcomes. Chesbrough (2011) found that a "strong and positive relationship existed between hours of service previously performed" and measures of cognitive development, skill development, and identity development. In a meta-analysis of service-learning studies, Warren (2012) supported the finding that service-learning has a positive influence on student learning, regardless of whether learning is measured through concrete measures or through student self-report assessments. In particular, service-learning led to increased multicultural awareness, enhanced social responsibility, and cognitive learning outcomes (Warren, 2012). Multicultural awareness and social justice are another common pedagogical outcome sought from service-learning.

Social Justice and Diversity

Social justice and diversity outcomes are often touted as important learning outcomes for service-learning, yet results from research provide mixed results. Einfield and Collins (2008) found that students in a university-sponsored service-learning program demonstrated increased awareness of inequality, but only some of the participants adopted a commitment to social justice. Participants also developed multicultural skills such as empathy, patience, reciprocity, trust, and respect through their work with community members. Beyond multicultural competence skills, Holsapple (2012) found a positive connection between service-learning and student diversity outcomes, which included tolerance of difference, stereotype confrontation, recognition of universality, knowledge about the served population, interactions across difference, and belief in the value of diversity.

In a quantitative study of service-learning courses at a medium-sized Catholic university in the Midwest, Bowman and colleagues (2010) found that participation in one-credit service-learning courses appeared to produce a positive impact on college learning and development. Students in the course gained significantly on equality, justice, and social responsibility outcomes. Course structure was an important criterion in yielding positive student outcomes, in addition to the amount of time spent in the community. In contrast, Mayhew and Engberg (2011) found that service-learning led to developmental gains in charitable responsibility, but not social justice responsibility. The mixed findings of social justice outcomes are often linked to the emphasis given to certain program components deemed necessary for effective service-learning practice.

Program Components That Lead to Learning Outcomes

Pascarella and Terenzini (2005) emphasized that research underscores the importance of quality service-learning placements and integrating service-learning and reflection. Pascarella and Terenzini tentatively concluded that integrated service-learning impacts student learning and development more than general community service or volunteer activities. The intensity and duration of the service-learning activity, use of reflection, quality of service placement, and preparation of students are all factors that impact learning outcomes (Bowman et al., 2010; Eyler & Giles, 1999; Pascarella & Terenzini, 2005). The more systematic and structured the experience, the stronger the effects of service-learning on students' civic attitudes, values, and orientations (Pascarella & Terenzini, 2005). Sustained immersion in the community, integrated into the course structure, appears to produce a positive impact on student learning and development (Bowman et al., 2010). Seider, Rabinowicz, and Gillmor (2012) found that students engaged in service programs demonstrated larger shifts in public service motivation and beliefs in a just world. This outcome was contingent on the type of service work in which students were engaged. Students working in adult-oriented services demonstrated stronger commitments and beliefs than students working in youth-oriented service sites.

When integrated with intentional reflection, service-learning also contributes to students' acquisition of subject matter, development of cognitive skills, development of moral and ethical reasoning, increases in social responsibility, and decreases in social prejudice (Pascarella & Terenzini, 2005). In their study, Eyler and Giles (1999) found that structured reflection opportunities, in addition to quality service-learning placements that provided meaningful responsibilities and interesting work, were key factors related to student learning outcomes. Reflection is a critical aspect of attaining service-learning outcomes such as applying knowledge and personal and cognitive development (Eyler & Giles, 1999; Hatcher, Bringle, & Muthiah, 2004). Reflection encourages students to examine the relationship between service activities, their academic knowledge, and their personal values and beliefs, leading to a broader and deeper understanding of "social, moral, personal, and civic dimensions" (Hatcher et al., 2004, p. 39).

Research shows that service-learning, particularly when connected to reflection and quality service placement, leads to positive student learning outcomes across various cognitive, affective, and interpersonal dimensions. Identity development and social justice are outcomes increasingly sought from students' engagement in service-learning. Although positive results exist related to the impact of service-learning, complexities also exist and are critically important for educators to acknowledge and address.

Complicating Issues in Service-Learning

Despite the many positive outcomes associated with service-learning, several complicating issues may emerge when centering student learning through service-learning. Butin (2010) argued that "service-learning is an experiential activity that is always already a culturally saturated, socially consequential, politically contested, and existentially defining experience" (p. 18). Butin (2007, 2010) advanced four conceptualizations of service-learning: technical, cultural, political, and anti-foundational. A technical conceptualization highlights best practices and focuses on increasing content knowledge in which service-learning is used to improve teaching effectiveness and learning outcomes. A cultural conceptualization emphasizes student meaning making and focuses on service-learning as a means of increasing tolerance for diversity and engagement with those who are "different." A political orientation emphasizes power relations and conceptualizes service-learning as either a tool for righting societal wrongs and empowering non-dominant voices or maintaining inequitable power relations. An anti-foundational conceptualization of service-learning disrupts the taken-for-granted assumptions in service-learning (for example, that all learning is transformational), recognizes that power relations are hidden, and questions the binaries that are used to make meaning of the world.

Situated in the context of student learning, confronting unacknowledged privilege and the challenges of changing social structures can lead to ambiguity and cognitive dissonance for students (Jones, Robbins, & LePeau, 2011). In service-learning that is anchored in an anti-foundational approach, working with communities produces an authentic pedagogical interaction in which students are forced to analyze their own biases and backgrounds. By embracing the complexity of service-learning, the anti-foundational framework has implications for the design, structure, and outcomes of service-learning. Specific implications, which we discuss in the following sections examining complexities associated with service-learning, call on practitioners to question the ways in which issues of power and community voice, racial identity, and student resistance are addressed for effective service-learning, which promotes intended student learning outcomes. We also explore the complicated impact of required service-learning and service tourism.

Issues of Power and Community Voice

Clark and Young (2005) suggested that service-learning practitioners must carefully attend to the power, privilege, and positioning of individuals within the service-learning setting, because service-learning is a complex task of "changing place" that can create tension. Jones, Gilbride-Brown, and Gasiorski (2005) cautioned that service-learning has the potential to result in going to a new place in order to "see" the poor or those affected by social issues. There remains little research on community participants' experiences with service-learning and what impact service-learning may have on communities (Jacoby, 2009; Stoecker & Tryon, 2009).

Given that there are often differences in power and privilege between the community and service-learners, forming reciprocal and equitable partnerships of colleges and communities through service-learning is a critical issue (Jacoby, 2009; Jones, 2003). Service-learning educators must avoid forging community partnerships with the sole goal of meeting desired student learning outcomes rather than seeking to address the root cause of the social issue (Jacoby, 1996). This point highlights a central tension in service-learning: that service-learning definitions emphasize mutually beneficial outcomes through reciprocal community partnerships, yet these may not always be conducive to student learning or compromised if student learning is at the foreground.

Engaging in reciprocal service-learning also has implications for student learning and development of critical consciousness. Cípolle (2010) asserted that "mainstream service-learning programs are primarily located at the initial stage of critical consciousness" (p. 55). Students do not question their assumptions and biases and apply the stereotypes they receive from media and individuals around them about the nature of social issues. As a result, they continue to operate with faulty opinions and judgments that reinforce racism, classism, sexism, and narrow-mindedness. Many White students engage in service with a colorblind approach in which they do not recognize their own White privilege or the role of discrimination (Cípolle, 2010). Cípolle (2010) advocated for greater critical awareness to move service-learning students from an ethic of charity to one of social justice. In order to develop the critical consciousness necessary for social justice, students must develop deeper self-awareness, broader perspectives on others, deeper understanding of social issues, and the potential to create change (Cípolle, 2010). Through an integration of critical reflection and action, students are able to develop a more critical and complex view of the world and recognize the power dynamics that oppress certain groups.

Racial Identity and Service-Learning

One of the complexities of service-learning is the role of racial identity, although the majority of service-learning literature focuses on the experiences of White students (Butin, 2005; Eyler & Giles, 1999; Jacoby, 2009). Dunlap, Scroggin, Green, and Davi (2007) developed a theoretical model from an analysis of reflections of students engaging in service-learning that illuminated the "process relatively privileged white students go through as they become more aware of their own socioeconomic and other advantages and come to terms with these within their community service learning placements" (p. 19). Trigger events occurred when students communicated with the "other" (Dunlap et al., 2007, p. 22). Through such trigger events, White students began to recognize the concept of privilege and challenged their understanding of what it meant to be White.

Green (2001) argued that considering the implications of White privilege in service-learning is crucial, particularly when most of the students are White and are engaging with mostly communities of color. Green (2001) noted that racial majority students were unable to avoid discussions of race when students of color were a part of the experience. The most productive way to get White students to recognize the factor of race in the service-learning setting was to engage them in discussions about Whiteness and White privilege (Green, 2001). The literature on White privilege and service-learning highlights the importance of recognizing the intersections of race and class in any service-learning context.

There is an absence of critical understanding about racially underrepresented students' experiences in service-learning (Gilbride-Brown, 2008). Butin (2006) commented that service-learning may be a luxury that many students, particularly underrepresented students, may not be able to afford because of financial situations or time. There are also challenges for students who may, through service-learning, be working in communities much like the ones in which they were raised. In Gilbride-Brown's (2008) study of the experiences of students of color in service-learning, students described service-learning as working "within" community and suggested that the experiences were an important reason for the college students and their high school mentees' academic persistence. Gilbride-Brown (2008) also indicated that students of color were less inclined to participate in community service because it was perceived as a White, do-gooder activity.

In another study, Conley and Hamlin (2009) found that a "justice-learning" curriculum in a service-learning course positively impacted academic and social engagement of students of color who identified as low income and first generation. Yeh (2010) studied the relationship between service-learning involvement and persistence of first-generation students of color and found that students experienced growth in academic, psychosocial, personal/spiritual, and sociocultural/sociopolitical dimensions. Students discussed their ability to build skills and understanding, develop resilience, find personal meaning, and develop critical consciousness. Finally, in a study of a diverse group of students involved in an alternative break experience, Jones, Robbins, and LePeau (2011) found that the learning outcomes associated with the trip were experienced differently for students of color and White students. For example, service-learning scholars often emphasize the "border crossing" that takes place as students engage in communities very different from their own. For the students of color in this study, borders were crossed but with much less angst and dissonance than the White students, because they crossed borders all the time (Jones et al., 2011).

Resistance and Dissonance

Through service-learning experiences, students encounter contexts that challenge their assumptions and previous experiences, which are situations necessary for growth (Eyler & Giles, 1999). Eyler and Giles identified these dissonant experiences as ill-structured problems through which students come to see the complex social system in which the problem exists. Students were then compelled to evaluate conflicting information on the ill-structured problem, for which there was no simple solution (Eyler & Giles, 1999). The cognitive dissonance that students experience can be made more complicated by their racial identity development and awareness of inequality and privilege.

Butin (2005) noted that White students often resort to ignorance or avoidance when issues of privilege and equity arise. Butin (2005) defined student resistance as the "rejection of one's own complicity in the culturally contentious issues under discussion, specifically in relation to one's privilege of Whiteness" (p. 116). Butin reconceptualized students' resistance as an attempt to maintain a particular identity and a refusal to see themselves in an alternate identity.

Jones, Gilbride-Brown, and Gasiorski (2005) conceptualized student resistance as "a process of struggle, negotiation, and meaning-making" (p. 7) and developed three profiles of student resistance: absence of critical thinking about connections and complexity, emerging recognition of the role of power and privilege, and disruptively resistant. They suggested creating communities of peer learners in order to expose students to different perspectives and stimulate greater self-awareness. Students are more likely to "take risks if they see their peers engaging in new ideas and different experiences" (Jones et al., 2005, p. 19).

Required Service-Learning

Because of the prevailing belief that service-learning yields student learning, many in education turn to requiring service-learning. Conflicting evidence exists about the benefits of service-learning as a course requirement or mandatory graduation component, and there is limited research on the impact of required—compared to optional—service-learning. Most of the literature on this topic emerges from research on high school graduation requirements. Several scholars have noted the problematic nature of requiring community service in high school, particularly the impact on the likelihood of volunteering in college (Helms, 2013; Jones & Hill, 2003; Jones, Segar, & Gasiorski, 2008; Marks & Jones, 2004). Jones and Hill (2003) found that college participation in service increased for students whose high school environment encouraged service. Voluntary community service that was "encouraged by family or friends, and made meaningful by teachers or others who helped explain why community service was important" (Jones & Hill, 2003, p. 534) was a key factor leading high school students to continue service after graduation. Jones and Hill (2003) further determined that high school requirements positioned service as "an obligation, with little thought given to the meaning of the service itself" (p. 534).

In a qualitative study of the perceived outcomes associated with a high school service-learning graduation requirement, Jones, Segar, and Gasiorski (2008) found that students resisted the forced nature of the requirement. While the structure of the requirement restricted their ability to engage in psychologically, cognitively, or civically meaningful activities, participants did acknowledge that the requirement likely led them and their peers to engage in service that they might not have without the requirement (Jones et al., 2008). In a recent quantitative study comparing the service activity of Maryland students before and after the passage of a high school service graduation requirement, Helms (2013) found that the high school requirement reduced volunteering among 12th-grade students and did not meet the goal of the requirement to create life-long volunteers. Twelfth graders initially increased their participation in volunteer activities but later reduced their participation, particularly once they had completed the requirement, which points to a negative effect of required service on students' continued participation in service (Helms, 2013).

The majority of higher education literature associated with the topic of required service focuses on the creation of required service-learning courses within programs of study (Haussamen, 1997; Jenkins, 2011; Reinders & Youniss, 2006; Saggers & Carrington, 2008). In a quantitative study of the impact of optional and required service-learning placements in 21 courses, Parker-Gwin and Mabry (1998) found that required participation in service-learning lowered students' perceptions of the importance of community service. Additionally, optional service-learning led to greater cognitive outcomes than required service-learning, particularly analytic, problem-solving, and critical thinking skills (Parker-Gwin & Mabry, 1998). Marks and Jones (2004) argued that institutions should invest in encouraging "faculty, staff, and students to engage in community-based teaching, learning, and service" (p. 335) rather than emphasize required community service for students. Another service-learning initiative growing in popularity and numbers on college campuses is that of short-term immersion programs, typically referred to as alternative breaks.

Short-Term Immersion Programs

Domestic and international service immersion is a burgeoning form of service-learning in higher education (Crabtree, 2008; Jones, Rowan-Kenyon, Ireland, Niehaus, & Skendall, 2012). Often these trips combine travel and community service either internationally or domestically through programs such as alternative breaks. Short-term immersion programs typically last 1–2 weeks, take place during academic breaks, incorporate service and immersion, and involve academic instruction and reflection (Cermak, Christiansen, Gleeson, White, & Leach, 2011). Research on the outcomes associated with these types of programs suggests that they have the potential to promote transformative learning, including challenging previously held beliefs and values, broadening career and educational perspectives, and increasing self-confidence (Kiely, 2004, 2005; Lewis & Niesenbaum, 2005).

In their multi-site case study investigating the experiences of students engaged in four week-long service-learning immersion programs, Jones, Rowan-Kenyon, Ireland, Niehaus, and Skendall (2012) found that students' experiences led to learning and meaning making, particularly focused on developing new understanding of social issues, privilege, and stereotypes, and led to shifts in sense of purpose and career planning. Upon their return from the experience, students reported a challenging process of reentry as they struggled to integrate what they learned into their lives back home. Surprisingly, many participants pointed to their immersion experience as their first intercultural learning experience, despite their enrollment in a fairly diverse student population (Jones et al., 2012). Participants' challenges with cross-racial interactions and developmental, physical, and cultural boundary crossings emphasized the need for critical reflection to promote transformative learning (Jones et al., 2012).

Not all findings, however, show a positive impact of short-term immersion on student learning outcomes. Cermak and fellow researchers (2011) studied undergraduates returning from international service trips to understand how students made meaning of service and activism within both personal and social contexts. It was found that students displaced activism with service as they experienced a sense of dissonance over how to respond to the injustices they witnessed and could not generate plans for strategic social change (Cermak et al., 2011). The Cermak study (2011) warned educators: "Our study shows that we cannot simply hope for the best from service programs to inspire students to develop change-making strategies" (p. 17).

We mention these complexities associated with service-learning not to dissuade those interested in service-learning from engaging in its practice, but more to suggest that student learning, despite positive outcomes, cannot be taken for granted. In fact, in many of these complexities lie the seeds for even deeper learning to occur through awareness of these issues and careful planning.

Conclusion

The links between service-learning and the kind of learning advocated as desirable to preparation for active involvement in a global world are evident. Service-learning opportunities provide rich contexts for transformational learning and the development of skills, dispositions, knowledge, and awareness that translate to civic and social responsibility. However, as we have pointed out in this chapter, such learning does not take place automatically. The learning outcomes intended will in part be anchored in one's definitions of service-learning, and the learning outcomes produced will in part depend upon the ways in which service-learning experiences are structured. Finally, complexities and issues will emerge from service-learning. If educators embrace these complexities rather than run from them, the potential for even greater, deeper, and longer-lasting student learning exists.

References

Association of American Colleges and Universities (AAC&U). (2005). *Liberal education outcomes: A preliminary report of student achievement in college.* Washington, DC: Author.

Association of American Colleges and Universities (AAC&U). (2007). *College learning for the new global century.* Washington, DC: Author.

Astin, A.W., & Sax, L.J. (1998). How undergraduates are affected by service participation. *Journal of College Student Development, 39*(3), 251–263.

Bowman, N.A., Brandenberger, J.W., Mick, C.S., & Toms Smedley, C. (2010). Sustained immersion courses and student orientations to equality, justice and social responsibility: The role of short-term service-learning. *Michigan Journal of Community Service Learning, 17*(1), 20–31.

Bringle, R.G., & Hatcher, J.A. (1996). Implementing service learning in higher education. *Journal of Higher Education, 67*(2), 221–239.

Butin, D.W. (2005). Identity (re)construction and student resistance. In D.W. Butin (Ed.), *Teaching social foundations of education: Contexts, theories, and issues* (pp. 109–126). Mahwah, NJ: Lawrence Erlbaum.

Butin, D.W. (2006). The limits of service-learning in higher education. *Review of Higher Education, 29*(4), 473–498.

Butin, D.W. (2007). Justice-learning: Service-learning as justice-oriented education. *Equity and Excellence in Education, 40*(2), 177–183.

Butin, D.W. (2010). *Service-learning in theory and practice: The future of community engagement in higher education.* New York, NY: Palgrave Macmillan.

Campus Compact. (2007). *President's declaration on the civic responsibilities of higher education.* Retrieved from http://www.compact.org/resources/declaration/Declaration_2007.pdf

Cermak, J.A., Christiansen, A.C., Gleeson, A.P., White, S.K., & Leach, D.K. (2011). Displaying activism? The impact of international service trips on understandings of social change. *Education, Citizenship and Social Justice, 6*(1), 5–19.

Chesbrough, R.D. (2011). College students and service: A mixed methods exploration of motivations, choices, and learning outcomes. *Journal of College Student Development, 52*(6), 687–705.

Christensen, C.M., Horn, M.B., Caldera, L., & Soares, L. (2011). *Disrupting college: How disruptive innovation can deliver quality and affordability to postsecondary education.* Washington, DC: Center for American Progress.

Cípolle, S.B. (2010). *Service-learning and social justice: Engaging students in social change.* Lanham, MD: Rowman and Littlefield.

Clark, C., & Young, M. (2005). Changing places: Theorizing space and power dynamics in service-learning. In D.W. Butin (Ed.), *Service-learning in higher education: Critical issues and directions* (pp. 3–24). New York, NY: Palgrave Macmillan.

Conley, P.A., & Hamlin, M.L. (2009). Justice-learning: Exploring the efficacy with low-income, first-generation college students. *Michigan Journal of Community Service Learning, 16*(1), 47–58.

Council for the Advancement of Standards (CAS). (2005). *Service-learning programs: CAS standards and guidelines.* Retrieved from http://www.kon.org/S-LP_standards.pdf

Crabtree, R.D. (2008). Theoretical foundations for international service-learning. *Michigan Journal of Community Service Learning, 14*(3), 18–36.

Dey, E.L., Ott, M.C., Antonaros, M., Barnhardt, C.L., & Holsapple, M.A. (2009). *Engaging diverse viewpoints: What is the campus climate for perspective-taking?* Washington, DC: Association of American Colleges and Universities.

Dunlap, M., Scroggin, J., Green, P., & Davi, A. (2007). White students' experiences of privilege and socioeconomic disparities: Toward a theoretical model. *Michigan Journal of Community Service Learning, 13*(2), 19–30.

Einfield, A., & Collins, D. (2008). The relationships between service-learning, social justice, multicultural competence, and civic engagement. *Journal of College Student Development, 49*(2), 95–109.

Eyler, J., & Giles, D.E. Jr. (1999). *Where's the learning in service-learning?* San Francisco, CA: Jossey-Bass.

Gilbride-Brown, J.K. (2008). *(E)racing service-learning as critical pedagogy: Race matters* (Unpublished doctoral dissertation). The Ohio State University, Columbus.

Green, A.E. (2001). But "you aren't white": Racial perceptions and service learning. *Michigan Journal of Community Service Learning, 8*(1), 18–26.

Hatcher, J.A., Bringle, R.G., & Muthiah, R. (2004). Designing effective reflection: What matters to service-learning. *Michigan Journal of Community Service Learning, 11*(1), 38–46.

Haussamen, B. (1997). Service learning and first-year composition. *Teaching English in the Two-Year College, 24*(3), 192–198.

Helms, S.E. (2013). Involuntary volunteering: The impact of mandated service in public schools. *Economics of Education Review, 36*(3), 295–310.

Holsapple, M.A. (2012). Service-learning and student diversity outcomes: Existing evidence and directions for future research. *Michigan Journal of Community Service Learning, 18*(2), 5–18.

Jacoby, B.A. (Ed.). (1996). *Service-learning in higher education: Concepts and practices.* San Francisco, CA: Jossey-Bass.

Jacoby, B.A. (Ed.). (2009). *Civic engagement in higher education.* San Francisco, CA: Jossey-Bass.

Jenkins, S. (2011). The impact of in-class service-learning projects. *Journal of Political Science Education, 7*(2), 196–207.

Jones, S.R. (2003). Principles and profiles of exemplary partnerships with community agencies. In B. Jacoby & Associates (Eds.), *Building partnerships for service-learning* (pp. 151–173). San Francisco, CA: Jossey-Bass.

Jones, S.R., & Abes, E.S. (2003). Developing student understanding of HIV/AIDS through community service-learning: A case study analysis. *Journal of College Student Development, 44*(4), 470–488.

Jones, S.R., & Abes, E.S. (2004). Enduring influences of service-learning on college students' identity development. *Journal of College Student Development, 45*(2), 149–166.

Jones, S.R., Gilbride-Brown, J., & Gasiorski, A. (2005). Getting inside the "underside" of service-learning: Student resistance and possibilities. In D.W. Butin (Ed.), *Service-learning in higher education: Critical issues and directions* (pp. 3–24). New York, NY: Palgrave Macmillan.

Jones, S.R., & Abes, E.S. (2013). *Identity development of college students: Advancing frameworks for multiple dimensions of identity.* San Francisco, CA: Jossey-Bass.

Jones, S.R., & Hill, K.E. (2001). Crossing High Street: Understanding diversity through community service-learning. *Journal of College Student Development, 42*(3), 204–216.

Jones, S.R., & Hill, K.E. (2003). Understanding patterns of commitment: Student motivation for community service involvement. *Journal of Higher Education, 74*(5), 516–539.

Jones, S.R., Robbins, C.K., & LePeau, L.A. (2011). Negotiating border crossing: Influences of social identity on service-learning outcomes. *Michigan Journal of Community Service Learning, 17*(2), 27–42.

Jones, S.R., Rowan-Kenyon, H.T., Ireland, S.M., Niehaus, E., & Skendall, K.C. (2012). The meaning students make as participants in short-term immersion programs. *Journal of College Student Development, 53*(2), 201–220.

Jones, S.R., Segar, T.C., & Gasiorski, A.L. (2008). "A double-edged sword": College student perceptions of required high school service-learning. *Michigan Journal of Community Service Learning, 15*(1), 5–17.

Kahne, J., & Westheimer, J. (1999). In the service of what? The politics of service-learning. In J. Claus & C. Ogden (Eds.), *Service-learning for youth empowerment and social change* (pp. 25–42). New York, NY: Peter Lang.

Keeling, R.P. (Ed.). (2004). *Learning reconsidered: A campus-wide focus on the student experience.* Washington, DC: American College Personnel Association & National Association of Student Personnel Administrators.

Kiely, R. (2004). A chameleon with a complex: Searching for transformation in international service-learning. *Michigan Journal of Community Service Learning, 10*(2), 5–20.

Kiely, R. (2005). A transformative learning model for service-learning: A longitudinal case study. *Michigan Journal of Community Service Learning, 12*(1), 5–22.

King, P.M., & Baxter Magolda, M.B. (1996). A developmental perspective on learning. *Journal of College Student Development, 37*(2), 163–173.

King, P.M., & Baxter Magolda, M.B. (2011). Student learning. In J.H. Schuh, S.R. Jones, & S.R. Harper (Eds.), *Student services: A handbook for the profession* (pp. 207–225). San Francisco, CA: Jossey-Bass.

Levine, A., & Dean, D.R. (2012). *Generation on a tightrope: A portrait of today's college student.* San Francisco, CA: Jossey-Bass.

Lewis, T.L., & Niesenbaum, R.A. (2005). Extending the stay: Using community-based research and service learning to enhance short-term study abroad. *Journal of Studies in International Education, 9*(3), 251–264.

Marks, H.M., & Jones, S.R. (2004). Community service in the transition: Shifts and continuities in participation from high school to college. *Journal of Higher Education, 75*(3), 307–339.

Mayhew, M.J., & Engberg, M.E. (2011). Promoting the development of civic responsibility: Infusing service-learning practices in first-year "success" courses. *Journal of College Student Development, 52*(1), 20–38.

Mitchell, T.D. (2008). Traditional vs. critical service-learning: Engaging the literature to differentiate the two models. *Michigan Journal of Community Service Learning, 14*(2), 50–65.

Morton, K. (1995). The irony of service: Charity, project, and social change in service learning. *Michigan Journal of Community Service Learning, 2*(1), 19–32.

National Center for Education Statistics. (2011). *Learning at a distance: Undergraduate enrollment in distance education courses and degree programs.* Retrieved from nces.ed.gov/pubs2012/2012154.pdf

Parker-Gwin, R., & Mabry, J.B. (1998). Service learning as pedagogy and civic education: Comparing outcomes for three models. *Teaching Sociology, 26*(4), 276–291.

Pascarella, E.T., & Terenzini, P.T. (2005). *How college affects students: A third decade of research.* San Francisco, CA: Jossey-Bass.

Pryor, J.H., Eagan, K., Palucki Blake, L., Hurtado, S., Berdan, J., & Case, M.H. (2012). *The American freshman: National norms Fall 2012.* Los Angeles, CA: Higher Education Research Institute, UCLA.

Reinders, H., & Youniss, J. (2006). School-based required community service and civic development in adolescents. *Applied Developmental Science, 10*(1), 2–12.

Saggers, B., & Carrington, S. (2008). Outcomes of a service-learning program for pre-service teachers: Links to Butin's conceptual model. *Teaching Education, 19*(1), 57–71.

Seider, S., Rabinowicz, S., & Gillmor, S. (2012). Differential outcomes for American college students engaged in community service-learning involving youth and adults. *Journal of Experiential Education, 35*(3), 447–463.

Stanton, T.K., Giles, D.E., & Cruz, N.I. (1999). *Service-learning: A movement's pioneers reflect on its origins, practice, and future.* San Francisco, CA: Jossey-Bass.

Steinberg, K.S., Hatcher, J.A., & Bringle, R.G. (2011). Civic-minded graduate: A north star. *Michigan Journal of Community Service Learning, 18*(1), 19–33.

Stoecker, R., & Tryon, E.A. (2009). *The unheard voices: Community organizations and service learning.* Philadelphia, PA: Temple University Press.

Vogelgesang, L.J. (2005). *Bridging from high school to college: Findings from the 2004 freshmen CIRP survey.* St. Paul, MN: National Youth Leadership Council.

Warren, J.L. (2012). Does service-learning increase student learning? A meta-analysis. *Michigan Journal of Community Service Learning, 18*(2), 56–61.

Yeh, T.L. (2010). Service-learning and persistence of low-income, first-generation college students: An exploratory study. *Michigan Journal of Community Service Learning, 16*(2), 50–65.

TWENTY EIGHT

Benefits of Outdoor Adventure Experiences on Student Learning and Transformation

Joseph A. Pate, Mallory A. Anderson, and Nathan Williams

Through the adventure week experiences of climbing and hiking, I have learned to be flexible—to roll with the challenges.... One shouldn't get mired down in self-doubt, but face them head on.... Pushing yourself is such an empowering thing. It has built and boosted the confidence I have in myself.... You have to learn to move beyond self-doubt, to leave it behind at the foot of the adventure. Through this you learn not only about yourself, but others and the world. And the best thing is the ability to take these experiences back and use them in "real life."[1]

Introduction

Each year, incoming college students are bombarded with marketing materials through mailings, websites, and admission offices aimed at presenting the myriad experiences awaiting them as they embark on this chapter of their lives. Most materials showcase potential academic disciplines and fields of study that will provide for their education, training, and skill development to help them meet workforce expectations and to succeed professionally beyond college. However, often coupled with this exposure to a diversity of academic and educational opportunities are intentionally placed images and language that highlight the student experience beyond the classroom. There are pictures of students participating in challenge courses, kayaking, rock climbing, or smiling and bonding with peers at a breathtaking overlook. In addition, many materials contain wording centered on outdoor concepts such as "adventure," "journeys," "challenges," "growth," and "transformation." These images and phrases demonstrate the potential these experiences have on attracting, engaging, and contributing to students' overall growth. Arguably steeped in an orientation and sentiment aimed at the development and learning of the whole student beyond mere academic endeavors during their collegiate years (American Council on Education, 1937, 1949) and actualized through the quotation above, these experiences provide a fertile and complementary platform for college professionals to promote and facilitate student learning, growth, and transformation.

Outdoor and adventure experiences make possible an engaging and transformative platform where students can grow, develop, and learn in novel, challenging, and unique contexts. Some of the promoted benefits and outcomes of outdoor and adventure experiences include successful orientation to college (Gass, 1999); understanding of both interpersonal and intrapersonal relationship dynamics (Stiehl & Parker, 2007); leadership skill acquisition (Ewert & Garvey, 2007; Martin, Cashel, Wagstaff, & Breunig, 2006; Panicucci, 2007); personally relevant and meaningful transformative and extraordinary experiences (Abrahams, 1986; Mezirow, 2000; Priest & Gass, 2005); spiritual, moral, ethical, and environmental stewardship development (Fox, 1999; Haluza-Delay, 1999; Henderson, 1999); as well as positive identity formation and increased perception of self-efficacy (Bandura, 1977; Priest & Gass, 2005; Stiehl & Parker, 2007). Outdoor adventure experiences are embedded with great potential.

In this chapter outdoor adventure experiences are promoted and defined as spaces for student development and transformation. Distinguishing these experiences from other possibilities and iterations, we intentionally ground them within the foundational philosophical tenets and theoretical underpinnings of experiential education and its elevation of the critical role that reflection plays in meaningful and personally relevant learning and growth. Through a focused overview of programmatic best practices grounded in student-centered initiatives, we then demonstrate how these experiences can be leveraged to celebrate and attend to the learning, development, and potential transformation of the whole person. We conclude with a synopsis and discussion of the salient benefits these experiences afford and direct readers to resources and assessment strategies that can be utilized to help evaluate their overall effectiveness. It is our hope that through this chapter we can provide insight into the student experience and learning attainable through purposeful, intentional, and well-developed outdoor adventure experiences.

Definitions

Becci had just left home. Far behind her was all she had known. In front of her she faced a new town, new people, new teachers, a new bed, and the reality of knowing no one. A month ago she had received a flyer in the mail advertising a whitewater adventure orientation program. She had never done anything like this before. The flyer promised good times and the opportunity to meet other new students, faculty, and staff at her new college. It also promised a thrilling experience of taking a raft down world class whitewater. As she looked down the long stretch of highway, her nervousness about all that was before her was tempered by the excitement of her first adventure rafting.

To better understand outdoor adventure experiences, it is necessary to define important terms and concepts, discuss their philosophical and theoretical origins, and to distinguish these experiences from other commonly used terms. We purposely have elected to use the phrasing outdoor adventure "experiences"—as opposed to activities or pursuits—to capture what is possible through these opportunities for students beyond just participating in the activity of rock climbing, skydiving, or hiking. Defining terms and understanding what is intended through their use helps to provide guidance, insight, and structure in the promotion and facilitation of student-centered experiences aimed at personally relevant and meaningful learning, transformation, and growth. In this section we define outdoor and adventure experiences, discuss the use of the word "experiences" to encompass *more than* activities or pursuits, and end by briefly grounding these experiences in the philosophical and theoretical tenets of experiential learning, highlighting the critical role of reflection.

Outdoor Adventure Experiences

For the purposes of this chapter, outdoor adventure experiences encompass the intentions, activities, reflections, benefits, and outcomes that occur through student involvement in contexts that are challenging, uncertain, novel, and potentially risk-filled. These experiences are primarily undertaken out-of-doors and are aimed at providing opportunities for groups and individuals to better understand themselves in relation to self, others, and the larger landscape and environment, ideally creating spaces for personally relevant and meaningful discovery, learning, growth, and transformation. One student described these types of experiences as "show[ing] me that there is more to college than just working to get grades—this trip helped me learn so much about myself and let me reevaluate the life I was living." Another student shared that "the expedition made me more confident and more comfortable stepping outside of my comfort zone, making my transition to student life here at college less stressful and allowed me to focus on growing from the change, instead of struggling with it." Finally, another student said, "because of adventure week, you grow and learn from the others in your group and learn about yourself." These experiences are potentially promoted through a variety of platforms on collegiate campuses (e.g., adventure orientations, campus recreation outdoor programs, challenge courses, etc.) but are seen to be separate from formalized, academic undertakings through specific course work or degree programs (e.g., a formalized major in outdoor education or outdoor leadership).

Steeped in the fields of adventure and outdoor education,[2] outdoor adventure experiences provide "non-traditional," active, and engaging contexts and opportunities for students to better understand who they are and what they are capable of in relation to an ever-evolving world full of challenges, tasks, and relational dynamics. In the opening vignette, Becci is afforded an opportunity to confront the transitional issues that many college students face when heading off to college. By participating in an adventure orientation program, Becci will challenge herself in a multitude of ways. First, she is in the adventure context of paddling world-class whitewater with others. Through this she has the opportunity to meet others, work toward completing a task, experience challenge and risk, and is potentially able to overcome her perceived fears and push through comfort zones. Many of these same tasks will be necessary as she navigates her new life at college.

Experiences, Pursuits, and Activities

Outdoor adventure programs are often actualized at colleges and universities through a variety of options and platforms. Understood in relation to theoretical concepts such as recreation (chosen activities that take place in order to restore or renew), leisure (intrinsically motivated experiences that are freely chosen and linked to a change in one's state of mind), and play (an activity undertaken for its own sake, where constraints are thrown off, and one experiences joy and freedom), outdoor adventure programs offer the potential for students to learn, become restored and rejuvenated, and engage relationally with themselves and others in deeply meaningful and transformative ways (Priest & Gass, 2005; Russell, 2009). Resisting limiting these programs by only focusing on the activity undertaken or defined by a general pursuit (e.g., rock climbing, hiking, or skydiving), we have elected to highlight the notion of *experiences* to emphasize the inherent benefits to individuals beyond merely the activity or pursuit. In order for outdoor adventure experiences to be actualized, facilitators and leaders must create spaces for students to reflect, helping them realize the latent potential these contexts afford for learning and growth beyond the activity or pursuit through direct, engaged, and experiential means.

Experiential Learning

Experiential learning is rooted in the pedagogical practices of experiential education. Experiential education relates not only to the activity or experience of a learner, but also how this experience is used. Doing the activity is essential, but reflecting on the activity and applying learning from the experience later is crucial, as in Kolb's (1984) experiential learning cycle. For Becci's school, the real power that emanates from the offering of adventure orientation experience comes in its ability to help Becci reflect on how her experiences during the whitewater rafting adventure can help in her transition to a new school. For example, through this experience Becci was able to meet challenges and push through her perceived comfort zones, much like attending a new school. She was also able to make essential and important connections to peers, as well as faculty, staff, and administration, which researchers have found ultimately helps in one's overall success at school (Gass, 1999).

Informed by Dewey's (1909/1998) educational philosophy highlighting the need for educators[3] to understand students as intellectual, social, moral, and physical "organic wholes" and not mere empty vessels where information is poured in only to be regurgitated and understood cognitively, experiential education seeks to engage the whole student in authentic experiences that have personally relevant and meaningful benefits and consequences. In concert with the *Student Personnel Point of View* of 1937 and 1949, experiential learning affords fertile contexts and opportunities to influence and celebrate the development of the whole student (American Council on Education, 1937, 1949). All outdoor adventure experiences fall under the theoretical and philosophical umbrella of experiential education and its assumptions grounded in the belief of the benefit that direct, purposeful experiences have on learning and growth (Dewey, 1938; Priest & Gass, 2005; Prouty, 2007).

According to the Association for Experiential Education (AEE), experiential education is "a process through which a learner constructs knowledge, skill, and value from direct experiences" (AEE, n.d., p. 3). Principles of experiential education practice established by AEE (Figure 1) highlight essential features and provide a clear picture of this educational approach. These features note the relational value within experiential education of the learner to self, learner to educator, and learner to the learning environment, as well as a focus on the mixture of content and process, an absence of excessive judgment, intentional engagement of learners in authentic and purposeful endeavors, the facilitation of students to take in larger, big-picture perspectives, a celebration of multiple styles of learning and knowing, the critical role of reflection, the need for learners to create an emotional investment in their experiences and growth, encouragement in one's re-examination of values, and the challenge to facilitate learning opportunities and experiences outside of one's perceived comfort zones (Chapman, McPhee, & Proudman, 2008).

Figure 1. Principles of Experiential Education Practice.

- Experiential learning occurs when carefully chosen experiences are supported by reflection, critical analysis, and synthesis.
- Experiences are structured to require the learner* to take the initiative, make decisions, and be accountable for the results.
- Throughout the experiential learning process, the learner is actively engaged in posting questions, investigating, experimenting, being curious, solving problems, assuming responsibility, being creative, and constructing meaning.
- Learners are engaged intellectually, emotionally, soulfully, and/or physically. This involvement produces a perception that the learning task is authentic.
- The results of the learning are personal and form the basis for future experience and learning.
- Relationships are developed and nurtured: learner to self, learner to others, and learner to the world at large.
- The educator** and learner may experience success, failure, adventure, risk taking, and uncertainty, since the outcomes of experience cannot be totally predicted.
- Opportunities are nurtured for learners and educators to explore and examine their own values.
- The educator's primary roles include selecting suitable experiences, posing problems, setting boundaries, supporting learners, insuring physical and emotional safety, and facilitating the learning process.
- The educator recognizes and encourages spontaneous opportunities for learning.
- Educators strive to be aware of their biases, judgments, and preconceptions and how they influence the learner.
- The design of the learning experience includes the possibility to learn from natural consequences, mistakes, and successes.

*There is no single term that encompasses all the roles of the participant within experiential education. Therefore, the term learner is meant to include student, client, trainee, participant, etc.

**There is no single term that encompasses all the roles of the professional within experiential education. Therefore, the term educator is meant to include therapist, facilitator, teacher, trainer, practitioner, counselor, etc.

Student-Centered, Engagement of the Whole Person, and Reflection

Extensive defining of and theorizing about experiential learning and education are beyond the scope of this chapter.[4] And, as some experiential educators quip, "of all things that might be true about experiential education, the one thing that is unassailably true is that you can't find out by defining it" (Huie, as cited in Chapman et al., 2008, p. 7). What is important to highlight is the central role of the student; the student experience through the engagement of the whole person cognitively, physically, and affectively; and the potential for student transformation and growth, in contrast to traditional didactic forms of education and learning, which are situated within and focused on the teacher and his or her knowledge and understanding (Freire, 1970/2000). Further, experiential learning and education move beyond a mere activity or pursuit and focus on the internal processes within students and their potential to make meaning and transfer relevancy through guided and critical reflection from the experience to their lives. Giving students an opportunity to construct their own meaning through experience and reflection lies at the heart of experiential education (Chapman et al., 2008; Itin, 1999). It is not simply participating in an activity; rather, it is an intentional process that transforms a mere activity or pursuit into an experience where facilitators create learner-centered environments that promote action followed by reflection (Berry, 2011; Breunig, 2005; Chapman et al., 2008; Itin, 1999). Reflection deepens student learning processes by providing opportunities for individuals to make relevant connections for future learning (Breunig, 2005; Chapman et al., 2008; Gass, 2008).

Opportunities for reflection are abundant in outdoor adventure programming. At the beginning of an outdoor orientation trip, for example, students can be asked to share with the group the things that informed their decision to attend the particular college or university, thus reflecting on this important piece of academic motivation. Later in the trip—possibly after students are frightened during a thunderstorm while camping on an isolated riverbank—the group can be invited to anonymously share fears about starting college through a popular "fears in a hat" activity. After the trip has ended and students are engaged in their first semester, the program can host a reunion dinner and invite students to reflect not only on what the trip means for their college experience but also on overcoming the challenge of the trip with a group of peers. This is just one example of a reflective progression, but numerous opportunities beyond this exist for journaling, individual solo reflection time in nature, artistic creation, post-trip evaluation surveys, guided discussion on trips, and other reflective opportunities.

Experiences

Raymond was on his fourth outing of the year. This time, the campus recreation program was leading a three-day fall break backpacking trip. Hiking by himself for part of the day, Raymond reflected on how different he felt about himself and life now as opposed to when he started school. He used to see commercials and students driving through campus with boats on their cars as "those people" who must be so much braver, adventurous, or competent than him. He thought of Katie, who was probably already at the shelter waiting for the group, and how she asked him if he wanted to go rock climbing at the recreation center. He decided to give it a go. He fell a lot, felt uncomfortable at times, but found a spark for pushing himself and trying new things. The coffee at sunrise this morning brought a sense of faith in his abilities to face challenges, even if he looked silly trying. Raymond also was so appreciative of Danae, the trip leader, and her continued presence and impact on his life.

As stated earlier, the central aspect of outdoor adventure experiences is the student: his or her learning, growth, development, and transformation as a whole person. Students entering colleges and universities encounter many challenges and uncertainties. They face meeting new people, learning new systems and roles, and engaging with academic content that challenges them to become divergent thinkers, reason critically, problem solve, make complex decisions lacking complete information, and become effective in both written and spoken communication. Outdoor adventure experiences have the potential to help students learn and develop in these areas. Further, they afford opportunities for students to get a better sense of who they are, their self-worth, and how this can be of use to their larger communities and world.

Currently, many outdoor adventure programmers tend to rely on a "black box" approach to programming, or the assumption that mere participation will lead to participant development (Sibthorp, Paisley, & Gookin, 2007). We contend that although learning, growth, and development may occur through mere participation, effective outdoor adventure experiences purposefully use outdoor contexts, adventure activities, and the critical role of reflection to help students come to understand the meaning they gain through these opportunities. Effective outdoor adventure programs have the hallmarks of being experiential, dramatic, novel, consequential, metaphoric, transferable, structured, voluntary, concrete, and holistic (Priest & Gass, 2005). Leaders of these experiences in higher education settings who intentionally focus on facilitating opportunities for student learning, growth, and transformation—beyond merely offering an activity or pursuit—create spaces for students to reflect on, gain, and leverage their new insights into other aspects of their lives.

Outdoor Adventure Programming in Higher Education

Students in today's universities and colleges are able to take advantage of outdoor adventure programming through a variety of opportunities and organizational contexts. Rather than attempt to encapsulate all outdoor adventure options available, this section provides examples of three major avenues of outdoor adventure experiences frequently available in higher education: outdoor orientation programs, outdoor recreation trips and associated programs, and leadership development opportunities for students as trip leaders and facilitators.

Outdoor Orientation Programs

Outdoor orientation programs, also called adventure orientation programs or wilderness orientation programs, are often the first programmatic outdoor adventure opportunity available to incoming college students. These programs vary greatly, but a traditional outdoor orientation program might offer incoming students a 5-day wilderness trip over the summer before their first semester. There could be one activity on the trip with a consistent group of peers (e.g., a backpacking trip with a small group of other new students on the Appalachian Trail) or multiple activities (e.g., starting the program with a large group of incoming students for opening icebreaker activities and then splitting up into smaller groups for kayak camping and whitewater rafting). Current research estimates that 185 of these programs exist in the United States (Bell & Starbuck, 2013). Historically, these programs started in small, private colleges in the Northeast, but they are currently available at many different types and sizes of institutions.

The Adventure WV program at West Virginia University is an example of a full-featured, mature outdoor orientation program. Using the mountainous setting of West Virginia and the Monongahela National Forest, Adventure WV offers both first-year and transfer students outdoor orientation programs, in addition to college and major-specific programs. The program also offers academic course credit to students who combine their outdoor experience with a follow-up course during the school year. Speaking about the benefits of this program, one participant said she was "nervous about moving to a new place, making friends and starting college classes. But the Adventure WV program gave me the opportunity to try something new while being supported by other students who felt just like I did. I learned so much about myself and the trip gave me the confidence to see that I really was ready for college."

While not all programs encompass as many options as Adventure WV, there are plenty of examples of other mature programs offering this experience to large numbers of students each year, among them the Outdoor Action program at Princeton University, Wisconsin Basecamp at the University of Wisconsin, and the LandSea program at Kalamazoo College, to name a few. Organizationally, these programs are often housed within recreational sports departments but may also be located within traditional student orientation areas, student unions, or academic programs and colleges. Current students will often serve as trip leaders for these experiences, and faculty, staff, and alumni may be involved in leadership or facilitation as well.

Outdoor Recreation Trips and Associated Programs

After coming to college, there are many chances for students to take advantage of outdoor adventure programming. These include outdoor adventure trips, indoor climbing walls, challenge and high-ropes courses, outdoor equipment rental, academic field courses, or other varieties of outdoor recreation. As with outdoor orientation programs, recreational sports departments might provide these opportunities, but students may also find that their university has a student-run outdoors club or a student activities office that offers trips, or that a faculty or staff member is passionate about the outdoors and invites students on occasional outdoor trips.

At the University of Georgia, the Outdoor Recreation program is housed within the Department of Recreational Sports. Outdoor adventure opportunities for students include whitewater rafting and backpacking trips in the Appalachian Mountains, SCUBA diving certification classes, caving trips, and outdoor climbing trips, among others. Students are also able to rent outdoor gear (e.g., tents, backpacks, and sleeping bags), climb at the recreation center's indoor climbing wall, or engage in a facilitated program at the on-campus high-ropes course. Students interested in earning academic credit can take advantage of the program's international trips that are collaboratively offered with academic departments on campus. This particular program also offers outdoor orientation trips to incoming first-year students. All of these opportunities are led by students with the support of three professional staff within the Outdoor Recreation program area.

Outdoor trips and associated programs are not always located within recreational sports departments. Some colleges and universities offer outdoor recreation as part of the student union (e.g., the Venture Out program at Virginia Tech University) or as a student organization or club (e.g., the Wisconsin Hoofers at the University of Wisconsin). Some institutions offer multiple avenues for students to take advantage of outdoor adventure programming. At Duke University, the Outdoor Adventures program offers trips, clinics, and equipment rentals within a recreational sports department, but there is also an active Duke Outing Club organized by students.

Leadership Development Opportunities for Students

Across many, if not all, of these programs, opportunities are abundant for students to develop leadership skills. Students often begin as participants in a program and progress to being leaders. Indeed, this is a function of many outdoor orientation programs: students attend an outdoor orientation trip as incoming, first-year participants, progress to a support staff role, and then lead these trips during their third or fourth years in college. Students may serve as trip leaders, challenge-course facilitators, climbing-wall staff, rental center attendants, or in other roles that provide leadership and other transferrable skills, in addition to valuable employment experience. For instance, it is not uncommon for a student leader and assistant leader to plan and facilitate a 6-day spring break backpacking trip or a three-day outdoor rock climbing trip that includes climbs to hundreds of feet.

Although research is not extensive on the benefits of leadership development for outdoor adventure staff members, anecdotal evidence is easy to find. When asked to compare outdoor leadership to other types of leadership opportunities, one student trip leader said: "The type of leadership that you have to be comfortable with on an outdoor recreation trip is you have to be comfortable making decisions that could seriously harm or potentially kill somebody if you make a poor decision. That puts an imperative on leadership that may not exist in other student leadership opportunities." Although not all outdoor adventure trips present a high level of risk, this aspect of a student leader being responsible for group safety creates an impactful developmental opportunity, particularly when reflection on leadership lessons is encouraged by professional staff members.

Benefits

Lela took a minute to reflect and watch the students walking back to their dorms, ready to take on their first year at school. She remembered how four short years ago she was one of them. Glowing in the aftermath of her adventure orientation program that took her rock climbing, hiking, and coastal marsh kayaking, she had decided at that moment that she wanted to one day be like her student trip leader, Bo. And today was the culmination of all the years and work. She knew the challenges that school would present, but she also knew that the experiences these students had faced, and the bond they had developed with one another and her, would help guide them as they began their new journey.

To maximize the potential learning, growth, and transformative outcomes for students, we recommend that administrators and facilitators focus on the benefits of outdoor adventure experiences. These benefits and outcomes originate at the intersection of the students, their experiences, and spaces for critical and intentional reflection. Assisting students in verbalizing and more deeply understanding and actualizing the transferable skills, insights, and meaning from outdoor adventure experiences makes possible the transcendent and transformational potential these opportunities afford. Although there are thematic benefits and outcomes found to be influenced by outdoor adventure experiences, personally relevant and student-specific understandings are also essential features born from these spaces. We have found students expressing meaning and insight gained from their participation in outdoor adventure experiences to be uniquely situated and centered in their own journey and life trajectories. In this final section, we briefly address some of the benefits and outcomes of outdoor adventure experiences on student learning, growth, development, and potential transformation. In addition, we provide assessment resources to help in the overall evaluation of these facilitated experiences. This section is by no means exhaustive. Professional associations such as the Association for Outdoor Recreation and Education (AORE), the National Intramural Recreational Sports Association (NIRSA), the Association for Experiential Education (AEE), and the Outdoor Orientation Program Symposium (OOPS) can provide further access to books, articles, and other outdoor adventure resources.

Research shows that qualities exhibited in outdoor adventure experiences lend themselves to creating opportunities for intrapersonal growth (student understanding self), enhanced interpersonal skills (student understanding others), and group development (Ewert & Garvey, 2007; Sibthorp & Arthur-Banning, 2004). Priest (1999) elaborated on potential areas of growth facilitated through outdoor adventure experiences by noting that through participants' responding to seemingly insurmountable tasks, groups and individuals learn to overcome almost any self-imposed perceptions of their capability to succeed. They are able to turn limitations into abilities, and, as a result, they learn a great deal about themselves and how they relate to others (p. 112).

These student-centered benefits relate directly to Bandura's (1977) social learning theory, self-efficacy. Self-efficacy is the belief or certainty that individuals hold with regard to their ability to successfully overcome a challenge or accomplish a task that tests their abilities. More than mere self-worth or self-confidence, increased perceptions of self-efficacy allow for students to believe they can perform and accomplish future tasks and challenges (Priest & Gass, 2005). Also, through such experiences, students working within groups gain an awareness of human interdependence, which in turn leads them to grow in "concern for those in danger and in need," inspiring a broader orientation toward civic engagement, service, and civility (Miner, 1999, p. 58). Using the challenges inherent in outdoor adventure experiences makes possible the development of skill sets useful in other arenas of a student's personal and communal life, allowing students to leverage their individualized insight and meaning to help navigate an unknown and uncertain future (Priest & Gass, 2005; Prouty, 2007).

Other benefits that arise from outdoor adventure experiences include academic outcomes such as increase in first-year student grade point averages, retention, and a contribution to greater levels of overall student development (Brown, 1998; Gass, 1987; Vlamis, Bell, & Gass, 2011). Students who participate in outdoor adventure experiences reported less stress and anxiety, as well as a greater ability to control their emotions (Frauman & Waryold, 2009; Kanters, Bristol, & Attariam, 2002). Students may gain increases in life effectiveness skills such as time management, task leadership, and achievement motivation (Flood, Gardner, & Cooper, 2009; Frauman & Waryold, 2009). Further, participation in these types of experiences results in students placing a higher lifelong importance on maintaining their health and wellness, in contrast to those who do not (Forrester, Arterberry, & Barcelona, 2006). Finally, through participating in outdoor adventure experiences, students tend to increase environmentally sustainable attitudes, behaviors, and actions (Jackson, 1986).

Outdoor adventure experiences appear to be especially beneficial to personal growth associated with the developmental stages occurring in traditional-age college students with regard to affective, cognitive, and psychosocial domains (Priest & Gass, 2005; Prouty, 2007). Interpreting Erikson's view of the exploration/commitment stage of development, Kleiber (1999) suggested that in leisure-based experiences like outdoor adventures, students can develop their emotional independence through exploration and by engaging in activities away from home prior to committing to more permanent courses of action and understanding, in similar or different contexts. Supporting this idea, Fine (1999) suggested that there was "probably no state in a person's life where adventure [was] more valuable than in the later adolescent years" (p. 196). Through outdoor adventure experiences, researchers found growth in the affective domain of student development through increased self-awareness, personal growth, motivation levels, interpersonal competence, and self-actualization in participants (Klint, 1999; Paisley, Furman, Sibthorp, & Gookin, 2008; Sibthorp et al., 2007). Further, development in the affective domain (especially interpersonal skill development) supports development in the cognitive domain as well (Zull, 2012). Outdoor adventure contexts "activate this synergistic system…[where] cognition and emotion work together" (Zull, 2012, p. 184) in a social context.

As noted in this section's opening vignette, through purposeful and well-designed outdoor adventure experiences, students are afforded opportunities to develop and hone leadership skills and competencies. In particular, these experiences allow for students to explore and test various leadership and group roles, such as designated leadership (appointed leadership role with majority of the responsibility housed within one or two designated individuals), active followership (supportive following and participating as an active and engaged group member), peer leadership (communal and shared responsibility for group functioning and success), and self-leadership (focused self-care and the importance this plays in overall group effectiveness) (Prouty, 2007). Not all outdoor adventure experiences have as their aim or goal to develop leaders, which is important to note. However, focusing on the benefits these experiences may have on student development, we note that leadership skills are all potential areas for growth and learning within students. These include establishing appropriate expeditionary behavior and group norms, technical and interpersonal skill mastery and competence, effective communication and empowerment of others through the development of their own personal expertise, and reflection on judgment and decision making. These should also include tolerance for ambiguity, adversity, diversity of opinions, and reflexive self-awareness and leading by example, challenging the status quo and making necessary changes, inspiring an agreed-upon and mutual vision, and implementing action (Johnson & Johnson, 2002; Prouty, 2007).

Finally, through outdoor adventure experiences, students are afforded spaces of transformation and *extraordinary* moments (Abrahams, 1986). In these spaces, students are absorbed in the experience and give a sense of "personal control, joy and valuing, a spontaneous letting be of the process, and a newness of [their own] perception and process" (Arnould & Price, 1993, p. 25). For the student, there arise feelings of harmony with nature, a connection to others, and personal growth and renewal, and in these "deeply emotional experiences that enchant and delight the participants...everything combines to make [the activity] one of the most memorable" (Wright & Larsen, 2012, pp. 130–131). Mezirow's (2000) transformational theory complements the idea of "change" found in these *extraordinary experiences*. Through these transformative experiences, the potential arises for individuals to change long-entrenched and unquestioned points of view and to open themselves up to creating new patterns of thought and habits of the mind. The themes that make up *extraordinary experiences* (harmony with nature, spontaneity, community, magic moments, and having a sense of personal control) mirror qualities researchers have found in outdoor adventure experiences (natural environment, sense of personal control, and an uncertain outcome) (Arnould & Price, 1993; Jefferies & Lepp, 2012; Priest, 1999; see also Csikszentmihalyi, 1990).

Assessment Resources

As with any program utilized to help facilitate and foster student learning, development, and growth, effective assessment and evaluation of that experience is paramount. Outdoor adventure experiences are no different. What is important to emphasize is the necessity of assessment strategies that actualize both qualitative and quantitative avenues to capture these experiences. Within the experiential learning profession, the website Wilderdom.com, and in particular its assessment resource page (www.wilderdom.com/tools.html), serves as a clearinghouse for a number of different assessment strategies, tools, and descriptions that can be incorporated by any number of programs or institutions to evaluate diverse outcomes and benefits of student participation.

Conclusion

In this chapter, outdoor adventure experiences have been advocated as a uniquely student-centered space where deeply meaningful and personally relevant learning, growth, and transformation are possible. These experiences have been conceptualized and defined as interactions between students with themselves, others, and the natural world, and include the presence of challenge, uncertainty, and the potential for development of the whole person. Informed by the philosophical tenets of experiential learning and the critical role of intentional reflection, we have presented a number of examples that focus on the overall student experience, as opposed to just the outdoor adventure activity or pursuit, resulting in the potential for transformation and growth within students. Empirical research and anecdotal evidence from students we have collectively led over the years indicate occurrences of learning and development in interpersonal and intrapersonal domains, in their skills and competencies as leaders, and through deeply meaningful, transformative, and extraordinary spaces and experiences. We have briefly suggested resources for assessment strategies and the provision of opportunities for critical and intentional reflection. Accessing the students' experiences and their voices highlights the potential power and transformational meaning afforded through outdoor adventure experiences.

In concert with the guiding spirit of student-centered and -voiced significance and meaning found within these spaces, we have elected to end this chapter with the words of one of the many students we have had the privilege to walk alongside. Student voice affords each of us a moment to experience the inspiring potential that purposeful programming makes possible:

> *I believe this [outdoor adventure experience] had one of the most important impacts on my college experience thus far. It showed me that there is more to college than just working to get good grades. It made me more confident and more comfortable stepping outside of my comfort zones. It brought me closer to some incredible people who are now some of my very best friends, and I'm not sure I could have gained this closeness any other way. And most importantly, it introduced me to new leadership strategies. In my past, I assumed leadership was as simple as showing up and allowing my voice to be heard. This experience demonstrated to me firsthand that leadership needs to be a far more nuanced skill that involves trust, reliability, communication, influence, and guidance, none of which come seamlessly or are developed overnight. For these lessons, I am forever grateful.*[5]

Notes

1. The student quotes in this chapter come from evaluations, surveys, and research spanning 14 years across the authors' collective experiences programming, facilitating, and leading a diverse range of outdoor and adventure experiences at colleges and institutions ranging from small, private, liberal arts colleges and mid-range state institutions, to large land-grant and research-based universities.
2. Outdoor and adventure education: Formalized use of outdoor adventure activities within educational programs can be dated back to 1861 (Raiola & O'Keefe, 1999), with the most recent developments in collegiate settings occurring within the past 80 years (Gass, 1999). Outdoor education is an engaged and active learning strategy that takes place primarily out of doors and involves direct interaction between individuals and groups with the natural environment (Priest & Gass, 2005; Prouty, 2007). Adventure education is situated under the definitional umbrella of outdoor educational initiatives, but is understood further as learning that involves the whole person and facilitates choices and actions with real consequences. A term that is closely associated with both outdoor and adventure education is environmental education. Through environmental education, the focus is specifically on ecosystemic (interdependence of living organisms within a larger ecological system) and ekistic (interactions and influence of humans on the natural environment) relationships (Priest & Gass, 2005). As formalized educational experiences, outdoor, adventure, and environmental education are typically associated with particular curricula and where student learning occurs through traditional academic mediums.
3. We have elected to use the term "educator" to encompass all of the personnel on a collegiate campus, including staff, administration, peers in leadership roles, and faculty.

4. See Warren, Mitten, & Loeffler (2008) for a far-reaching text on the theory and practice of experiential education.
5. We would like to thank Matt Marcus from the Georgia Institute of Technology and the Outdoor Recreation Program at Georgia Tech for ideas, student quotes, and insight into this chapter.

References

Abrahams, R.D. (1986). Ordinary and extraordinary experience. In V.W. Turner & E.M. Bruner (Eds.), *The anthropology of experience* (pp. 45–73). Urbana, IL: University of Illinois Press.

American Council on Education. (1937). *The student personnel point of view: A report of a conference on the philosophy and development of student personnel work in colleges and universities.* Washington, DC: Author. Retrieved from http://www.myacpa.org/pub/documents/1937.pdf

American Council on Education. (1949). *The student personnel point of view: A report of a conference on the philosophy and development of student personnel work in colleges and universities.* Washington, DC: Author. Retrieved from http://www.myacpa.org/pub/documents/1949.pdf

Arnould, E.J., & Price, L.L. (1993). River magic: Extraordinary experience and the extended service encounter. *Journal of Consumer Research, 20*(1), 24–45.

Association for Experiential Education (AEE). (n.d.). AEE definition of experiential education [Membership brochure]. Boulder, CO: Author.

Bandura, A. (1977). Self-efficacy: Toward a unifying theory for behavioral change. *Psychological Review, 84*(2), 191–215.

Bell, B.J., & Starbuck, D. (2013). Outdoor orientation program trends at colleges and universities in the United States. *Journal of Outdoor Recreation, Education, and Leadership, 5*(2), 111–114.

Berry, M. (2011). Learning and teaching in adventure education. In M. Berry & C. Hodgson (Eds.), *Adventure education: An introduction* (pp. 63–83). New York, NY: Routledge.

Breunig, M. (2005). Turning experiential education and critical pedagogy theory into praxis. *Journal of Experiential Education, 28*(2), 106–122.

Brown, D.A. (1998). Does an outdoor orientation program really work? *College and University, 73*(4), 17–23.

Chapman, S., McPhee, P., & Proudman, B. (2008). What is experiential education? In K. Warren, D. Mitten, & T.A. Loeffler (Eds.), *Theory and practice of experiential education* (pp. 3–15). Boulder, CO: Association for Experiential Education.

Csikszentmihalyi, M. (1990). *Flow: The psychology of optimal experience.* New York, NY: HarperCollins.

Dewey, J. (1938). *Experience & education.* New York, NY: Touchstone.

Dewey, J. (1998). The moral training given by the school community. In L.A. Hickman & T.M. Alexander (Eds.), *The essential Dewey, Vol. 1: Pragmatism, education, democracy* (pp. x–xx). Bloomington, IN: Indiana University Press.

Ewert, A., & Garvey, D. (2007). Philosophy and theory of adventure education. In D. Prouty, J. Panicucci, & R. Collinson (Eds.), *Adventure education theory and practice* (pp. 19–32). Champaign, IL: Human Kinetics.

Fine, L. (1999). Stage development theory in adventure programming. In J.C. Miles & S. Priest (Eds.), *Adventure programming* (pp. 193–199). State College, PA: Venture.

Flood, J.P., Gardner, E., & Cooper, N. (2009). One-day challenge course impact on student life effectiveness skills. *Journal of Outdoor Recreation, Education, and Leadership, 1*(1), 55–75.

Forrester, S., Arterberry, C., & Barcelona, B. (2006). Student attitudes toward sports and fitness activities after graduation. *Recreational Sports Journal, 30*(2), 87–99.

Fox, R. (1999). Enhancing spiritual experiences in adventure programs. In J.C. Miles & S. Priest (Eds.), *Adventure programming* (pp. 455–461). State College, PA: Venture.

Frauman, E., & Waryold, D. (2009). Impact of wilderness orientation program on college students' life effectiveness. *Journal of Outdoor Recreation, Education, and Leadership, 1*(2), 191–209.

Freire, P. (2000). *Pedagogy of the oppressed: 30th anniversary edition.* New York, NY: Continuum.

Gass, M.A. (1987). The effects of a wilderness orientation program on college students. *Journal of Experiential Education, 10*(2), 30–33.

Gass, M.A. (1999). Adventure programs in higher education. In J.C. Miles & S. Priest (Eds.), *Adventure programming* (pp. 373–383). State College, PA: Venture.

Gass, M.A. (2008). Programming the transfer of learning in adventure education. In K. Warren, D. Mitten, & T.A. Loeffler (Eds.), *Theory and practice of experiential education* (pp. 297–308). Boulder, CO: Association of Experiential Education.

Haluza-Delay, R.B. (1999). Navigating the terrain: Helping care for the earth. In J.C. Miles & S. Priest (Eds.), *Adventure programming* (pp. 445–454). State College, PA: Venture.

Henderson, R. (1999). The place of deep ecology and ecopsychology in adventure education. In J.C. Miles & S. Priest (Eds.), *Adventure programming* (pp. 439–444). State College, PA: Venture.

Itin, C.M. (1999). Reasserting the philosophy of experiential education as a vehicle for change in the 21st century. *Journal of Experiential Education, 22*(2), 91–98.

Jackson, E.L. (1986). Outdoor recreation participation and attitudes to the environment. *Leisure Studies, 5*(1), 1–23.

Jefferies, K., & Lepp, J. (2012). An investigation of extraordinary experiences. *Journal of Park and Recreation Administration, 30*(3), 37–51.

Johnson, D.W., & Johnson, F.P. (2002). *Joining together: Group theory and group skills* (8th ed.). Boston, MA: Allyn & Bacon.

Kanters, M.A., Bristol, D.C., & Attariam, A. (2002). The effects of outdoor experiential training on perceptions of college stress. *Journal of Experiential Education, 25*(2), 257–267.

Kleiber, D. (1999). Changes in leisure behavior over the life span. In D. Kleiber (Ed.), *Leisure experience and human development* (pp. 33–61). New York, NY: Basic Books.

Klint, K.A. (1999). New directions for inquiry into self-concept and adventure experiences. In J.C. Miles & S. Priest (Eds.), *Adventure programming* (pp. 193–199). State College, PA: Venture.

Kolb, D. (1984). *Experiential learning: Experience as the source of learning and development.* Englewood Cliffs, NJ: Prentice Hall.

Martin, B., Cashel, C., Wagstaff, M., & Breunig, M. (2006). *Outdoor leadership: Theory and practice.* Champaign, IL: Human Kinetics.

Mezirow, J. (2000). Learning to think like an adult: Core concepts of transformation theory. In J. Mezirow (Ed.), *Learning as transformation: Critical perspectives on a theory in progress* (pp. 35–69). San Francisco, CA: Jossey-Bass.

Miner, J.L. (1999). The creation of Outward Bound. In J.C. Miles & S. Priest (Eds.), *Adventure programming* (pp. 55–63). State College, PA: Venture.

Paisley, K., Furman, N., Sibthorp, J., & Gookin, J. (2008). Student learning in outdoor education: A case study from the national outdoor leadership school. *Journal of Experiential Education, 30*(1), 201–222.

Panicucci, J. (2007). Cornerstones of adventure education. In D. Prouty, J. Panicucci, & R. Collinson (Eds.), *Adventure education theory and practice* (pp. 33–48). Champaign, IL: Human Kinetics.

Priest, S. (1999). The semantics of adventure programming. In J.C. Miles & S. Priest (Eds.), *Adventure programming* (pp. 111–114). State College, PA: Venture.

Priest, S., & Gass, M.A. (2005). *Effective leadership in adventure programming* (2nd ed.). Champaign, IL: Human Kinetics.

Prouty, J. (2007). Introduction to adventure education. In D. Prouty, J. Panicucci, & R. Collinson (Eds.), *Adventure education theory and practice* (pp. 3–17). Champaign, IL: Human Kinetics.

Raiola, E., & O'Keefe, M. (1999). Philosophy in practice: A history of adventure programming. In J.C. Miles & S. Priest (Eds.), *Adventure programming* (pp. 45–53). State College, PA: Venture.

Russell, R.V. (2009). *Pastimes: The contest of contemporary leisure* (4th ed.). Champaign, IL: Sagamore.

Sibthorp, J., & Arthur-Banning, S. (2004). Developing life effectiveness through adventure education: The roles of participant expectations, perceptions of empowerment, and learning relevance. *Journal of Experiential Education, 27*(1), 32–50.

Sibthorp, J., Paisley, K., & Gookin, J. (2007). Exploring participant development through adventure-based programming: A model from the National Outdoor Leadership School. *Leisure Sciences, 29*(1), 1–18.

Stiehl, J., & Parker, M. (2007). Individual outcomes of participating in adventure. In D. Prouty, J. Panicucci, & R. Collinson (Eds.), *Adventure education theory and practice* (pp. 63–75). Champaign, IL: Human Kinetics.

Vlamis, E., Bell, B.J., & Gass, M. (2011). Effects of a college adventure orientation program on student development behaviors. *Journal of Experiential Education, 34*(2), 127–148.

Warren, K., Mitten, D., & Loeffler, T.A. (Eds.). (2008). *Theory and practice of experiential education.* Boulder, CO: Association for Experiential Education.

Wright, N.D., & Larsen, V. (2012). Every brick tells a story: Study abroad as extraordinary experience. *Marketing Education Review, 22*(2), 121–142.

Zull, J.E. (2012). The brain, learning, and study abroad. In M. Vande Berg, R.M. Paige, & K.H. Lou (Eds.), *Student learning abroad: What our students are learning, what they're not, and what we can do about it.* (pp. 162–187). Sterling, VA: Stylus.

TWENTY NINE

Study Abroad and Guided Reflections: How to Help Students Recognize the Personal Benefits of Their International Experience

Jennifer Giblin and Dennis E. Gregory

Introduction

Study abroad has been something that has been on the increase around the world. The United States is the host site for students from around the world who are seeking an experience to improve and broaden their academic experiences. While American students also study abroad, their numbers have been low but are now beginning to increase rapidly.

The 2011 academic year marked the greatest number of U.S. students studying abroad in any one year: 283,332. In addition, over the past 20 years, the number of U.S. students choosing to study abroad has increased by over 300% (Institute of International Education, 2013b). At the same time, however, only 1.4% of students enrolled in an institution of higher education in the United States studied abroad in the 2010 academic year (Institute of International Education, 2012), and over 90% of students do not study abroad at all in their academic careers (Institute of International Education, 2013b).

This long-term increase is promising because study abroad benefits students in many ways. Students who study abroad, when compared to students who do not, are more likely to remain enrolled at the same institution (Young, 2007), graduate (Redden, 2010), require fewer semesters to graduate (Ingraham & Peterson, 2004), see broader issues connected to concepts learned in class (Chieffo & Griffiths, 2004), and improve their oral language proficiency (Vande Berg, Connor-Linton, & Paige, 2009). They also are more open to (and appreciative of) diversity; global minded (see self as linked to world and committed to it) (Clarke, Flaherty, Wright, & McMillen, 2009; Golay, 2006); and able to recognize the differences in cultures (Clarke et al., 2009) than students who do not study abroad. Finally, students who study abroad, in contrast to students who do not, have a higher level of intercultural communication (Clarke et al., 2009; Williams, 2005) and intercultural competence (Clarke et al., 2009; Salisbury, 2011).

Institutions can help students who study abroad realize the skills they gain from the experience by requiring them to reflect on that experience. These reflections may dispel the myth that study abroad is an "extracurricular activity" (Posey, 2003, p. 5) or an "extended tourism experience" (Hovland, McTighe Musil, Skilton-Sylvester, & Jamison, 2009, p. 473). One group of students gained a greater understanding of the differences between the United States and their country of study by completing required reflective blogs while abroad (Lee, 2012). A different group of students who reflected on their experiences after completing them acquired this understanding and more independence, self-confidence, awareness, flexibility, tolerance, and curiosity from studying abroad (i.e., the reflections increased their intercultural competence; Williams, 2009). Before discussing ways in which institutions can help students realize these benefits through required reflections, this chapter will discuss some background information on who goes abroad and how those who go abroad benefit from the experience.

An Overview of Study Abroad

This section profiles many facets of study abroad. We begin with the demographics and then discuss the benefits of studying abroad. The section concludes with a discussion of one disadvantage of study abroad: reverse culture shock.

Demographics

Study abroad has grown markedly since the first non-summer American study abroad program began at the University of Delaware in 1923 (Hoffa, 2007; University of Delaware, n.d). In that year, eight male students in their junior year studied in France for a year. By contrast (and as mentioned earlier), in the 2011 academic year 283,332 U.S. students studied abroad (Institute of International Education, 2013b).

While the number of U.S. students studying abroad continues to increase, there are some aspects of the demographics of study abroad that resemble the trends from many years prior. The numbers documenting the early growth are somewhat unreliable because the Institute of International Education (IIE) surveyed only international institutions to gather its data before 1973, and before 1965 included only students who studied abroad for a full academic year (Stallman, Woodruff, Kasravi, & Comp, 2010). In the 1980 academic year, one of the first years in which the number included students from U.S. institutions studying abroad on programs sponsored by U.S. institutions, 30,613 students studied abroad. This number grew to 70,727 in 1989, 154,168 in 2000, and 223,534 in 2005 (Stallman et al., 2010).

As noted above, the demographic data regarding which U.S. students choose to study abroad are key to the understanding of the broader concept of U.S study abroad activities. This understanding is also necessary if U.S. institutions and the government wish to continue to put programs in place to support the diversity of those who undertake such study. The first demographic category is ethnic/racial breakdown. In the 1993 academic year—the first year in which the IIE included statistics of this sort in its report—83.8% of students who studied abroad were White, 5.0% Asian American, 5.0% Hispanic American, 2.8% African American, 3.1% multiracial, and 0.3% Native American (Stallman et al., 2010). In contrast, the percentages for the 2011 academic year were 76.4%, 7.7%, 7.6%, 5.3%, 2.5%, and 0.5% respectively (Institute of International Education, 2013c).

The second demographic category is the major of the students most likely to go abroad for study. In 1965, over half of the students studying abroad majored in the humanities, with social sciences the second most popular major and physical and natural sciences the third most popular major (Stallman et al., 2010). For the 2011 academic year, the most popular major was social sciences, followed by business and management, and then humanities (Institute of International Education, 2013a).

Two more demographic categories that have shown slight differences over a span of 20 or more years are class level and gender. A comparison of the students who studied abroad by class level for the 1989 and 2010 academic years shows that the greatest change was in the number of seniors studying abroad. For academic year 1989, 12.7% of the students going abroad were seniors; in the 2011 academic year, 24.4% of the students were seniors (Institute of International Education, 2013c; Stallman et al., 2010). There were slight increases in the numbers of freshmen and sophomores going abroad and a decrease of less than 1% in the number of juniors. (The drastic change in the number of seniors studying abroad despite small changes in the other numbers is likely due to the decrease in the percentage selecting "unspecified/other" over the years profiled.)

Finally, the gender gap—that is, the reality that females study abroad at a much greater rate than males—has persisted and, in fact, grown since the 1980 academic year. In that year, 61.3% of those who went abroad for study were females, and 38.7% were males (Stallman et al., 2010). For the 2011 academic year, those percentages were 64.8% and 35.2%, respectively (Institute of International Education, 2013c).

The most cited reason for why ethnic and racial minorities do not study abroad in the same numbers as White students is financial barriers (Salisbury, Paulsen, & Pascarella, 2011; Stallman et al., 2010; Van Der Meid, 2003). Salisbury and colleagues (2011) found that while receiving a grant increased the likelihood that Asian American and African American students would study abroad compared to White students, receipt of a loan decreased the likelihood that Hispanic students would study abroad in comparison to White students. While the past decade has seen a number of initiatives to increase the number of ethnic minorities who go abroad by providing them with more funding, the actual increase has been minimal (Stallman et al., 2010).

A second reason for the ethnic/racial disparity is reported to be fear, which is manifested in the stereotype threat. African Americans with high scores on the ACT were less likely to desire to study abroad, while the reverse was true for White students with high scores on this test (Salisbury et al., 2011). The researchers attributed this finding to the fact that African American students do not wish to expose themselves to a situation in which they may possibly fail, thus confirming the threat. They further mentioned that the majority of African Americans with high test scores in their study were at small, predominantly White liberal arts colleges where study abroad is more common than at larger institutions and where the pressure to overcome the threat is greater.

Flexibility in curriculum and emphasis of field are the main reasons for the pattern observed for field of study. Some majors, particularly those classified as STEM (science, technology, engineering, and math), do not have as much flexibility in terms of the selection of courses as other students do (NAFSA, 2008). In contrast, there are often fewer prerequisites in the social sciences and humanities, and courses offered abroad in these fields are usually comparable to those at institutions in the United States. Most notably, students in STEM fields are as interested as students in the humanities, fine arts, and modern languages in studying abroad, lending greater support to the hypothesis that curricular restriction is a viable explanation for their lower numbers in students who actually do study abroad (Salisbury, Umbach, Paulsen, & Pascarella, 2009).

STEM fields, unlike some of the other fields previously mentioned, do not traditionally emphasize global or international themes, a factor that decreases students' desire to seek out international experiences. Evidence for the effect that such an emphasis may have on the number of students going abroad can be seen in the increase in number of students majoring in business studying abroad over the last 45 years. When a greater emphasis began to be placed on the interconnectedness of the world in the business environment in the 1980s, the American Assembly of Collegiate Schools of Business, the accrediting body for business schools, implemented a requirement that all schools seeking accreditation must have a global component to their programs (Praetzel, Curcio, & DiLorenzo, 1996; Stallman et al., 2010). A natural outgrowth of this charge was programs' infusing study abroad into their newly global-focused business programs.

The final demographic trend related to study abroad for which an explanation has been offered by scholars is the gender gap. More women than men are currently receiving bachelor's degrees. In the 2009 academic year, women made up 57.4% of bachelor degree recipients and 63.5% of individuals who went abroad (Institute of International Education, 2013c; U.S. Department of Education, 2012). In addition, the fields in which men and women receive degrees are different. Men receive a greater percentage of degrees in STEM fields such as engineering and computer science—fields with a lower percentage of students going abroad. In contrast, women outnumber men in fields such as the humanities that send more students abroad. (Men outnumber women by less than 1% in the social sciences and history, the classification used by *Forbes* to measure the number of students studying the social sciences [Goudreau, 2010].)

Benefits of Studying Abroad

Efforts should be made to increase the number of minorities, students in majors not traditionally known for study abroad, and males who go abroad because of the positive effects these experiences have on students. The benefits are many and can be classified as personal, academic, and social. Some areas in which studying abroad has affected students positively include modern language development, global perspective, and involvement on campus. At the same time, the length of the study abroad experience has an effect on the strength of the benefits, and the benefits do not necessarily persist for months following the time spent abroad.

Modern Language Development

One oft-cited benefit of studying abroad is growth and development in a foreign language when one studies in a country where that language is the host language. Given that students are traveling to non-English speaking countries in larger numbers (more students studied in Italy, Spain, France, China, and Germany than in Australia in the 2011 academic year), the potential for language growth is high if students seek out opportunities to gain fluency in the host language while in the non-English-speaking country (Institute of International Education, 2013d). Aside from the extent to which students sought out opportunities to grow in language development, length of study abroad had an effect on the extent of gains students made.

Even though students on a 3-month excursion to the United Kingdom were able to improve their English skills (Mora & Valls-Ferrer, 2012), it was found that while studying abroad in general increases students' knowledge of a language, length of time abroad determines the extent of these gains (Dewey, Bown, & Eggett, 2012; Serrano, Tragant, & Llanes, 2012), a result that held when there were differences in the native language and the second language. Students who spent at least a year in the host nation made greater gains in vocabulary acquisition than students who spent 6 months in the country (Jiménez Jiménez, 2010). While all students in one study improved on writing ability compared to those who did not go abroad, the students who studied abroad for at least 4 months showed more improvement than the students who went abroad for 1½–2 months (Sasaki, 2011).

The amount of time spent speaking the host language also affected the language proficiency of students. Students in one study who spent more time speaking Japanese, the host language, made greater gains in speaking the language than those who spent less time speaking it. Conversely, students who spoke in English more than Japanese made fewer gains (Dewey et al., 2012). In addition, living with host families and living in the residence halls with native speakers resulted in language gains (Pérez-Vidal & Juan-Garau, 2011; Serrano et al., 2012). Engaging in sustained interactions with members of the host family has more of an effect on language development than merely living with a host family (Vande Berg, 2009).

A study abroad experience produces more benefit to students' vocabulary development than taking classes in the home country. Students who spent at least 6 months studying a language in another country grew in more areas of vocabulary development than students who stayed at home (Jiménez Jiménez, 2010). When compared to students who took a semi-intensive, at-home course that required 10 hours a week of instruction, study abroad students fared better on oral and written aspects of language growth after 2 months of study in the host country; no differences were observed for 2 weeks into the respective experiences (Serrano, Llanes, & Tragant, 2011). In a longitudinal study that compared gains in oral and written proficiency in a class with the gains these same students made after a study abroad experience, it was found that greater gains were made in multiple facets of oral and written proficiency only after the study abroad experience (Pérez-Vidal & Juan-Garau, 2011). Furthermore, upon their return, study abroad students (non-native speakers) were not significantly different from native speakers on the number of mistakes made in speaking and oral and written fluency.

Language gains of any sort are not guaranteed from a one-semester study abroad experience. According to Shi (2011), MBA students from China did not gain in communication competence from their semester in the United States. However, as Shi explains, there are many program-specific factors that may have contributed to this result. First, the students were not given a pre-departure orientation to help them understand cultural and linguistic nuances of their host country. Students who studied abroad and attended an orientation with an intercultural component made greater improvements in language skills than students who studied abroad but did not attend an orientation of this sort (Vande Berg, 2009). A program such as the one described in this study may increase students' engagement with the country to which they are heading, a factor shown to increase the gains students make while abroad (Yang &

Kim, 2011). Second, Shi (2011) found that students did not have any assistance with the language while in the United States. Third, they were not given structured opportunities to interact with Americans outside of the classroom, either through student organizations, organized intramural sports, or home-stays.

Academic and University-Based Gains

The academic gains made by students who studied abroad, when compared with students who did not, are many. Students who went abroad thought deeply about the material they discussed in their classes. Instead of taking the concepts at face value, these students questioned what they learned and sought to gain more from their classes (Ingraham & Peterson, 2004). In connection to this, they also integrated concepts they learned in one class into another and understood the importance of what they learned (Redden, 2010).

Objective quantitative measures further demonstrate the academic benefits of study abroad on students. Research has shown that students who study abroad have higher GPAs and graduation rates than students who do not (Ingraham & Peterson, 2004; Malmgren & Galvin, 2008; Redden, 2010). In conducting its analyses, the Georgia Learning Outcomes of Students Studying Abroad Research Initiative (GLOSSARI) created a control group of students that was similar to the students who go abroad. Not only did the GLOSSARI researchers witness the GPA/graduation benefits for the observed population as a whole, but they also found that the 4-year graduation rate was higher for African Americans and other minorities who went abroad (Redden, 2010). A similar result was found in observing the 4-, 5-, and 6-year graduation rates for students in three colleges at the University of Minnesota. Even though there were not significant results for all levels and all colleges, the data show that students who study abroad are more likely to graduate in a timely fashion than students who do not (Malmgren & Galvin, 2008).

Personal Growth

Study abroad not only has effects on academic variables related to students' performance, but also on their personal growth and career choice. The primary manner in which study abroad has an effect on students, that is, increasing their global perspective, will be discussed in the next section. This section will focus on personality development and career decisions.

The first area of personal growth relates to intangible aspects of personality development. Students considered themselves more self-reliant and confident as a result of studying abroad (Bender, Wright, & Lopatto, 2009; Ingraham & Peterson, 2004). They also viewed themselves as able to "go with the flow" upon return. In addition, they were more self-reflective about what they gained from the experience and how it helped them develop (Ingraham & Peterson, 2004). Finally, students who studied abroad gained greater self-understanding in comparison to those who did not (Bender et al., 2009).

Career aspects were another area in which study abroad had an effect on students. The experience aided students in discerning whether or not they were in the correct field, or helped them discover a new field that was a better fit for their personality (Ingraham & Peterson, 2004). In addition, the percentage of students who studied abroad and wished to work abroad was over 30 points higher than the students who did not study abroad who wished to do so (Orahood, Kruze, & Pearson, 2004). Sixty-two percent of students in a different study noted that their study abroad experience influenced their career choice (Norris & Gillespie, 2009).

Global Perspective Development

The primary benefit of study abroad mentioned in the literature is the development of global perspective and related terms such as global-mindedness and intercultural competence. Global perspective is the interconnection of the cognitive, intrapersonal, and intercultural domains as they relate to gaining an understanding of the world and the ability to communicate with individuals from different cultures (Braskamp, Braskamp, Carter Merrill, & Engberg, 2012). Gains were made in global perspective from short-term and long-term experiences. In addition, the gains persisted post-return, but only if the students continued to allow the experience to have an effect on their lives.

Short-term experiences have the ability to increase students' intercultural competence. Students who studied abroad on a 4-week excursion to one of two English-speaking nations improved in their intercultural competence, evidenced by a comparison of results on a pre- and a post-test (Anderson, Lawton, Rexeisen, & Hubbard, 2006). Three-week experiences in non-English-speaking nations also helped students to grow in intercultural competence and to desire more cross-cultural experiences (Hachtmann, 2012). A trip of 6–7 weeks' duration was found to positively influence students' intercultural competence (Martinsen, 2010). Martinsen's (2010) results resemble those of Williams (2005) in that interaction with natives was the only factor outside of study abroad experience to predict gains in intercultural competence. At the same time, when students who studied abroad for a semester are compared to students who studied abroad for 8 weeks or less, the semester students had a significantly greater gain in intercultural competence than the short-term students (Kehl & Morris, 2007).

Students who study abroad for a semester show improvement in a number of areas compared to students who stay in the United States. The first is global-mindedness (Clarke et al., 2009). Closely related to this are: the ability to successfully navigate in another country, cultural sensitivity, and knowledge of worldly current events, three additional areas in which study abroad students score higher than non-study abroad students (Bender et al., 2009; Redden, 2010). Clarke and fellow researchers (2009) also found differences between the two groups in openness to diversity. Finally, semester study abroad students in this study and another (Williams, 2005) were found to have higher scores on intercultural communication than students who did not go abroad. The latter study found that the greatest gains in this area were made by individuals who were exposed to other cultures. Country of study had a significant effect on students' world-mindedness. The greater the differences in culture between the students' home country and the students' host country, the greater the increase in world-mindedness (Douglas & Jones-Rikkers, 2001). While semester study abroad students show more improvements than students who do not go abroad, these effects are not as pronounced as the effects of a year-long experience (Engle & Engle, 2004).

Disadvantage of Studying Abroad

The primary disadvantage of studying abroad and one that affects students upon return is reverse culture shock (in-country disadvantages such as culture shock will not be included in this section). Reverse culture shock is defined as "the process of readjusting, reacculturating, and reassimilating into one's own home culture after living in a different culture for a significant period of time" (Gaw, 2000, pp. 83–84). Students who were able to easily adjust to their new country experienced more severe reverse culture shock than students who had a more difficult time adjusting to their host country (Davis et al., 2008). In addition, the length of the study abroad experience had an effect on the level of reverse culture shock students experienced. Students who studied abroad longer scored higher in reverse culture shock than students who studied abroad for a shorter amount of time. (In one study this consisted of students who studied on a 2-month program compared to students who studied on a semester program [Davis et al., 2008; Wielkiewicz & Turkowski, 2010].)

Reflections

One method that institutions or professors use to help students think about their study abroad experience is reflections. By making these a course requirement, educators ensure that the study abroad experience is more than a "nice field trip" with "little educational merit" (Braid & de Schrynemakers, 2011, p. 26). The methods of the reflections vary, but they usually include students writing about their experiences while abroad or once they return in the form of a journal or blog. Reflections benefit the reflectors because they help them examine and challenge their assumptions and beliefs (Carrington & Selva, 2010; Sharma, Phillion, & Malewski, 2011). Through these reflections students "assess" their experiences, "articulate" them, and gain "meaning and understanding" from them (Pagano & Roselle, 2009, p. 219; Pavlovich, 2007, p. 284). Without mandatory reflections, students may not analyze the experiences they gained while abroad (Laubscher, 1994). Instead, they will view the experiences through a preexisting lens and not learn from them (Sheckley, Allen, & Keeton, 1993).

Journal writing is one way in which students can document their study abroad experience. Peppas (2005) states that journals help students "organize, synthesize, retain, and reflect" on their experiences (p. 160). She found that when students write about experiences such as a conversation with a native or a trip to a museum and include their thoughts and feelings about the experience in the journal, it helps them grow in intercultural competence and increases their knowledge about the host culture (Peppas, 2005).

A more modern form of reflection employed by some professors is blogging. Students in one study who were required to complete free topic blogs and instructor-assigned topic blogs noted that one positive of the assignment was the requirement that they must interact with natives. They also liked how the blogs allowed them to reflect on their experiences and how they made them independent learners. Students were able to compare and contrast cultures in their writing and, by looking back at past blogs, learn how their thoughts about their host culture changed. The author mentions that one reason the blogs were effective was that students were assigned tasks for their blogs, which guided their thinking (Lee, 2012).

Pederson (2010) used a pre-/post-test quantitative methodology to study whether completing reflections while abroad increased students' intercultural competence. The intervention of interest to the researcher was a psychology course that included reflections and learning about other cultures. Three groups were included in the study: students enrolled in the evaluated class (Group 1); students who studied abroad through the same program as Group 1 but did not take the class (Group 2); and students interested in enrolling in the study abroad program the following year but were currently studying on the main campus (Group 3). The students who were in the class with the reflections grew in intercultural competence when compared to the students in the other two groups.

Engle and Engle (2002) noted that "cutting [students] loose and hoping for the best generally will not work" (p. 33). In the opinion of these authors, "sustained professional guidance," which includes guided reflection, is viewed as necessary to facilitate a "deeper cultural understanding" in students (p. 26).

The Internet and Study Abroad

One tool that has played a larger role in study abroad over the years is the Internet. As mentioned in the last section, students blog about their experiences abroad as a way to reflect on them. The Internet also has positive effects on study abroad because it allows students to communicate with those back home, and it acts as a tool to foster intercultural communication. However, students who use the Internet for the former purpose may impede their exploration of the host country.

One use of the Internet for students who are abroad is as a source of support. Students who received support through the Internet by means of Skype, social networking sites, and discussion boards reported feeling less stress, a desire to interact with host nationals, and a willingness to take risks. At the same time, too much support via the Internet may have an adverse effect on students. If students use the Internet as their sole means of reducing stress, they tend to report more stress than students who use a combination of the Internet and face-to-face methods to relieve stress (Mikal & Grace, 2012).

Another use of the Internet while abroad is to connect with the host culture. Students used the Internet to learn about the daily events taking place in the host country and the locations of tourist attractions. However, they did not use the Internet to connect with people from the host country while they were abroad (Mikal & Grace, 2012). The same is not true for students who studied abroad in the past. Over half of the students in one study remained in contact with at least one person they met during their study abroad experience because of social networking, and more used these means to keep in touch with host nationals for a time after leaving the country (Coleman & Chafer, 2010).

Some students who use the Internet to maintain contact with those back home actually jeopardize their ability to integrate into the host culture. One student profiled in Kinginger (2008) spent most of her time alone in her apartment speaking to family and friends back home because of the homesickness and isolation she felt while abroad. As a result, she did not engage with the host culture and made few gains in her language skills.

Integrating Reflection With Study Abroad—Curricular Examples

Institutions across the United States have devised programs that incorporate reflections to help students learn from their study abroad experiences. These include reflections concurrent with the study abroad experience and reflections upon return. Most of these programs have not been evaluated, and their effectiveness is therefore unknown.

Arcadia University in Glenside, Pennsylvania, requires all students to engage in a cross-cultural experience (the Global Connections Experience, or GCE). It may be completed by studying abroad or by taking designated courses offered at the university's Pennsylvania campuses that expose students to people from other cultures, such as senior citizens and inmates at a Philadelphia jail. While engaging in this experience, the students are required to simultaneously enroll in a two-credit reflection course (Global Connections Reflection, or GCR). For students who fulfill the GCE by taking a course, the reflections are usually built into this course. If the reflections are not part of the course, the students take an online GCR 101 class with students who are abroad. In the spring 2014 semester, Arcadia began face-to-face GCR 101 courses for students studying abroad in Chile, Greece, and South Africa. The class is taught by Arcadia staff in the host country (E. Skilton-Sylvester, personal communication, July 11, 2013; December 18, 2013).

From the fall of 2006 to the spring of 2008, the University of Minnesota had a similar requirement for all students who studied abroad for a semester or a full year through its Learning Abroad Center (Paige, Harvey, & McCleary, 2012). These students registered for the one-credit course "EdPA 3103: Maximizing Study Abroad (In-Country section)." This course was completed over the Internet while students were abroad. In the spring of 2008, an effort to redesign the course was begun. This redesign took place because student feedback about the course was not favorable. The result of the redesign efforts was "Global Identity: Connecting Your International Experience with Your Future." Like EdPA 3103, this is a one-credit course, but it is not mandatory (Paige et al., 2012).

Clemson University's Cultural Literacy Across Media is an optional, three-credit course available to all students who study abroad. They are required to keep a blog of their experience and produce a final project synthesizing this experience. For the project, students focus on an area of interest to them—such as gender dynamics in their country of study—and use various media forms to complete it. These projects and blogs extend beyond the class and are made available to the public (Kowarski, 2010).

An institution with a post-study abroad class is the University of the Pacific in Stockton, California. A pre-study abroad class is required of all students, whereas only students in the School of International Studies are required to take the post-study abroad class (though students outside this school who are not required to take the class sometimes enroll in it). Students are expected to take the post-study abroad class the semester after their study abroad experience. In this class the students cover the themes from the pre-study abroad class in greater detail (such as how to view concepts through a cultural lens and intercultural communication), and apply their experiences to these themes. A comparison of Intercultural Development Inventory scores of students who took both classes with students who took only the pre-study abroad course show that the scores of students who took both courses were significantly higher (Bathurst & La Brack, 2012).

Summary

This chapter began by noting that the demographic characteristics of students who study abroad have not changed much over the years. These students are more likely to be White females majoring in the humanities or social sciences in junior standing. By studying abroad, these students have the opportunity to improve their modern language skills and to gain the ability to integrate what they learned in one class into another. They are also more likely to graduate, become self-reliant and flexible, acquire insight into the career they wish to enter, and strengthen their global perspective. These effects are stronger for students who are abroad for a year rather than a semester.

Students learned how their views about the host culture changed and acquired more information about this culture by reflecting on their study abroad experience. The Internet offers students a way to gain support and knowledge about the host culture and connect with those they meet while abroad. However, the effects can be detrimental if students are too dependent on the Internet and engage in prolonged contact with those back home. Institutions from Pennsylvania to California offer students from all disciplines a way of thinking more deeply about their study abroad experience through reflections.

Study abroad can provide many benefits to those students who engage in such activities. As noted above, however, it is the responsibility of institutions of higher education and the U.S. government to seek ways to increase support for such study for all students, and particularly to find ways to broaden the demographic characteristics of those who can do so. Financial and counseling support to minority, low socioeconomic, and first-generation students is needed to continue and fuel the increases described for the recent past.

References

Anderson, P.H., Lawton, L., Rexeisen, R.J., & Hubbard, A.C. (2006). Short-term study abroad and intercultural sensitivity: A pilot study. *International Journal of Intercultural Relations, 30*(4), 457–469. doi: 10.1016/j.ijintrel.2005.10.004

Bathurst, L., & La Brack, B. (2012). Shifting the locus of intercultural learning: Intervening prior to and after student experiences abroad. In M. Vande Berg, R.M. Paige, & K. Hemming Lou (Eds.), *Student learning abroad: What our students are learning, what they're not, and what we can do about it* (pp. 261–283). Sterling, VA: Stylus.

Bender, C., Wright, D., & Lopatto, D. (2009). Students' self-reported changes in intercultural knowledge and competence associated with three undergraduate science experiences. *Frontiers: The Interdisciplinary Journal of Study Abroad, 18*, 307–321.

Braid, B., & de Schrynemakers, G.P. (2011). A case among cases. *Journal of the National Collegiate Honors Council, 12*(1), 25–32.

Braskamp, L.A., Braskamp, D.C., Carter Merrill, K., & Engberg, M. (2012). *The Global Perspective Inventory (GPI): Its purpose, construction, potential uses and psychometric characteristics.* Retrieved from https://gpi.central.edu/supportDocs/manual.pdf

Carrington, S., & Selva, G. (2010). Critical social theory and transformative learning: Evidence in pre-service teachers' service-learning reflection logs. *Higher Education Research & Development, 29*(1), 45–57. doi: 10.1080/07294360903421384

Chieffo, L., & Griffiths, L. (2004). Large-scale assessment of student attitudes after a short-term study abroad program. *Frontiers: The Interdisciplinary Journal of Study Abroad, 10*, 165–177.

Clarke III, I., Flaherty, T.B., Wright, N.D., & McMillen, R.M. (2009). Student intercultural proficiency from study abroad programs. *Journal of Marketing Education, 31*(2), 173–181. doi: 10.1177/0273475309335583

Coleman, J.A., & Chafer, T. (2010). Study abroad and the Internet: Physical and virtual context in an era of expanding telecommunications. *Frontiers: The Interdisciplinary Journal of Study Abroad, 19*, 151–167.

Davis, D., Chapman, D., Bohlin, B., Jaworski, B., Walley, C., Barton, D., & Ebner, N. (2008). Reverse culture shock: A comparison of United States and Japanese students' experiences returning from a study abroad sojourn. *Conference Papers—National Communication Association* (pp. 1–36).

Dewey, D.P., Bown, J., & Eggett, D. (2012). Japanese language proficiency, social networking, and language use during study abroad: Learners' perspectives. *Canadian Modern Language Review, 68*(2), 111–137. doi: 10.3138/cmlr.68.2.111

Douglas, C., & Jones-Rikkers, C.G. (2001). Study abroad programs and American student worldmindedness: An empirical analysis. *Journal of Teaching in International Business, 13*(1), 55–66.

Engle, J., & Engle, L. (2002). Neither international nor educative: Study abroad in the time of globalization. In W. Grünzweig & N. Rinehart (Eds.), *Rockin' in Red Square: Critical approaches to international education in the age of cyberculture* (pp. 25–40). New Brunswick, NJ: Transaction.

Engle, L., & Engle, J. (2004). Assessing language acquisition and intercultural sensitivity development in relation to study abroad program design. *Frontiers: The Interdisciplinary Journal of Study Abroad, 10*, 219–236.

Gaw, K. (2000). Reverse culture shock in students returning from overseas. *Journal of Intercultural Relations, 24*(1), 83–104. doi: 10.1016/S0147-1767(99)00024-3

Golay, P.A. (2006). *The effects of study abroad on the development of globalmindedness among students enrolled in international programs at Florida State University* (Doctoral dissertation). Retrieved from ProQuest Dissertations and Theses database. (UMI No. 3232382).

Goudreau, J. (2010, August 10). Most popular college majors for women. *Forbes*. Retrieved from www.forbes.com

Hachtmann, F. (2012). The effect of advertising-focused, short-term study abroad programs on students' worldviews. *Journal of Advertising Education, 16*(1), 19–29.

Hoffa, W.W. (2007). *A history of U.S. study abroad: Beginnings to 1965*. Carlisle, PA: Frontiers Journal.

Hovland, K., McTighe Musil, C., Skilton-Sylvester, E., & Jamison, A. (2009). It takes a curriculum: Bringing global mindedness home. In R. Lewin (Ed.), *The handbook of practice and research in study abroad: Higher education and the quest for global citizenship* (pp. 466–484). New York, NY: Routledge.

Ingraham, E.C., & Peterson, D.L. (2004). Assessing the impact of study abroad on student learning at Michigan State University. *Frontiers: The Interdisciplinary Journal of Study Abroad, 10*, 83–100.

Institute of International Education. (2012). *International education exchanges are at all-time high, strengthening economies and societies around the world* [Press release]. Retrieved from http://www.iie.org/Who-We-Are/News-and-Events/Press-Center/Press-Releases/2012/11-13-2012-Open-Doors-International-Students

Institute of International Education. (2013a). Fields of study of U.S. study abroad students, 2001/02–2011/12. *Open Doors report on international educational exchange*. Retrieved from http://www.iie.org/opendoors

Institute of International Education. (2013b). *International students in the United States and study abroad by American students are at all-time high* [Press release]. Retrieved from http://www.iie.org/en/Who-We-Are/News-and-Events/Press-Center/Press-Releases/2013/2013-11-11-Open-Doors-Data#.Uo1b98SThtg

Institute of International Education. (2013c). Profile of U.S. study abroad students, 2001/02–2011/12. *Open Doors report on international educational exchange*. Retrieved from http://www.iie.org/opendoors

Institute of International Education. (2013d). Top 25 destinations of U.S. study abroad students, 2010/11–2011/12. *Open Doors report on international educational exchange*. Retrieved from http://www.iie.org/opendoors

Jiménez Jiménez, A.F. (2010). A comparative study on second language vocabulary development: Study abroad vs classroom settings. *Frontiers: The Interdisciplinary Journal of Study Abroad, 19*, 105–123.

Kehl, K., & Morris, J. (2007). Differences in global-mindedness between short-term and semester-long study abroad participants at selected private universities. *Frontiers: The Interdisciplinary Journal of Study Abroad, 15*, 67–79.

Kinginger, C. (2008). Language learning in study abroad: Case studies of Americans in France. *Modern Language Journal, 92*(1), 1–124. doi: 10.1111/j.1540-4781.2008.00821.x

Kowarski, I. (2010, July 22). Colleges help students to translate the benefits of study abroad. *Chronicle of Higher Education*. Retrieved from http://www.chronicle.com

Laubscher, M.R. (1994). *Encounters with difference: Student perceptions of the role of out-of-class experiences in education abroad*. Westport, CT: Greenwood Press.

Lee, L. (2012). Engaging study abroad students in intercultural learning through blogging and ethnographic interviews. *Foreign Language Annals, 45*(1), 7–21. doi: 10.111/j.1944-9720. 2012.01164.x

Malmgren, J., & Galvin, J. (2008). Effects of study abroad participation on student graduation rates: A study of three incoming freshman cohorts at the University of Minnesota, Twin Cities. *NACADA Journal, 28*(1), 29–42.

Martinsen, R.A. (2010). Short-term study abroad: Predicting changes in oral skills. *Foreign Language Annals, 43*(3), 504–530. doi: 10.1111/j.1944-9720.2010.01095.x

Mikal, J.P., & Grace, K. (2012). Against abstinence-only education abroad: Viewing Internet use during study abroad as a possible experience enhancement. *Journal of Studies in International Education, 16*(3), 287–306. doi: 10.1177/1028315311423108

Mora, J.C., & Valls-Ferrer, M. (2012). Oral fluency, accuracy, and complexity in formal instruction and study abroad learning contexts. *TESOL Quarterly, 46*(4), 610–641. doi: 10.1002/tesq.34

NAFSA: Association of International Educators. (2008). *Strengthening study abroad: Recommendations for effective institutional management*. Report of the Task Force on Institutional Management of Study Abroad. Retrieved from http://www.nafsa.org/_/File/_/final_imsa_taskforce.pdf

Norris, E.M., & Gillespie, J. (2009). How study abroad shapes global careers: Evidence from the United States. *Journal of Studies in International Education, 13*(3), 382–397. doi: 10.1177/1028315308319740

Orahood, T., Kruze, L., & Pearson, D.E. (2004). The impact of study abroad on business students' career goals. *Frontiers: The Interdisciplinary Journal of Study Abroad, 10*, 117–130.

Pagano, M., & Roselle, L. (2009). Beyond reflection through an academic lens: Refraction and international experiential education. *Frontiers: The Interdisciplinary Journal of Study Abroad, 18*, 217–229.

Paige, R.M., Harvey, T.A., & McCleary, K.S. (2012). The maximizing study abroad project: Toward a pedagogy for culture and language learning. In M. Vande Berg, R.M. Paige, & K. Hemming Lou (Eds.), *Student learning abroad: What our students are learning, what they're not, and what we can do about it* (pp. 308–334). Sterling, VA: Stylus.

Pavlovich, K. (2007). The development of reflective practice through student journals. *Higher Education Research & Development, 26*(3), 281–295. doi: 10.1080/ 07294360701494302

Pederson, P.J. (2010). Assessing intercultural effectiveness outcomes in a year-long study abroad program. *International Journal of Intercultural Relations, 34*(1), 70–80. doi: 10.1016/j.ijintrel.2009.09.003

Peppas, S.C. (2005). Business study abroad tours for non-traditional students: An outcomes assessment. *Frontiers: The Interdisciplinary Journal of Study Abroad, 11*, 143–163.

Pérez-Vidal, C., & Juan-Garau, M. (2011). The effect of context and input conditions on oral and written development: A study abroad perspective. *IRAL: International Review of Applied Linguistics in Language Teaching, 49*(2), 157–185. doi: 10.1515/iral.2011.008

Posey, J.T. (2003). *Study abroad: Educational and employment outcomes of participants versus non participants* (Doctoral dissertation). Retrieved from ProQuest Dissertations and Theses database. (UMI No. 3137474).

Praetzel, G.D., Curcio, J., & DiLorenzo, J. (1996). Making study abroad a reality for all students. *International Advances in Economic Research, 2*(2), 174–182. doi: 10.1007/BF02295057

Redden, E. (2010, July 13). Academic outcomes of study abroad. *Inside Higher Ed*. Retrieved from http://www.insidehighered.com/

Salisbury, M.H. (2011). *The effect of study abroad on intercultural competence among undergraduate college students* (Unpublished doctoral dissertation). University of Iowa, Iowa City. Retrieved from http://ir.uiowa.edu/etd/1073

Salisbury, M.H., Paulsen, M.B., & Pascarella, E.T. (2011). Why do all the study abroad students look alike? Applying an integrated student choice model to explore differences in the factors that influence White and minority students' intent to study abroad. *Research in Higher Education, 52*(2), 123–150. doi: 10.1007/s11162-010-9191-2

Salisbury, M.H., Umbach, P.D., Paulsen, M.B., & Pascarella, E.T. (2009). Going global: Understanding the choice process of the intent to study abroad. *Research in Higher Education, 50*(2), 119–143. doi: 10.1007/s11162-008-9111-x

Sasaki, M. (2011). Effects of varying lengths of study-abroad experiences on Japanese EFL students' L2 writing ability and motivation: A longitudinal study. *TESOL Quarterly, 45*(1), 81–105. doi: 10.5054/tq.2011.240861

Serrano, R., Llanes, À., & Tragant, E. (2011). Analyzing the effect of context of second language learning: Domestic intensive and semi-intensive courses vs. study abroad in Europe. *System, 39*(2), 133–143. doi: 10.1016/j.system.2011.05.002

Serrano, R., Tragant, E., & Llanes, À. (2012). A longitudinal analysis of the effects of one year abroad. *Canadian Modern Language Review, 68*(2), 138–163. doi: 10.3138/cmlr.68.2.138

Sharma, S., Phillion, J., & Malewski, E. (2011). Examining the practice of critical reflection for developing preservice teachers' multicultural competencies: Findings from a study abroad program in Honduras. *Issues in Teacher Education, 20*(2), 9–22.

Sheckley, B.G., Allen, G.J., & Keeton, M.T. (1993). Adult learning as recursive process. *Journal of Cooperative Education, 28*(2), 56–67.

Shi, X. (2011). Negotiating power and access to second language resources: A study on short-term Chinese MBA students in America. *Modern Language Journal, 95*(4), 575–588. doi: 10.1111/j.1540-4781.2011.01245.x

Stallman, E., Woodruff, G.A., Kasravi, J., & Comp, D. (2010). The diversification of the student profile. In W.W. Hoffa & S.C. DePaul (Eds.), *A history of U.S. study abroad: 1965–present* (pp. 115–160). Carlisle, PA: Frontiers Journal.

University of Delaware. (n.d.). *Institute for Global Studies: Brief history*. Retrieved from http://www.udel.edu/global/studyabroad/information/brief_history.html

U.S. Department of Education, National Center for Education Statistics. (2012). *The condition of education 2012* (NCES 2012-045), Table A-47-2. Retrieved from http://nces.ed.gov/fastfacts/display.asp?id=72

Van Der Meid, J.S. (2003). Asian Americans: Factors influencing the decision to study abroad. *Frontiers: The Interdisciplinary Journal of Study Abroad, 9*, 71–110.

Vande Berg, M. (2009). Intervening in student learning abroad: A research-based inquiry. *Intercultural Education, 20*(1), S15–27. doi: 10.1177/1028315307303924

Vande Berg, M., Connor-Linton, J., & Paige, R.M. (2009). The Georgetown Consortium Project: Interventions for student learning abroad. *Frontiers: The Interdisciplinary Journal of Study Abroad, 18*, 1–75.

Wielkiewicz, R.M., & Turkowski, L.W. (2010). Reentry issues upon returning from study abroad programs. *Journal of College Student Development, 51*(6), 649–664. doi: 10.1353/csd.2010.0015

Williams, T.R. (2005). Exploring the impact of study abroad on students' intercultural communication skills: Adaptability and sensitivity. *Journal of Studies in International Education, 9*(4), 356–371. doi: 10.1177/1028315305277681

Williams, T.R. (2009). The reflective model of intercultural competency: A multidimensional, qualitative approach to study abroad assessment. *Frontiers: The Interdisciplinary Journal of Study Abroad, 18*, 289–306.

Yang, J-S., & Kim, T-Y. (2011). Sociocultural analysis of second language learner beliefs: A qualitative case study of two study-abroad ESL learners. *System, 39*(3), 325–334. doi: 10.1016/j.system.2011.07.005

Young, D.Y. (2007). Persistence at a liberal arts university and participation in a study abroad program. *Frontiers: The Interdisciplinary Journal of Study Abroad, 15*, 93–110.

Contributors

Ufuoma Abiola is an Ed.D. student in Higher Education at the University of Pennsylvania Graduate School of Education, where she also earned an M.S.Ed. in Higher Education. Her professional experience includes having worked as a counselor/therapist, adjunct professor, and higher education and student affairs administrator. Ufuoma's research interests involve college student affairs and increasing the persistence and success of students of color at higher education institutions. Ufuoma also earned an M.A. in Clinical Psychology, with a Graduate Certificate in Clinical Child and Family Studies, from Roosevelt University and a B.A. in Psychology, with a minor in African and African Diaspora Studies, from Boston College.

Mallory A. Anderson is a doctoral candidate in the Department of Counseling and Human Development Services with a concentration in Recreation and Leisure Studies at the University of Georgia. She has a M.Ed. in College Student Affairs Administration from the University of Georgia and a B.S. in Business Management from Appalachian State University. Mallory's career has included work in hospitality management, camps, orientation programming, curricular and co-curricular leadership development, outdoor programming, and study abroad education. Her research interests focus on adventure experiences and the development of college students.

Karen L. Archambault, Ed.D., is currently Executive Director of Drexel Central at Drexel University in Philadelphia, Pennsylvania. Her prior experience includes work in admissions, advising, and retention. She received her doctoral degree from Rowan University in New Jersey, where her research focused on community college students' preparation for transfer. Dr. Archambault is a past chair of NACADA's Advising Transfer Students Commission. Her current research and practice interests include the perceptions that advisors hold of students' preparation for transfer, as well as issues related to staff motivation and satisfaction in student service operations.

William Arnold currently serves as an assistant professor of educational administration at Michigan State University. He was a first-generation college student who went on to earn his master's degree from Michigan State University in 1995 and his Ph.D. from Bowling Green State University in 2002. In addition to first-generation students, his research interests include liberal arts colleges, leadership, and organizational development.

James P. Barber is an assistant professor of education at the College of William and Mary in Williamsburg, Virginia. He earned his Ph.D. in Higher Education Administration from the Center for the Study of Higher and Postsecondary Education at the University of Michigan. Dr. Barber's teaching and scholarship focus on college student learning and development, with a particular interest in integrative learning. His work has appeared in the *American Educational Research Journal*, *Journal of College Student Development*, and *Journal of Higher Education*. Barber is a member of Sigma Phi Epsilon fraternity and currently serves as the Faculty Fellow for the chapter at William and Mary.

Will Barratt received his master's degree from Miami University in 1973 and his Ph.D. from the University of Iowa in 1983. He has taught student affairs and higher education leadership at Indiana State University since 1988. He is currently the Coffman Distinguished Professor in the Department of Educational Leadership. His book *Social Class on Campus* was published in 2011, and his two blogs, on social class and first-generation students in student affairs, are widely read. He is a third-generation student and second-generation faculty member.

Mark Bauman is an assistant professor and program coordinator for the Counseling and College Student Affairs program at Bloomsburg University of Pennsylvania. Prior to assuming those positions, Mark spent 14 years in various student affairs roles at BU, including residence life and judicial affairs. Since 2009, Mark has focused his research and service efforts on student-veterans and was one of the first to write and speak about that population. Mark is currently a Boatswain's Mate First Class in the United States Coast Guard Reserve.

Mitsue Blythe is currently working toward a Ph.D. in Higher Education Administration at Old Dominion University. Blythe serves as a research administrator in the Office of Distance Learning and as a doctoral research assistant in the Office of Educational Foundations and Leadership. Prior to pursuing her doctoral degree, Blythe taught English in secondary and collegiate settings for 10 years. Blythe has extensive experience teaching students of diverse ages, ethnicities, and financial backgrounds. She holds an M.A. in Literature with a concentration in writing and a B.A. in English.

Daniel Bureau is the Director of Student Affairs Learning and Assessment at the University of Memphis. Over the course of his 16-year career in student affairs, Dan has worked with fraternity and sorority life programs at three different campuses and continues to consult with these organizations on a range of campuses. He has served as the 2004 President for the Association of Fraternity/Sorority Advisors as well as on other boards such as HazingPrevention.Org., the Center for the Study of the College Fraternity, and his fraternity, Phi Kappa Theta. He has also worked for the Center for Postsecondary Research and the National Survey of Student Engagement (NSSE) while doing his doctoral work in Higher Education and Student Affairs at Indiana University. His research interests include student affairs professional socialization, student learning and development, and fraternities and sororities.

Andy Casiello is Associate Vice President for the Office of Distance Learning at Old Dominion University in Norfolk, Virginia. Casiello is responsible for ODU's Distance Learning organization, which delivers 59 degree programs servicing one-fifth of the university's entire student population at 40 locations, and to homes, offices, military facilities, and other institutions worldwide. Casiello is currently working toward a Ph.D. in Higher Education Administration at Old Dominion. He holds an associate degree (A.S.) in Telecommunications Technology from Springfield (MA) Technical Community College, a B.S. degree in Communications from Fitchburg State College, and a Master of Science degree in Instructional Design and Technology from Old Dominion University. Casiello recently completed the Management Development Program at Harvard Graduate School of Education.

Keenan Y. Colquitt, Jr. is a doctoral student in the Department of Higher Education and Student Affairs at Bowling Green State University. Mr. Colquitt worked as a residence life professional for seven years prior to becoming a doctoral student. His research interests include gender identity development, specifically masculinity and gender role socialization in college men. In addition, Mr. Colquitt is interested in studying factors that affect high school graduation and college attrition in African American males.

Felecia Commodore is a third-year Ph.D. student in Higher Education at the University of Pennsylvania's Graduate School of Education. She has a background working as an admissions counselor and academic advisor at Trinity University, Washington, D.C., and the University of Maryland, College Park. She obtained an M.A. in Higher Education Administration from the University of Maryland, College Park, and a B.S. in Marketing with a minor in Sociology from Drexel University. She was a 2013 intern for the Southern Education Foundation. Her research focus areas are HBCU leadership, governance, and administrative practices.

Denise L. Davidson is an assistant professor in the Counseling and College Student Affairs program at Bloomsburg University of Pennsylvania. She completed her B.A. in Biology at Clark University, her M.S. in College Student Personnel Services at Miami University (Ohio), and her Ph.D. in Higher Education Administration at Bowling Green State University. Dr. Davidson has 20 years of experience with residence life, student conduct, academic advising, student financial aid, student activities, fraternity/sorority affairs, and alumni affairs. The recipient of two awards for outstanding teaching, Dr. Davidson's research interests include new professionals' job satisfaction and turnover, ROTC cadet constructions of identity, student affairs work at for-profit institutions, and the scholarship of teaching and learning.

Blair Dayton is a recent graduate of the Student Affairs and College Counseling master's program at Monmouth University. She received her bachelor's degree in Communications at the University of Rhode Island. Blair also studied at the American Comedy Institute in New York, where she honed her skills in comedy writing and stand-up. She is currently pursuing a career in academic advising and career services in higher education.

Joseph L. DeVitis has taught at five universities in his 40-year academic career. He is a prolific scholar and public intellectual in both the social foundations of education and higher education. He is the recipient of the Distinguished Alumni Award from the University of Illinois at Urbana-Champaign and is a past president of the American Educational Studies Association (AESA), the Council of Learned Societies in Education, and the Society of Professors of Education. Three of his recent books, *Critical Civic Literacy* (Peter Lang, 2011), *Character and Moral Education* (Peter Lang, 2011), and *Adolescent Education* (Peter Lang, 2010), won Critics Choice Awards from AESA as outstanding books of the year. His latest books, also published by Peter Lang, are *School Reform Critics: The Struggle for Democratic Schooling* (2014), *Contemporary Colleges and Universities* (2013), and *The College Curriculum* (2013).

Brighid Dwyer, Ph.D., is currently the Assistant Director for Research & Training at Villanova University. She also serves as one of the University's Ombudspersons for bias concerns. Dwyer teaches social justice courses in the Intergroup Relations Program and the Center for Peace and Justice Education at Villanova University and at Delaware County Community College. Her research focuses on minority-serving institutions, college access for underrepresented students, and college students' experiences interacting with diverse others.

Britni V. Epstein is a graduate student in Monmouth University's Student Affairs and College Counseling MS.Ed. program. She also works as a writing tutor and graduate assistant at Monmouth. Her professional interests include academic tutoring, advising, and mental health counseling. As a writing tutor, she has been trained as a Certified Reading and Learning Assistant.

Michelle M. Espino is an assistant professor of higher education in the Department of Student Affairs and International Education Policy at the University of Maryland, College Park. Her research centers on understanding community contexts and institutional responses associated with educational achievement and outcomes along the academic life course for racial/ethnic minorities, with particular focus on the experiences of Latina/o students, college administrators, and faculty. She has published articles in *The Review of Higher Education*, *Teachers College Record*, *Equity & Excellence in Education*, and *Qualitative Inquiry*. She was a 2011 Faculty Fellow for the American Association of Hispanics in Higher Education, the 2008 recipient of the Bobby Wright Dissertation of the Year Award from the Association of the Study of Higher Education, a 2007 Ford Foundation Dissertation Fellow, and is a member of Sigma Lambda Gamma National Sorority, Inc.

Jason Garvey is an assistant professor of higher education in the Department of Educational Leadership, Policy, and Technology Studies at the University of Alabama. He received his Ph.D. in college student-personnel administration from the University of Maryland with a certificate in Measurement, Statistics, and Evaluation. Jay holds his master's degree in school psychology from The Ohio State University, with a specialization in Sexuality Studies, and his bachelor's degree in educational studies from the University of Delaware. His research examines the experiences of diverse individuals in higher education primarily through the use of quantitative methodologies, with specific focus on LGBTQ students, faculty, and alumni.

Marybeth Gasman is a professor of higher education in the Graduate School of Education at the University of Pennsylvania. Her areas of expertise include minority-serving institutions and fundraising and philanthropy in communities of color. She has published numerous books in those academic areas, including *A Guide to Fundraising at Historically Black Colleges and Universities* (Routledge, 2011), *Understanding Minority-Serving Institutions* (Routledge, 2010),

Historically Black Colleges and Universities: Triumphs, Troubles, and Taboos (Palgrave Macmillan, 2008), and *Envisioning Black Colleges: A History of the United Negro College Fund* (Johns Hopkins University Press, 2007).

Jennifer Giblin is a doctoral candidate in the Higher Education Administration Program at Old Dominion University. Her research interests/professional areas of interest include study abroad, international students, and LGBTQ student affairs. She was the 2014 recipient of the Val DuMontier New Professional Award from ACPA's Standing Committee for Lesbian, Gay, Bisexual and Transgender Awareness for the online ally training she helped develop for ODU. She received her B.A. from Arcadia University and her M.S. from the University of Cincinnati. Both degrees are in criminal justice.

Chris R. Glass is an Assistant Professor of Educational Foundations and Leadership at Old Dominion University. His research examines the formation and evolution of the social networks of international students who attend U.S. colleges and universities. He has published in the *Journal of Educational Psychology*, the *International Journal of Intercultural Relations*, the *Journal of Studies in International Education*, *New Directions for Higher Education*, the *Journal of General Education*, the *Journal of Higher Education Outreach & Engagement*, and the *SAGE Handbook on Civic and Political Leadership.*

Kathleen M. Goodman is an assistant professor of student affairs in higher education at Miami University. She earned her Ph.D. at the University of Iowa in 2011. While at Iowa, she was a research assistant at the Center for Research on Undergraduate Education. Prior to that, she held an administrative position at the Association of American Colleges and Universities. Her research and teaching interests include the impact of college experiences on student development; diversity and equity in higher education; spirituality, life purpose, and atheist college students; and incorporating critical perspectives into quantitative research.

Véronique S. Grazioli is a doctoral student at the University of Lausanne (Switzerland) and is currently working as a graduate assistant at the Center for the Study of Health and Risk Behaviors at the University of Washington. Her research interests focus on alcohol-related harm reduction among the young population (e.g., college and high school students) and severely marginalized individuals with alcohol use disorders (e.g., chronically homeless individuals).

Dennis E. Gregory is an associate professor of higher education at Old Dominion University. He has served in numerous student affairs leadership roles, including as senior affairs officer. He has authored or co-authored over 50 publications, including a book on Greek life. Dr. Gregory has also made nearly 100 presentations on topics related to enrollment management, study abroad, and comparative education. He is a charter member and past president of the Association for Student Conduct Administration (ASCA) and the International Association of Student Affairs and Services (IASAS). He is a member of the editorial board of the *Journal of Counselling and Development in Higher Education, Southern Africa.*

Paige Haber-Curran is an assistant professor and program coordinator for the Student Affairs in Higher Education Master's Program at Texas State University. She earned her Ph.D. in Leadership Studies from the University of San Diego, her master's in College Student Personnel from the University of Maryland, and undergraduate degrees in Business Management and German Studies from the University of Arizona. Her research focuses on gender and the college experience, college student leadership development, student learning, women's leadership, and emotionally intelligent leadership.

Jeannie Hopper serves as the Assistant Director for University Housing at the University of Tennessee, Knoxville. She earned both her B.A. and M.A. in English Literature at the University of Tennessee, Knoxville, where she began working with University Housing as a freshman. Through her years as a resident assistant, graduate assistant for Living Learning Communities, hall director, and assistant director, she has worked with thousands of college students and gained vast experience as a residence life practitioner. Mrs. Hopper serves as the Feature Articles Editor for the Southeastern Association of Housing Officers (SEAHO) Report, and has presented and published on community building for upperclassmen in apartment-style halls, collaborating with campus and community partners, supervising graduate assistants and entry level professionals, and staff development.

Heather Huling is Assistant Vice President for Planning and Development in the Office of Distance Learning at Old Dominion University. Huling holds an associate degree from Jamestown Community College, Jamestown, New York, a bachelor's degree in International Economics and Business from the State University of New York at Brockport, and a master's degree in International Studies from Old Dominion University. Huling studied in Jonkoping, Sweden, for an academic semester and has recently completed the Management Development Program at Harvard Graduate School of Education.

S. Mei-Yen Ireland is a third-year Ph.D. student in the Higher Education and Student Affairs program in the Educational Studies Department at The Ohio State University. She received her B.A. in foreign languages from Lewis & Clark College and an M.A. in college student personnel from the University of Maryland. Her research on service-learning focuses on power and privilege in service-learning partnerships and the meaning students make of their experiences in short-term service-learning immersion programs. She is now engaged in research on undocumented students, identity development, and community colleges. Mei-Yen worked as the AmeriCorps Civic Engagement Coordinator at Lewis & Clark College, assisting faculty in incorporating service-learning and community-based research in the curriculum. She has also worked in the University of Maryland's Stamp Student Union as a coordinator of local community service-learning programs.

Susan R. Jones is Professor and Program Director in the Higher Education and Student Affairs program in the Educational Studies Department at The Ohio State University and previously served as Associate Professor and Director of the College Student Personnel Program at the University of Maryland, College Park. Her research interests include psychosocial perspectives on identity, intersectionality and multiple social identities, service-learning, and qualitative research methodologies. She is the co-author (with Dr. Elisa S. Abes) of books titled *Identity Development of College Students* (Jossey-Bass, 2013) and *Negotiating the Complexities of Qualitative Research: Fundamental Elements and Issues* (with Drs. Vasti Torres and Jan Arminio) (Routledge, 2006, 2nd edition published in 2013). Jones is one of the co-editors (with Schuh, Jones, & Harper) of the 5th edition of *Student Services: A Handbook for the Profession* (Jossey-Bass, 2011).

Sara R. Kaiser recently completed her doctorate in higher education at the University of Mississippi. Prior to graduate school she worked in student affairs, enrollment management, and parent programs. Her research interests include women in higher education, deans of women, and history of higher education.

Jason R. Kilmer is an assistant professor in the Department of Psychiatry and Behavioral Sciences at the University of Washington and has been an investigator on several studies evaluating prevention and intervention approaches for alcohol and marijuana use by college students. He is also the Assistant Director of Health and Wellness for Alcohol and Other Drug Education in the Division of Student Life, working with different areas across campus to increase student access to evidence-based approaches. He also serves as the chair of the College Coalition for Substance Abuse Prevention in the state of Washington. He has published several book chapters, and his research appears in such journals as *Addiction Theory and Research*, *Addictive Behaviors*, and the *Journal of Studies in Alcohol.*

Elizabeth J. Kociolek is an education advisor in the Education Abroad Program at the University of Kentucky and a doctoral student in higher education at Old Dominion University. Her research examines the impact of student-faculty interactions on international students' sense of belonging.

Chris Linder is assistant professor of College Student Affairs Administration at the University of Georgia. She earned her Ph.D. in higher education and student affairs leadership from the University of Northern Colorado. Her research interests include creating inclusive and effective campus learning environments, specifically related to race and gender. Additionally, she is interested in the influence of technology on campus environments and students' relationships to each other and their institutions.

Jose M. Maldonado has over 10 years of professional experience as a mental health clinician (LPC, NCC), psychotherapist, and middle and high school counselor in several school districts. His interests include the development and teaching of multicultural counseling, client advocacy, and clinical supervision. He holds a Ph.D. in counselor education from the University of Arkansas (2005).

Krista M. Malott is an associate professor in the Department of Education and Counseling at Villanova University. Her areas of research include Whiteness, racial and ethnic identity development, and multicultural counselor education. Her articles appear in such journals as the *Journal of Creativity in Mental Health*, *The Family Journal*, the *Journal of Multicultural Counseling and Development*, the *Journal of Social Action in Counseling*, the *Journal of Humanistic Counseling*, *Professional Counseling*, and the *Journal of School Counseling*.

Robin Minthorn, Ph.D., is a member of the Kiowa Tribe of Oklahoma and is also of Umatilla, Nez Perce, Assiniboine, and Apache descent. She is an assistant professor of educational leadership and Native American studies at the University of New Mexico. Her research interests include the Native American college student experiences on Non-Native College and University campuses, Native American college student and higher education leadership perspectives, Native American college students' participation in study abroad, and Native American women leaders' experiences. She is a former national chair of the Indigenous Peoples Knowledge

Community (IPKC) of NASPA and is a current board member of the National Indian Education Association.

Samuel D. Museus is an associate professor of higher education at the University of Denver. His research agenda focuses on examining the factors that affect college access and persistence among underrepresented students in the K–16 pipeline. His current research is focused on the impact of organizational environments on college success among racially diverse students. A prolific researcher, he is the recipient of the American College Personnel Association's Emerging Scholars Award, its Outstanding Contributor to Research Award, and the Association for the Study of Higher Education's Early Career Award.

Karen A. Myers is an associate professor and Director of the Higher Education Administration Graduate Program at Saint Louis University and Director of the award-winning international disability education project, *Allies for Inclusion: The Ability Exhibit.* She has been a college teacher and administrator since 1979 at nine institutions, is a national disability consultant and trainer, and teaches a self-designed graduate course, Disability in Higher Education and Society. She is the recipient of the ACPA College Student Educators International Voice of Inclusion Medallion, Annuit Coeptis Senior Professional Award, and the ACPA Foundation Diamond Honoree award. She is co-founder of the ACPA Standing Committee on Disability and co-author of the ASHE monograph *Allies for Inclusion: Disability and Equity in Higher Education* (Jossey-Bass, 2013).

Thai-Huy Nguyen is a Ph.D. candidate at the University of Pennsylvania's Graduate School of Education. His research interests include the diversification of the healthcare workforce as a means to narrow health disparities while addressing the shortage of primary healthcare providers and the promotion of URM students and professionals within STEM fields. Thai-Huy serves as the project manager for the national study on Models of Success at Minority-Serving Institutions.

Richard Overbaugh is a professor of teaching and learning at Old Dominion University, where he has taught since 1993. His major academic interests are instructional technology, design, and design theory. He teaches classes from the undergraduate to doctoral levels, specializing in the efficacy of technology-based instruction. He has also conducted evaluation work with WHRO, the Hampton Roads, Virginia, affiliate of the Corporation for Public Broadcasting.

Tina R. Paone is an associate professor and Chair of the Department of Educational Leadership, School Counseling, and Special Education at Monmouth University. She is engaged in multiple studies related to race, and she teaches primarily on groups and diversity. Dr. Paone also presents locally, regionally, and nationally on the topic of White Racial Identity Development (WRID) as well as on understanding and fighting racism.

Jeannette M. Passmore, M.A. is an academic advisor at James A. Rhodes State College in Lima, OH. She earned her M.A. in College Student Personnel from Bowling Green State University, where she focused on adult learners. She is currently pursuing an Ed.D. in higher education administration at the University of Nebraska at Lincoln and is focusing on community college leadership. Her focus on nontraditional students stems from her own experience as a nontraditional student.

Joseph A. Pate is an assistant professor of Outdoor Leadership at Young Harris College. Joseph's background in the philosophy and theory of experiential education, professional experiences in therapeutic uses of adventure, outdoor education, and environmental programming, and his research interests in qualitative inquiry, phenomenology, and creative pedagogical practices inform his orientation to teaching, facilitation, and scholarship. He earned a B.S. in Psychology from Presbyterian College, an M.Ed. in Outdoor Education Administration from Georgia College & State University, and a Ph.D. in Recreation and Leisure Studies from the University of Georgia.

Susan Rankin retired from the Pennsylvania State University in 2013, where she most recently served as an associate professor of education and senior research associate in PSU's Center for the Study of Higher Education. Dr. Rankin has presented and published widely on the intersections of identities and the impact of sexism, genderism, racism, and heterosexism in the academy and in intercollegiate athletics. Her most recent publications include the *2010 State of Higher Education for LGBT People*, *The Lives of Transgender People*, and the *2011 NCAA Student-Athlete Climate Study*. She has collaborated with over 100 institutions/organizations in implementing climate assessments and developing strategic initiatives regarding social justice issues.

Daniel Roesch is an assistant professor of education at Bloomsburg University. He has served as a middle school principal, high school principal, and science teacher in four different school districts. He has 20 years of diverse experience in public education, with 14 years as a building-level administrator. While serving as a middle school principal, he taught graduate courses for three different universities.

Stephanie Rosseter has a master's degree in Student Affairs and College Counseling from Monmouth University and a Bachelor's degree in Business Management from New Jersey City University. She previously worked for New York University in its Psychology Department and has a background in human resources. She was selected as a National Orientation Directors Association (NODA) intern for American University in the summer of 2012 and has interned at Brookdale Community College and Georgian Court University as well. She aspires to work in academic advising or career services.

Cristobal Salinas, Jr. is a research associate and doctoral student in higher education at Iowa State University. Cristobal has served as its College of Design's Multicultural Liaison Officer, where he provided assistance and guidance in understanding issues of diversity at Iowa State and beyond. He holds a B.A. in Spanish Education and ESL from the University of Nebraska at Kearney and an M.Ed. in Educational Leadership & Policy Studies from Iowa State University. His research explores the social and political context of educational opportunity for historically marginalized communities, with a focus on the Latina/o community.

Andrés Castro Samayoa is a Ph.D. student in Higher Education at the Graduate School of Education, University of Pennsylvania. Andrés has a background in queer methodologies, particularly historiographical research focused on narratives of sexual identities. His current research interests focus on the history of institutionalization of LGBTQ resource centers in U.S. colleges. He was a Gates Cambridge Scholar at the University of Cambridge, where he completed an M.Phil. in Multi-Disciplinary Gender Studies. Formerly, he worked as a Fellow for Student Life and Director of First-Year Community and Diversity Programming at Harvard University, where he also received a B.A. in Studies of Women, Gender, and Sexuality.

Pietro A. Sasso is an assistant professor of student affairs and college counseling at Monmouth University, where he is responsible for a related master's degree program. He holds a Ph.D. in higher education from Old Dominion University and a master's in student affairs and counseling from the University of Rochester. With over a decade of experience in postsecondary education spanning over five different functional areas, he has worked primarily in academic advising and alcohol education. Dr. Sasso has developed a research agenda focused on identity construction and college student development outcomes. He is a recipient of the Association of Fraternity/Sorority Advisors Research Award.

Alan M. Schwitzer is a licensed psychologist whose research encompasses more than 50 publications examining college student mental health. He is a professor of counseling at Old Dominion University. Dr. Schwitzer is past editor of the *Journal of College Counseling* and a department editor of *About Campus Magazine*. He is also an expert reviewer for the *Journal of College Student Development; Journal of American College Health;* and the *British Journal of Education, Society, and Behavioral Science.* He is a recipient of the Berdie Award for Research and Scholarship in the Field of College Student Affairs (American College Counseling Association), Outstanding Contribution to Professional Knowledge Award (American College Counseling Association), and the American College Counseling Association's Meritorious Service Award.

Heather J. Shotton, Ph.D., is a member of the Wichita & Affiliated Tribes, and is also Kiowa and Cheyenne. She is an assistant professor of Native American studies at the University of Oklahoma. Dr. Shotton's research areas include Native students' success in higher education, Native American student experiences in doctoral education, and Native American women leaders. She advocates for Native education issues nationally and is a past president of the National Indian Education Association and a past national chair of the Indigenous Peoples Knowledge Community (IPKC) of Student Affairs Administrators in Higher Education (NASPA).

Dafina-Lazarus Stewart has been an associate professor in the Department of Higher Education and Student Affairs at Bowling Green State University since 2005. Dr. Stewart's research interests are focused on issues of diversity and social justice, particularly related to student development and outcomes and institutional transformation. She publishes widely in higher education journals and regularly presents at conferences and workshops across the country. She recently published an edited volume on multicultural affairs, *Multicultural Student Services on Campus: Building Bridges, Re-visioning Community* (2011) through the American College Personnel Association's Books and Media in partnership with Stylus Publishing.

Daniel Tillapaugh, Ph.D., is a postdoctoral fellow in Higher Education at the University of Maine. He has his Ph.D. in Leadership Studies, with a specialization in Higher Education Leadership, from the University of San Diego and an M.Ed. from the Counseling and Personnel Services Program at the University of Maryland, College Park. Dan's research interests are intersectionality in higher education, particularly in student development theory work; college student leadership development; and the study of college men and masculinities. Currently he serves as the chair of the Standing Committee on Men and Masculinities for ACPA—College Student Educators International.

Brian Van Brunt is the Senior Vice President for Professional Program Development with the NCHERM Group. He is past president of the American College Counseling Association. Dr. Van Brunt is a frequent speaker at academic conferences around the world on the topics of threat assessment, mental health, and counselor education. He has served as the Director of Counseling at New England College and the Director of Counseling and Testing at Western Kentucky University. He is the author of several books, including *Ending Campus Violence: New Approaches in Prevention* (2012) and *A Faculty Guide to Addressing Disruptive and Dangerous Behavior in the Classroom* (2013).

Matthew Varga is an assistant professor of counselor education and college student affairs in the Department of Clinical and Professional Studies at the University of West Georgia. He holds a Ph.D. in Higher Education Administration. Dr. Varga's central research focus has emphasized exploring prescription drug abuse among graduate students. Other areas of focus include LGBTQ issues, campus climate perceptions, transition programs, and experiences and competencies of entry level professionals. As a former student affairs professional, working in the Department of University Housing at The University of Tennessee, Knoxville, he developed a passion for the success of not only higher education administration, but also for students.

Sudha Wadhwani, Psy.D., is a clinical psychologist and Coordinator of Outreach and Community Intervention at Montclair State University Counseling and Psychological Services (CAPS), where she specializes in the development and provision of community interventions to increase access for underserved student populations. She has also served as Multicultural Outreach Coordinator at Mount Holyoke College Counseling Center. She has served as co-chair of the New Jersey Psychological Association (NJPA) Diversity Committee; NJPA Diversity Delegate; and Steering Committee member for the National Association for University and College Counseling Center Outreach (AUCCCO).

Genevieve Weber is an associate professor of counselor education in the Department of Counseling and Mental Health Professions at Hofstra University, and a Licensed Mental Health Counselor in the State of New York with a specialization in Substance Abuse. At Hofstra, Dr. Weber teaches a variety of courses related to the training of professional counselors, including group counseling, multicultural counseling, psychopathology, and psychopharmacology and treatment planning. She was a Substance Abuse Counselor for 8 years at the Midtown Center for Treatment and Research, Weill Cornell Medical College. In her research and professional presentations, Dr. Weber focuses on the impact of homophobia and heterosexism on the lives of LGBT individuals, with particular attention to the relationship between homophobia, internalized homophobia, and substance abuse. She is involved in numerous projects related to campus climate assessment for LGBT people.

Amy E. Wells Dolan is Associate Dean of the School of Education at the University of Mississippi and an associate professor of higher education. Her research interests include the history of higher education in the South, especially historical analysis related to race, class, and gender. Her recent work has appeared in *Expanding the Donor Base in Higher Education* (2013), *Reflections on the 75th Anniversary of the Student Personnel Point of View* (2012), and *Higher*

Education: Handbook of Theory and Research (2012). At the University of Mississippi she has served as Chair of the Chancellor's Commission on the Status of Women and as a founding member of an interdisciplinary liberal arts working group on the Global South, among other leadership roles.

Nathan Williams serves as the Adventure Recreation Coordinator for Trips at the University of North Carolina, Wilmington. With a work and academic background in both outdoor education and student affairs, his work focuses on how outdoor recreation benefits students' leadership development and environmental awareness. He has presented on those topics at numerous national conferences, including the Association of Outdoor Recreation and Education (AORE), the National Intramural and Recreational Sports Association (NIRSA), and the American College Personnel Association (ACPA). Nathan has a B.Sc. in Outdoor Education from the University of Minnesota, Duluth, and an M.Ed. in College Student Affairs Administration from the University of Georgia.

Varaxy Yi is a doctoral student in Higher Education at the University of Denver. Her research interests include underrepresented and marginalized communities and their educational attainment, aspirations, and experiences. Specifically, she is interested in the experiences of Southeast Asian students as they navigate the postsecondary education system and encounter issues of access and degree completion. In addition, she is interested in examining the graduate student experience as these students navigate the complexities and intersections of academic, personal, and professional life.